Lecture Notes in Computer Science 14815

The series Lecture Notes in Computer Science (LNCS), including its subseries Lecture Notes in Artificial Intelligence (LNAI) and Lecture Notes in Bioinformatics (LNBI), has established itself as a medium for the publication of new developments in computer science and information technology research, teaching, and education.

LNCS enjoys close cooperation with the computer science R & D community, the series counts many renowned academics among its volume editors and paper authors, and collaborates with prestigious societies. Its mission is to serve this international community by providing an invaluable service, mainly focused on the publication of conference and workshop proceedings and postproceedings. LNCS commenced publication in 1973.

Osvaldo Gervasi · Beniamino Murgante ·
Chiara Garau · David Taniar ·
Ana Maria A. C. Rocha ·
Maria Noelia Faginas Lago
Editors

Computational Science and Its Applications – ICCSA 2024 Workshops

Hanoi, Vietnam, July 1–4, 2024
Proceedings, Part I

Springer

Editors
Osvaldo Gervasi
Department of Mathematics and Computer Science
University of Perugia
Perugia, Italy

Chiara Garau
Department of Civil and Environmental Engineering and Architecture
University of Cagliari
Cagliari, Italy

Ana Maria A. C. Rocha
Algoritmi Research Centre
University of Minho
Braga, Portugal

Beniamino Murgante
School of Engineering
University of Basilicata
Potenza, Italy

David Taniar
Faculty of Information Technology
Monash University Clayton Campus
Clayton, VIC, Australia

Maria Noelia Faginas Lago
Department of Chemistry, Biology and Biotechnology
University of Perugia
Perugia, Italy

ISSN 0302-9743 ISSN 1611-3349 (electronic)
Lecture Notes in Computer Science
ISBN 978-3-031-65153-3 ISBN 978-3-031-65154-0 (eBook)
https://doi.org/10.1007/978-3-031-65154-0

This Springer imprint is published by the registered company Springer Nature Switzerland AG
The registered company address is: Gewerbestrasse 11, 6330 Cham, Switzerland

Preface

These 11 volumes (LNCS volumes 14815–14825) consist of the peer-reviewed papers from the 55 Workshops of the 2024 International Conference on Computational Science and Its Applications (ICCSA 2024) which took place during July 1–4, 2024 in Hanoi (Vietnam). The peer-reviewed papers of the main conference tracks are published in a separate set consisting of two volumes (LNCS 14813–14814).

The conference was held in a hybrid form, with some participants present in person, hosted in Hanoi, Vietnam, by the Thuy Loi University. We enabled virtual participation for those who were unable to attend the event, due to logistical, political and economic problems, by adopting a technological infrastructure based on open source software (jitsi + riot), and a commercial Cloud infrastructure.

ICCSA 2024 was another successful event in the International Conference on Computational Science and Its Applications (ICCSA) conference series, previously held in Athens, Greece (2023), Malaga, Spain (2022), Cagliari, Italy (hybrid with few participants in presence in 2021 and completely online in 2020), whilst earlier editions took place in Saint Petersburg, Russia (2019), Melbourne, Australia (2018), Trieste, Italy (2017), Beijing. China (2016), Banff, Canada (2015), Guimaraes, Portugal (2014), Ho Chi Minh City, Vietnam (2013), Salvador, Brazil (2012), Santander, Spain (2011), Fukuoka, Japan (2010), Suwon, South Korea (2009), Perugia, Italy (2008), Kuala Lumpur, Malaysia (2007), Glasgow, UK (2006), Singapore (2005), Assisi, Italy (2004), Montreal, Canada (2003), and (as ICCS) Amsterdam, The Netherlands (2002) and San Francisco, USA (2001).

Computational Science is the main pillar of most of the present research, industrial and commercial applications, and plays a unique role in exploiting ICT innovative technologies, and the ICCSA conference series have been providing a venue to researchers and industry practitioners to discuss new ideas, to share complex problems and their solutions, and to shape new trends in Computational Science. As the conference mirrors society from a scientific point of view, this year's undoubtedly dominant theme was the machine learning and artificial intelligence and their applications in the most diverse economic and industrial fields.

The ICCSA 2024 conference is structured in 6 general tracks covering the fields of computational science and its applications: Computational Methods, Algorithms and Scientific Applications – High Performance Computing and Networks – Geometric Modeling, Graphics and Visualization – Advanced and Emerging Applications – Information Systems and Technologies – Urban and Regional Planning. In addition, the conference consisted of 55 workshops, focusing on very topical issues of importance to science, technology and society: from new mathematical approaches for solving complex computational systems, to information and knowledge in the Internet of Things, new statistical and optimization methods, several Artificial Intelligence approaches, sustainability issues, smart cities and related technologies.

In the Workshops proceedings we accepted 281 full papers, 17 short papers and 2 PhD Showcase papers. In the Main Conference Proceedings we accepted 53 full papers, 6 short papers and 3 PhD Showcase papers from 207 submissions to the General Tracks of the conference (acceptance rate 30%). We would like to express our appreciation to the workshops chairs and co-chairs for their hard work and dedication.

The success of the ICCSA conference series in general, and of ICCSA 2024 in particular, vitally depends on the support of many people: authors, presenters, participants, keynote speakers, workshop chairs, session chairs, organizing committee members, student volunteers, Program Committee members, Advisory Committee members, International Liaison chairs, reviewers and others in various roles. We take this opportunity to wholehartedly thank them all.

We also wish to thank our publisher, Springer, for their acceptance to publish the proceedings, for sponsoring part of the best papers awards and for their kind assistance and cooperation during the editing process.

We cordially invite you to visit the ICCSA website https://iccsa.org where you can find all the relevant information about this interesting and exciting event.

July 2024

Osvaldo Gervasi
Beniamino Murgante
Chiara Garau

Welcome Message from Organizers

After the very hard times of COVID, ICCSA continues its successful scientific endeavors in 2024, hosted in Hanoi, Vietnam. This time, ICCSA moved from the Mediterranean Region to Southeast Asia and was held in the metropolitan city of Hanoi, the capital of Vietnam. Hanoi is a vibrant urban environment known for the hospitality of its citizens, its rich history, vibrant culture, and dynamic urban life. Located in the northern part of the country, Hanoi is a bustling metropolis that combines the old with the new, offering a unique blend of ancient traditions and modern development.

ICCSA 2024 took place in a secure environment, allowing for safe and vibrant in-person participation. Combined with the active engagement of the ICCSA 2024 scientific community, this set the stage for highly motivating discussions and interactions regarding the latest developments in computer science and its applications in the real world for improving communities' quality of life.

Thuyloi University, also known as the Water Resources University, is a prominent institution in Hanoi, Vietnam, with a strong reputation in engineering and technical education, particularly in water resources and environmental engineering. In recent years, the University has expanded its academic offerings to include computer science, reflecting the growing importance of technology and digital skills in all sectors. This year, Thuyloi University had the honor of hosting ICCSA 2024. The Local Organizing Committee felt the burden and responsibility of such a demanding task and put all necessary energy into meeting participants' expectations and establishing a friendly, creative, and inspiring scientific and social/cultural environment that allowed for new ideas and perspectives to flourish.

Since all ICCSA participants, whether informatics-oriented or application-driven, realize the tremendous advancements in computer science over the last few decades and the huge potential these advancements offer in coping with the enormous challenges of humanity in a globalized, 'wired,' and highly competitive world, the expectations for ICCSA 2024 were high. The goal was to successfully match computer science progress with communities' aspirations, achieving progress that serves real, place- and people-based needs and paves the way towards a visionary, smart, sustainable, resilient, and inclusive future for both current and future generations.

On behalf of the Local Organizing Committee, I would like to sincerely thank all of you who contributed to ICCSA 2024.

Nguyen Canh Thai

Organization

ICCSA 2024 was organized by Thuyloi University (Vietnam), the University of Perugia (Italy), the University of Basilicata (Italy), Monash University (Australia), Kyushu Sangyo University (Japan), the University of Minho (Portugal), and the University of Cagliari (Italy).

Honorary General Chairs

Norio Shiratori	Chuo University, Japan
Kenneth C. J. Tan	Sardina Systems, UK

General Chairs

Nguyen Canh Thai	Thuyloi University, Vietnam
Osvaldo Gervasi	University of Perugia, Italy
David Taniar	Monash University, Australia

Program Committee Chairs

Beniamino Murgante	University of Basilicata, Italy
Chiara Garau	University of Cagliari, Italy
Ana Maria A. C. Rocha	University of Minho, Portugal
Bernady O. Apduhan	Kyushu Sangyo University, Japan

International Advisory Committee

Jemal Abawajy	Deakin University, Australia
Dharma P. Agarwal	University of Cincinnati, USA
Rajkumar Buyya	Melbourne University, Australia
Claudia Bauzer Medeiros	University of Campinas, Brazil
Manfred M. Fisher	Vienna University of Economics and Business, Austria
Pierre Frankhauser	University of Franche-Comté/CNRS, France
Marina L. Gavrilova	University of Calgary, Canada

Sumi Helal	University of Florida, USA & University of Lancaster, UK
Bin Jiang	University of Gävle, Sweden
Yee Leung	Chinese University of Hong Kong, China

International Liaison Chairs

Ivan Blečić	University of Cagliari, Italy
Giuseppe Borruso	University of Trieste, Italy
Elise De Donker	Western Michigan University, USA
Maria Noelia Faginas Lago	University of Perugia, Italy
Maria Irene Falcão	University of Minho, Portugal
Robert C. H. Hsu	Chung Hua University, Taiwan
Yeliz Karaca	University of Massachusetts Medical School, Worcester, USA
Tae-Hoon Kim	Zhejiang University of Science and Technology, China
Vladimir Korkhov	Saint Petersburg University, Russia
Takashi Naka	Kyushu Sangyo University, Japan
Rafael D. C. Santos	National Institute for Space Research, Brazil
Maribel Yasmina Santos	University of Minho, Portugal
Anastasia Stratigea	National Technical University of Athens, Greece

Workshop and Session Organizing Chairs

Beniamino Murgante	University of Basilicata, Italy
Chiara Garau	University of Cagliari, Italy

Award Chair

Wenny Rahayu	La Trobe University, Australia

Publicity Committee Chairs

Elmer Dadios	De La Salle University, Philippines
Nataliia Kulabukhova	Saint Petersburg University, Russia

Daisuke Takahashi	Tsukuba University, Japan
Shangwang Wang	Beijing University of Posts and Telecommunications, China

Local Organizing Committee Chairs

Doan Quang Tu	Academy of Military Science and Technology, Hanoi, Vietnam
Ho Sy Tam	Thuyloi University, Vietnam
Le Quang Tuan	Thuyloi University, Vietnam
Nguyen Huu Quynh	Thuyloi University, Vietnam
Ta Quang Chieu	Thuyloi University, Vietnam

Technology Chair

Damiano Perri	University of Perugia, Italy

Program Committee

Vera Afreixo	University of Aveiro, Portugal
Vladimir Alarcon	Northern Gulf Institute, USA
Filipe Alvelos	University of Minho, Portugal
Debora Anelli	Polytechnic University of Bari, Italy
Hartmut Asche	Hasso-Plattner-Institut für Digital Engineering, Germany
Ginevra Balletto	University of Cagliari, Italy
Socrates Basbas	Aristotle University of Thessaloniki, Greece
David Berti	ART SpA, Italy
Michela Bertolotto	University College Dublin, Ireland
Debnath Bhattacharyya	Koneru Lakshmaiah University, India
Sandro Bimonte	CEMAGREF, TSCF, France
Ana Cristina Braga	University of Minho, Portugal
Tiziana Campisi	Kore University of Enna, Italy
Yves Caniou	Lyon University, France
José A. Cardoso e Cunha	Universidade Nova de Lisboa, Portugal
Rui Cardoso	University of Beira Interior, Portugal
Leocadio G. Casado	University of Almeria, Spain
Mete Celik	Erciyes University, Turkey
Maria Cerreta	University of Naples Federico II, Italy
Mauro Coni	University of Cagliari, Italy

Eric Pardede	La Trobe University, Australia
Ana Isabel Pereira	Polytechnic Institute of Bragança, Portugal
Damiano Perri	University of Perugia, Italy
Massimiliano Petri	University of Pisa, Italy
Telmo Pinto	University of Coimbra, Portugal
Maurizio Pollino	ENEA, Italy
Alenka Poplin	Iowa State University, USA
Marcos Quiles	Federal University of São Paulo, Brazil
Humberto Rocha	University of Coimbra, Portugal
Marzio Rosi	University of Perugia, Italy
Manna Sheela Rani Chetty	Koneru Lakshmaiah University, India
Lucia Saganeiti	University of L'Aquila, Italy
Tamie Salter	Citizen Alerts Inc., Canada
Francesco Scorza	University of Basilicata, Italy
Marco Paulo Seabra dos Reis	University of Coimbra, Portugal
Jie Shen	University of Michigan, USA
Chien Sing Lee	Sunway University, Malaysia
Francesco Tajani	Sapienza University of Rome, Italy
Rodrigo Tapia-McClung	Centro de Investigación en Ciencias de Información Geoespacial, Mexico
Eufemia Tarantino	Polytechnic of Bari, Italy
Sergio Tasso	University of Perugia, Italy
Ana Paula Teixeira	Universidade do Minho, Portugal
Maria Filomena Teodoro	IST ID, Instituto Superior Técnico, Portugal
Yiota Theodora	National Technical University of Athens, Greece
Carmelo Torre	Polytechnic of Bari, Italy
Giuseppe A. Trunfio	University of Sassari, Italy
Toshihiro Uchibayashi	Kyushu University, Japan
Marco Vizzari	University of Perugia, Italy
Frank Westad	Norwegian University of Science and Technology, Norway
Fukuko Yuasa	High Energy Accelerator Research Organization, Japan
Ljiljana Zivkovic	Republic Geodetic Authority, Serbia

Workshops

Advances in Artificial Intelligence Learning Technologies: Blended Learning, STEM, Computational Thinking and Coding (AAILT 2024)

Workshop Organizers

Alfredo Milani	University of Perugia, Italy
Valentina Franzoni	University of Perugia, Italy
Sergio Tasso	University of Perugia, Italy

Workshop Program Committee Members

Li Yuanxi	Hong Kong Baptist University, Hong Kong, China
Valentino Santucci	University for Foreigners, Perugia, Italy
Krassimir Markov	Institute of Information Theories and Applications, Sofia, Bulgaria
Clement Leung	Chinese University of Hong Kong, China
Rajdeep Niyogi	Indian Institute of Technology, Rooorkee, India

Advanced and Innovative Web Apps 2024 (AIWA 2024)

Workshop Organizers

Osvaldo Gervasi	University of Perugia, Italy
Damiano Perri	University of Perugia, Italy

Workshop Program Committee Members

Tamie Salter	Citizen Alert Inc., Canada
Paolo Nesi	University of Florence, Italy
Tae Hoon Kim	Zhejiang University of Science and Technology, China
Debnath Bhattacharyya	Koneru Lakshmaiah Education Foundation, India
David Berti	ART SpA, Italy

Advanced Processes of Mathematics and Computing Models in Complex Computational Systems (ACMC 2024)

Workshop Organizers

Yeliz Karaca	University of Massachusetts Chan Medical School and Massachusetts Institute of Technology, USA
Dumitru Baleanu	Cankaya University, Turkey
Osvaldo Gervasi	University of Perugia, Italy
Yudong Zhang	University of Leicester, UK
Majaz Moonis	University of Massachusetts Medical School, USA

Workshop Program Committee Members

Tamie Salter	Citizen Alert Inc., Canada
TaiHoon Kim	Konkuk University, South Korea
Debnath Bhattacharyya	Koneru Lakshmaiah Education Foundation, India
Massimiliano Nicolini	OliTec Foundation, Italy
Martin Bohner	Missouri University of Science and Technology, Missouri, USA
René Lozi	Université Côte d'Azur, France
Ravi P. Agarwal	Texas A&M University-Kingsville, USA
Aziz Dursun	Virginia Tech, USA
Muhammad Attique Khan	HITEC University, Pakistan and Lebanese American University, Lebanon
Rasulova Mukhayo	National University Uzbekistan, Uzbekistan

Advances in Information Systems and Technologies for Emergency Management, Risk Assessment and Mitigation Based on the Resilience Concepts (ASTER 2024)

Workshop Organizers

Maurizio Pollino	Italian National Agency for New Technologies, Energy and Sustainable Economic Development, Italy
Marco Vona	University of Basilicata, Italy

Alessandro Giocoli	Italian National Agency for New Technologies, Energyand Sustainable Economic Development, Italy
Chiara Ormando	Italian National Agency for New Technologies, Energy and Sustainable Economic Development, Italy
Angelo Anelli	Italian National Research Council, Italy

Workshop Program Committee Members

Gregorio D'Agostino	Italian National Agency for New Technologies, Energy and Sustainable Economic Development, Italy
Christian Bignami	INGV, Italy
Paolo Clemente	Anti-Seismic Systems International Society, ASSISI, USA
Sonia Giovinazzi	Italian National Agency for New Technologies, Energy and Sustainable Economic Development, Italy

Advances in Web-Based Learning 2024 (AWBL 2024)

Workshop Organizers

Mustafa Inceoglu	Ege University, Turkey
Birol Ciloglugil	Ege University, Turkey

Workshop Program Committee Members

Birim Balci	Celal Bayar University, Turkey
Burak Galip Aslan	Izmir Yuksek Teknoloji University, Turkey
Mahmut Unan	University of Alabama, USA
Nisha S. Raj	Global Indian International School, Japan
Oylum Alatlı	Ege University, Turkey

Blockchain and Distributed Ledgers: Technologies and Applications (BDLTA 2024)

Workshop Organizers

Vladimir Korkhov	Saint Petersburg State University, Russia
Elena Stankova	Saint Petersburg State University, Russia
Nataliia Kulabukhova	Saint Petersburg State University, Russia

Workshop Program Committee Members

Vasily Solodkov	Higher School of Economics Banking Institute
Alexander Bogdanov	St. Petersburg State University, Russia
Alexander Degtyarev	St. Petersburg State University, Russia
Dmitry Vasiunin	Deutsche Telekom Cloud Services E.P.E., Greece
Serob Balyan	National Academy of Sciences of Armenia, Armenia
Suren Abrahamyan	Osensus Arm LLC, Armenia
Ashot Gevorkyan	National Academy of Sciences of Armenia, Armenia
Martin Vala	Univerzita Pavla Jozefa Šafárika Košiciach, Košice, Slovakia
Nodir Zaynalov	Tashkent University of Information Technologies, Uzbekistan
Michail Panteleyev	St. Petersburg Electrotecnical University, Russia
Nikolay Peryazev	Irkutsk State University, Irkutsk, Russia

Computational and Applied Mathematics (CAM 2024)

Workshop Organizers

Maria Irene Falcao	University of Minho, Portugal
Fernando Miranda	University of Minho, Portugal

Workshop Program Committee Members

Ricardo Severino	University of Minho, Portugal
Helmuth Malonek	University of Aveiro, Portugal
Isabel Cacao	University of Aveiro, Portugal
Graça Tomaz	Polytechnic of Guarda, Portugal

Rosário Fernandes	University of Minho, Portugal
Lidia Aceto	University of Piedmont Oriental, Italy
Patrícia Beites	University of Beira Interior, Portugal
Regina de Almeida	University of Trás-os-Montes e Alto Douro, Portugal
Luís Ferrás	University of Porto, Portugal
Helmuth Malonek	University of Aveiro, Portugal
João Morais	Autonomous Technological Institute of Mexico, Mexico
Yilmaz Simsek	Akdeniz University, Turkey

Computational and Applied Statistics (CAS 2024)

Workshop Organizer

Ana Cristina Braga	University of Minho, Portugal

Workshop Program Committee Member

Adelaide Freitas	University of Aveiro, Portugal
Ângela Silva	University of Minho, Portugal
Arminda Manuela Gonçalves	University of Minho, Portugal
Arunasalam Rahunanthan	Central State University, USA
Elisete Correia	University of Trás-os-Montes e Alto Douro, Portugal
Frank Westad	Norwegian University of Science and Technology, Norway
Humberto Rocha	University of Coimbra, Portugal
Ivan Rodriguez Conde	University of Arkansas, USA
Lino Costa	University of Minho, Portugal
Marco Reis	University of Coimbra, Portugal
Maria Filipa Mourão	Polytechnic Institute of Viana do Castelo, Portugal
Martín Pérez Pérez	University of Vigo, Spain
Michal Abrahamowicz	McGill University, Canada
Vanda Lourenço	New University of Lisbon, Portugal
Vera Afreixo	University of Aveiro, Portugal

Cyber Intelligence and Applications (CIA 2024)

Workshop Organizer

Gianni D'Angelo	University of Salerno, Italy

Workshop Program Committee Members

Massimo Ficco	University of Salerno, Italy
Marcello Trovati	Edge Hill University, UK
Michal Choras	Bydgoszcz University of Science and Technology, Poland

Computational Methods, Statistics and Industrial Mathematics (CMSIM 2024)

Workshop Organizers

Maria Filomena Teodoro	University of Lisbon and Portuguese Naval Academy, Portugal
Marina A. P. Andrade	University Institute of Lisbon, Portugal
Maria de Fátima Alves de Pina	University Institute of Lisbon, Portugal

Workshop Program Committee Members

Ricardo Moura	University of Lisboa and FCT, Portugal
Aldina Correia	Escola Superior de Tecnologia e Gestão, Portugal
Eliana Costa	Escola Superior de Tecnologia e Gestão, Portugal
Ana Borges	Escola Superior de Tecnologia e Gestão, Portugal
Cristina Lopes	ISCAP, Portugal
Fernando Carapau	University of Evora, Portugal
Fernanda Costa	University of Minho, Portugal
Maria Luísa Morgado	University of Trás os Montes e Alto Douro and University of Lisboa, Portugal
Ana Isabel Pereira	Instituto Politécnico de Bragança, Portugal
Bruna Ramos	University of Minho, Portugal
Rosário Ramos	Universidade Aberta, Portugal
Elisabete Carolino	Escola Superior da Saúde de Lisboa, Portugal
Sofia Rézio	Instituto Politécnico de Lisboa, Portugal
Matteo Sacchet	University of Turin, Italy

Marina Marchisio Conte	University of Turin, Italy
António Seijas-Macias	University of Coruña, Spain
Luís F. A. Teodoro	University of Glasgow, UK and University of Oslo, Norway
Christos Kitsos	University of West Attica, Greece

Computational Optimization and Applications (COA 2024)

Workshop Organizers

Ana Maria A. C. Rocha	University of Minho, Portugal
Humberto Rocha	University of Coimbra, Portugal

Workshop Program Committee Members

Eligius M. T. Hendrix	University of Málaga, Spain
Joana Matos Dias	University of Coimbra, Portugal
Ana Isabel Pereira	Polytechnic Institute of Bragança, Portugal
Filipe Alvelos	Univeristy of Minho, Portugal
Emerson José de Paiva	Federal University of Itajubá, Brazil

Computational Astrochemistry (CompAstro 2024)

Workshop Organizers

Marzio Rosi	University of Perugia, Italy
Nadia Balucani	University of Perugia, Italy
Daniela Ascenzi	University of Trento, Italy
Stefano Falcinelli	University of Perugia, Italy

Workshop Program Committee Members

Albert Rimola	Universitat Autònoma de Barcelona, Spain
Dimitrios Skouteris	Master-Tec, Perugia, Italy
Piero Ugliengo	University of Turin, Italy
Andrea Lombardi	University of Perugia, Italy
Piergiorgio Casavecchia	University of Perugia, Italy
Fernando Pirani	University of Perugia, Italy
Costanza Borghesi	University of Perugia, Italy

Gabriella Digenova	University of Perugia, Italy
Lisa Giani	Grenoble Alpes University, France
Marco Parriani	University of Perugia, Italy
Cecilia Coletti	University of Chieti, Italy
Massimiliano Aschi	University of L'Aquila, Italy
Emilia Dearagao	University of Perugia, Italy
Giacomo Pannacci	University of Perugia, Italy
Gianmarco Vanuzzo	University of Perugia, Italy

Computational Methods for Porous Geomaterials (CompPor 2024)

Workshop Organizers

Vadim Lisitsa	Russian Academy of Science, Russia
Evgeniy Romenski	Russian Academy of Science, Russia

Workshop Program Committee Members

Kirill Gadylshin	Russian Academy of Science, Russia
Tayana Khachkova	Russian Academy of Science, Russia
Dmitri Prokhorov	Russian Academy of Science, Russia
Mikahil Novikov	Russian Academy of Science, Russia

Workshop on Computational Science and HPC (CSHPC 2024)

Workshop Organizers

Elise De Doncker	Western Michigan University, USA
Fukuko Yuasa	High Energy Accelerator Research Organization, Japan
Hideo Matsufuru	High Energy Accelerator Research Organization, Japan

Workshop Program Committee Members

Tadashi Ishikawa	High Energy Accelerator Research Organization, Japan
Hiroshi Daisaka	Hitotsubashi University, Japan
Naohito Nakasato	University Aizu, Japan

Takahiro Ueda	Juntendo University, Japan
Khiem Hong Phan	Duy Tan University, Vietnam
Naohito Nakasato	University Aizu, Japan
Tasnim Gharaibeh	Kalamazoo College, USA
Robert Makin	Western Michigan University, USA

Cities, Technologies and Planning (CTP 2024)

Workshop Organizers

Beniamino Murgante	University of Basilicata, Italy
Giuseppe Borruso	University of Trieste, Italy
Malgorzata Hanzl	Lodz University of Technology, Poland
Anastasia Stratigea	National Technical University of Athens, Greece
Ljiljana Zivkovic	Republic Geodetic Authority, Serbia
Ginevra Balletto	University of Cagliari, Italy

Workshop Program Committee Members

Silvia Battino	University of Sassari, Italy
Mara Ladu	University of Cagliari, Italy
Maria del Mar Munoz Leonisio	University of Cadiz, Spain
Ahinoa Amaro Garcia	Univeristy of Las Palmas of Gran Canaria, Spain
Maria Attard	University of Malta, Malta
Enrico Dagostini	University of Malta, Malta
Francesca Krasna	University of Trieste, Italy
Brisol García García	Polytechnic University of Quintana Roo, Mexico
Tu Anh Trinh	College of Technology and Design for UEH University, Vietnam
Giovanni Mauro	University of Campania Luigi Vanvitelli, Italy
Maria Ronza	University of Naples, Federico II, Italy
Massimiliano Bencardino	University of Salerno, Italy

Sustainable Digital Circular Economy (DiCE 2024)

Workshop Organizers

Ginevra Balletto	University of Cagliari, Italy
Stefano Epifani	Digital Sustainability Foundation, Italy

Stefano Carboni	University of Sassari, Italy
Francesca Sinatra	University of Cagliari, Italy
Salvatore Dore	University of Sassari, Italy
Andrea Gallo	University of Trieste, Italy

Workshop Program Committee Members

Giuseppe Borruso	University of Trieste, Italy
Silvia Battino	University of Sassari, Italy
Beniamino Murgante	University of Basilicata, Italy
Mara Ladu	University of Cagliari, Italy
Luigi Mundula	University of Perugia, Italy
Maria Attard	University of Malta, Malta
Enrico Dagostini	University of Malta, Malta
Emilio Ghiani	University of Cagliari, Italy
Marco Naseddu	University of Cagliari, Italy
Balázs Kulcsaár	University of Debrecen, Hungary
Tu Anh Trinh	College of Technology and Design for UEH University, Vietnam
Giovanni Mauro	University of Campania Luigi Vanvitelli, Italy
Maria Ronza	University of Naples, Federico II, Italy
Massimiliano Bencardino	University of Salerno, Italy

Evaluating Inner Areas Potentials (EIAP 2024)

Workshop Organizers

Diana Rolando	Polytechnic of Turin, Italy
Alice Barreca	Polytechnic of Turin, Italy
Manuela Rebaudengo	Polytechnic of Turin, Italy
Giorgia Malavasi	Polytechnic of Turin, Italy

Workshop Program Committee Members

John Accordino	Virginia Commonwealth University, USA
Sara Favargiotti	University of Trento, Italy
Maddalena Ferretti	Polytechnic University of Marche, Italy
Daniel Laven	Mid Sweden University, Sweden
Barbara Lino	University of Palermo, Italy
Umberto Mecca	Polytechnic University of Turin, Italy

Lorenzo Savio	Polytechnic University of Turin, Italy
Asja Aulisio	Polytechnic University of Turin, Italy

Econometrics and Multidimensional Evaluation of Urban Environment (EMEUE 2024)

Workshop Organizers

Carmelo Maria Torre	Polytechnic of Bari, Italy
Francesco Tajani	Sapienza University of Rome, Italy
Pierluigi Morano	Polytechnic of Bari, Italy
Simona Panaro	University of Sussex, UK
Maria Cerreta	University of Naples Federico II, Italy
Debora Anelli	Polytechnic of Bari, Italy

Workshop Program Committee Members

Pierfrancesco de Paola	University of Naples Federico II, Italy
Daniela Tavano	University of Calabria, Italy
Giuseppe Cerullo	Sapienza University of Rome, Italy
Francesco Paolo del Giudice	Sapienza University of Rome, Italy
Marco Locurcio	Polytechnic University of Bari, Italy
Maria Rosa Trovato	University of Catania, Italy
Felicia di Liddo	Polytechnic University of Bari, Italy
Maria Paz Saez Perez	University of Granada, Spain
Yasmine Selim	Ain Shams University, Cairo
Hasan Mara	Indian Institute of Technology Roorkee, India
Philipp Wiesner	Technical University of Berlin, Germany
Maria Gamboa Perez	Complutense University of Madrid, Spain
Manuel Yanez	Universidad Autónoma de Madrid, Spain
Lucia Ika Fitriastuti	Solusi Bisnis Indonesia, Indonesia
Frank Devai	London South Bank University, UK
Frank Westad	Norwegian University of Science and Technology, Norway
Eugenio Muccio	University of Naples Federico II, Italy
Chiara Mazzarella	TU Delft, The Netherlands
Daniele Cannatella	TU Delft, The Netherlands
Sabrina Sacco	University of Naples Federico II, Italy
Piero Zizzania	University of Naples Federico II, Italy
Stefano Cuntò	University of Naples Federico II, Italy

Sveva Ventre	University of Naples Federico II, Italy
Caterina Loffredo	University of Naples Federico II, Italy
Giuseppe Ciciriello	University of Naples Federico II, Italy
Maria Somma	University of Naples Federico II, Italy
Ludovica La Rocca	University of Naples Federico II, Italy
Gaia Daldanise	National Research Council, Italy
Giuliano Poli	University of Naples Federico II, Italy

Environmental, Social, Governance of Energy Planning (ESGEP 2024)

Workshop Organizers

Ginevra Balletto	University of Cagliari, Italy
Emilio Ghiani	University of Cagliari, Italy
Roberto De Lotto	University of Pavia, Italy
Alessandra Marra	University of Salerno, Italy
Riccardo Trevisan	University of Cagliari, Italy
Balázs Kulcsár	University of Debrecen, Hungary

Workshop Program Committee Members

Jacopo Torriti	University of Reading, UK
Roberto Gerundo	University of Salerno, Italy
Luigi Mundula	University of Perugia, Italy
Mara Ladu	University of Cagliari, Italy
Giuseppe Borruso	University of Trieste, Italy
Tu Anh Trinh	College of Technology and Design for UEH University, Vietnam
Giovanni Mauro	University of Campania Luigi Vanvitelli, Italy
Maria Ronza	University of Naples, Federico II, Italy
Massimiliano Bencardino	University of Salerno, Italy

Ecosystem Services in Spatial Planning for Resilient Urban and Rural Areas (ESSP 2024)

Workshop Organizers

Sabrina Lai	University of Cagliari, Italy
Corrado Zoppi	University of Cagliari, Italy
Francesco Scorza	University of Basilicata, Italy

Beniamino Murgante	University of Basilicata, Italy
Floriana Zucaro	University of Naples Federico II, Italy
Carmela Gargiulo	University of Naples Federico II, Italy

Workshop Program Committee Members

Carmen Guida	University of Naples Federico II, Italy
Irina Di Ruocco	Insubria University, Italy
Silvia Rossetti	University of Parma, Italy
Barbara Caselli	University of Parma, Italy
Gloria Pellicelli	University of Parma, Italy
Federica Leone	University of Cagliari, Italy
Federica Isola	University of Cagliari, Italy
Francesca Leccis	University of Cagliari, Italy
Francesca Perrone	Sapienza University of Rome, Italy
Angela Pilogallo	Italian National Research Council, Italy
Alfonso Annunziata	University of Basilicata, Italy
Alessandro Marucci	University of L'Aquila, Italy
Francesco Zullo	University of L'Aquila, Italy
Gizem Dinç	Süleyman Demirel University, Turkey
Atila Gul	Süleyman Demirel University, Turkey
Sarah Scheiber	University of Malta, Malta
Matteo Caglioni	Université Côte d'Azur, France

Ethical AI Applications for a Human-Centered Cyber Society (EthicAI 2024)

Workshop Organizers

Valentina Franzoni	University of Perugia, Italy
Alfredo Milani	University of Perugia, Italy
Jordi Vallverdu	University Autonoma Barcelona, Spain

Workshop Program Committee Members

Sergio Tasso	University of Perugia, Italy
Yuanxi Li	Hong Kong Baptist University, Hong Kong, China
Daniele Mezzetti	Santa Maria della Misericordia Hospital of Perugia, Italy
Abeer Dyoub	L'Aquila University, Italy

14th International Workshop on Future Computing System Technologies and Applications (FiSTA 2024)

Workshop Organizers

Bernady Apduhan	Kyushu Sangyo University, Japan
Rafael Santos	National Institute for Space Research, Brazil

Workshop Program Committee Members

Agustinus Borgy Waluyo	Monash University, Australia
Andre Ricardo Abed Grégio	Federal University of Parana, Brazil
Earl Ryan Aleluya	MSU-Iligan Institute of Technology, Philippines
Kai Cheng	Kyushu Sangyo University, Japan
Alvaro Fazenda	Federal University of São Paulo, Brazil
Yusuke Gotoh	Okayama University, Japan
Eric Pardede	La Trobe University, Australia
Yasuaki Sumida	Kyushu Sangyo University, Japan
Kazuaki Tanaka	Kyushu Institute of Technology, Japan
Toshihiro Uchibayashi	Kyushu University, Japan
Toshihiro Yamauchi	Okayama University, Japan
Fenghui Yao	Tennessee State University, USA

Geographical Analysis, Urban Modeling, Spatial Statistics (Geog-An-Mod 2024)

Workshop Organizers

Beniamino Murgante	University of Basilicata, Italy
Giuseppe Borruso	University of Trieste, Italy
Harmut Asche	Hasso-Plattner-Institut für Digital Engineering, Germany
Andreas Fricke	Hasso-Plattner-Institut für Digital Engineering, Germany
Rodrigo Tapia McClung	Centro de Investigación en Ciencias de Información Geoespacial, Mexico

Workshop Program Committee Members

Ginevra Balletto	University of Cagliari, Italy
Silvia Battino	University of Sassari, Italy
Mara Ladu	University of Cagliari, Italy
Marco Mazzarino	IUAV Univeristy Venice, Italy
Maria del Mar Munoz Leonisio	Univeristy of Cadiz, Spain
Ahinoa Amaro Garcia	University of Las Palmas of Gran Canaria, Spain
Veronica Camerada	University of Sassari, Italy
Maria Attard	University of Malta, Malta
Enrico Dagostini	University of Malta, Malta
Francesca Krasna	University of Trieste, Italy
Malgorzata Hanzl	Lodz University of Technology, Poland
Anastasia Stratigea	National Technical University of Athens, Greece
Tu Anh Trinh	College of Technology and Design for UEH University, Vietnam
Giovanni Mauro	University of Campania Luigi Vanvitelli, Italy
Maria Ronza	University of Naples, Federico II, Italy
Massimiliano Bencardino	University of Salerno, Italy

Geomatics for Resource Monitoring and Management (GRMM 2024)

Workshop Organizers

Alessandra Capolupo	Polytechnic of Bari, Italy
Eufemia Tarantino	Polytechnic of Bari, Italy
Alberico Sonnessa	Polytechnic of Bari, Italy

Workshop Program Committee Members

Umberto Fratino	Polytechnic of Bari, Italy
Valeria Monno	Polytechnic of Bari, Italy
Antonino Maltese	University of Palermo, Italy
Athos Agapiou	Cyprus University of Technology, Cyprus
Michele Mangiameli	University of Catania, Italy
Angela Gorgoglione	University of la República de Uruguay, Uruguay
Roberta Ravanelli	Sapienza University of Rome, Italy
Alessandra Mascitelli	D'Annunzio University of Chieti–Pescara, Italy
Ester Scotto di Perta	University of Naples, Federico II, Italy

Giacomo Caporusso	National Research Council, Italy
Andrea Montanino	University of Naples, Federico II, Italy
Antonino Iannuzzo	University of Sannio, Benevento, Italy
Silvano Dal Sasso	University of Basilicata, Potenza, Italy
Laura Mirra	National Research Council, Water Research Institute, Italy
Alessandro Pagano	National Research Council, Water Research Institute, Italy
Francesco Chiaravalloti	National Research Council, Water Research Institute, Italy
Francesco Di Capua	University of Basilicata, Italy
Stefania Santoro	National Research Council, Water Research Institute, Italy
Cinzia Albertini	National Research Council, IREA, Italy
Alessandra Saponieri	University of Salento, Italy

International Workshop on Information and Knowledge in the Internet of Things (IKIT 2024)

Workshop Organizers

Teresa Guarda	Peninsula State University of Santa Elena, Ecuador
José María Díaz Nafría	Madrid Open University, Spain
Filipe Portela	University of Minho, Portugal

Workshop Program Committee Members

Arnulfo Alanis	Instituto Tecnologico de Tijuana, Mexico
Bruno Sousa	University of Coimbra, Portugal
Carlos Balsa	Instituto Politécnico de Bragança, Portugal
Filipe Mota Pinto	Instituto Politécnico de Leiria, Portugal
Gustavo Gatica	Universidad Andrés Bello, Chile
Isabel Lopes	Instituto Politécnico de Bragança, Portugal
José María Díaz Nafría	Universidad a Distancia, Spain
Maria Fernanda Augusto	BiTrum Research Group, Spain
Maria Isabel Ribeiro	Instituto Politécnico Bragança, Portugal
Modestos Stavrakis	University of the Aegean, Greece
Simone Belli	Universidad Complutense de MadridSpain
Walter Lopes Neto	Instituto Federal de Educação, Brazil

Regenerating Brownfields Enhancing Urban Resilience Appeal (INFERENCE 2024)

Workshop Organizers

Francesca Moraci	Mediterranea University of Reggio Calabria, Italy
Maurizio Oddo	University of Enna Kore, Italy
Antonella Versaci	University of Enna Kore, Italy
Celestina Fazia	University of Enna Kore, Italy
Tiziana Campisi	University of Enna Kore, Italy
Kh Md Nahiduzzaman	University of British Columbia, Canada

Workshop Program Committee Members

Alessandro Baracco	University of Enna Kore, Italy
Kaoutare Amini Alaoui	Mohammed VI Polytechnic University, UM6P, Morocco
Maurizio Errigo	Sapienza University of Rome, Italy
Marsia Marino	Sapienza University of Rome, Italy
Nessrine Moumen	Mohammed VI Polytechnic University, UM6P, Morocco
Francesca Perrone	Sapienza University of Rome, Italy
Pasquale Pizzimenti	Mediterranea University of Reggio Calabria, Italy
Barbara Scala	University of Brescia, Italy
Clarastella Vicari Aversa	Mediterranea University of Reggio Calabria, Italy

International Workshop on Territorial Planning to Integrate Risk and Urban Ontologies (IWPRO 2024)

Workshop Organizers

Elisabetta Maria Venco	University of Pavia, Italy
Beniamino Murgante	University of Basilicata, Italy
Roberto De Lotto	University of Pavia, Italy
Caterina Pietra	University of Pavia, Italy

Workshop Program Committee Members

Stefano Borgo	National Research Council, Italy
Valentina Costa	University of Genoa, Italy
Pajouh Danesh	Middle East Technical University, Turkey

Ilaria Delponte	University of Genoa, Italy
Lorena Fiorini	University of L'Aquila, Italy
Veronica Gazzola	Polytechnic of Milan, Italy
Ghazaleh Goodarzi	Islamic Azad University, Iran
Michele Grimaldi	University of Salerno, Italy
Alessandra Marra	University of Salerno, Italy
Naghmeh Mohammadpourlima	Akademi University, Finland
Francesca Pirlone	University of Genoa, Italy
Silvia Rossetti	University of Parma, Italy
Lucia Saganeiti	University of L'Aquila, Italy
Bahareh Shahsavari	University of Minnesota, USA
Ilenia Spadaro	University of Genoa, Italy
Maria Rosaria Stufano Melone	Polytechnic of Bari, Italy

MaaS Solutions for Airports, Cities and Regional Connectivity (MaaS 2024)

Workshop Organizers

Gianfranco Fancello	University of Cagliari, Italy
Francesco Piras	University of Cagliari, Italy
Tanja Congiu	University of Sassari, Italy
Mara Ladu	University of Cagliari, Italy
Martina Sinatra	University of Cagliari, Italy
Ginevra Balletto	University of Cagliari, Italy

Workshop Program Committee Members

Italo Meloni	University of Cagliari, Italy
Tu Anh Trinh	College of Technology and Design for UEH University, Vietnam
Giuseppe Borruso	University of Trieste, Italy
Luigi Mundula	University of Perugia, Italy
Francesca Sinatra	University of Trieste, Italy
Salvatore Dore	University of Trieste, Italy
Andrea Gallo	University of Trieste, Italy
Marcello Tadini	University of Eastern Piedmont, Italy
Marco Mazzarino	IUAV Univeristy Venice, Italy
Maria del Mar Munoz Leonisio	University of Cadiz, Spain
Veronica Camerada	Univeristy of Sassari, Italy

Brunella Brundu	Univerisity of Sassari, Italy
Maria Attard	University of Malta, Malta
Enrico Dagostini	University of Malta, Malta
Giovanni Mauro	University of Campania Luigi Vanvitelli, Italy
Maria Ronza	University of Naples, Federico II, Italy
Massimiliano Bencardino	University of Salerno, Italy

Development of Urban Mobility Management and Risk Assessment (MAINTAIN 2024)

Workshop Organizers

Tiziana Campisi	University of Enna Kore, Italy
Massimo Di Gangi	University of Messina, Italy
Antonio Comi	University of Rome Tor Vergata, Italy
Grigorios Fountas	Aristotle University of Thessaloniki, Greece
Jesús González-Feliu	Excelia Business School, La Rochelle, France

Workshop Program Committee Members

Paola Panuccio	Mediterranea University of Reggio Calabria, Italy
Domenica Savia Pellicano	Mediterranean University of Reggio Calabria, Italy
Alexandros Nikitas	University of Huddersfield, UK
Antonio Polimeni	University of Messina, Italy
Orlando Belcore	University of Messina, Italy
Marinella Giunta	Mediterranea University of Reggio Calabria, Italy
Borja Alonso	University of Cantabria, Spain
Luigi Dall'Olio	University of Cantabria, Santander, Spain
Kh Md Nahiduzzaman	UBC, Canada

Multidimensional Evolutionary Evaluations for Transformative Approaches (MEETA 2024)

Workshop Organizers

Maria Cerreta	University of Naples Federico II, Italy
Giuliano Poli	University of Naples Federico II, Italy
Daniele Cannatella	TU Delft, The Netherlands

Ludovica Larocca	University of Naples Federico II, Italy
Maria Somma	University of Naples Federico II, Italy
Gaia Daldanise	National Research Council, Italy

Workshop Program Committee Members

Maria Lucia Raiola	University of Naples Federico II, Italy
Eugenio Muccio	University of Naples Federico II, Italy
Chiara Mazzarella	TU Delft, The Netherlands
Sabrina Sacco	University of Naples Federico II, Italy
Piero Zizzania	University of Naples Federico II, Italy
Stefano Cuntò	University of Naples Federico II, Italy
Sveva Ventre	University of Naples Federico II, Italy
Caterina Loffredo	University of Naples Federico II, Italy
Giuseppe Ciciriello	University of Naples Federico II, Italy
Laura Di Tommaso	University of Naples Federico II, Italy
Benedetta Grieco	University of Naples Federico II, Italy
Simona Panaro	University of Sussex, UK

Building Multi-dimensional Models for Assessing Complex Environmental Systems (MES 2024)

Workshop Organizers

Vanessa Assumma	University of Bologna, Italy
Caterina Caprioli	Politechnic of Turin, Italy
Giulia Datola	Politechnic of Turin, Italy
Federico Dell'Anna	Politechnic of Turin, Italy
Marta Dell'Ovo	Politechnic of Milan, Italy
Marco Rossitti	Politechnic of Milan, Italy

Workshop Program Committee Members

Maksims Feofilovs	Riga Technical University, Latvia
Ossama Abdelwahab	University of Bari, Italy
Mariarosaria Angrisano	Pegaso Telematic University, Italy
Francesca Torrieri	Polytechnic of Milan, Italy
Maurizio Pioletti	University of Padua, Italy
Daniela Tavano	University of Calabria, Italy
Simone Persico	Polytechnic of Turin, Italy

Chiara D'Alpaos	University of Padua, Italy
Ezgi Şahin	Mersin University, Turkey
Giorgia Sugoni	LINKS Foundation, Italy
Rubina Canesi	University of Padua, Italy
Giulia Marzani	University of Bologna, Italy
Danny Casprini	Polytechnic of Milan, Italy
Simona Barbaro	University of Palermo, Italy
Giulio Cavana	Polytechnic of Turin, Italy
Diana Rolando	Polytechnic of Turin, Italy
Giuliano Poli	University of Naples Federico II, Italy
Francesco Sica	University of Rome La Sapienza, Italy
Sabrina Lai	University of Cagliari, Italy

Models and Indicators for Assessing and Measuring the Urban Settlement Development in the View of Zero Net Land Take by 2050 (MOVEto0 2024)

Workshop Organizers

Lucia Saganeiti	University of L'Aquila, Italy
Lorena Fiorini	University of L'Aquila, Italy
Angela Pilogallo	University of L'Aquila, Italy
Francesco Zullo	University of L'Aquila, Italy
Alessandro Marucci	University of L'Aquila, Italy

Workshop Program Committee Members

Ginevra Balletto	University of Cagliari, Italy
Giuseppe Borruso	University of Trieste, Italy
Chiara Garau	University of Cagliari, Italy
Beniamino Murgante	University of Basilicata, Italy
Ljiljana Zivkovic	MBA, Republic Geodetic Authority, Serbia
Ilaria Del Ponte	University of Genoa, Italy
Carmen Guida	University of Naples Federico II, Italy
Chiara Di Dato	University of L'Aquila, Italy

4th Workshop on Privacy in the Cloud/Edge/IoT World (PCEIoT 2024)

Workshop Organizers

Michele Mastroianni	University of Salerno, Italy
Mauro Iacono	University of Campania Luigi Vanvitelli, Italy
Lelio Campanile	University of Campania Luigi Vanvitelli, Italy

Workshop Program Committee Members

Maria Ganzha	Warsaw University of Technology, Poland
Armando Tacchella	University of Genoa, Italy
Alessio Merlo	School for Advanced Defense Studies, Italy
Antonio Iannuzzi	Roma Tre University, Italy
Arcangelo Castiglione	University of Salerno, Italy
Daniel Grzonka	Cracow University of Technology, Poland
Davide Cerotti	University of Piedmont Oriental, Italy

Scientific Computing Infrastructure (SCI 2024)

Workshop Organizers

Vladimir Korkhov	St. Petersburg University, Russia
Elena Stankova	St. Petersburg State University, Russia

Workshop Program Committee Members

Adam Belloum	University of Amsterdam, the Netherlands
Dmitry Vasiunin	Deutsche Telekom Cloud Services E.P.E., Greece
Serob Balyan	National Academy of Sciences of Armenia, Armenia
Suren Abrahamyan	Osensus Arm LLC, Armenia
Ashot Gevorkyan	National Academy of Sciences of Armenia, Armenia
Michal Hnatic	Univerzita Pavla Jozefa Šafárika v Košiciach, Slovakia
Martin Vala	Univerzita Pavla Jozefa Šafárika v Košiciach, Slovakia
Nodir Zaynalov	Tashkent University of Information Technologies, Uzbekistan
Michail Panteleyev	St. Petersburg Electrotecnical University, Russia

Nikolay Peryazev	Irkutsk State University, Irkutsk, Russia
Alexander Degtyarev	St. Petersburg State University, Russia
Alexander Bogdanov	St. Petersburg State University, Russia
Nataliia Kulabukhova	SberAutoTech, Russia

Downscale Agenda 2030 (SDGscale 2024)

Workshop Organizers

Anna Richiedei	University of Brescia, Italy
Michele Pezzagno	University of Brescia, Italy
Ginevra Balletto	University of Cagliari, Italy
Francesca Sinatra	University of Trieste, Italy
Federico Martellozzo	University of Florence, Italy
Tú Anh Trinh	University of Economics Ho Chi Minh City, Vietnam

Workshop Program Committee Members

Giuseppe Borruso	University of Trieste, Italy
Elisabetta Maria Venco	University of Pavia, Italy
Riccardo Privitera	University of Catania, Italy
Elisa Conticelli	University of Bologna, Italy
Giovanni Marinelli	Polytechnic University of Marche, Italy
Francesca Sinatra	University of Trieste, Italy
Salvatore Dore	University of Trieste, Italy
Maria Attard	University of Malta, Malta
Giovanni Mauro	University of Campania Luigi Vanvitelli, Italy
Maria Ronza	University of Naples, Federico II, Italy
Massimiliano Bencardino	University of Salerno, Italy

Socio-Economic and Environmental Models for Land Use Management (SEMLUM 2024)

Workshop Organizers

Debora Anelli	Polytechnic of Bari, Italy
Pierluigi Morano	Polytechnic of Bari, Italy
Benedetto Manganelli	University of Basilicata, Italy
Francesco Paolo Del Giudice	Sapienza University of Rome, Italy

Workshop Program Committee Members

Laura Gabrielli	University of Ferrara, Italy
Sergio Copiello	University of Venice, Italy
Antonio Nesticò	University of Salerno, Italy
Pierfrancesco De Paola	University of Napoli, Italy
Elena Fregonara	Polytechnic of Turin, Italy
Paola Amoruso	LUM, Italy

Ports of the Future - Smartness and Sustainability (SmartPorts 2024)

Workshop Organizers

Giuseppe Borruso	University of Trieste, Italy
Gianfranco Fancello	University of Cagliari, Italy
Patrizia Serra	University of Cagliari, Italy
Silvia Battino	University of Sassari, Italy
Marco Petrelli	Roma Tre University, Italy

Workshop Program Committee Members

Ginevra Balletto	University of Cagliari, Italy
Beniamino Murgante	University of Basilicata, Italy
Marco Mazzarino	IUAV University Venice, Italy
Maria del Mar Munoz Leonisio	University of Cadiz, Spain
Ahinoa Amaro Garcia	University of Las Palmas of Gran Canaria, Spain
Veronica Camerada	University of Sassari, Italy
Brunella Brundu	University of Sassari, Italy
Maria Attard	University of Malta, Malta
Enrico Dagostini	University of Malta, Malta
Tu Anh Trinh	College of Technology and Design for UEH University, Vietnam
Giovanni Mauro	University of Campania Luigi Vanvitelli, Italy
Maria Ronza	University of Naples, Federico II, Italy
Massimiliano Bencardino	University of Salerno, Italy

Smart Transport and Logistics - Smart Supply Chains (SmarTransLog 2024)

Workshop Organizers

Giuseppe Borruso	University of Trieste, Italy
Marcello Tadini	University of Eastern Piedmont, Italy
Maria del Mar Munoz Leonisio	University of Cádiz, Spain
Maria Attard	University of Malta, Malta
Veronica Camerada	University of Sassari, Italy
Brunella Brundu	University of Sassari, Italy

Workshop Program Committee Members

Ginevra Balletto	University of Cagliari, Italy
Silvia Battino	University of Sassari, Italy
Gianfranco Fancello	University of Cagliari, Italy
Mara Ladu	University of Cagliari, Italy
Martina Sinatra	University of Cagliari, Italy
Francesca Sinatra	University of Trieste, Italy
Salvatore Dore	University of Trieste, Italy
Andrea Gallo	University of Trieste, Italy
Marco Mazzarino	IUAV University Venice, Italy
Enrico Dagostini	University of Malta, Malta
Marco Naseddu	University of Cagliari, Italy
José Ángel Hernández Luis	University of Las Palmas de Gran Canaria, Spain
Maurizio Cociancich	Adriafer, Italy
Giovanni Longo	University of Trieste, Italy
Luca Toneatti	University of Trieste, Italy
Giovanni Mauro	University of Campania Luigi Vanvitelli, Italy
Maria Ronza	University of Naples, Federico II, Italy
Massimiliano Bencardino	University of Salerno, Italy

Smart Tourism (SmartTourism 2024)

Workshop Organizers

Silvia Battino	University of Sassari, Italy
Francesca Krasna	University of Trieste, Italy
Maria del Mar Munoz Leonisio	University of Cadiz, Spain

Ginevra Balletto	University of Cagliari, Italy
Brisol García García	Polytechnic University of Quintana Roo, Mexico
Ainhoa Amaro Garcia	University of Las Palmas of Gran Canarias, Spain

Workshop Program Committee Members

Giuseppe Borruso	University of Trieste, Italy
Beniamino Murgante	University of Basilicata, Italy
Gianfranco Fancello	University of Cagliari, Italy
Mara Ladu	University of Cagliari, Italy
Martina Sinatra	University of Cagliari, Italy
Salvatore Dore	University of Trieste, Italy
Veronica Camerada	University of Sassari, Italy
Brunella Brundu	University of Sassari, Italy
Maria Attard	University of Malta, Malta
Tu Anh Trinh	College of Technology and Design for UEH University, Vietnam
Giovanni Mauro	University of Campania Luigi Vanvitelli, Italy
Maria Ronza	University of Naples, Federico II, Italy
Massimiliano Bencardino	University of Salerno, Italy

Sustainable Evolution of Long-Distance Freight Passenger Transport (SOLIDEST 2024)

Workshop Organizers

Tiziana Campisi	University of Enna Kore, Italy
Socrates Basbas	Aristotle University of Thessaloniki, Greece
Massimo Di Gangi	University of Messina, Italy
Antonio Comi	University of Rome Tor Vergata, Italy
Francesco Russo	Mediterranea University of Reggio Calabria, Italy
Giovanni Tesoriere	University of Enna Kore, Italy

Workshop Program Committee Members

Antonio Polimeni	University of Messina, Italy
Orlando Belcore	University of Messina, Italy
Filippo G. Praticò	Mediterranea University of Reggio Calabria, Italy
Borja Alonso	University of Cantabria, Spain
Luigi Dall'Olio	University of Cantabria, Spain
Antonio Russo	University of Enna Kore, Italy

Sustainability Performance Assessment: Models, Approaches, and Applications Toward Interdisciplinary and Integrated Solutions (SPA 2024)

Workshop Organizers

Francesco Scorza	University of Basilicata, Italy
Sabrina Lai	University of Cagliari, Italy
Jolanta Dvarioniene	Kaunas University of Technology, Lithuania

Workshop Program Committee Members

Carmela Gargiulo	University of Naples Federico II, Italy
Floriana Zucaro	University of Naples Federico II, Italy
Corrado Zoppi	University of Cagliari, Italy
Federica Leone	University of Cagliari, Italy
Federica Isola	University of Cagliari, Italy
Francesca Leccis	University of Cagliari, Italy
Francesca Perrone	Sapienza University of Rome, Italy
Angela Pilogallo	Italian National Research Council, Italy
Alfonso Annunziata	University of Basilicata, Italy
Luigi Santopietro	Italian National Research Council, Italy
Beniamino Murgante	University of Basilicata, Italy
Alessandro Marucci	University of L'Aquila, Italy
Francesco Zullo	University of L'Aquila, Italy
Monica Salvia	Italian National Research Council, Italy
Fulvia Pietrapertosa	Italian National Research Council, Italy
Valentin Grecu	Lucian Blaga University, Romania
Georgia Pozoukidou	Aristotle University of Thessaloniki, Greece
Giampiero Lombardini	University of Genoa, Italy

Specifics of Smart Cities Development in Europe (SPEED 2024)

Workshop Organizers

Chiara Garau	University of Cagliari, Italy
Katarína Vitálišová	Matej Bel University, Slovakia
Paolo Nesi	University of Florence, Italy
Anna Vaňová	Matej Bel University, Slovakia
Kamila Borsekova	Matej Bel University, Slovakia
Paola Zamperlin	University of Florence, Italy

Workshop Program Committee Members

Tiziana Campisi	University of Enna Kore, Italy
Giovanna Concu	University of Cagliari, Italy
Claudia Loggia	University of KwaZulu-Natal, South Africa
Alessandro Plaisant	University of Sassari, Italy
Francesca Maltinti	University of Cagliari, Italy
Silvia Rossetti	University of Parma, Italy
Gerardo Carpentieri	University of Naples Federico II, Italy
Carmen Guida	University of Naples Federico II, Italy
Anastasia Stratigea	National Technical University of Athens, Greece
Yiota Theodora	National Technical University of Athens, Greece
Marco Fanfani	University of Florence, Italy
Emanuele Bellini	University of Rome 3, Italy

Smart, Safe and Health Cities (SSHC 2024)

Workshop Organizers

Chiara Garau	University of Cagliari, Italy
Gerardo Carpentieri	University of Naples Federico II, Italy
Carmen Guida	University of Naples Federico II, Italy
Floriana Zucaro	University of Naples Federico II, Italy
Tanja Congiu	University of Sassari, Italy
Martina Carra	University of Brescia, Italy
Benedetto Barabino	University of Brescia, Italy

Workshop Program Committee Members

Rosaria Battarra	Italian National Research Council, Italy
Barbara Caselli	University of Parma, Italy
Francesca Maltinti	University of Cagliari, Italy
Romano Fistola	University of Naples Federico II, Italy
Sabrina Lai	University of Cagliari, Italy
Claudia Loggia	University of KwaZulu-Natal, South Africa
Alessandro Plaisant	University of Sassari, Italy
Silvia Rossetti	University of Parma, Italy
Michela Tiboni	University of Brescia, Italy
John Zacharias	Peking University, China
Thomas Buhler	University of Franche-Comté, France

Aynaz Lotfata	University of California, USA
Lucia Saganeiti	University of L'Aquila, Italy
Francesco Zullo	University of L'Aquila, Italy
Paola Zamperlin	University of Florence, Italy
Katarína Vitálišová	Matej Bel University, Faculty of Economics, Slovakia
Tiziana Campisi	University of Enna Kore, Italy
Caterina Pietra	University of Pavia, Italy
Elisabetta Maria Venco	University of Pavia, Italy
Vincenza Torrisi	University of Catania, Italy

Smart and Sustainable Island Communities (SSIC 2024)

Workshop Organizers

Chiara Garau	University of Cagliari, Italy
Anastasia Stratigea	National Technical University of Athens, Greece
Yiota Theodora	National Technical University of Athens, Greece
Giovanna Concu	University of Cagliari, Italy

Workshop Program Committee Members

Milena Metalkova-Markova	University of Portsmouth, UK
Tarek Teba	University of Portsmouth, UK
Despina Dimelli	Technical University of Crete, Greece
Gerardo Carpentieri	University of Naples Federico II, Italy
Carmen Guida	University of Naples Federico II, Italy
Floriana Zucaro	University of Naples Federico II, Italy
Anestis Gourgiotis	University of Thessaly, Greece
George Tsilimigkas	University of the Aegean, Greece
Maria Panagiotopoulou	National Technical University of Athens, Greece
George Somarakis	National Technical University of Athens, Greece
Harry Kyriakidis	National Technical University of Athens, Greece
Apostolos Lagarias	Univ. of Thessaly, Greece
Paola Zamperlin	University of Florence, Italy
Giuseppina Vacca	University of Cagliari, Italy
Roberto Minunno	Curtin University, Perth, Australia
Claudia Loggia	University of KwaZulu-Natal, South Africa
Francesca Maltinti	University of Cagliari, Italy
Elisabetta Maria Venco	University of Pavia, Italy

From Street Experiments to Planned Solutions (STEPS 2024)

Workshop Organizers

Silvia Rossetti	University of Parma, Italy
Angela Ricciardello	University of Enna Kore, Italy
Francesco Pinna	University of Cagliari, Italy
Chiara Garau	University of Cagliari, Italy
Tiziana Campisi	University of Enna Kore, Italy
Vincenza Torrisi	University of Catania, Italy

Workshop Program Committee Members

Martina Carra	University of Brescia, Italy
Barbara Caselli	University of Parma, Italy
Tanja Congiu	University of Sassari, Italy
Gabriele D'Orso	University of Palermo, Italy
Matteo Ignaccolo	University of Catania, Italy
Md Kh Nahiduzzaman	University of British Columbia, Canada
Muhammad Ahmad Al-Rashid	University of Malaya, Malesia
Alessandro Plaisant	University of Sassari, Italy
Marianna Ruggieri	University of Enna Kore, Italy
Michele Zazzi	University of Parma, Italy

Sustainable Development of Ports (SUSTAINABLEPORTS 2024)

Workshop Organizers

Giuseppe Musolino	Mediterranea University of Reggio Calabria, Italy
Tiziana Campisi	University of Enna Kore, Italy
Efstathios Bouhouras	Aristotle University of Thessaloniki, Greece
Elena Cocuzza	University of Catania, Italy
Gianfranco Fancello	University of Cagliari, Italy
Massimo Di Gangi	University of Messina, Italy

Workshop Program Committee Members

Georgios Vaggelas	National and Kapodistrian University of Athens, Greece
Antonio Polimeni	University of Messina, Italy

Orlando Belcore	University of Messina, Italy
Lucia Dalla Spina	Mediterranea University of Reggio Calabria, Italy
Elen Twerdy	University of Lubljana, Slovenia
Claudia Caballini	Polytechnic University of Turin, Italy

Theoretical and Computational Chemistry and Its Applications (TCCMA 2024)

Workshop Organizers

Noelia Faginas-Lago	University of Perugia, Italy
Andrea Lombardi	University of Perugia, Italy
Marcos Mandado	University of Vigo, Spain

Workshop Program Committee Members

Ángel Martín Pendás	University of Oviedo, Spain
Ernesto Garcia Para	University of Basque Country, Spain
Giovanni Bistoni	University of Perugia, Italy
Juan Jose Nogueira Perez	University Autonoma of Madrid, Spain
Jose Hermida	Universidade di Vigo, Spain
Luca Mancini	University of Perugia, Italy

Transport Infrastructures for Smart Cities (TISC 2024)

Workshop Organizers

Francesca Maltinti	University of Cagliari, Italy
Mauro Coni	University of Cagliari, Italy
Francesco Pinna	University of Cagliari, Italy
Chiara Garau	University of Cagliari, Italy
Nicoletta Rassu	University of Cagliari, Italy
James Rombi	University of Cagliari, Italy

Workshop Program Committee Members

Benedetto Barabino	University of Brescia, Italy
Martina Carra	University of Brescia, Italy

Mauro D'Apuzzo	University of Cassino, Italy
Roberto Minunno	Curtin University, Australia
Claudia Loggia	University of KwaZulu-Natal, South Africa
Amir Kavussi	Tarbiat Modares University, Iran
Tiziana Campisi	University of Enna Kore, Italy
Alessandro Plaisant	University of Sassari, Italy
Elena Cocuzza	University of Catania, Italy
Vincenza Torrisi	University of Catania, Italy

From Structural to Transformative-Change of City Environment: Challenges and Solutions and Perspectives (TRACE 2024)

Workshop Organizers

Maria Rosaria Guarini	Sapienza University of Rome, Italy
Francesco Sica	Sapienza University of Rome, Italy
Carmelo Maria Torre	Polytechnic University of Bari, Italy
Francesco Tajani	Polytechnic University of Bari, Italy

Workshop Program Committee Members

Angela Pilogallo	Italian National Research Council, Italy
Maria Cerreta	University of Naples Federico II, Italy
Giuseppe Cerullo	Sapienza University of Rome, Italy

Transport and Digital Multiscale Sustainable Network for Circular Economy (TransNet 2024)

Workshop Organizers

Andrea Gallo	University of Trieste, Italy
Mara Ladu	University of Cagliari, Italy
Enrico Dagostini	University of Malta, Malta
Salvatore Dore	University of Trieste, Italy
Martina Sinatra	University of Cagliari, Italy
Francesca Sinatra	University of Trieste, Italy

Workshop Program Committee Members

Martina Carra	University of Brescia, Italy
Ginevra Baletto	University of Cagliari, Italy
Giuseppe Borruso	University of Trieste, Italy
Beniamino Murgante	University of Basilicata, Italy
Maria del Mar Munoz Leonisio	Univeristy of Cadiz, Spain
Ahinoa Amaro Garcia	Univeristy of Las Palmas of Gran Canaria, Spain
Malgorzata Hanzl	Lodz University of Technology, Poland
Balázs Kulcsár	University of Debrecen, Hungary

Temporary Real Estate Management: Approaches and Methods for Time-Integrated Impact Assessments and Evaluations (TREAT 2024)

Workshop Organizers

Chiara Mazzarella	TU Delft, The Netherlands
Hilde Remoy	TU Delft, The Netherlands
Maria Cerreta	University of Naples Federico II, Italy

Workshop Program Committee Members

Maria Lucia Raiola	University of Naples Federico II, Italy
Eugenio Muccio	University of Naples Federico II, Italy
Daniele Cannatella	TU Delft, The Netherlands
Sabrina Sacco	University of Naples Federico II, Italy
Piero Zizzania	University of Naples Federico II, Italy
Stefano Cuntò	University of Naples Federico II, Italy
Sveva Ventre	University of Naples Federico II, Italy
Caterina Loffredo	University of Naples Federico II, Italy
Giuseppe Ciciriello	University of Naples Federico II, Italy
Maria Somma	University of Naples Federico II, Italy
Ludovica La Rocca	University of Naples Federico II, Italy
Laura Di Tommaso	University of Naples Federico II, Italy
Benedetta Grieco	University of Naples Federico II, Italy
Gaia Daldanise	National Research Council, Italy
Simona Panaro	University of Sussex, UK
Giuliano Poli	University of Naples Federico II, Italy

Urban Regeneration: Innovative Tools and Evaluation Model (URITEM 2024)

Workshop Organizers

Fabrizio Battisti	University of Florence, Italy
Giovanna Acampa	University of Florence and University of Enna Kore, Italy
Orazio Campo	La Sapienza University of Rome, Italy

Workshop Program Committee Members

Alice Barreca	Polytechnic of Turin, Italy
Marco Rossitti	Polytechnic of Milan, Italy
Celestina Fazia	University of Enna Kore, Italy

Urban Space Accessibility and Mobilities (USAM 2024)

Workshop Organizers

Chiara Garau	University of Cagliari, Italy
Alessandro Plaisant	University of Sassari, Italy
Barbara Caselli	University of Parma, Italy
Gabriele D'Orso	University of Palermo, Italy
Mauro D'Apuzzo	University of Cassino, Italy
Matteo Ignaccolo	University of Catania, Italy

Workshop Program Committee Members

Ivan Blečić	University of Cagliari, Italy
Mauro Coni	University of Cagliari, Italy
Martina Carra	University of Brescia, Italy
Tiziana Campisi	University of Enna Kore, Italy
Tanja Congiu	University of Sassari, Italy
Francesca Maltinti	University of Cagliari, Italy
Silvia Rossetti	University of Parma, Italy
Angela Pilogallo	Italian National Research Council, Italy
Lorena Fiorini	University of L'Aquila, Italy
Francesco Pinna	University of Cagliari, Italy

Aime Tsinda	University of Rwanda, Rwanda
Nicoletta Rassu	University of Cagliari, Italy
Youssef El Ganadi	International University of Rabat, Morocco
Marco Migliore	University of Palermo, Italy
Elena Cocuzza	University of Catania, Italy
Alessio Salvatore	Italian National Research Council, Italy
Giuseppe Stecca	Italian National Research Council, Italy
Gerardo Carpentieri	University of Naples Federico II, Italy
Carmen Guida	University of Naples Federico II, Italy
Floriana Zucaro	University of Naples Federico II, Italy

Virtual Reality and Augmented Reality and Applications (VRA 2024)

Workshop Organizers

Osvaldo Gervasi	University of Perugia, Italy
Damiano Perri	University of Florence, Italy
Sergio Tasso	University of Perugia, Italy

Workshop Program Committee Members

Massimiliano Nicolini	OliTec Foundation, Italy
JungYoon Kim	Gachon University, South Korea
Paolo Nesi	University of Florence, Italy
David Berti	ART SpA, Italy
Tamie Salter	Citizen Alert Inc., Canada
Marcelo Guimarães	Federal University of São Paulo, Brazil

Workshop on Advanced and Computational Methods for Earth Science Applications (WACM4ES 2024)

Workshop Organizers

Luca Piroddi	University of Malta, Malta
Patrizia Capizzi	University of Palermo, Italy
Marilena Cozzolino	Università Del Molise, Italy
Sebastiano D'Amico	University of Malta, Malta
Chiara Garau	University of Cagliari, Italy
Giuseppina Vacca	University of Cagliari, Italy

Workshop Program Committee Members

Andrea Angelini	ISPC, CNR, Italy
Raffaele Martorana	University of Palermo, Italy
Paolo Mauriello	University of Molise, Italy
Raffaele Persico	University of Calabria, Italy
Eufemia Tarantino	Polytechnic of Bari, Italy
Roberto Ricciu	University of Cagliari, Italy
Stefano Sfarra	University of L'Aquila, Italy
Peter Iregbeyen	University of Malta, Malta
Elisa Pilia	University of Cagliari, Italy
Emanuele Colica	Ministry for Transport, Infrastructure and Public Works, Malta
Luciano Galone	University of Malta, Malta
Sergio Vincenzo Calcina	University of Cagliari, Italy
Maria Brovelli	Polytechnic of Milan, Italy
Francesca Trevisiol	University of Bologna, Italy

Additional Reviewers

Burak Aslan	Izmir Institute of Technology, Turkey
Birim Balcı	Manisa Celal Bayar University, Turkey
Atrin Barzegar	Università degli Studi della Campania L. Vanvitelli, Italy
Manuel Carlos Figueiredo	University of Minho, Portugal
Chiara Chioni	University of Trento, Italy
Annalisa Contato	University of Palermo, Italy
Aurora Costales	Universidad de Oviedo, Spain
Hamid Daneshpajouh	Middle East Technical University, Turkey
Vito Dario Camiola	Università di Catania, Italy
Roberta De Fazio	Università degli Studi della Campania Luigi Vanvitelli, Italy
Michele Di Giovanni	Università degli Studi della Campania, Italy
David Ferro Costas	University of Santiago de Compostela, Spain
Michal Hnatič	P.J. Šafarik University in Košice, Slovak Republic
Francesco Loddo	Henge S.r.l., Italy
Caterina Loffredo	University of Naples Federico II, Italy
Vanda Lourenco	Universidade Nova de Lisboa, Portugal
Ángel Martín Pendás	Universidad de Oviedo, Spain
Maria Mourao	Polytechnic Institute of Viana do Castelo, Portugal

Martin Perez Perez	University of Vigo, Spain
Marco Pezzella	University of Perugia, Italy
Maria Polidoro	ESTG IPP, Portugal
Josef Rebenda	Brno University of Technology, Czech Republic
Donatella Rita Fiorino	University of Cagliari, Italy
Evgeniy Romenskiy	Sobolev Institute of Mathematics, Russia
Ezgi Sahin Toptal	Mersin University, Turkey
Domenica Savia Pellicanò	Mediterranean University of Reggio Calabria, Italy
Carina Silva	ESTeSL-IPL, Portugal
Paula Simões	CMA FCT UNL CINAMIL, Portugal
Francesca Sinatra	University of Trieste, Italy
Ana Sofia Rézio	Iscal, Portugal
Alexandra Stankulova	Politecnico di Torino, Italy
Maria Stella De Biase	Università della Campania Luigi Vanvitelli, Italy
Guan Yue Hong	Western Michigan University, USA

Sponsoring Organizations

ICCSA 2024 would not have been possible without the tremendous support of many organizations and institutions, for which all organizers and participants of ICCSA 2024 express their sincere gratitude:

Springer

Springer Nature Switzerland AG, Switzerland
(https://www.springer.com)

computers

Computers Open Access Journal
(https://www.mdpi.com/journal/computers)

Thuyloi University, Hanoi, Vietnam
(https://en.tlu.edu.vn/)

University of Perugia, Italy
(https://www.unipg.it)

University of Basilicata, Italy
(http://www.unibas.it)

Monash University, Australia
(https://www.monash.edu/)

Kyushu Sangyo University, Japan
(https://www.kyusan-u.ac.jp/)

Universidade do Minho
Escola de Engenharia

University of Minho, Portugal
(https://www.uminho.pt/)

University of Cagliari, Italy
(https://en.unica.it/en)

Venue

ICCSA 2024 took place on the main campus of Thuyloi University in Hanoi, Vietnam.

Plenary Lectures

Harnessing Artificial Intelligence for Enhanced Spatial Analysis of Natural Hazard Assessments

Prof. Dr. Biswajeet Pradhan

Director - Centre for Advanced Modelling and Geospatial Information Systems (CAMGIS), School of Civil and Environmental Engineering, Faculty of Engineering and IT, University of Technology Sydney, Australia

Abstract. In the realm of natural hazard assessments within spatial domains, the advent of Artificial Intelligence (AI) represents a paradigm shift, revolutionizing the way we conceptualize, model, and interpret environmental risks. This keynote address illuminates the profound impact of AI technologies, particularly machine learning algorithms and data-driven approaches, in reshaping our understanding and prediction capabilities concerning natural disasters.

By assimilating and scrutinizing vast spatial datasets, AI-driven models offer unparalleled accuracy and efficiency, facilitating timely and precise hazard assessments. Real-time processing of geospatial information not only enables rapid predictions but also forms the cornerstone of proactive disaster management strategies. Furthermore, AI's capacity lies in its adeptness at deciphering intricate spatial patterns inherent to natural hazards, unraveling subtle cues and previously unnoticed correlations within the data fabric.

This keynote delves into how AI's nuanced interpretation, coupled with advanced algorithms, elevates hazard modeling, providing deeper insights into the spatial dynamics of environmental risks. By augmenting traditional methodologies and revealing hidden patterns, AI fosters comprehensive risk assessments, fostering informed decision-making processes. The fusion of AI and natural hazard assessments in spatial domains heralds a more resilient approach to disaster preparedness and response.

Join us in embracing this transformative era, where AI's sophisticated modeling techniques and precise spatial interpretations converge, heralding proactive and effective mitigation strategies amidst the ever-evolving landscape of environmental challenges.

Short Bio. Distinguished Professor Dr. Biswajeet Pradhan is an internationally established scientist in the field of Geospatial Information Systems (GIS), remote sensing and image processing, complex modelling/geo-computing, machine learning and soft-computing applications, natural hazards and environmental modelling. He is the Director of the Centre for Advanced Modelling and Geospatial Information Systems (CAMGIS) at the Faculty of Engineering and IT at the University of Technology, Sydney (Australia). He was listed as the World's Most Highly Cited Researcher by the Clarivate Analytics Report for five consecutive years, 2016–2020, as one of the world's most influential minds.

He ranked number one (1) in the field of "Geological & Geomatics Engineering" during the calendar year 2021–2023, according to the list published by Stanford University Researchers, USA. This list ranks the world's top 2% most highly cited researchers based on Scopus data. In 2018–2020, he was awarded as World Class Professor by the Ministry of Research, Technology and Higher Education, Indonesia. He is a recipient of the Alexander von Humboldt Research Fellowship from Germany. Between 2015–2021, he served as "Ambassador Scientist" for the Alexander Humboldt Foundation, Germany.

Professor Pradhan has received 58 awards since 2006 in recognition of his excellence in teaching, service and research. Out of his more than 850 articles (Google Scholar citation: 70,000, H-index: 129), more than 750 have been published in science citation index (SCI/SCIE) technical journals. He has authored/co-authored ten books and thirteen book chapters.

Software Engineering Research in a New Situation

Prof. Carl K. Chang

Professor Emeritus, Iowa State University, USA

Abstract. With the rise of Generative Artificial Intelligence (GAI), epitomized by Large Language Models (LLMs), a profound shift has unfolded in software engineering research. In this presentation, I will traverse my four-decade journey in software engineering research, focusing on situational awareness in the era of the Internet of Things (IoT). I have witnessed the turbulence brought forth by the AI community that demands changes in our approaches. Meanwhile, owing to the pervasiveness of services computing, services became the first-class citizen in modern-day software engineering methodologies.

I argue that situational awareness must permeate the entire lifecycle to consistently deliver software services that align with the dynamic needs of users and the ever-evolving environments. I will elucidate this argument by reviewing the Situ framework, offering a comprehensive illustration of my perspective. Furthermore, I will outline my vision regarding the formidable research challenges considering the rapidly shifting landscape dominated by an irresistible and profoundly disruptive generative AI tsunami.

Short Bio. Carl K. Chang is a former department chair and Professor Emeritus of Computer Science at Iowa State University. His research interests include requirements engineering, net-centric computing, situational software engineering and digital health. Chang was the 2004 President of the IEEE Computer Society. Previously he served as the Editor-in-Chief for IEEE Software (1991–1994), and as the Editor-in-Chief of IEEE Computer (2007–2010). He was the 2012 recipient of the Richard E. Merwin Medal from the IEEE Computer Society. Chang is a Life Fellow of IEEE, a Fellow of AAAS, and a Life Member of the European Academy of Sciences (EurASc).

Interpretability and Privacy Preservation in Large Language Models (LLMs)

Prof. My Thai

University of Florida (UF) Research Foundation Professor
Associate Director of UF Nelms Institute for the Connected World

Abstract. Large Language Models (LLMs) have transformed the AI landscape, captivating researchers and practitioners with their remarkable ability to generate human-like text and perform complex tasks. However, this transformative power comes with a set of critical challenges, particularly in the realms of interpretability and privacy preservation. In this keynote, we embark on an exploration of these pressing issues, shedding light on how LLMs operate, their limitations, and the strategies we can employ to mitigate risks. We begin by examining the interpretability in LLMs, which often function as enigmatic "black boxes." Their complex neural architectures make it challenging to understand how they arrive at specific outputs. This lack of transparency raises questions of trust and accountability. When deploying LLMs in real-world applications—whether for chatbots, content generation, or decision-making—it becomes crucial to demystify their decision paths.

We will use explainable AI (XAI) to offer faithful explanations, from the black-box to white-box models, and from feature-based [1, 2] to neuron circuits-based [3, 4] explanations. By visualizing attention mechanisms, feature importance, and saliency maps, we empower users to comprehend LLM predictions. XAI not only fosters trust but also encourages responsible utilization of LLMs.

We next turn our attention to one of the utmost concerns and challenges: data privacy. LLMs process vast amounts of data, raising risks of data leakage, model inversion, the right to be forgotten, and inadvertent exposure of sensitive information. Furthermore, the integration of LLMs into diverse applications also significantly brings these challenges to the next level [5]. This talk explores strategies to protect privacy, including differential privacy, federated learning, and data encryption.

Short Bio. My T. Thai is a University of Florida (UF) Research Foundation Professor, Associate Director of UF Nelms Institute for the Connected World, and a Fellow of IEEE and AAIA. Dr. Thai is a leading authority who has done transformative research in Trustworthy AI and Optimization, especially for complex systems with applications to healthcare, social media, critical networking infrastructure, and cybersecurity. The results of her work have led to 7 books and 350+ publications in highly ranked international journals and conferences, including several best paper awards from the IEEE, ACM, and AAAI.

In responding to a world-wide call for responsible and safe AI, Dr. Thai is a pioneer in designing deep explanations for black-box ML models, while defending against explanation-guided attacks, evident by her Distinguished Papers Award at the Association for the Advancement of Artificial Intelligence (AAAI) conference in 2023. At the same year, she was also awarded an ACM Web Science Trust Test-of-Time award, for her landmark work on combating misinformation in social media. In 2022, she received an IEEE Big Data Security Women of Achievement Award. In 2009, she was awarded the Young Investigator (YIP) from the Defense Threat Reduction Agency (DTRA), and in 2010 she won the NSF CAREER Award. She is presently the Editor-in-Chief of the Springer Journal of Combinatorial Optimization and the IET Blockchain Journal, and editor of the Springer book series Optimization and Its Applications.

References

1. Vu, M., Thai, M.T.: PGM-explainer: probabilistic graphical model explanations for graph neural networks. In: Advances in Neural Information Processing Systems (NeurIPS) (2020)
2. Nguyen, T., Lai, P., Phan, H., Thai, M.T.: XRand: differentially private defense against explanation-guided attacks. In: AAAI Conference on Artificial Intelligence (AAAI) (2023)
3. Vu, N., Nguyen, T., Thai, M.T.: NeuCEPT: learn neural networks' mechanism via critical neurons with precision guarantee. In: IEEE International Conference on Data Mining (ICDM) (2022)

4. Conmy, A., Mavor-Parker, A., Heimersheim, S., Garriga-Alonso, A.: Towards automated circuit discovery for mechanistic interpretability. In: Advances in Neural Information Processing Systems (NeurIPS) (2023)
5. Vu, M., Nguyen, T., Jeter, T., Thai, M.T.: Analysis of privacy leakages in federated large language models. In: International Conference on Artificial Intelligence and Statistics (AISTATS) (2023)

Contents – Part I

Blockchain and Distributed Ledgers: Technologies and Applications (BDLTA 2024)

Computational and Applied Mathematics (CAM 2024)

Advances in Artificial Intelligence Learning Technologies: Blended Learning, STEM, Computational Thinking and Coding (AAILT 2024)

Large Language Models for Emotion Evolution Prediction

Clement Leung[1(✉)] and Zhifei Xu[2]

[1] School of Science and Engineering and Guangdong Provincial Key Laboratory of Future Networks of Intelligence, Chinese University of Hong Kong, Shenzhen, China
clementleung@cuhk.edu.cn

[2] School of Science and Engineering, Chinese University of Hong Kong, Shenzhen, China
zhifeixu@link.cuhk.edu.cn

Abstract. In numerous tasks, especially those of critical safety importance, it is essential that the human participants maintain appropriate emotional states. Recognizing these emotional states accurately has become a key focus, with mainstream approaches typically leveraging Pre-trained Language Models (PLMs) to integrate emotional insights. Recent advancements in Large Language Models (LLMs), like ChatGPT, have shown impressive proficiency in a range of natural language processing applications. Yet, the exploration into ChatGPT's zero-shot capabilities in the realm of image-based emotion recognition and analysis has been notably under-examined. In our research, we study the classification and prediction of emotions, distinguishing between positive and negative states, and we critically assess the ability of ChatGPT4 to recognize emotions from images, putting a spotlight on its potential in this area. The experimental results show that ChatGPT4 can effectively predict the evolution of emotion, and the accuracy of the evolution of positive and negative emotions is more than expected. However, ChatGPT4's prediction of specific negative emotions has gaps.

Keywords: image emotion prediction · Large Language Model · ChatGPT4 · zero-shot

1 Introduction and Related Works

In the complex landscape of human interactions, the nuanced portrayal and perception of emotions are fundamental. They not only facilitate meaningful connections but also serve as crucial indicators of well-being and intent. Meanwhile, research on how to imbue human-computer dialogue systems with emotions has It has been going on for ten years [3,4,12]. Furthermore, given the current perception of ChatGPT [14] and Instruct-GPT [18] as potent and versatile tools across various domains, we aim to explore their potential in facilitating accurate emotion recognition. Emotional support is increasingly becoming essential in numerous conversational contexts, including social interactions, mental

O. Gervasi et al. (Eds.): ICCSA 2024 Workshops, LNCS 14815, pp. 3–19, 2024.
https://doi.org/10.1007/978-3-031-65154-0_1

health assistance, and customer service chats. Thus, our research study assesses ChatGPT4's [1] efficiency and capability in identifying emotions through facial expressions.

Emotion recognition and prediction have garnered significant attention for their potential to enhance safety, support mental health, and improve user experiences. Emotion recognition and prediction have been recognized to be a significant factor affecting human safety and have been widely studied [2,27]. There exist in general multiple ways for people to express their emotions or feelings naturally, such as voice, text, video, facial expressions, and physical language.

In the modern world, where technology is ever more entwined with our daily activities, the ability of artificial intelligence to perceive and understand human emotions is becoming indispensable [22]. The importance of emotionally aware AI is magnified across various applications, reflecting the increasing pressures society faces today-ranging from criticism from superiors and unfair treatment to the pain of romantic separations [13,23]. Such stressors can push individuals to the brink, leading to a loss of emotional control. This, in turn, might result in harmful behaviors towards oneself or others. The evidence of emotional distress manifesting in severe outcomes is abundant: individuals grappling with suicidal ideation amidst academic or professional pressures [23]; the distressing prevalence of school shootings in the United States; or catastrophic accidents caused by road rage. Furthermore, in certain professions, emotional stability is critically important-consider the roles of surgeons, pilots, or truck drivers. For instance, there was a disturbing case where a pilot, suffering from depression, attempted to disable the plane's engines mid-flight [13]. This underscores the vital necessity for advancements in emotion recognition and prediction technologies in our lives [7].

In Recent years, generating emotional responses using neural networks has become a research hotspot [26], credit to the rapid development of online social networks and deep learning. In addition, with the continuous emergence of large language model technology and its rapid iterative development, many Human-computer interaction robots and artificial intelligence have brought a new technological revolution in the field of dialogue represented by ChatGPT4. At the same time, they demonstrate powerful general-purpose language processing capabilities and bring unprecedented human semantic understanding and response generation capabilities. Since their emergence, the interaction experience with human users has been greatly improved. However the question of whether emotions are shown in conversations has not yet been explored, and we are interested in developing effective conversation techniques in ChatGPT4. At the same time, we hope to explore the research progress, advantage analysis, and shortcomings [11,24,29] of ChatGPT4's multi-modal task emotion recognition and prediction fields. Moreover, the use of ChatGPT-4 for emotion recognition and prediction is deemed to enhance the fairness of experimental procedures. This is attributed to ChatGPT-4's ability as a large language model to analyze data without the bias and subjectivity often inherent in human judgment. The paragraph underscores the importance of this approach not only for maintaining fairness but also for focusing on safety and well-being. By accurately identifying emotional states, interventions can be better tailored and more effectively implemented, thereby safeguarding participants and ensuring ethical standards are met within experimental frameworks.

In addition, in the field of emotion recognition and prediction, the main methods are studied by Ekman [5] and is one of the most famous classification models. He identified six basic emotions: joy, sadness, fear, anger, surprise, and disgust, which are considered universally identifiable. Plutchik has since expanded Ekman's model to propose eight major emotions [20] structured in a wheel format, including joy, trust, fear, surprise, sadness, disgust, anger, and anticipation. The model they proposed is a classification model, one of the two main framework models. Categorical models, also known as discrete emotion models, assume that there are a certain number of primary or basic emotions that are universally recognized and experienced by humans, regardless of cultural or individual differences. The other is the continuum model, which conceptualizes emotions as a spectrum or continuum [9,10], allowing for Valence (the positive or negative nature of the emotion), Arousal (the level of excitement or calmness), and Dominance (the level of excitement or calmness in a situation), degree of control or influence felt.

Studying emotion recognition and prediction has traditionally focused on a singular mode of expression. However, humans communicate emotions through various channels, including voice, text, video, facial expressions, and physical gestures, making it challenging to accurately discern emotions from a single source. The practice of multimodal sentiment classification, which merges information from multiple sources such as audio, dynamic shape, and global appearance features [17], addresses this complexity. This approach leverages the combined use of multi-modal datasets, incorporating both text and images, along with advanced analytical techniques like convolutional neural networks (CNNs) [8,28] or transforms for enhanced emotion recognition and classification. Given that emotions typically evolve in real-life situations, it is also crucial to predict their progression.

2 Methodology

Because in our real world, people's emotions are usually continuous, transitioning from one emotional state to another [15,21]. Depending on the actual situation, it is often necessary to predict and identify the emotional state of relevant personnel, for example: arranging surgeries in hospitals, pilots flying airplanes, scheduling work in high-risk industries, etc. As mentioned earlier, people may behave emotionally if they are tired or have been treated unfairly. In safety-critical jobs, we want the person doing the work to be in a sound emotional state [13]. In other words, people who work in high-risk industries can endanger the safety of others if they have emotional problems.

In this article, we focus on analyzing the classification model, while adopting the Ekman model, for Ekman's categories using the six primary emotions of happiness, sadness, fear, anger, surprise, and disgust, we also group these into positive and negative emotions. We group the states happiness and surprise as positive (+1) emotions and group sadness, fear, anger, and disgust as negative (−1) emotions. As a variation, for safety-critical jobs, we may wish to be extra safe and more strict concerning positive emotion, and we may take surprise out from the positive emotion category, and place it in the negative emotion category. Here, though, we place surprise in the positive emotion category.

The model $S(t)$ encapsulates the emotional dynamics of an individual over time, where t represents the temporal dimension and $S(t)$ reflects shifts in emotional states due to time's passage. Specifically, the model assigns a value of 1 to denote positive emotions and −1 for negative emotions. The complexity of human emotions stems from an array of external stimuli that individuals have little to no control over. These stimuli can originate from numerous aspects of life such as financial status, personal relationships, health conditions, professional environments, the stock market, and family dynamics. It is the interplay of these factors that can prompt a shift from a state of positive to negative emotions, or the reverse.

Initially, we set $S(0) = 1$. Next, we model the moments of transition (switching from +1 to −1 or vice versa) using a Poisson Process. Consequently, $S(t)$ will equal 1 when the count of transitions within the period $(0, t)$ is an even number, and $S(t)$ will be −1 whenever this count is odd. Thus,

$$P[S(t) = 1|S(0) = 1] = p_0 + p_2 + p_4 + ... + ..., \tag{1}$$

where p_k is the number of Poisson points in $(0, t)$ with parameter λ. That is,

$$\begin{aligned} P[S(t) = 1|S(0) = 1] &= e^{-\lambda t}[1 + \frac{(\lambda t)^2}{2!} + \frac{(\lambda t)^4}{4!} ... + ...] \\ &= e^{-\lambda t} \cosh \lambda t \end{aligned} \tag{2}$$

Now, $S(t) = -1$ if the number of points in the time interval $(0, t)$ is odd; that is,

$$\begin{aligned} P[S(t) = -1|S(0) = 1]] &= e^{-\lambda t}[1 + \frac{(\lambda t)^3}{3!} + \frac{(\lambda t)^5}{5!} ... + ...] \\ &= e^{-\lambda t} \sinh \lambda t \end{aligned} \tag{3}$$

Equation 2 represents the probability that the emotion is still positive at time t given that it was positive at time 0. Equation 3 gives the probability that the emotion is negative at time t given that it was positive at time 0. The parameter λ in both expressions represents a rate at which emotions change or decay over time. A larger value of λ would mean emotions change more rapidly, while a smaller value would mean they change more slowly. This is where we mathematically analyze possible emotional changes and predict them. Also, to verify the idea, we use ChatGPT. As for the experimental evaluation part, the Receiver Operating Characteristic (ROC) method was adopted to analyze the experimental results, and a specific explanation was placed in the experimental part.

Here we briefly explain the above equation, first, we assume that lambda is 0.3, 0.6, 0.9. Meanwhile, The figure, labeled as Fig. 1, displays the function $e^{-\lambda t}\sinh(\lambda t)$ with λ values of 0.3, 0.6, and 0.9, Displaying the function $e^{-\lambda t}\sinh(\lambda t)$with λvalues of 0.3, 0.6, and 0.9, provides insightful observations about the temporal changes in probabilities, especially relevant to emotional states or comparable processes that may either diminish or progress over time. It is evident from the visualization that varying the decay constants (λ) significantly affects how long and intensely certain states persist across several days.

With a decay constant of $\lambda = 0.3$, the probability initially is high but diminishes gradually, indicating a persistent or slowly fading condition. For example, maintaining a negative emotional state translates to a higher likelihood of remaining in this state longer. Within the initial day, the probability stays well above 60%, denoting a strong endurance of the state. By day three, it hovers around 50%, showing a steady, yet noticeable decline. This gradual reduction might symbolize scenarios where the causes behind the emotional state are slow to be addressed or alleviated.

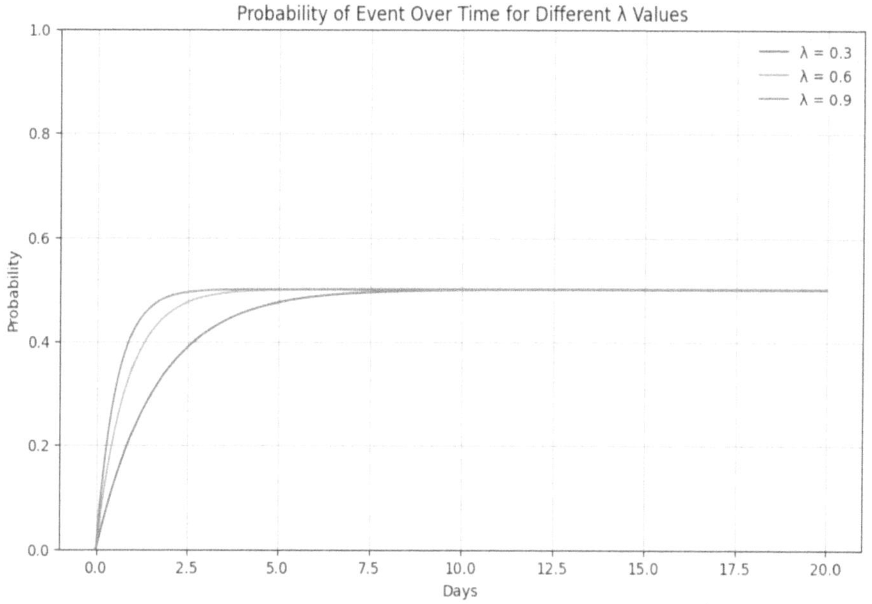

Fig. 1. Different λ of the Eq. 3

Increasing the decay constant to $\lambda = 0.6$ accelerates the probability's decline. This faster fall suggests a quicker fading of the emotional intensity or the likelihood of sustaining the same state. On the first day, the probability remains elevated but swiftly falls below 60%, nearing 50% by the close of the second day. This quicker reduction may be associated with effective interventions or environmental changes, or possibly better coping strategies that shorten the duration of the negative condition.

At $\lambda = 0.9$, the probability decreases even more swiftly. The graph shows a sharp descent, indicative of scenarios where negative emotional states or similar conditions dissipate very quickly. The probability does not stay above 50% beyond two days, dropping near this mark by the end of the first day. This rapid decline could point to highly effective external support or events that inherently do not have prolonged effects.

By analyzing these curves, one can determine how various strategies or intrinsic elements affect the control or maintenance of specific states-be they emotional, physical, or of another nature. The differing λ values symbolically illustrate the varied speeds at which environments, individuals, or systems either normalize or transition from one state to another. This knowledge is essential in areas such as psychology, where predicting the duration of an individual's negative emotional state is key to developing timely and effective interventions. Insights into these temporal patterns are invaluable for customizing interventions or supports that are sensitive to timing and more closely correspond to the observed rates of change.

3 Experimentation

Emotion prediction in conversation is the convergence area of artificial intelligence and natural language processing. It involves analyzing data from text, images, and even audio to identify and predict the emotional state of participants during a conversation. This is useful for a variety of applications, such as improving customer service interactions, supporting mental health assessments, and enhancing human-computer interaction. In addition, conversational emotion recognition predictions can be analyzed and judged by chatbots to assess the current user's emotional state and responses to emotion drivers. From the above, ChatGPT4 is a form of conversational robot, and we hope to explore and analyze whether it can usefully predict changes in emotions.

3.1 Emotion Prediction with Different Situations

For the experimental part, we chose three Data sets from Kaggle which are Emotion Detection, Facial Expressions Training Data, and Natural Human Face Images for Emotion Recognition.

Dataset Emotion Detection. This dataset is the same as the FER-2013 [25] dataset. The collection features 35,685 grayscale images, each 48×48 pixels, organized into two sections: training and testing. Each section hosts a variety of images representing different emotional states. The images have been categorized by the creators into several emotions, namely anger, disgust, fear, happiness, neutrality, sadness, and surprise, providing a comprehensive basis for emotion detection tasks.

Table 1. Sample of Four Different Situations

Dataset	Question 1	Question 2	Question 3	Question 4
	what emotion of this person? If they are about to be praised by their boss or their parents respectively, what do you think their emotions become?	If they were to be criticized separately, what do you think their emotions would be?	If they were to each receive a $1,000 reward, what do you think their emotions would be?	If they were to break up, what do you think their emotions would be?
	what emotion of this person? If they are about to be praised by their boss or their parents respectively, what do you think their emotions become?	If they were to be criticized separately, what do you think their emotions would be?	If they were to each receive a $1,000 reward, what do you think their emotions would be?	If they were to break up, what do you think their emotions would be?
	what emotion of this person? If they are about to be praised by their boss or their parents respectively, what do you think their emotions become?	If they were to be criticized separately, what do you think their emotions would be?	If they were to each receive a $1,000 reward, what do you think their emotions would be?	If they were to break up, what do you think their emotions would be?

Facial Expression Training Data. The AffectNet [16] database, a substantial compilation of facial images annotated with expressions, serves as the foundation for this dataset. To adapt to typical memory constraints, image resolution is scaled down to 96×96 pixels. The dataset employs Principal Component Analysis, specifically focusing on the Singular Value Decomposition method, to enhance image processing efficiency. A threshold is applied to ensure the Principal Component's percentage remains below 90%, primarily excluding monochrome images. The dataset, derived from the high-quality AffectNet repository and refined using advanced Facial Expression Recognition technology, spans eight emotional categories: anger, contempt, disgust, fear, happiness, neutrality, sadness, and surprise.

Natural Human Face Images for Emotion Recognition. Unlike traditional datasets used in facial expression recognition like Facial Expression Recognition dataset (FER), Extended Cohn-Kanade dataset (CK+), and Karolinska Directed Emotional Faces dataset (KDEF), this unique dataset is curated from the internet, encompassing over 5,500 images manually labeled for eight emotional expressions: anger, contempt, disgust, fear, happiness, neutrality, sadness, and surprise. Each image, capturing real human expressions in 224×224 pixel grayscale format, is meticulously selected from various online sources, including Google, Unsplash, and Flickr, ensuring a wide array of natural facial expressions for enhanced learning and recognition tasks.

Task Definition of Emotion Prediction with Four Situations. According to the above description, we use three data sets and select 6 types anger, disgust, happiness, neutral, sadness, and surprise in the data set. In each data set, 10 images of 6 emotions are randomly selected and put into ChatGPT4 for judgment. As for the prompt words in Table 1, we want to preliminarily explore and predict the changes of emotion, so we choose four scenarios that are most likely to produce emotional changes in real life. At the same time, we artificially provide 4 situation simulations for each image, two positive situations, and two negative situations. (For details of specific questions see Table 1)

Predict the emotional changes of the image based on the simulated situation. Since ChatGPT4 will be released in 2023, the above experiments were all conducted using ChatGPT4. We use supervised learning and evaluate the performance of ChatGPT4 in a zero-shot prompt setting for the above tasks. After the judgment of ChatGPT4, if the result is the same as our cognitive result, it is recorded as 1, if the result is different, it is recorded as 0, in other words, the predicted results must be consistent with the logical results of most cognitive and emotional changes in real society and be consistent with common sense and recorded as positive or negative according to the emotion according to the description of ChatGPT4. Moreover, we construct a Receiver Operating Characteristic (ROC) [6] curve utilizing the outcomes we have documented. Within this curve, positive emotions such as happiness, neutrality, or surprise are assigned a value of 1, while negative emotions like anger, disgust, or sadness are designated with a value of 0. ChatGPT4's predictions for positive emotions are marked as 1 when they align with the actual outcomes, and as 0 when they do not. Similarly, for negative emotions, a matching prediction is indicated by a 0, and a mismatching one by a 1. The confidence level of these predictions is categorized on a scale from 1 to 3, where 1 indicates low confidence, 2 signifies moderate confidence, and 3 represents high confidence.

Table 2. Result of Four Different Situations

Emotion	Parameter	Positive Situation	Negative Situation
Anger	accuracy	68.30%	73.30%
	sensitivity	NaN	NaN
	specificity	68.30%	73.30%
Disgust	accuracy	78.30%	85.00%
	sensitivity	NaN	NaN
	specificity	78.30%	85.00%
Happiness	accuracy	91.70%	83.30%
	sensitivity	91.70%	83.30%
	specificity	NaN	NaN
Neutral	accuracy	86.70%	83.30%
	sensitivity	86.70%	83.30%
	specificity	NaN	NaN
Sad	accuracy	71.70%	80.00%
	sensitivity	NaN	NaN
	specificity	71.70%	80.00%
Surprise	accuracy	85.00%	90.00%
	sensitivity	85.00%	90.00%
	specificity	NaN	NaN
Negative	accuracy	72.80%	79.40%
	sensitivity	NaN	NaN
	specificity	72.80%	79.40%
Positive	accuracy	87.80%	85.60%
	sensitivity	87.80%	85.60%
	specificity	NaN	NaN

Preliminary Results. In the context of data presented in Table 2, the True Positive Rate (TPR), also referred to as Sensitivity, is a metric that quantifies the fraction of true positive instances accurately identified by the predictive model. Conversely, the False Positive Rate (FPR), also known as the complement of Specificity (1-Specificity), represents the proportion of negative cases that are mistakenly identified as positive by the model. The Observed Operating Points on the Receiver Operating Characteristic (ROC) curve signify the various thresholds applied within the classifier. Each of these points illustrates the equilibrium achieved between TPR and FPR at a given threshold setting. To elucidate, setting a higher threshold might lead to a reduction in FPR but at the cost of diminishing TPR, whereas a lower threshold setting is likely to elevate both TPR and FPR. These critical points are instrumental in assessing the model's efficacy and in determining the optimal threshold for the task at hand, highlighting the inherent compromise between maximizing the detection of positive instances (achieving a higher TPR) and minimizing the occurrence of false positives (achieving a lower FPR).

Table 2 shows the prediction results of ChatGPT4 for the evolution of emotions after initially identifying negative and positive emotions and describing them through two positive situations and two negative situations respectively. For images initially identified as negative emotions, we found that their ChatGPT4 prediction accuracy in negative contexts was 79.4%. However, if the situation was positive, the predicted evolution of emotion was 72.8%. In contrast, for images initially identified as having positive emotions, their response accuracy was higher in positive contexts than in negative contexts. We think that it may be due to ChatGPT4, the possibility of negative emotions turning into positive emotions when encountering a positive environment is lower than the possibility of remaining negative in a negative environment. Positive emotions have the same result. This result shows that the prediction results of ChatGPT4 are consistent with the changes in our cognitive emotions since we want to preliminary explore and predict the changes in emotion, we choose four scenarios that are most likely to produce emotional changes in real life. For details in Table 2. The explanation is that the six categories of emotions were initially explored and analyzed separately, so when calculating the ROC, we also calculated the six categories of emotions separately to obtain the experimental results. According to the above description, positive emotions are recorded as 1 and negative emotions are recorded as 0. This means that when the six types of emotions are analyzed separately, they will lack the other half of the records. In other words, if the positive emotions are calculated as ROC When, it does not contain negative emotions, which is why there is a situation where specificity is *NaN*. Vice versa is also true.

Table 4 corresponds to the prediction results of emotional changes corresponding to different events that will occur under each different emotion. First, we preliminary observe that in the case of images depicting surprise or astonishment, GPT4 demonstrates a notable capability in recognizing these emotions as such. However, it encounters difficulty in discerning whether the surprise conveys a positive or negative sentiment, leading to a tendency to classify the emotion of surprise as predominantly neutral. Consequently, this is the reason why the outcomes for surprise closely mirror those associated with neutral expressions.

In order to avoid the harm caused by negative emotions to high-risk industries or high-risk groups, we mainly look at three types of emotions: anger, disgust, and sadness. We observe that in negative emotions, if the upcoming event is positive, then the accuracy of ChatGPT4 in predicting the emotion evolution from high to low in zero-shot is disgust, sad, and anger; FPR is 78.3%, 71.7%, and 68.3% respectively. Anger is the strongest of negative emotions and the lowest in response to positive events. At the same time, because disgust is the most complex of negative emotions, including disgust, unhappiness, contempt, etc., it ranks the highest. Furthermore, the precision in identifying negative emotions falls short of expectations, suggesting that GPT4 could benefit from the inclusion of additional descriptive cues to enhance its decision-making process. Presently, in a zero-shot scenario, GPT4 is adept at recognizing the presence of negative emotions in individuals; however, it struggles with the accurate classification of specific emotions such as disgust, contempt, or anger. This is why negative predictions are less accurate than positive ones.

Analysis and Discussion. Throughout the training phase, it is common to encounter discrepancies between the emotions depicted in certain dataset images and our real-world perceptions. Due to the subjective nature of emotional interpretation, there is a possibility of encountering biases in recognizing the emotions conveyed by some images. In such instances, we rely on our judgment as the ultimate criterion and compare it to the interpretations provided by ChatGPT4.

Moreover, we have identified an additional complication: a misalignment between ChatGPT4's interpretations and the dataset's guidelines. A closer look at the specific examples of ChatGPT4's predictions highlights a fundamental issue-the disparity between the model's understanding and the dataset's standard. While the dataset might categorize an image as portraying anger based on its guidelines, ChatGPT4 might interpret the same expression as sadness or confusion. This discrepancy is not a matter of accuracy but rather an indication of differing standards used to classify negative emotions. Upon analysis, this divergence seems not solely a limitation of ChatGPT4 but could also stem from inadequate prompting. As the complexity of prompt instructions increases, expecting comprehensive coverage with minimal input becomes impractical. This realization opens up avenues for future improvements: if adhering strictly to the dataset's criteria is not mandatory, then refining the model based on broad prompt adjustments (like specifying the depicted emotions) might be viable. Yet, evaluating based on the dataset's labels could prove unsuitable, necessitating a more thorough manual review. On the contrary, if strict conformity to the dataset's guidelines is essential, relying on a multitude of prompt adjustments may fall short, making the supervised model fine-tuning a more effective strategy.

3.2 Emotion Prediction with Different Categories of Emotional Sentences

Dataset. First, we continue to use the same images as the previous task. They are still from emotion detection, facial expressions training data, and natural human faces. Each data set is still the same 10 images. But in the second task, we added a data set called MELD [19].

MELD. The Multimodal EmotionLines Dataset (MELD) builds upon and enriches the original EmotionLines dataset by incorporating additional modalities such as audio and visual elements alongside text. MELD features over 1,400 dialogue sequences and 13,000 spoken exchanges drawn from the "Friends" TV series, with various characters contributing to the conversations. Every piece of dialogue within MELD is categorized under one of seven possible emotions: Anger, Disgust, Sadness, Joy, Neutral, Surprise, and Fear. Additionally, MELD assigns a sentiment classification-positive, negative, or neutral-to each utterance, further enhancing its utility for emotion and sentiment analysis research.

Task Definition. The tasks in Part Two are partially similar to those in Part One. They all use the same images from the same dataset. However, each picture uses 6 categories of sentences full of different emotions 1. Anger, 2. Disgust, 3. Happiness, 4. Neutral, 5. Sad, 6. Surprise; think of these statements as what the character in the image is going to say. The input images and sentences are then analyzed using ChatGPT4 and the emotional evolution of any image is predicted and judged. (For details of specific questions see Table 3)

Preliminary Results. The abscissa of Table 5 represents the image of the dataset, and the ordinate represents the evolution of ChatGPT4's prediction of emotions after inputting 6 different emotional sentences. We can observe that the prediction accuracy of ChatGPT4 from high to low is: happiness, surprise, neutral, anger, sad, disgust. Among the three positive emotions, according to ChatGPT4 prediction, except for the happiness emotion that is directly converted into anger, which has the lowest accuracy, happiness is the highest for the others. At the same time, we observe that according to the description of ChatGPT4, when defining surprise and neutral, because they can be regarded as positive or negative, the results of the two are very similar. In the prediction of negative emotions, according to the above explanation of the FPR index, it shows that the disgust emotion is the least accurate to identify, and the emotion of the disgust category is the most difficult to judge among the six types of emotions. At the same time, still the same as the previous task, ChatGPT4 requires more prompts to achieve the accuracy of negative emotions. In the case of zero-shot, ChatGPT4 is not as good at predicting the evolution of emotions as in the case of positive emotions.

The vertical axis of the ROC curve denotes sensitivity, with its value directly proportional to the accuracy of diagnosis. Conversely, the horizontal axis signifies 1-specificity, where a lower value indicates a reduced rate of false positives. Generally, a point nearer to the upper left quadrant of the ROC space signals superior diagnostic performance, implying that a sensitivity approaching 1 correlates with enhanced predictive accuracy of the model. Before starting, we need to build on the explanation of partial definitions given earlier, this section

Table 3. Example of Six Different Categories Emotional Sentences

Dataset	Question 1	Question 2	Question 3	Question 4	Question 5	Question 6
	what emotion of these person? If the next thing they say is, "Well, why don't you tell her to stop being silly!" What do you think their emotions will become?	If the next sentence they say is, "Say it louder, I don't think the guy in the back heard you!" What do you think their emotions will become?	If the next sentence they say is, "Guess what, I got an audition!" What do you think their emotions will become?	If the next sentence they say is, "Great. He's doing great. Don't you worry about him?" What do you think their emotions will become?	If the next sentence they say is, "Yeah but we won't be able to like to get up in the middle of the night and have those long talks about our feelings and the future." What do you think their emotions will become?	If the next sentence they say is, "Look what I got! Look what I got! Can you believe they make these for little people?" What do you think their emotions will become?
	what emotion of these person? If the next thing they say is, "Well, why don't you tell her to stop being silly!" What do you think their emotions will become?	If the next sentence they say is, "Say it louder, I don't think the guy in the back heard you!" What do you think their emotions will become?	If the next sentence they say is, "Guess what, I got an audition!" What do you think their emotions will become?	If the next sentence they say is, "Great. He's doing great. Don't you worry about him?" What do you think their emotions will become?	If the next sentence they say is, "Yeah but we won't be able to like to get up in the middle of the night and have those long talks about our feelings and the future." What do you think their emotions will become?	If the next sentence they say is, "Look what I got! Look what I got! Can you believe they make these for little people?" What do you think their emotions will become?

focuses on the concepts of the Empirical ROC Area. The Empirical ROC Area, commonly known as the Area Under the Curve (AUC), quantifies the model's discriminative power directly from raw data by constructing an empirical ROC curve. This curve plots the True Positive Rate (TPR) against the False Pos-

Table 4. Result of Six Different Categories Emotional Sentences

Emotion	Anger sentence	disgust Sentence	Happiness sentence	Neutral Sentence	Sad sentence	Surprise sentence
Anger	70.00%	86.70%	86.70%	86.70%	86.70%	83.30%
Disgust	60.00%	70.00%	60.00%	56.70%	83.30%	56.70%
Happiness	70.00%	96.70%	1	96.70%	96.70%	96.70%
Neutral	76.70%	86.70%	96.70%	96.70%	90.00%	90.00%
Sad	63.30%	76.70%	76.70%	76.70%	86.70%	86.70%
Surprise	73.30%	86.70%	96.70%	96.70%	93.30%	96.70%

Table 5. Result of Dataset for Six Different Categories Emotional Sentences

Dataset	Parameter	Anger Sentence	Disgust Sentence	Happiness Sentence	Neutral Sentence	Sad Sentence	Surprise Sentence
Emotion Dection	accuracy	88.30%	53.30%	93.30%	90.00%	71.70%	91.70%
	sensitivity	83.30%	30.00%	96.70%	96.70%	70.00%	93.30%
	specificity	93.30%	76.70%	90.00%	83.30%	73.30%	90.00%
	Empiric ROC Area	0.989	0.837	0.997	0.994	0.92	0.993
Facial Expression	accuracy	81.70%	58.30%	93.30%	91.70%	78.30%	95.00%
	sensitivity	83.30%	46.70%	100	100	83.30%	96.70%
	specificity	80.00%	70.00%	86.70%	83.30%	73.30%	93.30%
	Empiric ROC Area	0.967	0.84	1	1	0.956	0.998
Neutral Human	accuracy	73.30%	58.30%	93.30%	93.30%	79.70%	85.00%
	sensitivity	76.70%	50.00%	100	100	79.30%	100
	specificity	70.00%	66.70%	66.70%	86.70%	80.00%	70.00%
	Empiric ROC Area	0.93	0.833	1	1	0.959	1

itive Rate (FPR) across a spectrum of decision thresholds. The AUC metric evaluates the model's efficacy in distinguishing between positive and negative classes' overall threshold values, with a larger AUC indicating superior model performance. An AUC value of 0.5 suggests no better than random class differentiation, while a value of 1.0 represents flawless discrimination. According to the table, we think that it may be due to the sensitivities of the three data sets being very close, except in the disgust statement. Because when the initial state has different emotions, it is difficult for ChatGPT4 to judge disgust. For example, in a positive situation, it will judge the disgusting statement as a joke or a prank, so the accuracy is not high. In terms of specificity, the prediction results of ChatGPT4 are beyond expectations, especially under the initial positive sentiment, the prediction accuracy is very high, almost close to being completely correct. Judging from the accuracy and ROC curve, ChatGPT4's performance in sentence prediction for different emotions exceeded expectations.

4 Conclusion

In this paper, we study the zero-shot capabilities of ChatGPT4 in sentiment reasoning and prediction based on multi-modal image text. The experimental results show that the prediction ability of ChatGPT4 is unexpectedly good and the accuracy is high. Since our goal is to analyze limitations, for example, ChatGPT4 can analyze that images have negative emotions, but it will incorrectly judge disgust as depression, etc., resulting in inaccurate prediction results. However, with more prompt words and mental health analysis, ChatGPT4 has the ability and potential to improve inferences. Our findings indicate that tasks requiring subjective interpretation, like mental health assessments and understanding emotions in image-based conversations, pose significant challenges for ChatGPT. By enhancing the strategy for creating prompts and selecting relevant contextual examples, we posit that substantial further work is essential to boost ChatGPT's effectiveness and overcome its current shortcomings. This effort is crucial for its practical deployment in real-world scenarios about mental health and analogous fields.

5 Limitations and Future Work

In this paper, we evaluate sentiment primarily based on static inputs (images or single text inputs). In real-life scenarios, emotions are dynamic and can change rapidly based on ongoing interactions that current experimental setups may not fully capture. On the one hand, the lack of real-time feedback mechanisms to adjust model predictions based on user interactions limits the practical applicability of adaptive systems such as interactive chatbots or mental health monitoring tools. This article only focuses on the functions of ChatGPT4 in image-based emotion recognition. In the future, it may be extended to different large language models, such as Claude3, to discuss and compare the potential advantages and disadvantages of different large language models. On the other hand, an in-depth evaluation of performance in real-world scenarios is missing, raising questions about the robustness and generalization of the models beyond experimental settings. In the future, we can continue to explore and discuss how ChatGPT4 derives predictions or performs analytical observations by fine-tuning and adding prompt words, thereby improving the transparency and interpretability of the model's decision-making process at the same time. Judging based on emotional changes in perceived reality may bias the experiment. Since ChatGPT is a probabilistic model, even if the same result is given in the operation, it may give different results. Therefore, the next step might be to average the results over the dataset by running the same input multiple times, based on the disadvantage that a single experiment on the input is not sufficiently correlated.

References

1. OpenAI: GPT 4. https://openai.com/gpt-4
2. Ciraolo, D., Celesti, A., Fazio, M., Bonanno, M., Villari, M., Calabrò, R.S.: Emotional artificial intelligence enabled facial expression recognition for tele-rehabilitation: a preliminary study. In: 2023 IEEE Symposium on Computers and Communications (ISCC), pp. 1–6. IEEE (2023)
3. Deng, J.J., Leung, C.H.C.: Towards learning a joint representation from transformer in multimodal emotion recognition. In: Mahmud, M., Kaiser, M.S., Vassanelli, S., Dai, Q., Zhong, N. (eds.) BI 2021. LNCS (LNAI), vol. 12960, pp. 179–188. Springer, Cham (2021). https://doi.org/10.1007/978-3-030-86993-9_17
4. Deng, J.J., Leung, C.H.C., Li, Y.: Multimodal emotion recognition using transfer learning on audio and text data. In: Gervasi, O., et al. (eds.) ICCSA 2021. LNCS, vol. 12951, pp. 552–563. Springer, Cham (2021). https://doi.org/10.1007/978-3-030-86970-0_39
5. Ekman, P.: Facial expressions of emotion: New findings, new questions (1992)
6. Fawcett, T.: An introduction to ROC analysis. Pattern Recogn. Lett. **27**(8), 861–874 (2006)
7. Geetha, A., Mala, T., Priyanka, D., Uma, E.: Multimodal emotion recognition with deep learning: advancements, challenges, and future directions. Inf. Fusion **105**, 102218 (2024)
8. Issa, D., Demirci, M.F., Yazici, A.: Speech emotion recognition with deep convolutional neural networks. Biomed. Signal Process. Control **59**, 101894 (2020)
9. Kosti, R., Alvarez, J.M., Recasens, A., Lapedriza, A.: Emotion recognition in context. In: Proceedings of the IEEE Conference on Computer Vision and Pattern Recognition, pp. 1667–1675 (2017)
10. Kosti, R., Alvarez, J.M., Recasens, A., Lapedriza, A.: Context based emotion recognition using emotic dataset. IEEE Trans. Pattern Anal. Mach. Intell. **42**(11), 2755–2766 (2019)
11. Le, H.D., Lee, G.S., Kim, S.H., Kim, S., Yang, H.J.: Multi-label multimodal emotion recognition with transformer-based fusion and emotion-level representation learning. IEEE Access **11**, 14742–14751 (2023)
12. Leung, C.H., Deng, J.J., Li, Y.: Enhanced human-machine interactive learning for multimodal emotion recognition in dialogue system. In: Proceedings of the 2022 5th International Conference on Algorithms, Computing and Artificial Intelligence, pp. 1–7 (2022)
13. Lewis, R., Rose, J.: 'i'm not okay,' off-duty alaska pilot allegedly said before trying to cut the engines (OCTOBER 25, 2023, 11:55 AM ET). https://www.npr.org/2023/10/24/1208244311/alaska-airlines-off-duty-pilot-switch-off-engines
14. Mann, B., et al.: Language models are few-shot learners. arXiv preprint arXiv:2005.14165 (2020)
15. Metallinou, A., Narayanan, S.: Annotation and processing of continuous emotional attributes: challenges and opportunities. In: 2013 10th IEEE International Conference and Workshops on Automatic Face and Gesture Recognition (FG), pp. 1–8. IEEE (2013)
16. Mollahosseini, A., Hasani, B., Mahoor, M.H.: Affectnet: a database for facial expression, valence, and arousal computing in the wild. IEEE Trans. Affect. Comput. **10**(1), 18–31 (2017)

17. Nicolle, J., Rapp, V., Bailly, K., Prevost, L., Chetouani, M.: Robust continuous prediction of human emotions using multiscale dynamic cues. In: Proceedings of the 14th ACM International Conference on Multimodal Interaction, pp. 501–508 (2012)
18. Ouyang, L., et al.: Training language models to follow instructions with human feedback. Adv. Neural. Inf. Process. Syst. **35**, 27730–27744 (2022)
19. Poria, S., Hazarika, D., Majumder, N., Naik, G., Cambria, E., Mihalcea, R.: Meld: a multimodal multi-party dataset for emotion recognition in conversations. arXiv preprint arXiv:1810.02508 (2018)
20. Robert, P.: Emotion: Theory, Research, and Experience, Volume 1: Theories of Emotion (1980)
21. SAMHSA: Warning signs and risk factors for emotional distress. https://www.samhsa.gov/find-help/disaster-distress-helpline/warning-signs-risk-factors
22. Shank, D.B., Graves, C., Gott, A., Gamez, P., Rodriguez, S.: Feeling our way to machine minds: people's emotions when perceiving mind in artificial intelligence. Comput. Hum. Behav. **98**, 256–266 (2019)
23. Fat cat incident. https://sports.sohu.com/a/776021122_121856967
24. Yang, K., Ji, S., Zhang, T., Xie, Q., Ananiadou, S.: On the evaluations of chatgpt and emotion-enhanced prompting for mental health analysis. arXiv preprint arXiv:2304.03347 (2023)
25. Zahara, L., Musa, P., Wibowo, E.P., Karim, I., Musa, S.B.: The facial emotion recognition (FER-2013) dataset for prediction system of micro-expressions face using the convolutional neural network (CNN) algorithm based raspberry PI. In: 2020 Fifth International Conference on Informatics and Computing (ICIC), pp. 1–9. IEEE (2020)
26. Zhang, R., Wang, Z., Huang, Z., Li, L., Zheng, M.: Predicting emotion reactions for human-computer conversation: a variational approach. IEEE Trans. Hum.-Mach. Syst. **51**(4), 279–287 (2021)
27. Zhang, T., Schoene, A.M., Ji, S., Ananiadou, S.: Natural language processing applied to mental illness detection: a narrative review. NPJ Digit. Med. **5**(1), 46 (2022)
28. Zhang, W., He, X., Lu, W.: Exploring discriminative representations for image emotion recognition with CNNs. IEEE Trans. Multimedia **22**(2), 515–523 (2019)
29. Zhao, W., Zhao, Y., Lu, X., Wang, S., Tong, Y., Qin, B.: Is chatgpt equipped with emotional dialogue capabilities? arXiv preprint arXiv:2304.09582 (2023)

Advanced and Innovative Web Apps (AIWA 2024)

SEMG-Based Prosthetic Hand with an Integrated Mobile Application

Ma Thi Chau(✉) and Bui Danh Hung

HMI Lab, University of Engineering and Technology, Hanoi, Vietnam
chaumt@vnu.edu.vn

Abstract. The main focus of this study was to design and develop an assistive device in the form of a low-cost prototype prosthetic hand that utilizes cords as tendons, inexpensive servos, and a simplified actuation method. Additionally, the objective was to create a neural network using only two surface electromyography (sEMG) sensors. Various methods were experimented with to achieve the desired outcome, including transfer learning with RESNET50 and the implementation of a Convolutional Neural Network. The UCI-sEMG dataset was used to train the proposed model for hand movements. Furthermore, a mobile application was developed to control the prosthetic hand, aiming to enhance interactivity and expand the range of control. The entire system communicates through gRPC. The results demonstrate the feasibility of creating a prosthetic hand that internally stores all the cords and servos, while still providing a satisfactory range of motion for each finger. The evaluation process also indicates the algorithm's ability to predict hand gestures, although its performance may not be on par with state-of-the-art models. Nevertheless, considering the limited number of sensors used, the achieved accuracy of 58% shows promise. Additionally, the mobile application features a simple yet functional design that meets the requirements for support, ease of use, and flexibility.

Keywords: Prosthetic hand · sEMG · Convolutional Neural Network

1 Introduction

Hand amputations or loss affect nearly four million individuals globally, with causes ranging from infections, congenital absence, diabetes, cancer, and other conditions [1]. Partial amputations make up the majority, accounting for over 75% of these cases. The loss of a hand significantly impacts the functional abilities of individuals. Fortunately, prosthetic hands offer the opportunity to restore some functionality.

A typical prosthetic hand consists of three main interconnected parts: an input signal acquisition unit, a processing and control unit, and an end effector. The cost of a prosthetic device is quite expensive, ranging from 30,000 to 40,000 USD. However, a low-cost prosthetic hand prototype was designed in [14],

O. Gervasi et al. (Eds.): ICCSA 2024 Workshops, LNCS 14815, pp. 23–38, 2024.
https://doi.org/10.1007/978-3-031-65154-0_2

with a cost of only 1,000 USD, and a commercial version priced at 7,000 USD. Nowadays, high-performing artificial hands (or prostheses) commonly use surface electromyography signals (sEMG or myosignals) for control. sEMG records the electrical muscle movements from the surface of muscle cells when they are electrically or neurologically activated. The amplitude of sEMG signals ranges from 0 to 10 mV (peak to peak). Collecting sEMG signals requires the proper placement of EMG electrodes after applying a layer of gel on the skin surface.

Traditional prosthetic hands based on sEMG typically require more than 6 channels of data for accurate classification of control signals. However, using multiple sensors to capture EMG signals can lead to muscle fatigue during hand operation. In the study [11], the authors successfully classified 4 control signals using only 3 channels of data.

In this study, we conducted research and designed a prototype of a prosthetic hand called HMI Prosthetic Hand, based on 2 channels of EMG signals, aiming to provide an affordable solution suitable for the Vietnamese market. Our contributions include: (1) designing a flexible and expandable prosthetic hand with 4 fingers, (2) conducting tests and mapping the control device to finger rotations corresponding to 6 basic hand movements, and (3) applying a CNN network to classify the 2-channel sEMG signals into 6 classes corresponding to the 6 basic hand movements.

2 Backgrounds and Related Works

2.1 Backgrounds

The human hand is composed of 27 bones that can be divided into 3 main groups [3]:

- Wrist: Consists of 8 carpal bones.
- Palm: Comprises 5 metacarpal bones.
- Fingers: Contains 14 phalanges.

To delve deeper, each finger consists of 3 bones: the Distal Interphalangeal Joint (DIP), the Proximal Interphalangeal Joint (PIP), and the Metacarpophalangeal Joint (MCP). The DIP joint is situated at the fingertip, just before the fingernail. The PIP joint is the first joint of the finger and is located between the first two bones, allowing the bending and extending of the finger. The MCP joint is where the hand bone, known as the metacarpal, connects with the finger bones, known as the phalanges. Aside from the bones and muscles, the human body also comprises fibrous connective tissues like tendons and ligaments. Tendons play the role of connecting bone to bone and can be replicated using mechanical joints. Ligaments, on the other hand, serve as attachments between muscles and bones, enabling finger movements such as bending and straightening. So, the human finger consists of 3 joints: MCP, PIP, DIP. In terms of the human anatomy aspect that the prosthetic hand needs to replicate, it is the finger movement, which can be compared and evaluated by the trajectory of the fingertip.

Below is the formula to determine the trajectory of fingertip movement.

$$\begin{aligned} x &= lph_1 \times cos(\theta_1) + lph_2 \times cos(\theta_1 + \theta_2) + lph_3 \times cos(\theta_1 + \theta_2 + \theta_3) \\ y &= lph_1 \times sin(\theta_1) + lph_2 \times sin(\theta_1 + \theta_2) + lph_3 \times sin(\theta_1 + \theta_2 + \theta_3) \end{aligned} \tag{1}$$

where, lph_1, lph_2, and lph_3 are the length of Proximal phalanx, Middle Phalanx, and Distal Phalanx respectively. θ_1, θ_2, θ_3 is the rotation angle (from 0^0 - 90^0) of MCP, PIP, DIP in that order.

There are six basic types of hand movements (Fig. 1): *spherical*, *pinch*, *palmar*, *lateral*, *cylindrical*, and *hook*.

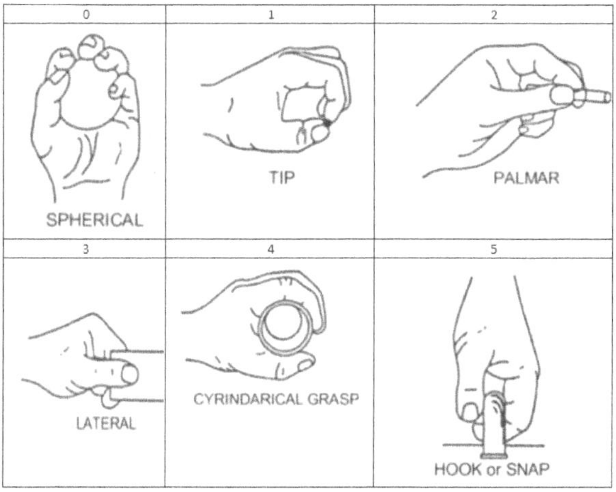

Fig. 1. Six basic hand movements

Over the years, there has been significant advancement in prosthetic hands, offering a wide range of applications and types. These hands can be categorized as passive or active artificial hands, providing replacements for different levels of amputation. Moreover, they can replicate human movements. Passive prosthetic hands encompass both prosthetic hands and tools. They can either be completely static or adjustable. Generally, they are designed with a specific purpose in mind and cannot dynamically adapt to the user's needs. In contrast, active prosthetic hands are bio-compatible mechatronic or mechanical devices that provide a broad range of functionalities. These prostheses can be mechanically powered by the user's body or rely on an external power source and control module for operation. Each type has its advantages and disadvantages. Body-powered prostheses, though not requiring an external power source like a battery, rely on the user's physical strength, which can lead to fatigue over time. On the other hand, externally powered prostheses can assist users in conserving energy and offer a strong grip for prosthetic hands or the ability to handle heavy loads for prosthetic arms.

2.2 Related Works

The LUKE arm/Deka arm system[1] is considered one of the most advanced mechatronic devices ever created. While it has received approval from the United States Food and Drug Administration, it is currently not available for commercial use. To obtain one, buyers must comply with Federal law, which requires the involvement of a licensed healthcare professional in the ordering process. Additionally, this equipment comes with a price tag of around $100,000 or more.

Open Bionics[2] is a UK-based company known for offering a diverse range of products including Hero arm. The Hero arm, which shares a similar design principle to the Brunel hand, is priced between $3,000 and $20,000. Although their products are open-source, acquiring the specific materials required for their Brunel hand, such as sheets of elastic material, can be challenging.

Currently, the field of sEMG signal classification lacks state-of-the-art models compared to image classification, despite its active nature. Among the existing models, the generative flow model (GFM) [2] stands out as one of the most effective models for hand gesture recognition. It achieves an accuracy of $63.86 \pm 5.12\%$ when classifying 53 different hand gestures in the popular NinaPro 5 database, which employs multiple sensors including 2 Thalmic Myo armbands.

Moreover, the MYO armband with 8 channels has been extensively used in numerous datasets and research studies. However, the limited accessibility of this equipment poses additional challenges in the field. The nature of sEMG signals makes generalization challenging, even with a large amount of data. These signals are susceptible to various factors, such as electrode relocation, user fatigue, and inter-subject variability. Technological advancements have greatly improved the field of prosthetic hands and machine learning algorithms for hand gesture classification. However, accessibility remains a challenge in certain regions due to the high cost and limited availability of prosthetic manufacturers and vendors. Various designs of robotic/prosthetic hands have been developed, especially those inspired by human anatomy, where the fingers are controlled by synthetic tendons instead of gears. Nevertheless, most of these designs still place the cords and actuators in the forearm, mimicking the positioning of tendons and muscles in the human body. While this approach is effective, it limits the storage capacity and functionality of the hand module. Additionally, implementing cutting-edge machine learning models with bionic limbs often requires expensive and difficult-to-obtain high-channel datasets and specific use cases. The studies [5–11] utilized sEMG signals to control prosthetic hands; however, these studies used a minimum of 6 sEMG channels. In [12], only 3 sEMG channels were used, but they classified only 4 control signals corresponding to 4 hand movements. The authors in [13] also highlighted that muscle fatigue can occur at the sensor placement locations for signal acquisition. Therefore, using fewer channels of sEMG data, if possible, would be a good choice.

The authors in [4] also aim to design an affordable prosthetic arm for the Indian market, using EMG signals and 5 servo motors. However, the implemen-

[1] https://mobiusbionics.com/.
[2] https://openbionics.com/en/.

tation of EMG signal analysis has not been specified, and the design prototype has been noted to require several improvements to be better suited for real-life usage.

3 Our Method

We have developed a prosthetic hand and its operation based on the process depicted in Fig. 2, which consists of four modules: (1) Prosthetic hand shape design, (2) Basic hand movement learning (optional), (3) Servo parameter estimation, and (4) Control module. In the Prosthetic hand shape design module, we simulated a flexible 4-finger hand design, taking inspiration from the biological structure of the human hand. This design is capable of performing the six basic hand movements mentioned in Sect. 2.1. Subsequently, we fabricated and assembled the hand according to this design.

In the Basic hand movement learning module, we employed a CNN network to classify the six basic hand movements based on SEMG signals. If the user prefers to provide the basic hand movements themselves, we offer the option to perform them through a mobile application. Building upon the prosthetic hand shape and the basic hand movements, we conducted experiments to establish a mapping between hand movements and servo control parameters for each finger in the prosthetic hand. This mapping was accomplished in the servo parameter estimation module. Finally, we programmed the Arduino+ circuit to control the servo operation and activate the finger movements corresponding to each basic hand movement in the control module. Detailed explanations of each module will be provided in the subsequent sections.

4 Prosthetic Hand Design

4.1 Prosthetic Hand Shape Design

We have designed a HMI 4-finger mechanical hand (refer to Fig. 3) that utilizes a combination of servo actuators for joint movement and synthetic tendons to connect the joints. The four fingers included are the Thumb, Index, Middle, and Pinkie. Each finger consists of three joints: MCP, PIP, and DIP. The components that form the shape of the prosthetic hand are described in detail in Fig. 4. These components include (0) connector, which connects each phalanx; (1) string port, where the string or cable passes through; (2) cap, which prevents the finger from falling out; (3) pin, which connects the finger to the hand; (4) fingertip, which represents the distal phalanx; (5) intermediate phalanx (longer); (6) intermediate phalanx (shorter); (7) finger base, which represents the proximal phalanx; (8) hand; and (9) thumb base.

The necessary electronic components for the project include: Arduino Nano; Potentiometers; 3-pin switches; Pins push button; LED (optional); Servos; and Resistors

In particular, four servos are utilized to control the movements of the four fingers (refer to Fig. 5).

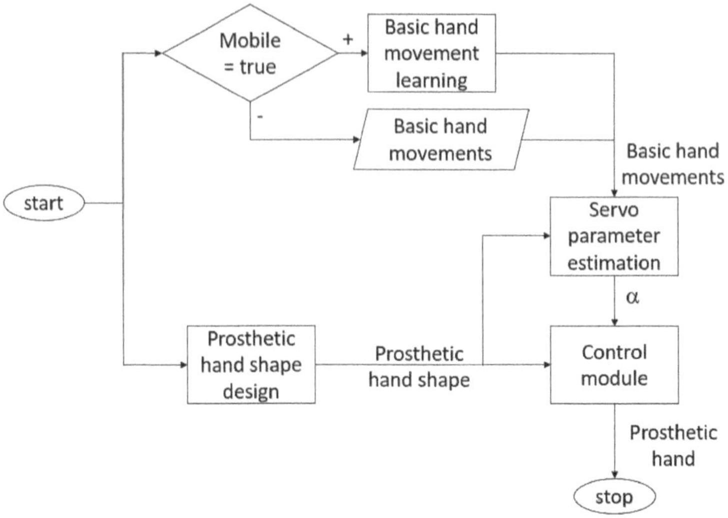

Fig. 2. Our proposal

4.2 Servo Parameter Estimation and Control Module

Experimental validation has confirmed that the maximum identification delay does not exceed $180ms$. Each finger position, ranging from Thumb to Pinkie, corresponds to a specific servo rotation angle. The corresponding angles for the proposed prototype are provided in Table 1 and Fig. 6. In addition to the six basic hand movements mentioned earlier (which are detailed in the first six rows of the table), we have defined additional common hand movements. These movements include Flip off (fully extending the middle finger), Peace (fully extending the index and middle fingers), Point (fully extending the index finger), Open (fully extending all four fingers), and Close (fully flexing all four fingers). The mapping of servo angles concerning finger positions is referred to as the Lookup Table ($LookupTab$). Let α be the rotation angle that activates the servo. We have the following formula to calculate α:

$$\alpha = (Degree - om) \times (iM - im)/(oM - om) + im \tag{2}$$

where, $im = 0$, $iM = 1023$ are the minimum and maximum of the servo rotation angle. $om = 0$, $oM = 180$ are the minimum and maximum of the finger rotation angle.

After the sEMG signals are classified (Sect. 5) into one of the six classes (β ranging from 0 to 5) corresponding to the six basic hand movements (Fig. 1), the parameter α, representing the servo rotation angle for each finger, is estimated and activated.

Input: β $//0 - 5$ basic hand movements
Output: Activated hand

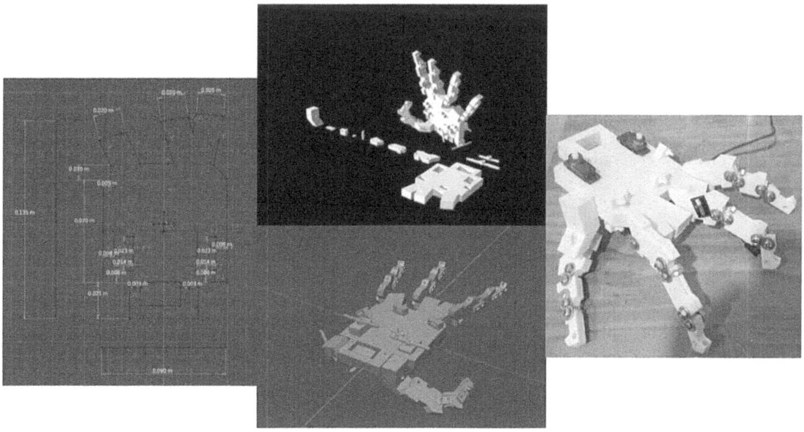

Fig. 3. Detail of the HMI prosthetic hand shape design

Table 1. Mapping servo angle with respect to finger position.

Movements	Thumb	Index	Middle	Pinkie	Movements	Thumb	Index	Middle	Pinkie
Spherical	70	90	40	40	Flip off	0	180	0	0
Tip	100	60	50	50	Peace	0	180	180	0
Palma	40	90	0	0	Point	0	180	0	0
Lateral	40	40	0	0	Open	180	180	180	180
Cylinder	65	45	45	45	Close	0	0	0	0
Hook	180	100	90	90					

Begin
For each finger
α=ServoParEstimation(β,$LookupTab$);
ServoActivation(α);
End

5 SEMG Based Basic Hand Movement Classification

5.1 Dataset

UCI sEMG[3], which stands for surface electromyography, is a dataset named "sEMG for Basic Hand Movements." This dataset comprises surface electromyographic signals (sEMG) recorded during the execution of six fundamental hand movements using the Delsys EMG System. The data was collected from healthy participants while they performed every day grasping actions.

[3] https://archive.ics.uci.edu/dataset/313/semg+for+basic+hand+movements.

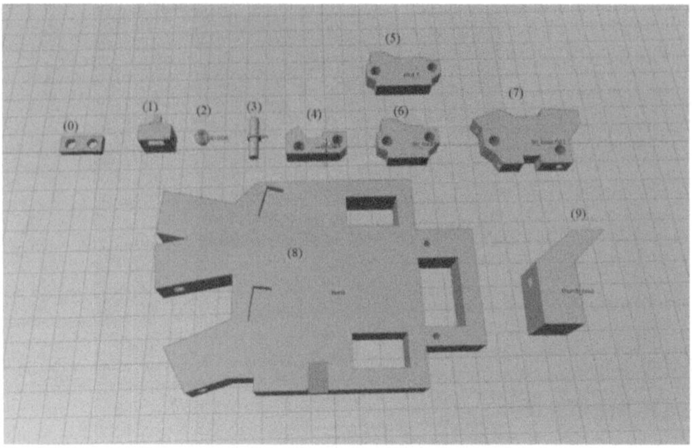

Fig. 4. Detail of the HMI prosthetic hand shape components

The data, stored in MATLAB (.mat) files, with separate tables for each grasping technique and each channel, and each row of these tables represents a trial and contains voltage values of the signals, possesses the following characteristics:

- Data type: Time-series
- Topic domain: Health and Medicine
- Related tasks: Classification
- Feature type: Real numbers
- Number of examples: 3000
- Number of features: 2500

The dataset is divided into two parts:

- Part 1 includes data from five healthy participants (two males and three females) within a similar age range (20 to 22 years old). Each participant performed six hand movements 30 times, with each trial lasting 6 s.
- Part 2 contains data from a single healthy participant (a 22-year-old male) performing six hand movements, repeated 100 times per movement over three consecutive days. The duration of each trial in this part is 5 s.

The data was gathered at a sampling rate of 500 Hz using National Instrument's (NI) Labview as the programming framework. The signals underwent filtering through a Butterworth Band Pass filter and a notch filter to eliminate power line interference. The hardware employed was an NI analog-to-digital conversion card connected to a personal computer, and the signals were captured from two differential voltage EMG electrodes and transmitted to the dual-channel EMG system using Delsys Bagnoli™ Handheld EMG Systems.

The experiments involved both voluntary and repetitive grasping of various objects, enabling participants to independently determine the speed and force of their movements. Surface EMG electrodes placed on the forearm were used to

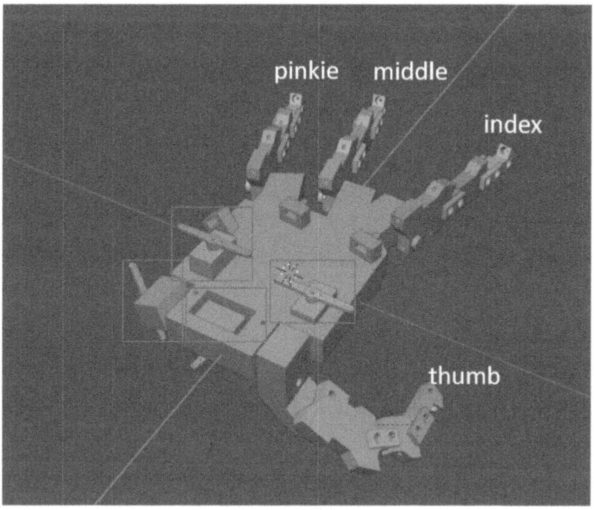

Fig. 5. Servo positions for the fingers.

collect muscle activity information. The dataset encompasses six types of hand movements: *spherical*, *pinch*, *palmar*, *lateral*, *cylindrical*, and *hook* Fig. 1, each corresponding to distinct grasping techniques.

5.2 Data Normalization

To facilitate the use of the Convolutional Layer and ResNet50 in transfer learning, the data is reshaped into an n × n array while preserving its sequential nature. This is achieved by extracting an equal number of samples from both channels and reshaping them according to their sequence position.

With a sampling rate of $500Hz$ and a duration of 6 s, there are 3000 data samples per action. Although we have only two channels, creating a neural network with only two inputs $[chn_1, chn_2]$ is not advisable. This approach is prone to overfitting due to the limited information provided to the network and does not accurately represent the nature of the signal. Muscle signals exhibit time-related properties, so grouping samples together enhances training success and enables effective utilization of CNNs and pre-trained models like ResNet50, which are typically designed for image data.

To ensure compatibility with training and resemble real sensor data, the acquired dataset is reformatted into pairs of channels accompanied by their corresponding labels. Following that, the signals need to be normalized. The signal $x_{1.T}$ can be represented as $(x_{11}, x_{12}, ..., x_{1n})$, and similarly, $x_{2.T}$ can be expressed as $(x_{21}, x_{22}, ..., x_{2n})$,. Both signals are then normalized.

Figure 7 illustrates the process of signal normalization. Subsequently, the normalized data is obtained by extracting n samples from *channel*1 and n samples from *channel*2. This acquired data can be represented as an image (Fig. 7) with

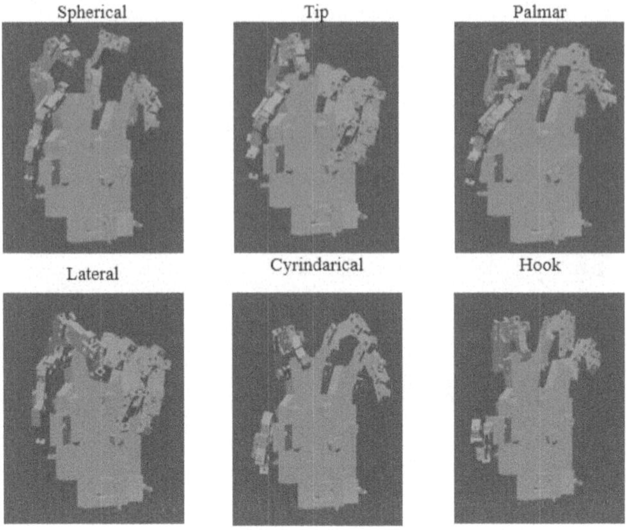

Fig. 6. Six defined basic prosthetic hand movements.

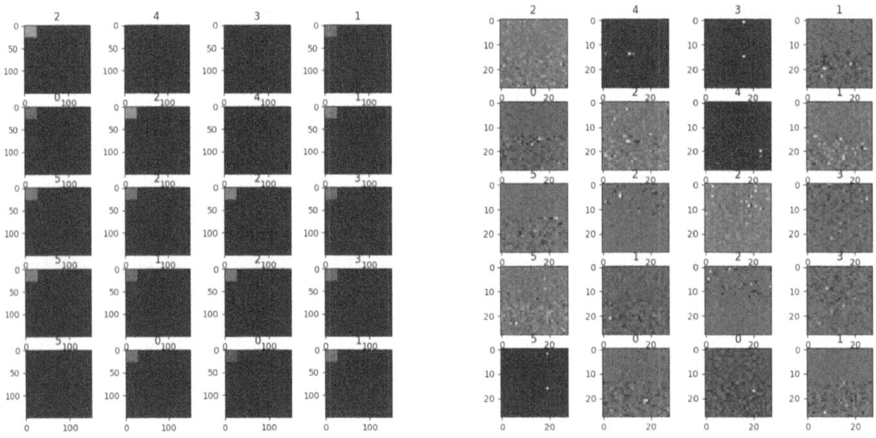

Fig. 7. Signals in discrete space

a 40 × 40 shape (image on the right). To align with the requirements of transfer learning using ResNet50, it can be padded with zeros (image on the left) to achieve a suitable dimension, typically 224 × 224.

5.3 CNN Model

We trained a CNN model structure (as shown in Fig. 9) that achieved the best performance. The best-performing model achieved a loss of 0.7 and an accuracy of 0.7 (on a scale of 0 to 1) during evaluation. The training process history is depicted in Fig. 8, where a learning rate (LR) of 0.03 was used.

Using the same model but training it with a different number of epochs and a lower learning rate (LR = 0.01), we obtained a second model with a loss of 0.4 and an accuracy of 0.2.

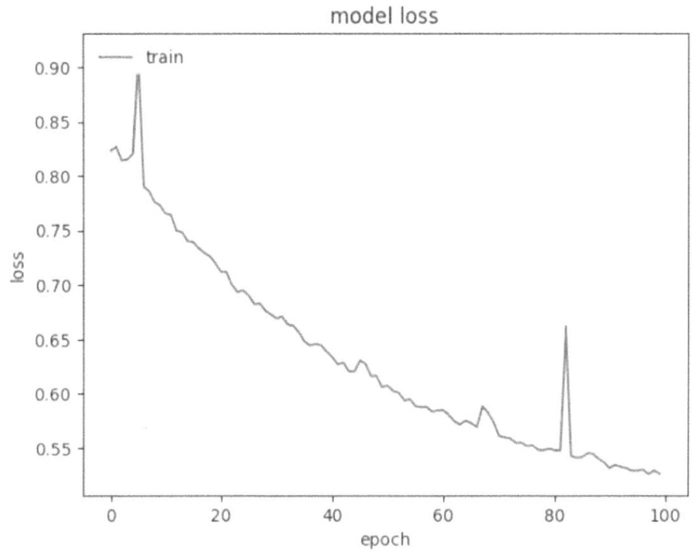

Fig. 8. A training session history.

Using the Keras Tuner, a Keras model with optimal layers and a hyperparameter-like learning rate is set.

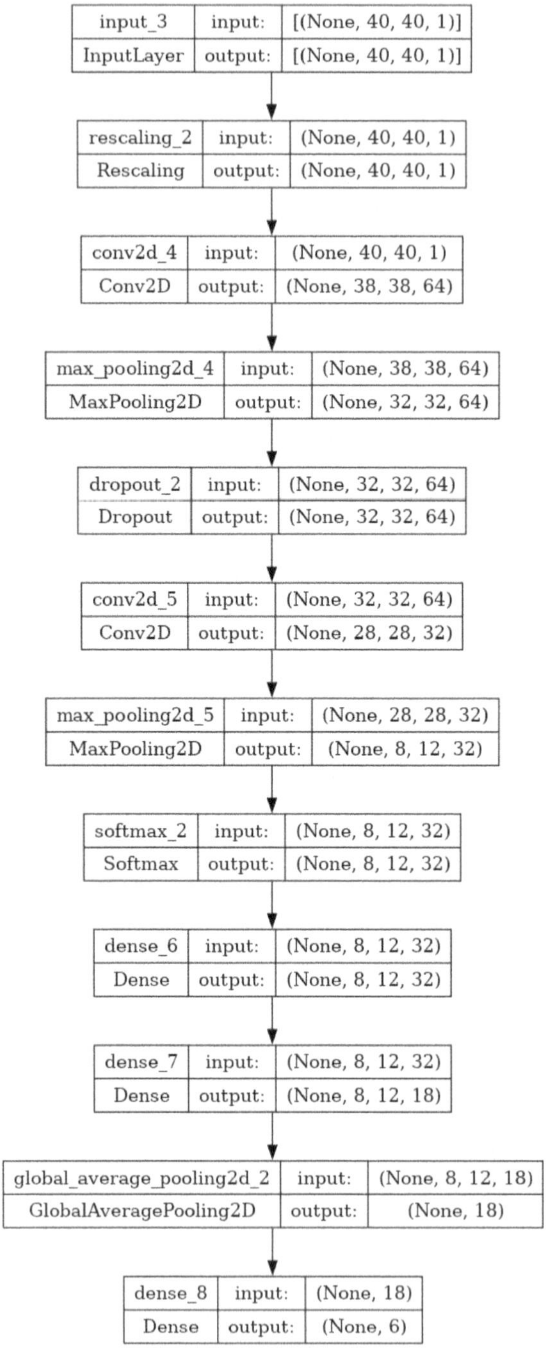

Fig. 9. CNN model architecture.

6 Experiments and Evaluations

We have successfully designed HMI prosthetic hand - a cost-effective 4-finger prosthetic hand with 4 DOF (Degrees Of Freedom). Some technical comparisons regarding the hand's design are illustrated in Table 2 and Fig. 10. The HMI prosthetic hand also demonstrates the potential for expanding hand designs with more fingers and greater degrees of freedom at an affordable price.

Fig. 10. Movement of prosthetic hand.

Table 2. Technical comparison.

Names	Branches	No of joints	Methods	DOF
Bebionic stepper	RSL	11	DC motor lead screw	6
HeroArm	Open bionhics	10	Linear actuator screw	6
Brunel	Open bionics	9	Linear actuator screw	5
Luke arm	Mobius Bionics	14	Not given	7
HMIhand	Ours	12	180°C Servo screw	4

We have developed a control mechanism for the HMI hand using sEMG signals from the forearm muscles for individuals with hand disabilities. The signals are captured through sensors and fed into a CNN network that we have built to recognize the intended hand movements for controlling the HMI hand. With Dataset UCI sEMG (ratio 80:20 for training and testing, respectively), we have successfully trained the initial model with 2 input channels and 6 basic hand movements. The accuracy is illustrated in Fig. 11 more than 58%, where movement Hook exhibits the highest accuracy around 66%. Additionally, we have expanded the mechanism to provide hand movement input through a mobile application, enhancing the flexibility of using the HMI hand. As mentioned before, we have also experimented and developed additional hand movements beyond the 6 basic gestures, including Flip of, Peace, Point, Open, and Close. This highlights the significant potential for expansion and adaptability of the hand, opening up possibilities for affordable robotic arms in various fields.

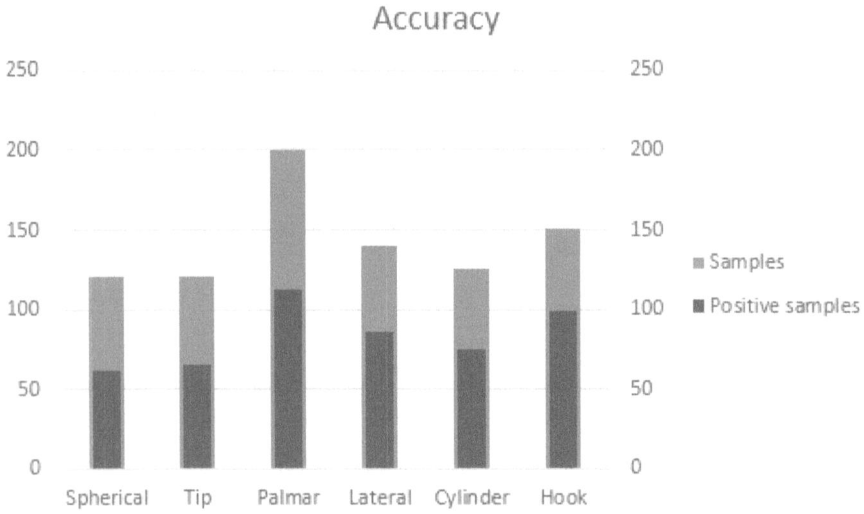

Fig. 11. Prediction result of fine tune model.

7 Conclusion

We have successfully designed and developed an advanced prosthetic hand with four fingers, incorporating state-of-the-art technology that enables it to perform six fundamental movements based on SEMG signals. In addition to the prosthetic hand, we have also developed a user-friendly mobile application that allows for a broader range of gestures, significantly enhancing the flexibility and assistance provided by the robotic arm.

Our groundbreaking research findings present a practical and affordable solution for individuals who have lost their hands and lack access to specialized devices for their daily activities. By utilizing cutting-edge technology, we have overcome numerous challenges to create a device that not only meets the functional needs of users but also addresses the financial constraints that often accompany such devices.

Although our work faced certain limitations, including challenges in data collection and limited testing opportunities, our prosthetic hand stands as a valuable support system for individuals with disabilities and offers a means of controlling robots. By continually refining our design and addressing these limitations, we aim to improve the functionality and accessibility of prosthetics, ultimately enhancing the quality of life for individuals with limb loss.

References

1. O&P Almanac Amputation data from community hospitals. O&P Almanac (2022)
2. Sun, W., Liu, H., Tang, R., Lang, Y., He, J,. Huang, Q.: sEMG-based hand-gesture classification using a generative flow model. Sensors (Basel) **19**(8), 1952 (2019). https://doi.org/10.3390/s19081952, PMID: 31027292; PMCID: PMC6515175
3. Arias, D.G., Varacallo, M.: Anatomy, shoulder and upper limb, hand bones. In: StatPearls. StatPearls Publishing, Treasure Island (FL) (2022). PMID: 31613464
4. Selvan, M.P., et al.: Prosthetic hand using EMG. J. Phys. Conf. Ser. (2021)
5. Naik, G.R., Al-Timemy, A.H., Nguyen, H.T.: Transradial amputee gesture classification using an optimal number of sEMG sensors: an approach using ICA clustering. IEEE Trans. Neural Syst. Rehabil. Eng. **24**, 837–846 (2016). https://doi.org/10.1109/TNSRE.2015.2478138
6. Al-Timemy, A.H., Bugmann, G., Escudero, J., Outram, N.: Classification of finger movements for the dexterous hand prosthesis control with surface electromyography. IEEE J. Biomed. Health Inform. **17**, 608–618 (2013). https://doi.org/10.1109/JBHI.2013.2249590
7. Pan, L., Zhang, D., Liu, J., Sheng, X., Zhu, X.: Continuous estimation of finger joint angles under different static wrist motions from surface EMG signals. Biomed. Sig. Process. Control **14**, 265–271 (2014). https://doi.org/10.1016/j.bspc.2014.08.004
8. Riilloa, F., et al.: Optimization of EMG-based hand gesture recognition: supervised vs. unsupervised data preprocessing on healthy subjects and transradial amputees. Biomed. Sig. Process. Control. **14**, 117–125 (2014). https://doi.org/10.1016/j.bspc.2014.07.007

9. Stango, A., Member, S., Negro, F., Farina, D., Member, S.: Spatial correlation of high density EMG signals provides features robust to electrode number and shift in pattern recognition for Myocontrol. IEEE Trans. Neural Syst. Rehabil. Eng. **23**, 189–198 (2015). https://doi.org/10.1109/TNSRE.2014.2366752
10. Kawasaki, H., Kayukawa, M., Sakaeda, H., Mouri, T.: Learning system for myoelectric prosthetic hand control by forearm amputees. In: Proceedings of the 23rd IEEE International Symposium on Robot and Human Interactive Communication; Edinburgh, UK, 25–29 August 2014, pp. 899–904 (2014)
11. Pancholi, S., Joshi, A.M.: Electromyography-based hand gesture recognition system for upper limb amputees. IEEE Sens. Lett. **3**, 1–4 (2019). https://doi.org/10.1109/LSENS.2019.2898257
12. Momen, K., Krishnan, S., Chau, T.: Real-time classification of forearm electromyographic signals corresponding to user-selected intentional movements for multifunction prosthesis control. IEEE Trans. Neural Syst. Rehabil. Eng. **15**, 535–542 (2007). https://doi.org/10.1109/TNSRE.2007.908376
13. Parajuli, N., et al.: Real-time EMG based pattern recognition control for hand prostheses: a review on existing methods, challenges and future implementation. Sensors (Basel) **19**(20), 4596 (2019). https://doi.org/10.3390/s19204596, PMID: 31652616; PMCID: PMC6832440
14. Unanyan, N.N., Belov, A.A.: Low-price prosthetic hand controlled by EMG signals. IFAC-PapersOnLine **54**(13), pp. 299–304 (2021). ISSN 2405-8963, https://doi.org/10.1016/j.ifacol.2021.10.463

Integration of an Artificial Intelligence Model into a Smartphone Flutter Application to Solve a Live Image Classification Problem

Sergio Tasso(✉), Simone Calò, Osvaldo Gervasi, and Damiano Perri

Department of Mathematics and Computer Science, University of Perugia, via Vanvitelli, 1, 06123 Perugia, Italy
{sergio.tasso,osvaldo.gervasi,damiano.perri}@unipg.it

Abstract. The object of study consists of solving a live image classification problem in the mobile environment and the subsequent implementation of mechanisms to integrate an image classification model, leveraging TensorFlow Lite, within a smartphone application built with Google's Flutter framework and written in Dart code. The functionality has been implemented within a cultural outreach application and allows the user, during an art visit, to use the camera on his or her device to frame the artwork and get its name on the screen in real time. Each captured frame is in fact sent as input to the classifier, which, after performing the classification, returns as output the associated label (the name of the artwork) that is finally displayed on the screen. After briefly introducing the preliminary knowledge necessary for the complete understanding of the object of study (implementation of the camera in the app and conversion of the classification model into Tensorflow Lite format), the tools used for the implementation of the functionality are described, which exploit the main plugin used, namely tflite_flutter. Finally, to ensure that the performance of the feature is optimal in devices, it is presented the concept of Isolate in the flutter framework and described the mechanisms for creating a new Isolate within which to perform the classification operation and how to communicate between them in order to display in the application user interface the output returned by the image classifier.

Keywords: Mobile Developing · Image Classification · Artificial Intelligence · Convolutional Neural Network

1 Introduction

The idea behind this study is to use technology intelligently to encourage the dissemination of art and culture. In fact, technology can be used not only to experiment with new artistic possibilities and forms, but also as a means of dissemination and a tool for popularising all those pre-existing traditional cultural and artistic forms [1,2].

O. Gervasi et al. (Eds.): ICCSA 2024 Workshops, LNCS 14815, pp. 39–55, 2024.
https://doi.org/10.1007/978-3-031-65154-0_3

Technologies using virtual and augmented reality quickly and affordably allow users to fully immerse themselves [3–6] in the works of art they are viewing in real time during an artistic visit. In fact, using an AR application on their smartphones, viewers can explore artworks in a three-dimensional way, often with interactive elements that enrich the experience, or by viewing information or trivia about the framed artwork in a contextual way [7]. The visit then becomes interactive, viewers are actively involved, and as they contemplate the artwork, they can view contextual information that enriches and embellishes the experience as if they were part of the artwork itself [8–10].

Another example are apps dedicated to art and culture [11], such as complementary museum apps, with which viewers can experience features such as camera recognition of artworks and view detailed information about the artworks, stories, and trivia about the artists on their smartphone screen, all in real time as they continue their art visit.

In other words, technology can thus be used to culturally enrich and supplement the art visit [12,13], in real time and without sacrificing contact with reality [14]. This is where the *Lions Umbria Art*[1] cultural outreach app and its live image classification feature, which is the subject of the following article, was born.

2 Mobile Developing

To implement this functionality, it is first necessary to create a flutter design of a smartphone app and create an image classifier.

2.1 Development of the Classification Model

A common Convolutional Neural Network can be used to develop an image classification model [15]. First, it is necessary to create an appropriate dataset with which to train the model later. In this case, the dataset consists of a set of images depicting some artistic paintings dating back to the early/late Middle Ages in the Italian region of Umbria.

For the definition of the Convolutional Neural Network, Tensorflow's Keras API[2] of the Python programming language and the *Sequential* model were used, to which the appropriate convolutional and downsampling layers were added [16]. It should be noted that the input model receives 3 maps of size 256×256 (one for each of the 3 RGB colors) whose values are normalised. This is an important step since, then, within the *dart* code of the application, the image captured by the camera must first also be normalised. In output, however, the model returns an array of decimal values, each of which expresses the probability of belonging to that specific class (each value is then between 0 and 1, and the length of the output array is equal to the number of classes with which the model is trained).

[1] https://www.lions108l.com/.

[2] https://keras.io/api/.

After compiling the model, we continue with its training from the dataset appropriately created earlier [17,18]. At the end of this phase, you have obtained a Keras model of image classification ready to make possible predictions.

Before it can be used in the mobile environment, the newly created Keras model must be converted to the Tensorflow Lite format [19].

2.2 Conversion of Image Classification Model to Tensorflow Lite Format

In fact, converting the model to the *.tflite* format is necessary because Tensorflow Lite[3] guarantees excellent model execution performance within mobile environments [20].

To convert a classification model, it is first necessary to identify the format with which it was stored. In this case, the newly created model is a Keras model, so the corresponding Python API for[4] conversion is used, as shown in Listing 1.1.

```
converter = tf.lite.TFLiteConverter.from_keras_model(model)
converter.optimizations = [tf.lite.Optimize.DEFAULT]
```

Listing 1.1. Conversion by *from_keras_model().*

After storing the newly converted model with the appropriate function shown in Listing 1.2, we obtain the file *.tflite* that coincides with the classification model that will be used by the flutter application.

```
with open('model.tflite', 'wb') as f:
  f.write(tflite_model)
```

Listing 1.2. Storage of the *.tflite* model.

2.3 Creating a Flutter App that Uses the Camera

This Section briefly describes the creation of a simple Flutter[5] application that, when opened, opens the device's camera.

First, a Flutter project must be created [21]. In this case, the development environment is Windows 11 and the project was created via Android Studio, as described in depth in the official documentation[6].

Within the **directory *root*** of the **project**, the elements that are most involved are as follows:

- **directory *assets***
  - This directory is used to store all those assets that the application needs, such as static files like images, fonts, and JSON data. Usually the contents of the assets directory can be organised into subdirectories to have more sorting by file types.

[3] https://www.tensorflow.org/lite.
[4] https://www.tensorflow.org/lite/models/convert.
[5] https://docs.flutter.dev/.
[6] https://docs.flutter.dev/get-started/install/windows/mobile.

- In this directory are stored:
  * *model.tflite*, which is the model of image classifications.
  * *labels.txt*, which is the file containing the list of labels involved in the classification problem (each line contains one label).

- **directory *lib***
  - It is the heart of a project developed with Flutter as it contains all the *.dart* files that allow the definition of the application's Dart code[7]. In fact, this directory contains the *main.dart* file with which you can launch the execution of the application. All classes, widgets and graphical objects will be defined within this directory. In other words, the source code written by the developer resides entirely in this folder.
- **file *pubspec.yaml***
  - The file *pubspec.yaml* is the second most important file within the project. It is located in the project's root directory and is used to manage the project's *dependencies*, define metadata and application assets. It has **3 key elements** of the *pubspec.yaml* file:
    * ***dependencies***: within this section are declared all the external packages that the application uses. Flutter packages can be obtained from the official website *pub.dev*[8], where examples, versions, and instructions for installation and use can be found for each package.
    * ***assets***: this section declares the resources used by the application, such as images, icons, fonts. Paths to subdirectories or files within the *assets* folder are then specified.

Presented in Listing 1.3, the first file involved is ***main.dart***, which contains the ***main()*** function, whose job is to launch the execution of the app.

In the context of Flutter, central is the concept of **widget**[9]. The **widgets**, in fact, are the **elements** of a Flutter **application**, and similar to the bricks forming a wall, the widgets are **aggregated inside each other** creating a **structure** called *Widget Tree* with which the user interface is identified. Thus, the design of the **user interface** in Flutter involves the **assembly** and/or creation of several **widgets**, building more complex widgets by combining many simpler ones. In Flutter, moreover, a **widget** represents an immutable **description** of the **user interface**: graphics, text, shapes, animations, and in general **any graphic object** that appears on the screen are created using **widgets**.

To actually define the content of a custom widget (i.e., a custom class that extends *StatelessWidget* or *StatefulWidget*), must be executed *override* of the inherited **build()** method, the return of which is what will be displayed. In fact, the ***build()*** method is responsible for building the widget and displaying it.

So in this case the largest container is the custom widget *MyFlutterApp* that is launched by the function *main()*. In fact, its method *build()* returns the widget *MaterialApp* which has as its child the custom widget *CameraScreen*, described in Sect. 3.2.

[7] https://dart.dev/guides/.

[8] At the following link https://pub.dev/packages the entire library of Dart packages that can be used with the Fluter framework can be consulted.

[9] https://docs.flutter.dev/.

```
import 'package:flutter/material.dart';

void main() async {
  runApp(const MyFlutterApp());
}

class MyFlutterApp extends StatelessWidget {
  const MyFlutterApp({super.key});

  @override
  Widget build(BuildContext context) {
    return MaterialApp(
      title: 'Flutter␣App',
      debugShowCheckedModeBanner: false,
      theme: ThemeData(
        colorScheme: ColorScheme.fromSeed(seedColor: Colors.green),
        useMaterial3: true,
      ),
      home: const CameraScreen(),
    );
  }
}
```

Listing 1.3. *main()* function and *MyFlutterApp* class.

Figure 1 shows the widget tree of the entire application.

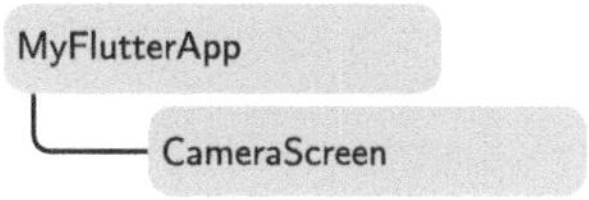

Fig. 1. Application Widget Tree.

3 Architecture of the System

In order for them to be effectively used by the classifier, frames captured by the camera must be converted into objects of **class** ***Image***[10]. In order to use the latter class, it is necessary to import the **package** ***image*** within the app.

3.1 Class *ImageUtils*

Within the class ***ImageUtils*** are then defined the **functions** that allow the conversion of **objects** of **class** ***CameraImage*** (i.e., frames captured by the ***camera***) to **objects** of the **class** ***Image***. Depending on the device used (Android or iOS), the *CameraImage* class object coincides with two different types of images: bgra8888 for iOS and YUV420 for Android.

Therefore, the functions to be implemented are as follows:

- *convertBGRA8888ToImage()*
- *convertYUV420ToImage()*

[10] https://pub.dev/documentation/image/latest/.

3.2 Class *CameraScreen*

This custom widget takes care of camera management through the use of the package ***camera***[11].

In fact, the *camera* package was imported to be able to use the ***CameraPreview*** widget, which allows the display of a screen where the camera is active. The two main objects that were used are the class ***controller*** and the function ***availableCameras()***, which is needed to get the list of all the cameras in the device. In addition, the following functions were also used:

- ***getMinZoomLevel()*** and ***getMaxZoomLevel()***, which allow capturing the minimum and maximum zoom value of the camera used, respectively.
- ***getMinExposureOffset()*** and ***getMaxExposureOffset()***, which respectively allow capturing the minimum and maximum exposure value of the camera used.
- ***takePicture()***, which allows you to take a picture.

The screen interface, whose widget tree is shown in Fig. 2, is made possible from the widget ***Stack***, which allows multiple widgets to be stacked on top of each other.

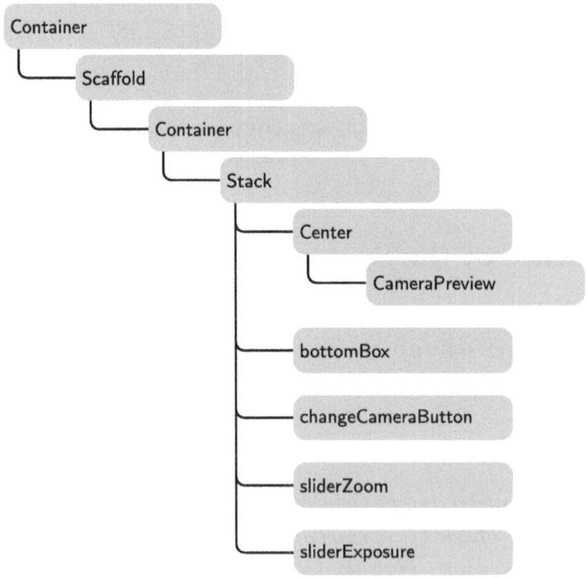

Fig. 2. *CameraScreen* Widget Tree.

[11] https://pub.dev/documentation/camera/latest/.

In fact, the following custom widgets are placed above the main widget:

- widget returned by the function ***bottomBox()***, positioned **at the bottom of the screen** and within which appear the **information** obtained through the **classification** of the **image framed** by the user.
- widget returned by the function ***sliderZoom()***, which realizes a slider to increase or decrease the zoom.
    - The slider is made with the widget ***Slider***, at whose **field** ***onChanged*** is assigned an **anonymous function** that **updates** the **current zoom value** with the one set by the user by calling the ***setState()*** function to update the widget display.
- widget returned by the function ***sliderExposure()***, which makes a slider to increase or decrease the display.
    - The slider is made with the widget ***Slider***, at whose **field** ***onChanged*** is assigned an **anonymous function** that **updates** the **current display value** with the one set by the user by calling the function ***setState()*** to update the display of the widget.

The function *initCamera*
The function ***initCamera()***, shown in Listing 1.4 has the simple task of initializing the widget ***CameraView***, by performing the following operations:

- **captures** all the **cameras** available in the **device** via the ***availableCameras()*** function of the **package camera**, assigning them to a list of class ***List<CameraDescription>***.
- calls the function ***initController()***, described in the next Sect. 3.2.

```
void initCamera() async {
    if (camerasList.isEmpty) {
      camerasList = await availableCameras();
    }
    for (var i = 0; i < camerasList.length; i++) {
      if (listaCamere[i].lensDirection == widget.initialCameraLensDirection)
          {
        currentCameraIndex = i;
        break;
      }
    }
    if (currentCameraIndex != -1) {
      initController();
    }
  }
```

Listing 1.4. *initCamera* function of *CameraScreen*.

It should be noted that the function ***initCamera()*** is **recalled** by the function ***initState()*** of the widget ***CameraScreen***.

The function *initController*
The function ***initController()*** deals with the **creation** of the **controller** class ***CameraController***, to which are given as input, for example, one of the **cameras** class ***CameraDescription*** captured earlier in the *initCamera()* function, or the resolution with which it will be used and disabling audio while using the camera as it is not necessary.

After **istanced** the **controller**, you perform the following operations, as shown in the code excerpt contained in Listing 1.5:

1. You start the procedure that allows the execution of the function ***imageAnalysis()*** with each captured frame.
2. You **create** the class object ***ImageClassificationHelper*** to create the classifier.
3. You execute ***initHelper()*** to actually load the classification model.
4. The operations of capturing the maximum and mini zoom and exposure values with the appropriate functions provided by **package** ***camera*** are executed.

```
Future initController() async {
        final camera = cameraList[currentCamera];
        controller = CameraController(
        camera,
        ResolutionPreset.high,
        enableAudio: false,
        imageFormatGroup: Platform.isAndroid ? ImageFormatGroup.yuv420 :
            ImageFormatGroup.bgra8888,
        );
        controller?.initialize().then((_) {

                //1
                controller!.startImageStream(imageAnalysis);


                //2
                imageClassificationHelper = ImageClassificationHelper();

                //3
                imageClassificationHelper.initHelper();

                ...
        });
}
```

Listing 1.5. Excerpt from the function *initController* of *CameraScreen*.

The function *imageAnalysis()*

The ***imageAnalysis()*** function, presented in Listing 1.6, is the most important function of the *CameraScreen* widget since it is executed for each frame that the *CameraView* widget captures when the camera is active and if the analysis operation is not currently active. The function ***imageAnalysis()*** calls the function ***inferenceCameraFrame()*** on the object of class ***ImageClassificationHelper***, passing to it as the **parameter** the **frame** of class ***CameraImage***.

```
Future<void> imageAnalysis(CameraImage cameraImage) async {
        if (_isProcessing) {
                return;
        }
        _isProcessing = true;

        try {
                classification = await imageClassificationHelper.
                    inferenceCameraFrame(cameraImage);
        } catch (e) {
                print(
                ''Late Inizialization Exception.  imageClassificationHelper
                    not yet initialized.'');
        }
```

```
        _isProcessing = false;
        if (mounted) {
                setState(() {});
        }
}
```

Listing 1.6. *imageAnalysis* function of *CameraScreen.*

3.3 Creation of a Second *Isolate*

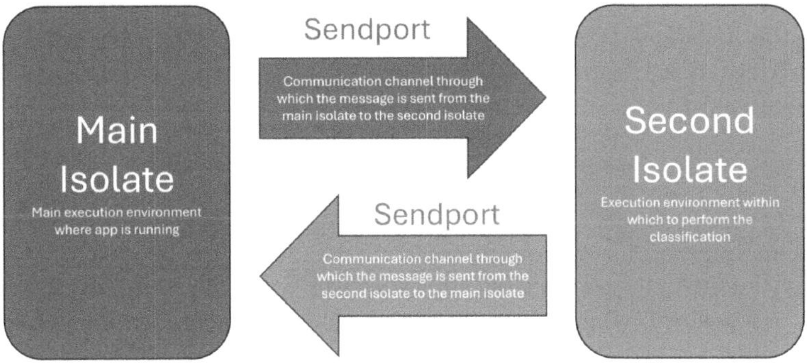

Fig. 3. Scheme of operation of the *Isolates* and the communication mechanism between them.

***Isolates* e communication mechanism**
The classification operation takes a lot of resources to perform, so it makes sense to separate it from the one environment currently running that manages the entire application. The *main()* method launches the execution of the app within the ***MainIsolate***[12], which basically consists of an isolated execution environment similar to a java thread. To separate the classification operation from the rest, one must then initialize a new *Isolate*, within which one must execute everything necessary to classify the frame captured by the camera.

In order then for the output of the classifier to be shown on the screen at the end of the classification operation, it is necessary for the second *Isolate* to communicate the label to the *MainIsolate*. As shown schematically in Fig. 3, one must then implement the unique **mechanism** of **communication between *Isolates*** that initiates via **message exchange**. In particular, the main objects with which a communication channel is realized are *ReceivePort* and *SendPort*:

- ***ReceivePort*** is the object from which an *Isolate* receives messages, listening to the corresponding *SendPort*.

[12] https://docs.flutter.dev/perf/isolates.

- ***SendPort***, on the other hand, represents the actual communication channel and is created with the *sendPort()* method of ***ReceivePort***.
  - A ***SendPort*** is then always instantiated starting with the creation of a ***ReceivePort*** via the *send()* method.

Therefore, the creation of the class ***IsolateInference*** is indispensable.

IsolateInference **class**
The class ***IsolateInference*** is basically identified with the second *Isolate* within which to perform the classification operation and has associated **3 fields** that are extremely important:

- the **2 objects** of class ***ReceivePort*** and ***SendPort*** for the **communication** with the *MainIsolate*.
- the **object** class ***Isolate*** that coincides with the actual **second execution environment**.

In addition, it is essential to define the following **functions**:

1. ***start()***
   - This function has the simple of:
     (a) **create** the **istance** of class ***Isolate*** with the appropriate function ***spawn()***, which allows the creation of the second execution environment.
     (b) listens to the second *Isolate* to receive the message from the *MainIsolate*.
2. ***close()***
   - This function has the simple of:
     (a) **destroy** the **istance** of class *Isolate* with the appropriate function ***kill()*** called on the class object *Isolate*.
     (b) **close** also the **communication channel** by means of the ***close()*** function called on the ***ReceivePort***.
3. ***entryPoint()***
   - This function, shown in Listing 1.7, is executed whenever the ***Isolate*** receives a message from the ***MainIsolate*** and is responsible for the actual classification of the frame. The ***message*** that it receives is the ***InferenceModel*** class object[13] which is appropriately **created with each frame captured by the camera** and which contains everything needed to perform the classification.
     (a) After converting the *CameraFrame* to an object of class *Image* and appropriately generating the 3-dimensional matrix (remember that, in the example, the model receives a matrix with normalised values, thus divided by 255) and appropriately setting the *shape* of the model input and output, the function loads the classification model and performs the classification, obtaining the output.

[13] The class ***InferenceModel*** is described in more detail in Sect. 3.4.

(b) Finally, after appropriately transforming the output of the model into a map of the type ***label: value*** (where *value* is a decimal number from 0 to 1 expressing the probability of belonging to that class), the function sends the result to the *MainIsolate* exploiting the *SendPort* associated with the *InferenceModel*.

```
static void entryPoint(SendPort sendPort) async {
    final port = ReceivePort();
    sendPort.send(port.sendPort);

    await for (final InferenceModel isolateModel in port) {
      image_lib.Image? img;

      img = ImageUtils.convertCameraImage(isolateModel.cameraImage!);

      image_lib.Image imageInput = image_lib.copyResize(
        img!,
        width: isolateModel.inputShape[1],
        height: isolateModel.inputShape[2],
      );

      imageInput = image_lib.copyRotate(imageInput, angle: 90);

      final imageMatrix = List.generate(
        imageInput.height,
        (y) => List.generate(
          imageInput.width,
          (x) {
            final pixel = imageInput.getPixel(x, y);
            return [pixel.r / 255, pixel.g / 255, pixel.b / 255];
          },
        ),
      );

      final input = [imageMatrix];

      final output = [List<double>.filled(isolateModel.outputShape[1], 0.0)];

      Interpreter interpreter = Interpreter.fromAddress(isolateModel.
          interpreterAddress);
      interpreter.run(input, output);

      final result = output.first;

      double maxScore = result.reduce((a, b) => a + b);

      var classification = <String, double>{};
      for (var i = 0; i < result.length; i++) {
        if (result[i] != 0) {
          classification[isolateModel.labels[i]] = result[i].toDouble() /
              maxScore.toDouble();
        }
      }
      isolateModel.responsePort.send(classification);
    }
  }
```

Listing 1.7. *entryPoint* function of *ImageClassificationHelper*.

3.4 *InferenceModel* Class

The class ***InferenceModel*** has the sole purpose of enabling the **communication** between the *MainIsolate* and the second *Isolate*. As already specified, the

MainIsolate class object is in fact the **content** of the **message** that the *MainIsolate* sends to the second *Isolate* whenever the device's camera captures a frame. This class, in fact, contains only a **set** of **fields necessary** for **classification**:

- class object *CameraImage* captured by the camera.
- object of class *Image*.
- integer value specifying the address of class object *Interpreter* (the classifier).
- list of type *List<String>* that contains the labels involved in the classification.
- list of type *List<int>* that contains the *shape* of the classifier input (in this case it is [1, 256, 256, 3], i.e., a vector containing 3 256×256 matrices).
- list of type *List<int>* that contains the *shape* of the classifier's output (in this case it is [1, 4], i.e., a vector containing 4 decimal values from 0 to 1, each associated with its respective label).
- object of class *SendPort* for communication between the *MainIsolate* and the second *Isolate*.

3.5 *ImageClassificationHelper* Class

Within this class are defined the **functions** that deal with the **management** of the **model *.tflite***, among which we emphasize:

- ***loadModel()***
  - It is responsible for loading the model (***.tflite*** stored in the **folder *assets***) into the class variable ***Interpreter*** (the use of which is allowed through the package ***tflite_flutter***[14]).
- ***loadLabels()***
  - It provides the loading of labels (*labels*) stored in the corresponding text file *.txt*.
- ***initHelper()***
  - It takes care of initiating the procedures for the creation of the second *Isolate*, in particular it provides:
    1. create the class object ***IsolateInference***.
    2. call the function ***start()*** on the newly created class object ***IsolateInference***, which, as already described in Sect. 3.3, listens for the message containing the class object ***InferenceModel***.
- ***inferenceCameraFrame()***
  - As visible in Listing 1.8, it takes care of creating the class object ***InferenceModel*** which is the object that the *MainIsolate* exchanges in the communication channel with the other *Isolate*. Specifically, it performs the following operations:
    1. first creates the class object ***ReceivePort***, the only means of communication (along with ***SendPort***) between ***Isolate***.

[14] https://www.tensorflow.org/lite.

2. connects the ***SendPort*** class objects of the ***MainIsolate*** and the second ***Isolate***.
3. opens a *listener* such that it waits for the **response** of the second *Isolate*.
4. returns as a result the response sent by the second *Isolate* to the *MainIsolate*, that is, the label that the classifier assigned to the frame captured by the device camera.

– ***close()***
  • Instead, it deals with the closure of the second *Isolate*, thus executing the function ***close()*** on the class object ***IsolateInference***.
    * It is pointed out that the function ***close()*** of the class *ImageClassificationHelper* is ***dispose()*** by the function ***dispose()*** of the widget ***CameraScreen***. When the ***CameraScreen*** widget is closed, the second execution space reserved for the classification operation is then also closed.

```
Future<Map<String, double>> inferenceCameraFrame(CameraImage cameraImage)
    async {


    var inferenceModel = InferenceModel(cameraImage, null, interpreter.
        address, labels, inputTensor.shape, outputTensor.shape);

    ReceivePort responsePort = ReceivePort();
    isolateInference.sendPort.send(inferenceModel..responsePort =
        responsePort.sendPort);

    var results = await responsePort.first;
    return results;
  }
```

Listing 1.8. *inferenceCameraFrame* function of *ImageClassificationHelper*.

4 Feature Applications: *Lions Umbria Art*, Cultural Outreach App

The functionality analysed and developed in this paper was realised for the cultural outreach application *Lions Umbria Art*. As visible in Fig. 4, the user can open the camera of his or her device whenever he or she wants to take pictures of the works he or she is viewing during the art visit. Taking a cue from cultural museum applications and simple basic virtual reality features, the user, while taking the photo, has the possibility in real time to read on the screen some information associated with the work he or she is framing, such as its name and author. In this way, as anticipated within the Introduction, the user actively participates in the artistic visit, intelligently using the smartphone enriching the experience without, however, sacrificing contact with reality.

Fig. 4. Screenshot that allows the user to read the associated information in real time as they are framing the work with their smartphone.

5 Conclusions

The use of development frameworks such as Flutter and programming languages highly expressive such as Dart has made it possible to ascertain the feasibility practicality of developing sufficiently complex and feature-rich software integrating an artificial intelligence model.

First, it was indeed possible to see the enormous advantage of writing of the only source code, thus halving the entire app development. The management and integration of the classification model is uniquely implementable for both target platforms (iOS and Android), with rare exceptions of single management (such as the conversion of the *CameraImage* object, which depending on the device is in bgra8888 format for iOS and YUV420 for Android and thus requires writing 2 conversion functions).

Second, the excellent execution performance of the classification model could be ascertained. Indeed, the separate handling of the operation within the second *Isolate* ensures that there is no loss of smoothness in the user interface. In addition, the Flutter framework together with the Tensorflow Lite format guarantees excellent performance, especially from the point of view of classification timing. In fact, the latter is substantially immediate, ensuring maximum responsiveness and ease of use by the user. It is also pointed out that the quality of the classification is obviously not taken into account, since the latter depends on the goodness of the construction of the classification model and the appropriate training of the latter, providing an adequate dataset in order to avoid overfitting or underfitting. Also significant is the mechanism for handling Isolates provided by the Flutter framework, which allows the application (both the simplified version just described and *Lions Umbria Art*) to be extremely responsive, both on devices equipped with high-end hardware and software optimizations such as Google Pixel 8, and on more modest devices such as Nothing Phone (1). Finally, also not to be forgotten is the final size of the application, which, despite the packages used and the presence of a classification model, is nevertheless sufficiently contained without therefore being a real disadvantage for users who will wish to download it to their smartphones.

Acronyms

The following acronyms are used in this manuscript:

API	Application Programming Interface
AR	Augmented Reality
iOS	iPhone Operating System
JS	JavaScript
JSON	JavaScript Object Notation
RGB	Red Green e Blue

References

1. Pellas, N., Dengel, A., Christopoulos, A.: A scoping review of immersive virtual reality in STEM education. IEEE Trans. Learn. Technol. **13**(4), pp. 748–761 (2020). https://doi.org/10.1109/TLT.2020.3019405
2. Buragohain, D., Deng, C., Sharma, A., Chaudhary, S.: The impact of immersive learning on teacher effectiveness: a systematic study. IEEE Access **12**, 35924–35933 (2024). https://doi.org/10.1109/ACCESS.2024.3373541
3. Zhang, X.: The college english teaching reform supported by multimedia teaching technology and immersive virtual reality technology. In: 2019 International Conference on Virtual Reality and Intelligent Systems (ICVRIS), pp. 77–80 (2019). https://doi.org/10.1109/ICVRIS.2019.00028
4. Han, H., Lu, A., Wells, U.: Under the movement of head: evaluating visual attention in immersive virtual reality environment. In: 2017 International Conference on Virtual Reality and Visualization (ICVRV), pp. 294–295 (2017). https://doi.org/10.1109/ICVRV.2017.00067
5. Perri, D., Fortunelli, M., Simonetti, M., Magni, R., Carloni, J., Gervasi, O.: Rapid prototyping of virtual reality cognitive exercises in a tele-rehabilitation context. In: Electron. (Switz.) **10**(4) (2021). Cited by: 6; All Open Access, Gold Open Access, Green Open Access, pp. 1–16. https://doi.org/10.3390/electronics10040457
6. Rajasagi, D.P.: Immersive health data visualization in virtual reality. In: 2023 IEEE Conference on Virtual Reality and 3D User Interfaces Abstracts and Workshops (VRW), pp. 971–972 (2023). https://doi.org/10.1109/VRW58643.2023.00328
7. Gervasi, O., Perri, D., Simonetti, M.: Empowering knowledge with virtual and augmented reality. IEEE Access **11**, 144649–144662 (2023). https://doi.org/10.1109/ACCESS.2023.3342116
8. Qu, M., Sun, Y., Feng, Y.: Digital media and VR art creation for metaverse. In: 2022 2nd Asia Conference on Information Engineering (ACIE), pp. 48–51 (2022). https://doi.org/10.1109/ACIE55485.2022.00018
9. Gervasi, O., Perri, D., Simonetti, M., Tasso, S.: Strategies for the digitalization of cultural heritage. In: Gervasi, O., Murgante, B., Misra, S., Rocha, A.M.A.C., Garau, C. (eds.) Computational Science and Its Applications – ICCSA 2022 Workshops. ICCSA 2022. LNCS, vol. 13382. Springer, Cham. https://doi.org/10.1007/978-3-031-10592-0_35
10. Hong, R., He, H.: Interference and consultation in virtual public space: the practice of intermedia art in metaverse. In: 2021 17th International Conference on Mobility, Sensing and Networking (MSN), pp. 792–797 (2021). https://doi.org/10.1109/MSN53354.2021.00124
11. Perri, D., Simonetti, M., Tasso, S., Gervasi, O.: Open metaverse with open software. In: Gervasi, O., et al. Computational Science and Its Applications – ICCSA 2023 Workshops. ICCSA 2023. LNCS, vol. 14111. Springer, Cham (2023). https://doi.org/10.1007/978-3-031-37126-4_37
12. Li, X., Li, K., Zhao, H., Lou, Y., Geng, X., Huang, W.: Virtual reality custom interactive art space. In: 2020 International Conference on Virtual Reality and Visualization (ICVRV), pp. 365–366 (2020). https://doi.org/10.1109/ICVRV51359.2020.00104
13. Liu, Q.: The virtual reality technology in art design. In: 2012 2nd International Conference on Consumer Electronics, Communications and Networks (CECNet), pp. 2226–2228 (2012). https://doi.org/10.1109/CECNet.2012.6201444

14. Wu, X., Yuan, X.: Innovation system of film art creation based on virtual reality technology. In: 2021 6th International Conference on Smart Grid and Electrical Automation (ICSGEA), pp. 231–234 (2021). https://doi.org/10.1109/ICSGEA53208.2021.00057
15. Kumar, G., Kumar, P., Kumar, D.: Brain tumor detection using convolutional neural network. In: 2021 IEEE International Conference on Mobile Networks and Wireless Communications (ICMNWC), pp. 1–6 (2021). https://doi.org/10.1109/ICMNWC52512.2021.9688460
16. Perri, D., Simonetti, M., Lombardi, A., Faginas-Lago, N., Gervasi, O.: Binary classification of proteins by a machine learning approach. In: Gervasi, O., et al (eds.). Computational Science and Its Applications – ICCSA 2020. ICCSA 2020, vol. 12255. Springer, Cham (2020). https://doi.org/10.1007/978-3-030-58820-5_41
17. Tseng, C.C., Lee, S.L.: Design of digital differentiator using supervised learning on keras framework. In: 2019 IEEE 8th Global Conference on Consumer Electronics (GCCE), pp. 162–163 (2019). https://doi.org/10.1109/GCCE46687.2019.9014634
18. Joshi, S., Owens, J.A., Shah, S., Munasinghe, T.: Analysis of preprocessing techniques, keras tuner, and transfer learning on cloud street image data. In: 2021 IEEE International Conference on Big Data (Big Data), pp. 4165–4168 (2021). https://doi.org/10.1109/BigData52589.2021.9671878
19. Konaite, M., et al.: Smart hat for the blind with real-time object detection using raspberry pi and tensor- flow lite. In: Proceedings of the International Conference on Artificial Intelligence and Its Applications. icARTi '21. Virtual Event, Mauritius: Association for Computing Machinery, pp. 1–6 (2021). isbn: 9781450385756. https://doi.org/10.1145/3487923.3487929
20. Ahmed, S., Bons, M.: Edge computed NILM: a phone-based implementation using MobileNet compressed by Tensorflow Lite. In: Proceedings of the 5th International Workshop on Non-Intrusive Load Monitoring. NILM'20. Virtual Event, Japan: Association for Computing Machinery, 2020, pp. 44–48. isbn: 9781450381918. https://doi.org/10.1145/3427771.3427852. url: https://doi.org/10.1145/3427771.3427852
21. Lohani, D.: Taking Flutter to the Web: Learn How to Build Crossplatform UIs For Web and Mobile Platforms Using Flutter For Web. Packt Publishing (2022). isbn: 1801817715

Advanced Processes of Mathematics and Computing Models in Complex Computational Systems (AMCM 2024)

Mental Health News Coverage in Turkish National Newspapers with Respect to Episodic and Thematic Framing: A Retrospective Content Analysis

Ahu Dereli Dursun[1](✉) and Aslı Tunç[2]

[1] Institute of Social Sciences, Communication Studies, Istanbul Bilgi University, Istanbul, Türkiye
ahu.dereli.dursun@bilgiedu.net
[2] Faculty of Communication, Department of Media, Istanbul Bilgi University, Istanbul, Türkiye
asli.tunc@bilgi.edu.tr

Abstract. News framing is a process by which news media highlight, emphasize and place prominence to a certain aspect of a news story. This process is comprised of constructing news narratives to shape the perceptions and attitudes of the audience within the context of communication studies. Thereby, news framing is stated to shape public opinion and understanding through its emphasis of particular aspects of news stories, which may come to mean subtle guiding of the audience interpretations. Episodic and thematic framing constitute two approaches in news frames as suggested by Iyengar. If news is expressed as an episodic event, its focus is on discrete and individual cases, specific incidents, or personal aspects of issues. In contrast, thematically framed news points to a broader trend over time, background information or expert opinions provided concerning the issue being handled. Accordingly, this study aims to elucidate episodic and thematic framing approaches in the news items covered in Turkish print media over a five-year period (2014–2018). A total of 577 news items on mental health and psychological problems published in six Turkish daily newspapers constitute the sample dataset of the study on which the content analyses of framing approaches are conducted. In addition, frequency distributions calculated present the measurement of the most frequently occurring frame types in the newspaper items by the newspaper and year. The results of the study provide an extract of the portrayal of mental health-related news in in Türkiye, while attempting to point a way toward addressing news on a pressing social issue, namely mental health, from a systemic perspective. Based on these considerations and validation through the statistical frequency measurements and framing methods, the study aims at contributing to the understanding of how mental health issues are framed within the theoretical framework of social constructionism and framing applications.

Keywords: News Framing · Episodic and Thematic Framing Approaches · Mental Health News · Content Analysis · Framing Theory Applications · Textual News Data Analysis · Computational Statistical Frequency Measurements · Print News Media · Ethical Journalism · Journalistic Practices · News Media Framing

O. Gervasi et al. (Eds.): ICCSA 2024 Workshops, LNCS 14815, pp. 59–71, 2024.
https://doi.org/10.1007/978-3-031-65154-0_4

Analysis · Frames as Dependent Variables · Qualitative and Quantitative Techniques of Content Analysis · Expert Opinion

1 Introduction

Social constructionism, pioneered by sociologist Berger and philosopher Luckman (1966), is a theory of knowledge and approach in social sciences which in brief states that people develop knowledge of the work in social contexts and much of what they perceive as reality depends on shared assumptions [1]. This theoretical position, which upholds that learning and knowledge are socially created, has become influential towards making sense of reality and social world by questioning the existence of rational and objective knowledge. In that regard, characteristics which are considered to be solely biological (i.e. class, ability, race, gender, and so forth) and immutable are products of definitions and interpretations made by humans and shaped by historical and cultural contexts. Social constructionism, therefore, challenges positivist positions as it is not possible for reality to be self-evident or stable. It cannot be an objective truth either since reality is a product of humans' activities, and their experiences are mediated historically, culturally and linguistically. The last note is related to the view that humans' understanding of the world is influenced by language, symbols and discourse, which also emphasizes the social nature of reality. Along this view, mental distress would be regarded as being situated within specific cultural and historical moments where society's language is the part of the creation of a given 'disorder' [2]. Regarding news, social construction of news perspective relinquishes handling news as an entirely formed and stable thing. Rather, it acknowledges that news is a dynamic entity shaped by the environment. This means that a journalist's personal and education background, workplace arrangements and interactions with society at large over the particular period of time could all affect the construction of news [3]. Based on the social constructionist perspective, different sorts of societal activities and interactions are at the center of how reality is perceived and understood. As a consequence, journalism can be conceptualized as a social practice, with journalists acting as critical social actors who influence the way news stories are represented [4]. Other factors like ideological impacts, professional values and organizational cultures also need to be taken into consideration in the process of construction [5]. In short, the news as is reported in the media is less a reflection of the reality and significance of a situation than a contested space in which the inclusion or exclusion of certain social actors in a story, as well as impacts of journalists themselves, conscious or else, are crucial [6]. These indicate the relevance of social constructionism to different disciplines such as philosophy, sociology, psychology, anthropology education and communication. Correspondingly, social construction of news assumes a sociological standpoint to examine the way working arrangements in the news organizations and professional beliefs shape the expectations for news production.

Framing, in communication, describes the process in which certain aspects of an issue are emphasized, while others are excluded, as put by Entman [7]. Essentially involving selection and salience, to frame refers to select some aspects of a perceived reality and to make them more salient in a communicating text so that a particular problem definition, causal interpretation, moral evaluation and/or treatment recommendation for the item described can be promoted. Framing is regarded as one of the ways by which media messages assign meanings to issues, linking them with the broader environment. A frame suggests how the issue should be thought about and understood [8]. More concisely, framing has a function of shaping the way the public thinks about an issue through proposing what the issue is about, who the cause is and what is required to be done as a remedy or solution. It is reported that news media can frame the question of responsibility, causing the audience to conclude the reasons for and solutions to social problems [9]. As a consequence of the function of the frames in terms of shaping individual understanding and opinion about an issue by highlighting the specific elements of a broader controversy, a generally complex issue can be reduced down to one or two central aspects [10]. At the previous stages of framing theory, Goffman assumed that framing is an analytical tool through which individuals can actively get engaged in the classification of different events and interpret the meanings of those events [11]. Further on, Gamson developed this concept into the structure of the basic point of practice providing meaning or the formation of a story line with meaningful interpretation [12, 13]. As Goffman states, frames generate a mechanism that enables us to store the realities in our minds in order that we can retrieve them as needed. Through this mechanism, the reality that focuses on a certain frame is contained, whereas the other realities are left out [11]. Besides its classification and simplification function, which is cognitive, all these definitions and explanations also indicate the subtle function of framing mechanism and its somehow manipulative aspect when selective emphasis and attribution of responsibility are at stake in particular. Another argument pointed out is that framing as a part of the culture may guide elites to construct information and influence journalists to select information and present that information in the text, which impacts the attitude and cognition of the audience [14]. Framing, noticeably, relies on the basis of social consensus whose exploration is helpful for having a more profound interpretation of the formation mechanism of frames. In addition, the basis of social consensus holds significance to refine and analyze frames [15]. When all these aforementioned cultural, contextual and linguistic aspects are considered, it can be noted that both social construction and framing consider the role of language and impact of communication in shaping perceptions of reality.

Episodic and thematic approaches to news framing as a model were suggested by Iyengar who stated that news could be expressed as an episodic event or thematic event. The former refers to the conveying of the events as isolated, one-time individual cases with a focus on the personal aspects of the issue. In episodic framing, the individual's experience or a specific event is used for the illustration of the issue. Thematic framing, on the other hand, addresses the part of a broader trend or background information on the topic, which brings up the portrayal of issues through information related to the systemic causes, consequences and trends [9]. Regarding the health problems' coverage, thematic framing would then include statistical trends, expert analyses of contextual conditions, reports on research related to disease prevention and treatment, widespread outcomes as well as presentation of remedies at community level and based on policies to be implemented [16–18].

A large body of communication research has examined how responsibility is attributed for social problems, oriented towards societal- and personal-level consequences of the responsibility attribution since Iyengar's study on responsibility framing [9] and Weiner's work on attribution theory in which the question of responsibility has been among the fundamental notions in understanding human interactions, evaluation of other people as well as policy making processes [19]. The interest in research concerned with frames and responsibility in health communication has been due to their importance in shaping public opinion. Responsibility frames are stated to have the potential to shape the public perception of health issues like diabetes, obesity or mental illness, concerning responsibility attributions for their causes and treatment in particular. To illustrate, the systematic review applied a quantitative content analysis on the published literature, namely articles in peer-reviewed scientific journals, about framing in the field of health communication to provide the description of common topics, characteristics and the use of different types of frames besides the sociological and psychological tendency of framing [20]. The review also addressed the framing effect studies to examine if they contained competitive frames along with gain and loss framing. The way news stories report about health is stated to generate shifts in the perceptions of readers pertaining to problems of health problems. Another review on the studies published between 2004 and 2019 employs different methodological approaches [21]. The content analyses conducted demonstrate that different media attribute frequently (not exclusively) health responsibility to individuals. On the effect scale, despite not being clear-cut pertaining to affective and behavioral outcomes, experimental studies show that policy support is reduced by individual responsibility frames. Another finding of the review is its revealing of some research gaps on responsibility frames related to health since the effects of responsibility frames are understudied and the focus is on noncommunicable diseases like obesity and depression with communicable diseases being paid less attention. The authors also share the finding that the conceptual focus on individual versus societal responsibility based on episodic versus thematic framing could be problematic due to inhibiting a more nuanced understanding of responsibility frames and their effects. An inductive mixed-method computational approach was presented in another study which proposed novel computational tools as for inductive frame identification in another study where the frame elements were demonstrated to be identified through topic modeling, being automatically grouped into frame packages [22].

Continuing with the effects of episodic and thematic framing, the authors of a related study manipulated two variables in a controlled experiment [23]. These variables were the number of sources with their expertise and the framing. The framing was changed from an episodic frame, which is said to be traditional, to thematic frame including information related to context, risk factors, prevention strategies as well as attributions of responsibility. The results of the study indicated that the use of a thematic frame enabled readers to be more supportive regarding public policy changes, prompting them to improve their own health behaviors. Even though the study showed that no change was seen in the attribution of responsibility for health problems, it revealed the positive effect of thematic framing on the perceptions scale of the readers with regard to health problems. The findings of these studies underscore the importance of thematic framing in terms of reflecting a wide-angle lens considering the broader context. Regarding the attributions of responsibility, the study points towards the concept of audience awareness in thematic framing, which is stated to treat the audience as informed citizens, bringing out critical mode of thinking about societal issues. Framing perspective makes up the topic of another study which examined the coverage of television news about autism based on issues, sources, personal and social responsibility [24]. The last two components mentioned refer to episodic and thematic aspects, respectively. The content analysis covering two decades (from 1990 to 2010) identified that the top three key issues were personal stories, children and cause. As source, doctors were the most interviewed sources that were followed by family and people with autism. As for episodic and thematic aspects, personal (episodic) responsibility frames were more in number compared to the social (thematic) ones.

Regarding the news media coverage of mental health news, there is often association with negative elements. Linking the individuals who experience mental health problems with criminality, violence, unpredictability, unusual acts, irrecoverability, and so on has been shown to be among the common trends in such news media coverage [25–29]. Motivated by the fact that portrayal of mental illnesses negatively by media may contribute to the mental illness stigmatization, while objective portrayals could help improve mental health literacy and reduce stigma, a narrative review of studies on mental illnesses in media is provided and important gaps in research are identified [30].

As an important source of information on different topics, particularly the ones about which individuals have no direct experience or knowledge, newspapers are considered to one of the primary sources of information on different topics. As evidenced by different work, the news items on mental health and psychological problems display negative frames (dangerousness being a very common theme) more compared to positive ones (stories of recovery or accomplishment) [31]. Negative depictions may be influential on different parties and stakeholders since the coverage of health-related information by media is stated to have impact on patients, families, medical professionals, and government officials to a significant extent [32]. In addition, the way news stories report on health issues has the potential of generating shifts in the readers' perceptions of problems [23]. The studies analyzing the depiction of mental health disorders in media in Turkish context seem to be limited in number. One retrospective scanning study deals with the investigation of the perception of the word schizophrenia in 12 Turkish newspapers (2001–2006), revealing that the word is attributed with strong negative perception [33]. Another retrospective study assesses the articles in Turkish newspapers mentioning individuals with mental disorders, presenting the way scope of the news relates to people with mental disorders. The results show that nearly all the reviewed articles were negative toward people with mental disorders with forensic, criminalization and victimization themes being dominant [34]. As shown by research, there needs to be more studies to determine the situation with regard to news media portrayal of mental health and those with mental disorders. Against this motivational aspect and need, the current study has the aim of providing information on the episodic and thematic framing approaches in the national newspapers of Türkiye so that dynamic processes underlying frames and their development can be presented.

The rest of the paper is organized as follows. Section 2 provides information on the materials and methods. Section 3 addresses the experimental results and discussion. Section 4 presents the conclusion and future directions.

2 Materials and Methods

2.1 Mental Health News Dataset

The newspaper stories about mental health and psychological problems printed over a five-year period (2014–2018) in six daily national newspapers of Türkiye, which are *Hürriyet*, *Milliyet*, *Cumhuriyet*, *Posta*, *Sabah* and *Sözcü*, accessible through their electronic databases comprise the dataset of this study. The total number of the newspaper stories analyzed corresponds to 577 with the following distribution across the newspapers: *Hürriyet* (n = 187), *Milliyet* (n = 131), *Cumhuriyet* (n = 28), *Posta* (n = 14), *Sabah* (n = 131) and *Sözcü* (n = 86). The number of newspaper stories analyzed by year is as follows: 75 stories in 2014, 127 in 2015, 113 in 2016, 126 in 2017 and 136 in 2018. The newspaper items were selected from the regular news stories related to mental health and psychological issues. The dataset belongs to the dissertation named "News Media Portrayal of Mental Health and Psychological Problems: An Analysis of Daily Newspapers in Turkey". The focus of the news stories is on the portrayal of mental health and those living with this particular condition.

2.2 Methods

Media framing for the current research involves the analysis of media by employing qualitative and quantitative content analysis techniques to assess and describe the frames in the news. Media frames have been treated as a dependent variable to examine how different frames have been used by the newspapers so that specific issues can be presented. It has been analyzed whether a news item has been predominantly presented episodically and thematically, which is Iyengar's concept forming the foundation of the content analysis of the study. The news item was coded as episodically framed if individual-focused matters were foregrounded and as thematically if systemic and societal factors were predominant. If the content covered both aspects of the issue with equal amounts of episodic and thematic content, it was coded mutually episodic and thematic. For cases when no such focus was able to be captured, it was coded as non-applicable (NA).

2.2.1 Media Framing Theory and Methods Related to Frames

Framing analysis is presented as a constructivist approach for the examination of news discourse with the principal focus on news texts' conceptualization into empirically operationalizable dimensions (i.e. script, syntactical, thematic and rhetorical structures) so that proof of the news media's framing pertaining to issues in news texts may be gathered [13]. Media framing involves a process of developing certain interpretation based on problem definition, cause, moral judgment and solution, so it may provide an appropriate method to the question regarding media. In making sense of the real world and everyday life situations, frame analysis provides a systematic account of the way humans use expectations, which is known as the framing process [35]. According to Goffman, daily life encompasses numerous shifts in frames which are negotiated through the use of social cues [11]. These show the discursive and dynamic aspects of frames. Along these lines, framing research suggests that a symbiotic relationship exists between journalists using frames to support the status quo and news consumers that typically want to be reassured that the status quo will endure with problems being only temporary. This relationship between journalists and consumers may be particularly strong during times when the status quo is challenged severely [35]. The potential of framing theory rests on the focus on communicative processes, and rather than being stable, communication is a dynamic process which include the elements of frame building (how frames emerge) and frame setting (the reciprocal interaction between media frames and audience inclinations) [36].

2.2.2 Textual News Data Analysis with Statistical Frequency Measurements

Textual data signifies the systematically collected materials that are made up of printed, written or electronically published words. Data gathering process for the analysis of text data is a methodology which provides the examination of the content, structure and meaning of a text.

In addition to content analysis, the methods of descriptive statistics have also been used to summarize the sample of this study. To this end, frequency distributions were employed to measure the most frequently occurring frame types in the newspaper items by newspapers and years of publication. The frequency distributions were calculated based on the following formula:

$$P = \frac{F}{N} \times 100\%$$

P refers to the percentage, F denotes the frequency and N is the total number of respondents' frequency. P is obtained by dividing F by N with the result being multiplied by 100 [37–39]. Statistical Package for the Social Sciences (SPSS) software program (IBM SPSS Version 26.0) was used for the data analyses of this study [40].

3 Experimental Results and Discussion

The distinction between "episodic" and "thematic" news framing based on Iyengar's classification puts forward that episodic framing presents a concrete event, whereas thematic framing provides the presentation of the story within a context relating to broader social trends and factors [9]. Accordingly, the unit of analysis concerning the news coverage concerning mental health and psychological problems of six national newspapers (*Hürriyet, Milliyet*, *Cumhuriyet*, *Posta*, *Sabah* and *Sözcü*) published in Türkiye over a five-year period (2014–2018) reveals the news stories' episodic and thematic framing modes. Table 1 shows the frequency of episodic and thematic frames in the newspaper items analyzed for the purposes of the study.

As indicated in Table 1, while the frequency of episodic framing corresponds to 44.2%, that of thematic framing is 42.5%. The number of episodic frames is slightly

Table 1. Frequency of episodic and thematic framing.

variable	frequency (f)	percentage (%)
Episodic frames	255	44.2
Thematic frames	245	42.5
Both	72	12.5
Non-applicable	5	0.9

more than that of thematic frames by a difference of 1.7%. Both kinds of frames are seen in 72 of the news items analyzed, corresponding to 12.5%. 5 news items could not be identified as to whether episodic and thematic framing was used.

The type of framing, namely episodic and thematic, analyzed in the newspaper content by the newspapers and the related publication years is depicted in Fig. 1.

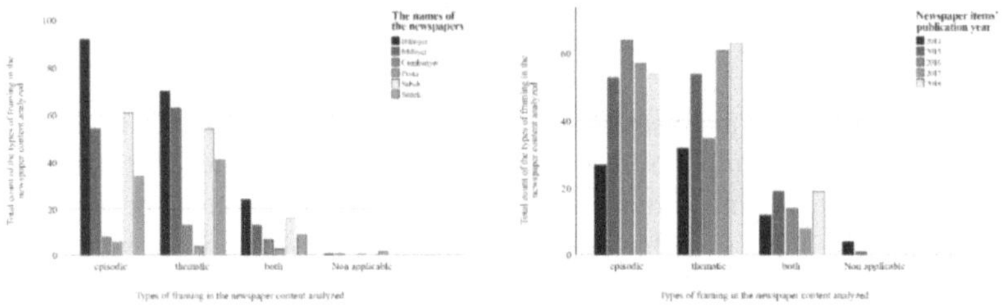

Fig. 1. Histogram depictions of type of framing by the newspapers and publication years.

The year with the highest frequency of episodic framing is 2016 with a percentage of 56.6%, while the year when the highest frequency of thematic framing is observed is 2018 with a percentage of 46.3%. There is no evident upward or downward trend in episodic or thematic framing over the years, which shows that the distribution is stable.

As indicated previously, thematic frames are defined as texts which focus on reports, background data, contextualizing information as well as expert opinion. The inclusion of expert opinions was also analyzed in the study, and the related frequency results are presented in Table 2.

As Table 2 presents, psychiatrists make up the highest frequency. Their opinions were provided in 99 of the newspaper items analyzed, which corresponds to 17.2%. Legal professionals' opinions follow those of psychiatrists with a percentage of 6.9%. Medical doctors' opinions (5%) are slightly more than the ones of psychologists or psychological counselors (3.6%). Opinions of the academics were observed to be the lowest (1.2%) based on the frequency analyses conducted. Although not indicated in Table 2, it can additionally be noted that in 381 of the news items analyzed which make up 66% of the dataset, no expert opinion was included.

Previous research on news media coverage demonstrates that public health issues are generally framed episodically as individual problems which can be solved by individual action [16, 17, 41–43]. These studies are concerned with childhood nutrition

Table 2. Frequency of expert opinions.

expert	frequency (f)	percentage (%)
Psychiatrist	99	17.2
Legal professional	40	6.9
Academic	7	1.2
Psychologist/Counselor	21	3.6
Physician (MD)	29	5.0

policies, obesity, public health advocacy and intimate violence reporting. Parallel with these findings, episodic framing is stated to be more common in the news coverage of social issues, and Western news media are observed to be using episodic framing frequently while covering social problems [44]. Poverty is the social problem addressed in the aforementioned study. Regarding mental health problems, it is shown that depression has been framed more thematically in Chinese newspapers compared to American newspapers [18]. The results of the current study are in line with the findings that Western media use more episodic frames while addressing social issues. The frequency of episodic framing is at 44.2%, corresponding to 255 in a total of 577 news items. This frequency is slightly more than that of thematic framing at 42.5%, corresponding to 245 news items (see Table 1). Even though the difference is not significant, episodic framing is found to be more frequent statistically, which supports the findings of the previous literature.

It is recommended by the World Health Organization (WHO) that mental health should be integrated into primary care, and such integration would be successful if mental health can be incorporated into health policy and legislative frameworks with the support of senior leadership, ongoing governance and adequate resources. It is further noted that primary care for mental health requires coordination with a network of services on different care levels to be complemented by broader health system development. This last note on 'broader' is reflected in thematic framing of news which has a systemic outlook toward social issues addressing the background data, expert opinion and contextualization of information. Even though episodic stories are said to initially grab the readers' attention, it is the thematic stories that are better to confer information and suggest policy solutions to the readers. As demonstrated through the research on alcohol problem, thematically-framed stories can lead the readers to focus on solutions that involve policy makers and public institutions [45]. Regarding problems like immigrant health, smoking, obesity and diabetes, another study revealed that a thematic frame, including information on context, prevention strategies, risk factors, and social attributions of responsibility, made readers be more supportive of public policy changes, while also encouraging them to improve their own health behaviors [23].

With regard to sources, medical experts, nonmedical experts and research documents are stated to be significantly more likely to be used as sources in thematic stories than in episodic ones [46]. As demonstrated by earlier research, more medical experts are used as sources than nonmedical experts [31], which supports the concept of medicalization of mental health news. A relevant content analysis of newspapers revealed that nearly all expert medical opinions were from psychiatrists, and a strong emphasis was placed on hospitalization and medication as treatments [25]. This observation is also in line with the findings obtained by the present research whose frequency analyses have shown that the psychiatrists' expert opinions were used most as sources in 99 of the news items (17.2%). Physicians' opinions ranked the third mostly occurring source in 29 new items (5%) (see Table 2). Since health information is complex, journalists rely on sources for explanations if they lack adequate background. In addition, sources are used for giving perspective and balance to a news story in the building of frames and for the generation of story ideas. Overall, experts, sources and referrals are employed as important elements of responsible journalism in order that unbiased and accurate news can be generated.

4 Conclusion and Future Directions

Media framing helps to shape our understanding of the meaning of news events, often problematically. Considering that health information is sensitive and not easy to address, it is important to build frames by giving an unbiased perspective and balance to a news item. Yet, it is not always possible to achieve this kind of accuracy and balance since news framing by journalists is every so often dependent on the availability of various sources of information and specific attributes thereof, which are subject to shifts over time, influenced by new events and changing conditions. Amid these multiple factors, journalists are encouraged to develop comprehensive and informative presentations related to mental issues surrounding the mental system so that readers can be provided with accurate information within the context of general social trends and relevant expert opinions [47]. This point is related to presenting news thematically within context, pointing to a broader trend over time, background information or expert opinions provided concerning the issue at hand. Accordingly, this study has attempted to reveal episodic and thematic framing approaches in the news items covered in six Turkish daily newspapers over a five-year period between 2014 and 2018 through content analysis based on Iyengar's concept. A total of 577 news items have been analyzed, and frequency distributions have presented the measurement of the most frequently occurring frame types in the newspaper items by the newspaper and years. Episodic framing has been found to be slightly more frequent than thematic framing by a difference of 1.7%. Related to expert opinions, which is an important part of thematically framed news, it has been revealed that 381 of the news items analyzed, making up 66% of the dataset, has included no expert opinion. Among the experts, psychiatrists' opinions (17.2%) have been included more than the opinions of other sources, which reveals the medicalization of mental health news. The results of this research can provide an extract of the portrayal of mental health-related news in Türkiye to point a way toward addressing news on pressing social issues, like mental health in this case, from a systemic perspective. Based on these considerations and validations enabled by the statistical frequency measurements and framing methods employed, the study can contribute to the understanding of how mental health issues are framed within the theoretical framework of social constructionism and framing applications.

Mental health disorders affect millions of people worldwide, and they may lead to permanent harm if left untreated. Negative media portrayals may perpetuate stigma and discourage some individuals from seeking treatment. On the other hand, media can also serve as a collaborator to challenge public prejudices by reflecting positive portrayals on people with mental illness, providing factual information based on the analyses of contextual conditions, accurate data and experts' opinions as well as reports on research concerning disease prevention, treatment, remedies and policies that can be implemented. Future work can be directed to focus on nuances of framing and their effects on the audiences so that guidelines can be prepared in detail for the presentation of mental health-related news. Based on the findings to be obtained from further work, application-oriented research can open up new directions towards responsible and ethical journalistic practices.

References

1. Berger, P.L., Luckmann, T.: The Social Construction of Reality: A Treatise in the Sociology of Knowledge, 1st edn. Doubleday, Garden City (1966)
2. O'Reilly, M., Lester, J.N.: Introduction: the social construction of normality and pathology. In: The Palgrave handbook of Adult Mental Health: Discourse and Conversation Studies, pp. 1–19. Palgrave Macmillan, London (2016)
3. Paul, S., Berkowitz, D.: Social construction of news. Int. Encycl. Journal. Stud. 1–6 (2019)
4. Van Gorp, B.: Strategies to take subjectivity out of framing analysis. In: Doing News Framing Analysis, pp. 100–125. Routledge (2010)
5. Hall, S., Critcher, C., Jefferson, T., Clarke, J., Roberts, B.: Policing the Crisis: Mugging, the State and Law and Order. Bloomsbury Publishing (2017)
6. Galvin, A., Quinn, F., Cleary, Y.: Shaping the 'inexplicable': a social constructionist analysis of news reporting of familicide-suicide. Journalism **24**(7), 1499–1517 (2023)
7. Entman, R.M.: Framing: toward clarification of a fractured paradigm. J. Commun. **43**(4), 51–58 (1993)
8. Nelson, T.E., Kinder, D.R.: Issue frames and group-centrism in American public opinion. J. Polit. **58**(4), 1055–1078 (1996)
9. Iyengar, S.: Is Anyone Responsible?: How Television Frames Political İssues. University of Chicago Press (1991)
10. Nelson, T.E., Clawson, R.A., Oxley, Z.M.: Media framing of a civil liberties conflict and its effect on tolerance. Am. Polit. Sci. Rev. **91**(3), 567–583 (1997)
11. Goffman, E.: Frame Analysis: An Essay on the Organization of Experience. Harvard University Press (1974)
12. Gamson, W.A., Modigliani, A.: The changing culture of affirmative action. Res. Polit. Sociol. **3**(1), 137–177 (1987)
13. Pan, Z., Kosicki, G.M.: Framing analysis: an approach to news discourse. Polit. Commun. **10**(1), 55–75 (1993)
14. Matthes, J.: Framing politics: an integrative approach. Am. Behav. Sci. **56**(3), 247–259 (2012)
15. Wang, H.: Linguistic analysis of news title strategies in media frame—a case study of "the mueller ınvestigation" in the news titles of the new york times and fox news. Journal. Media **5**(1), 342–358 (2024)
16. Kim, S.-H., Willis, A.L.: Talking about obesity: news framing of who is responsible for causing and fixing the problem. J. Health Commun. **12**(4), 359–376 (2007)
17. Lawrence, R.G.: Framing obesity: the evolution of news discourse on a public health issue. Harvard Int. J. Press/Politics **9**(3), 56–75 (2004)

18. Zhang, Y., Jin, Y.: Thematic and episodic framing of depression: how Chinese and American newspapers framed a major public health threat. Athens J. Mass Media Commun. **3**(2), 91–106 (2017)
19. Weiner, B.: Judgments of Responsibility: A Foundation for a Theory of Social Conduct. Guilford Press (1995)
20. Guenther, L., Gaertner, M., Zeitz, J.: Framing as a concept for health communication: a systematic review. Health Commun. **36**(7), 891–899 (2021)
21. Temmann, L.J., Wiedicke, A., Schaller, S., Scherr, S., Reifegesrte, D.: A systematic review of responsibility frames and their effects in the health context. J. Health Commun. **26**(12), 828–838 (2021)
22. Walter, D., Ophir, Y.: News frame analysis: an inductive mixed-method computational approach. Commun. Methods Measures **13**(4), 248–266 (2019)
23. Coleman, R., Thorson, E., Wilkins, L.: Testing the effect of framing and sourcing in health news stories. J. Health Commun. **16**(9), 941–954 (2011)
24. Kang, S.: Coverage of autism spectrum disorder in the US television news: an analysis of framing. Disabil. Soc. **28**(2), 245–259 (2013)
25. Wahl, O.E., Wood, A., Richards, R.: Newspaper coverage of mental illness: is it changing? Psychiatr. Rehabil. Skills **6**(1), 9–31 (2002)
26. Wahl, O.F.: Mass media images of mental illness: a review of the literature. J. Commun. Psychol. **20**(4), 343–352 (1992)
27. Wahl, O.F.: Depictions of mental illnesses in children's media. J. Ment. Health **12**(3), 249–258 (2003)
28. Wilcox, S.: Media and the Criminalization of Mental Illness: The Impact of Stigma Reduction Videos (2016)
29. McGinty, E.E., Kennedy-Hendricks, A., Choksy, S., Barry, C.L.: Trends in news media coverage of mental illness in the United States: 1995–2014. Health Aff. **35**(6), 1121–1129 (2016)
30. Ma, Z.: How the media cover mental illnesses: a review. Health Educ. **117**(1), 90–109 (2017)
31. Wahl, O.F.: News media portrayal of mental illness: implications for public policy. Am. Behav. Sci. **46**(12), 1594–1600 (2003)
32. Atkin, C.K., McFeters, C., Ferguson, V.: A comprehensive analysis of breast cancer news coverage in leading media outlets focusing on environmental risks and prevention. J. Health Commun. **13**(1), 3–19 (2008)
33. Boke, O., Aker, S., Aker, A.A., Sarısoy, G.: Schizophrenia in Turkish newspapers: retrospective scanning study. Soc. Psychiatry Psychiatr. Epidemiol. **42**, 457–461 (2007)
34. Aci, O.S., Ciydem, E., Bilgin, H., Ozaslan, Z., Tek, S.: Turkish newspaper articles mentioning people with mental illness: a retrospective study. Int. J. Soc. Psychiatry **66**(3), 215–224 (2020)
35. Baran, S.J., Davis, D.K., Striby, K.: Mass Communication Theory: Foundations, Ferment, and Future, 6th edn. Wadsworth Publishing (2011)
36. De Vreese, C.: News framing: theory and typology. Inf. Des. J. Doc. Des. **13**(1), 51–62 (2005)
37. Gravetter, F.J., Wallnau, L.B.: Statistics for the Behavioral Sciences. Cengage (2012)
38. Guilford, J.P.: Fundamental Statistics in Psychology and Education. Mc-Graw Hill (1956)
39. Tunc, A., Arsan, E.: Gazetelerde Seçim Var: 2002 Genel Seçimlerinin Yazılı Basında Sunumu: Bir İçerik Analizi. Yalın Yayıncılık (2007)
40. IBM Corp. Released 2019. IBM SPSS Statistics for Windows, Version 26.0. IBM Corp., Armonk
41. Woodruff, K., Dorfman, L., Berends, V., Agron, P.: Coverage of childhood nutrition policies in California newspapers. J. Public Health Policy **24**(2), 150–158 (2003)
42. Dorfman, L., Wallack, L., Woodruff, K.: More than a message: framing public health advocacy to change corporate practices. Health Educ. Behav. **32**(3), 320–336 (2005)

43. McManus, J., Dorfman, L.: Functional truth or sexist distortion? Assessing a feminist critique of intimate violence reporting. Journalism **6**(1), 43–65 (2005)
44. Kim, S.-H., Carvalho, J.P., Davis, A.C.: Talking about poverty: news framing of who is responsible for causing and fixing the problem. Journal. Mass Commun. Q. **87**(3–4), 563–581 (2010)
45. Myhre, S.L., Saphir, M.N., Flora, J.A., Howard, K.A., Gonzalez, E.M.: Alcohol coverage in California newspapers: frequency, prominence, and framing. J. Public Health Policy **23**, 172–190 (2002)
46. Myrick, J.G., Major, L.H., Jankowski, S.: The sources and frames used to tell stories about depression and anxiety: a content analysis of 18 years of national television news coverage. Electron. News **8**(1), 49–63 (2014)
47. Slopen, N.B., Watson, A.C., Gracia, G., Corrigan, P.W.: Age analysis of newspaper coverage of mental illness. J. Health Commun. **12**(1), 3–15 (2007)

Secure Image Encryption Using Single-Mode Fiber and Dense Wavelength Division Multiplexing in Chaotic Systems

Nadia M. G. Al-Saidi[1], Suzan J. Obaiys[2](✉), Nawras A. Alwan[2], Arkan J. Mohammed[3], Alaa Kadhim Farhan[4], and Yeliz Karaca[5]

[1] Department of Applied Sciences, University of Technology, Baghdad, Iraq
[2] Department of Computer System and Technology, Faculty of Computer Science and, Information Technology, University of Malaya, Kuala Lumpur, Malaysia
suzan@um.edu.my
[3] Department of Mathematics, College of Science, Mustansiriyah University, Baghdad, Iraq
[4] Department of Computer Sciences, University of Technology, Baghdad 110066, Iraq
[5] Chan Medical School, University of Massachusetts (UMass), 55 Lake Avenue North, Worcester, MA, 01655, USA

Abstract. The integration of the advanced technologies of the current landscape (The Internet of Things (IoT), Artificial Intelligence (AI), smart devices, and so forth) has converted the security issue into a significant matter, particularly in cases, when the data is transferred through different insecure channels. However, the necessity for robust and innovative security of data through transmission is still a challenge. The sensitivity of the chaotic systems to their initial conditions and control parameters makes them a reasonable choice for such purposes. This application for Dense Wavelength Division Multiplexing (DWDM) is designed to enhance long-distance communication by increasing the transmission capacity. Our design uses four channels each with a bit rate of 10 Gbs. To ensure the security of the data sent through this method, a novel 5D-chaotic system serves as an encryption key for images. This approach enables the safe transmission of images over a 150 km distance at a capacity of 40 Gbps. The simulation results are obtained by hybridizing Matlab and Optisystem software. Accordingly, the study evaluates the encryption's security using measures such as histogram analysis, correlation coefficient analysis, and information entropy. Findings show enhanced security and efficiency across longer distances.

Keywords: Dense Wavelength Division Multiplexing · Chaotic Encryption · Information Entropy · Chaotic System · Fiber Networks · Chaotic Encryption · Complex oscillations · Lyapunov Exponents · Bifurcations of 5D System · Optical Communication System · Shannon Entropy

O. Gervasi et al. (Eds.): ICCSA 2024 Workshops, LNCS 14815, pp. 72–90, 2024.
https://doi.org/10.1007/978-3-031-65154-0_5

1 Introduction

In the fast-emerging era of the technology and internet, dealing with and sharing thousands of images at times may lead to the disclosure of some private information unknowingly. Their large size, high redundancy, and pixel interconnectivity require diverse structural approaches for encryption that process the given image data into a form almost unreadable to unauthorized readers. Thus, they are needed for securing information and ensuring their integrity. Image encryption is the instance of the strategies for transforming image data to the encoded format since it contains information about privacy and integrity of the data. Many encryption techniques based on diverse technologies have therefore been developed to serve this purpose, such as chaos-based, S-Box-based, optical compression, frequency-domain, DNA-based encryption, and many others [1–3].

Chaotic systems, with their complicated dynamics, present a chance to boost the security of communication systems. The characteristics are therefore rather unpredictable, which makes them very suitable for an encryption process and serves to provide protection against intrusion and interception. Chaotic systems are characterized by their sensitivity to initial conditions, their irregular patterns, and their nonlinearity. These systems yield many studies in the field of nonlinear dynamics due to their complex, unpredictable nature and have found broad applications across many fields. They can be used to model behaviors in the market and develop trading strategies in finance [4], examine population dynamics in biology and the behavior of biological systems in pharmacology [5, 6], model neurons and advance machine learning and AI algorithms in neural networks, and through their structural similarities they can be used to create secure communication systems in cryptography [7]. The concept of "chaotic encryption" was first introduced by Robert Matthews in 1989 [8], since then there have been significant studies on using encryption methods based on chaos to convert the systems from order to chaos [9].

Continuous chaotic systems offer the benefit of exhibiting more complex dynamic behaviors and enhanced adaptability. However, they come with the drawbacks of needing more computational resources and intricate mathematical models. Additionally, they require discretization to fit real-world applications. In this paper, we present a system that builds upon the well-known Lorenz model [10]. This system is defined by a series of equations and positive variables. We extensively investigate the dynamics of this system using techniques, including phase plane analysis Lyapunov exponent calculations and bifurcation diagrams. Through these analyses, we uncover the behavior and significant level of chaos displayed by the system which is essential for its potential use in secure communications.

The proposed system is practically employed in communication in a setup called Dense Wavelength Division Multiplexing (DWDM) channel in Single Mode Fiber (SMF). It performs well in long-distance communication by improving the bandwidth and thereby increasing the transmission capacity. The paper provides information, about the design of both the transmitter, which consists of a pseudo random bit generator and a Mach Zehnder Modulator (MZM) and the receiver equipped with a PIN photodiode, low pass filter, 3R regenerator, and bit error rate analyzer [11–13]. A significant aspect of this study involves utilizing chaotic Stream Segmentation (CSS) technology for transmitting data over distances [14]. The effectiveness and security of the system are thoroughly assessed using metrics such as histogram analysis, correlation coefficient and information entropy evaluations. These assessments confirm that both the system and its encryption algorithm are secure and efficient for transmitting data over distances.

The available works in this regard were devoted to using the signals of semiconductor lasers to ensure the reliability of communication. It should be noted that in 1992 Mork et.al.[15] performed a study that proves the real possibility of using semiconductor lasers, that is the starting point of chaos-aided communication. The next work appeared in 2005 by Argyris et. al. [16] was directed towards the development of encryption and decryption algorithms for signals transmitted using diode lasers in fiber optics. The work on the technology Dense Wavelength Division Multiplexing was continued [17]. In 13 years later since the last publication, they showed, for example, that Zhou et al. [18] proved that DWDM has the ability to increase the data capacity of fiber optic systems. Their work extensively examined the effectiveness of DWDM in managing large-scale data transmission an aspect of our study. Moreover, in 2018, Simarpreet, and Singh [19] explored encryption techniques including algorithms, within the context of fiber optics. Their findings emphasized the vital role encryption plays in ensuring the security of data transmitted over distances. In 2016 Huang et. al. [20] worked on optimizing signal integrity and security over extended distances. Their findings provided insights, into managing signal degradation and preventing security breaches in transmissions.

Given the inputs of the previous studies, the aim of this study emphasizes on proposing of a new 5D chaotic system, which is designed specifically to be implemented in a DWDM Single Mode Fiber system. Through this integration, security is enhanced and the problem of optical communication over long distances and high capacity is overcome. Moreover, the security and efficiency of fiber optic communication will be enhanced too.

The remainder of this paper is organized as follows: In addition to this section that represents the introduction to chaos-based image encryption in optical communications, this work includes another five sections. Section 2 proposes a new 5D-Chaotic system and discusses its dynamic properties. Section 3 introduces the technology of optical communication as a multiplexing operation in fiber networks using DWDM technology. Section 4 four evaluates the effectiveness of the proposed encryption method based on some performance metrics. The transmission of the image data over a long distance is shown as a result of the optical setup in Sect. 5. Finally, the conclusion about the efficiency and security of the proposed system along with the future directions are provided in Sect. 6.

2 The Proposed Chaotic System

In this section, we proposed a 5D-chaotic system to be used for generating high random sequences to encrypt images and ensure safe transitions. The proposed system is given in (1).

$$\begin{aligned} x_1' &= (y - w)u - x + a \\ y_1' &= (z - u)x - y + b \\ z_1' &= (w - x)y - z + c \\ w_1' &= (u - y)z - w + d \\ u_1' &= (x - z)w - u + e \end{aligned} \tag{1}$$

where a, b, c, d, and e are positive variables and x, y, z, w, and u are the main parameters.

3 Numerical Analysis of System (1)

The behavior of system (1) is investigated through some numerical simulations such as; trajectory (Fig. 1), phase space (Fig. 2), Sensitivity parameter (Fig. 3), Lyapunov exponent (Fig. 4), and bifurcation diagram (Fig. 5). This simulation is also important for choosing the control parameters that ensure a high chaosity range [21]. The simulation results have been obtained by hybridizing Matlab [22] and Optisystem software [23].

A. System Attractor

The complex attractor in phase space is an indicator of an efficient chaotic system. Figure 1 displays the attractor diagrams and time series for system (1), which are generated under varying parameter values of $a = 6$, $b = 10$, $c = 0.85$, $d = 2$, and $e = 0.1$. And an initial state of $(x,\ y,\ z,\ w,\ u) = (1, 1, 1, 1, 1)$. Figure 2 illustrating the phase space of a system (1) -specifically through the direct trajectories between the variable pairs (x vs y, y vs z, z vs w, and w vs u) -we capture the essence of the system's complex dynamics, with the control parameters $a = 6$, $b = 10$, $c = 0.85$, $d = 2$, and $e = 0.1$. These visualizations reveal the interplay and feedback mechanisms among the variables, showcasing the chaotic system's sensitivity to initial conditions and parameter changes. By examining the figures, we observe how each pair of variables interacts within the larger system, offering insights into the unpredictable and aperiodic paths that characterize the system's evolution. The detailed exploration of these phase space plots deepens our understanding of the dynamical processes controlling the chaotic behavior, providing invaluable information for theoretical and practical applications aimed in various fields. Figure 3 show demonstrates profound sensitivity to parameter changes of system (1), based on the change parameter b (10:11) significantly impacts both the attractor structure and the time series of state variables, which shows the system's responsiveness. This sensitivity reveals itself through changes in the attractor's geometry in phase space a visual representation of the system's state evolution over time and in the aperiodic, complex oscillations observed in the time series plots for variables (x,y,z,w) and (u).

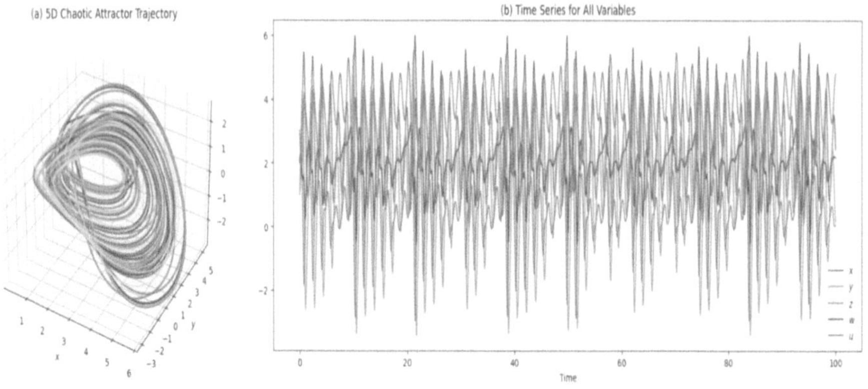

Fig. 1. Attractors and time series of system (1)

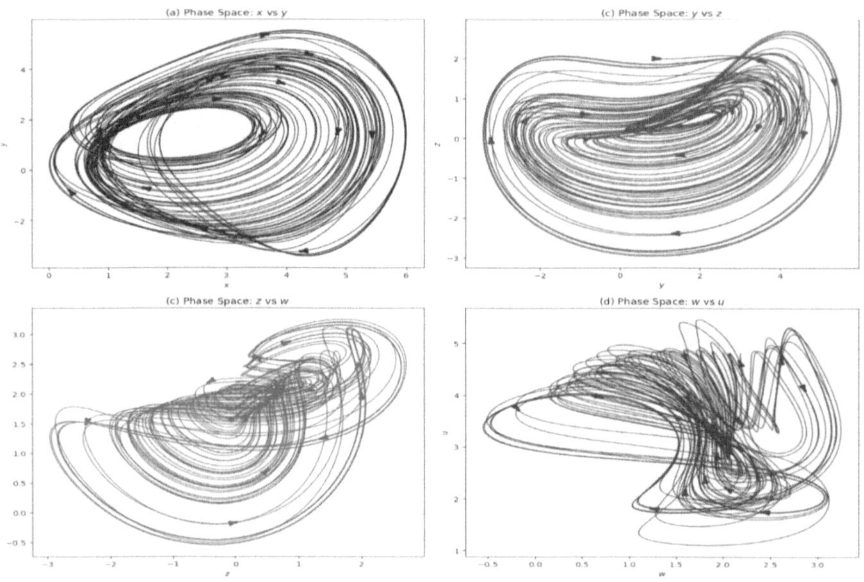

Fig. 2. Phase space of system (1) with the control parameters a = 6; b = 10; c = 0.85; d = 2; e = 0.1, as shown in (a),(b),(c), and (d)

B. Lyapunov Exponents

Lyapunov Exponent (LE) is an important measure used to demonstrate the chaotic behavior of the nonlinear dynamical system. It is a method employed to show that, when two starting values that differ slightly are introduced into the same chaotic system, the paths they create diverge exponentially as time increases. The Lyapunov exponents of the system (1) are given by: LE1 = 0.256625, LE2 = 0, LE3 = -0.647382, LE4 = -1.852560, LE5 = -2.756661. Figure 4 depicts the LE of hyperchaotic behavior of system (1).

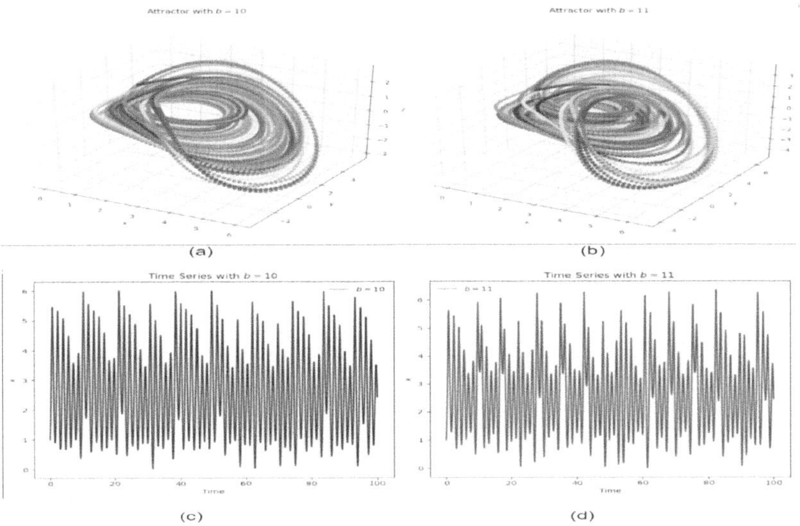

Fig. 3. Sensitivity parameter

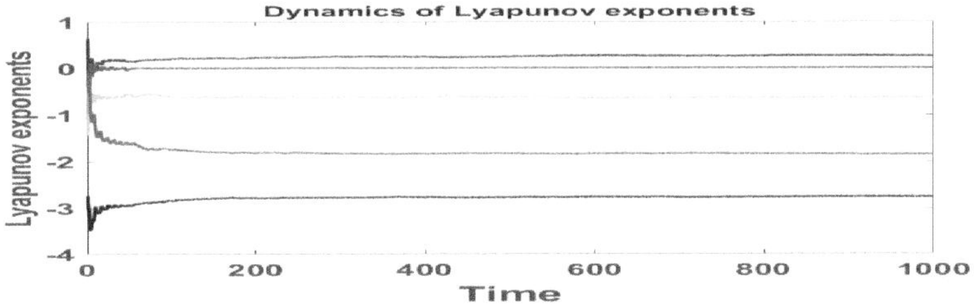

Fig. 4. Lyapunov exponent of system (1)

III. Bifurcations of 5D propose system

The term "bifurcation" is utilized to describe the behavior variation as a result of a small change in a system parameter. The correlation between the control parameters and the features of the chaotic system can be illustrated by a diagram known as a bifurcation diagram. It shows how system performance changes as parameters vary and indicates sudden changes in performance as critical parameters are reached. Bifurcations are essential in the evaluation of dynamic systems in a variety of fields, including physics, engineering, biology, and economics. The bifurcation diagram in Fig. 5 illustrates the long-term behavior of the x variable in a system (1) as a function of the parameter a, which varies from (1: 0.1: 10). Despite the system (1) having 5D $(x,\ y,\ z,\ w,\ u)$, we actually focusing on variable x, which allows us to understand how this component of the system (1) stay stabilizes or varies over time, based on some variables or parameters. The bifurcation refers to the point on the diagram representing the state of the x variable after the system has evolved or changed time, during the interval [90,100], indicating the system's steady-state or periodic behavior at different values of a. We take this interval

[90,100] to ensure that the system has had sufficient time to evolve into its steady state or a characteristic periodic orbit if one exists. Now, the color of points changes from dark purple to bright yellow based on the value of the parameter a increases, facilitating a clear visual distinction between different regions of the parameter space. This change of color allows for an immediate visual to understand the bit change in the parameter a how long influence the system's dynamics over time, highlighting regions where changes lead to significant changes in the system's behavior. These bifurcations point to the sensitivity of the chaotic system to initial conditions and parameters.

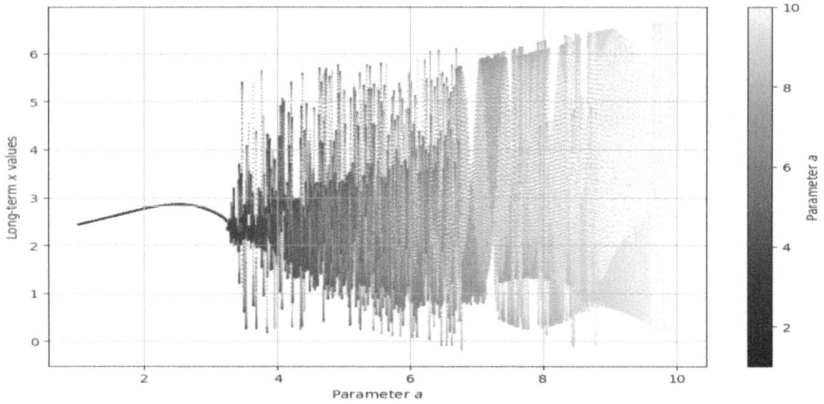

Fig. 5. Bifurcations diagram of system (1)

4 Optical Communication System

The multiplexing operation in optical networks is a technology utilized to improve their bandwidth. This is done through the DWDM technology. DWDM is an optical fiber multiplexing technology which can deliver multiple signals simultaneously and raise the information capacity, which is transferred through optical fibers, so that it can reach higher bandwidth and transmission capability [24]. This technology makes it perfect for high-speed applications such as broadband, video conferences and cloud computing. Moreover, it is appropriate for telecom networks, which need to transmit data over long distances. Furthermore, DWDM enables numerous data signals to be transmitted in various wavelength channels. The following are three main components of the proposed system;

i. The transmitter: The suggested transmitter has four parts, which are:
   1. The pseudo-random bit sequence generator (PRSG) is to be used as input to the Matlab connector.
   2. Matlab connector: used to encrypt the input image.
   3. The input image data is carried by a nonreturn to zero (NRZ) generator [25].

4. A continuous laser (CW) with a power of 5 dBm modulates the data optically at wavelengths between 193.1 and 193.8 THz with a Mach-Zehnder-Modulator (MZM) [24].

ii. Optical fiber: The single-mode fiber (SMF) is used to transmit the plain and encrypted image. The attenuation and dispersion are considered challenges in communications-based optical fiber. The dispersion compensating fiber (DCF) can be used to overcome image dispersion, while an Erbium-Doped Fiber Amplifier (EDFA) is used to amplify the signal strength [11].

iii. The receiver section: Consists of a PIN photodiode for data detection, a filter of low-pass Bassel, a 3R regenerator for signal reshaping, and the Matlab implementation for image decryption. A bit error rate (BER) analyzer receives and examines the delivered data. Table 1, and Figs. 4 and 5, display the input parameters that were utilized to define the system in more detail.

Table 1. SMF system components

	Component	Specifications
Transmitter part	Pseudo random bits generator	Bit Rate: 5E + 9 bps
	MATLAB connector	Used to encrypt/decrypt the signal message
	CW Laser	Power = 5dBm, wavelength:193.1 THz-193.8 THZ,linewidth: 10 MHz
	RZ	Amplitude = 5
	MZM	Extinction ratio = 30db
	Wavelength division multiplexing	WDM 4 × 1 channel, bandwidth = 30 Ghz
Channel	SMF	Length = 100km, Attenuation = 0.2dB/km
	DCF	Length = 15.22, Dispersion = -110 ps/ns/km, Attenuation = 0.44 dB/km
	EDFA	Gain = 31 dB, Wavelength = 980nm Noise figures = 3 dB
Receiving part	PIN Photodetector	Responsivity = 1 A/W
	Low pass Bessel filter	Cutoff frequency = 0.75xBit rate, depth: 100 dB
	3R Regenerator	WDM 4 × 1 channel, bandwidth = 30 GHz,

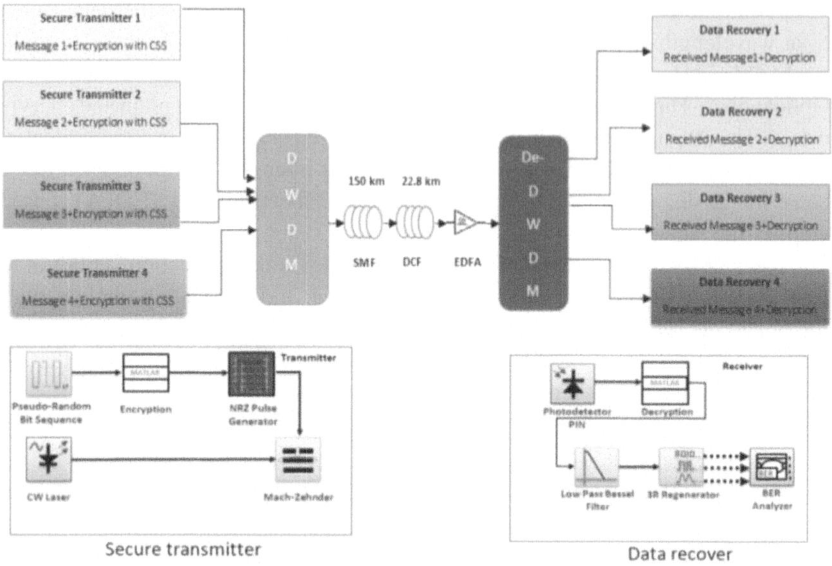

Fig. 6. Schematic diagram of the proposed DWDM system

5 Security Evaluation and Experimental Results

In this part, the effectiveness of implementation results are evaluated using some performance metrics. The system of encryption is used for color and grayscale images [26].

5.1 Histogram

The histogram of an image is a graphical representation of the distribution of pixel intensities in the image. It is a useful tool for image analysis because it provides information about the distribution of pixel values and can reveal important characteristics of an image, such as its contrast, brightness, and color balance. The encrypted image whose histogram is as uniform as possible, meaning that all pixel values should have approximately the same frequency of occurrence, making it difficult for an attacker to extract any meaningful information from the histogram. If the histogram of the encrypted image appears to be quite uniform, it is a good indication that the encryption has been successful in hiding the information. Figure 8 shows the histogram of the original image (b), the encrypted images (d), and the decryption image (f). The histogram of the cipher image appears to be quite uniform, whereas the histograms of the original and decipher images are different.

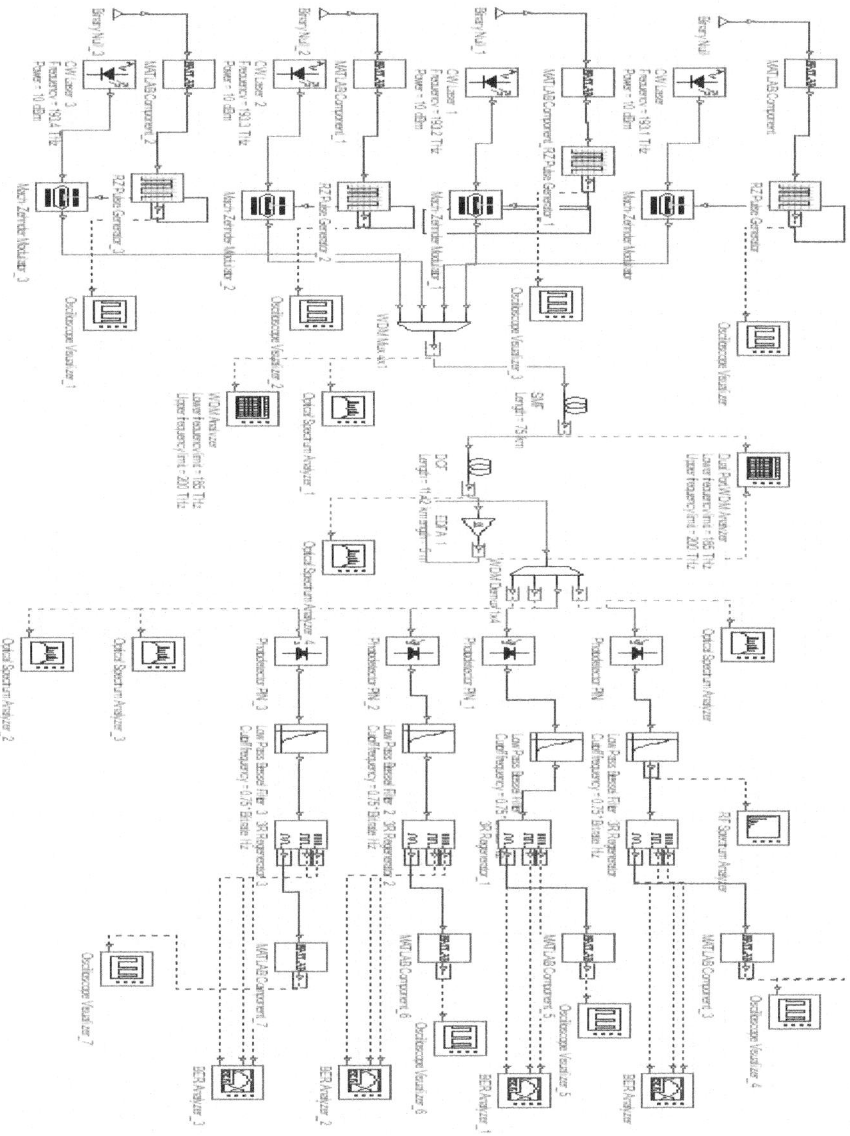

Fig. 7. The implemented DWDM system via Optisystem

5.2 Correlation Coefficient Analysis

In a plain image, if the correlation value is close to 1, it means that the adjacent pixel, whether it is vertical, horizontal, or diagonal, has a high correlation with each other. So, a close to 1 correlation value, is an indication of a high correlation in the image, whereas, a close to zero value is an indicator for high randomly distributed pixels. Therefore, the strong correlation between the adjacent pixels needs to be eliminated by a good encryption method. The results of the Sunflower image correlation are shown in Fig. 9 in three different directions (horizontal (b), vertical (c), and diagonal (d) for the plain and cipher images shown in (a)). Table 2, shows the correlation between adjacent pixels in plain and cipher images using (2), which indicates that adjacent pixels in the plain image have a correlation value near 1, while adjacent pixels in the encrypted image have a correlation value close to 0, which lead us to conclude that the cipher image pixels are randomly distributed.

The correlation coefficient is calculated by:

$$\mathrm{CC} = \frac{E(X - E(X))E(Y - E(Y))}{\sqrt{D(X)}\sqrt{D(Y)}} \tag{2}$$

$$\text{where } E(X) = \frac{1}{N}\sum_{i=1}^{N} x_i \text{ and } D(X) = \frac{1}{N}\sum_{i=1}^{N}(x_i - E(x))^2$$

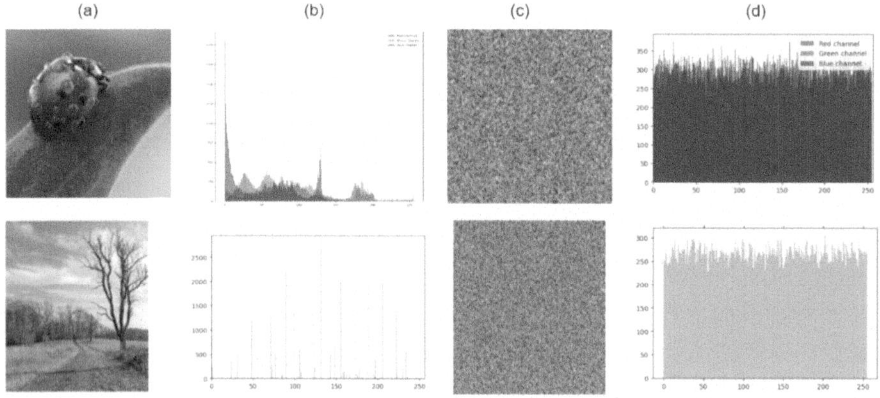

Fig. 8. Histogram of some color and grayscale images before and after the encryption process

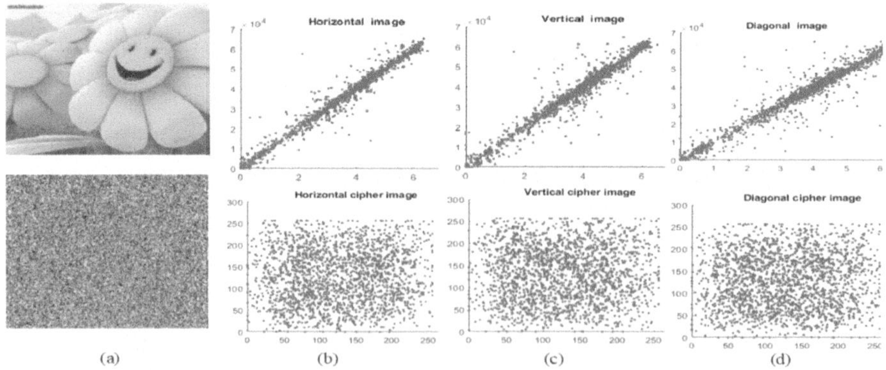

Fig. 9. The correlation between pixels before and after the encryption process

5.3 Information entropy

Shannon's entropy is a measure of the randomness or unpredictability of an information source, and it is commonly used in image analysis to quantify the degree of randomness in an image (3). Which can be calculated as:

$$H(e) = -\sum_{i=0}^{2N-1} P(e_i) \log_2 P(e_i) \quad (3)$$

where (e) is the source, N is the grey-level number with a probability P(ei). The recommended value for H(e) for entirely random images is equal to 8. Table 3, shows the entropies of some images before and after the encryption process.

As a conclusion, from the histogram in Fig. 6, it is evident that the encrypted image has a distribution indicating the concealment of features from the original image. This uniformity plays a role in preventing attackers from gaining insights into data. The correlation measure for the neighbouring pixels in the encrypted image indicates an efficient encryption method that successfully disrupts the patterns of the original image as shown in Fig. 7, and Table 2. The results of information entropy (Table 3) approach the value for random images indicating a high degree of randomness and unpredictability in the encrypted images.

6 Results of the Optical Setup

This work aims to secure the transmission of data at a rate of Gb/s over longer distances using Chaotic Stream Segmentation (CSS) technology [14]. The input signal is generated from a pseudo-random bit sequence generator at a rate of 10 Gbps and fed into a nonreturn to zero (NRZ) pulse generator. The output from the NRZ is then modulated with a Mach-Zehnder modulator (MZM) and transmitted via a continuous wave (CW) laser. The performance of the proposed system was evaluated based on Q-factor and bit error rate (BER) as a function of link distance, with andwithout encryption, across four different channels at varying wavelengths (1550 nm, 1550.8 nm, 1551.6 nm, 1552.4 nm).

The results of the study are presented in two figures: Fig. 7 shows the system's performance without encryption, while Fig. 8 shows its encryption performance with the help of EDFA, and Fig. 10 shows the performance with encryption using DCF and EDFA together. The maximum link distance achieved without encryption was 110 km, with encryption was 69.5 km, and with encryption using DCF and EDFA was 150 km. The Q-factor and BER values are displayed in Tables 4, 5, 6, 7, 8, 9 sequentially.The quality factor (Q-factor) of a plain image for several wavelengths is depicted in (a). Whereas, (b) depicts the bit error rate (BER) for the same wavelengths as shown in Fig. 10, and Tables 4 and 5. The system achieved a link distance of approximately 110 km.

Table 2. Correlation analysis

Image	Correlation coefficient
	0.9841
	0.0039
	0.9823
	0.0035

The quality factor (Q-factor) for several wavelengths of an encrypted image is shown in Fig. 11 (a), while (b) depicts the bit error rate (BER) for the same wavelengths with EDFA. The system achieved a link distance of approximately 69.5 km as shown in Tables 6 and 7.

The quality factor and bit error rate for different wavelengths of the communication system. The system incorporates encryption, with the help of dispersion compensation fiber (DCF), and erbium-doped fiber amplifiers (EDFAs) to enhance transmission distance as shown in Fig. 12, and Tables 8 and 9. The system realized a link distance of about 150 km.

Table 3. Information entropy analysis

Plain image	Entropy	Cipher image	Entropy
	7.7087		7.9679
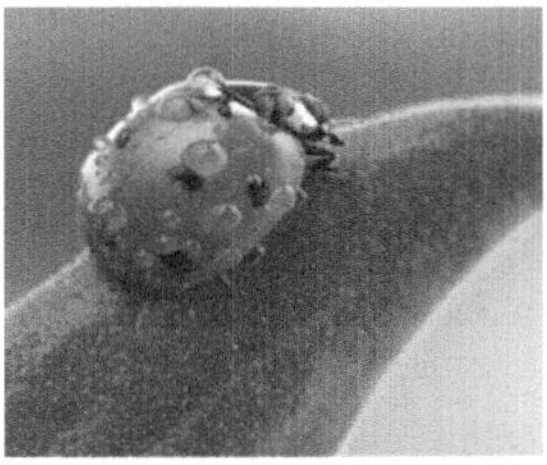	7.4499		7.9683
	6.0733		7.9563

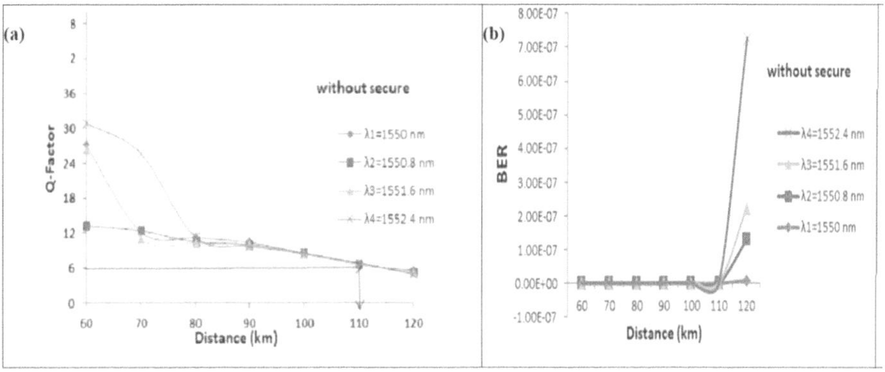

Fig. 10. (a) The quality factor (Q-factor) for several wavelengths, (b) the bit error rate (BER) for plain image.

Table 4. The Q-factor values of various distances for plain image

Length	$\lambda 1 = 1550nm$	$\lambda 2 = 1550.8nm$	$\lambda 3 = 1551.6nm$	$\lambda 4 = 1552.4nm$
60	27.1324	13.2877	26.4014	30.9064
70	12.2056	12.4228	11.1756	25.6449
80	11.2365	10.5183	10.2846	11.2532
90	10.4468	10.0459	9.91854	9.76129
100	8.56135	8.60103	8.41555	8.53719
110	6.51525	6.69968	6.57875	6.893
120	5.62462	5.14927	5.19446	4.88372

Table 5. The BER value of various distances for a plain image

Length	$\lambda 1 = 1550nm$	$\lambda 2 = 1550.8nm$	$\lambda 3 = 1551.6nm$	$\lambda 4 = 1552.4nm$
60	1.40E-162	1.33E-40	4.35E-154	3.60E-210
70	1.41E-34	9.34E-36	2.46E-29	1.83E-145
80	1.29E-29	3.38E-26	3.94E-25	1.06E-29
90	7.48E-26	4.78E-24	1.69E-23	7.55E-23
100	5.45E-18	3.64E-18	1.81E-17	6.62E-18
110	3.45E-11	9.59E-12	2.11E-11	2.66E-12
120	9.02E-09	1.21E-07	9.44E-08	5.02E-07

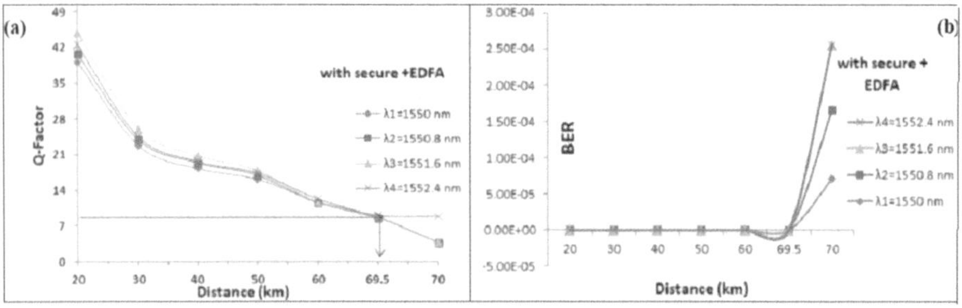

Fig. 11. (a) The quality factor (Q-factor) for several wavelengths of an encrypted image, while (b) shows the bit error rate (BER) for the same wavelengths with EDFA.

The system's performance is evaluated by measuring the Q-factor and bit error rate (BER) at distances of various wavelengths (Figs. 10, 11 and 12; Tables 4, 5, 6, 7, 8, 9). Without using the encryption process, we were able to achieve a link distance of 110 km. Whereas, when the encryption process was implemented, this distance was reduced to 69.5 km due to dispersion effects caused by the encryption process. To

Table 6. Q-factor values of various distances for the encrypted images with EDFA

Length	$\lambda 1 = 1550nm$	$\lambda 2 = 1550.8nm$	$\lambda 3 = 1551.6nm$	$\lambda 4 = 1552.4nm$
20	39.0983	40.6591	44.998	42.4285
30	22.791	23.9233	26.0789	24.535
40	18.3037	19.4257	20.8236	19.6616
50	16.1195	16.9178	17.8958	17.3363
60	11.715	11.531	11.671	12.3529
69.5	8.73365	8.56599	8.70018	9.09824
70	3.80227	3.73188	3.74327	8.96017

Table 7. BER values of various distances for the encrypted images with EDFA

Length	$\lambda 1 = 1550nm$	$\lambda 2 = 1550.8nm$	$\lambda 3 = 1551.6nm$	$\lambda 4 = 1552.4nm$
20	0.00E + 00	0.00E + 00	0.00E + 00	0.00E + 00
30	2.79E-115	8.70E-127	3.16E-150	3.12E-133
40	3.85E-75	2.31E-84	1.29E-96	2.27E-86
50	8.64E-59	1.51E-64	5.63E-72	1.13E-67
60	5.03E-32	4.38E-31	8.58E-32	2.18E-35
69.5	1.20E-18	5.21E-18	1.62E-18	4.45E-20
70	7.15E-05	9.45E-05	9.03E-05	1.57E-19

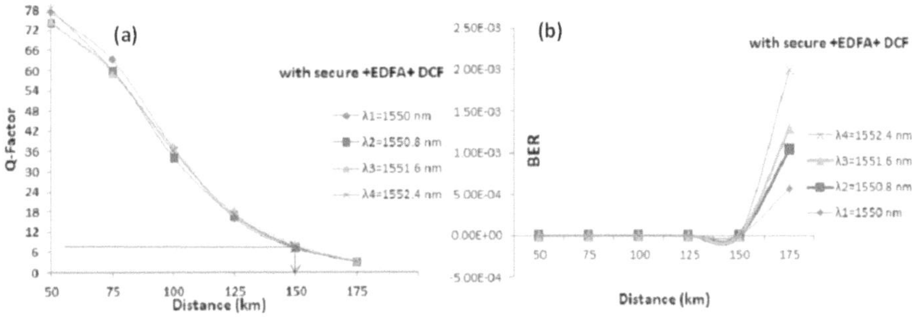

Fig. 12. (a) The quality factor for different wavelengths with (DCF), and (EDFAs), (b) the BER for different wavelengths with (DCF), and (EDFAs).

counteract this reduction in link distance caused by encryption effects we incorporated dispersion compensation fibers (DCF) and erbium-doped fiber amplifiers (EDFA) into our system. This resulted in an improvement in link distance up to approximately 150 km.

Table 8. The Q-factor values for various distances for encrypted images with EDFA and DCF

Length	$\lambda 1 = 1550nm$	$\lambda 2 = 1550.8nm$	$\lambda 3 = 1551.6nm$	$\lambda 4 = 1552.4nm$
50	77.286	74.1772	74.769	78.3244
75	63.2239	59.8862	58.9592	60.1082
100	37.1807	34.3323	37.2323	36.2179
125	16.0668	16.6539	18.3037	17.2585
150	7.131	7.32753	8.24748	7.62268
175	3.21525	3.2846	3.45289	3.1555

Table 9. The BER values for various distances for encrypted images with EDFA and DCF

Length	$\lambda 1 = 1550nm$	$\lambda 2 = 1550.8nm$	$\lambda 3 = 1551.6nm$	$\lambda 4 = 1552.4nm$
50	0.00E + 00	0.00E + 00	0.00E + 00	0.00E + 00
75	0.00E + 00	0.00E + 00	0.00E + 00	0.00E + 00
100	5.11E-303	9.37E-259	7.43E-304	1.11E-287
125	1.51E-58	1.00E-62	2.82E-75	3.34E-67
150	3.84E-13	9.00E-14	6.49E-17	9.45E-15
175	5.71E-04	4.65E-04	2.55E-04	6.99E-04

This improvement demonstrates that we can effectively mitigate any impacts, on signal quality caused by encryption through compensatory mechanisms.

In general, the findings of this research indicate that incorporating the system into the DWDM SMF system greatly improves security while maintaining the overall performance of the system. By utilizing CSS technology for encryption data transmission over distances can be effectivelyprotected by employing DCF and EDFA. The potential issues related to signal integrity arising from encryption can be successfully addressed. This study presents a method, for achieving high-capacity and long-range optical communication.

7 Conclusion

The advanced information technologies in the current time entail the sharing of voluminous digital data through both public and private networks. These developments pose a challenge and an essential task in terms of protecting the data from vulnerable access. This paper tries to enrich the field of optical communication by focusing on security and data transmission efficiency. By incorporating a chaotic system into the DWDM-SMF system, it offers an approach to achieving high bandwidth and long-distance data communication. System (1) has a complex and unpredictable nature. By implementing CSS technology within the DWDM-SMF system, data encryption is effectively carried out over extended distances. By using encryption, the link distance is lowered from 100 km to 69.5 km due to dispersion effects, but the issue is addressed through the use of DCF to achieve a 150 km link distance. According to the study, DWDM can be used to increase the transmitted bit rate, which can be considered to be an input obtained as a result of our analyses. The security analysis is demonstrated using measures like histogram uniformity, correlation coefficient and information entropy to ensure that the system exhibits a level of security. This robustness makes it resilient, against attacks, and with the utilization of DCF and EDFA, there emerges a significant impact on the performance of the system ensuring that the integrity of signals is maintained even over distances as long as 150 km. Notwithstanding, this study not only enhances data transmission security but also ensures high efficiency and performance over extended distances, which can pave the way for more sophisticated and advanced applications in various fields for the attainment of optimized solutions.

Acknowledgments. This work was accomplished at the University of Technology, Iraq, and the Faculty of Computer Science and Information Technology, Universiti Malaya, Malaysia and it is funded by the Universiti Malaya RMFI2067-2021 Grant.

References

1. Wazi, M.T., Ali, D.S., Al-Saidi, N.M., Alawn, N.A.: A secure image cryptosystem via multiple chaotic maps. Discrete Math. Algorithms Appl. **14**(4), 2150141 (2021)
2. Veeman, D., Natiq, H., Al-Saidi, N.M., Rajagopal, K., Jafari, S., Hussain, I.: A new megastable chaotic oscillator with blinking oscillation terms. Complexity **2021**(1), 5518633 (2021)
3. Al-Saidi, N.M.G., Younus, D., Natiq, H., Ariffin, M.R.K., Asbullah, M.A., Mahad, Z.: A new hyperchaotic map for a secure communication scheme with an experimental realization. Symmetry **12**(11), 2021 (1881)
4. Vogl, M.: Chaos measure dynamics in a multifactor model for financial market predictions. Commun. Nonlinear Sci. Numer. Simul. Nonlinear Sci. Numer. Simul. **130**, 107760 (2024)
5. Salih, S.H., Al-Saidi, N.M.G.: 3D-Chaotic discrete system of vector borne disease using environment factor with deep analysis. AIMS Math. **7**(3), 3972–3987 (2022)
6. Sadkhan Al Maliky, S.B.(ed.) Multidisciplinary Perspectives in Cryptology and Information Security. IGI Global (2014)
7. Balakrishnan, H.N., et al.: ChaosNet: a chaos based artificial neural network architecture for classification. Chaos Interdisc. J. Nonlinear Sci. **29**(11) (2019)
8. Matthews, R.: On the derivation of a "chaotic" encryption algorithm. Cryptologia **13**(1), 29–42 (1989)
9. Natiq, H., Al-Saidi, N.M., Obaiys, S.J., Mahdi, M.N., Farhan, A.K.: Image encryption based on local fractional derivative complex logistic map. Symmetry **14**(9), 2022 (1874)
10. Lorenz, E.N.: Designing chaotic models J. Atmos. Sci. **62**(5), 1574–1587 (2005)
11. Abdulsatar, S.M., Saleh, M.A., Abass, A.K., Ali, M.H., Yaseen, M.A.: Bidirectional hybrid optical communication system based on wavelength division multiplexing for outdoor applications. Opt. Quantum Electron. **53**(10), 1–11 (2021)
12. Khadir, A.A., Dhahir, B.F., Fu, X.: Achieving optical fiber communication experiments by optisystem. Int. J. Comput. Sci. Mob. Comput.Comput. Sci. Mob. Comput. **3**(6), 42–53 (2014)
13. Mohammed, S.H., Abass, A.K., Ali, M.H., Rashid, F.F.: Design and simulation of secure fiber optic communication system utilizing hill cipher algorithm. J. Opt. **53**(2), 1499–1507 (2023). https://doi.org/10.1007/s12596-023-01313-8

14. Al-Saidi, N.M. and Ali, M.H.: Assessment of highly performance secure optical communication systems based on chaotic design. Al-Iraqia J. Sci. Eng. Res. **1**(1), 109–123 (2022)
15. Mork, J., Tromborg, B., Mark, J.: Chaos in semiconductor lasers with optical feedback: theory and experiment. IEEE J. Quantum Electron. **28**(1), 93–108 (1992)
16. Argyris, A., et al.: Chaos-based communications at high bit rates using commercial fibre-optic links. Nature **438**(7066), 343–3466 (2005)
17. Qiao, J.: Dense wavelength division multiplexing (DWDM) for optical networks. The University of Texas at Austin (2001)
18. Zhou, R., et al.: 80-km coherent DWDM-PON on 20-GHz grid with injected gain switched comb source. IEEE Photonics Technol. Lett. **26**(4), 364–367 (2013)
19. Kaur, S., Singh, S.: Review on developments in all-optical spectral amplitude coding techniques. Opt. Eng. **57**(11), 116102 (2018)
20. Huang, C., et al.: A bounded model of the communication delay for system integrity protection schemes. IEEE Trans. Power Delivery **31**(4), 1921–1933 (2016)
21. Al-Saidi, N.M., et al.: The dynamic and discrete systems of variable fractional order in the sense of the Lozi structure map. AIMS Math. **8**(1), 733–751 (2023)
22. The MathWorks, Inc.: MATLAB 2023 version 9.12.0(R2023a), Software, Natick, MA (2023)
23. Atieh, A., Mirza, J., Ghafoor, S.: Optical fiber sources design in OptiSystem software. Photonics North (PN) (cdn.optiwave.com, 2022). https://cdn.optiwave.com/wp-content/uploads/2022/05/Photonics-North-2022_May-25-2022.pdf. Accessed 25 May 2022
24. Cheung, N.K., Nosu, K., Winzer, G.: Dense wavelength division multiplexing techniques for high capacity and multiple access communication systems. IEEE J. Sel. Areas Commun. **8**(6) (1990)
25. Xu, L., Li, Z., Li, J., Hua, W.: A novel bit-level image encryption algorithm based on chaotic maps. Opt. Lasers Eng. **78**, 17–25 (2016)
26. Al-Saidi, N.M., Yahya, H., Obaiys, S.J.: Discrete dynamic model of a disease-causing organism caused by 2D-quantum Tsallis entropy. Symmetry **14**(8), 1677 (2022)

A Pseudo Random Number Generator Based on 4D Hyperchaotic Systems, Riddled Basins of Attraction and Advanced Microfluidic Technology

Nawres A. Alwan[1], Suzan J. Obaiys[1(✉)], Nadia M. G. Al-Saidi[2], Nurul Fazmidar Binti Mohd Noor[1], and Yeliz Karaca[3,4]

[1] Department of Computer System and Technology, Faculty of Computer Science and Information Technology, University of Malaya, Kuala Lumpur, Malaysia
s2000740@siswa.um.edu.my, {suzan,fazmidar}@um.edu.my

[2] Department of Applied Sciences, University of Technology, Baghdad, Iraq
nadia.m.ghanim@uotechnology.edu.iq

[3] University of Massachusetts (UMass) Chan Medical School, 55 Lake Avenue North, Worcester, MA 01655, USA
yeliz.karaca@ieee.org

[4] Massachusetts Institute of Technology (MIT), 77 Massachusetts Avenue, Cambridge, MA 02139, USA

Abstract. A pseudo random number generator (PRNG), also referred to as a deterministic random bit generator (DRGB) is an algorithm utilized to generate a sequence of numbers which have approximate properties pertaining to those of sequences in random numbers. The current PRNGs can be exemplified as linear congruence generators, inverse congruence generators as well as PRNGs that are based on chaotic systems which have benefits like pseudorandom behavior, sensitivity to initial conditions, ergodicity and high complexity. Accordingly, this paper presents a new mode of PRNG sequences by combining microfluidic (MF) techniques with hyper-chaotic systems of n-dimension. The proposed system offers complex behavior, wide distribution, and plausible ergodicity. This interdisciplinary technique combines engineering, physics, and mathematics to create a random sequence. The mixture of the four outcome sequences generated from the 4 dimensions (4D) hyperchaotic system and the Fisher-Yates Shuffle algorithm is used to generate the PRNG. The algorithmic process is designed to rearrange the sequence elements in a random order. Statistical analysis of the NIST test, key sensitivity, auto-correlation and cross-correlation, and entropy are also presented that play a significant role in demonstrating the PRNG methods.

Keywords: Hyperchaotic · Chaos · Pseudo Random Number Generator (PRNG) · Randomness analysis · Microfluidic · Auto-correlation and cross-correlation tests · Entropy · Permutation entropy · Fisher-Yates Shuffle algorithm · Riddled basins of attraction · Chaotic systems · Fixed point analysis · Conservation system · Bifurcation diagrams of systems

O. Gervasi et al. (Eds.): ICCSA 2024 Workshops, LNCS 14815, pp. 91–109, 2024.
https://doi.org/10.1007/978-3-031-65154-0_6

1 Introduction

Pseudo-random number generators (PRNG) are widely utilized across various disciplines such as statistics, computer science, cryptography, and gaming [1]. These generators produce random number series that are derived from a specific starting point through a mathematical formula. In the field of cryptography, the efficacy of PRNG is crucial due to the security process of cryptosystems relies on the randomness and unpredictability of the key generations. A high-quality PRNG must embody some essential attributes to guarantee the security and integrity of the outputs, such as; stochasticity, erraticism, periodicity, security, and efficiency [3]. Typically, PRNGs can be classified into two categories: linear and nonlinear. Linear PRNGs utilize methods such as linear congruential generators (LCGs) and linear feedback shift registers (LFSRs) to produce pseudorandom sequences [4]. However, these methods have limitations, including shorter periods and reduced randomness. Further, the nonlinear PRNG employs nonlinear transition functions or output functions to convert a linear system to nonlinear ones. This approach is increasingly preferred in cryptography due to its superior randomness [5]. Chaotic nonlinear systems are known for several distinctive features including ergodicity, initial condition to sensitivity, seemingly random actions, and a wide spectrum of behaviors [6]. Since Lorenz discovered chaos in 1963, there has been significant research on chaos and the hyper-chaos phenomena. In 1982, Oishi et al. [7] introduced the first pseudorandom sequence generator using a chaotic system. Then, Liu et al. [8] employed a chaotic system for a binary pseudorandom sequence generation. These efforts incorporated a single chaotic system into the PRNG design. Subsequently, many scholars have proposed various algorithms for designing new PRNGs [9–14]. To improve the unpredictability of the sequences created, several security measures were put in place, demonstrating the capability of the generator to produce secure pseudo-random number sequences (PRNS). In 2021, Yu et al. [12] introduced a PRNG based on a chaotic system with an enhanced Hopfield neural network, aimed at reducing chaotic degradation's effects and improving PRNS quality. In 2022, Zang and team [14] proposed a method for PRNS generation based on complex polynomial chaotic maps, exhibiting strong randomness in the PRNS and susceptibility to differential attacks. A notable drawback of chaos-based cryptographic methods is their reliance on chaotic maps that operate with real numbers, which are not ideal for finite numbers cryptographic uses. The quantization of real numbers to round-off values can lead to issues, including the creation of non-reversible functions, thus rendering decryption unfeasible. In 2023, Li et al. published a new PRNG based on a 4D discrete system that has been developed to address issues found in previous literature, including a focus on continuous or low-dimensional chaotic systems characterized by strong temporal correlations and a lack of complex nonlinear dynamics [15]. Haider et al. [16] introduced a novel PRNG based on multivariable optimization for image-cryptographic algorithms. While Shunsuke et al. [17] presented a novel design of random number generators based on chaos-based extremum coding. The security flaws of PRNGs established in linear systems are primarily due to their brief cycle lengths. This shortcoming is exacerbated by the rapid deterioration seen in low-dimensional chaotic systems, which further diminishes the period and randomness of PRNG constructions. The simultaneous presence of chaotic attractors and periodic points in conservative hyper-chaotic systems makes them

less suitable for pseudo-random number generator (PRNG) design due to inherent predictability and difficulty in control [16]. Instead, attention has shifted towards dissipative hyper-chaotic systems within the nonlinear system-based PRNGs era. The robustness of PRNGs derived from these systems hinges on their complexity and the extent of chaotic breakdown. Chaotic systems that exhibit complex dynamic behaviors are known for their enhanced randomness [5]. One of the most critical measures of this randomness is the Lyapunov exponent (LE), with the maximum LE being particularly indicative of the system sensitivity to initial conditions, the higher the exponent the more rapidly trajectories diverge, indicating greater system sensitivity. The weakness of conventional PRNG methodologies, attributed to the simplistic nature of chaotic systems, is evidenced by phenomena such as discontinuous chaotic domains, constricted chaos boundaries, and suboptimal obfuscation and diffusion capabilities [18–20]. Hence, the inception of a novel PRNG approach, characterized by enhanced complexity and stochastic properties, is advocated. Consequently, this paper introduces a new hyperchaotic system, inspired by prior investigations and conceptualizations, demonstrating significantly augmented dynamic complexity. This newly devised chaotic system manifests across a broad continuum of parameters sans periodic windows, exhibiting heightened sensitivity to infinitesimal variances in initial conditions and displaying intricate dynamic behaviors with hyperchaotic attributes, thereby ensuring robust ergodicity. By considering these characteristics, they are considered important for many applications (e.g., image encryption [6]).
Herein, a new PRNG technique commences from the random sequences (SQ) emanating from the newly developed hyperchaotic system of microfluidic (MF) properties is presented. This technique distinguishes itself by utilizing a dynamic MF, engendered from the hyperchaotic scheme. Then, we use the FYS algorithm [21] to shuffle the SQ and randomly distribute its elements to produce the new PRNG is sequence. The converted 32-bit binary representation SQ outcome from the last 16 bits is extracted and presented in a decimal number. This decimal number is then subjected to a modulo 256 operation, aligning the output with the requirements of cryptographic applications and simulations necessitating high-quality randomness. The performance of the proposed mode is evaluated using statistical analysis of the NIST test, key sensitivity, auto-correlation & cross-correlation, and Entropy.

The literature review conducted reveals that numerous PRNG techniques, which utilize one or more chaotic maps, have been introduced. However, there is a notable redundancy in the application of these maps and their combinations. This sort of negligence compromises the PRNG security and robustness. Accordingly, the key contributions of this work include the following aspects: 1) A new 4D hyperchaotic system is developed. 2) Verification of the proposed system's effectiveness through passing all dynamical analyses is ensured. 3) A new method to generate PRNG that employs the 4D hyperchaotic system and Microfluidic technical is provided. 4) Verification of the proposed method is effectiveness through passing all tests in the NIST SP 800 analysis suite is presented.

The paper is structured as follows: Sect. 2 describes the proposed dynamical system and analysis of it. Afterwards, Sect. 3 provides the details of the proposed PRNG methodology. Section 4 evaluates the performance and discusses the results obtained from the various analyses. Finally, Sect. 5 concludes the paper.

2 Proposed Dynamical System

This section presents the new 4D- hyperchaotic system which is designed for random SQ generation. The 4D-hyperchaotic system can be described as follows:

$$\frac{dx_1}{dt} = (\beta x_2 - \gamma x_3)\, x_4; \quad \frac{dx_2}{dt} = (\gamma x_3 - \delta x_4)\, x_1; \frac{dx_3}{dt} = (\delta x_4 - \alpha x_1)\, x_2; \\ \frac{dx_4}{dt} = (\alpha x_1 - \beta x_2)\, x_3; \tag{1}$$

where x_1, x_2, x_3 and x_4 are initial state, and α, β, γ, and δ are parameters. The electrical circuit corresponding to system 1 is depicted in Fig. 1(a), indicating its real-life applicability. Figure 1(b) shows the phase spaces of system 1 for x_1 vs. x_2 using the electrical circuit shown in Fig. 1 of x_1 vs. x_2.

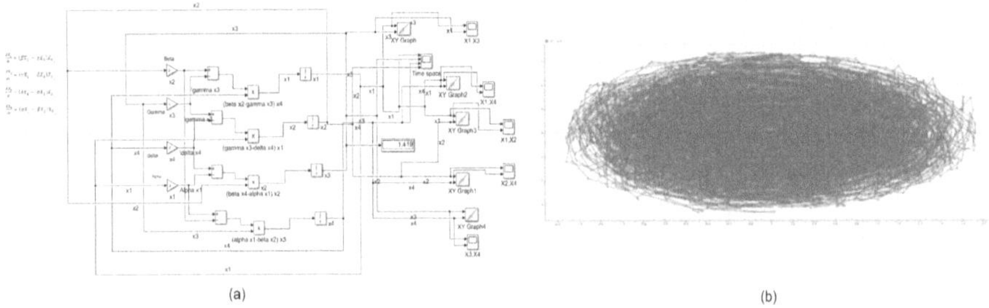

Fig. 1. System 1 (a) circuit using MATLAB Simulink, (b) The phase space of system 1 using MATLAB Simulink of x_1 vs. x_2.

2.1 The Attractor

System 1 attractor is described as a collection of points or a sequence of values within the state space, illustrating the trajectory followed by the system's output. Figure 2(a)–(b) displays the attractor diagrams and time series for the 4D-hyperchaotic system, which are generated under varying parameter values of $\alpha, \beta,\ \gamma,\ \delta$ to $60, 40, 8, 20$ and an initial state of (x_1, x_2, x_3, x_4) to $(1, 1, 2, 2)$. This visualization captures the dynamic behavior and the complexity of the system's evolution over time based on these specific settings. Figure 2(c) shows the sensitivity of the attractor diagrams of the system 1 based on different values of the parameters $(\alpha, \beta,\ \gamma,\ \delta)$ and initial state $(x_1,\ x_2,\ x_3,\ x_4\ )$, where parameters are fixed $\alpha = 40$; $\beta = 60$; $\gamma = 8$; and the value of δ is change into three values $\delta = 3$, and $\delta = 3.2$ corresponding the attractor diagram with different values of the initial states (x_1, x_2, x_3, x_4)= (1, 1, 2, 2), (1, 1, 2, 2.2), and (1, 1, 2, 2.4) as blue, red, and green, respectively. Analysis of the sensitivity to initial conditions and parameters in any chaotic map reveals a critical dependence on both aspects. Sensitivity to the initial conditions sensitivity demonstrated notable reaction to minimal alterations, with the initial condition x_4 adjusting to merely 0.1 and the parameter δ by 0.2. Subsequent examination and comparison of the resulting trajectories have emphasized this observation.

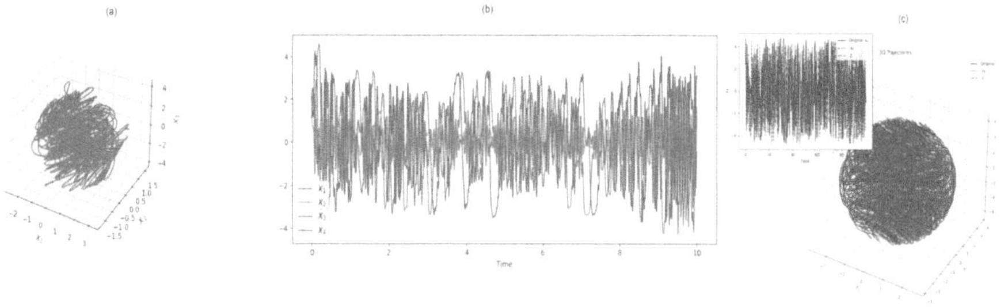

Fig. 2. (a)–(b) Attractors and time series of 4D- hyperchaotic system, respectively, (c) The sensitivity of the system 1 for the Parameters x_4 and b.

Figure 3 shows the phase portraits for pairs of state variables from system 1, (a) x_1 vs. x_2, and (b) x_3 vs. x_4. These plots provide a visual dynamical representation of the system in phase space, illustrating how the state variables interact with each other over the time frame.

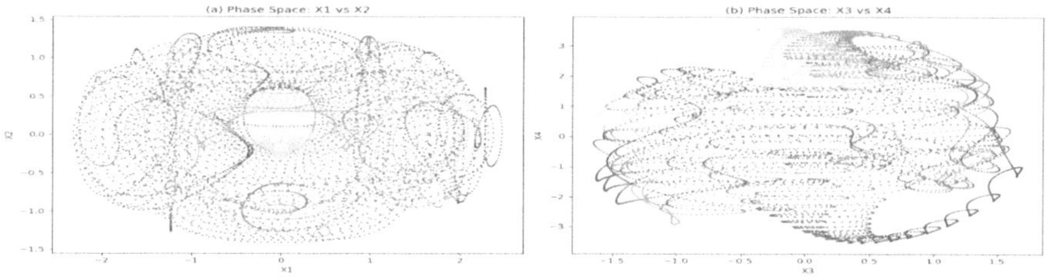

Fig. 3. Phase space of system 1 (a) x_1 vs. x_2, and (b) x_3 vs. x_4.

2.2 Bifurcation Diagram

In the field of dynamic systems, a bifurcation diagram represents a situation in which new behaviors arise when parameters are altered. The diagram serves as a visual representation of the number of possible states that a system can have under various parameter conditions. It uses dots for chaotic behavior and lines for non-chaotic behavior.

Figure 4 (a, b, c, d) depicts the bifurcation diagrams of the system 1 respectively, where $(x(1), x(2), x(3), x(4) = (1, 0.1, 0, 1))$ and various parameters $\alpha \in (60 : 0.01 : 61)$,$\beta \in (40 : 0.01 : 41)$, $\gamma \in (7 : 0.01 : 8)$ and $\delta \in (20 : 0.01 : 21)$.

2.3 Lyapunov Exponent

Lyapunov exponents (LE) serve as a measure for the rate at which trajectories in a system either diverge or converge. These exponents can be mathematically represented as follows [6]:

$$\lambda \approx \frac{1}{t} \ln \frac{||\delta x(t)||}{||\delta x(0)||}$$

Here, the term $\frac{||\delta x(t)||}{||\delta x(0)||}$ denotes the relative distance between two distinct trajectories. Figure 5, depict (a), (b), and (c), the hyperchaotic behavior of a system (1) is illustrated using LE, particularly for the parameter sets ($\alpha = 40; \beta = 60; \gamma = 8; \delta = 20$), ($\alpha = 40; \beta = 60; \gamma = 8; \delta = 20$) and ($\alpha = 40; \beta = 60; \gamma = 8; \delta = 20$), respectively.

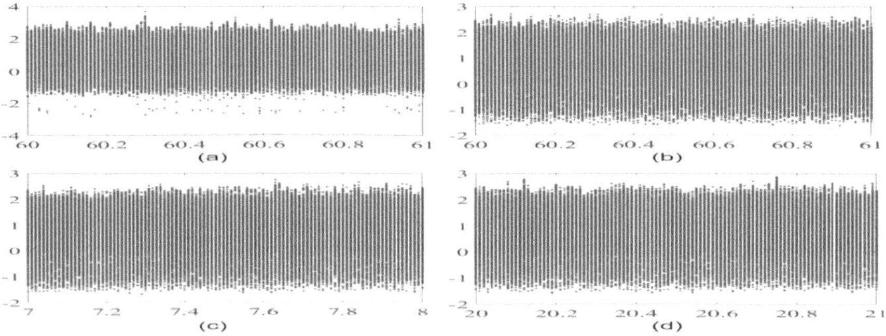

Fig. 4. Bifurcation diagrams of system 1 where the initial state $(x(1), x(2), x(3), x(4) = (1, 0.1, 0, 1))$ and various parameters (a) $\alpha \in (60 : 0.01 : 61)$,(b) $\beta \in (40 : 0.01 : 41)$,(c) $\gamma \in (7 : 0.01 : 8)$, and (d) $\delta \in (20 : 0.01 : 21)$.

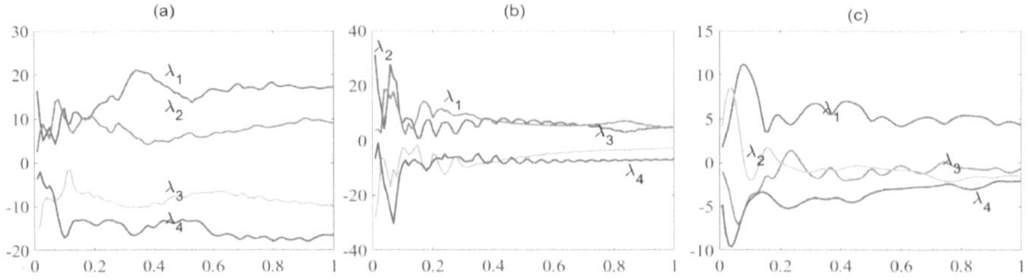

Fig. 5. The Lyapunov exponents of system 1 where the initial state $(x(1), x(2), x(3), x(4) = (1, 0.1, 0, 1))$ and various parameters $(\alpha, \beta, \gamma, \delta)$ (a) (60, 40, 8, 20), (b) (90, 40, 7, 3), and (c) (60, 30, 3, 10).

2.4 Permutation Entropy

Permutation entropy (PE) [22] serves as a crucial measure for assessing the complexity level of time series. It indicates how closely the behavior of chaotic maps mimics pseudo-random sequences. A higher complexity score suggests a closer resemblance to pseudo-random sequences, thereby implying enhanced security. Figure 6 shows the PE for all variables.

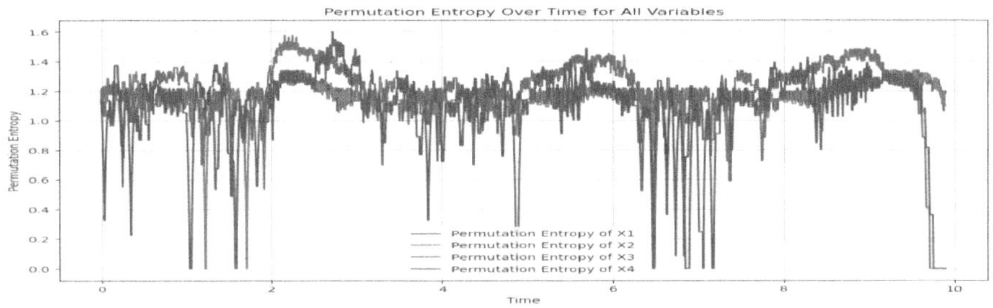

Fig. 6. PE Over Time for All Variables

2.5 Poincaré map

The Poincaré section, also known as the Poincaré map [22], is a crucial tool in the study of dynamical systems, particularly in the analysis of chaotic systems. It provides a way to reduce the dimensionality of a system by taking a cross-section of the phase space, which can simplify the visualization and understanding of the system's dynamics. By studying the intersections of a trajectory with the Poincaré section, one can observe patterns that reveal the underlying structure of the chaotic system. Figure 7(a) shows the simplified Poincaré section of the system 1, focusing on the periodic nature of the dynamics. Two distinct points are shown in red on the section plane, indicating where the system's trajectory intersects the plane in opposite directions. This pattern of intersections suggests a potential periodic orbit within the chaotic system. The semi-transparent grey plane represents the chosen Poincaré section for this analysis, providing a backdrop for the intersection points. In Fig. 7(b), a 2D projection of a Poincaré section is shown for the system 1. The section reveals a series of points where the system's trajectory crosses the section plane, with blue dots indicating the 'in' direction and red dots the 'out' direction of the flow. This differentiation helps to distinguish between the points where the trajectory enters and exits the section plane, respectively. The clustered nature of the points around the central region suggests a looping pattern, characteristic of periodic orbits embedded within the chaotic attractor. Figure 7(c) shows a 2D of the Poincaré section points in and out-direction, where in-direction will be where the sign of x_4 changes from negative to positive, and out-direction will be where the sign changes from positive to negative. Figure 7 (d) illustrates the Poincaré section points with a linear regression line fitted to them. The fitted line equation is $y= -0.0335x+0.5136$, with a very low of coefficient of determination R^2 value of 0.0012. The Poincaré section points are shown in blue color, which representing their position in the three-dimensional space. The red plane represents the linear regression fit extended into this space, with the x_1 and x_2 variables.

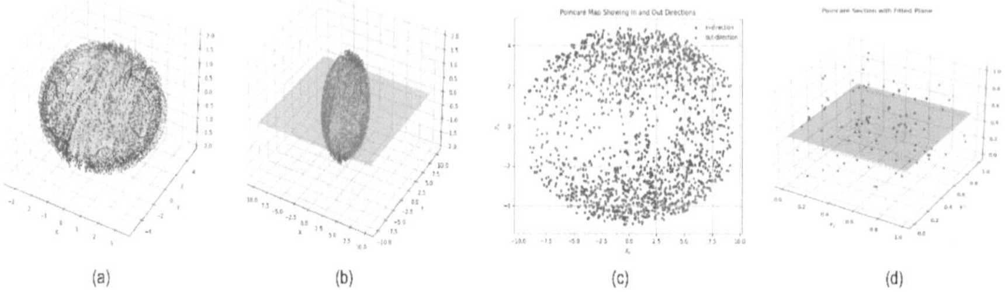

Fig. 7. (a) chaotic flow of system 1 intersecting the Poincaré section, (b) its corresponding Poincaré map, (c) 2D of Poincaré map and (d) Poincaré map

2.6 Conservation and Fixed Points and Basin of Attractor

Conservation: To assess whether the phase space volume of the system exhibits conservative or dissipative characteristics, it is necessary to compute the conservative of the system described in 1. The divergence of the vector field $\mathbb{C}\mathbf{F}$, denoted by $(\nabla\cdot\mathbb{C}\mathbf{F})$ is determined by the aggregate of the partial derivatives associated with each equation in 1, which can be expressed as:

$$\nabla\cdot\mathbb{C}\mathbf{F}=\sum_{i=1}^{4}\frac{\partial}{\partial X_i}\text{ (RHS of the } i\text{–th equation)}$$

where $\frac{\partial}{\partial X_i}$ is applied to the corresponding right-hand side of the i-th differential equation of system 1, which is expanded as.

$$\nabla\cdot\mathbf{CF} = \frac{\partial}{\partial x_1}(\beta x_2 - \gamma x_3)\,x_4 + \frac{\partial}{\partial x_2}(\gamma x_3 - \delta x_4)\,x_1 + \frac{\partial}{\partial x_3}(\delta x_4 - \alpha x_1)\,x_2 + \frac{\partial}{\partial x_4}(\alpha x_1 - \beta x_2)\,x_3 \tag{2}$$

It is obvious that the first term $\frac{\partial}{\partial x_1}(\beta x_2 - \gamma x_3)\,x_4= 0$, and the second term $\frac{\partial}{\partial x_2}(\gamma x_3 - \delta x_4)\,x_1= 0$, since x_1 and x_2 do not appear in the expansion, and so on for the other terms. Then we have;

$$\nabla\cdot\mathbb{C}\mathbf{F}= 0 + 0 + 0 + 0 = 0.$$

Since the $\nabla \cdot \mathbb{C}\mathbf{F} = 0$, this indicates that system 1 holds to conservation laws, indicative of Hamiltonian or conservative systems. According to Liouville's theorem [23], such a condition ensures that the phase space density, along with the system's trajectories, remains constant over time. This indicates that the volume of the phase space is invariant under the system's dynamics, marking a significant contrast to dissipative systems, in which the phase space volume typically decreases over time. Therefore, a system meeting the condition $\nabla \cdot \mathbb{C}\mathbf{F} = 0$ is classified as a conservative dynamical system, characterized by the conservation of energy or analogous quantities, devoid of dissipative effects.

Fixed Points: To determine the equilibrium points, we set the derivatives of all variables to zero. Therefore, applying $\frac{dx_i}{dt} = 0; i = 1, 2, 3, 4$, we get the following equations:

$$(\alpha x_2 - \gamma x_3)\, x_4 = 0; \quad (\beta x_3 - \delta x_4)\, x_1 = 0; (\gamma x_4 - \alpha x_1)\, x_2 = 0; \quad (\delta x_1 - \beta x_2)\, x_3 = 0;$$

This implies that one set of equilibrium points is $x_1 = x_2 = x_3 = x_4 = 0$, while $x_1 = \frac{\beta x_2}{\delta}; x_2 = \frac{\beta x_3}{\alpha}; x_3 = \frac{\gamma x_4}{\beta}; x_4 = \frac{\alpha x_1}{\gamma}$. Figure 8(a) shows the equilibrium points (E_1, E_2) and trajectory of system 1, where the parameter sets ($\alpha = 40; \beta = 60; \gamma = 8; \delta = 20$) and initial state sets ($x_1 = 1; x_2 = 1; x_3 = 1; x_4 = 1$).

Basins of Attraction: Riddled basins of attraction represent a complex structure within the phase space of multistable chaotic systems, where the regions of convergence towards different attractors intricately intermingle. This intricate pattern signifies that infinitesimally close initial conditions can result in divergent long-term behaviors, leading to unpredictable transitions between attractors. The presence of riddled basins underscores the sensitivity of the system's ultimate state to its initial conditions, a hallmark of chaotic dynamics. Such behavior has profound implications for predicting the long-term behavior of physical, biological, and engineering systems, as it highlights the limitations posed by inherent unpredictability [24]. Figure 8(b) shows the riddled basins of attraction for a dynamical system. Where the different colors in the plot represent different basins of attraction. The basins of different attractors are intricately interwoven, such that a very small change in initial conditions represented by the x_1 and x_2 axes can lead to convergence to a different attractor. This characteristic makes predicting the long-term behavior of the system quite challenging and is a hallmark of chaotic systems with sensitive dependence on initial conditions.

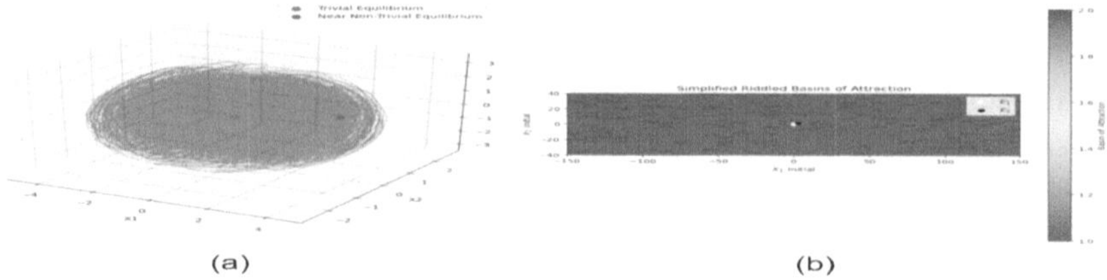

Fig. 8. (a) Equilibrium points and attractor trajectory and (b) Riddled basins of attraction in $x_1(0)$ – $x_2(0)$, and the equilibrium points E_1 and E_2.

3 Proposed Method

3.1 Microfluidic Technology

Microfluidics (MF)refers to a system that manipulates a little amount of fluid by the use of small canals in a specific dimension, and based on this, microfluidic technology is stated to be potentially employed as a platform for the investigation of interactions between drug carriers and cells as well as the treatment implications of active compounds and drugs. Thus, it provides the possibility of analyzing the response of multiple cells, tissues or organs, which can pave the way for the development of novel treatments. MF is one of the important field of science, particularly in, chemical analysis, biological research, diagnostics and the development of new materials [25]. MF deals with the processing of fluids on a very small scale, typically in channels with dimensions ranging from tens to hundreds of micrometers. The principal work of MF is on controlling the behavior, manipulation, and analysis of very small volumes of fluids. Moreover, it enhances some physical properties such as laminar flow, surface tension, fluidic resistance and others. MF technology allows for the miniaturization of laboratory processes, reducing the need for large volumes of reagents and samples, speeding up experiments, and enabling high-throughput testing and analysis with increased efficiency and lower costs, in many scientific areas such as genomics, proteomics, drug discovery and environmental monitoring [25]. Based on this technology, we suggest using this MF technology to mix multiple sequences of random numbers derived from a chaotic dynamical system Instead of fluids, like those in MF. Here are some techniques inspired by MF mixing methods that could be applied to mix random sequences: such as; Serial Dilution, Droplet-Based mixing, Split-and-Recombine (SAR) method, and Fisher-Yates Shuffle algorithm [21].

3.2 Fisher-Yates Shuffle Algorithm

In the technique proposed in this study, we used the Fisher-Yates Shuffle (FYS) algorithm also known as the Knuth shuffle, which is used in MF to mixture the fluids. FYS is an algorithmic process designed to rearrange the elements of the sequence in a random order, which is considered one of the most important methods of shuffling. The FYS algorithm stands as a cornerstone in the domain of random permutations, this is due to its strong mathematical basis and optimal efficiency in generating uniformly distributed sequences. FYS mathematically can be explained as follows, suppose a sequence S with length n, the first step of the process is starting from the last element and proceeding to the second element in the sequence. At each iteration i, generates random index j is chosen where $1 \leq j \leq i$ and the elements at positions i and j are swapped. Such that, this operation guarantees that each permutation of the sequence has the same probability, establishing the uniform randomness of the algorithm's output. The swap operation is an essential component of the FYS, and involves exchanging the values of two elements within the sequence. For elements at positions i and j, the value at i is temporarily stored, the value at j is placed in position i, and the stored value is then moved to position j. This simple yet effective operation is important for the algorithm's ability to randomize a sequence where each element has the same probability without bias. Based on system 1 and the FSY algorithm, we propose a novel algorithm for generating PRNG sequences. The proposed method begins with the generation of initial values derived from a set of parameters of system 1, and key blocks $K_1, K_2, \ldots, K_{15}$, employing a chaotic system to produce a random sequence of values. These sequences are generated based on system 1 denoted as $SQ(i)$ where i ranges from 1 to 4. Subsequently, these sequences are concatenated into a single sequence SQ, to which the FYS is applied to ensure a uniform distribution of the elements. The final step in the algorithm involves processing the shuffled sequence to produce the PRNG sequence. Each number in the random sequence SQ is converted into a 32-bit binary representation, from which the last 16 bits, which leads to requirements for cryptographic applications and simulations that require high-quality randomness. Through this method, we leverage the deterministic chaos of MF-inspired systems and the confirmatory randomness of FYS to generate PRNG sequences. This approach not only ensures the uniformity and unpredictability essential for cryptographic security but also introduces a novel application of chaos theory in the field of encryption security and random number generation (Fig. 9).

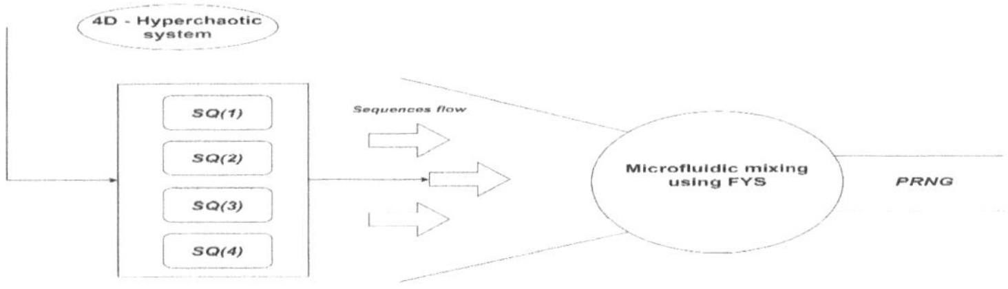

Fig. 9. MF technical to generate PRNG

3.3 Generating Pseudo Random Number Sequences Based on the 4D-Hyperchaotic System in (1)

In this subsection, we discussed the generation of PRNG utilizing systems 1. The initial step involves creating an initial state (x_1, x_2, x_3, x_4) and parameters α, β, γ, and δ of the system 1. The process for computing new initial values given a set of original initial states and parameters $(x_1, x_2, x_3, x_4, \alpha, \beta, \gamma, \delta)$ along with key blocks $(K_1, K_2, \ldots, K_{15})$. The objective is to produce updated initial values $\left(x_1', x_2', x_3', x_4', \alpha', \beta', \gamma', \delta'\right)$. This is achieved by adjusting each of the original states and parameters by adding the binary-to-decimal conversion of the exclusive or (XOR) operation between specific pairs of key blocks, with a small constant $(1e-6)$ to ensure a minor but significant change. Specifically, $\left(x_1'\right)$ is recalculated by adding (x_1) to the binary-to-decimal conversion of (K_1) XOR (K_2), and similar operations are performed for $\left(x_2'\right), \left(x_3'\right), \left(x_4'\right), (\alpha'), (\beta'), (\gamma')$, and (δ') with their respective key blocks. Such modifications are crucial for boosting the randomness and unpredictability of the initial state (x_0). Algorithm 1 shows the process for generating the initial state (x_0).

Algorithm 1. Generating Initial Values

Input: Original initial states and parameters: $x_1, x_2, x_3, x_4, \alpha, \beta, \gamma, \delta$, Key blocks: $K_1, K_2, \ldots, K_{15}$;
Output: New initial values: $x_1', x_2', x_3', x_4', \alpha', \beta', \gamma', \delta'$;

function $\left[x_1', x_2', x_3' x_4', a', b', c', d'\right]$ = INITIAL VALUES $(x_1, x_2, x_3 x_4, \alpha, \beta, \gamma, \delta, K_1, K_2, \ldots, K_{15})$ % Calculate the new initial values
    $x_1' = x_1 + \text{bin}\,2\,\text{dec}\,(K_1 \; bitxor \; K_2)\,1e-6;$
    $x_2' = x_2 + \text{bin}\,2\,\text{dec}\,(K_3 \; bitxor \; K_4)\,1e-6;$
    $x_3' = x_3 + \text{bin}\,2\,\text{dec}\,(K_5 \; bitxor \; K_6)\,1e-6;$
    $x_4' = x_4 + \text{bin}\,2\,\text{dec}\,(K_7 \; bitxor \; K_8)\,1e-6;$
    $\alpha' = \alpha + \text{bin}\,2\,\text{dec}\,(K_9 \; bitxor \; K_2)\,1e-6;$
    $\beta' = \beta + \text{bin}\,2\,\text{dec}\,(K_{10} \; bitxor \; K_{11})\,1e-6;$
    $\gamma' = \gamma + \text{bin2dec}\,(K_{12} \; bitxor \; K_{13})\,1e-6;$
    $\delta' = \delta + \text{bin}\,2\,\text{dec}\,(K_{14} \; bitxor \; K_{15})\,1e-6;$
    Return the new initial values: $x_1', x_2', x_3' x_4', \alpha', \beta', \gamma', \delta'$;
end function

The next stage is the generation of PRNG based on system (1) and MF technique as shown in **Algorithm 4** and Fig. 10, but before that, we introduce some algorithms that should be applied to generate PRNG. In our work, we employed MATLAB 2022b, and we validated the suggested proposed scheme on a personal computer device, powered by CPU 11th Gen Intel(R) Core(TM) i7-11370H @ 3.30GHz 3.30 GHz, and 16.0 GB of RAM.

Where the combine all sequences generated based on system 1 $SQ(1), SQ(2)$, $SQ(3)$, and $SQ(4)$ into a single sequence SQ is a step designed to increase the randomness produced from each iteration, creating a unified sequence that benefits from the complexity and variability inherent in each $SQ(i)$, where $i = 1:4$.

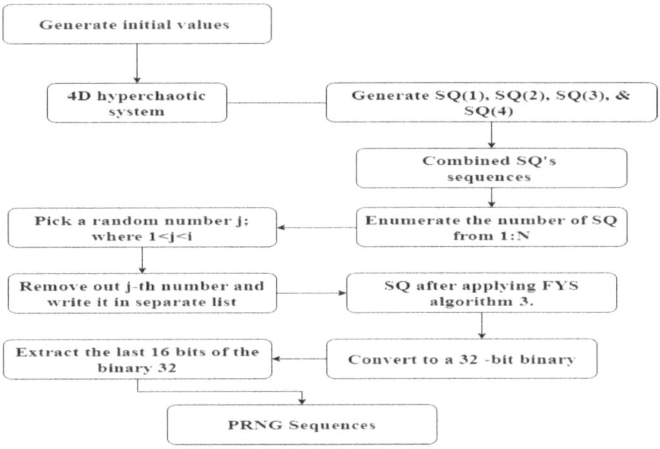

Fig. 10. The PRNG Algorithm

4 Randomness Analysis

4.1 The NIST Test of the System

The National Institute of Standards and Technology (NIST) from the United States offers a standard software package for testing the random behavior of time series.

Algorithm 2. Generation and Combination of Chaotic Sequences

Input: New initial values from Algorithm 1;
Output: Combined sequence SQ

Initialize SQ as empty
for $i = 1:4$ **do**
  $\left[x_1', x_2', x_3' x_4', a', b', c', d'\right]$ = Initial Values $(x_1, x_2, x_3 x_4, \alpha, \beta, \gamma, \delta, K_1, K_2, \ldots, K_{15})$;
  sx_1, sx_2, sx_3, sx_4 % be sequences of equal length n generated from system 1, and let *combined* be the sequence resulting from their zigzag combination.
  combined = [], % an empty sequence;
  for $j = 1, 2, \ldots, n$ **do**% n length of sx_1
    combined = *combined* $\oplus [sx_1[j]]$
    combined = *combined* $\oplus [sx_2[j]]$ % Where $\oplus$ denotes the concatenation of elements from each sequence in order.
    combined = *combined* $\oplus [sx_3[j]]$
    combined = *combined* $\oplus [sx_4[j]]$
  end for
  $SQ(j)$ = *combined*;
end for
for $i = 1:4$ **do**
  $SQ \leftarrow SQ \oplus SQ(i)$% where $\oplus$ denotes the concatenation operation, combining the sequences end-to-end.
end for
return SQ

This package is used to assess the stochastic performance of time series data. The testing process involves evaluating multiple sequences, each consisting of $1,000,000$ bits. NIST employs two key performance metrics, namely the P value and the pass rate, to gauge the randomness of these time series. By default, NIST sets the significance level (α) to 0.01. The pass rate is assessed using a confidence interval formula: $1-\alpha\pm3\sqrt{\alpha(1-\alpha)/m}$. In this formula, m represents the number of groups of bit sequences. For instance, when α is 0.01 and m is 100, the resulting confidence interval becomes 1 $0.01 \pm 3\sqrt{0.01\times0.99/100}= 0.99\pm0.0094393$, which simplifies to the range $[0.9602, 1.0198]$. This implies that the pass rate of the sequence must exceed 0.9602 to meet the required criteria.
We generated a PRNG sequences where the parameters of system 1 are set as $\alpha=$ 50, $\beta=$ 20, $\gamma=$ 8, and δ = 20. A length of 1000000×16 bits binary sequence is obtained, which is divided into 100 groups and each group has a length of 10^6 bits for the NIST test. The outcomes of the experiments are detailed in Table 1. The test results indicate that all P-values exceed 0.01, demonstrating the successful passage of the NIST test by the generated hyperchaotic sequence and comparison with some other works.

Table 1. NIST Statistical test results for the generated hyperchaotic sequences in comparison to some previous methods.

NIST statistical test item	P-value					Results
	Proposed	Ref. [26]	Ref. [16]	Ref. [5]	Ref. [27]	
Block-Frequency	0.3032	0.2028	0.0062	0.5850	0.5852	True
Frequency (Monobit)	0.6240	0.1428	0.6371	0.3939	0.0741	True
Discrete Fourier Transform	0.7721	0.1729	0.9463	0.5456	0.9319	True
Approximate Entropy	0.2352	0.0216	0.0308	0.4444	0.2228	True
Cumulative Sums (Forward)	0.6513	0.2666	0.0757	0.8483	0.0513	True
Cumulative Sums (Reverse)	0.7321	-	0.7399	-	-	True
Serial-1	0.7123	0.3608	0.4373	0.3917	0.3241	True
Serial-2	0.6121	0.4480	0.0329	-	-	True
Runs	0.3312	0.2859	0.1626	0.3504	0.9808	True
Longest Run of Ones	0.7662	0.8303	0.6163	0.8138	0.3781	True
Overlapping Template	0.9717	0.5782	0.0712	0.6066	0.9705	True
Non-overlapping Template	0.3378	0.00001	0.9558	0.6977	0.7727	True
Linear Complexity	0.5341	0.9511	0.1719	0.4091	0.0487	True
Binary Matrix Rank	0.6773	0.8813	0.1296	0.6993	0.2133	True
Maurer's universal statistical	0.4468	0.6342	0.0966	0.4190	0.3371	True
Random Excursions	0.5867	0.7147	0.8195	0.7787	0.4372	True
Random Excursions Variant	0.5778	0.5142	0.8195	0.6815	0.7061	True

4.2 Key Sensitivity Analysis

Key sensitivity analysis evaluates the impact of minor changes in input on the resultant outputs. A system demonstrates high sensitivity if small alterations in the input lead to significant differences in the output. The bit change rate (BCR) is a critical metric for gauging the sensitivity of a system, such as a PRNG, to its initial settings. This concept quantifies the extent of variation between outputs generated from the original and slightly modified inputs. In this study, the initial parameter δ of the hyperchaotic system is increased by 0.1. The PRNG output based on this initial setting is then compared with the output derived from the adjusted value. The BCR evaluating the sensitivity of a PRNG to its initial conditions, measures the proportion of bytes that change between two sequences generated with slightly different initial inputs. This analysis is crucial for assessing the sensitivity of cryptographic systems, where high sensitivity to initial conditions is often desirable for security reasons. The formula for calculating the (BCR) can be defined as:

$$BCR = \left(\frac{\text{Number of differing bytes}}{\text{Total number of bytes}} \right) \times 100\%$$

In our experiment, the (BCR) stands at 99.50% which highlights the system's high sensitivity to initial conditions. Figure 11 shows the key sensitivity analysis of two PRNG sequences, where the PRNG sequence 1 with $\delta = 20$, and sequence 2 with $\delta = 20.1$, which means any tiny change in system 1 leads to the generation of a new PRNG.

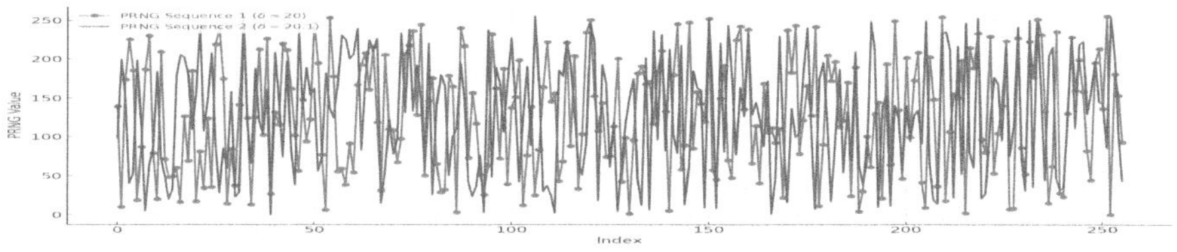

Fig. 11. Key sensitivity analysis of two PRNG sequences.

4.3 Auto-correlation and Cross-correlation

Auto-correlation and cross-correlation tests are statistical tools used to analyze sequences for patterns and relationships. Auto-correlation tests the similarity between a sequence $\{S_i\}_{i=1}^{N}$ and its shifted counterpart $\{S_i\}_{i=j}^{N+j}$, where j ranges from 0 to $N-1$. The auto-correlation at lag k for a sequence S of length N is calculated as:

$$R_s(k) = \frac{1}{(N-k)\sigma^2} \sum_{i=1}^{N-k} (s_i - \mu)(s_{i+k} - \mu)$$

where μ is the mean of x and σ^2 is its variance.

similarly, Cross-correlation, assesses the similarity between two distinct sequences. Employing the same formula, it allows for the comparison of different sequences generated by the scheme in question. The cross-correlation at lag k between sequences S_1 and S_2 of equal length N is:

$$R_{S_1S_2}(k) = \frac{1}{(N-k)\sigma_{S_1}\sigma_{S_2}} \sum_{i=1}^{N-k} (\mathrm{S}_{1_i} - \mu_{s_1})(S_{2i+k} - \mu_{S_2})$$

where μ_{S_1} and μ_{S_1} are the means of S_1 and S_2, and σ_{S_1} and σ_{S_2} are their standard deviations.

In this study, both auto-correlation and cross-correlation of sequences produced by the proposed method are examined to assess their similarity and randomness characteristics. Figure 12 shows the auto-correlation and cross-correlation of two PRNG sequences with a length sequence off 200 bits.

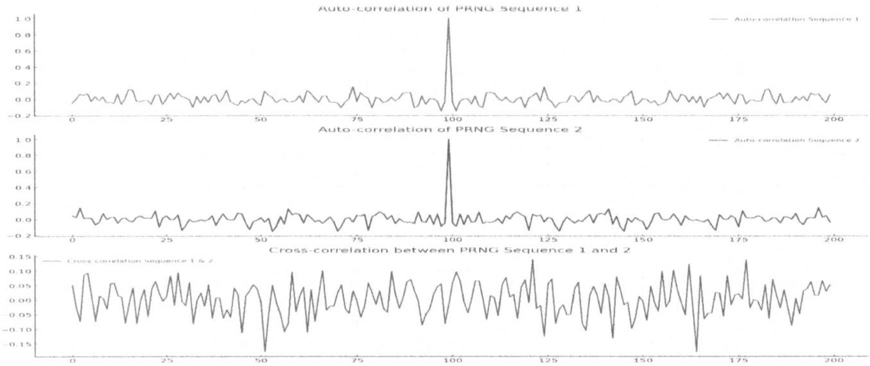

Fig. 12. The auto-correlation test and cross-correlation test of PRNG sequences 1 and 2.

4.4 Entropy

Information entropy is a measure of the unpredictability or randomness of a data source. For a discrete random variable S with possible values $\{s_1, s_2, \ldots, s_n\}$ and probability mass function $P(S = s_i) = p_i$, the entropy $Entropy(S)$ is defined as:

$$Entropy(S) = -\sum_{i=1}^{n} p_i \log_2(p_i)$$

For PRNG sequences, we are interested in the entropy of the distribution of their values. Higher entropy indicates greater randomness and the values of $Entropy(S)$ must be between 1 to 8 indicating a significant level of randomness in both sequences. The closer the $Entropy(S)$ value is to 8, the higher the randomness and unpredictability of the sequence. To obtain the $Entropy(S)$ of PRNG Sequences, we will first need to estimate the probability distribution of their values. One common approach is to use histogram bins to approximate these probabilities. Table 2 shows the entropy values of our scheme and some other methods, the comparison is based on entropy analysis.

Table 2. Entropy and comparison with other methods.

Scheme	Proposed	Ref. [5]	Ref. [11]	Ref. [28]	Ref. [29]	Ref. [30]	Ref. [31]
Entropy Value	7.975	7.9896	7.9980	7.9985	7.9864	7.9937	7.9692

5 Conclusion and Future Directions

Microfluidics (MF) is a system directing a little amount of fluid through small canals in the dimension ranging from tens to hundreds of micrometers. Based on microfluidics, microfluidic technology can serve as an effective platform to investigate interactions between drug carriers and cells as well as the treatment implications of active compounds and drugs. In addition, a pseudo random number generator (PRNG), which is also known as a deterministic random bit generator (DRGB) is an algorithm which can employed for the generation of a sequence of numbers with approximate properties pertaining to the sequences in random numbers. Accordingly, this paper presents a new mode of PRNG sequences by combining microfluidic (MF) techniques with hyperchaotic systems of n-dimension. Hence, a novel PRNG is proposed based on an MF, and chaotic system. A PRNG algorithm based on a hyperchaotic system is used for this purpose. It uses two main steps, the first of which is generating a hyperchaotic system, and the second step is mixing the SQ used FYS algorithm of MF. The PRNG approach demonstrated outstanding performance through simulation tests, such as, the NIST test, key sensitivity, auto-correlation and cross- correlation and entropy. Furthermore, the result of the BCR stands at 99.50% highlighting the system's high sensitivity to initial conditions. As future directions, the proposed scheme in this study can be extended and developed in a way to provides the possibility of analyzing the response of multiple cells, tissues or organs, which can pave the way for the development of novel treatments while having extensive application areas in applied sciences, engineering and other related realms.

Acknowledgments. This work was accomplished at the University of Technology, Iraq, and the Faculty of Computer Science and Information Technology, Universiti Malaya, Malaysia and it is funded by the Universiti Malaya RMFI2067-2021 Grant.

References

1. Luby, M.G.: Pseudorandomness and cryptographic applications. Princeton University Press (1996)

2. Menezes, A.J., Van Oorschot, P.C., and Vanstone, S.A.: Handbook of applied cryptography. CRC Press (2018)
3. Knuth, D.E.: Art of computer programming, volume 2: Seminumerical algorithms. Addison-Wesley Professional (2014)
4. L"Ecuyer, P.: Random number generation. Springer (2012)
5. Zhao, Y., Gao, C., Liu, J., Dong, S.: A self-perturbed pseudo-random sequence generator based on hyperchaos. Chaos, Solitons Fractals: X **4**, 100023 (2019)
6. Wazi, M.T., Ali, D.S., Al-Saidi, N.M., Alawn, N.A.: A secure image cryptosystem via multiple chaotic maps. Discrete Math. Algorithms Appl. **14**(04), 2150141 (2022)
7. Oishi, S.i., Inoue, H.: Pseudo-random number generators and chaos. IEICE Trans. (1976-1990) **65**(9), 534–541 (1982)
8. Liu, Z., Tang, J., Yu, J.: An application of chaos: generating binary pseudo-random sequences. In: Editor (Ed.) Book An application of chaos: generating binary pseudo-random sequences (IEEE, 1988, edn.), pp. 1–3
9. Akif, Omar Z., et al.: A new pseudorandom bits generator based on a 2D-chaotic system and diffusion property. Bull. Electr. Eng. Inform. **10**(3), 1580–1588 (2021)
10. Al Maliky, S.S.B.: Multidisciplinary perspectives in cryptology and information security. IGI Global (2014)
11. Ullah, I., Azam, N.A., Hayat, U.: Efficient and secure substitution box and random number generators over Mordell elliptic curves. J. Inf. Secur. Appl. **56**, 102619 (2021)
12. Yu, F., et al.: Design and FPGA implementation of a pseudo-random number generator based on a Hopfield neural network under electromagnetic radiation. Front. Phys. **9**, 690651 (2021)
13. Al-Khedhairi, A., Elsonbaty, A., Elsadany, A.A., Hagras, E.A.: Hybrid cryptosystem based on pseudo chaos of novel fractional order map and elliptic curves. IEEE Access **8**, 57733–57748 (2020)
14. Natiq, H., Al-Saidi, N.M., Obaiys, S.J., Mahdi, M.N., Farhan, A.K.: Image encryption based on local fractional derivative complex logistic map. Symmetry **14**(9), 2022 (1874)
15. Li, S., et al.: A high throughput pseudo random number generator driven by four dimensional discrete hyper chaotic system. Electron. Lett. **59**(18), el2950 (2023)
16. Haider, T., Blanco, S.A., Hayat, U.: A novel pseudo-random number generator based on multivariable optimization for image-cryptographic applications. Expert Syst. Appl. **240**, 122446 (2024)
17. Araki, S., Wu, J.-H., Yan, J.-J.: A novel design of random number generators using chaos-based extremum coding. IEEE Access **12**, 24039–24047 (2024)
18. Al-Saidi, N.M.G., Younus, D., Natiq, H., Ariffin, M.R.K., Asbullah, M.A., Mahad, Z.: A new hyperchaotic map for a secure communication scheme with an experimental realization. Symmetry **12**(11), 2021 (1881)
19. Liu, L., Wang, J.: A cluster of 1D quadratic chaotic map and its applications in image encryption. Math. Comput. Simul. **204**, 89–114 (2023)
20. Ali, D.S., Alwan, N.A., Al-Saidi, N.M.G.: Image encryption based on highly sensitive chaotic system. In: AIP Conference Proceedings, vol. 2183. No. 1. AIP Publishing (2019)
21. Tabeling, P.: Introduction to Microfluidics Oxford University Press. In: Editor (Ed.) Book Introduction to Microfluidics Oxford University Press (Oxford, England ISBN, 2005, edn.), pp. 978–970
22. Veeman, D., et al.: A new megastable chaotic oscillator with blinking oscillation terms. Complexity **2021**, 1–12 (2021)
23. Goldstein, H., Poole, C., Safko, J.: Classical mechanics. In: Editor (Ed.) Book Classical mechanics' (American Association of Physics Teachers, 2002, edn.), pp. 782–783
24. Chazottes, J.-R., Fernandez, B., Ashwin, P.: Riddled basins and coupled dynamical systems. In: Dynamics of Coupled Map Lattices and of Related Spatially Extended Systems, pp. 181–207 (2005)

25. Whitesides, G.M.: The origins and the future of microfluidics. Nature **442**(7101), 368–373 (2006)
26. Hamza, R.: A novel pseudo random sequence generator for image-cryptographic applications. J. Inf. Secur. Appl. **35**, 119–127 (2017)
27. Chen, X., et al.: Pseudorandom number generator based on three kinds of four-wing memristive hyperchaotic system and its application in image encryption. Complexity **2020**, 1–17 (2020)
28. Shi, Y., Deng, Y.: Hybrid control of digital Baker map with application to pseudo-random number generator. Entropy **23**(5), 578 (2021)
29. Agarwal, S.: Designing a pseudo-random bit generator using generalized cascade fractal function. Chaos Theory Appl. **3**(1), 11–19 (2021)
30. Barani, M.J., Ayubi, P., Valandar, M.Y., Irani, B.Y.: A new Pseudo random number generator based on generalized Newton complex map with dynamic key. J. Inf. Secur. Appl. **53**, 102509 (2020)
31. Wang, L., Cheng, H.: Pseudo-random number generator based on logistic chaotic system. Entropy **21**(10), 960 (2019)

Designing and Implementing a 2D Integer DCT Hardware Accelerator Fully Compatible with Versatile Video Coding

Nhu-Hoang Nguyen[1,2], Tan-Phat Dang[1,2], Thanh-Dat Bui[1,2], Trong-Thuc Hoang[3], Cong-Kha Pham[3], and Huu-Thuan Huynh[1,2(✉)]

[1] University of Science, Ho Chi Minh City, Vietnam
hhthuan@hcmus.edu.vn
[2] Vietnam National University, Ho Chi Minh City, Vietnam
[3] University of Electro-Communications (UEC), Tokyo, Japan

Abstract. This paper focuses on implementing and optimizing a 2D Integer Discrete Cosine Transform (DCT) hardware accelerator to provide an efficient and flexible solution for the H.266 video compression standard. Unlike previous standards, H.266 introduces additional complexities in the 2D DCT computation, such as support for non-square blocks and high frequency removal. Our proposed design offers a versatile implementation method for the 2D Integer DCT hardware at very high speed. Our approach aims to provide a flexible and efficient solution, achieving better results than other methods. The results were tested on the Stratix 10 FPGA, utilizing 35,799 ALMs at the frequency of 353.23 MHz, and throughput reached 11,482.77 Mega pixels/s supporting video resolutions up to 16K@60fps. The data was also verified by using VTM reference software [1].

Keywords: Integer DCT · VVC · Hardware Accelerator

1 Introduction

The demand for efficient and high-quality video compression is increasing in today's digital age, especially in communication and entertainment applications. Versatile Video Coding (VVC) [2–4] was finalized in July 2020 as the latest international video encoding standard. It was developed by the Joint Video Experts Team (JVET) of the ITU-T Video Coding Experts Group (VCEG) and the ISO/IEC Moving Picture Experts Group (MPEG). VVC represents a significant advancement in this field and promises data bandwidth savings and improves image quality. To implement an effective hardware architecture for the H.266 encoder, algorithms requiring computational complexity, such as Discrete Cosine Transform (DCT) [5–7], Context-Based Adaptive Binary Arithmetic Coding (CABAC) [8–10], and so on, must be efficiently designed and optimized.

There are many researches focusing on the hardware design with efficient architectures, such as a reusable architecture for various Transform Unit (TU)

O. Gervasi et al. (Eds.): ICCSA 2024 Workshops, LNCS 14815, pp. 110–121, 2024.
https://doi.org/10.1007/978-3-031-65154-0_7

sizes [11] or integrating forward and inverse transforms [12] and so on. However, the new features of H.266, such as non-square blocks and high-frequency removal, have not been solved yet. In this context, our research aims to provide efficient and flexible hardware for the 2D DCT. This DCT hardware architecture supports all previous video compression standards, including Advanced Video Coding (AVC) and High Efficiency Video Coding (HEVC) standards. Additionally, it accommodates new features of H.266, such as square and rectangular block sizes and high-frequency removal.

This paper is structured as follows: Sect. 2 presents related work on integer DCT implemented on hardware, serving as essential references for our research. Section 3 provides fundamental knowledge about integer DCT, including key features and the method for decomposing the kernel matrix. Our proposed architecture is reviewed in Sect. 4, covering the general architecture and detailed structures of each component. Section 5 presents the synthesis results of the proposed architecture, which was verified by version 9.0 of the VVC reference software called VVC Test Model (VTM). And compares them with those of other architectures. Finally, Sect. 6 concludes the paper.

2 Related Works

In the fields of hardware implementation of Integer DCT, there have been several prior researches aimed at optimizing performance and integration into modern video compression standards. The research [13] proposed a new hardware architecture for 2D DCT computation on Xilinx Artix-7 FPGA (Zynq-7000). Their proposal utilizes accelerated integer 2-D hardware, with 34421 LUTs and 8729 flip-flops (FF). The maximum clock frequency achieved is 289 MHz, supporting the HEVC standard and capable of processing up to 30 frames for 8K resolution. In [14], the authors presented a novel architecture structure for 2D integer DCT computation. Their architecture was described in VHDL language and synthesized on the Intel FPGA device. The hardware architecture throughput reaches processing speeds of up to 52 million pixels per second at a clock frequency of 90 MHz. The intellectual property (IP) core is implemented and verified using a system-on-chip (SoC) embedded video system. In [15], the authors introduced a hardware architecture for a 2D discrete cosine transform dedicated to the HEVC standard. This architecture supports 4K@30 frames per second with hardware cost reduction ranging from 31–64%. The hardware architecture of 2D DCT with a Compression Ratio of 5:3 was proposed in [16] with the purpose reduces computational complexity and power consumption. Specifically, a compression ratio of approximately 5:3 is used to reduce area as well as power consumption. A proposed algorithm for determining the number of DCT Output Coefficients was mentioned in [17]. This study proposes an algorithm to determine the number of DCT output coefficients such that the peak signal-to-noise ratio (PSNR) decreases by less than 0.15 dB. This algorithm can process up to 4K@288fps. These researches have contributed to the efficient implementation of Integer DCT on hardware, and they are essential references for our work.

3 Basic Knowledge

To reduce discrepancies between encoding and decoding during the 2D DCT computation and simplify hardware implementation, some researchers have applied matrix multiplication and partial butterfly implementation for DCT calculation [11,18,19]. This section outlines the essential characteristics of integer DCT and the matrix decomposition approach to enhance hardware efficiency.

3.1 Key Feature of Integer DCT

The key feature of the Integer DCT is its ability to perform lossy compression of digital images or video signals while preserving crucial visual information. Unlike the traditional DCT, which operates on floating-point numbers, the Integer DCT processes integer-valued input data. This property makes it suitable for implementation on hardware platforms, where integer arithmetic operations are more efficient than floating-point operations.

The formula (1) can generalize the Integer DCT:

$$X = C_N \times x \tag{1}$$

In which X is the coefficient after the DCT transformation, C_N is the kernel matrix, and x is the input coefficient for the DCT.

Additionally, the N-point integer DCT can be computed by utilizing $N/2$ point DCT and a vector of size $N/2$ using the butterfly method proposed in [19,20], represented by the formula (2):

$$\begin{aligned} X_{Even} &= C_{N/2} \times a \\ X_{Odd} &= M_{N/2} \times b \\ a_i &= x_i + x_{N-1-i} \quad \text{Where } 0 \le i \le N/2 - 1 \\ b_i &= x_i - x_{N-1-i} \quad \text{Where } 0 \le i \le N/2 - 1 \end{aligned} \tag{2}$$

X_{Even} and X_{Odd} denote the output coefficients of even and odd rows. $C_{N/2}$ is the left half of the even row of the matrix C_N, while $M_{N/2}$ is the matrix that has unique coefficients represented in Table 1.

Table 1. The table presents the coefficients of the DCT matrix.

Type	Unique coefficient
DCT 2	64
DCT 4	83, 36
DCT 8	89, 75, 50, 18
DCT 16	90, 87, 80, 70, 57, 43, 25, 9
DCT 32	90, 88, 85, 82, 78, 73, 67, 61, 54, 46, 38, 31, 22, 13, 4
DCT 64	91, 90, 88, 87, 86, 84, 83, 81, 79, 77, 73, 71, 69, 65, 62, 59, 56, 52, 48, 44, 41, 37, 33, 28, 24, 20, 15, 11, 7, 2

3.2 Matrix Decomposition

Each TU block size in the Integer DCT transformation has a distinct kernel matrix with corresponding coefficients listed in Table 1. These matrices share a common property: even rows are symmetric about the center, while odd rows are symmetric but flipped around the center. Additionally, larger-sized matrices' even rows contain matrices of smaller sizes. Based on these characteristics, during computation, we can decompose the matrix into smaller ones to reduce complexity and reuse architecture for smaller-sized DCTs to compute larger-sized ones, thereby optimizing hardware resources.

The kernel matrices for 4, 8, 16, and 32 points integer DCTs are provided in [19]. Applying this kernel matrix to compute the 8-point DCT, we obtain Eq. (3).

$$\begin{bmatrix} X_0 \\ X_1 \\ X_2 \\ X_3 \\ X_4 \\ X_5 \\ X_6 \\ X_7 \end{bmatrix} = \begin{bmatrix} 64 & 64 & 64 & 64 & 64 & 64 & 64 & 64 \\ 89 & 75 & 50 & 18 & -18 & -50 & -75 & -89 \\ 83 & 36 & -36 & -83 & -83 & -36 & 36 & -83 \\ 75 & -18 & -89 & -50 & 50 & 89 & 18 & -75 \\ 64 & -64 & -64 & 64 & 64 & -64 & -64 & 64 \\ 50 & -89 & 18 & 75 & -75 & -18 & -89 & -50 \\ 36 & -83 & 83 & -36 & -36 & 83 & -83 & 36 \\ 18 & -50 & 75 & -89 & 89 & -75 & 50 & -18 \end{bmatrix} \times \begin{bmatrix} x_0 \\ x_1 \\ x_2 \\ x_3 \\ x_4 \\ x_5 \\ x_6 \\ x_7 \end{bmatrix} \quad (3)$$

This multiplication can be decomposed into two simpler multiplications as (4a) and (4b).

$$\begin{bmatrix} X_0 \\ X_2 \\ X_4 \\ X_6 \end{bmatrix} = \begin{bmatrix} 64 & 64 & 64 & 64 \\ 83 & 36 & -36 & -83 \\ 64 & -64 & -64 & 64 \\ 36 & -83 & 83 & -36 \end{bmatrix} \times \begin{bmatrix} x_0 + x_7 \\ x_1 + x_6 \\ x_2 + x_5 \\ x_3 + x_4 \end{bmatrix} \quad (4a)$$

$$\begin{bmatrix} X_1 \\ X_3 \\ X_5 \\ X_7 \end{bmatrix} = \begin{bmatrix} 89 & 75 & 50 & 18 \\ 75 & -18 & -89 & -50 \\ 50 & -89 & 18 & 75 \\ 18 & -50 & 75 & -89 \end{bmatrix} \times \begin{bmatrix} x_0 - x_7 \\ x_1 - x_6 \\ x_2 - x_5 \\ x_3 - x_4 \end{bmatrix} \quad (4b)$$

In which the computation of X_0, X_2, X_4, and X_6 can be further decomposed into two multiplications of smaller matrices (5a) and (5b).

$$\begin{bmatrix} X_0 \\ X_4 \end{bmatrix} = \begin{bmatrix} 64 & 64 \\ 64 & -64 \end{bmatrix} \times \begin{bmatrix} (x_0 + x_7) + (x_3 + x_4) \\ (x_1 + x_6) + (x_2 + x_5) \end{bmatrix} \quad (5a)$$

$$\begin{bmatrix} X_2 \\ X_6 \end{bmatrix} = \begin{bmatrix} 83 & 36 \\ 36 & -83 \end{bmatrix} \times \begin{bmatrix} (x_0 + x_7) - (x_3 + x_4) \\ (x_1 + x_6) - (x_2 + x_5) \end{bmatrix} \quad (5b)$$

Applying this matrix decomposition approach, we can compute a 64-point integer DCT using 32, 16, 8, 4, and 2-point integer DCTs.

4 Proposed Architecture

This section introduces the proposed architecture for computing the integer DCT. It aims to reduce the number of operations by replacing multiplications with shifts and additions. Moreover, this architecture utilizes the pipeline technique to improve processing throughput.

4.1 The General Architecture

Our general architecture is illustrated in Fig. 1, the control unit oversees the overall DCT process. Specifically, when a *start* signal is triggered, the control unit decodes the *width* and *height* of the input coefficients to generate *Idx* value for the next steps including the DCT and the Transpose Memory (TM) to operate correctly with the input matrix size. Additionally, the control unit creates *shift* signal for rounding and converting the output coefficients to a 16-bit size at the end of the 1D DCT calculation step. Furthermore, the control unit transmits logic "0" to the MUX to select the data stream into the DCT as the input coefficients. After 11 clock cycles, the control unit generates a *write* signal to store the DCT result of the first row in the TM. Since our architecture utilizes pipeline techniques, the result of one row is computed after each clock cycle. Therefore, after the subsequent N clock cycles, the 1D DCT computation is completed, and all the results are stored in the TM row by row. Next, the control unit sends logic "1" to the MUX to multiply the DCT value from the TM while simultaneously sending a *read* signal to the TM to retrieve the data and pass it to the 1D DCT. After 11 clock cycles, the *Datavalid* signal is activated to indicate the availability of output data. In the following N clock cycles, all output data will be retrieved until the *done* signal is activated.

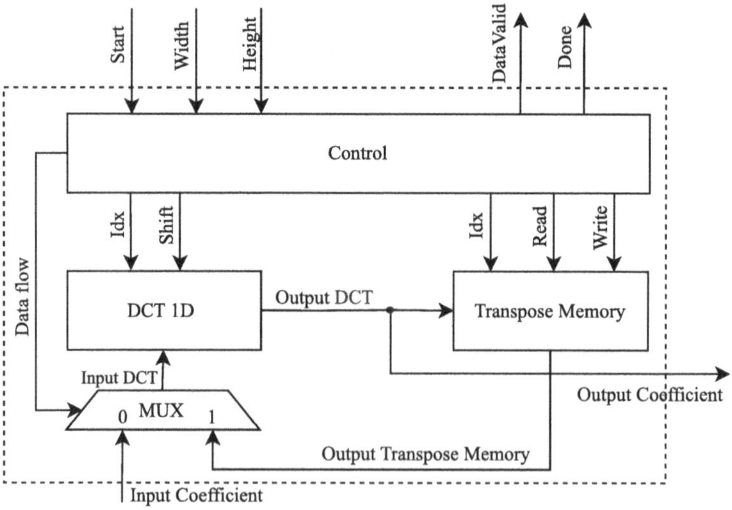

Fig. 1. The general architecture.

4.2 1D DCT Architecture

In this section, the architecture for implementing the integer DCT on hardware was introduced. This architecture consists of three main steps including Add/Sub, Odd, and Add steps, each responsible for a specific part of the computation process as shown in Fig. 2.

Add/Sub Step: This step performs addition and subtraction operations between the input coefficients following a predefined sequence [11]. As shown in Fig. 3, the resulting data from the Add/Sub step is divided into two parts: one is sent to the odd block, and the other is directed to N/2 point DCT block, which is the same 1D DCT architecture but smaller in size (N/2). For example as mentioned in Sect. 3.2, the first part is matrix b in formula 2, and this matrix is used in formula 4b. The remaining part is put into a smaller 1D DCT block to continue decomposing in the form of formulas 5a and 5b.

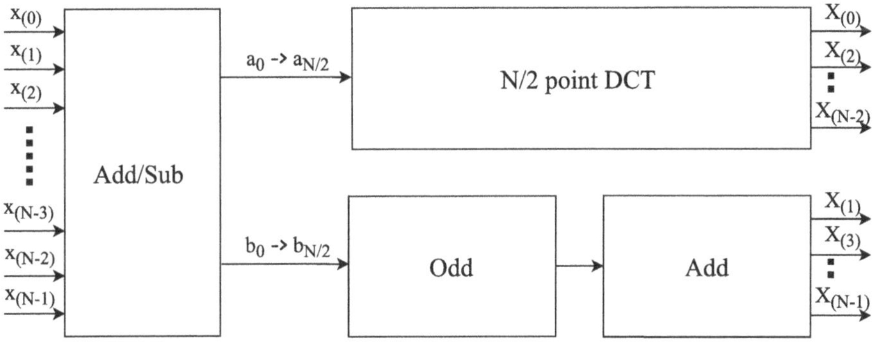

Fig. 2. 1D DCT architecture.

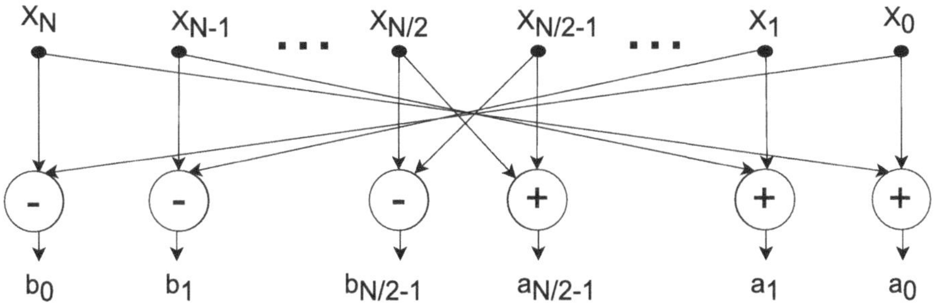

Fig. 3. Add Sub architecture.

Odd Step: This step receives the results from the Add/Sub step. Instead of performing matrix multiplication, we employ shifting and addition operations to simplify hardware complexity. Additionally, we integrate pipelining techniques during the 1D DCT calculation. To achieve this, we design an Odd architecture to ensure all outputs appear after two addition operations. Specific coefficient values in the kernel matrix are changed in sign to meet this requirement. Figure 4 illustrates our proposed architecture for the Odd block of the 16-point DCT, where 90x and 87x are replaced with −90x and −87x, respectively. This approach is also applied to all Odd blocks of varying sizes.

Add Step: The Add step conducts addition or subtraction operations between the elements of the result matrix from the Odd step in a specific sequence. Because we reversed the signs of some coefficients in the Odd step, our architecture reversed them back before performing addition along the binary tree. Additionally, we merge the subtraction operations to minimize the number of subtractions in the circuit, aiming to optimize the circuit size during synthesis. So, each output result is computed from a different Adder circuit. An example of the Add block in the 16-point DCT is depicted in Fig. 5. The result of this step is the final result of the integer DCT. By combining the Odd and Add steps, The multiplication as in formula 4b can calculated by using only shift and addition operations. Furthermore, the proposed architecture also minimizes the number of calculation cycles of this step.

Moreover, the proposed architecture includes a smaller module that performs similar computations to the overall structure but on a smaller scale. The X_{Even} in Eq. 2 was calculated by this module, and it can be decomposed into two simpler multiplications as 5a and 5b.

Pipeline Architecture: To reduce the number of clock cycles consumed during the 1D DCT calculation, the proposed architecture employs pipeline techniques. This way, our architecture can finish the 1D DCT for the first 64 points using only ten cycles (as illustrated in Fig. 6). After the subsequent 64 cycles, the entire 64×64 block is computed. In this pipeline architecture, the Add/Sub step takes one clock cycle, and the Odd step takes two clock cycles for all N-point integer DCT operations. The number of clock cycles for the Add step increases incrementally with the size of the kernel matrix. Additionally, our architecture includes an additional rounding stage to round and resize the output coefficients to 16 bits.

4.3 Transpose Memory Architecture

Our proposal utilizes N single-port RAMs arranged in an array to optimize memory access. By organizing the write addresses of the RAM, our architecture enables reading/writing 64 coefficients in a single cycle. Figure 7 illustrates an example of the TM block used for DCT 8×8, comprising eight separate single-port RAMs. During the writing process to TM, each row of the 1D DCT

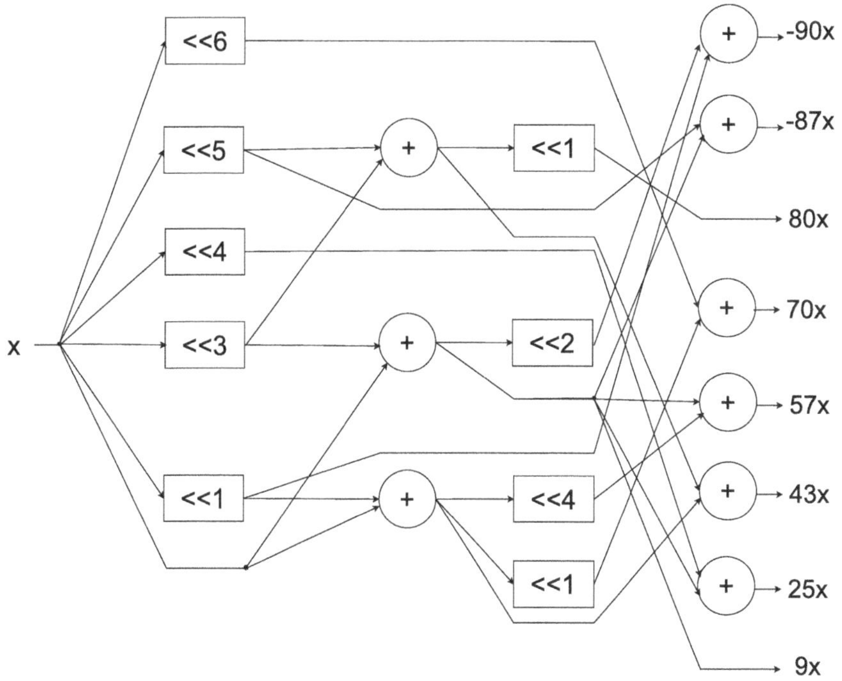

Fig. 4. The Odd architecture for the 16-point DCT.

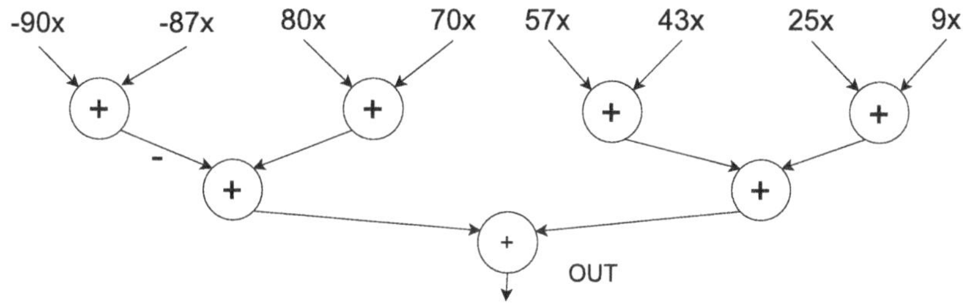

Fig. 5. An example of the Add architecture for the 16-point DCT.

result is sequentially written into TM along the forward diagonals, starting from the main diagonal. When reading from TM for the second round of 1D DCT calculation, all 8 RAMs are simultaneously read at the same address.

5 Results

In this section, our architecture was implemented and evaluated in two parts. The first part only supports a maximum size of 32×32 for easier comparison with previous studies, as those studies were applied only to the H.265 compression standard, where the DCT is applied up to a maximum block size of 32.

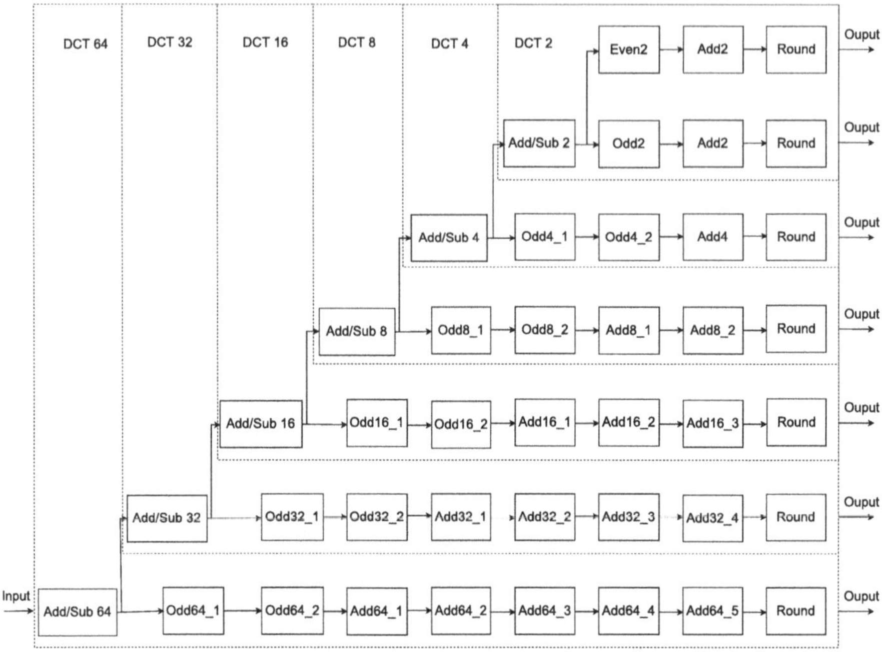

Fig. 6. Pipeline architecture.

MEM 0	Y00	Y71	Y62	Y53	Y44	Y35	Y26	Y17
MEM 1	Y10	Y01	Y72	Y63	Y54	Y45	Y36	Y27
MEM 2	Y20	Y11	Y02	Y73	Y64	Y55	Y46	Y37
MEM 3	Y30	Y21	Y12	Y03	Y74	Y65	Y56	Y47
MEM 4	Y40	Y31	Y22	Y13	Y04	Y75	Y66	Y57
MEM 5	Y50	Y41	Y32	Y23	Y14	Y05	Y76	Y67
MEM 6	Y60	Y51	Y42	Y33	Y24	Y15	Y06	Y77
MEM 7	Y70	Y61	Y52	Y43	Y34	Y25	Y16	Y07

Fig. 7. Transpose Memory Architecture for DCT 8×8.

Second one supports a size of 64×64 to accommodate all new video compression standards. All results were verified by compare with output of VTM.

5.1 The Comparison with the Same DCT Size

In this comparison, our proposed architecture only supports sizes ranging from 2 to 32 for comparison with other architectures. The Odd and Add steps are designed to minimize the number of clock cycles. This architecture also uses the pipeline technique to speed up the 1D DCT step, and the control unit

Table 2. The synthesis results on Xilinx's boards utilizing identical TU size.

	FPGA	Resources				F (Mhz)	Throughput (Mega pixels/s)
		R	LUT	Slice	DSP		
Our work	Virtex 7	27147	27723	8341	0	172	1918
[13]	Artix-7	8729	34421	N/A	N/A	289	1541
[15]	Virtex 7	N/A	5 600	N/A	128	177	361

Table 3. The synthesis results on Intel's boards utilizing identical TU size.

	FPGA	Resources (ALUT)	F (Mhz)	Throughput (Mega pixels/s)
Our work	Stratix III	25 692	316	3520
[15]	Stratix III	52 000	206	421

is used to handle non-square blocks. We conducted comparisons across Xilinx and Intel platforms, and the results show that our architecture consumes more resources but achieves higher throughput, as shown in Table 2 and Table 3. In the design [13], they achieve a higher frequency but with lower throughput because they propose utilizing a processing element (PE) architecture for computing the Odd block, where each PE block requires six clocks to produce a result. Our Odd architecture only takes two clocks to return a result. Consequently, this research has lower throughput compared to our architecture. In the design [15], they consume many clocks for computing the 1D integer DCT, specifically 256 clocks for the 32×32 block. In contrast, our design employs pipeline techniques, requiring only 42 clocks to complete the 1D integer DCT computation for the 32×32 block. Thus, it achieves relatively limited throughput compared to our design.

5.2 The 64×64 Block Results

Our proposed architecture applies pipelining techniques, so it has a larger hardware resource when implemented. Furthermore, our design utilizes fewer clock cycles to compute the 2D DCT, requiring only 126 clock cycles for a 64×64 block. The implementation results on various chips are demonstrated in Table 4.

Table 4. The experimentation results of our proposed architecture at size 64×64.

FPGA	Resources	F (Mhz)	Throughput (Mega pixels/s)
Stratix III	55 061 ALUT	260	8450
Cyclone IV	64 828 LE	117	3815
Stratix 10	35 799 ALM	352	11482
Artix-7	47472 R, 59573 LUT, 17102 Slice	107	3505

When implemented on an Intel Stratix 10 chip, the maximum frequency achieved is 352 MHz, with a throughput of 11482 Mega pixels/s, supporting video resolutions up to 16k@60fps.

6 Conclusion

In conclusion, the 2D integer DCT Hardware Accelerator was implemented and optimized on an FPGA, focusing on supporting the H.266 video compression standard. Our proposed design has demonstrated efficiency and flexibility in handling the complexities introduced by H.266, such as non-square blocks and high-frequency removal. The design was tested on Stratix 10 FPGA at a throughput of 11,482.77 Mega pixels/s and ready for 16K@60fps. Our design also supports previous video compression standards and accommodates the advanced features of H.266, making it a versatile solution for various video compression applications.

Acknowledgments. This research is funded by University of Science, VNU-HCM under grant number ĐT-VT 2023-06.

References

1. The VTM reference software. https://vcgit.hhi.fraunhofer.de/jvet/VVCSoftware_VTM. Accessed 25 Mar 2024
2. Bross, B., et al.: Overview of the versatile video coding (VVC) standard and its applications. IEEE Trans. Circuits Syst. Video Technol. **31**(10), 3736–3764 (2021). https://doi.org/10.1109/TCSVT.2021.3101953
3. Wieckowski, A., Brandenburg, J., Bross, B., Marpe, D.: VVC search space analysis including an open, optimized implementation. IEEE Trans. Consum. Electron. **68**(2), 127–138 (2022). https://doi.org/10.1109/TCE.2022.3148813
4. Bossen, F., Sühring, K., Wieckowski, A., Liu, S.: VVC complexity and software implementation analysis. IEEE Trans. Circuits Syst. Video Technol. **31**(10), 3765–3778 (2021). https://doi.org/10.1109/TCSVT.2021.3072204
5. Zhao, X., et al.: Transform coding in the VVC standard. IEEE Trans. Circuits Syst. Video Technol. **31**(10), 3878–3890 (2021). https://doi.org/10.1109/TCSVT.2021.3087706
6. Mukherjee, D., Mukhopadhyay, S.: hardware efficient architecture for 2D DCT and IDCT using taylor-series expansion of trigonometric functions. IEEE Trans. Circuits Syst. Video Technol. **30**(8), 2723–2735 (2020). https://doi.org/10.1109/TCSVT.2019.2928045
7. Masera, M., Masera, G., Martina, M.: An area-efficient variable-size fixed-point DCT architecture for HEVC encoding. IEEE Trans. Circuits Syst. Video Technol. **30**(1), 232–242 (2020). https://doi.org/10.1109/TCSVT.2018.2886736
8. Ramos, F.L.L., Saggiorato, A.V.P., Zatt, B., Porto, M., Bampi, S.: Residual syntax elements analysis and design targeting high-throughput HEVC CABAC. IEEE Trans. Circuits Syst. I Regul. Pap. **67**(2), 475–488 (2020). https://doi.org/10.1109/TCSI.2019.2932891

9. Zhang, Y., Lu, C.: A highly parallel hardware architecture of table-based CABAC bit rate estimator in an HEVC intra encoder. IEEE Trans. Circuits Syst. Video Technol. **29**(5), 1544–1558 (2019). https://doi.org/10.1109/TCSVT.2018.2830126
10. Karwowski, D.: Precise estimation of probabilities in CABAC using the cauchy optimization method. IEEE Access **8**, 32088–32099 (2020). https://doi.org/10.1109/ACCESS.2020.2973549
11. Meher, P.K., Park, S.Y., Mohanty, B.K., Lim, K.S., Yeo, C.: Efficient integer DCT architectures for hevc. IEEE Trans. Circuits Syst. Video Technol. **24**(1), 168–178 (2014). https://doi.org/10.1109/TCSVT.2013.2276862
12. Budagavi, M., Sze, V.: Unified forward+inverse transform architecture for hevc. In: 2012 19th IEEE International Conference on Image Processing, pp. 209–212 (2012). https://doi.org/10.1109/ICIP.2012.6466832
13. Ansari, A.E., Mansouri, A., Ahaitouf, A.: An efficient VLSI architecture design for integer DCT in hevc standard. In: 2016 IEEE/ACS 13th International Conference of Computer Systems and Applications (AICCSA), pp. 1-5 (2016). https://doi.org/10.1109/AICCSA.2016.7945747
14. Loukil, H., Masmoudi, N.: A novel architecture design for VLSI implementation of integer DCT in HEVC standard. Multimed. Tools Appl. **79**, 23977–23993 (2020). https://doi.org/api.semanticscholar.org/CorpusID:219710153
15. Chen, M., Zhang, Y., Lu, C.: Efficient architecture of variable size hevc 2d- dct for fpga platforms. AEU - Int. J. Electron. Commun. **73**, 1–8 (2017). https://doi.org/10.1016/j.aeue.2016.12.024
16. Akman, A., Cekli, S.: Efficient 2d DCT architecture based on approximate compressors for image compression with HEVC intra-prediction. J. Real-Time Image Proc. **20**(2), 22 (2023)
17. Singhadia, A., Mamillapalli, M., Chakrabarti, I.: Hardware-efficient 2D-DCT/IDCT architecture for portable HEVC-compliant devices. IEEE Trans. Consum. Electron. **66**(3), 203–212 (2020)
18. Abdelrasoul, M., Sayed, M.S., Goulart, V.: Scalable integer DCT architecture for HEVC encoder. In: 2016 IEEE Computer Society Annual Symposium on VLSI (ISVLSI), pp. 314–318 (2016). https://doi.org/10.1109/ISVLSI.2016.98
19. Budagavi, M., Fuldseth, A., Bjøntegaard, G., Sze, V., Sadafale, M.: Core transform design in the high efficiency video coding (HEVC) standard. IEEE J. Sel. Top. Signal Process. **7**(6), 1029–1041 (2013). https://doi.org/10.1109/JSTSP.2013.2270429
20. Chen, W.-H., Smith, C., Fralick, S.: A fast computational algorithm for the discrete cosine transform. IEEE Trans. Commun. **25**(9), 1004–1009 (1977). https://doi.org/10.1109/TCOM.1977.1093941

Blockchain and Distributed Ledgers: Technologies and Applications (BDLTA 2024)

Revolutionizing Payment Systems: Integrating RSA-Encrypted NFTs in Blockchain for Cash-on-Delivery Transactions

L. K. Bang[1], P. H. T. Trung[1(✉)], T. P. Nghiem[1], D. P. N. Trong[1], N. T. K. Ngan[2], L. T. Nhi[1], N. H. Kha[1], and T. N. Anh[1]

[1] FPT University, Can Tho City, Vietnam
banglkce160155@fpt.edu.vn, trungpht@fe.edu.vn
[2] FPT Polytecnic, Can Tho City, Vietnam

Abstract. In the e-commerce fields, our approaches consider to address the enhance security, trust, and transparency issues in cash-on-delivery (COD) systems. Handling the traditional risks and inefficiencies of current COD processes (e.g., cross-border transactions between the shipper and buyer/purchaser), this paper present an encryption-powered (i.e., RSA encryption) with Non-Fungible Tokens (NFTs) within a blockchain platform. This approach not only benefits the decentralized, immutable, and transparent as a nature of blockchain-supported technology but also protects the sensitive info with the added security layer of RSA encryption. The NFTs usages ensure the uniqueness and irreplaceability of each transaction, thereby offering a system that is secure, private, and efficient compared to the central-based storage in the current system. This paper represents a our effort in digital payment systems, providing a comprehensive solution that responds to the evolving challenges in e-commerce and sets new benchmarks for digital transaction security, privacy, and efficiency.

Keywords: RSA-Encrypted · Blockchain · cash-on-delivery (COD) · NFT · Smart contract

1 Introduction

In the upgrading of the e-commerce approach to address the traditional limitation, the blockchain-exploited technology has become an important factor, addressing the steps in which transactions are processed [14]. In particular, smart contracts usage as well as decentralized-based consideration are considered to handle some challenges and problems regarding payment processes, for example, trust, transparency, and security [13]. In the same benefit, our proposed model refines payment systems via blockchain-baed techniques, moreover to protect the personal information in the transaction the RSA-powered on Non-Fungible

O. Gervasi et al. (Eds.): ICCSA 2024 Workshops, LNCS 14815, pp. 125–141, 2024.
https://doi.org/10.1007/978-3-031-65154-0_8

Tokens (NFTs) release layer to enhance both the security and efficiency of Cash on Delivery (COD) transactions is the necessary consideration. This means that our paper is an effort for the preparation step in addressing both privacy concerns and operational challenges in e-commerce platforms before considering the blockchain-deployed system in the real environment.

The basis of our research is built on the effort presented in prior work. In practice, Son et al. [15] and Le et al. [9] have deployed a framework for secure transactional ecosystems using blockchain technology in the initial steps. These systems protect the interests of sellers in COD transactions by proposing several roles of the stakeholder via the definition of rules and responsibilities through smart contracts. Although these studies have improved transactional transparency and privacy (i.e., based on the role/permission definition) some personal information is still released to the unexpected stakeholders. To this end, our approach changes the focus from not only the transparency of the transaction among the users (e.g., shipper vs buyers/purchasers) to the privacy of sensitive user data through RSA encryption, addressing a key shortfall in previous frameworks which often place the security of transactional details above the protection of personal information.

Furthermore, our research expands upon the ideas presented by Ha et al. [5] and Quoc et al. [12], who have explored decentralized marketplace mechanisms and the challenges in cross-border e-commerce exchanges. Additionally, the other approaches build on ideas from several aspects (e.g., Ha et al. [5]; Quoc et al. [12]) that have examined decentralized marketplace mechanisms as well as the challenges of cross-border e-commerce exchanges. While these studies provide robust solutions for maintaining integrity and fostering trust in transactions, our work goes a step further. We implement a multi-platform blockchain deployment strategy, assessing and comparing the suitability of various EVM-supported blockchain environments for our e-commerce solution. This methodology provides a comprehensive analysis of each platform's strengths and limitations, allowing for a more informed choice of blockchain technology tailored to specific e-commerce requirements. We apply not only a multi-platform blockchain deployment strategy to evaluate and compare different EVM-supported blockchain environments for our e-commerce solution but also analysis of each platform's strengths and weaknesses as the original approach of [3].

For the encryption-based approaches on the blockchain platform, sensitive info sharing is not a strong point consideration in traditional e-commerce systems. In fact, the background section, in this paper, summarized the traditional considerations that focus on transparency, decentralization, and immutable improvement by applying the blockchain characteristic technique. By ensuring that personal and sensitive information is encrypted and secure via RSA strategy, we address an important issue that has previously been somewhat neglected in blockchain-based e-commerce solutions [13]. The use of RSA-encrypted NFTs stored on IPFS networks ensures that transaction details remain transparent and immutable, while personal and sensitive data are kept confidential and secure.

The rest of our paper is structured as follows: the first two sections provide background on traditional approaches and review existing literature on blockchain applications in e-commerce. The sections on system architecture and implementation, detailed in Sect. 4 and Sect. 5, outline our methodology and the implementation points for our proposed model. The evaluation of our system, including performance, cost, and efficiency, is discussed in Sect. 6. The discussion section explores the implications of our findings and potential directions for future research. Finally, the conclusion highlights our key contributions and the potential impact of our work in this paper.

2 Background

2.1 The Traditional Approach - Post-office Transportation

The traditional model for COD transactions is a sequential, five-step process encompassing activities from the seller's preparation of the package to the final delivery and payment collection by the buyer. This model serves as the foundation for understanding the subsequent integration of RSA-Encrypted NFTs in blockchain technology (Fig. 1).

Fig. 1. The post-office case for transporting goods

Step 1 - Seller Preparation: The COD process commences with the seller preparing the item for dispatch. This initial step involves meticulous packaging and the completion of all necessary documentation to ensure the item's security and provide clear delivery instructions. This meticulous preparation is essential to mitigate potential delays or complications in the later stages of the delivery process.

Step 2 - District Post Office Handling: Following the seller's preparation, the package is transferred to the district-level post office. Here, postal workers assume responsibility for the package, processing it in accordance with postal regulations. Activities in this stage include sorting based on destination, address verification, and logging the package into the postal tracking system. The district post office acts as an intermediary, preparing the package for its onward journey to a city or provincial-level facility.

Step 3 - City/Provincial Post Office Processing: The package, upon reaching the city or provincial post office, undergoes additional sorting. These larger facilities are equipped to handle greater volumes, enabling efficient sorting based on the final delivery areas. At this juncture, packages are grouped according to their destinations, and logistics for the last part of the delivery are organized to guarantee timely and efficient delivery.

Step 4 - Delivery by Postal Staff: In the fourth stage, the postal delivery staff, often referred to as shippers, are tasked with the final delivery. They ensure the package is loaded onto the delivery vehicle and transported to the recipient's address. This phase is critical, as it tests the postal service's reliability and timeliness, with shippers navigating various routes to deliver the package safely.

Step 5 - Buyer Receives Package: The delivery process culminates with the buyer receiving the package. In COD transactions, the buyer pays the postal delivery staff the owed amount upon delivery. This exchange marks the completion of the transaction, with the buyer confirming receipt in satisfactory condition, and the seller's obligation considered fulfilled following successful delivery and payment.

The traditional model for cash-on-delivery transactions, when viewed through the lens of a shipping company's involvement, presents a comprehensive and multi-faceted process. This integrated approach marries the detailed steps of seller preparation, postal handling, and delivery with the logistical prowess of a transportation company.

2.2 The Traditional Approach - Transportation Company Case

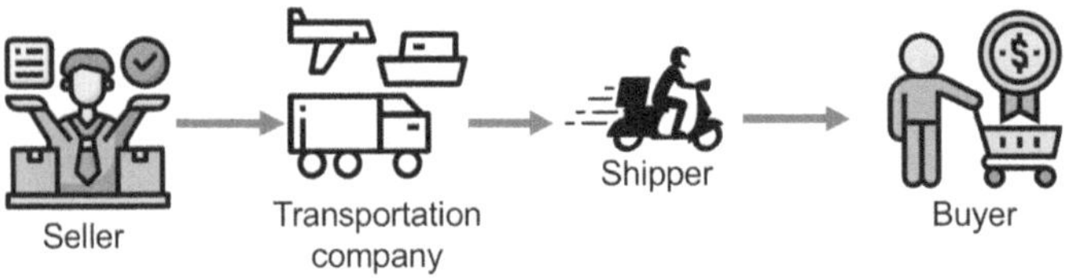

Fig. 2. The transportation company case for transporting goods

Step 1 - Seller's Preparation: The process begins with the seller preparing to package the product and prepare it for shipping through the shipping service. This preparation is based on the product packaging steps, depending on the size and material the seller will package them differently. For example, the steps involved include selecting appropriate packaging materials to protect the item during shipping and preparing the necessary documents to provide to the partner, such as shipping labels, pricing, etc. name, destination and delivery address or customs form for long-distance orders (e.g. international orders). After the sealing and labeling stage, the package is ready for pickup, and the seller selects the shipping company to deliver the goods to the buyer. Depending on the needs as well as the price, the companies are chosen (Fig. 2).

Step 2 - Transportation Company's Involvement: Once the shipping company takes care of the package, they will begin a journey that may include multiple forms of transportation by different means, e.g., motorbike, truck, plane, or ship. Depending on the distance, the shipper's vehicle will change accordingly. The key requirement at this stage is to use a tracking system (e.g. GPS) to provide updates and assurance to both sellers and buyers, thereby instilling customer confidence. This advanced tracking feature builds on traditional postal services, providing delivery reliability and consistency. Taking advantage of transportation through traditional postal systems also contributes to the benefits of this approach. Specifically, as the package moves through different stages, especially when it is close to the recipient's location, messages will be sent including the time and location of delivery.

Step 3 - Shipper's Role: The final delivery phase is managed by a shipper, a dedicated individual responsible for the last segment of the package's journey. Their role, navigating through local terrains, is a testament to the adaptability and customer-centric focus of the delivery process. Here, the traditional postal approach and modern shipping methodologies converge, ensuring the package reaches its intended recipient efficiently and securely.

Step 4 - Buyer's Receipt: The culmination of this integrated process is marked by the buyer receiving the package. This final interaction, whether it includes a cash-on-delivery transaction or simply a confirmation of receipt, is a critical touchpoint in the logistics chain. It signifies the successful collaboration between traditional postal services and modern transportation logistics, wrapping up the delivery process with customer satisfaction as the ultimate goal.

3 Related Work

3.1 Smart Contract-Based Solutions for Cash on Delivery (COD) and E-Commerce

In the realm of Cash-on-Delivery (COD) transactions, blockchain technology and smart contracts are paving the way for secure and efficient processes. Son et al. (2019) developed a blockchain-based payment system that safeguards sellers by enforcing a predefined set of transaction rules through smart contracts [15]. This system ensures transparency and minimizes risk by requiring adherence to agreed delivery times, places, and costs. Similarly, Le et al. (2019) propose a multi-shipper mechanism using blockchain and smart contracts to instill trust and prevent fraud in decentralized markets, demonstrating the practicality of their approach with case studies and open-source code for community enhancement [9].

Further advancing COD security, Le et al. (2019) introduce a framework involving double smart contracts to mitigate fraudulent transactions. This innovative approach, leveraging Ethereum blockchain, requires both buyers and shippers to place a mortgage, ensuring reliability and imposing penalties for any breaches of contract [10]. Ha et al. (2020) contribute to the field with DEM-COD, a decentralized marketplace mechanism designed to promote integrity and robustness in COD transactions through smart contracts, enhancing participant trust and privacy while offering a comprehensive code solution for adoption and improvement [5]. These studies collectively highlight the transformative impact of blockchain and smart contracts in enhancing the security and efficiency of COD transactions.

3.2 Security, Trust, and Transparency in E-Commerce and Delivery Systems

Ha et al. [6] scrutinize the existing decentralized blockchain approaches, identifying key areas needing improvement for efficiency and completion in COD systems. The paper highlights the lack of motivation for honest participation among sellers, buyers, and shippers, and the over-reliance on a trusted third party or arbitrator. To address these issues, they propose a novel solution using Hyperledger Composer to protect merchant rights and smart contracts to eliminate the need for any third party or arbitrator. This approach aims to enhance trust and transparency in the transaction process, mitigating the risks associated with dishonesty and disputes.

Duong et al. [3], on the other hand, tackle the operational inefficiencies in COD systems, particularly in handling multiple delivery sessions. They observe that existing models support only a single delivery session at a time, leading to inefficiencies when buyers are unavailable to receive goods. To overcome this challenge, they propose a multi-session mechanism that leverages blockchain technology, smart contracts, and the hyperledger fabric platform. This mechanism ensures distributed and transparent operations across multiple delivery sessions in decentralized markets, significantly improving the efficiency of the delivery process. The authors also release their source codes to encourage further development and reproducibility in this field.

3.3 Decentralized Marketplaces and Peer-to-Peer E-Commerce

Quoc et al. [12] introduce the Safe Seller Safe Buyer (SSSB) system, an innovative approach utilizing blockchain technology and smart contracts to insure cross-border exchanges. They identify key challenges in traditional commercial systems, such as transportation issues, information latency, and reliability, which affect the overall trading process. The SSSB system addresses these issues by storing all relevant information about packages and orders in a distributed ledger, allowing both sellers and buyers to access necessary data about their transactions. This system significantly differs from traditional international trading systems by reducing the need for a middleman or arbitrator in conflict resolution.

The authors also implement the SSSB system on various platforms supporting Ethereum's ERC20, like Ethereum, BNB Smart Chain, and Fantom, and provide an analysis of the implementation costs on these platforms, encouraging further research in this area.

Dragomir et al. [2] focus on the logistics aspect of online second-hand marketplaces, particularly the pickup and delivery problem (PDP) with alternative locations and overlapping time windows. They aim to facilitate transportation providers in expanding their services by addressing the complexities of serving a fleet of vehicles to multiple roaming pickup and delivery locations. The proposed solution approach is based on a multi-start, adaptive, large neighborhood search with specific operators tailored to solve the PDP with alternative locations. By examining different scenarios based on real data from an Austrian logistics provider, Dragomir et al. demonstrate that increased flexibility and convenience for customers can lead to significant cost savings for carriers, up to 30% in some cases.

3.4 Revolutionizing Cash-on-Delivery Systems: The Transformative Role of Blockchain and Smart Contracts

The integration of blockchain technology and smart contracts into various sectors is revolutionizing traditional processes, enhancing security, efficiency, and trust. Son et al. (2019) proposed a novel payment system based on smart contracts implemented on blockchain technology to protect sellers' interests in cash-on-delivery transactions, showcasing the use of Hyperledger to minimize risks for parties involved [15]. Similarly, Le et al. (2019) introduced double smart contracts to assure non-fraudulent transactions in cash-on-delivery systems, presenting a framework that prevents fraud by shippers and buyers [10]. Hasan and Salah (2018) proposed a decentralized solution for the proof of delivery of digital assets using blockchain and smart contracts, leveraging Ethereum to provide immutable, tamper-proof logs, and accountability [7]. To address security concerns, Mohammed et al. (2023) developed a secure smart contract based on blockchain to prevent the non-repudiation phenomenon, focusing on enhancing transaction security [11]. Ahmadieh and El Madhoun (2023) explored the potential of NFTs in online trading and transaction cancellation, demonstrating how smart contracts can facilitate the creation, trading, and ownership transfer of digital artworks [1]. Jha et al. (2023) proposed a blockchain-based transaction system using smart contracts to eliminate the need for bank and third-party verification in transactions, thereby improving the speed and security of payments [8]. Lastly, Elghaish et al. (2020) integrated project delivery with blockchain in the construction industry, developing an automated financial system that leverages smart contracts for financial transactions, which could significantly improve project delivery outcomes [4]. These studies collectively highlight the transformative potential of blockchain and smart contracts across various domains, from ensuring secure and efficient transactions to revolutionizing digital marketplaces and project delivery systems.

4 Approach

We present the traditional model as well as the analysis in appendix A. In the ever-evolving landscape of digital transactions, the need for more secure, transparent, and efficient systems is paramount, especially in the context of cash-on-delivery (COD) operations. This proposed architecture aims to revolutionize COD transactions by enhancing security, ensuring authenticity, and fostering trust among all stakeholders. In the realm of modern logistics and supply chain management, the integration of RSA-Encrypted Non-Fungible Tokens (NFTs) into blockchain technology represents a revolutionary stride, especially in the context of cash-on-delivery transactions. This approach involves a multi-step process that seamlessly combines traditional logistics with cutting-edge blockchain technology, offering unprecedented levels of transparency, security, and efficiency. It is shown in Fig. 3.

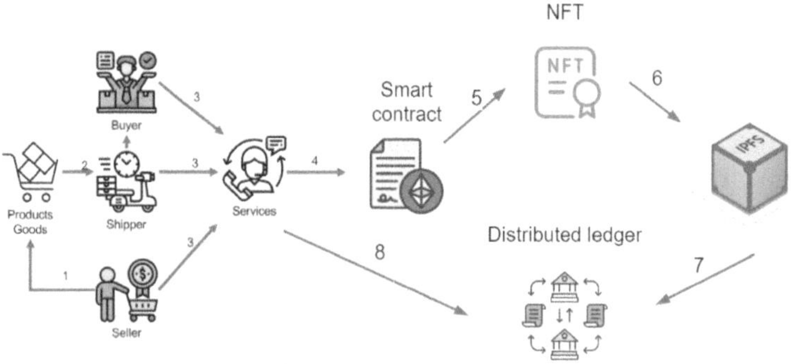

Fig. 3. The process of transporting goods based on blockchain technology, smart contract, NFT and IPFS

The Seller's Pivotal Role: The journey of a product in this innovative system commences with the seller. Beyond merely selling the product, the seller interacts with a sophisticated service system, marking the transaction's completion. This interaction is crucial, as it involves the seller using the system interface to register the product information, subsequently transforming it into an NFT. This step is not just a digital representation of the product but a significant leap in ensuring its uniqueness, security, and traceability. The initiation of a smart contract on the blockchain at this point is pivotal, setting in motion the delivery chain that is both transparent and immutable.

The Journey of Products/Goods: Once the transaction is completed and the product information is securely embedded in the blockchain, the physical goods embark on their journey. This transition from a digital entry to physical logistics is where the model integrates traditional shipping methods. The product, now linked to its digital counterpart, is handed over to shipping personnel, maintaining a tangible connection between the physical item and its digital representation.

The Interplay of Shipper and Buyer: The shipper plays a crucial role in this ecosystem. Upon receiving the product from the seller, the shipper updates the order status through the same system interface, ensuring every step of the delivery process is transparently recorded on the blockchain. This transparency extends to the buyer, who actively participates by tracking the progress of the order through the system interface. The culmination of this process is marked by the buyer confirming the receipt of the goods. In scenarios involving cash-on-delivery, this step is also recorded and confirmed through the interface, adding an extra layer of security and trust to the transaction.

The Central Role of Smart Contracts and NFTs: The smart contract, embedded within the blockchain, is the backbone of this model. It automates the transaction terms and executes only when predefined conditions, such as the buyer's confirmation of receipt, are met. The representation of each product or good as an NFT is a game-changer. It ensures the product's uniqueness and irreplaceability, further solidifying the process's security and authenticity. This digital representation also plays a vital role in verifying ownership, a crucial aspect in cash-on-delivery transactions.

The Distributed Ledger: A Record of Transparency: Every interaction, from the issuance of the NFT to updates made by the seller, shipper, or buyer, is meticulously recorded on a distributed ledger. This ledger forms an immutable and fully transparent record of the entire product delivery process. The immutability of this ledger means that once a transaction is recorded, it cannot be altered, providing a trustworthy and transparent account of the entire process.

The Service Interface: The Unifying Element: At the heart of this model lies the service component, represented by the system interface. This interface is integral to the service and supply chain management system, offering tools for tracking, confirming, and managing order information. It is through this interface that all stakeholders - the seller, the buyer, and the shipper - interact. From updating the order status to confirming the delivery, every interaction is facilitated through this interface, ensuring a seamless and integrated experience for all parties involved.

The second phase of our proposed approach introduces a sophisticated (Fig. 4, secure transaction process within the blockchain environment, leveraging the power of RSA encryption and Non-Fungible Tokens (NFTs). This phase is centered around ensuring the security and integrity of the transaction between the seller and buyer, facilitated through a smart contract.

The process begins with the seller, who is integral to initializing the transaction. The seller possesses a unique identifier in the form of a public key, hereafter

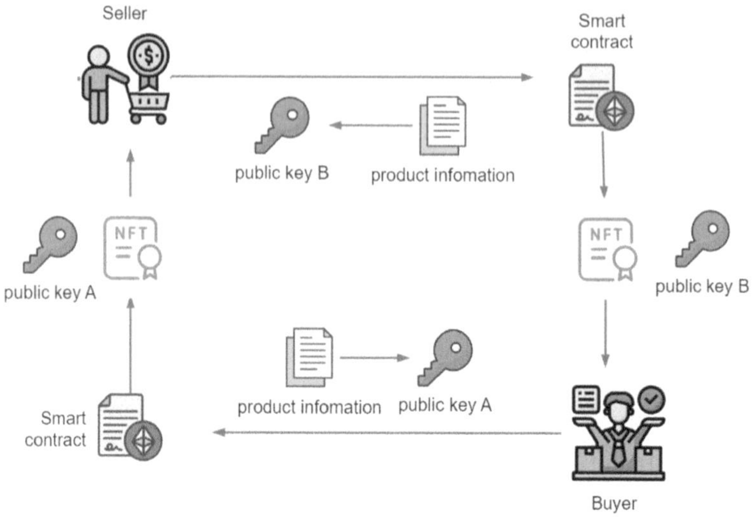

Fig. 4. RSA Encryption Model for Secure NFT Transactions

referred to as public key A. When the seller decides to create an NFT that represents a product, the product's information, including details like description, price, and ownership data, is first encrypted using public key A. In step 2, the smart contract in our architecture plays a pivotal role in facilitating the transaction. Upon receiving the encrypted product information from the seller, the smart contract securely stores this data. It is designed to interact with potential buyers who express interest in purchasing the product. When a buyer steps into the transaction process, they engage with the smart contract using their distinct public key, referred to as public key B. This interaction is a key element of our architecture, as it enables a secure and direct communication channel between the buyer and the smart contract.

After that, the encrypted product information is transferred to them via this smart contract. This transfer ensures that the integrity and confidentiality of the product information are maintained, as only the holder of the private key corresponding to the public key used for encryption (in this case, the buyer) can decrypt and access this information. Finally, the buyer's role in this phase is not just limited to expressing interest in the product but also extends to the decryption and verification of the product information. Using their public key B, the buyer receives the encrypted product information from the smart contract.

5 Implementation

This section presents the implementation process of our proposed model which exploits the RSA-encrypted for the NFTs (called the proof-of-delivery) as well as stores in the IPFS. The next four steps will detail our implementation in the proof-of-concept.

Figure 5 illustrates the benchmarking of NFT-related operations in a testing environment (step 1). It specifically highlights the time efficiency of two critical operations: minting the NFT, which is completed in 2151 ms, and decrypting the NFT's URI, which takes 3329 milliseconds. The tests are conducted to assess the performance and reliability of the NFT creation and retrieval process, which is fundamental to ensuring a seamless COD system. The sub-7-s total time for completing all tests indicates a swift execution conducive to real-world applications where transaction speed is essential.

In second step, Fig. 6 delves into the technical implementation of the minting function. The code snippet shows a JavaScript function utilizing asynchronous execution to handle the NFT creation process. The data structure includes various fields such as product information, price, weight, and transaction details. This structured data is essential for creating a comprehensive and descriptive NFT. Moreover, the metadata options specify the file name "COD_RSA.json", suggesting the NFT's metadata will be in a format compatible with the RSA encryption scheme, further underpinning the security aspect of the NFT.

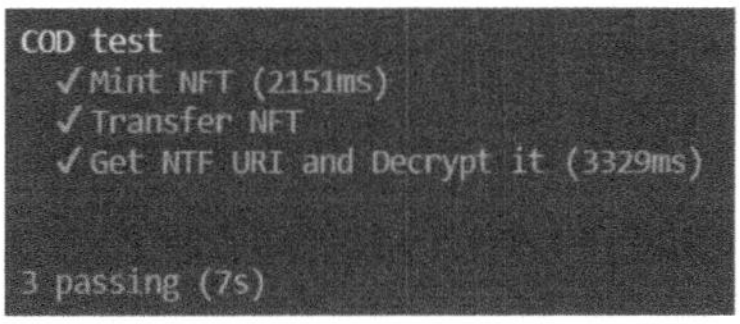

Fig. 5. NFT Minting and Decryption Test Benchmarks

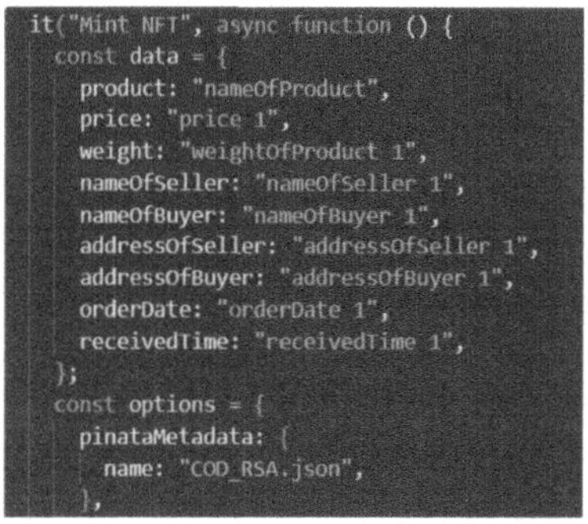

Fig. 6. Minting NFT Function Implementation

Figure 7, we see the Pinata cloud interface, which is used for hosting the NFT data (step 3). The file "COD_RSA.json" appears to have been successfully uploaded to the IPFS through Pinata, as indicated by its presence in the files list. The use of Pinata suggests an intention to leverage decentralized storage solutions for maintaining the NFT metadata, which not only provides redundancy and persistence but also aligns with the decentralized nature of blockchain technology.

Finally, Fig. 7 showcases the actual encrypted data as it is stored on the IPFS, retrieved via a specific IPFS gateway. The data is displayed as an encrypted string, representing the secure storage of the NFT's content. This level of encryption is critical to protect sensitive transaction data from unauthorized access, and it requires the corresponding private key for decryption, ensuring that only authorized participants can access the transaction's details (Fig. 8).

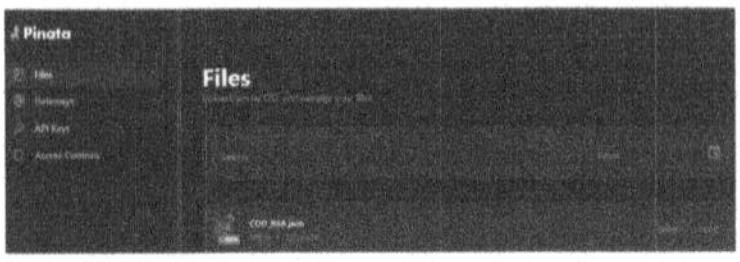

Fig. 7. Pinata Cloud Storage Interface

Fig. 8. Encrypted NFT Data Retrieval from IPFS

The detailed analysis of the performance and the secure handling of data through encryption and storage reveals a system designed with security and efficiency at its core. The time taken for minting and decrypting NFTs demonstrates the feasibility of integrating such a system into real-world COD transactions, where the balance between security measures and performance is critical. The implementation of RSA encryption within this context not only safeguards against potential data breaches but also ensures the privacy and integrity of the transactions, thus addressing two of the most significant concerns in e-commerce today. This intricate process, from minting to encryption and secure storage, forms a comprehensive solution poised to enhance the COD payment landscape significantly.

6 Evaluation

6.1 Performance Evaluation of RSA-Encrypted NFT Framework

The evaluation of our work involved a thorough analysis of the performance of RSA encryption and decryption in two distinct scenarios: encryption of a 120 KB image and encryption of the text presented in Fig. 6 The experiments were structured into three stages: Generating the RSA key, Encrypting, and Decrypting. The outcomes are elucidated in a structured format below.

For the image encryption scenario, the process times across ten trials showed notable consistency and variation in performance. The average time taken for generating the RSA key was approximately 2,461 ms, highlighting a relatively high computational demand in the key generation phase. This duration is crucial as it underpins the security of the RSA algorithm, with longer key generation times often correlating with increased security strength. The encryption times averaged around 1,156 ms, indicating a faster process compared to key generation. This quicker encryption process is beneficial in real-world applications where rapid response times are desired. Decrypting the image, however, took an average of 3,442 ms, the longest duration among the three stages. This longer decryption time is attributed to the computational complexity involved in the RSA decryption process, underscoring the trade-off between security and computational efficiency (Table 1).

Table 1. Time Analysis for RSA Processes in Image Data Encryption and Decryption Scenario

RSA with image(ms)	1	2	3	4	5	6	7	8	9	10
Generating RSA key	2330	2206	2750	2314	2480	2218	2526	3790	2773	2378
Encrypting image	1436	848	913	890	1141	1422	1025	1036	1397	1355
Decrypting image	3234	3946	3337	3796	3379	3360	2449	3174	3830	3267

In the text encryption scenario, similar patterns were observed. The RSA key generation time averaged around 2,413 ms, aligning closely with the image encryption scenario and reaffirming the computational intensity of this stage. Encrypting the text (Fig. 6) took an average of 1,167 ms, comparable to the image encryption, suggesting that the RSA encryption algorithm maintains a consistent performance regardless of the data type. The decryption time for the text averaged around 3,561 ms, slightly higher than that for the image decryption. This increment might be due to variations in the data structure of the text compared to the image, affecting the decryption complexity (Table 2).

Table 2. Evaluation of RSA Key Generation, Encryption, and Decryption Timings for Text Data Scenario

RSA with Text(ms)	1	2	3	4	5	6	7	8	9	10
Generating RSA key	2332	2257	2368	2259	2866	2736	2442	1947	2689	2151
Encrypting Text	1496	933	1363	1523	888	781	1483	825	1030	1520
Decrypting Text	3172	3810	3269	3218	4246	3483	4075	3228	3281	3329

Analyzing the performance, it is evident that the RSA encryption process is relatively efficient and consistent across different data types. However, the key generation and decryption processes are computationally intensive, a characteristic inherent to RSA due to its high security standards. The decryption time, being the longest, highlights the computational costs associated with secure data retrieval in RSA-encrypted systems. This trade-off between security and efficiency is a critical consideration in the deployment of RSA-encrypted systems in real-world applications, especially in e-commerce scenarios where both security and speed are paramount.

In conclusion, the evaluation demonstrates that while the RSA encryption method in our proposed system ensures a high level of security, it does so at the expense of increased computational time, especially in key generation and decryption phases. This insight is essential for optimizing and balancing the security and efficiency of payment systems in e-commerce, particularly in scenarios demanding rapid transaction processing without compromising data security.

6.2 Economic Efficiency of Smart Contract Deployment for RSA-Encrypted NFTs

Smart Contract Deployment on EVM-Compatible Platforms. In the quest to revolutionize payment systems, we explored the deployment of smart contracts on four eminent Ethereum Virtual Machine (EVM)-compatible platforms. Binance Smart Chain (BNB Smart Chain), Polygon, Fantom, and Celo were selected due to their prominence and innovative contributions to the blockchain ecosystem. These platforms, while ensuring compatibility with Ethereum, offer distinct advantages and cost structures, making them suitable candidates for our implementation.

Our research involved deploying and examining the performance of smart contracts-specifically their transaction creation, NFT minting, and transfer capabilities-within real-estate transaction scenarios on these platforms, ensuring the integrity and functionality of our RSA-encrypted NFT framework.

Comparative Transaction Fee Analysis. The operational costs associated with blockchain technologies are a critical factor, especially in the adoption of smart contracts for commercial applications like cash-on-delivery transactions. We conducted a meticulous analysis of the transaction fees required for deploying smart contracts and executing their functions on each platform, as shown in Table 3. This assessment was vital for understanding the financial feasibility of our proposed payment system across different blockchain networks.

Table 3. Transaction fee

	Contract Creation	Create NFT	Transfer NFT
BNB Smart Chain	0.027311 BNB ($8.33)	0.00109162 BNB ($0.33)	0.00056991 BNB ($0.17)
Fantom	0.0095767 FTM ($0.003)	0.000405167 FTM ($0.000127)	0.0002380105 FTM ($0.000075)
Polygon	0.0068405000328344 MATIC ($0.01)	0.000289405001273382 MATIC ($0.00)	0.000170007500748033 MATIC ($0.00)
Celo	0.00709722 CELO ($0.004)	0.0002840812 CELO ($0.000)	0.0001554878 CELO ($0.000)

The findings from our examination revealed Fantom as the optimal platform for deploying our smart contract for RSA-encrypted NFTs, particularly considering the economic efficiency. The transaction fees on Fantom, as detailed in Table 3, were substantially lower compared to the other platforms. Such cost-effectiveness, paired with robust functionality, positions Fantom as a leading choice for our application, which demands frequent and economically feasible smart contract interactions. The reduced costs of NFT minting and transfer on Fantom are conducive to the broad-scale implementation of blockchain solutions in payment systems, particularly in the real estate sector where multiple, frequent transactions are the norm.

This comparative analysis underscores our commitment to not only enhancing the security and efficiency of COD transactions but also ensuring the economic viability of our solutions in real-world applications. By selecting a platform that aligns with our performance and cost-efficiency criteria, we lay the groundwork for a more accessible and practical adoption of blockchain technology in the transformation of payment systems.

7 Discussion

In discussing the validity of our study on integrating RSA-Encrypted NFTs in blockchain for cash-on-delivery transactions, it's crucial to acknowledge the inherent limitations and potential threats to the validity of our proposed model. One of the primary concerns is the computational demand of RSA encryption, which, while providing a high level of security, imposes a significant processing overhead. This could potentially limit the scalability of our system, especially in scenarios with a high volume of transactions or where rapid transaction processing is required.

Another threat to validity is the assumption of consistent network conditions. The performance evaluation was conducted in a controlled environment, which may not accurately reflect the real-world conditions where network latency and varying loads could affect the transaction times. Additionally, the deployment of smart contracts across multiple blockchain platforms may encounter unforeseen challenges due to platform-specific constraints or incompatibilities, which could hinder the practical implementation of our model.

Furthermore, the ever-present risk of evolving security threats, particularly in the realm of blockchain and encryption technologies, cannot be overlooked. Our system's reliance on RSA encryption may be robust against current threats, but the development of quantum computing and other advanced cryptographic attack methods could pose significant risks in the future. This necessitates ongoing research and updates to our encryption mechanisms to maintain the integrity and security of the transactions.

The economic feasibility of deploying our model is also subject to the volatile nature of transaction fees within the blockchain ecosystem. The cost-effectiveness of our approach today might be challenged by fluctuating transaction fees, affecting the overall sustainability of the model. As such, continuous monitoring of the economic landscape and the integration of adaptive fee management strategies are essential for the long-term viability of the proposed system.

Lastly, the adoption of our RSA-Encrypted NFT framework depends heavily on the end-user acceptance and the perceived complexity of the system. Despite its technical merits, the practical deployment may face resistance due to the technology's complexity and the potential reluctance of users to transition from traditional payment systems to a blockchain-based model.

Addressing these threats to validity and acknowledging the limitations of our deployment strategy is critical for the refinement and successful implementation of our proposed model. Future work will need to focus on optimizing the encryption process for better performance, designing robust systems capable of adapting to changing network conditions and security landscapes, and ensuring economic and user-centric feasibility to facilitate widespread adoption.

8 Conclusion

The research presented a pivotal advancement in the landscape of digital payment systems. By intricately combining RSA encryption with NFTs in a blockchain-based environment, this paper addresses the critical challenges of traditional COD systems, offering a solution that is not only secure and transparent but also efficient. This innovative approach transcends the limitations of existing payment systems, particularly in securing and streamlining cross-border transactions. The integration of advanced cryptographic techniques with blockchain technology in our model sets a new standard in the realm of e-commerce transactions, emphasizing security, privacy, and transactional integrity. This contribution is poised to have a substantial impact on the future of digital transactions, potentially revolutionizing the way COD transactions are conducted and perceived in the digital era. It is a forward-looking solution that signals a new era of trust and reliability in e-commerce, catering to the dynamic needs of a rapidly evolving digital economy.

References

1. Ahmadieh, E., El Madhoun, N.: Artwork NFTS for online trading and transaction cancellation. In: 2023 Fifth International Conference on Blockchain Computing and Applications (BCCA), pp. 235–239 (2023)
2. Dragomir, A.G., Van Woensel, T., Doerner, K.F.: The pickup and delivery problem with alternative locations and overlapping time windows. Comput. Oper. Res. **143**, 105758 (2022)
3. Duong-Trung, N., et al.: Multi-sessions mechanism for decentralized cash on delivery system. Int. J. Adv. Comput. Sci. Appl. **10**(9) (2019)
4. Elghaish, F., Abrishami, S., Hosseini, M.: Integrated project delivery with blockchain: an automated financial system. Autom. Constr. **114**, 103182 (2020)
5. Ha, X.S., et al.: Dem-cod: novel access-control-based cash on delivery mechanism for decentralized marketplace. In: 2020 IEEE 19th International Conference on Trust, Security and Privacy in Computing and Communications (TrustCom), pp. 71–78. IEEE (2020)
6. Ha, X.S., Le, T.H., Phan, T.T., Nguyen, H.H.D., Vo, H.K., Duong-Trung, N.: Scrutinizing trust and transparency in cash on delivery systems. In: Wang, G., Chen, B., Li, W., Di Pietro, R., Yan, X., Han, H. (eds.) SpaCCS 2020. LNCS, vol. 12382, pp. 214–227. Springer, Cham (2021). https://doi.org/10.1007/978-3-030-68851-6_15

7. Hasan, H.R., Salah, K.: Proof of delivery of digital assets using blockchain and smart contracts. IEEE Access **6**, 65439–65448 (2018)
8. Jha, A., Dubey, S., Kumar, H.U.: Transaction system based on blockchain technology using smart contract. Int. J. Sci. Res. Eng. Manag. (2023)
9. Le, H.T., et al.: Introducing multi shippers mechanism for decentralized cash on delivery system. Int. J. Adv. Comput. Sci. Appl. **10**(6) (2019)
10. Le, N.T.T., et al.: Assuring non-fraudulent transactions in cash on delivery by introducing double smart contracts. Int. J. Adv. Comput. Sci. Appl. **10**(5), 677–684 (2019)
11. Mohammed, N.S., Dawood, O., Sagheer, A., Nafea, A.A.: Secure smart contract based on blockchain to prevent the non-repudiation phenomenon. Baghdad Sci. J. (2023)
12. Quoc, K.L., et al.: SSSB: an approach to insurance for cross-border exchange by using smart contracts. In: Awan, I., Younas, M., Poniszewska-Marańda, A. (eds.) MobiWIS 2022. LNCS, vol. 13475, pp. 179–192. Springer, Cham (2022). https://doi.org/10.1007/978-3-031-14391-5_14
13. Raj, P.V.R.P., Jauhar, S.K., Ramkumar, M., Pratap, S.: Procurement, traceability and advance cash credit payment transactions in supply chain using blockchain smart contracts. Comput. Ind. Eng. **167**, 108038 (2022)
14. Sikder, A.S.: Blockchain-empowered e-commerce: Redefining trust, security, and efficiency in digital marketplaces in the context of Bangladesh. Blockchain-empowered e-commerce. Int. J. Imminent Sci. Technol. **1**(1), 216–235 (2023)
15. Son, H.X., et al.: Towards a mechanism for protecting seller's interest of cash on delivery by using smart contract in hyperledger. Int. J. Adv. Comput. Sci. Appl. **10**(4) (2019)

Virtual Blockchain Network for Secure Financial and Industrial Applications

Alexander Bogdanov[1], Valery Khvatov[2], Alexei Uteshev[1], and Nadezhda Shchegoleva[1](✉)

[1] St. Petersburg University, Saint Petersburg, Russia
{a.v.bogdanov,a.uteshev,n.shchegoleva}@spbu.ru
[2] DGT Technologies AG, Toronto, Canada

Abstract. This study introduces blockchain virtualization as a solution to tackle modern challenges. Evaluating the DGT network as a model, experiments probe the impact of virtualization (network-of-networks) on scaling and latency, shedding light on its potential for enhanced performance. Conclusively, the study emphasizes the significance of blockchain virtualization for enhancing blockchain performance and scalability. Future directions of research are discussed, including testing of security and privacy within virtualized environments and the potential of virtualization in shaping cloud-based blockchain-as-a-service solutions. In sum, blockchain virtualization emerges as a pivotal innovation poised to redefine the landscape of blockchain technology and its applications.

Keywords: DGT · Layer 1 digital platform · multi-party computation over blockchain · decentralization

1 Introduction

More than a decade has passed since Satoshi Nakamoto introduced the groundbreaking concept of blockchain, revolutionizing the way we perceive decentralized transactions and particularly cryptocurrencies. Despite this initial innovation, the blockchain landscape remains relatively stagnant. Initiatives like Ethereum, Algorand, Ripple, and Stellar have contributed their unique features, yet the underlying architecture largely echoes Nakamoto's original design. While blockchain has immense potential, its broader adoption has been hampered by persistent challenges that seem to demand a reevaluation of its architecture.

A closer examination of the current state of blockchain technology reveals several bottlenecks that have hindered its widespread acceptance:

- **Scalability Woes**: As participation in blockchain networks grows, the speed of transaction processing tends to decrease. This phenomenon stems from the communication-intensive nature of peer-to-peer solutions and the trade-offs presented by the "blockchain trilemma" 1 (also known as CAP theorem). It dictates that decentralized solutions can prioritize two out of three traits: decentralization, scalability, and security.

O. Gervasi et al. (Eds.): ICCSA 2024 Workshops, LNCS 14815, pp. 142–161, 2024.
https://doi.org/10.1007/978-3-031-65154-0_9

- **Escalating Transaction Costs**: High transaction costs, often unrelated to cryptocurrencies, arise from redundancy and communication inefficiency within the blockchain network 2. This, in turn, affects the overall efficiency of the solution.
- **Confidentiality Gaps**: While public blockchains offer anonymous ownership, transaction details remain transparent. The absence of built-in private transactions prevents blockchain technology from being embraced by enterprises, including financial institutions, due to privacy concerns 3.
- **Smart Contract Insecurities**: Vulnerabilities within smart contracts, though enabling customization, expose the network to security threats 4. Simultaneously, the computational complexity of executing these contracts raises communication costs and limits efficiency.
- **Interoperability Impediments**: The blockchain ecosystem's lack of seamless integration between networks has prevented the technology from realizing its full potential. Solutions like Polkadot, Cosmos, and Avalanche have attempted to address this, yet the overall architecture has limited their effectiveness 5.

In response to these challenges, this work introduces the concept of the Virtual Blockchain Network, which amalgamates the best architectural practices from various distributed solutions 6. This paradigm envisions a revamped approach to blockchain architecture that promises to surmount the limitations inherent in traditional blockchains.

Blockchain virtualization is rethought in terms of key architectural solutions that allow participants in information exchange to interact effectively, including launching their own ecosystems. Blockchain virtualization entails abstracting the blockchain infrastructure, enabling the creation and management of multiple virtual instances within a shared physical blockchain network. This novel approach offers enhanced scalability, isolation, and resource allocation. By deploying tailored blockchain networks that cater to specific organizational requirements, the Virtual Blockchain Network overcomes the constraints imposed by a single, communal blockchain.

At its core, this virtualization leverages a hybrid architecture in which clusters mimic independent blockchain ecosystems. A two-layer consensus mechanism underpins this arrangement, ensuring consensus both at the cluster level and across the broader network. This innovative architecture effectively addresses scalability constraints while bolstering transaction processing speed and preserving decentralization.

The transformative potential of the Virtual Blockchain Network becomes evident in its capability to rectify the existing limitations of classical blockchain architectures. This advancement, characterized by an efficient and scalable consensus mechanism, integration of Directed Acyclic Graph (DAG) technology, and a hybrid cluster-segment structure, paves the way for a blockchain ecosystem that is more scalable, cost-effective, and suitable for broader adoption.

To illustrate the practical application of this concept, the DGT network is employed as a testament to the real-world viability of virtualized networks. DGT, with its hybrid approach 15, exemplifies how a Virtual Blockchain Network can transcend traditional barriers and catalyze the evolution of blockchain technology.

The versatility of the Virtual Blockchain Network concept extends to various use cases 7:

- **Financial Processing**: Virtual blockchain networks offer a platform for efficient, secure, and cost-effective financial transactions. Smart contracts executed on the network facilitate seamless cross-border payments, trade settlements, and supply chain finance while ensuring transparency and immutability.
- **Distributed Identity**: Virtualized blockchains enhance identity management by allowing users to control their digital identities securely. Utilizing self-sovereign identity solutions, individuals can manage and share personal information while maintaining privacy.
- **Secure Data Sharing**: Organizations can utilize virtual blockchain networks to securely share sensitive data across partners, customers, and stakeholders. The integration of cryptographic techniques ensures data integrity and confidentiality throughout the sharing process
- **Industrial Coo**peration: Virtualized blockchain networks pave the way for enhanced collaboration within industries. Consortiums can establish their own dedicated blockchains, enabling streamlined supply chain management, data exchange, and interoperability between diverse stakeholders
- **Virtual Data Networks**: Virtual blockchain networks can act as frameworks for the creation of decentralized data marketplaces. Such platforms allow users to share and monetize their data while maintaining control over its usage and ownership.

Each of these use cases harnesses the potential of virtualized blockchain networks to overcome traditional limitations and drive innovation across industries. By offering improved scalability, enhanced security, and tailored functionality, these networks facilitate the integration of blockchain technology into diverse applications.

2 Evolving the Blockchain Blueprint: Architectural Innovations and Concepts

The evolution of blockchain technology has been driven by the constant pursuit of addressing its inherent challenges and limitations. In this article, we delve into the fundamental aspects of blockchain solutions, explore the layered approach to blockchain architecture, and shed light on the paradigm-shifting concepts of Web 3 and tokenomics. We also delve into the emerging need for virtualized blockchains and the critical importance of striking the right balance between centralization and decentralization.

2.1 Foundations of Blockchain Architecture

At the heart of any blockchain architecture lies a distributed ledger that forms the foundation for recording transactions in a secure and transparent manner. This ledger, often referred to as the blockchain, consists of a chronological chain of blocks, with each block containing a set of transactions. The architecture encompasses various components and mechanisms that collectively ensure the integrity and immutability of the data stored within the blockchain. NISTIR 8202 8 and ITU-T 9 guidelines offer foundational insights into understanding this intricate architecture (Fig. 1).

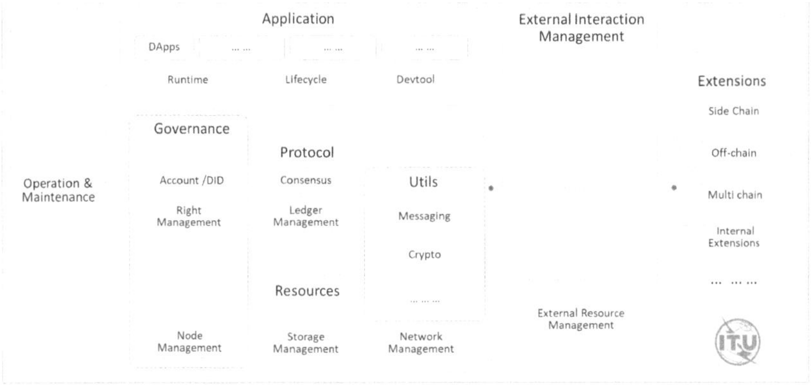

Fig. 1. TU's DLT Reference Architecture.

Main Components of Classical Blockchain Architecture:

- Transactions: Transactions are the fundamental units of data in a blockchain. They represent actions or events that alter the state of the system. Transactions can include financial transfers, smart contract executions, or any action that requires recording.
- **Blocks**: Blocks are containers that group a set of transactions together. Each block includes a reference to the previous block (creating a chain), a timestamp, and a cryptographic hash of its contents. The hash ensures the integrity of the data within the block and establishes a strong link to the previous block.
- **Decentralized Network**: A network of nodes maintains and verifies the blockchain. Each node has a copy of the entire blockchain. The decentralized nature ensures that no single entity has control over the network, enhancing security and preventing single points of failure.
- **Consensus Mechanism**: Consensus mechanisms determine how transactions are validated and added to the blockchain. Traditional mechanisms include Proof of Work (PoW), where nodes compete to solve complex puzzles to validate transactions, and Proof of Stake (PoS), where validators are chosen based on the number of tokens they hold.
- **Smart Contracts**: Smart contracts are self-executing contracts with predefined rules and conditions. They automatically execute when certain conditions are met, eliminating the need for intermediaries, and enhancing automation.
- **Cryptography**: Cryptography plays a pivotal role in blockchain security. It ensures the privacy of transactions, verifies identities, and secures communication between nodes.
- **Public and Private Keys**: Users have a pair of cryptographic keys – a public key for identification and a private key for signing transactions. The private key is kept secret and is used to prove ownership of assets.
- **Hashing**: Cryptographic hash functions generate fixed-length strings of characters (hashes) from variable-length input. Hashes are used to ensure the integrity of data and create the linkage between blocks.
- **Security and transparency** are the cornerstones of any blockchain architecture, establishing a foundation of trust in a decentralized environment. These mechanisms

work in tandem to safeguard the integrity of data, prevent tampering, and promote openness throughout the network. By combining cryptographic techniques, decentralized consensus, and immutability, blockchain architecture ensures that information remains unalterable, transactions are verified, and participants can have confidence in the validity of the recorded data. This short article delves into the essential mechanisms that underpin security and transparency within blockchain systems, shedding light on their crucial roles in shaping the future of secure, trustworthy transactions.

2.2 Permission Network Design

Blockchain networks exhibit a versatile range of designs to accommodate different use cases and requirements. These designs can be broadly categorized into three main types: public networks, private networks, and consortium networks. Each variant caters to distinct scenarios, offering tailored solutions for various entities and collaborations.

- **Public Networks**: Public blockchain networks, exemplified by pioneers like Bitcoin and Ethereum, uphold the essence of decentralization and inclusivity. These networks are open to all participants, irrespective of their identity or affiliation. Transactions are validated and recorded by a distributed network of nodes, ensuring transparency and consensus through protocols such as Proof of Work (PoW) and Proof of Stake (PoS). Public networks emphasize transparency, as all transactions are visible to anyone and can be independently verified.
- **Private Networks**: In contrast, private blockchain networks are designed for specific entities seeking a controlled and confidential environment. These networks restrict participation to pre-approved participants, ensuring a closed ecosystem. Private networks are well-suited for enterprises or organizations that require a secure platform for internal processes, supply chain management, or inter-departmental interactions. The degree of decentralization and transparency may vary, and participants typically have more control over consensus mechanisms.
- **Consortium Networks**: Consortium networks strike a balance between public and private designs, representing a collaborative effort among multiple entities. These networks are governed by a group of organizations with shared interests, making them suitable for industries or sectors where cooperation and data sharing are pivotal. Consortium networks offer more decentralization and transparency compared to private networks, while maintaining some level of controlled access.

2.3 Consensus Mechanisms and Network Hierarchies: Ensuring Agreement and Efficiency

The essence of blockchain technology rests upon consensus mechanisms, the mechanisms by which network participants achieve agreement on the state of the shared ledger 10. These mechanisms play a pivotal role in maintaining the integrity and trustworthiness of distributed ledgers. Diverse consensus algorithms such as Proof of Work (PoW), Proof of Stake (PoS), and Byzantine Fault Tolerance (BFT) share the common objective of achieving consensus through various means, while simultaneously exhibiting their unique strengths and limitations.

PoW, the algorithm underpinning Bitcoin and several other networks, demands computational effort as a proof of commitment. While it ensures robust security by requiring miners to compete for block validation, its energy consumption and slow transaction finality are notable drawbacks. The energy-intensive nature of PoW raises environmental concerns and constrains scalability.

On the other hand, PoS assigns the block validation privilege to participants who hold a significant stake in the network's native cryptocurrency. This approach mitigates the energy inefficiency of PoW, but introduces challenges related to centralization risks and the "nothing at stake" problem, where validators might support multiple chains simultaneously.

BFT consensus mechanisms aim for fast and deterministic finality by requiring network participants to agree on each transaction's validity before appending it to the blockchain. While offering quick transactions, BFT algorithms face challenges in terms of scalability and communication cost.

Consensus mechanisms differ in their consensus determination methods: deterministic (BFT) or probabilistic (PoW and PoS). Deterministic consensus ensures finality with high certainty, while probabilistic consensus offers statistical finality. The trade-off lies between absolute certainty and faster confirmation times.

The GOSSIP protocol 11, commonly employed for node communication, employs a peer-to-peer approach where nodes spread information to their peers. While simple and decentralized, GOSSIP's efficiency diminishes as the network scales due to communication redundancy, latency, and potential data loss.

Hierarchical network 12 designs provide an innovative alternative to address these challenges. By segmenting nodes into clusters, hierarchical networks reduce the direct communication required among all nodes. This structure enhances scalability and performance, tackling the communication bottleneck of flat P2P architectures.

2.4 Layered Architectural Approach

To address the inherent limitations of blockchain technology, a common approach is to break down the architecture into separate functional layers 13. This allows for more efficient and effective management of the triple limitations of blockchain, as well as addressing key characteristics like security, scalability, and functionality. The decomposition of complex systems into layers is a widely accepted approach and can vary in emphasis. In some cases, the decomposition is used to highlight the fundamental conceptual entities of the technology, including a data layer, network layer, and application layer.

Such approaches inherit the classical network model known as the Open Systems Interconnection model (OSI model, 16). The approach describes the component structure of the system well but avoids the issues of decentralization that are essential for the blockchain.

Within the framework of this approach, the following components can be distinguished (Fig. 2):

- **Layer 0 (L0)** represents the physical layer of the blockchain, which includes hardware, Internet protocols, cloud solutions, and protocols that facilitate interaction between different protocols at the architecture level. It also encompasses Blockchain as a Service (BaaS) solutions and Blockchain DevOps infrastructure.

- **Layer 1 (L1)** is the base protocol layer of the blockchain architecture, responsible for fundamental blockchain functionality, such as transaction validation and network consensus. Layer 1 prioritizes security, particularly the consensus mechanism. Common Layer 1 blockchain solutions include Bitcoin, Ethereum, Binance Smart Chain (BSC), and Algorand.
- **Layer 2 (L2)** solutions work in conjunction with Layer 1 to provide additional features or improvements without compromising the security and scalability of the underlying blockchain network. Examples of L2 solutions include payment channels (Lightning Network, Raiden Network, and Polygon), sidechains, Plasma, sharding, and rollups.
- **Layer 3 (L3)** focuses on enabling interoperability, supporting decentralized identity, and providing off-chain computation capabilities. This layer ensures different blockchain networks and systems can communicate and interact seamlessly. It also includes the development of decentralized data storage and exchange solutions, such as IPFS, and off-chain computation solutions like Quant and Chainlink.
- **Layer 4 (L4)**, also known as the Application and Blockchain API layer, is the topmost layer of the blockchain architecture. This layer includes applications that use the blockchain network and APIs that allow developers to build decentralized applications (DApps) on top of the blockchain. It is responsible for providing a user interface for accessing blockchain features and interacting with the blockchain network. Examples of applications in Layer 4 include decentralized exchanges, digital asset marketplaces, and voting systems. Blockchain APIs, such as Ethereum's Web3.js and Bitcoin's JSON-RPC API, also operate in Layer 4.

It is important to understand that the layered blockchain architecture model presented is a logical interpretation and that final solutions can span across multiple layers. Moreover, different layers can be utilized for data exchange, considering the workload profiles and specific characteristics such as the amount and dynamics of data transferred, and the required level of security. In the following examples, the DGT platform will be presented as an integrated system, utilizing mechanisms from different layers.

WEB 3 and Tokenomics

The evolution of the internet has brought us to the cusp of a new era known as Web 3.0 17, where blockchain technology plays a pivotal role in redefining online interactions. Web 3.0 (Web 3) envisions a decentralized digital landscape that prioritizes privacy, security, and user empowerment. At its core, Web 3 leverages blockchain's unique attributes to enhance data ownership, privacy, and interoperability. Tokenomics, a fundamental aspect of Web 3, introduces a paradigm shift in how value is generated and distributed across digital ecosystems. By seamlessly integrating tokens into various aspects of the online experience, tokenomics reshapes the dynamics of digital economies, fostering innovation, inclusivity, and sustainable growth.

Web 3 Paradigm: Web 3 introduces a user-centric internet, enabling individuals to regain control over their data and identity. It emphasizes peer-to-peer interactions, decentralization, and data ownership. The foremost contribution of the Web 3 concept to network evolution lies in introducing tokenomics and privacy-by-design. Both aspects necessitate a profound shift in blockchain architecture.

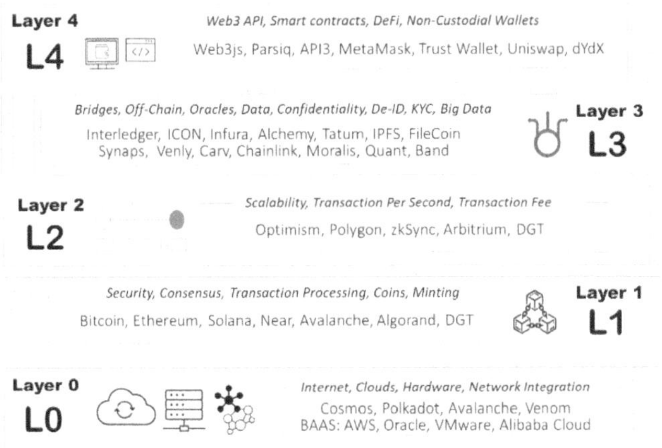

Fig. 2. TU's DLT Reference Architecture Layered Blockchain Solutions Model.

Tokenomics and Hybrid Approach: Tokens serve as the lifeblood of the blockchain ecosystem, representing value and enabling participation. They incentivize network contributors, facilitate governance, and streamline transactions. While tokens are intrinsic to public blockchains, even private blockchain systems like Hyperledger Fabric benefit from tokenization. The hybrid approach, combining public and private features, addresses redundancy and infrastructure limitations.

2.5 Requirements for a Virtualized Blockchain: Orchestrating Seamless Connectivity

In the pursuit of constructing a virtualized blockchain ecosystem, a set of critical requirements emerges to ensure its effectiveness, adaptability, and utility 18. These requirements are aimed at facilitating the creation and management of multiple interconnected blockchain instances, fostering collaboration and interoperability among diverse networks. As a network of networks, a virtualized blockchain must meet several key prerequisites:

- **Scalability and Performance Enhancement**: A virtualized blockchain should transcend the limitations of individual blockchains by enabling horizontal and vertical scaling. This ensures that the ecosystem can accommodate a multitude of interconnected networks without compromising transaction speed or network performance.
- **Isolation and Customization**: Each blockchain instance within the virtualized environment should maintain its own characteristics, allowing for tailored customization and specialization according to unique use cases, regulatory frameworks, and business requirements.
- **Interoperability**: An essential feature of virtualized blockchains is the seamless exchange of data, assets, and value across instances. The architecture should facilitate

communication and collaboration among disparate networks, fostering an ecosystem of interconnectedness.

- **Security and Privacy**: Ensuring data confidentiality, integrity, and privacy across interconnected blockchains is paramount. Strong cryptographic mechanisms, Zero-Knowledge Proofs, and advanced privacy-preserving technologies should be incorporated to safeguard sensitive information.
- **Consensus Flexibility**: The architecture should support multiple consensus mechanisms to accommodate various use cases and network requirements. This includes Proof of Work (PoW), Proof of Stake (PoS), Byzantine Fault Tolerance (BFT), and more, enabling the selection of the most suitable consensus for each instance.
- **Resource Allocation and Optimization**: Efficient resource allocation ensures that the virtualized blockchain network operates optimally, avoiding overutilization or underutilization of resources. Dynamic allocation mechanisms can ensure fairness and efficient utilization across instances.
- **Decentralized Governance**: A decentralized governance model should guide decision-making processes across the virtualized environment. Clear rules and protocols for network upgrades, maintenance, and dispute resolution should be established to maintain the integrity of the ecosystem.
- **Adaptive Protocol Framework**: The architecture should allow for seamless protocol upgrades and enhancements to accommodate evolving technological standards, security measures, and industry best practices.
- **Ease of Use and Accessibility**: User-friendly interfaces, developer-friendly APIs, and comprehensive documentation should simplify the deployment, management, and interaction with virtualized blockchain instances.
- **Economic Sustainability**: The economic model should incentivize participation and contributions across interconnected networks. Tokenomics should be designed to reward validators, developers, and participants, ensuring long-term sustainability.
- **Cross-Chain Communication**: A standardized protocol for cross-chain communication and asset exchange should be established, facilitating frictionless value transfer between different blockchain instances.
- **Compliance and Regulation**: The architecture should support compliance with regulatory frameworks in various jurisdictions, enabling businesses to operate within legal boundaries while benefiting from the advantages of a virtualized blockchain network.

By meeting these requirements, this network of networks can unlock a new era of connectivity, collaboration, and innovation in the world of distributed ledger technology. The architecture should be rooted in Layer 1 networks while incorporating essential components from Layer 0 and Layer 2, offering a comprehensive and effective solution for a dynamic virtualized blockchain ecosystem.

2.6 Decentralization Issues in Virtualized Blockchain Ecosystems: Navigating the Spectrum

Decentralization, a foundational principle of blockchain technology, remains a cornerstone in the design of virtualized blockchain ecosystems 19. However, the quest for an optimal level of decentralization presents a multifaceted challenge that requires a nuanced approach. While a fully decentralized network offers unparalleled security and resilience, it may not always align with practical implementation and performance demands.

The conventional metric for decentralization calculates the number of independent nodes participating in a network. Yet, this metric doesn't account for broader aspects that influence the degree of decentralization and its implications for practical applications. Factors like governance, token distribution, and network influence also contribute significantly to the architecture's decentralization.

A central issue in the realm of decentralization is the concept of "51% attack," whereby a single entity or coalition acquires majority control over the network's computational power. This concern highlights the need for mechanisms that safeguard against centralization of power, both in terms of computational resources and decision-making authority.

Striking a balance between full centralization and decentralization has led to the emergence of hybrid solutions. These hybrid approaches leverage the benefits of both centralized and decentralized architectures to create flexible, modular, and adaptive systems. Such hybrid models offer a higher degree of security compared to fully centralized systems while retaining a level of efficiency and scalability often associated with centralized setups.

The advantages of decentralized hybrid solutions are manifold. They encompass enhanced security, enabling resistance against single points of failure and malicious attacks. Scalability is another benefit, as decentralization allows the network to scale horizontally by adding nodes and instances as needed. This modular design fosters adaptability, making it possible to tailor solutions to specific use cases while maintaining interoperability.

Furthermore, decentralized hybrid architectures can mitigate latency issues that arise due to geographical distribution and network propagation delays. The architecture's modular nature enables strategic placement of nodes and instances to optimize communication paths and reduce latency.

Importantly, such architectures pave the way for smoother regulatory compliance. By striking a balance between decentralization and centralization, they can navigate the intricate regulatory landscape while upholding data integrity and security.

3 DGT as a Framework for Virtualization

In the pursuit of an optimal architectural solution for virtualized blockchain ecosystems, the DGT platform 15 stands as a testament to innovation and adaptability. Built upon a hybrid architecture, DGT presents a formidable framework that not only embraces decentralization principles but also offers a set of features tailored to engage institutional players, thereby fostering widespread adoption and usability.

DGT Digital Platform

The DGT platform is a pioneering blockchain solution characterized by its innovative Hybrid-Network Architecture (H-NET). This architecture 15 leverages a combination of clusters and segments to establish an interconnected network of networks, enabling enhanced scalability, privacy, and customized consensus mechanisms. DGT empowers various blockchain instances within a unified ecosystem, supporting decentralized applications, secure data exchange, and efficient financial transactions. DGT provides a robust and reliable framework for decentralized data exchange, embracing the Web 3.0 principles of decentralization, sovereignty, and user empowerment. It fosters a new era of internet interactions, where users have greater control over their data, participate actively in network governance, and contribute to a more inclusive and decentralized digital ecosystem:

DGT is moving forward within the D3 paradigm:

- **Data integration** based on an innovative consensus mechanism.
- **Data management** through the entire life cycle.
- **Data delivery** enabling data presentation for any user in real time.

This allows DGT to implement applied innovative products within a single paradigm and in a short time. Features of the DGT solution include:

- **H-NET Architecture**: At the heart of DGT's design lies the innovative H-NET architecture. This architecture envisions the network as an amalgamation of interconnected clusters and segments. Each cluster functions as an independent entity with its own nodes, leaders, and arbitrators, fostering modularity and scalability.
- **Two-Level Consensus**: DGT leverages a two-level consensus mechanism called the F-BFT Consensus 20. At the cluster level, a Byzantine Fault Tolerant (BFT) consensus, such as the P-BFT, Hot-Stuff, or Lagrange Construction 24, ensures agreement within clusters. At the higher level, a ring of arbitrators employs a Proof-of-Stake (PoS) or an anchor mechanism (certified arbitrators) to finalize decisions and resolve inter-cluster conflicts.
- **Transaction Families**: DGT introduces the concept of transaction families, akin to smart contracts. These transaction processors handle transactions based on predefined validation rules, offering versatility and optimized execution.
- **Hybrid Ledger:** DGT's ledger combines the conventional block structure with a Directed Acyclic Graph (DAG). This innovative approach not only maintains transaction connections but also facilitates independent network time through the Heartbeat mechanism, enhancing both structural integrity and synchronization.
- **Off-Chain Notaries**: DGT incorporates specialized nodes known as Notaries to address functions unsuited for on-chain execution. These Notaries function as oracles, accessing extensive data and supporting Zero-Knowledge Proof (ZKP) mechanisms 22, thus enabling private transactions, and enhancing data confidentiality. They also play a crucial role in decentralized identification and verification processes.
- **DEC Processing Family**: DGT features a dedicated DEC processing family that includes comprehensive tokenization functionalities, adhering to the ISO 20022 21 compliance standards. This family enables the issuance and management of internal DEC tokens, streamlining financial operations and supporting a robust token economy.

3.1 Basic Network Design

In the ever-evolving landscape of blockchain technology, the concept of virtualized blockchain networks has emerged as a promising frontier. These networks transcend the traditional notion of individual nodes to encompass entire network instances. However, achieving such a feat requires a departure from the conventional flat peer-to-peer (p2p) structure facilitated by the GOSSIP protocol.

The DGT Platform strides boldly into this realm of innovation by adopting a sophisticated topology, moving beyond the limitations of simple p2p frameworks. Central to this advancement is the H-NET network model 15, a cornerstone of DGT's architecture. H-NET introduces a revolutionary paradigm wherein networks are not just clusters of nodes but are orchestrated as a synergy of diverse fragments or segments. These segments offer the flexibility to establish unique rules for node behavior, local transaction families, and even custom consensus mechanisms. This distinctive approach serves as the bedrock for crafting hybrid network environments, accommodating diverse permission design models under a single cohesive framework.

3.2 Hierarchical Structure: Redefining Scalability

H-NET's hierarchical architecture addresses one of the blockchain ecosystem's pressing challenges: scalability. By organizing clusters into segments, which in turn form a hierarchical network, DGT achieves a scalable structure that can handle increasing transaction volumes without compromising performance.

The hierarchy ensures that individual clusters manage their transactions seamlessly, minimizing communication bottlenecks. At the same time, segments permit cross-cluster interactions, granting the flexibility to cater to diverse applications. This synergy between clusters and segments paves the way for a network that can evolve in tandem with growing demands Fig. 3.

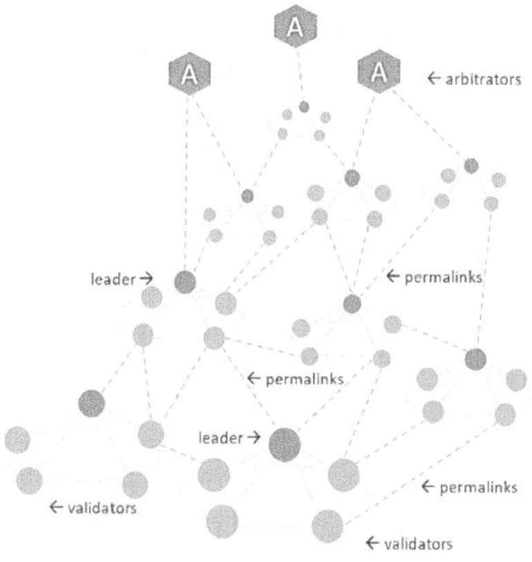

Fig. 3. H-Net Architecture.

3.3 Efficiency and Modularity: A Harmonious Balance

The H-NET architecture emphasizes modularity, enabling easy integration of new clusters and segments to accommodate evolving requirements. Each cluster operates with minimal interdependence, fostering rapid innovation and experimentation. This modularity translates into efficient upgrades, reduced maintenance downtime, and a seamless user experience.

Additionally, the H-NET architecture prioritizes resource optimization by distributing computational tasks across clusters and segments. This design promotes parallel processing, resulting in faster transaction validation and enhanced network responsiveness.

3.4 Adaptive Consensus Mechanisms: Tailored for Excellence

The DGT platform has several technical solutions that define the approach to decentralized and distributed computing:

- **Permalinks:** Unlike classical p2p networks, DGT supports communication between nodes through routes called permalinks. Each node can have several connections, one main one, and multiple reserve ones in case of loss of the main channel. Such networking allows for a reduced cost of communication through the entire network.
- **Layered Ledger**: The ledger has a block structure, on top of which a directed graph (DAG) is built. The block approach allows for the formation of the classic blockchain structure. The DAG supports additional connections between transactions, while also allowing to set characteristic network time based on the topological sorting property of the directional graph. Such network time (implemented by a special Heartbeat Mechanism) is the basis of relatively static network configurations – Network Eras.

In contrast, at the network level, a ring of arbitrators employs Proof-of-Stake (PoS) or anchor mechanisms to finalize decisions. This two-level consensus approach harmonizes efficiency and security, ensuring that both cluster-level and network-wide consensus are achieved seamlessly.

While the cluster and data transfer layer use a BFT (F-BFT) approach, arbitrators represent a critical part of the DGT infrastructure and defend against Sybil-type attacks with a second layer of a PoS consensus 15.

- **Initiation**. Transactions are initiated on a client (computer, phone) communicating with a node through a standardized service API layer.
- **Components**. Each transaction consists of a header and the main body of the transaction (payload). A header contains the digital signature of the customer who created the transaction and the input and output (address) fields for the transactions.
- **Processing**. The transaction processor provides capabilities for processing individual transaction families and validating transaction properties. The Journal component, which is separate from the business logic of transactions, provides parallel processing and advanced batching management [10].
- **Stages**. All transactions are wrapped in batches before being sent to the ledger, which allows for additional processing acceleration. Below are the main steps of transaction formation.

- **Validation**. At this stage of processing, the nodes in the cluster "vote" for transactions, forming the usual quorum for BFT. The immediate BFT consensus mechanism can use the options P-BFT ("Lazy Mode"), Pipelined Fast-HotStuff ("Fast- Run"), or Lagrange Construction ("Alpine") 24.
- **Arbitration**. Maintaining the integrity of the network combined by the ledger is carried out through the second layer of transaction processing, when the nodes included in the so-called "ring of arbitrators" consider transactions, check for integrity, and directly place them in blocks and branches of the DAG. As noted above, the PoS mechanism (or a similar "anchor" principle) is used at this level. Arbitrators are delegates who implement an increased level of security.

Cluster-Based BFT Consensus

In the pursuit of optimizing the functionality and performance of a hybrid network, this section delves into the implementation and functioning of a cluster-based consensus mechanism known as Fast-RUN. It is important to note that Fast-RUN represents just one among several consensus options that can be employed within a cluster-based environment. In this context, the Fast-HotStuff consensus algorithm will be elucidated as a notable choice, showcasing its advantages and operational intricacies.

Fast-RUN Consensus Implementation with Fast-HotStuff

Fast-RUN, operating within the realm of cluster-based consensus, is characterized by its integration of the Fast-HotStuff consensus algorithm 23. This integration is achieved through the development of a dedicated plugin within a transaction family, granting validation capabilities to the transaction body. Importantly, this plugin is accessible across all nodes within the cluster, enabling seamless consensus implementation.

The core principle of the Fast-RUN algorithm revolves around enhancing the performance of Practical Byzantine Fault Tolerance (PBFT) consensus by incorporating Quorum Certificates at the cluster level. This innovative approach significantly bolsters security and concurrently minimizes communication costs associated with leader changes, specifically the Change View process 23.

Fast-Run Algorithm Workflow

- **The Fast-HotStuff** consensus algorithm, operational within the Fast-RUN framework, orchestrates its workflow through a series of distinct steps:
- **Leader Proposes a Block**: At the onset, a designated leader node undertakes the responsibility of proposing a block, housing a collection of transactions. The leader accompanies the block proposal with a certificate, attesting to the block's validity.
- **Block Validation by Nodes**: Validators, encompassing nodes engaged in the consensus, conduct a comprehensive validation of the proposed block and its corresponding certificate. Upon consensus regarding the block's legitimacy, validators append their signatures to the certificate.
- **Certificate Broadcast by Leader**: After securing enough validator signatures, the leader disseminates the certificate across the network.
- **Block Commitment by Nodes**: Receiving validators ascertain the authenticity of the certificate, scrutinizing its endorsement by fellow validators and the inclusion of

a bona fide block proposal. Upon verification, validators incorporate the block into their localized states.

- **Pipelined Block Proposals**: During the block commitment phase, the leader initiates the proposal of the subsequent block. This overlapping of proposal and commitment phases accelerates the consensus process, augmenting overall efficiency.

3.5 Transaction Families: DEC Processing

The DEC (Digital Economic Component) transaction family constitutes a pivotal element within the DGT platform 15, essential for its functional model. Unlike conventional solutions, DGT employs a unified transaction structure emphasizing headers and payloads. This design allows the network to efficiently process diverse transactions, both token-based and token-less, concurrently. In particular, the DEC transaction family assumes prominence in the DGT ecosystem due to its multifaceted nature and pivotal role in assessing the virtualized structure's performance.

Key Functions of the DEC Transaction Family

- **Token Issuance and Management**: The DEC transaction family facilitates the creation and management of DEC tokens. This encompasses mechanisms for minting new tokens and dynamically adjusting the token supply to align with network demands and token circulation.
- **Transfers**: It enables secure and seamless transfers of DEC tokens between accounts, forming the core of the DGT economic model. Participants within the network can engage in transactions, leveraging DEC tokens as the medium of exchange.
- **Banking Operations**: The DEC family extends its capabilities to support banking operations, encompassing tasks such as generating and overseeing invoices and virtual cards. This expansion broadens the utility of DEC tokens, enabling their use in various applications across the DGT platform.
- **Secondary Token Support**: Beyond the native DEC tokens, this transaction family accommodates the issuance and management of secondary tokens. This functionality fosters a diversified token landscape within the DGT ecosystem, enabling the creation of custom tokens tailored to specific use cases.
- **Security and Compliance**: The DEC transaction family prioritizes security and compliance (ISO 20022). It incorporates robust cryptographic techniques to safeguard transactions while integrating mechanisms to ensure adherence to pertinent regulatory frameworks.

4 Experiments and Comparisons

4.1 Empirical Evaluation of Blockchain Virtualization: Performance Analysis and Insights

Virtualization serves as a pivotal tool in addressing diverse challenges within the blockchain domain. Among these challenges, one significant task involves examining the hypothesis of heightened network performance within segmented networks, where communication complexity is constrained. To investigate this, a series of experiments were conducted on the DGT platform, targeting latency measurement as the number of nodes increased under virtualization (cluster and segment allocation). Additionally, a comparison was made with non-virtualized conditions using the conventional GOSSIP protocol.

Experimental Design

The study utilized the H-NET architecture of DGT to configure the network. Seven physical machines, each running Ubuntu 20.04, were employed, varying in RAM from 2 GB to 64 GB. These physical machines collectively hosted 15 virtual machines, organized into three clusters based on the initial configuration. An extra network segment was introduced, containing virtual nodes ranging from 15 to 30. This segment mimicked a scalable virtual blockchain network.

Methodology

Transaction Generation: An API-based transaction generator emulated authentic blockchain activity. Transactions of varying complexity, including basic transfers, digital object registrations, and DEC processing family-based account attribute alterations, were executed. Each transaction was tagged with size and type, simultaneously integrated into both the DAG structure and the 1 MB limited block.

Network Configuration: The DGT network was orchestrated with the stipulated physical and virtual machines, clusters, and segments. This ensured seamless synchronization and interaction between the nodes. The node count spanned from 10 to 60 across different consensus mechanisms (configured via an independent microservice). In the virtualized context, up to 25% of nodes formed the arbitrator ring, significantly influencing overall performance.

Consensus Mechanisms: Five consensus scenarios were tailored for each cluster:

- PBFT (universally across all nodes)
- SBFT (Extended Consensus, No Blockchain Virtualization)
- HotStuff for virtualized blockchain (segments and clusters)
- F-BFT (Lazy Path), an enhanced PBFT for virtualized blockchain
- F-BFT (FAST-RUN), Fast-HotStuff pipeline atop the virtualized blockchain system.

Data Collection Transactions were generated through APIs, and latency was gauged from transaction submission to consensus confirmation. Multiple iterations were executed for each scenario to ensure statistical robustness.

Performance Metrics: Latency, quantified in milliseconds, served as the primary performance metric. Additionally, CPU and memory usage were closely monitored for comprehensive resource consumption insights.

Outcomes: The results, graphically illustrated below, affirm the constructive impact of virtualization on performance enhancement. Latency was markedly curtailed compared to the use of non-virtualized P-BFT, with the best-case scenario demonstrating latency reduction by 5–6 times.

4.2 Comparative Analysis of Blockchain Virtualization Approaches

Blockchain virtualization, involving the creation of a "network of networks," has led to the emergence of various approaches aimed at improving scalability and interoperability. In addition to DGT's hierarchical network structure, other notable initiatives in this space include the Polkadot's parachains-based model 25 and Avalanche's multi-chain architecture 26. This section provides a comparative overview of these approaches, highlighting their distinctive features and potential implications (Table 1).

Discussion

While DGT introduces a novel approach by using clusters and segments for virtualized blockchain instances, Polkadot's parachains and Avalanche's multi-chain architecture also offer innovative solutions. Each approach has its own strengths and limitations, which need to be carefully considered based on the specific use case requirements. DGT's use of arbitrators to form segments represents an interesting departure from the conventional models, promising efficient resource utilization and tailored solutions for various applications. On the other hand, Polkadot's parachain model ensures strong interoperability, while Avalanche's multi-chain architecture capitalizes on the Avalanche protocol's strengths to enhance throughput and latency. The choice between these approaches ultimately depends on factors such as scalability needs, interoperability goals, and the nature of the applications to be supported.

Table 1. Comparative Overview.

Aspect	DGT	Polkadot	Avalanche
Network Topology	Hierarchical structure with clusters and segments forming independent blockchain instances	Central relay chain (parachains) communicating with heterogeneous and independent sharded chains	Multi-chain architecture comprising Exchange Chain (X-Chain), Contract Chain (C-Chain), and Platform Chain (P-Chain)
Consensus Mechanism	Two-level consensus with BFT clusters and PoS-based arbitrators	Relay chain using nominated Proof-of-Stake (NPoS) consensus	Avalanche protocol with multiple sub-protocols
Node Connection	Clusters and segments based on arbitration	Parachains connected to relay chain	Chains connected via the Avalanche protocol
Strengths	Efficient resource utilization due to arbitration-based segment formation	Strong interoperability between parachains	High throughput and low latency through Avalanche protocol

(continued)

Table 1. (*continued*)

Aspect	DGT	Polkadot	Avalanche
Limitations	Complexity in managing arbitrator rings	Dependency on the relay chain's availability	Sub-protocols can increase communication complexity
Prospects	Potential for diverse application scenarios with clusters and segments	Enhanced scalability through parallel processing	Continued protocol enhancements for improved performance

5 Conclusions and Future Directions: Unleashing the Potential of Blockchain Virtualization

In the journey to redefine the landscape of blockchain technology, this article has extensively explored the realm of blockchain virtualization with the Distributed Governance Technology (DGT) platform as a pivotal example. The innovative concept of blockchain virtualization, particularly in the context of hybrid networks, presents a transformative solution to the critical challenges facing traditional blockchain architectures. By abstracting the blockchain infrastructure, DGT introduces a paradigm shift that enables the creation and management of multiple virtual instances of blockchains on a shared physical blockchain network. This unique approach facilitates improved scalability, isolation, and resource allocation, addressing the limitations of conventional single-blockchain networks.

Experiment and Implications

The experiment conducted within the DGT environment provided illuminating insights into the tangible benefits of blockchain virtualization. The demonstration of reduced latency through virtualization, especially when implementing the Fast-RUN consensus option, showcased the potential to significantly enhance blockchain performance. This empirical evidence substantiates the promise of virtualization in ameliorating latency issues and thus cultivating a more efficient blockchain ecosystem.

Future Works

Moving forward, this exploration gives rise to new research objectives:

- **Security and Privacy Testing**: Future research should encompass rigorous testing of security and privacy aspects within a virtualized blockchain environment. As virtualization introduces novel dynamics, evaluating these dimensions becomes paramount to ensure the robustness and confidentiality of the system.
- **Impact on Deployment and Cloud Solutions**: The influence of blockchain virtualization on deployment methodologies and the evolution of cloud-based Blockchain-as-a-Service (BaaS) solutions presents a promising avenue. Virtualization enables more versatile and customized blockchain networks, propelling the evolution of cloud-based services and their alignment with diverse enterprise needs.

- **Interoperability and Network Compatibility**: Exploring the interplay of virtualized networks within a broader ecosystem remains an area of interest. How virtualized instances interact with other blockchain networks and legacy systems, and how standards are upheld, warrant comprehensive study.
- **Evolving Ecosystem**: As blockchain virtualization fosters scalability, reduces entry barriers for institutions, and introduces private transaction capabilities, it has the potential to revolutionize the blockchain landscape. Its adoption paves the way for more widespread institutional participation and real-world enterprise use cases.

References

1. Carrara, G.R., Burle, L.M., Medeiros, D.S.V., et al.: Consistency, availability, and partition tolerance in blockchain: a survey on the consensus mechanism over peer-to-peer networking. Ann. Telecommun. **75**, 163–174 (2020). https://doi.org/10.1007/s12243-020-00751-w
2. Fang, M., Liu, J.: Toward low-cost and stable blockchain networks. In: ICC 2020 - 2020 IEEE International Conference on Communications (ICC), Dublin, Ireland, 2020, pp. 1–6 (2020). https://doi.org/10.1109/ICC40277.2020.9148615
3. Zhang, R., Xue, R., Liu, L.: Security and Privacy on Blockchain. ACM Comput. Surv. **52**(3), 1−34 (2019). https://doi.org/10.1145/3316481
4. Khan, S.N., Loukil, F., Ghedira-Guegan, C., et al.: Blockchain smart contracts: applications, challenges, and future trends. Peer-to-Peer Netw. Appl. **14**, 2901–2925 (2021). https://doi.org/10.1007/s12083-021-01127-0
5. Wang, G., Wang, Q., Chen, S.: Exploring blockchains interoperability: a systematic survey. ACM Comput. Surv. **55**(13s), 1−38 (2023). https://doi.org/10.1145/3582882
6. Taskou, S.K., Rasti, M., Nardelli, P.H.J.: Blockchain function virtualization: a new approach for mobile networks beyond 5G. IEEE Netw. **36**(6), 134–141 (2022). https://doi.org/10.1109/MNET.009.2100473
7. Sharma, A.: Beyond Cryptocurrency - More To Blockchain (2020). https://doi.org/10.13140/RG.2.2.24976.23049
8. Yaga, D., Mell, P., Roby, N., Scarfone, K.: Blockchain Technology Overview, NISTIR 8202 (2019). https://doi.org/10.6028/NIST.IR.8202
9. ITU-T Focus Group on Application of Distributed Ledger Technology, Technical Specification FG DLT D3.1, Distributed ledger technology reference architecture (2019)
10. Khobragade, P., Turuk, A.K.: Blockchain consensus algorithms: a survey. In: Prieto, J., Benítez Martínez, F.L., Ferretti, S., Arroyo Guardeño, D., Tomás Nevado-Batalla, P. (eds.) Blockchain and Applications, 4th International Congress. BLOCKCHAIN 2022. Lecture Notes in Networks and Systems, vol. 595. Springer, Cham (2023). https://doi.org/10.1007/978-3-031-21229-1_19
11. Attamah, M., van Ditmarsch, H., Grossi, D., van der Hoek, W.: A framework for epistemic gossip protocols. In: Bulling, N. (eds.) Multi-Agent Systems. EUMAS 2014. LNCS, vol. 8953. Springer, Cham (2015). https://doi.org/10.1007/978-3-319-17130-2_13
12. Sahoo, S., Fajge, A.M., Halder, R., Cortesi, A.: A hierarchical and abstraction-based blockchain model. Appl. Sci. **9**(11), 2343 (2019). https://doi.org/10.3390/app9112343
13. Newell, J., Mamun, Q., Rehman, S., Islam, Md.: A Generalised Logical Layered Architecture for Blockchain Technology (2021)
14. Deloitte 2021 Global Blockchain Survey: Global Financial Services Industry Undergoing Seismic Shift; Banks Must Embrace Inevitable Digital Future
15. DGT Technical Documentation, Revision 21, (2023). https://dgtnetwork.gitbook.io/dgt-docs

16. Hammoudi, A., Khanfar, K.: OSI Model (2022)
17. Wang, Q., Li, R., Wang, Q., Chen, S., Ryan, M., Hardjono, T.: Exploring Web3 From the View of Blockchain (2022)
18. Uddin, M., Khalique, A., Jumani, A., Ullah, S.S.: Next-generation blockchain-enabled virtualized cloud security solutions: review and open challenges. Electron. **10**, 1–23 (2021). https://doi.org/10.3390/electronics10202493
19. Di Bona, G., Bracci, A., Perra, N., Latora, V., Baronchelli, A.: The decentralized evolution of decentralization across fields: from Governance to Blockchain (2022). https://doi.org/10.48550/arXiv.2207.14260
20. Bogdanov, A., et al.: Testing and comparative analysis of the F-BFT-based DLT solution. In: Gervasi, O., et al. Computational Science and Its Applications – ICCSA 2021. ICCSA 2021. LNCS, vol.12952. Springer, Cham (2021). https://doi.org/10.1007/978-3-030-86973-1_3
21. ISO 20022, Universal financial industry message scheme. https://www.iso20022.org/
22. Buchanan, W.: Zero-knowledge Proof (ZKP) and Privacy Preserving (2022). https://doi.org/10.1201/9781003337751-12
23. Jalalzai, M.M., Niu, J., Feng, C.: Fast-HotStuff: A Fast and Resilient HotStuff Protocol (2020)
24. Bogdanov A., Uteshev A., Khvatov V.: Error Detection in the Decentralized Voting Protocol, Computational Science and Its Applications – ICCSA 2019, https://doi.org/10.1007/978-3-030-24296-1_38
25. Abbas, H., Caprolu, M., Pietro, R.: Analysis of Polkadot: Architecture, Internals, and Contradictions (2022). https://doi.org/10.48550/arXiv.2207.14128
26. Tanana, D.: Avalanche blockchain protocol for distributed computing security. In: 2019 IEEE International Black Sea Conference on Communications and Networking (BlackSeaCom), pp.1–3. (2019) https://doi.org/10.1109/BlackSeaCom.2019.8812863

Property and Pixels: Redefining Real Estate in the Digital Era

Bang L. Khanh[1(✉)], Trinh. D. Phung[1], Triet M. Nguyen[1], Hong K. Vo[1], Khoa T. Dang[1], Phuc N. Trong[1], Ngan N. T. Kim[2], and N. H. Kha[2]

[1] FPT University, Can Tho city, Vietnam
banglkce160155@fpt.edu.vn
[2] FPT Polytecnic, Can Tho city, Vietnam

Abstract. This paper addresses the systemic inefficiencies of the traditional real estate system, such as manual processes, intermediary reliance, and lack of transparency, by exploring the integration of blockchain technology. We propose a paradigm shift in real estate transactions management through blockchain's decentralized nature, which enhances transparency, security, and efficiency. Our significant contribution is the development of an RSA-encrypted Non-Fungible Token (NFT) framework tailored for real estate transactions. This framework prioritizes security and privacy by using RSA encryption to protect sensitive transaction data and personal information, ensuring access only to authorized entities with corresponding private keys. We extend this security to image and text-based NFTs, ensuring robust property representation. Additionally, the framework's deployment across multiple Ethereum Virtual Machine (EVM)-supported platforms demonstrates its versatility and adaptability. Our research presents a groundbreaking approach in blockchain-based real estate transactions, offering a novel solution that mitigates risks associated with both traditional and digital methods in the real estate sector.

Keywords: Blockchain · Non-Fungible Tokens (NFTs) · Real Estate Management · RSA Encryption · Social Computing · InterPlanetary File System (IPFS) · Smart Contracts

1 Introduction

The traditional real estate system, while foundational to property ownership and transfer, has long been encumbered by a variety of systemic inefficiencies. At its core, the conventional process is mired in manual documentation, intermediaries, and a lack of transparency that often leads to protracted transaction times and increased susceptibility to fraud [4]. The reliance on paper-based records and in-person verifications not only adds layers of complexity but also creates opportunities for discrepancies and manipulation of critical documents. Such constraints not only impede the fluidity of property transactions but also

O. Gervasi et al. (Eds.): ICCSA 2024 Workshops, LNCS 14815, pp. 162–177, 2024.
https://doi.org/10.1007/978-3-031-65154-0_10

impact the overall dynamism of the real estate market [6]. Moreover, the traditional system's limitations are further exacerbated when it comes to cross-border transactions, where the involvement of multiple intermediaries, each with their own sets of rules and regulations, can significantly escalate costs and complicate due diligence processers [5]. In an increasingly globalized economy, these barriers present substantial challenges for investors and buyers looking to operate in international markets. The opacity of transactions and the centralized nature of record-keeping in such a system can also result in a lack of trust between parties, making the need for innovation in this sector both urgent and clear [21].

The advent of blockchain technology offers a promising solution to these entrenched challenges, presenting a paradigm shift in how real estate transactions can be managed. The decentralized nature of blockchain introduces a level of transparency and security hitherto unattainable, paving the way for a system where transactions are immutable, verifiable, and executed with unparalleled efficiency [13]. The integration of blockchain into real estate has the potential to not only streamline processes but also reduce the risk of fraud, eliminate unnecessary intermediaries, and open up the market to a broader range of participants on a global scale [2].

The intersection of blockchain technology and real estate has catalyzed a paradigm shift in how property transactions are conducted, managed, and recorded [10]. Emergent studies have been pivotal in mapping the contours of this transformation, delineating the benefits and outlining the challenges associated with blockchain implementation in the real estate domain. The pioneering work of [2,16,17], and [8] has collectively underscored the potential for blockchain to revolutionize real estate transactions by enhancing transparency, efficiency, and security, while simultaneously grappling with the impediments posed by inadequate legislative infrastructures and the complex technicalities of blockchain integration. These studies contribute to a nuanced understanding of blockchain's capabilities to facilitate more streamlined, secure, and cost-effective real estate transactions.

In tandem with these technological advancements, the realm of secure transactions and data storage in real estate has been the focus of significant scholarly attention. Innovations proposed by [1,9] have demonstrated the efficacy of integrating blockchain with cutting-edge encryption algorithms to create secure platforms for peer-to-peer real estate transactions. This body of work underpins the creation of a secure, interoperable framework that upholds the confidentiality of personal and financial details, a crucial consideration in the real estate sector. Adding to the corpus of blockchain real estate literature, [20,21], and [11] have introduced systems like 'BlockYards' and blockchain-based authentication schemes that aim to eradicate traditional land registry and contract management system inefficiencies. These systems are designed to ensure the integrity and immutability of asset transactions, fostering a conducive environment for trustworthy and transparent real estate dealings.

As the concept of tokenization and the use of Non-Fungible Tokens (NFTs) in real estate gain traction, studies such as [7,19], and [14] have become increasingly pertinent. They have laid the groundwork for frameworks that utilize blockchain technology to inject liquidity, transparency, and security into real estate investments and transactions, reshaping the industry to accommodate a more open, efficient, and secure market.

Amidst this backdrop of innovative research, our contribution stands out by addressing the imperative need for security and privacy in blockchain-based real estate platforms. Our study introduces an RSA-encrypted NFT framework for real estate transactions, aiming to bolster anonymity, transaction confidentiality, and interoperability. By leveraging RSA's cryptographic strength, we ensure that such data are securely encrypted, rendering them accessible only to authorized parties who possess the corresponding private keys. This methodology is crucial in mitigating risks such as data breaches and unauthorized access, which are prevalent concerns in digital transactions. Furthermore, our framework extends its security measures to the two most common types of NFTs used in real estate: images and text. By providing a detailed encryption process for both, we cater to the diverse needs of the real estate market, ensuring that all forms of property representation are securely managed and transferred. In addition to enhancing security and privacy, our use of NFTs in representing property titles offers several benefits. Each NFT serves as a unique and tamper-evident digital record of property titles, ensuring the authenticity and provenance of assets in the blockchain ledger. This approach significantly reinforces the trustworthiness and reliability of digital property records, a critical factor in real estate transactions. Moreover, to ascertain the effectiveness and applicability of our RSA-encrypted NFT framework, we conduct a comprehensive deployment across four Ethereum Virtual Machine (EVM)-supported platforms (i.e., BNB, Fantom, Celo, and Polygon). This extensive testing aims to identify the most suitable platform that aligns with our framework's objectives, taking into account factors such as transaction speed, cost-efficiency, and platform stability. By doing so, we provide a practical and versatile solution that can be adapted to various blockchain ecosystems, further emphasizing our framework's flexibility and adaptability.

Concluding our introduction, in the rest of the paper, the following sections of this paper will critically examine related work to position our contribution within the existing body of research; delineate our approach by detailing the RSA-encrypted NFT framework in Sect. 3; rigorously evaluate its performance across varied scenarios in Sect. 4; discuss the potential threats to its validity, and finally, synthesize our findings to draw meaningful conclusions in the last two sections.

2 Related Work

2.1 Blockchain Technology Implementation in Real Estate

In the burgeoning field of blockchain application in real estate, several studies have laid the groundwork for understanding and overcoming the challenges inherent in implementing this technology. The study by [2] delves into the potential for blockchain to enhance public administration, particularly in real estate registration in Kazakhstan. It underscores the technology's capacity to bolster transparency and efficiency while also serving as a tool to curb corruption and reduce transaction costs. However, the paper brings to light significant impediments such as inadequate legislative frameworks and the technical complexities of integrating blockchain with existing systems. Complementing this analysis, [17] argues for a balanced approach between public and private interests in the realm of real estate registration. The proposed measures aim to augment the reliability of real estate registers and secure property circulation through wider blockchain adoption. This study employs comparative legal research, legal modeling, and economic analysis of law to propose modernization vectors for real estate registration, including the innovative use of virtual and augmented reality technologies for property accounting.

Meanwhile, [16] provides an empirical basis for the discussion, examining the application of blockchain in the real estate sector through the study of existing practices and specific cases. This paper articulates the advantages and potential pitfalls of blockchain, highlighting the efficiency and security it brings to real estate transactions and its role in financing mechanisms. It suggests that blockchain technology streamlines real estate transactions, rendering them faster, more secure, and cost-effective. Lastly, [8] offers a unique perspective from Kosovo, exploring the factors that influence the adoption of blockchain in real estate transactions. Through a quantitative methodology involving a stratified probability sample of buyers and sellers, the study reveals that transparency and cost reduction are the most significant factors driving the intention to adopt blockchain. The paper posits that blockchain can facilitate transparent and errorless interactions in the real estate market, reduce costs by eliminating intermediaries, and increase trust between parties, thereby serving as a deterrent against corruption and money laundering in property investments.

These studies collectively indicate a growing recognition of blockchain's transformative potential in real estate transactions, while also acknowledging the challenges that need to be addressed for its successful implementation. They contribute to a comprehensive understanding of how blockchain technology can revolutionize the real estate sector by making transactions more transparent, secure, and efficient.

2.2 Blockchain for Secure Transactions and Data Storage

The integration of blockchain technology for enhancing security and data storage in real estate transactions has been a focal point of research, as evidenced by several studies that propose innovative solutions to address these challenges. In the work presented by [9], the fusion of blockchain with artificial intelligence is explored to develop a secure platform for peer-to-peer (P2P) real estate transactions. This study ventures into creating an encryption algorithm that is validated through blockchain's consensus process, specifically the practical Byzantine fault tolerance (PBFT) algorithm of Hyperledger, to safeguard the contract verification process. The utilization of virtual machines for blockchain real estate contracts and quantum cryptography for communication are among the methods applied to automate and test the security features. Additionally, [1] identifies the risk involved in sharing private and financial details within the real estate sector and proposes a blockchain architecture integrated with an optimized attribute-based encryption technique, termed as geometric octal zones distance estimation (GOZDE), to secure real estate information. The paper demonstrates the effectiveness of combining blockchain with the ABE technique to provide a potent solution for storing and transferring sensitive data securely.

Further contributions from [20] introduce 'BlockYards', a blockchain-powered system that seeks to establish a publicly accessible platform for verified real estate transactions on the Ethereum Blockchain. This system aims to address property scams and unauthorized claims by ensuring the integrity and immutability of asset transactions using consensus mechanisms. BlockYards also incorporates Machine Learning decision models to predict the real value of properties, thereby promoting accurate real estate price estimations and transparency in the online property market. The research presented by [21] delves into the authentication threats prevalent in traditional land registry systems and proposes a blockchain-based security scheme to enhance the authenticity and security of real estate land transaction data. By focusing on the shortcomings of centralized systems, the study suggests blockchain as a viable solution to the inherent issues of authentication in land transactions. Also, [11] addresses the risks associated with real estate contracts, especially online, by implementing a blockchain-based system using the zero-knowledge proof algorithm. The system aims to maintain the low cost and high efficiency of online transactions while ensuring the reliability and confidentiality of the contract information. By solving scalability issues with blockchain technology, this system offers a secure online contract management system that prevents fraud throughout the contract lifecycle.

These studies collectively underscore the potential of blockchain technology to revolutionize the security and data storage aspects of real estate transactions. They demonstrate how blockchain can be leveraged to develop secure, efficient, and transparent systems for managing sensitive transaction data in the real estate sector.

2.3 Blockchain and Real Estate Market/Platform Development

The transformative potential of blockchain technology in the real estate sector, specifically through the use of smart contracts, has been a significant point of focus in recent literature. The studies by [5,22], and [13] explore various facets of this integration, from conceptual frameworks to legal challenges and the broader implications for property rights. In the same spirit, The adoption of blockchain for market and platform development in real estate is not just theoretical but increasingly practical, as evidenced by recent research contributions in the field. These studies offer innovative approaches to redefining the real estate market, addressing long-standing challenges such as inefficiency, lack of transparency, and the high cost of transactions.

In the work of [3], blockchain technology is touted as a transformative force in real estate document storage. The study highlights the vulnerabilities of paper-based documentation to forgery and manipulation, especially in high-profile real estate transactions. The paper champions blockchain as a solution that maintains a complete history of real estate transactions and registrations via smart contracts. By digitizing property records, blockchain promises to expedite transaction times from months to mere seconds, heralding significant societal impacts. Building on this foundation, [12] proposes a Real Estate Transaction Trace (RETT) system model that revolutionizes the traditional real estate transaction process in Vietnam. The RETT model facilitates the management and tracking of real estate transactions across all participants, leveraging a blockchain network architecture, distributed ledger, and smart contracts. This system model aims to digitize assets, store decentralized transaction histories, and provide direct transactions between parties, thereby eliminating intermediaries and fostering mutual trust. Also, [18] presents a systematic literature review and thematic content analysis to understand recent blockchain developments and real-world applications in real estate. While the conceptual literature predicts blockchain as a disruptive technology for real estate, empirical applications suggest its incremental adoption in hybrid settings. The paper reveals that blockchain's conceptual benefits are yet to be fully realized empirically but notes the technology's potential to enhance efficiency, reduce transaction times, and increase security and trust, even in smaller-scale applications. Lastly, [15] explores the potential of blockchain in the commercial real estate market, recognizing the liquidity and global access issues that currently limit investor participation. The study concludes that blockchain and smart contracts can resolve classical real estate challenges, proposing a more stable-priced market that benefits tenants, owners, and investors alike.

2.4 Tokenization and NFTs in Real Estate

The topic of tokenization and the use of Non-Fungible Tokens (NFTs) in real estate has been a novel area of exploration, seeking to address the inherent limitations of real estate transactions and ownership records. The studies by [7,19], and [14] have contributed significantly to this emerging field, proposing frameworks that utilize blockchain technology to bring liquidity, transparency, and security to real estate investments and transactions.

[19] introduces a crypto NFT framework specifically tailored for real estate, aiming to tackle the prevalent issues of data availability and veracity. Traditional real estate transactions often suffer from outdated or manipulated data, which can lead to economic disparities. In a similar vein, [7] addresses the issue of liquidity in real estate investments. Real estate assets are typically illiquid compared to stocks, deterring many potential investors. The paper advocates for the tokenization of real estate using blockchain technology, which can transform real estate into a more liquid investment through the creation of security tokens representing fractional ownership. Finaly, [14] envisions a reshaped real estate industry through blockchain adoption. The current real estate industry,

while significant for economic growth, is riddled with complexities and a lack of transparency in transactions. Blockchain technology offers a solution by digitizing property-related information and hosting it on a decentralized database, reducing fraud and inaccuracies. This transformative approach aims to eliminate the potential for deception during sales, rentals, and leases, thereby achieving a digitized and trustworthy environment for all real estate operations.

2.5 Our Contribution

Security and privacy are paramount concerns in blockchain-based real estate platforms, where sensitive data and high-value transactions necessitate robust protection mechanisms. The study by [1] acknowledges the critical importance of preserving user identity and transaction confidentiality.

Our contribution to this landscape of blockchain real estate solutions lies in fortifying the security and privacy foundation laid by prior research. We introduce an RSA-encrypted NFT framework for real estate transactions that not only builds upon the necessity for anonymity and transaction confidentiality but also integrates the dimension of interoperability and transparency. In this version, we deploy the two versions of the NFT - image and text for the encryption process. By employing RSA encryption, our approach ensures that sensitive transaction data and personal information are securely encrypted and accessible only to authorized parties holding the corresponding private keys. Furthermore, the use of NFTs for property representation adds an extra layer of security, as each NFT is unique and tamper-evident within the blockchain, thereby ensuring the authenticity and provenance of property titles.

The combination of RSA encryption and NFTs creates a dual shield against both identity theft and transaction fraud, addressing the urgent need for enhanced security measures in the rapidly evolving real estate sector. Our methodology's deployment in a blockchain-based real estate platform not only promises improved privacy and security but also introduces benefits such as copyright protection and anti-tampering features. The result is a sophisticated, secure, and user-centric platform that significantly reduces the risks associated with traditional and digital real estate transactions.

3 Approach

Incorporating the principles of blockchain technology into real estate transaction processes, we introduce an approach that caters to the three main players: the landowner, agency, and buyer. Within this scheme, the agency acts as a trusted entity, orchestrating smart contracts and managing public keys, ensuring a seamless and secure transaction environment. The approach is divided into two intricate phases.

3.1 Phase 1: Blockchain-Based Identification of Prospective Buyers

Figure 1a presents our proposed architecture for the first phase real estate transactions by integrating blockchain technology and smart contracts, depicting a shift from the traditional model to a more streamlined and secure approach. The proposed architecture demonstrates a decentralized system where various stakeholders interact through a blockchain-enabled platform, fundamentally transforming the way property sales are conducted.

At the outset of the transaction, we have the land indicating its intrinsic and appreciative value. The owners, denoted as 'Owners A', initiate the sale. Unlike the traditional process, the owners here are equipped with digital tools that empower them to manage their transaction (i.e., generating as an NFT digital asset) with greater autonomy and efficiency. The central node in this architecture is the 'Agency', which, unlike traditional agencies, operates within a blockchain framework. The agency's role is redefined from being a mere intermediary to a facilitator of the smart contract execution. It provides the platform and the necessary blockchain infrastructure to execute the transaction, ensuring compliance, due diligence, and enforceability of the contract terms.

'Buyers B' are the counterparts in the transaction, seeking ownership of the land. In this new model, buyers interact with the blockchain-based system, where they can verify property details, ownership history, and transaction validity in a transparent and immutable manner. The buyer's engagement with the blockchain platform streamlines the process, enabling a faster and more secure transaction. A key component of this architecture is the 'Smart Contract', which encodes the terms of the sale agreed upon by the buyer and the seller. Smart contracts automate the transaction process, executing predefined conditions without the need for intermediary verification. This contract acts as a self-enforcing agreement that triggers actions such as transfer of ownership and release of funds upon satisfaction of contractual terms.

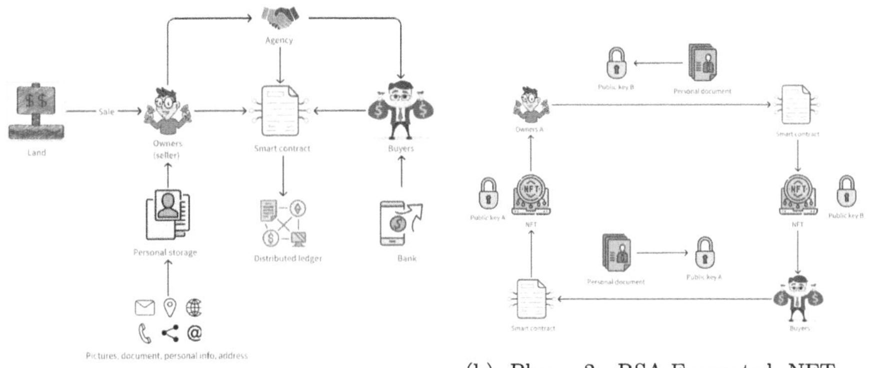

(a) Phase 1: Prospective buyer identification process

(b) Phase 2: RSA-Encrypted NFT Framework for Real Estate Transactions

Fig. 1. RSA&Blockchain-Enhanced Real Estate Transaction Architecture

Underpinning the entire system is the 'Distributed Ledger', a decentralized database that records all transactions across multiple sites, countries, or institutions. All participants have access to the distributed ledger and its immutable record of transactions, ensuring transparency and trust in the system. The ledger records every aspect of the transaction from the initial listing to the final transfer of ownership, including any amendments or disclosures required by law. The 'Personal Storage' represents a secure repository for the sellers, where they can store their personal information, property documents, pictures, and more. This storage is linked to the blockchain, providing a secure way to access and share information as needed for the transaction while maintaining privacy and control over personal data.

The architecture also includes traditional financial institutions like banks, which are now integrated into the blockchain system. Banks facilitate the financial aspect of the transaction, processing payments through secure channels that interface with the blockchain platform. The integration ensures that funds are transferred only upon fulfillment of the smart contract terms, thus safeguarding the interests of all parties involved.

3.2 Phase 2: Facilitating the Transaction Between Owner and Buyer

Figure 1b illustrates the second phase of our proposed approach to secure real estate transactions using a blockchain-based architecture that incorporates Non-Fungible Tokens (NFTs) encrypted with RSA public-key cryptography. This phase represents an advanced progression in the transaction process, harnessing the capabilities of blockchain to enhance security, transparency, and trust between parties involved in the real estate market.

The architecture delineates a flow of information and value facilitated by cryptographic principles and smart contract automation. At the beginning of this process, we see the owners, labeled 'Owners A', who are ready to engage in the sale of their property. They hold the initial key to unlocking the transaction process - their public key, symbolized by a lock with a keyhole. This public key is part of the RSA encryption mechanism that secures the transaction, ensuring that only the intended parties can access the sensitive information involved in the deal.

The owners' first step in this digital transaction is to encrypt their personal documents, which likely include identity verification, proof of property ownership, and legal documents that substantiate their right to sell the property. These documents are encrypted using the public key of the prospective buyer ('Public key B'), guaranteeing that the sensitive information contained within can only be decrypted and viewed by the holder of the corresponding private key, ensuring confidentiality and data protection. Once the personal documents are encrypted and thus secured, they are then tied to a smart contract. This smart contract is a self-executing contract with the terms of the agreement directly written into lines of code. It exists across the blockchain network; it is distributed and replicated on each node, making it immutable and tamper-proof. The smart contract contains logic that dictates the conditions under which the property will be sold, including verification of payment, transfer of ownership, and release of the encrypted documents to the buyer.

Central to this architecture is the use of NFTs. Here, an NFT is created to represent the property, which is a unique and non-interchangeable unit of data stored on the blockchain that certifies a digital asset to be unique and therefore not interchangeable. The NFT can represent the property's title deed, embodying the ownership rights that will be transferred from the seller to the buyer. The creation of the NFT itself is an action triggered by the smart contract, once all predefined conditions are met.

The NFT, once created, is encrypted using the seller's public key ('Public key A') to ensure that it remains secure and tamper-proof until the transaction conditions are fulfilled. This NFT is then sent to the buyer, but it remains encrypted - and thus, inaccessible - until the buyer fulfills their part of the contract, such as making the payment. The smart contract monitors for the fulfillment of these conditions and, upon their completion, will execute the transfer of the NFT to the buyer's control, simultaneously decrypting the NFT so that the buyer can assume ownership of the property. 'Buyers B' is depicted receiving the NFT, which signifies the completion of the transaction. At this point, the buyer has assurance of the authenticity and uniqueness of their new asset thanks to the blockchain's transparency and the NFT's non-fungibility. The RSA encryption ensures that during this transaction, the integrity and security of the personal documents and property rights were maintained.

This phase of the architecture showcases a sophisticated blend of blockchain technology, RSA encryption, and NFTs to create a seamless, secure real estate transaction process. It not only simplifies the transaction but also introduces a level of security and trust that traditional methods struggle to provide. By leveraging these technologies, we see the potential for a significant reduction in fraud, an increase in transaction speed, and a marked improvement in the accuracy of record-keeping within the real estate domain.

4 Evaluation Scenarios

4.1 Performance Evaluation of RSA-Encrypted NFT Framework

The evaluation of our RSA-encrypted NFT framework for real estate transactions, focusing on two distinct scenarios—a 120 KB image and the text "Hello, RSA encryption!"—offers an in-depth look into the framework's performance across three critical experiments: Generating RSA key, Encrypting, and Decrypting. This performance analysis provides valuable insights into the framework's efficiency and robustness, particularly when handling diverse data types commonly encountered in real estate transactions.

For the image data (Table 1), the RSA key generation process exhibited a consistent performance, with an average time of approximately 101.87 ms and a relatively stable standard deviation of 6.05 ms. This consistency in key generation is crucial, as it lays the foundation for a secure encryption environment. The

Table 1. RSA Key Generation, Encrypting, and Decrypting for Image Data

RSA with image (ms)	1	2	3	4	5	6	7	8	9	10
Generating RSA key	99.142	94.958	100.969	105.679	106.379	110.745	96.81	105.778	106.355	91.907
Encrypting image	77.859	72.325	70.633	80.696	73.735	70.382	74.502	78.371	77.778	77.077
Decrypting image	590.165	617.779	620.544	645.72	666.376	674.631	647.898	585.451	680.482	681.03

encryption of the image data, averaging around 75.34 ms, and a standard deviation of 3.53 ms, further demonstrates the framework's capability to efficiently handle larger and more complex data types. However, the decryption time for the image data was significantly higher, averaging at 641.01 ms. The higher standard deviation of 35.95 ms in this phase indicates a greater variability in processing times, likely attributable to the complexity and size of the image file.

In stark contrast, the text data "Hello, RSA encryption!" was processed much more swiftly, with an average processing time of just 5.50 ms (see Table 2). The standard deviation, although proportionally large relative to the mean time, was minimal in absolute terms at 3.03 ms, suggesting a fairly consistent performance across different instances.

Table 2. RSA Key Generation, Encrypting, and Decrypting for text

RSA with text (ms)	1	2	3	4	5	6	7	8	9	10
Generating RSA key	72.36	99.867	96.377	107.134	82.157	73.38	76.844	100.155	78.44	84.858
Encrypting text	0.162	0.166	0.175	0.157	0.18	0.159	0.137	0.147	0.145	0.151
Decrypting text	1.036	1.049	0.854	0.915	1.143	0.999	0.862	1.182	0.939	1.171

These findings underscore the framework's adaptability and scalability. The substantial disparity in processing times between the image and text data highlights the impact of data size on encryption and decryption efficiency. While the framework demonstrates excellent performance in key generation and text data processing, it also capably handles the more resource-intensive image data encryption and decryption processes. This balance of efficiency and reliability in handling varying data sizes is pivotal for its application in real estate transactions, where both images and textual data play significant roles.

Overall, the RSA-encrypted NFT framework presents a promising solution for securing real estate transactions, showcasing the ability to effectively manage diverse data types with varying complexities. Its performance in these evaluations indicates its potential to transform the landscape of real estate transactions, making them more secure, efficient, and adaptable to the evolving needs of the industry.

4.2 Land Certificate (i.e., NFT) Journey

As illustrated in Fig. 2, the first step involves the creation of the NFT corresponding to a real-estate certificate. During this phase, a smart contract function is called upon to mint the NFT, encapsulating within it all the relevant

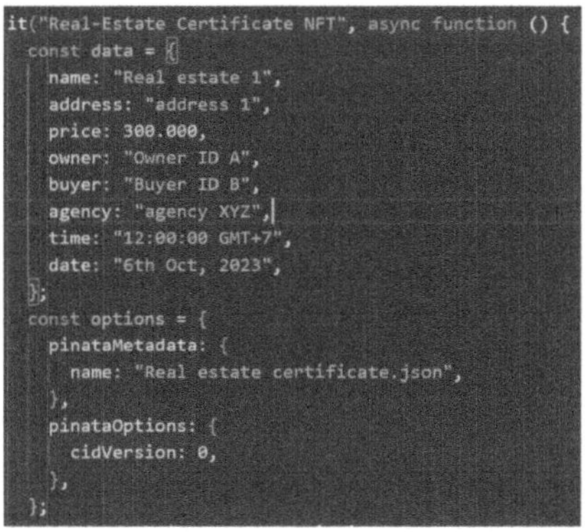

Fig. 2. Step 1: Real-Estate Certificate NFT

property information and attributes. The minting process is integral, serving as the genesis of the digital certificate that will represent the real estate asset on the blockchain.

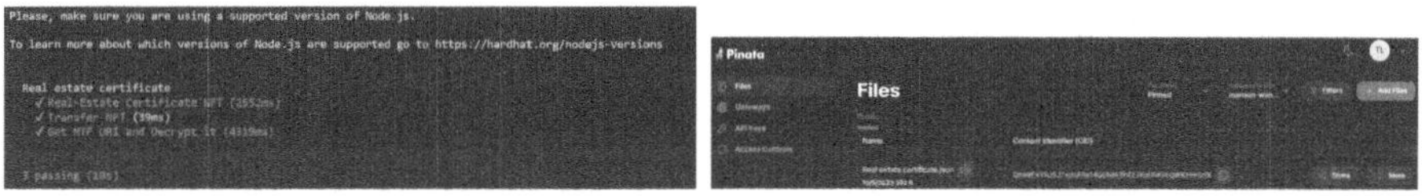

(a) Step 2: Hash key generation (b) Step 3: Uploading NFT to IPFS

Fig. 3. Land certificate (i.e., NFT) Journey in IPFS

In second step, Fig. 3a depicts the subsequent step where a unique hash key is generated. This hash key is fundamental to the NFT's identity, acting as a digital fingerprint that ensures the token's uniqueness and authenticity. The process of hash generation is a cryptographic measure that adds a layer of security, making it computationally infeasible to reverse-engineer or duplicate the NFT.

The journey continues with step three, as shown in Fig. 3b, where the NFT, now associated with a unique hash key, is uploaded to the IPFS[1]. This decentralized storage solution ensures that the NFT's data remains persistent and tamper-proof. By leveraging the IPFS, we ensure that the real estate certificate's digital representation is not confined to a single point of failure and is resilient against data loss or censorship.

Finally, as visualized in Fig. 4, addresses the security concerns related to unauthorized access. In this step, mechanisms are put in place to prevent unauthorized parties from accessing the NFT data stored on IPFS platforms like Pinata. This is achieved through access control measures that restrict data

[1] Pinata platform: https://www.pinata.cloud/.

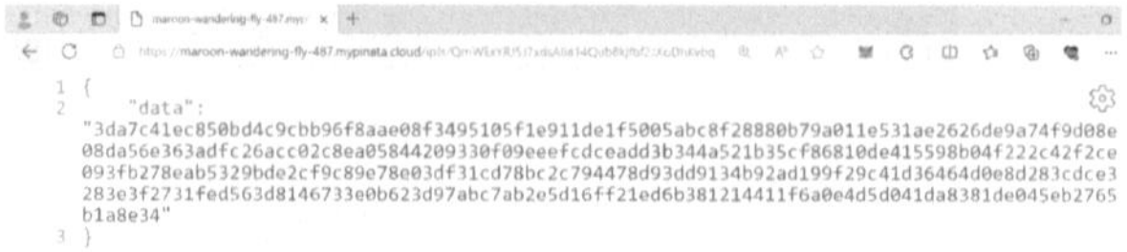

Fig. 4. Step 4: The unauthorized on IPFS - e.g., Pinata

retrieval to entities possessing the correct authorization credentials, such as private keys or access tokens. For the proof-of-concept, our code for implementation and deployment is presented in our GitHub repositories[2].

4.3 Smart Contract Deployment on the Four EVM-Supported Platforms

Smart Contract Deployment. The landscape of blockchain technology has seen the emergence of various platforms, each with distinct offerings and enhancements. Platforms compatible with the Ethereum Virtual Machine (EVM) stand out for their widespread adoption and unique attributes. These platforms, while maintaining Ethereum's compatibility, distinguish themselves with specialized features and economic frameworks.

In our research, we selected four leading EVM-compatible platforms for the deployment of our smart contract: Binance Smart Chain (BNB Smart Chain), Polygon, Fantom, and Celo. These platforms were chosen based on their prominence and potential within the blockchain environment. The deployment process across these platforms is transparent and can be verified through their respective blockchain explorers. In each platform, e scrutinized three core functionalities (transaction/data creation, mint, and transfer NFT) of the smart contract in real-estate scenarios.

Transaction Fee Analysis. Although the functionalities were consistent across all platforms, the cost implications varied. A key factor in determining a platform's economic suitability is its transaction fee structure. We conducted a detailed comparative analysis of these fees, examining the cost of deploying smart contracts and executing specific functions on each platform. This analysis provides a critical overview of the financial aspects of utilizing these blockchain environments for real estate-related smart contracts.

Among the evaluated EVM-supported platforms shown in Table 3, Fantom emerges as the most suitable for our RSA-encrypted NFT framework when considering the balance between cost-efficiency and functionality. The transaction fees on Fantom for contract creation, NFT minting, and NFT transfers are significantly lower than those on the BNB Smart Chain, Polygon, and Celo, with costs being mere fractions of a dollar. This economical fee structure makes Fantom an

[2] Since the double-blind of the manuscript, we will provide our code when it's public.

Table 3. Transaction fee

	Contract Creation	Create NFT	Transfer NFT
BNB Smart Chain	0.027311 BNB ($8.33)	0.00109162 BNB ($0.33)	0.00056991 BNB ($0.17)
Fantom	0.0095767 FTM ($0.003)	0.000405167 FTM ($0.000127)	0.0002380105 FTM ($0.000075)
Polygon	0.0068405000328344 MATIC ($0.01)	0.000289405001273382 MATIC($0.00)	0.000170007500748033 MATIC ($0.00)
Celo	0.00709722 CELO ($0.004)	0.0002840812 CELO ($0.000)	0.0001554878 CELO ($0.000)

attractive option for deploying smart contracts, particularly in scenarios where multiple transactions and operations are anticipated. Furthermore, the minimal fees associated with NFT creation and transfer on Fantom can facilitate a more accessible and widespread adoption of blockchain technology in the real estate domain.

5 Threats to Validity

The performance evaluation, while comprehensive, points to potential constraints that could influence the framework's applicability in real-world scenarios.

Firstly, the variability in decryption times, especially for image data, may present a threat to the framework's validity. This variability could stem from factors such as computational limitations of the test environment, network latency, or inefficiencies in the encryption algorithm itself when scaling to larger data sets. Such discrepancies could impact the user experience, particularly in real estate transactions where time-sensitive operations are common. Secondly, the framework's reliance on the RSA encryption algorithm, while robust, may not be as efficient when compared to more contemporary cryptographic methods. RSA, being one of the earliest public-key cryptosystems, may not offer the same level of performance as newer algorithms designed with modern computational capabilities and security threats in mind. This aspect suggests a potential limitation in the framework's long-term viability as cryptographic standards evolve.

Furthermore, the deployment of smart contracts across various EVM-supported platforms revealed significant differences in transaction fees, which translate to economic implications for users. While Fantom emerged as the most cost-effective platform, this may not hold true under all conditions, especially as network congestion and demand for blockchain space fluctuate. The economic viability of deploying our framework is thus subject to market dynamics and platform-specific fee structures, which could limit its accessibility for some users. Another limitation pertains to the generalizability of our findings. The platforms selected for this study were chosen based on their prominence within the blockchain ecosystem. However, there are numerous other platforms with different configurations and consensus mechanisms that may offer distinct advantages or drawbacks. The performance and economic feasibility of deploying our framework on these alternative platforms remain untested, which poses a limitation to the universal applicability of our results. Lastly, as blockchain technology rapidly evolves, there may be unforeseen advancements or shifts in the regulatory landscape that could affect the deployment and functionality of our framework. Legal and compliance issues, particularly in the complex and regionally diverse field of real estate, may present additional hurdles that need to be navigated carefully.

In future work, addressing these threats to validity and limitations will be crucial. This may involve optimizing the encryption process for large datasets, exploring alternative cryptographic solutions, and expanding the scope of deployment platforms for broader testing. Additionally, staying abreast of regulatory changes and market conditions will be vital to ensure the framework remains both compliant and economically viable for widespread adoption.

6 Conclusion

Our study introduces an approach in blockchain applications for real estate as well as an RSA-encrypted NFT framework that addresses critical needs for security, privacy, and interoperability in real estate transactions. By integrating RSA encryption, we ensure the secure encryption of sensitive data, accessible exclusively to entities with the corresponding private keys. This approach not only enhances data protection but also supports the diverse needs of the real estate market through the encryption of both image and text-based NFTs. The use of NFTs in our framework further strengthens the system, offering a secure and transparent method for representing property titles digitally. Our extensive testing across various EVM-supported platforms demonstrates the framework's adaptability and efficiency, highlighting its potential to be a versatile solution in different blockchain ecosystems. This research contributes to the growing body of literature on blockchain technology in real estate and sets a new standard for secure, efficient, and transparent real estate transactions.

References

1. AbdulKader, M.M., et al.: An efficient geometric octal zones distance estimation and attribute-based encryption for secure transfer of sensitive data. Telecommun. Syst. **84**(2), 251–270 (2023)
2. Akhmetbek, Y., et al.: Opportunities and barriers of using blockchain in public administration: the case of real estate registration in Kazakhstan. Network of Institutes and Schools of Public Administration in Central and Eastern Europe. NISPAcee J. Publ. Adm. Policy **14**(2), 41–64 (2021)
3. Anandan, A.K., et al.: Revamping real estate document storage with blockchain. Int. J. Blockchains Cryptocurr. **1**(4), 342–364 (2020)
4. Djursén, L., Björk, T.: Blockchain adoption is an evolution–not a revolution:: advantages and challenges of blockchain in real estate transaction in Sweden (2022)
5. Garcia-Teruel, R.M.: Legal challenges and opportunities of blockchain technology in the real estate sector. J. Property Plann. Environ. Law **12**(2), 129–145 (2020)
6. Gotham, K.F.: The secondary circuit of capital reconsidered: globalization and the us real estate sector. Am. J. Sociol. **112**(1), 231–275 (2006)

7. Gupta, A., Rathod, J., Patel, D., Bothra, J., Shanbhag, S., Bhalerao, T.: Tokenization of real estate using blockchain technology. In: Zhou, J., et al. (eds.) ACNS 2020. LNCS, vol. 12418, pp. 77–90. Springer, Cham (2020). https://doi.org/10.1007/978-3-030-61638-0_5
8. Hoxha, V., Sadiku, S.: Study of factors influencing the decision to adopt the blockchain technology in real estate transactions in Kosovo. Property Manag. **37**(5), 684–700 (2019)
9. Huh, J.H., et al.: Verification plan using neural algorithm blockchain smart contract for secure p2p real estate transactions. Electronics **9**(6) (2020)
10. Hung, N., et al.: Revolutionizing real estate: a blockchain, NFT, and IPFS multi-platform approach. In: Delir Haghighi, P., et al. (eds.) iiWAS 2023. LNCS, vol. 14416, pp. 68–73. Springer, Cham (2023). https://doi.org/10.1007/978-3-031-48316-5_10
11. Jeong, S., Ahn, B.: Implementation of real estate contract system using zero knowledge proof algorithm based blockchain. J. Supercomputing **77**(10), 11881–11893 (2021)
12. Khoa Tan, V., Nguyen, T.: The real estate transaction trace system model based on ethereum blockchain platform. In: 2022 14th International Conference on Computer and Automation Engineering (ICCAE), pp. 173–177 (2022)
13. Konashevych, O.: Constraints and benefits of the blockchain use for real estate and property rights. J. Property Plann. Environ. Law **12**(2), 109–127 (2020)
14. Krupa, K.S.J., Akhil, M.S.: Reshaping the real estate industry using blockchain. In: Sridhar, V., Padma, M.C., Rao, K.A.R. (eds.) Emerging Research in Electronics, Computer Science and Technology. LNEE, vol. 545, pp. 255–263. Springer, Singapore (2019). https://doi.org/10.1007/978-981-13-5802-9_24
15. Latifi, S., et al.: Blockchain-based real estate market: One method for applying blockchain technology in commercial real estate market. In: 2019 IEEE International Conference on Blockchain (Blockchain), pp. 528–535 (2019)
16. Pankratov, E., et al.: The blockchain technology in real estate sector: experience and prospects. IOP Conf. Ser. Mater. Sci. Eng. **869**(6), 062010 (2020)
17. Podshivalov, T.P.: Improving implementation of the blockchain technology in real estate registration. J. High Technol. Manag. Res. **33**(2), 100440 (2022)
18. Saari, A., et al.: Blockchain in real estate: recent developments and empirical applications. Land Use Policy **121**, 106334 (2022)
19. Serrano, W.: Real estate tokenisation via non fungible tokens. In: The 2022 4th International Conference on Blockchain Technology, pp. 81–87. Association for Computing Machinery (2022)
20. Sheikh, A., et al.: Blockyards: a blockchain-powered system for secure real estate transactions. Int. J. Emerg. Eng. Technol. **2**(1), 30–34 (2023)
21. Shuaib, M., Alam, S., Daud, S.M.: Improving the authenticity of real estate land transaction data using blockchain-based security scheme. In: Anbar, M., Abdullah, N., Manickam, S. (eds.) ACeS 2020. CCIS, vol. 1347, pp. 3–10. Springer, Singapore (2021). https://doi.org/10.1007/978-981-33-6835-4_1
22. Ullah, F., et al.: A conceptual framework for blockchain smart contract adoption to manage real estate deals in smart cities. Neural Comput. Appl. **35**(7), 5033–5054 (2023)

Systematic Mapping Study: Blockchain Applied to Healthcare

Vitor Gonçalez Lindbergh(✉) and Itamir de Morais Barroca Filho

Federal University of Rio Grande do Norte, Digital Metropolis Institute, Natal, Rio Grande do Norte, Brazil

vitor.goncalez.054@ufrn.edu.br, itamir.filho@ufrn.br

Abstract. This study presents a systematic mapping of Blockchain technology in healthcare, aiming to provide an overview of the field and identify areas for future research. The research focuses on blockchain's characteristics, problems, platforms, and challenges in healthcare applications. An extensive search in the Scopus database resulted in 35 selected publications, which were analyzed to extract data. Findings highlight blockchain's transformative potential in healthcare, characterized by decentralized architecture, data security, and interoperability. The extracted data includes platforms and technologies used for architecture, engineering, and development of blockchain applications. Key challenges identified are scalability, interoperability, privacy concerns, and regulatory compliance. The study underscores blockchain's promise to improve healthcare data storage, sharing, and management but also emphasizes the need to address technical and regulatory challenges. It suggests a collaborative approach involving diverse stakeholders to optimize blockchain's healthcare implementation. The research is limited by its technical focus, potentially overlooking broader challenges in policy and regulations.

Keywords: Blockchain Healthcare · Blockchain Technology · Smart Contracts · DLT in Medicine · EHR Blockchain · Medical Data Interoperability · Healthcare Data Privacy

1 Introduction

The healthcare sector, a prime target for cybercriminals, has seen costly cyberattacks in the U.S., with breaches like Anthem Inc.'s affecting 78.8 million records. These attacks cause financial loss and jeopardize patient health when medical records become inaccessible. Healthcare organizations globally face numerous cyberattacks, particularly on networks and applications. Small healthcare entities often underestimate cybercrime risks and neglect cybersecurity, making them more susceptible. According to 2022 research, small healthcare organizations were twice as likely to be hit with cyberattacks. The most frequent causes of healthcare data breaches in the U.S. are hacking and IT security incidents, followed by unauthorized access or disclosure of sensitive information [31].

O. Gervasi et al. (Eds.): ICCSA 2024 Workshops, LNCS 14815, pp. 178–195, 2024.
https://doi.org/10.1007/978-3-031-65154-0_11

With the advent of big data, the size and complexity of healthcare records are increasing, and they are still not optimized. The security of healthcare records is becoming increasingly crucial for protecting data from security breaches and criminal activity. If unauthorized users can gain access to patient data, it can be sold or leaked to the market, with patients' personal information being revealed to anyone with access [40].

Healthcare data requires a high level of security and privacy. Privacy refers to persons having the right to allow or disclose personal information to others. Data must always be free of threats and secure at all times. If these conditions are not met, the technologies used may not function correctly or be deemed reliable [40].

In this current context, constant care and attention to the data involved in the health sector are necessary. Technology advancement must benefit society. The application and feasibility of these new technologies must be studied and tested to bring greater security to all parties involved, be they hospitals, patients, doctors, or employees.

Blockchain is a technology that ensures data storage and transmission, is transparent and secure, and works without a central control entity. Being secured, decentralized, and distributed, Blockchain has become extremely popular in practically all domains. There is no need for a central authority to govern the network because it is decentralized. To obtain agreement among nodes, data are archived via a consensus process. The ledger is distributed, and it is maintained by all of the network's nodes. Blockchain security is achieved by many concepts, including cryptography, consensus mechanisms, immutability, replication, and data traceability [3].

In this research, a systematic mapping study is utilized to explore the use of Blockchain technology in Healthcare. While a systematic review is recommended to understand the current evidence on the subject, we initiate with a systematic mapping to gain a broad understanding of the field, as proposed by Petersen et al. [30].

Systematic Mapping Studies are designed to provide a broad overview of a research area, establish if research evidence exists on a topic, and indicate the quantity of the evidence. The mapping study results can identify areas suitable for conducting Systematic Literature Reviews and areas where a primary study is more appropriate [19].

The main goal of a Systematic Mapping study is to provide an overview of a research area and identify the quantity and type of research and results available within it [30]. Therefore, the systematic study encompasses a broader scope, making it suitable for preliminary exploration of a particular topic. Filtering research and papers based on research questions to extract, classify, and categorize data.

2 Method

This study aims to collect information regarding the use of blockchain technology in healthcare. This information is collected through previously defined research questions, which will direct the data collection to answer them. In this way, we seek to develop a state-of-the-art regarding the technology applied in the area and its future trends.

The methodology proposed [30] is applied to this study, which consists of developing a systematic mapping. A systematic mapping study provides a structure of the type of research reports and results that have been published by categorizing them. It often gives a visual summary, the map, of its results. It requires less effort while providing a more coarse-grained overview.

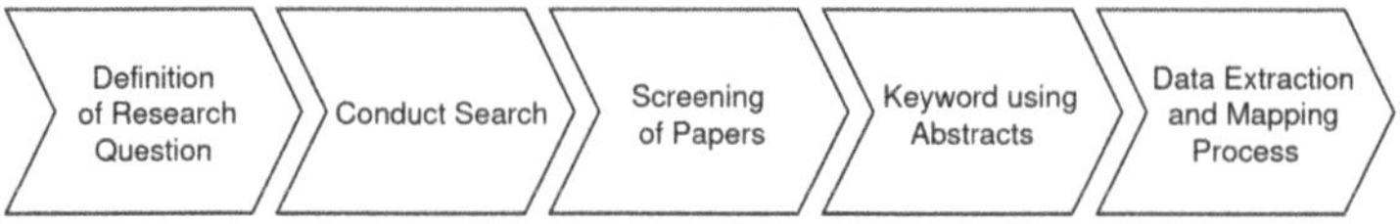

Fig. 1. The Systematic Mapping Process.

In the model presented in Fig. 1, the first step consists of defining the research questions. The second step is to query a database using a search string. Third, with a number of results returned, papers are screened. Fourth, a selection is done by reading research abstracts without going deeper into the work. Finally, data extraction is done with analysis and deepening in the remaining selected research.

Following this process, divided into stages, the search is expected to be directed to papers, works, and research that will accurately answer the defined questions.

2.1 Research Questions

Research questions must be elaborated as the first step to achieving the main objectives of systematic mapping research. These will serve as a study guide in search of the answers. The research questions addressed by this study are:

RQ1: *What are the main characteristics of healthcare applications based on blockchain?*

RQ2: *What problems do blockchain-based applications try to solve in healthcare?*

RQ3: *What are the blockchain platforms used in blockchain applications for healthcare?*

RQ4: *What are the challenges related to healthcare applications based on blockchain?*

While RQ1 and RQ2 are more general regarding the state of blockchain technologies today and what is expected in the future, RQ3 and RQ4 focus on more technical requirements regarding application development.

Search Process. The Scopus search base was used because it is one of the main research sources for the Computer Science subject area. Using the search string, quantitative information was collected regarding the area, type, and year of publication.

The search string filter was entered with search within Keywords. Results include publications in conferences, books, journals, magazines, etc. No year of publication range was added.

Despite having generic questions regarding definitions and challenges, the objective was to restrict the search through keywords to practical work involving architecture, engineering, and software development. For this, keyword categories were divided and defined:

- Technology.
  - Goal of Search: Related to blockchain technology.
  - Keywords: "blockchain" OR "DLT" OR "distributed ledger" OR "distributed ledger technology" OR "shared ledger"
- Development.
  - Goal of Search: Development-related search.
  - Keywords: "application" OR "architecture" OR "software" OR "system" OR "technology"
- Programming.
  - Goal of Search: Technical details of blockchain development and programming.
  - Keywords: "smart contract" OR "chaincode"
- Area.
  - Goal of Search: Related to the healthcare.
  - Keywords: "healthcare" OR "EHR" OR "EMR" OR "PHR" OR "electronic health record" OR "electronic medical records" OR "health" OR "personal health record"

The technology and area keyword categories must be clear, as they are the main themes of this work. The development category focuses on practical articles that encompass engineering and development. Programming focuses on specific technical details of blockchain development.

Contextualizing the keywords in the programming category: A smart contract is a computer program that stores rules for negotiating the terms of a contract. Programs can autonomously verify and execute contract-related agreements, reducing the cost of constructing and managing a centralized database [16]. In other words, smart contracts are how to program business rules on the blockchain. These rules run automatically as scheduled events and triggers occur. Chaincode is how smart contracts are called on the Hyperledger blockchain platforms. Smart contracts and chaincode are synonymous.

The search string is defined: ("blockchain" OR "DLT" OR "distributed ledger" OR "distributed ledger technology" OR "shared ledger") AND ("application" OR "architecture" OR "software" OR "system" OR "technology") AND ("smart contract" OR "chaincode") AND ("healthcare" OR "EHR" OR "EMR" OR "PHR" OR "electronic health record" OR "electronic medical records" OR "health" OR "personal health record")

Inclusion and Exclusion Criteria. The process of selecting articles involved eliminating those that did not fully address the research questions, aiming to curate a collection that aligns with the goals of this study. For this to be achieved, the exclusion criteria used were removing articles that do not address the search string, are not written in English, are not focused on infrastructure or blockchain technology, and have fewer than 5 pages. No date filter was applied, as the work intends to be as broad as possible, and the blockchain technology is still very recent [26].

Quality Assessment. According to CRD Guidelines and the Cochrane Reviewers' Handbook [19], the purpose of asserting a quality level for the studies is to minimize bias and maximize internal and external validity. Presenting the following points:

- Bias (Systematic error): A tendency to produce results that depart systematically from the 'true' results. Unbiased results are internally valid.
- Internal validity (Validity): The extent to which the design and conduct of the study are likely to prevent systematic error. Internal validity is a prerequisite for external validity.
- External validity (Applicability): The extent to which the effects observed in the study apply outside the study.

Detailed quality assessments are usually based on "quality instruments," which are checklists of factors that must be evaluated for each study. If quality items within a checklist are assigned numerical scales, numerical quality assessments can be obtained. Checklists are also developed by considering bias and validity problems that can occur at the different stages in an empirical study: Design, Conduct, Analysis, and Conclusions [19].

For the quality checklist, the following questions are defined [25]:

- Does the article clearly describe the purpose of the research?
- Does the article describe the literature review, background, or context?
- Does the article present related work?
- Does the article present an architecture proposal or a research methodology?
- Does the article contain research results?
- Does the article present a conclusion?

Data Collection. The data extracted to categorize the articles were authors, application context, publication year, journal, and keywords. As inputs for the research questions, the extracted data includes modern healthcare applications problems and challenges, blockchain platforms experimented with, blockchain applications and architecture definition and main characteristics, the technologies and frameworks used for developing blockchain in healthcare, and blockchain challenges that are yet to be overcome.

3 Results

This topic provides a comprehensive summary of the study's outcomes. It details every phase of its implementation and offers a broad summary of the articles and papers that were fundamental in addressing the research questions. That includes the stages for the selection, the articles list, publication year, and the word cloud of the articles' keywords.

3.1 Search Results

The research process is divided into 4 stages, as shown in Fig. 2.

In the first stage of the research, 364 works were obtained in the query result. In these, we applied the exclusion criteria of less than 5 pages, duplicated, not written in English, and out of the blockchain technology application context. In the second stage, the titles and abstracts of 190 works were read and analyzed, returning 46 publications to stage 3. In stage 3, the quality checklist was applied with a score, and 1 point was assigned to each question. Only studies that completed the entire quality checklist, with maximum marks (score = 6), were selected.

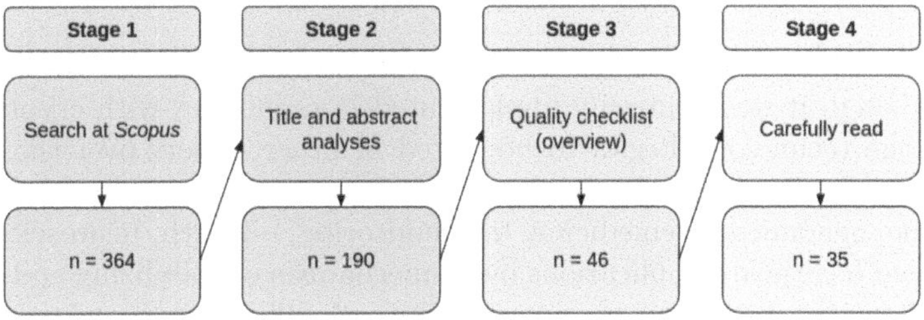

Fig. 2. Stages of the paper selection process.

In stage 4, the last one, all 35 selected articles and conference papers were carefully read and used to answer the defined research questions.

Articles list: Google sheets docs

3.2 Papers Overview

After 4 stages of the research process, this topic provides information about the 35 selected works.

Regarding the publication type of the papers, 86% of them are articles, and 14% are conference papers. As presented in Fig. 3, the data covers articles and papers from 2018 to 2023, reflecting a small range of publication timelines. Notably, there is a progressive increase in the number of publications each year from 2018 through 2022, starting with one article in 2018 and peaking at twelve in 2022. It is worth noting that this research was carried out in the second half of 2023. This must be considered when analyzing the number of articles selected from 2023.

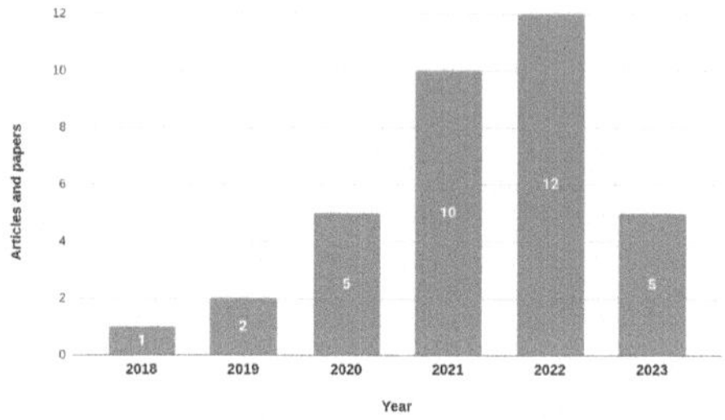

Fig. 3. Distribution of the selected works by year of publication.

Remarkably, the number of publications on the subject has increased in recent years. Although it was primarily implemented in economics with cryptocurrencies [26], the technology began to be tested in other sectors over the last few years, including the biomedical area. Blockchain technology can be witnessed in medicine, genomics, telemedicine, telemonitoring, e-health, neuroscience, and personalized healthcare applications by its mechanism of stabilizing and securing the data set with which users can interact through different types of transactions [32]. With greater popularity in the sector, more use cases are discovered, and technologies, frameworks, and tools are developed.

A word cloud was created with all the keywords extracted from the selected articles, shown in Fig. 4.

All works were developed in the health area and classified by specific themes to address blockchain technology, as shown in Table 1: Data storage and sharing, Internet of Things (IoT), 5G network, and machine learning.

This classification was made to categorize areas of blockchain research in healthcare: Research focused on blockchain and its data storage and sharing characteristics or its joint application with other information technology topics, such as networks or artificial intelligence. It is categorized by the level of detail that each work addresses each of these topics. As blockchain technology, all articles deal with security and data sharing, but if emphasis is placed on applications focused on sensors, for example, the research was classified in the IoT category.

Fig. 4. Word cloud generated from the keywords of all selected works.

The works in the"Data storage and sharing" category address the development of applications in healthcare and specific characteristics of blockchain. These characteristics deal with how data is stored and shared in blockchain systems, permissions and access control, encryption, consensus mechanism, and network performance.

The articles categorized as "Internet of Things (IoT)" address blockchain-based applications and architecture to process, store, and manage healthcare data from sensors and devices. The article [13] approaches blockchain to secure network slicing (NS) in e-health environments and [38] attends a blockchain-based privacy-preserving support vector machine (SVM) classification for a COVID-19 Healthcare System, a machine learning topic.

4 Discussion

This research focused on the architecture, engineering, and development of blockchain applications in healthcare. In addition to answering blockchain's definitions, problems, and challenges, we sought information about how and what is being used in its development, obtaining details of applied technologies.

Table 1. Selected articles categories by the context of the application.

Category	Articles
Data storage and sharing	[1,2,4–12,15–18,23,24,27,29,34,35,37,39–41].
Internet of Things (IoT)	[3,14,20–22,28,33,36].
5G network	[13].
Machine learning	[38]

RQ1: What Are the Main Characteristics of Healthcare Applications Based on Blockchain? The main characteristics of healthcare applications based on blockchain, as derived from the provided answers, can be summarized under several key themes as follows.

Distributed Architecture and Decentralization: Blockchain's decentralized nature eliminates reliance on central authorities, reducing single points of failure and bottlenecks [5,15,36,39]. This architecture ensures data consistency and integrity by storing copies of data across multiple nodes [13,39].

Data Security and Privacy: Blockchain technology enhances data security through cryptographic algorithms and secure, tamper-proof data storage [9,23,34,41]. Smart contracts and distributed ledgers provide robust access control, ensuring that only authorized entities can access sensitive medical data [7,29,35,38].

Immutability and Traceability: Once data is recorded on a blockchain, it cannot be altered or deleted, ensuring the integrity and non-repudiation of medical records [6,8,17,28]. This feature is crucial for the provenance of records and patient-doctor interactions [23,27].

Data Sharing and Interoperability: Blockchain facilitates the secure and efficient exchange of health records among various stakeholders, promoting interoperability and patient-centric data management [8,10,14,16]. This aspect is especially relevant for integrating disparate systems and devices in the Internet of Medical Things (IoMT) [3,20,33].

Real-time Processing and Efficiency: Blockchain applications can support real-time disease detection, process scheduling, and efficient management of medical data [18,21,40]. The use of smart contracts automates various processes in the blockchain, enhancing the overall efficiency of healthcare systems [11,22,24].

Compliance and Legal Considerations: Blockchain applications can aid in meeting compliance requirements, such as those under the General Data Protection Regulation (GDPR), by providing transparent, verifiable, and secure data handling mechanisms [1,4,12].

Cost-Effectiveness and Scalability: By eliminating intermediaries and administrative overhead, blockchain can reduce operational costs and optimize processes in healthcare [2,8,40]. Combining blockchain with technologies like IPFS (InterPlanetary File System) addresses scalability issues [2,3,17].

Support for Clinical Research and Trials: Blockchain can facilitate clinical trial accountability, auditability, and data sharing, offering a trusted environment for medical research and large-scale data analysis [12,15].

Healthcare applications based on blockchain offer a transformative approach to managing health data. They enhance data security, integrity, and accessibility while providing a decentralized framework that fosters interoperability, real-time processing, cost-effectiveness, and support for legal compliance and research initiatives.

RQ2: What Problems Do Blockchain-Based Applications Try to Solve in Healthcare? Blockchain-based applications in healthcare are designed to address a variety of critical issues:

Privacy and Data Transparency: One of the primary issues blockchain aims to solve is the lack of transparency in how health data is collected, stored, and used [5,23]. This includes addressing the need for privacy and security in health data sharing and ensuring individual consent is explicitly obtained [5,36].

Fragmentation of Health Data: Patient information is often scattered across different locations and organizations, leading to fragmented, duplicated, and mismatched records [7,15,37]. Blockchain seeks to unify these disparate data sources, allowing for more coherent and efficient data management.

Security Concerns in Data Sharing: The theft of Electronic Health Records (EHRs) and data breaches are significant concerns in the current system due to poor security and policy enforcement [8,10,16]. Blockchain provides a more secure and reliable platform for sharing sensitive health information.

Centralization and Single Points of Failure: Traditional health informatics systems and IoT networks suffer from centralization, leading to single points of failure and control, which blockchain technology aims to eliminate [3,9,11,12,20,27,35,39].

Interoperability and Standardization Issues: Existing systems often lack uniform storage standards and efficient data exchange methods, resulting in silos of healthcare information [14,17,37,39]. Blockchain facilitates better interoperability and standardization across different healthcare systems.

Authenticity and Integrity of Medical Records: Blockchain applications strive to ensure the integrity and authenticity of medical records and prescriptions to prevent illegal or unauthorized use [1,6,11,29].

Efficiency and Cost-Effectiveness in Health Care Management: Issues like the high cost of healthcare services, inefficient task scheduling, and resource allocation in IoMT systems are addressed using blockchain for more secure, efficient, and cost-effective management [21,22,40].

Trust Issues, Verification, and Compliance with Legal and Regulatory Standards: Blockchain technology is applied to overcome trust and verification issues in health data sharing and transactions [1,2,14]. Blockchain applications can help ensure compliance with privacy laws such as GDPR, addressing concerns about data protection, minimization, transfer, and storage [4].

Scalability and Performance Challenges: With the growing volume of healthcare data and increased use of IoMT devices, scalability becomes a critical issue, which blockchain technology addresses through decentralized data management [13,24,36].

Blockchain-based applications in healthcare seek to improve data transparency, security, interoperability, and efficiency while addressing the challenges of data fragmentation, centralization, compliance, and trust in the healthcare sector.

RQ3: What Are the Blockchain Platforms Used in Blockchain Applications for Healthcare? Various blockchain platforms and technologies are utilized in blockchain applications for healthcare, each offering specific features and capabilities suitable for different healthcare needs. Data extracted regarding platforms and technologies are listed below and in Table 2, highlighting the main ones mentioned.

Hyperledger Fabric: Widely used for its modular and versatile framework, Hyperledger Fabric is a preferred choice for many healthcare applications [5,7,8,11,12,15,28,39,40]. It often employs smart contracts (Chaincode) and integrates with other technologies like IPFS for decentralized file storage and Docker for containerization.

Ethereum: Ethereum is another popular platform due to its robust smart contract capabilities and Ethereum Virtual Machine (EVM) [1–4,6,9,10,13,14,16,17,20,22–24,27,29,33–36,41]. It is frequently used alongside IPFS for decentralized storage and tools like Remix IDE, MetaMask, Truffle for development and deployment, and Ganache for blockchain network setup [4,35,36].

InterPlanetary File System (IPFS): IPFS is widely used in conjunction with blockchain platforms like Ethereum and Hyperledger Fabric for efficient and secure decentralized storage of healthcare data [1–3,5,7–9,13,16,17,20,23,24,27,29,35,37,39]. It is a protocol and is commonly used for data storage, while blockchain stores the address for the data in a hash format, responsible for accessing the data.

Hyperledger Indy, Aries, and Ursa: These Hyperledger frameworks are used for identity management and transaction interactions, providing tools for storing, transmitting, and verifying digital credentials [34].

Oracles: Oracles like Chainlink insert real-world data into the blockchain [13].

Cryptography and Security Protocols: Technologies like Threshold Proxy Re-Encryption (TPRE) and public key encryption are used for enhancing data security and privacy [5,8,23,24].

Cloud Computing and Virtualization: Platforms like Amazon Web Services (AWS) are used for cloud computing (Virtual machines, Function-as-a-Service, etc.) and deploying blockchain nodes [4,9,12,27], while virtualization tools like

Kubernetes facilitate the dynamic use of resources [13,24]. Docker and Docker Compose are used for containerization and deployment [13,24,28,34,39,40].

Consensus Mechanisms: Various consensus algorithms like Proof of Work (PoW), Proof of Stake (PoS), and Byzantine Fault Tolerant (BFT) mechanisms are employed for securing transactions and maintaining the blockchain [13,21, 24,37]. The choice of the consensus algorithm is based on business logic and technical architecture. It influences the speed of validation and inclusion of new data (blocks) into the blockchain, affecting the system's scalability.

Programming Languages and Custom Solutions: For smart contract development, Solidity programming language [1,2,4,6,9,10,13,14,16,17,20,24,27,29, 33–36,41], Go and Rust [5,8,11,12,28]. Custom blockchain solutions are developed in other programming languages, like Python [38] and Java [27,37], and are tailored to specific healthcare needs. Additional tools and frameworks include Node.js for backend development and interaction with the blockchain [3,13,34,36,39].

Blockchain applications in healthcare leverage various platforms and technologies, each contributing unique features such as secure data handling, smart contract functionality, decentralized storage, and identity management. These technologies are integrated to create robust, secure, and efficient systems for managing healthcare data and processes.

RQ4: What Are the Challenges Related to Healthcare Applications Based on Blockchain? Healthcare applications based on blockchain face several challenges that impact their scalability, efficiency, and practical implementation.

Scalability and Data Management: A significant challenge is handling the increasing volume of data on the blockchain, which can burden the system and affect scalability. This issue is aggravated by blockchain's data redundancy and the need for modern large-scale data processing [1,35,39,41]. Storing large amounts of data directly on the blockchain is often impractical [10,14,16,27].

Interoperability and Integration: Ensuring interoperability among different blockchain systems and integrating them with existing health IT systems is a significant challenge [20,23,36,37]. The lack of interoperability between different blockchain networks and the challenge of synchronizing interacting blockchains are significant, especially in multi-blockchain architectures [18,24,27]. This includes the difficulty of managing multiple deployments of smart contracts and achieving seamless communication between various blockchain platforms and healthcare applications.

Security and Privacy Concerns: While blockchain enhances data security, there are concerns about maintaining the privacy of sensitive health information. This includes the risk of privacy leakage when using public blockchains [2,6,9,27] and the challenges in device authentication and protecting data from unauthorized access [1,33].

Smart Contract Complexity and Limitations: The complexity of writing and managing smart contracts, particularly in terms of encoding complex data access

Table 2. Main blockchain technologies used on healthcare applications.

Category	Technology	Papers
Platform	Ethereum	[1–4,6,9,10, 13,14,16, 17,20,22–24,27,29, 33–36,41].
Platform	Hyperledger Fabric	[5,7,8,11, 12,15,28, 39,40].
Protocol	InterPlanetary File System (IPFS)	[1–3,5,7–9,13,16,17, 20,23,24, 27,29,35, 37,39].
Smart contracts programming language	Solidity	[1,2,4,6,9, 10,13,14, 16,17,20, 24,27,29, 33–36,41].
Smart contracts programming language	Go and Rust[a]	[5,8,11,12, 28].
Application programming language	Node.js	[3,13,34,36, 39].
Application programming language	Python and Java[a]	[27,37,38]

[a] A few papers deploy those languages; some use both in the same research, so they were put in the same category.

policies, is a challenge [5,11,38,41]. Moreover, the immutable nature of smart contracts raises issues regarding their upgradability and flexibility [23,29].

Regulatory and Compliance Issues: Ensuring compliance with laws and regulations such as GDPR is a challenge, especially considering the immutable nature of blockchain, which can conflict with data removal requests [18,23,24]. Meeting governmental policies and standards also adds complexity to blockchain implementations in healthcare [36].

Resource Efficiency, Energy Consumption, and Economic Considerations: Blockchain networks, particularly those using consensus mechanisms like Proof of Work, can be resource-intensive and require significant computational power [1,13,21,34]. The economic costs associated with transactions on the blockchain and the need for appropriate incentive models for participation are concerns, especially in public blockchains [1,13,28,29]. Furthermore, writing data to public blockchains can be expensive due to limited space and high transaction costs. This has led to the exploration of off-chain storage solutions like IPFS, but balancing cost and speed remains a critical point [1,13,16].

Technical Challenges, User-Friendly Features, and Patient-Centric Control Trade-offs: The lack of user-friendly features for key management and the potential for users to forget their credentials pose challenges [23]. There are also technical hurdles in terms of integrating blockchain with mobile applications and other healthcare technologies [5,13,34]. Additionally, in patient-centric solutions, the trade-off between patient controllability and the overhead of managing data-sharing requests is a notable challenge [12].

While blockchain technology offers significant advantages for healthcare applications, such as enhanced security and decentralized data management, it also presents scalability, interoperability, privacy, technical complexity, regulatory compliance, and resource consumption challenges. Addressing these challenges is crucial for the successful implementation and widespread adoption of blockchain in healthcare.

5 Conclusion

The exploration of blockchain applications in the healthcare sector, as delineated through research questions RQ1 to RQ4, unveils a multifaceted landscape of opportunities and challenges. Blockchain technology, primarily recognized for its foundational role in cryptocurrencies, emerges as a transformative force in healthcare, offering novel approaches to data management, security, and interoperability.

The fundamental attractiveness of blockchain in the healthcare sector lies in its capacity to foster decentralized, transparent, and immutable record-keeping, guaranteeing system trustworthiness and integrity. As highlighted in RQ1, key characteristics of blockchain applications in healthcare include enhanced data security, improved interoperability, and patient-centric data management. The technology facilitates secure, real-time data exchange, reducing errors and discrepancies while combating fraud and operational inefficiencies. Smart contracts, integral to blockchain healthcare platforms, include business logic and automated processes, further enhancing system efficiency.

However, the implementation of blockchain in healthcare presents some challenges. RQ4 reveals that scalability is a significant hurdle, particularly in handling vast amounts of healthcare data. The immutability of blockchain, while advantageous for data integrity, complicates compliance with regulations like the GDPR, which mandates the right to be forgotten. This immutability brings logic complexity to engineering and development, summed up to the complexity of smart contracts development and deployment. Additionally, there are challenges in integrating blockchain with existing healthcare IT systems.

Despite these challenges, the potential of blockchain to revolutionize healthcare data management is evident. Blockchain applications can potentially mitigate the fragmentation of patient data between different organizations, enhance the security and privacy of medical records, and improve the overall efficiency of healthcare systems. To fully realize this potential, however, there is a need for concerted efforts to address the identified challenges. This includes developing scalable blockchain solutions, creating user-friendly interfaces for key management, and ensuring compliance with privacy regulations.

In conclusion, blockchain technology is a healthcare innovation, promising a paradigm shift in storing, managing, accessing, and utilizing patient data. While the path forward is filled with technical, regulatory, and operational challenges, the intersection of blockchain with healthcare holds immense promise. Navigating the complexities and unlocking the full potential of blockchain in healthcare necessitates a collaborative approach involving technologists, healthcare professionals, policymakers, and patients.

6 Limitations of This Study

The search keywords can be considered a limitation in the study in the context that with the addition of words such as "smart contract" and "chaincode", the search is directed to papers that involve development. This work sought to extract information about platforms, technologies, and development in blockchain, analyzing their application goals and challenges through research questions. Focusing on the technical part can be a limitation when the challenges of implementing blockchain systems include a broader scope, such as policy, legislation, and societal impacts.

7 Future Works

Despite these limitations, the use of blockchain technology in healthcare reveals a promising scenario that encourages cooperation between institutions and participants. It is a technically viable system that can bring positive returns to its users regarding the security and usability of their data. Therefore, we intend to continue our research and future work on data storage performance on blockchains compared to traditional database systems. We must analyze the new possibilities and challenges of working with data in a distributed and decentralized way, including ways of using this data as models for artificial intelligence.

References

1. Akkaoui, R., Hei, X., Cheng, W.: EdgeMediChain: a hybrid edge blockchain-based framework for health data exchange. IEEE Access **8**, 113467–113486 (2020)
2. Alnuaimi, A., Alshehhi, A., Salah, K., Jayaraman, R., Omar, I.A., Battah, A.: Blockchain-based processing of health insurance claims for prescription drugs. IEEE Access **10**, 118093–118107 (2022)
3. Azbeg, K., Ouchetto, O., Andaloussi, S.J.: Access control and privacy-preserving blockchain-based system for diseases management. IEEE Trans. Comput. Soc. Syst. **10**(4), 1515–1527 (2022)
4. Barati, M., et al.: Privacy-aware cloud auditing for GDPR compliance verification in online healthcare. IEEE Trans. Industr. Inf. **18**(7), 4808–4819 (2021)
5. Bigini, G., Zichichi, M., Lattanzi, E., Ferretti, S., D'Angelo, G.: Decentralized health data distribution: A DLT-based architecture for data protection. In: 2022 IEEE International Conference on Blockchain (Blockchain), pp. 97–104. IEEE (2022)
6. Cao, S., Zhang, Q., Wang, D., Xiangli, P., Zhang, X.: Hybrid smart contracts for privacy-preserving-aware insurance compensation. In: 2022 IEEE Wireless Communications and Networking Conference (WCNC), pp. 1533–1538. IEEE (2022)
7. Chelladurai, M.U., Pandian, S., Ramasamy, K.: A blockchain based patient centric electronic health record storage and integrity management for e-health systems. Health Policy Technol. **10**(4), 100513 (2021)
8. Chenthara, S., Ahmed, K., Wang, H., Whittaker, F.: A Novel Blockchain Based Smart Contract System for eReferral in Healthcare: HealthChain. In: Huang, Z., Siuly, S., Wang, H., Zhou, R., Zhang, Y. (eds.) Health Information Science. HIS 2020. LNCS, vol. 12435. Springer, Cham (2020). https://doi.org/10.1007/978-3-030-61951-0_9
9. Chinnasamy, P., Albakri, A., Khan, M., Raja, A.A., Kiran, A., Babu, J.C.: Smart contract-enabled secure sharing of health data for a mobile cloud-based e-health system. Appl. Sci. **13**(6), 3970 (2023)
10. Dagher, G.G., Mohler, J., Milojkovic, M., Marella, P.B.: Ancile: Privacy-preserving framework for access control and interoperability of electronic health records using blockchain technology. Sustain. Urban Areas **39**, 283–297 (2018)
11. Garcia, R.D., Zutião, G.A., Ramachandran, G., Ueyama, J.: Towards a decentralized e-prescription system using smart contracts. In: 2021 IEEE 34th International Symposium on Computer-Based Medical Systems (CBMS), pp. 556–561. IEEE (2021)
12. Gohar, A.N., Abdelmawgoud, S.A., Farhan, M.S.: A patient-centric healthcare framework reference architecture for better semantic interoperability based on blockchain, cloud, and IOT. IEEE Access **10**, 92137–92157 (2022)
13. Gonçalves, J.P.d.B., de Resende, H.C., Villaca, R.d.S., Municio, E., Both, C.B., Marquez-Barja, J.M.: Distributed network slicing management using blockchains in e-health environments. Mob. Netw. Appl. **26**(5), 2111–2122 (2021)
14. Hasan, K., Chowdhury, M.J.M., Biswas, K., Ahmed, K., Islam, M.S., Usman, M.: A blockchain-based secure data-sharing framework for software defined wireless body area networks. Comput. Netw. **211**, 109004 (2022)
15. Hylock, R.H., Zeng, X.: A blockchain framework for patient-centered health records and exchange (HealthChain): evaluation and proof-of-concept study. J. Med. Internet Res. **21**(8), e13592 (2019)

16. Jabarulla, M.Y., Lee, H.N.: Blockchain-based distributed patient-centric image management system. Appl. Sci. **11**(1), 196 (2020)
17. Kaur, J., Rani, R., Kalra, N.: Attribute-based access control scheme for secure storage and sharing of EHRs using blockchain and IPFS. Cluster Comput. **27**(1), 1–15 (2023)
18. Khan, A.A., et al.: QoS-Ledger: smart contracts and metaheuristic for secure quality-of-service and cost-efficient scheduling of medical-data processing. Electronics **10**(24), 3083 (2021)
19. Kitchenham, B., Charters, S.: Guidelines for performing systematic literature reviews in software engineering. Technical Report EBSE-2007-01, School of Computer Science and Mathematics, Keele University (2007)
20. Kumar, R., Tripathi, R.: Towards design and implementation of security and privacy framework for internet of medical things (IoMT) by leveraging blockchain and IPFS technology. J. Supercomputing 1–40 (2021)
21. Lakhan, A., Mohammed, M.A., Elhoseny, M., Alshehri, M.D., Abdulkareem, K.H.: Blockchain multi-objective optimization approach-enabled secure and cost-efficient scheduling for the internet of medical things (IoMT) in fog-cloud system. Soft. Comput. **26**(13), 6429–6442 (2022)
22. Lakhan, A., et al.: Smart-contract aware ethereum and client-fog-cloud healthcare system. Sensors **21**(12), 4093 (2021)
23. Madine, M.M., et al.: Blockchain for giving patients control over their medical records. IEEE Access **8**, 193102–193115 (2020)
24. Malamas, V., Kotzanikolaou, P., Dasaklis, T.K., Burmester, M.: A hierarchical multi blockchain for fine grained access to medical data. Ieee Access **8**, 134393–134412 (2020)
25. Mayer, A.H., Da Costa, C.A., Righi, R.d.R.: Electronic health records in a blockchain: a systematic review. Health Inf. J. **26**(2), 1273–1288 (2020)
26. Nakamoto, S.: Bitcoin: A peer-to-peer electronic cash system (2008). https://bitcoin.org/bitcoin.pdf
27. Nguyen, D.C., Pathirana, P.N., Ding, M., Seneviratne, A.: Blockchain for secure EHRs sharing of mobile cloud based e-health systems. IEEE Access **7**, 66792–66806 (2019)
28. Nie, Z., Long, Y., Zhang, S., Lu, Y.: A controllable privacy data transmission mechanism for internet of things system based on blockchain. Int. J. Distrib. Sens. Netw. **18**(3), 15501329221088450 (2022)
29. Pericàs-Gornals, R., Mut-Puigserver, M., Payeras-Capellà, M.M.: Highly private blockchain-based management system for digital COVID-19 certificates. Int. J. Inf. Secur. **21**(5), 1069–1090 (2022)
30. Petersen, K., et al.: Systematic mapping studies in software engineering. In: 12th International Conference on Evaluation and Assessment in Software Engineering (EASE), pp. 1–10 (2008)
31. Petrosyan, A.: Healthcare and cyber security in the u.s. (2023). https://www.statista.com/topics/8795/healthcare-and-cyber-security-in-the-us/#topicOverview. Accessed 23 Jan 2024
32. Rabah, K.: Challenges and opportunities for blockchain powered healthcare systems: a review. Mara res. j. med. health sci. **1**(1), 45–52 (2017)
33. Rahman, M.Z.U., Surekha, S., Satamraju, K.P., Mirza, S.S., Lay-Ekuakille, A.: A collateral sensor data sharing framework for decentralized healthcare systems. IEEE Sens. J. **21**(24), 27848–27857 (2021)

34. Saidi, H., Labraoui, N., Ari, A.A.A., Maglaras, L.A., Emati, J.H.M.: DSMAC: privacy-aware decentralized self-management of data access control based on blockchain for health data. IEEE Access **10**, 101011–101028 (2022)
35. Sharma, P., Borah, M.D., Namasudra, S.: Improving security of medical big data by using blockchain technology. Comput. Electr. Eng. **96**, 107529 (2021)
36. Sharma, P., Namasudra, S., Chilamkurti, N., Kim, B.G., Gonzalez Crespo, R.: Blockchain-based privacy preservation for IOT-enabled healthcare system. ACM Trans. Sens. Netw. **19**(3), 1–17 (2023)
37. Shuaib, K., Abdella, J., Sallabi, F., Serhani, M.A.: Secure decentralized electronic health records sharing system based on blockchains. J. King Saud Univ. Comput. Inf. Sci. **34**(8), 5045–5058 (2022)
38. Smahi, A., Xia, Q., Gao, J., Xia, H.: An efficient and secure blockchain-based SVM classification for a COVID-19 healthcare system. In: 2021 6th International Conference on Mathematics and Artificial Intelligence, pp. 122–129 (2021)
39. Sun, Z., Han, D., Li, D., Weng, T.H., Li, K.C., Mei, X.: MedRSS: a blockchain-based scheme for secure storage and sharing of medical records. Comput. Ind. Eng. **183**, 109521 (2023)
40. Tanwar, S., Parekh, K., Evans, R.: Blockchain-based electronic healthcare record system for healthcare 4.0 applications. J. Inf. Secur. Appl. **50**, 102407 (2020)
41. Xu, B., Xu, L.D., Wang, Y., Cai, H.: A distributed dynamic authorisation method for internet+ medical & healthcare data access based on consortium blockchain. Enterp. Inf. Syst. **16**(12), 1922757 (2022)

Ethereum Marketplace Creation: Scaling, FT vs NFT in Theory, Cross-Chain and Splitting Experiments

Anastasiya Lavrova[1,2], Vladimir Korkhov[1(✉)], and Albina Lavrova[3]

[1] Saint Petersburg State University, St. Petersburg, Russia
{a.k.lavrova,v.korkhov}@spbu.ru
[2] ITMO University, St. Petersburg, Russia
[3] Lanit-Tercom Italia SRL, Bari, Italy

Abstract. Ethereum is the most popular altcoin today. It is a platform for large decentralized platforms and thousands of DApps. It was this blockchain that gave the crypto community such technologies as NFT and DAO. On September 15, 2022, Ethereum switched to the Proof-Of-Stake consensus algorithm. In this article, we review the existing blockchain architecture and token standards, compare the difference before and after the transition, identify existing problems, and review existing solutions. We evaluate the performance of FT and NFT creation; consider the solution to the Ethereum scaling with ZkSync; evaluate alternative platforms for creating tokens such as Open Sea or switching to other blockchains like Polygon, Fantom or Binance Smart Chain using cross-chain bridges.

Keywords: blockchain · distributed ledger · token · Ethereum · marketplace · solidity · smart-contracts · decentralized finances · cross-chain

1 Introduction

Blockchain technology has revolutionized various industries, offering unparalleled transparency, security, and efficiency. In its essence, the blockchain is a specialized database transforming how we store and manage data. Unlike traditional databases, the blockchain structure consists of a chain of blocks added to this database.

The initial iterations of blockchain, exemplified by Bitcoin, primarily function as decentralized payment systems possessing relatively limited functionalities. However, the advent of the second generation of blockchains, such as Ethereum, has ushered in a new era of possibilities, offering an all-encompassing digital ecosystem rather than merely a cryptocurrency. These advanced blockchains serve as the foundational infrastructure for the creation and execution of decentralized projects. Notably, the key distinguishing feature of this generation is

O. Gervasi et al. (Eds.): ICCSA 2024 Workshops, LNCS 14815, pp. 196–213, 2024.
https://doi.org/10.1007/978-3-031-65154-0_12

the integration of smart contracts and computer protocols designed to facilitate the management of specific entities, such as cryptocurrencies, specialized tokens, and more. Ethereum, for instance, leverages Solidity as its Turing-complete Programming Language for interacting with smart contracts.

One of Ethereum's significant contributions to the crypto community is the invention of crypto tokens. These digital assets exist on specific blockchains and have revolutionized various sectors, including finance, gaming, and art. Crypto tokens can be categorized into fungible and non-fungible tokens (NFTs). Fungible tokens, known as FT, are identical and interchangeable, serving as a form of currency within the blockchain ecosystem. On the other hand, non-fungible tokens, or NFTs, represent unique objects, such as digital art, collectibles, or virtual real estate, bringing scarcity and ownership rights to the digital world.

As we mentioned, blockchain technology's emergence and rapid advancement have transformed various industries. One of the most groundbreaking applications of blockchain is the creation and management of non-fungible tokens (NFTs), which have gained significant attention in recent years. NFTs have revolutionized digital asset ownership by providing a unique identifier and proof of authenticity for digital assets, ranging from artworks and collectibles to music and virtual real estate.

In this article, we have developed a platform Art Space Marketplace [1] for creating and managing fungible and non-fungible tokens. But also, during our work, we delved into the nuances of blockchain technology. We closely studied the second generation of blockchains, theirs scaling and problems and have developed a platform that solves these issues.

Section 2 gives an overview of existing literature and research related to blockchain technology and NFT marketplaces. We highlight the essential findings and insights from previous studies, setting the context for the subsequent sections.

Section 3 delves into the various scaling solutions proposed and implemented to address the challenges faced by the Ethereum network. It explores technologies such as sharding, plasma chains, and state channels, which aim to enhance the throughput and performance of the blockchain.

Section 4 overviews the primary existing ETH token standards, shows the difference between fungible and non-fungible tokens, and emphasizes the importance of choosing the suitable token standard for the proper operation of a decentralized application.

Section 5 discusses the lifecycle of fungible tokens and also covers AMM principle of work.

Section 6 focuses specifically on NFTs. It explores the structure and architecture of NFTs. It also explains the various ways to view NFT assets and introduces the concept of cross-chain bridges and their operation scheme.

Section 7 identifies and describes the main technological challenges and issues present in the current architecture of tokens. It highlights areas that require further improvement and development to enhance the functionality and usability of tokens within the blockchain ecosystem.

The Sect. 8 presents the developed project. We provide a detailed description of the decentralized application, as well as compare it with well-known operating marketplaces such as OpenSea and Rarible.

2 Related Work

Blockchain technology attracts a lot of attention. The article [2] considers the difference between the two most popular blockchains - Bitcoin and Ethereum. The authors compare network architectures and their main characteristics.

Recognizing the distinction between cryptocurrencies and tokens is crucial for researchers, investors, and developers, as it enables a clear understanding of their respective functionalities, use cases, and regulatory considerations. The difference between NFT and cryptocurrency is presented in [3]. In this article, the authors compare NFT, Ethereum cryptocurrency, CryptoCoin, Bitcoin and the relationship between their prices.

The article [5] introduces a comprehensive overview of NFT and its underlying core technologies: blockchain and Ethereum. The authors present an analysis of marketplaces for NFT exchange, NFT dApps in different categories, and challenges that the authors see in NFT technology from the perspective of security, privacy, environmental impact, ownership, governance, and property rights.

Paper [6] overviews state-of-the-art NFT solutions and analyzes their technical components, protocols, standards, and desired proprieties. The authors consider a security evolution, with discussions on the perspectives of their design models, opportunities, and challenges.

Research on measurement of Ethereum-Based ERC20 Token Networks is introduced in [7]. The authors present a descriptive measurement study to characterize token networks quantitatively. Based on the first 6.3 million blocks of the Ethereum blockchain, they provide an overview of more than 64,000 ERC20 token networks and analyze the top 1,000 from a graph perspective.

3 Blockchain Scaling

Over a million transactions occur on the Ethereum network every day [8]. So, scaling mechanisms play a key role in modern blockchain architecture, ensuring efficient transaction processing and reducing the load on the main chain. Architectural solutions at the blockchain level may face performance constraints and high fees, which complicates the process of trading and managing NFT. Using L2 solutions when creating a marketplace for NFT can provide more efficient and cost-effective trading, as well as increase the accessibility of the platform for users with different levels of financial capabilities.

On-chain scaling and off-chain scaling are the two categories of scaling for Ethereum.

1. On-Chain Scaling
   This solution entails reconfiguring the main Ethereum network. Scaling is achieved using Sharding technology. Segmenting transactions enables each node of the network to handle just a portion of a block rather than the complete transaction.
2. Off-Chain Scaling
   This solution suggests the creation of a distinct solution from the Mainnet. Depending on the protocol, security is provided directly by the Ethereum Mainnet consensus algorithms (Optimistic Rollups, zkRollups) or independently (sidechains, plasma).
   - **Optimistic Rollups**
     The fundamental premise of the approach is that L2 transactions are valid by default. Calculations will only be made if fraud is suspected.
   - **Zero Knowledge Rollups**
     Such a method combines off-chain transactions and uses zero-disclosure SNARK to produce a specific cryptographic proof. Without having to provide the information, it enables the proving party to verify its accuracy. One of the most popular Ethereum scaling solutions, zkSync, is based on this method. It is with the help of it that further research related to Ethereum L2 will be conducted.
   - **Side-Chains**
     This solution uses a separate blockchain. It is functionally equivalent to the Mainnet Ethereum, allowing the transfer of assets between networks. Assets are frozen in the original blockchain as soon as they are in a different one.
   - **Plasma**
     A separate blockchain connected to the main network serves as the solution. It enables chain creation within the primary networks, enabling scalability. The subsidiary "root contracts," which are Ethereum smart contracts, are linked to the main Ethereum network and contain the fundamental guidelines for running each subsidiary chain.

We conducted a study of scalable Ethereum using ZKSync. And also testing ZkSync, it was found that although the execution of operations on L2 occurs almost instantly, their confirmation and output to L1 takes a lot of time, since these operations are processed through a single L1 blockchain network for all users. Despite the fact that such a solution will significantly reduce gas costs and time to create tokens, it will also significantly complicate the ability of users to log in. An analysis of the creation of tokens in the zkSync Testnet is presented in Fig. 1.

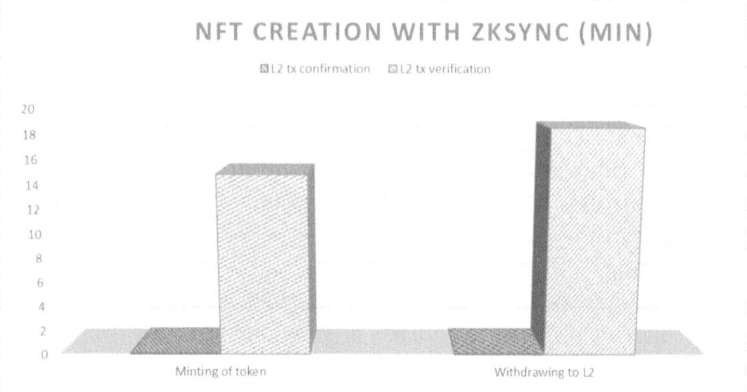

	Minting of token	Withdrawing to L2
L2 tx confirmation	0,057	0,047
L2 tx verification	14,79	18,49

Fig. 1. The time of token generation with ZkSync on 16.10.2023

4 Fungible and Non-fungible Tokens. the Main Ethereum Token Standards

As we have already mentioned, Ethereum is a decentralized platform on the basis of which various decentralized applications can be created. These applications are based on a special script called a smart contract. A large number of smart contracts are based on the same scheme, called the standard. Each standard specifies the minimum set of functions required to regulate tokens in the blockchain.

Ethereum is an open-source project, so any user can propose a new standard. If such a standard turns out to be really useful, then it can become the official Ethereum standard [13].

To create the right smart contract for token management, it is necessary to determine in advance the basic token standard. As was stated before, tokens can be fungible (FT) and non-fungible (NFT). Their main difference is that each NFT token is unique, that is, suitable for identifying something. Therefore, while the NFT encodes a digital object, the FT encodes a digital currency.

There are three main token standards in the Ethereum network: ERC20 ([15]), ERC721 ([16]), and ERC1155 ([17]).

- ERC20 is a protocol integrated into Ethereum in 2017. It is used to manage FT tokens. One smart contract of such a protocol encodes one such FT, which can denote a fiat currency, ounces of gold, or units of experience in a certain gaming platform. That is, 10 different smart contracts are required to work with 10 different types of tokens.
- ERC721 was also introduced in 2017, however, tokens of this standard are NFT. They can encode fragments of digital art, music, unique game objects, domain names ([4]), and even physical objects ([9]). Each such token is

assigned an identifier, so a single smart contract allows you to manage several types of tokens presented in a single instance.

- ERC1155 is a standard released in 2018. It is a mixture of ERC20 and ERC721, which allows managing both FT and NFT on a single smart contract by assigning a unique identifier to each token. An important feature of this protocol is the ability to transfer multiple tokens in a single transaction.

5 Fungible Tokens

As shown above, the FT token can be controlled by the ERC20 and ERC1155 protocols.

Our platform will have to support not only NFT, but also FT. Therefore, it is necessary to give users the opportunity to exchange tokens. The process of exchanging these tokens is usually performed by exchanges called Automated market makers (AMM). AMM is based on a simple mathematical formula that takes various forms. The most common of them is

$$aTokenBalance * bTokenBalance = k, \tag{1}$$

where k characterizes a constant balance of assets that determines the price of tokens in the liquidity pool and multipliers show how many tokens used for exchange are currently in the pool. For example, if AMM has ether (ETH) and bitcoin (BTC), every time ETH is bought, the price of ETH rises because there is less ETH in the pool than before the purchase. Conversely, the price of BTC decreases as there is more BTC in the pool. The pool remains in a constant balance, while the total value of ETH in the pool will always be equal to the total value of BTC in the pool.

6 Non-fungible Tokens

6.1 NFT's Structure

In order to give the user the opportunity to mint NFT using our platform, it is necessary to understand this technology in more detail. NFT allows people to secure the ownership of some digital object in the blockchain. However, data storage in the blockchain is very expensive, so in fact, only a link to JSON with the characteristics of a digital asset is stored in the blockchain. The existing NFT architecture looks like this: a smart contract is stored in the blockchain, in which each NFT has a unique identifier. According to this identifier, the smart contract issues a link to the corresponding JSON, which, in turn, stores links to the corresponding metadata.

A more detailed architecture of all NFT components we present in Fig. 2.

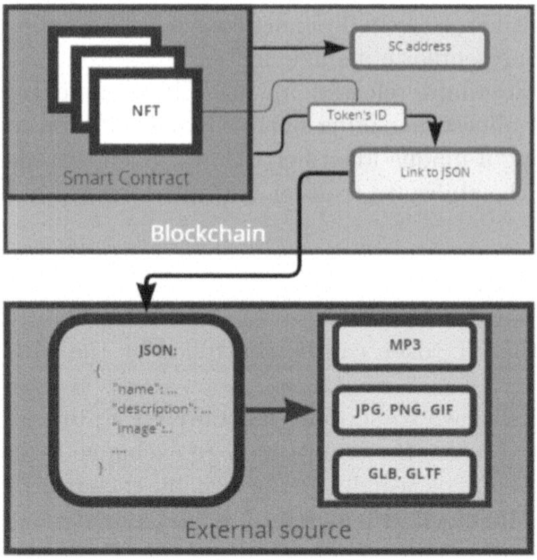

Fig. 2. Architecture of NFT components

NFT Minting. The creation of an NFT is the main operation related to the life of the token. It can be carried out in two ways

- **On-Chain** minting - the most common option. In this case, the creation of the NFT takes place in the blockchain. It meains that each user can see creation transaction, and any third-party service (another market place or crypto wallet) will be able to get information about this token.
- **Off-Chain** minting - the method of creation takes place outside the blockchain. This type of minting is less common, but it can increase the creation speed and reduce the cost. Usually, creating such an NFT directly in the blockchain occurs at the buyer's expense when buying a token on the marketplace.

Comparing these two types of minting, it is worth noting that on-chain minting is a more reliable and secure method since transactions occur in a decentralized network. It also allows you to see the entire transaction history, which may be necessary when selling NFT in the future.

Off-chain minting can provide convenience and time savings when creating an NFT. However, this method may need to be more transparent and guarantees that all processes will be carried out correctly and without the possibility of change.

Art Space marketplace strives to achieve the highest level of decentralization, so it will use only on-chain minting.

NFT Trading. The NFT can also be put up for sale in two ways:

1. Storing the order book inside the blockchain. This method ensures transparency of all operations and guarantees the impossibility of substituting information about the lot being sold. However, this approach increases the transaction costs for the user since it forces him to pay for the transaction in a distributed ledger.
2. Storing the order book on a centralized server. This solution saves users money but allows deleting or replacing information about the lot being sold.

Most popular marketplaces, like Opensea [10] or Rarible [11], store order books on centralized servers. But, as mentioned, our goal is to make the platform as decentralized as possible, so we store order book in a special smart-contract.

6.2 Metadata Storage

Since both the JSON file and the corresponding metadata are stored outside the blockchain, 3 options for their placement are considered [12]:

- Personal HTTPS file server.
  The disadvantage of this method is the possibility of changing or deleting data by any user with access to the server.
- A decentralized network for storing files - IPFS.
  This service provides the user with a unique link containing a hash of the data. This makes it impossible to change/replace the file. However, it is necessary to consider that when deleting media data from all network nodes, the user will receive an error when trying to view his NFT. The solution to this problem is to deploy your IPFS network node, which will guarantee the availability of downloaded files.
- Specialized blockchains for storing files.
  In this case, fragments from several old ones will be saved when a new data block appears. Thus, thanks to consensus algorithms and the replication of old files, the data cannot be changed or deleted. However, the problem of the solution under consideration is their low prevalence. For example, a strong reduction in blockchain users can cause uncontrolled data loss.

Table 1 shows the results of the comparison this storage methods.

Table 1. Characteristics of storage methods

	Personal Server	IPFS	Blockchain
Data changing	YES	NO	NO
Data deletion	YES	YES	NO
Distribution	NO	YES	YES

It is also necessary to take into account that links to media files and metadata contain a domain name, which guarantees a loss of access when the corresponding domain is blocked.

7 Main Token Issues

In the context of creating a marketplace, it is important to highlight the main problems of tokens and try to solve them.

7.1 Slow Processing of Operations

Transactions on the Ethereum network take quite a long time, even with high gas prices. For example, we tested the creation rates of FT and NFT in the tightness of Ethereum with Gas Price = 40 Gwei, when the average price was 34 Gwei. The result is shown in Fig. 3.

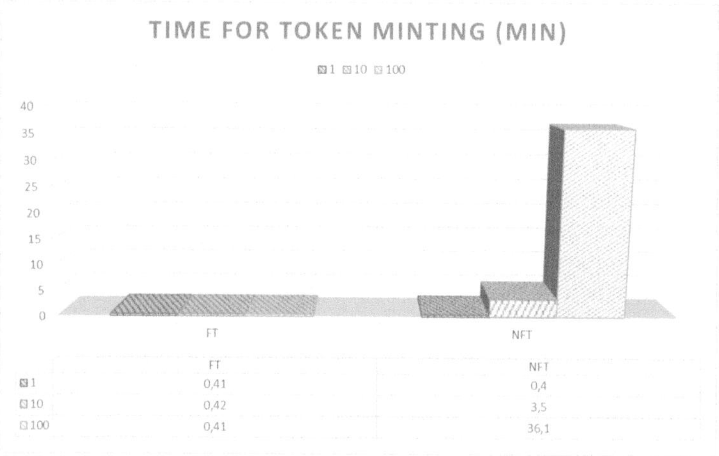

Fig. 3. The time of token generation in Ethereum Sepolia testnet on 16.10.2023

To solve this problem, version 2 plans to transfer the order book to L2, while only purchase transactions will be placed on L1.

7.2 Lack of Tracking of NFT's Creators

One of the ideas underlying NFT technology is to enable the creators of tokens to make a profit by reselling their creations. Since the entire history of transactions related to a certain token is recorded in the distributed ledger, the original creator can be easily found.

The current royalties system implies that the author of the token must manually indicate on the platform selected for sale what amount of commission he would like to receive from resales.

The problem arises when the buyer of the token resells it on another platform. In this case, if the author of the token did not register his contract there, he will not be able to receive any commission. This arises due to the fact that smart contracts of marketplaces use only a universal transfer function in the token smart contract.

Let's denote through A - the smart contract of the marketplace, through B - the smart contract of the token and consider the approximate algorithm of the purchase function is shown on Fig. 4.

1. Receipt of token value in the contract A
2. Calling the token transfer function in Contract B
3. Receiving the specified royalties in contract A
4. Calculation of commissions and transfer of funds taking into account the received data

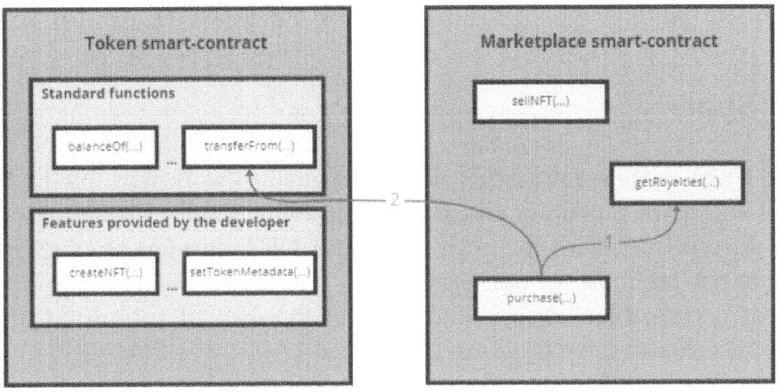

Fig. 4. Approximate algorithm of the purchase function

To solve this problem, a new standard EIP2981 [14] was introduced. It provides a function that takes the token ID and the sale price as input and returns the recipient and the desired commission. In this case, the algorithm will look like this:

1. Receipt of A token value in the contract A
2. Receiving the specified royalties in a contract B
3. Calling the token transfer function in Contract B
4. Calculation of commissions and transfer of funds taking into account the received data

This scheme is presented in Fig. 5.

However, this solution also has drawbacks. The standard assumes that the marketplace will voluntarily turn to this function and transfer part of its profits. Currently, only one of the popular marketplaces adheres to this policy - Rarible.

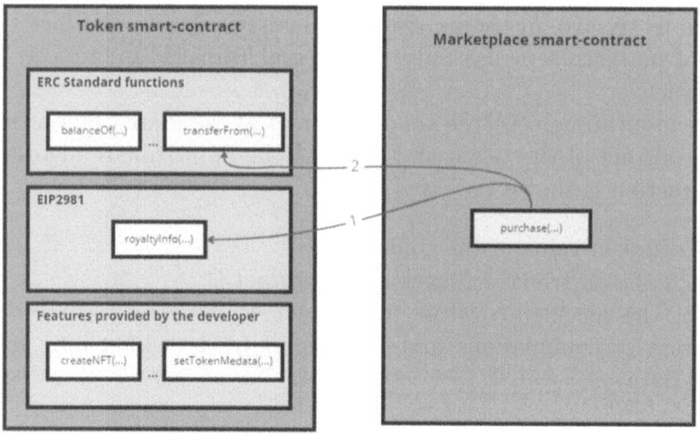

Fig. 5. Approximate algorithm of the purchase function with EIP2981

8 Art Space

Currently, there are several marketplaces designed to work with NFT. The most popular of these are OpenSea and Raible. However, each of these marketplaces has some unresolved issues for both users and NFT developers. Such problems may include the high cost of operations with tokens, the lack of support for test networks or certain blockchains, and the insufficiency of submitted operations to work with tokens.

Cross-Chain Bridges. Since users were given an opportunity to mint the NFT on various blockchains, it was decided to implement cross-chain NFT bridge for transferring assets. This can be useful, for example, when a user created his/her NFT based on Ethereum, but was tired of paying for expensive transactions, then he could transfer his NFT, for example, to Polygon, where the cost of transactions is much lower. (Comparison of transaction prices will be presented below). Currently there are many ready-made solutions for transferring FT between the blockchains, but the transfer of NFT has not been implemented, as there are some difficulties with transferring of metadata and burning of tokens.

To understand NFT problem, let's go a little bit deeper into the smart contracts theory. As we discussed above, there are special standards for smart contracts. They represent a list of functions with a predetermined name and argument. It is this predestination that tells the developer for transferring certain token, for example, of ERC-1155 standard it will be needed to call a function, named *SafeTransferFrom()* and pass in it 4 parameters - the address of the sender, the address of the recipient, the token and the number of

1. From whom token will be transferred
2. Address of recipient
3. ID of that token

4. Amount of transferring tokens

However, in the development process, the creator of the smart contract extends the list of functions predefined by the standard. The most common such extension is the function of token minting. This is where we are faced with a problem. The developer can give such a function the name “mintNFT” or “mint” or “createTokens” or some other. Thus, if we want to create a token on a pre-existing contract, we don’t know if there is a function like this, how it is called and what arguments it takes.

To create a mechanism that would transfer a token belonging to a smart contract in blockchain A on smart contract in blockchain B, you need:

1. Burn a token in blockchain A.
   But the combustion function is not a standard and is added to the contract developer as an extension. It follows that if a user comes to our platform to transfer his or her token to another blockchain, it may be that parent smart contract does not provide a burning feature. Even in case it exists, we still don’t know exactly what it’s called.
2. Create a pair smart contract, token ID in smart contract B.

Thus, if developers need to create cross-chain bridge for tokens, they will have to develop an individual solution based on the characteristics of a written certain smart-contract. We have made such a bridge built on the basis of our smart-contracts, in which we added the possibility of burning tokens. This solution will allow users to move between the supported blockchains all the tokens minting on our platform. However, the user who created NFT somewhere outside will not be able to transfer it’s asset.

Also, the main value of NFT is the number of transactions carried out with it. Accordingly, with the transition to a new blockchain, it is impossible to transfer the entire history of operations. This problem is solved by storing each NFT in the database its pair address of the smart contract, token ID for each blockchain and displaying the complete transaction history of one token on all distributed registries.

The algorithm of the bridge presented by the Art Space team is as follows:

1. ERC-1155 contracts are created on each selected blockchain.
2. The user selects the token to transfer and the blockchain to which the token will be transferred. Then, it starts the transfer process on the oracle (in this case, a web page).
3. Oracle receives the NFT metadata reference.
4. The user signs a transfer transaction in blockchain A. This transaction unlocks metadata from the original token and transfers it to a temporary storage wallet.
5. The Oracle checks whether there is a “twin” in the database for chosen token on the selected blockchain.
6. The user signs the creation transaction if there is no “twin” for the token in blockchain B. As a result of this transaction, a new token is created in

blockchain B, linked to the metadata obtained in step 3. If the "double" is detected, the unfreezing transaction will be signed, which will fix the metadata of the token in the blockchain and transfer it from the storage wallet to the user's wallet.
7. In the database, if the "twin" of the token has not been found, then a new bundle smart contract address, token ID is added for the NFT on the blockchain B. Then the bundle of the "twin" is marked active.

Thus, NFT retains information about previous transactions on all blockchains supported by the marketplace, and, in the case of transferring the token to the original blockchain, the original token with its entire history will be returned to the user. Unpinning metadata at the transfer stage to the repository ensures that tokens with the same parameters cannot be found on third-party marketplaces.

NFT Splitting. Imagine a situation where the NFT is a large expanse of land, for example, a park in virtual reality. The owner of this park wants to place a kiosk with the sale of certain digital objects on it. However, in order to transfer NFT of certain part to the seller's ownership, it is necessary to transfer the NFT of the entire park and lose ownership of another territory.

In this case, the owner of the NFT will be able to turn to our platform to cut the token into two parts. Then the NFT part for the kiosk will be transferred to the ownership of the tenant, and the rest of the NFT part of the park will remain with the original owner. Parent NFT of the ownership of the entire park in this case will be frozen. With this tool, we provide an opportunity for the landlord to significantly increase the potential income. This feature also helps to provide more flexible conditions for tenants and simplifies the process of managing virtual real estate.

A unique feature of our token division is also the ability to combine child elements into the original token. So, after the lease ends, the owner of the park will be able to burn the issued child NFTs and unfreeze his original asset.

8.1 Infrastructure Design

For the client, the Art Space ecosystem will be presented in two forms:

- Mobile Unity application;
- website.

Thus, the platform becomes universal for the user: it can be used from desktop or mobile devices.

However, it is crucial to have a well-planned ecosystem of servers, in addition to smart contracts, to ensure correct functionality. They face the following class of tasks:

1. Getting information from the selected distributed ledger:
   - Getting the current gas price of the selected blockchain;

  - Getting a list of wallet transactions in the selected blockchain;
  - Getting the transaction execution status;
  - Getting the owner of the selected token;
  - Getting the metadata of the token when importing it in the application.
2. Token maintenance:
  - Uploading image/video files to IPFS;
  - Generating token metadata in a JSON file and uploading it to IPFS;
  - Maintaining an IPFS node.

These functions were implemented in JavaScript. Their representation in the form of an API is performed using the AXIOS library [19]. To reduce the cost of implementing functions, we utilized two pre-built solutions:

1. It is important for the marketplace to have the current state of the blockchain at the time of the user's request. Deploying a local block browser requires high costs for sorting and storing all transactions related to tokens in a distributed ledger. Therefore, to obtain up-to-date data from a distributed ledger the Moralis NFT API is used [20], which supports such popular blockchains such as Ethereum, Polygon, Binance SC, Solana, Fantom et al.
2. To ensure the safety of data on the IPFS network, a data pinning process is required on a specific network node. This prevents important data from being deleted from the node during the cleanup process. However, data control and consolidation are possible only on own nodes: it is impossible to force other network nodes to consolidate personal data. Thus, to ensure the safety of metadata in IPFS, it is necessary to start own node of this system. Tracking pinned content and managing large amounts of pinned data requires investing in the creation of additional tools to work with the local IPFS node. In addition, accessing content through a shared gateway *https://ipfs.io/ipfs/${CID}* sets a limit on the number of requests per hour. For these reasons, the Infura pinning service is used IPFS, which allocates its gateway for receiving data, as well as tools for working with uploaded files.

During the development of application, one of the tasks is to develop database that stores information about tokens, smart contracts, users, and user exhibitions. The Django framework (Python) was used for this task.

The general scheme of the developed solution is shown on Fig. 6.

At the moment, Art Space mobile application is available to users in the Play Market [21] and App Store [22]. The website is in the final stages of development.

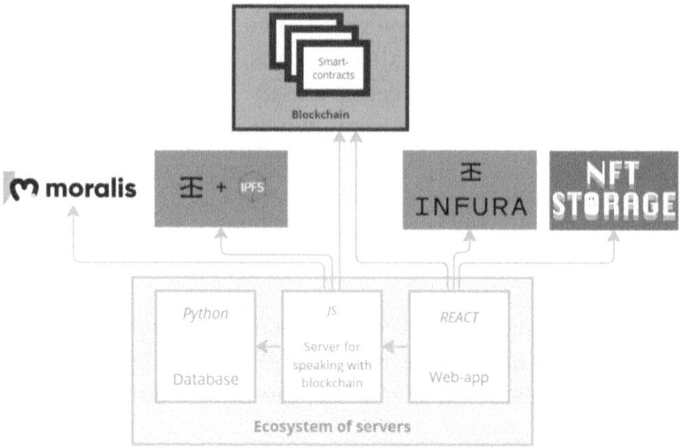

Fig. 6. Approximate algorithm of the purchase function with EIP2981

8.2 Comparison with Existing Solutions

One of the important steps in this process is to compare the resulting solution with analogs on the market. This approach allows you to evaluate the advantages and disadvantages of a new product and determine its competitiveness. In this part, the Art Space Marketplace will be compared with the most popular analogs, namely OpenSea and Raible. We will compare basic operations with NFT: minting, selling, and buying. Since the cost of transactions may differ at different times due to changes in the price of gas, the comparison of the cost of transactions will be carried out in units of gas. This will help you accurately compare the amount of computing resources needed to interact with smart contracts, without reference to a time interval. The results of comparison are presented in Table 2.

The first thing worth noting is that ArtSpace Marketplace smart contracts require less gas to function, but they need to be paid for creating an NFT and putting it up for sale. This payment ensures transparency and security of transactions. Figure 7 shows a comparison of basic operations in gas units on 3 platforms.

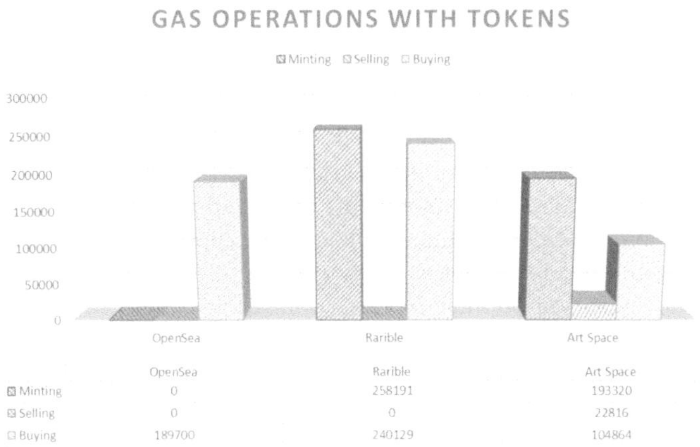

Fig. 7. Comparison of the labor costs of operations for working with NFT on the marketplaces selected for the study.

Table 2. Characteristics of storage methods

	OpenSea	Rarible	Art Space
Way of minting	off-chain	off-chain and on-chain	on-chain
Token standards	ERC1155	ERC721	ERC1155 and ERC721
Support of EIP2981	NO	NO	YES
Supported blockchains	1 Ethereum, Polygon, Klaytn, Solana, Arbitrum, Optimism, Avalanche, and BNB	Ethereum, Polygon, Tezos	1 stage: Polygon, Ethereum; 2 stage: zkSync, BSC, Fantom, Harmony, Polka dot, Avalanche
Storing the order book	centralized	centralized	decentralized

9 Conclusion

In this article, we have extensively examined the creation of a decentralized application tailored for second-generation blockchains. Throughout the development process, we have thoroughly investigated the intricate architecture of blockchains and their distinctions. Also, our focus of study in this article revolves around exploring tokens. This examination encompasses their diverse types, the stages they undergo throughout their lifecycle, the encoding standards, the methodologies for observing them, and finally, the techniques employed for storing their metadata.

As a direct outcome of our meticulous research and articulation throughout this article, we have successfully conceived and established an ecosystem of two innovative applications. The first application is an online platform, currently undergoing its final stages of development, poised to provide useful services in alignment with our research findings. The second application complements the initial platform and has been meticulously crafted to cater to mobile users. It is available for download on popular mobile application stores.

Acknowledgements. Partially supported by Saint Petersburg State University, project ID: 95438429.

References

1. Art Space Marketplace Info page. https://lanit-tercom.ru/art-space. Accessed 01 Dec 2023
2. Vujičić, D., Jagodić, D., Ranđić, S.: Blockchain technology, bitcoin, and Ethereum: a brief overview. In: 17th International Symposium INFOTEH-JAHORINA, East Sarajevo, Bosnia and Herzegovina, March 2018. IEEE (2018). https://doi.org/10.1109/INFOTEH.2018.8345547
3. Apostu, S.A., Panait, M., Vasa, L., Mihaescu, C., Dobrowolski, Z.: NFTs and cryptocurrencies-the metamorphosis of the economy under the sign of blockchain: a time series approach. Mathematics **10**(17), 3218 (2022). https://doi.org/10.3390/math10173218
4. Unstoppable domains. https://unstoppabledomains.com/. Accessed 1 Dec 2023
5. Rehman, W., Zainab, H.; Imran, J., Bawany, N.Z.: NFTs: applications and challenges. In: 22nd International Arab Conference on Information Technology (ACIT), December 2021. IEEE (2021). http://dx.doi.org/10.1109/ACIT53391.2021.9677260
6. Wang, Q., Li, R., Wang, Q., Chen, S.: Non-Fungible Token (NFT): overview, evaluation, opportunities and challenges. Cryptography and Security (cs.CR), FOS: Computer and Information Sciences, FOS: Computer and information sciences (2021). https://doi.org/10.48550/ARXIV.2105.07447
7. Victor, F., Lüders, B.K.: Measuring Ethereum-based ERC20 token networks. In: Goldberg, I., Moore, T. (eds.) FC 2019. LNCS, vol. 11598, pp. 113–129. Springer, Cham (2019). https://doi.org/10.1007/978-3-030-32101-7_8
8. Ethereum Daily Transactions Chart. https://etherscan.io/chart/tx. Accessed 01 Dec 2023
9. Patent NIKE CryptoKickss. https://patft.uspto.gov/netacgi/nph-Parser?Sect1=PTO2&Sect2=HITOFF&p=1&u=/netahtml/PTO/search-bool.html&r=1&f=G&l=50&co1=AND&d=PTXT&s1=Nike&s2=Crypto&OS=Nike+AND+Crypto&RS=Nike+AND+Crypto. Accessed 01 Dec 2023
10. OpenSea marketplace web. https://opensea.io/. Accessed 01 Dec 2023
11. Rarible marketplace web. https://rarible.com/. Accessed 01 Dec 2023
12. Lavrova, A., Iakushkin, O.: NFT performance and security review. In: Gervasi, O., Murgante, B., Misra, S., Rocha, A.M.A.C., Garau, C. (eds.) ICCSA 2022.

LNCS, pp. 217–228. Springer, Cham (2022). https://doi.org/10.1007/978-3-031-10536-4_15
13. Official Ethereum standards. https://eips.ethereum.org/erc. Accessed 01 Dec 2023
14. EIP2981 standard description. https://eips.ethereum.org/EIPS/eip-2981. Accessed 01 Dec 2023
15. EIP20 standard description. https://eips.ethereum.org/EIPS/eip-20. Accessed 01 Dec 2023
16. EIP721 standard description. https://eips.ethereum.org/EIPS/eip-721. Accessed 01 Dec 2023
17. EIP1155 standard description. https://eips.ethereum.org/EIPS/eip-1155. Accessed 01 Dec 2023
18. Mohan, V.: Automated market makers and decentralized exchanges: a DeFi primer. Financ. Innov. **8**, 20 (2022)
19. Link to axios web. https://axios-http.com/. Accessed 01 Dec 2023
20. Link to Moralis web. https://moralis.io/. Accessed 01 Dec 2023
21. Link to mobile app Art Space in Google Play. https://play.google.com/store/apps/details?id=com.lanittercom.artspace. Accessed 01 Jun 2023
22. Link to mobile app Art Space in App Store. https://apps.apple.com/us/app/art-space/id6444775365/. Accessed 01 Dec 2023

The Impact of Ethereum Node Service Centralization on the Security and Efficiency of Blockchain

Denis Sinkevich, Anton Anikin(✉), Alexey Chibrikov, and Dmitry Rak

Volgograd State Technical University, Volgograd, Russia
anton@anikin.name

Abstract. The purpose of this article is to analyze the impact of centralization of node services on the security and efficiency of smart contracts in the Ethereum network, taking into account the massive scale and importance of cloud services in modern blockchain architecture. A key aspect of this analysis is the use of relevant data and academic sources, including information from Ethernodes.org and publications published on sites such as MDPI, Ethereum.org, CoinDesk and CoinMarketCap. This research aims to identify the risks and benefits associated with centralization of node services in the context of cloud technologies and develop recommendations to minimize potential threats to the Ethereum blockchain system. In the course of achieving this goal, all necessary steps are performed, such as analyzing and studying the impact of cloud services on the availability, scalability, reliability and security of the Ethereum network, assessing issues related to governance and trust in decentralized networks. The analysis shows that the process of centralizing node services exposes the network to security and censorship risks. Despite the advantages of cloud platforms, such as affordable and fast scalability of the system and accessibility to the consumer, in order to preserve the basic idea of blockchain decentralization, it is necessary to increase the security of smart contracts and reduce the level of centralization, this article suggests techniques and solutions. The study analyzes the complexity of building a relationship between the basic principles of blockchain and the advantage of cloud technologies and offers recommendations to cloud service providers, network users and developers on how to find a balance between decentralization, efficiency and security.

Keywords: Blockchain · Ethereum · Smart contract · Cloud technologies

1 Introduction

Ethereum is an open and decentralized blockchain system (launched in 2015) offered a unique opportunity - the creation and execution of smart contracts. These contracts are some kind of programs that automatically fulfill the previously prescribed legal conditions avoiding the influence of interested third parties

O. Gervasi et al. (Eds.): ICCSA 2024 Workshops, LNCS 14815, pp. 214–225, 2024.
https://doi.org/10.1007/978-3-031-65154-0_13

after agreement. Due to this, the platform gained popularity and mass popularity among developers.

With the help of smart contracts, users can develop complex contract execution scenarios using code, without resorting to control from a third, possibly interested, party for their execution. This became possible due to the fact that the program code runs on the Ethereum network, where the results follow the basic principles in the blockchain. When such an architecture is implemented into the network, it guarantees the immutability of the terms of the contract, security and transparency [3, 10].

The role of smart contracts in the Ethereum ecosystem is high. They have become the basis for the development and operation of many applications: decentralized financial services (DeFi), games, tokenized assets and others. Smart contracts automate the execution of transactions and agreements, providing a high degree of trust and reliability without the need to involve intermediaries [11–13].

The Ethereum blockchain platform is a powerful and high-performance platform for concluding smart contracts. It improves and modernizes business practices, data management, and application development in the digital world. This approach not only provides a secure and transparent environment for the execution of contracts, but also opens up new opportunities for creating complex decentralized systems that are less subject to control or management by third parties [2].

In recent times, blockchain platforms are being heavily influenced by cloud services, which are noticeably changing the behavior and development of these platforms, including Ethereum. The cloud computing model provides developers and enterprises with reliable computing resources, data storage capabilities, and a set of tools for development, testing, and deployment. This approach helps to reduce complexity and costs for many projects in the field of blockchain technology. Studying the aspects allows us to highlight several key points:

- Accessibility and scalability. Cloud services allow companies to develop their blockchain solutions or buy ready-made ones and adapt to changing needs without having to spend additional resources on long-term scaling of infrastructure or new equipment. This makes it easier to launch new projects and guarantees high availability and reliability of the network, since cloud platforms often provide distributed computing resources and data storage on a global scale.
- Simplify development and deployment. Cloud computing platforms offer a range of tools and services that facilitate the creation, testing and implementation of blockchain applications. Using the provided templates, developers can focus on creating targeted applications without worrying about the basic functionality.
- Increase efficiency and reduce costs. The development and implementation of blockchain applications using cloud services allows you to reduce the cost of purchasing and maintaining the necessary infrastructure. Moreover, there are many designers, thanks to which consumers can choose the best tariff plan for themselves.

- Potential Risks and Challenges: Despite the apparent advantages, the use of cloud services in blockchain infrastructure carries potential risks, especially related to centralization and security. Dependence on cloud providers can lead to vulnerabilities in the event of hacking of their systems or sudden shutdown of services. In addition, the centralization of nodes from a single cloud provider is more at risk of attacks, such as distributed denial-of-service (DDoS).

On the one hand, cloud services participate in the development and expansion of blockchain platforms - offering developers and companies a number of significant advantages. On the other hand, it is necessary to carefully analyze potential risks and develop strategies to minimize them in order to ensure the security and stability of blockchain systems.

The purpose of this article is to explore the disadvantages of using cloud services to service nodes on the Ethereum network. Special attention is paid to the security and effectiveness of smart contracts in the context of popularization of cloud technologies. It is necessary to identify potential risks and vulnerabilities that arise due to centralization and dependence on cloud providers.

2 Cloud Computing and Its Impact on Ethereum's Infrastructure: Analyzing Scalability, Security, and Centralization Challenges

Cloud computing is the concept of distributing various computing resources and services (such as servers, storage, databases, network components and software) over the Internet on a consumer basis. Thanks to this paradigm, enterprises do not need to invest in internal IT infrastructure to take advantage of reliable computing capabilities. Platform as a Service (PaaS), software as a Service (SaaS), and Infrastructure as a Service (IaaS) are just a few examples of several types of cloud services, each offering different levels of management, flexibility, and scalability.

The role of cloud computing in blockchain:

1. Flexibility and scalability: cloud services enable efficient scaling of blockchain systems, which allows them to be rapidly expanded by adding additional resources in response to growing demand. Because cloud solutions provide flexible resource management, enterprises can reduce costs while increasing productivity;
2. Cloud services simplify development and implementation by providing programmers with access to environments and tools for creating, testing and deploying blockchain applications. This reduces the technical barriers associated with the creation and implementation of new businesses, making blockchain technology available to a wider range of developers;
3. Reliability and availability - the use of cloud services can enhance the reliability and availability of blockchain systems. The distributed architecture of cloud platforms ensures a high level of fault tolerance and guarantees continuous operation of services even in the event of failures at individual nodes;

4. Security - despite concerns related to centralization and control by cloud service providers, many cloud platforms offer advanced security solutions. This includes data encryption, access and identity management, and regular security audits.

But even with all the advantages, the use of cloud computing in the blockchain also entails certain risks related to data security, dependence on specific service providers and potential vulnerability to centralized attacks [1]. It is very important to carefully assess these risks and develop strategies to mitigate them in order to fully exploit the potential of cloud technologies for the development and support blockchain infrastructure.

Centralization of node maintenance in the Ethereum network is a serious problem, as it contradicts the basic principles of security and decentralization of blockchain technology. Nodes are autonomous computers or servers that participate in the Ethereum blockchain, performing transactions and/or verifying blocks. When a significant portion of these nodes are supported by a small number of cloud service providers, centralization occurs. This raises concerns about network administration, security, and trust:

1. Distributed Denial of Service (DDoS) attacks. If most nodes are located in the infrastructure of several cloud providers, DDoS attacks on these providers can temporarily disable a significant part of the network;
2. Censorship of transactions. Because nodes are centralized, it is easier for cloud service providers working under external pressure to censor or block transactions;
3. A security breach. In centralized systems, the likelihood of data compromise and network manipulation increases due to the presence of individual points of failure.

The centralization of nodes also calls into question the principles of trust and management in the Ethereum network:

1. Dependency on cloud service providers. A strong reliance on a few cloud providers reduces the degree of decentralization and increases the risks associated with external management and control;
2. Reduced resistance to censorship. One of the primary objectives of blockchain is its resistance to censorship and external control. The centralization of nodes threatens this objective by simplifying the potential for blocking or restricting access to the network;
3. Loss of trust. An increase in centralization can undermine the network participants' trust, as one of the key advantages of blockchain over traditional financial systems is its decentralized nature.

The centralization of node maintenance in the Ethereum network poses a serious problem for the security, trust and sustainability of the ecosystem [4]. It is extremely important to look for strategies and solutions aimed at reducing the degree of centralization, for example, to encourage the deployment of nodes within a diverse and distributed infrastructure. The development and application of such strategies will help preserve the fundamental principles of decentralization and security of the Ethereum blockchain, ensuring its long-term functioning and sustainability.

Analysis of the current state of Ethereum infrastructure.

Statistical analysis of the proportion of Ethereum nodes serviced through cloud platforms (2022–2024). The study used data from several sources, such as direct requests to Ethereum nodes and information received from large cloud service providers. The information was collected in order to find out how many nodes of the Ethereum network are currently in use in general, what proportion of nodes are hosted in cloud services such as Microsoft Azure, Amazon Web Services (AWS), Google Cloud Platform (GCP) and others, and where these nodes are located.

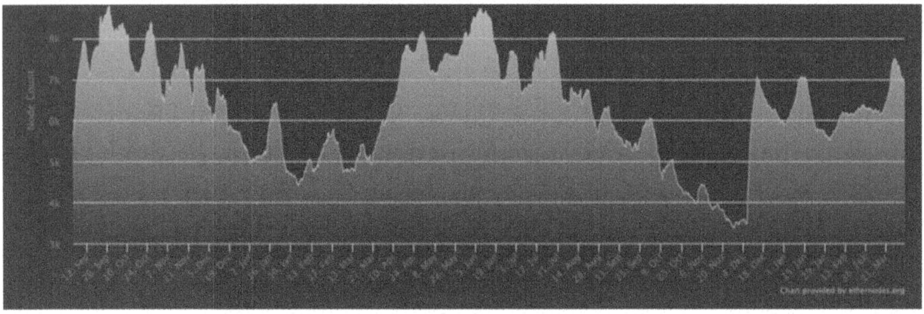

Fig. 1. Distribution of node count by time.

The analysis yielded the following conclusions:

1. The total number of active nodes in the Ethereum network fluctuated between 8700 and 3390 from 2022 to 2024, and as of March 2024, it returned to the figures of September 2022 - the moment of the network's transition to PoS (Fig. 1) [5].
2. The share of nodes on cloud platforms in 2022 accounted for approximately 60% of all Ethereum nodes, with AWS dominating at 40%, followed by GCP at 12% and Azure at 8%. By 2023, there was a slight increase to 65%, indicating a continuing trend towards centralization. In 2024, the proportion of cloud-hosted nodes decreased to 47% (Fig. 2), which may suggest the beginning of distribution and diversification of infrastructure among developers and network users [7].
   The diversity of cloud providers (Fig. 3) and the significant proportion of non-cloud nodes highlight the move towards diversification and distribution of the Ethereum infrastructure [7].
3. Geographic Distribution. Nodes situated on cloud platforms were predominantly concentrated in North America and Europe (Fig. 4), highlighting the

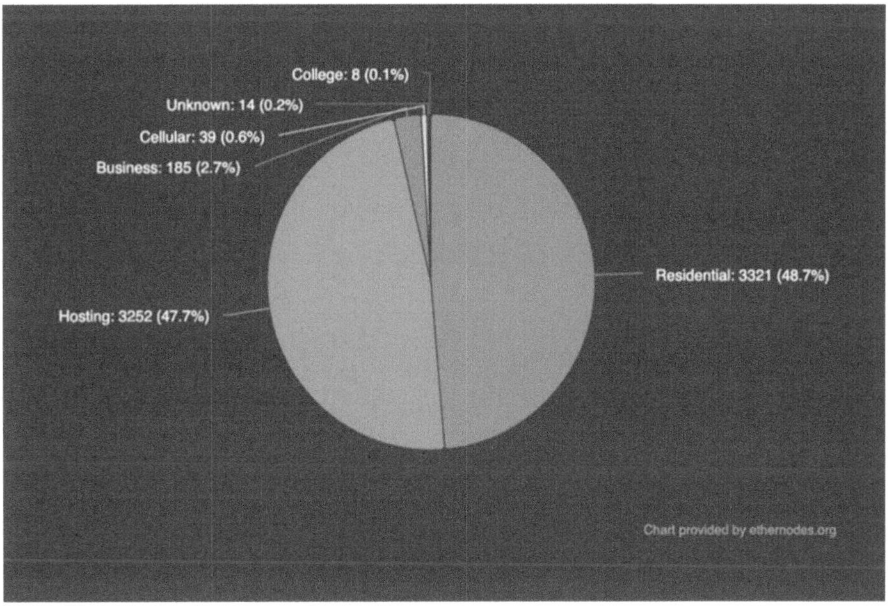

Fig. 2. Distribution of nodes by hosting type.

geopolitical and economic factors influencing the distribution of blockchain infrastructure [6].

Statistics show that a significant percentage of Etherium nodes are hosted in cloud services, which contributes to centralization. The situation may improve in 2024 if there is a slight trend towards decentralization, but there are still significant threats to network security and reliability when using large cloud providers. These results highlight the need for additional research and strategies to promote more dispersed and decentralized node hosting. This may include improving the availability and usability of nodes on personal computers and in small data centers, as well as developing tools and incentives for deploying local nodes.

As shown, a significant part of the Ethereum nodes are hosted on the internal servers of well-known cloud providers. The centralization of nodes affects the structure and functionality of the network, which raises security concerns and threatens the concept of decentralization underlying blockchain technology. One of the main security concerns is that any flaws or failures in cloud services can have far-reaching consequences for the Ethereum network as a whole. A careful strategy is required to reduce the degree of centralization and the associated security risks:

1. Expanding the range of cloud service providers. Encouraging the installation of nodes on other cloud platforms, such as standalone small cloud services;

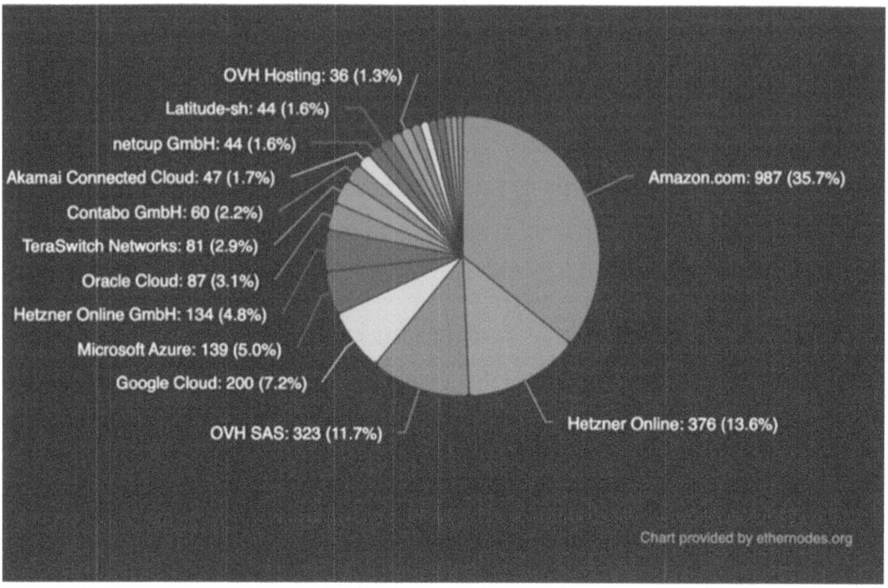

Fig. 3. Distribution of nodes across cloud services.

2. Deployment of local nodes. Encouraging local node deployment by network users and developers to reduce reliance on centralized cloud infrastructures;
3. Enhancing security measures. Implementing advanced security measures, including encryption, authentication, and regular audits, to reduce the vulnerabilities of nodes hosted on cloud platforms;
4. Regulatory support and standardization. Developing standards and regulatory frameworks to ensure the security and resilience of cloud services used for maintaining blockchain infrastructure.

Reducing the level of centralization in the Ethereum network and improving its security require joint efforts from the community, developers, and cloud providers. Maintaining decentralization not only contributes to the networks security and resilience but also ensures adherence to its fundamental principles.

3 The Block Censorship Problem in Ethereum and the Role of Flashbots

In Ethereum the ability of some parties, such as miners or validators, to choose which transactions to reject is known as blocking censorship. This possibility raises questions about the transparency and fairness of the Ethereum network, especially in light of the decentralized nature of blockchain technology; One of the key players in this scene is Flashbots, a research and development company whose goal is to prevent the centralization risks associated with MEV, mitigate

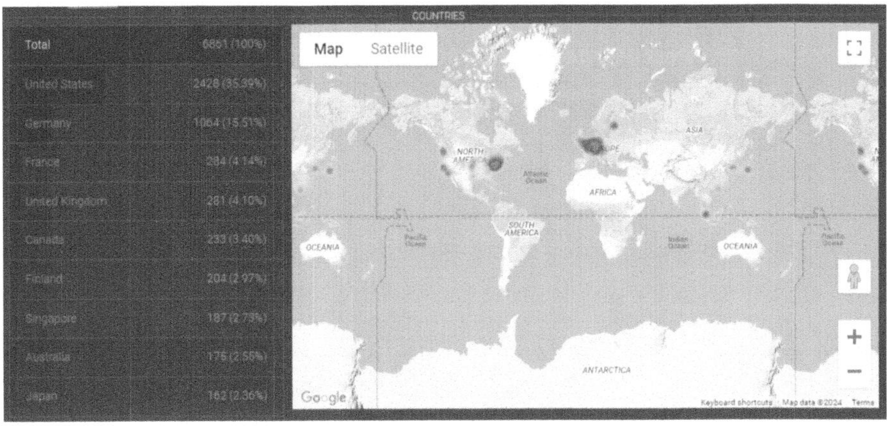

Fig. 4. Geography of node distribution.

the negative effects of existing mining (MEV) strategies (such as gas auction wars, which can lead to the strangulation of the network).

Flashbots introduced MEV-Boost [8], a protocol that allows validators to outsource the construction of blocks to specialized builders, which include Flashbots and others, in a sealed-bid auction format. While this system was designed to make the MEV extraction process more efficient and reduce network congestion, it inadvertently introduced a potential vector for censorship, especially concerning transactions associated with certain protocols or wallets.

A significant portion of Ethereum blocks processed with MEV-Boost is attributed to flashbots. The obtained data suggests that a significant portion of transactions in Ethereum can and has been censored. So the situation in 2022 was critical, the share of censored blocks amounted to 80% (Fig. 5). This high level of censorship raises critical questions about the integrity and censorship-resistant stability of the Ethereum network. It is important to realize that although Flash bots aim to improve network efficiency and reduce MEV issues, but the concentration of power in a few blockchain builders can lead to censorship vulnerabilities [9].

The central role of flashbots in block production and related censorship issues highlight the contradiction between improving the effectiveness of specialized MEV strategies and the fundamental principles of decentralization and anti-censorship in Ethereum. Depending on a limited number of block developers, even with the intention of optimizing MEV extraction, can lead to a scenario in which transactions are excluded based on criteria set by several organizations, thereby jeopardizing the open and non-permissive nature of the network. In addition, the current situation sheds light on the broader problem of reconciling the technical and economic optimization provided by solutions such as flashbots with the ethical and philosophical foundations of blockchain technology. As Ethereum continues to evolve, especially with its transition to Proof of Stake - (PoS) and

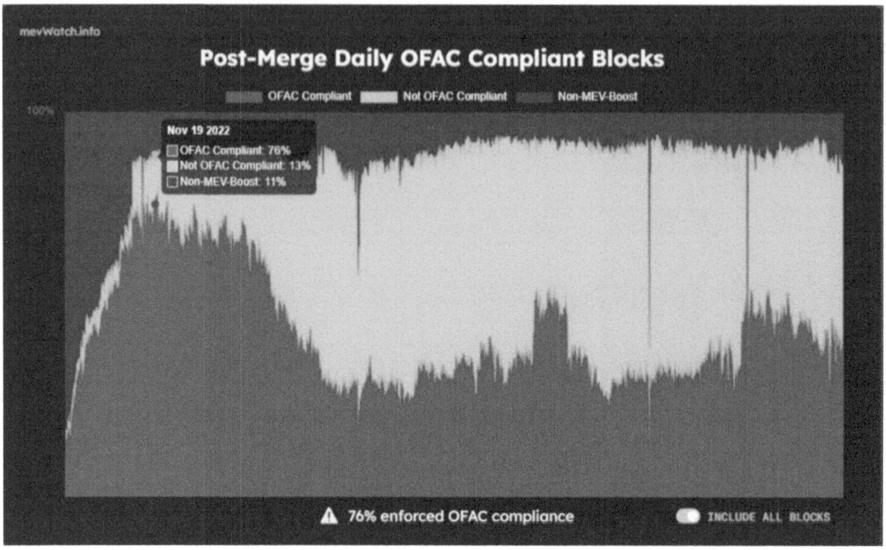

Fig. 5. Percentage of censored blocks 2022

increased focus on scalability and efficiency, the community faces an important challenge to address the issues of centralization and censorship.

To solve the block censorship problem by taking advantage of flash bots and similar MEV-related innovations, several strategies can be considered:

1. Diversification of block developers. Encouraging a wider range of participants to participate in the development of blocks can help reduce the risks of censorship and centralization. This includes encouraging small operators and ensuring transparency and fairness in the selection process for block developers.
2. Transparent censorship policy. Implementing clear guidelines and transparency measures regarding the reasons for excluding transactions can help maintain trust in the ecosystem. This transparency should extend to the criteria used by blockchain developers to censor transactions.
3. Supervision and management by the community. Creating mechanisms for public oversight and contributing to the practice of MEV extraction and block creation can enhance accountability. This may include management proposals and voting procedures that allow stakeholders to voice their concerns and influence the direction of MEV-related development.
4. Technical solutions to counter censorship. Research and development of technical solutions that make it difficult or economically impractical to censor certain transactions or types of transactions can provide better protection against censorship.

Thanks to the aforementioned methods, the share of censored blocks has begun to decrease. As of March 2024, the share of such blocks is around 50%

(Fig. 6), which is almost twice as low as in 2022 [9]. This indicates that society is striving to return to one of the fundamental principles of blockchain - decentralization.

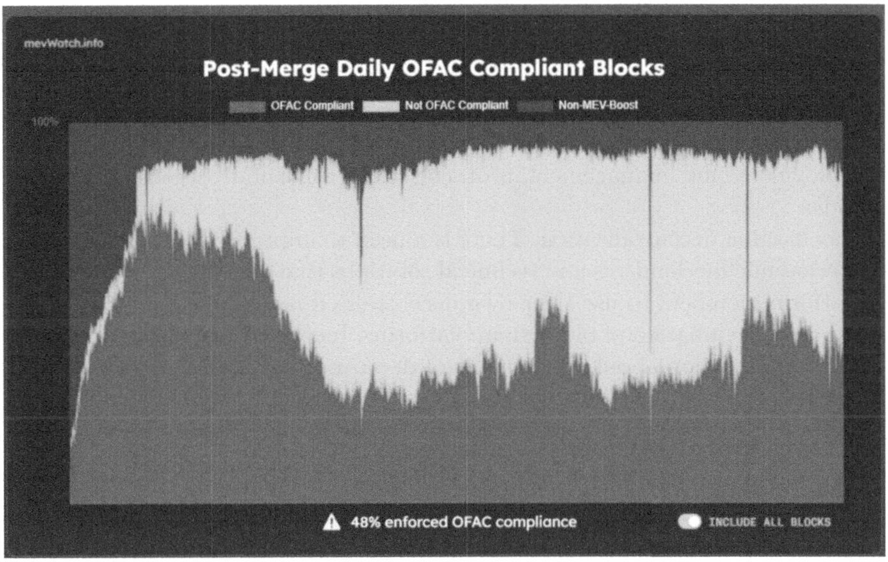

Fig. 6. Percentage of censored blocks 2024

4 Conclusion

This research shows that hosting blockchain nodes on cloud platforms significantly increases the security and transparency risks of smart contracts, making them more vulnerable to cyber-attacks, data leaks, and third-party interference. This paper analyzes the impact of the centralization process on the security, efficiency, and transparency of smart contracts hosted on the Ethereum network. As a result, the data obtained demonstrates the problem of violation of one of the fundamental principles of blockchain technology - decentralisation. The following conclusions can be drawn:

1. Impact on performance parameters. The analysis revealed that using centralised cloud services can have a negative impact on transaction execution time and cost on the Ethereum blockchain, which affects overall network performance.
2. Security. The study found that centralisation increases the security risk of smart contracts, exposing them more privately to cyberattacks, data breaches and third-party interference.

3. Decentralisation. The process of centralising the maintenance of blockchain platform nodes contradicts one of the main approaches of the technology, compromising its reliability and openness.

The results of this research work reflect the need to move away from the massive use of cloud servers, which is a centralised service model to a more decentralised one:

1. Development of new technological solutions. Introducing innovations that aim to simplify the process of building proprietary platforms, including improved deployment and management protocols that will entail decentralisation of nodes.
2. Encouraging decentralisation. There is a need to improve the implementation of economic mechanisms and technical solutions that will explicitly encourage platform members to use their own decentralised nodes.
3. Increase the inflation of blockchain platforms. Increase the quantity and quality of information about the benefits of decentralisation and the risks of centralisation, which will generate ideas to support the principle of decentralisation.

Decentralisation is not just a technical challenge, it is an important aspect on which blockchain systems are based. By adhering to this principle and moving to more decentralised service models, openness, transparency and trustworthiness can be strengthened in the system.

The realization of this transformation requires collective efforts from researchers, developers, and users to explore and implement innovative solutions that contribute to genuine decentralization.

References

1. CoinMarketCap. A Deep Dive Into Infrastructure Centralization in Ethereum. https://coinmarketcap.com/academy/article/a-deep-dive-into-infrastructure-centralization-in-ethereum
2. Ethereum. Nodes and Clients. https://ethereum.org/en/developers/docs/nodes-and-clients/
3. Ethereum. Security Considerations for Smart Contracts. https://ethereum.org/en/developers/docs/smart-contracts/security/
4. CoinDesk. ETH May Already Be Showcasing Increased Signs of Centralization (2022). https://www.coindesk.com/tech/2022/09/15/eth-may-already-be-showcasing-increased-signs-of-centralization/
5. Ethernodes. Ethereum Node History (2024). https://ethernodes.org/history
6. Ethernodes. Ethereum Nodes Geographic Distribution (2024). https://ethernodes.org/countries
7. Ethernodes. Network Types (2024). https://ethernodes.org/network-types
8. MEV-Boost (2024). https://github.com/flashbots/mev-boost
9. MEV Watch. Post-Merge Daily OFAC Compliant Blocks (2024). https://www.mevwatch.info/

10. Dostov, V., Krivoruchko, S., Shust, P., Titov, V.: Are digital signatures in blockchain functionally equivalent to handwritten signatures? In: Gervasi, O., et al. (eds.) Computational Science and Its Applications - ICCSA 2023 Workshops - Athens, Greece, July 3–6, 2023, Proceedings, Part I. Lecture Notes in Computer Science, vol. 14104, pp. 527–537. Springer, Cham (2023). https://doi.org/10.1007/978-3-031-37105-9_35
11. Sinkevich, D., Anikin, A., Smirnov, V.: Embracing Blockchain technology in logistics. In: Kabassi, K., Mylonas, P., Caro, J. (eds.) NiDS 2023. LNCS, vol. 784, pp. 127–133. Springer, Cham (2023). https://doi.org/10.1007/978-3-031-44146-2_13
12. Sychev, O., Denisov, M., Anikin, A.: Verifying algorithm traces and fault reason determining using ontology reasoning. In: Taylor, K.L., Gonçalves, R., Lécué, F., Yan, J. (eds.) Proceedings of the ISWC 2020 Demos and Industry Tracks: From Novel Ideas to Industrial Practice co-located with 19th International Semantic Web Conference (ISWC 2020), Globally online, November 1-6, 2020 (UTC). CEUR Workshop Proceedings, vol. 2721, pp. 49–54. CEUR-WS.org (2020). http://ceur-ws.org/Vol-2721/paper495.pdf
13. Zhou, H., Milani Fard, A., Makanju, A.: The state of Ethereum smart contracts security: vulnerabilities, countermeasures, and tool support. J. Cybersecur. Priv. **2**(2), 358–378 (2022)

Integration of PBFT and Raft Algorithms with Recurrent Neural Networks to Improve the Reliability of Distributed Systems

Alexander Bogdanov[1], Nadezhda Shchegoleva[1,2], Valery Khvatov[3], Jasur Kiyamov[1,5](✉), Gennady Dik[1,4], Ilkhom Rakhmatullayev[5], Shakhboz Ergashev[6], and Oybek Umurzakov[5]

[1] St. Petersburg University, Saint Petersburg, Russia
{a.v.bogdanov,n.shchegoleva,z.kiyamov}@spbu.ru
[2] St. Petersburg State Marine Technical University, Saint Petersburg, Russia
[3] DGT Technologies AG, Lachine, Canada
[4] St. Petersburg LLC "System Technologies", Saint Petersburg, Russia
g.dick@systechnologies.ru
[5] Samarkand Branch of Tashkent University of Information Technologies, Samarkand, Uzbekistan
[6] Millitary Institute of Information and Communication Technologies, Tashkent, Uzbekistan

Abstract. The combined approach proposes the use of PBFT and Raft to ensure data consistency and fault tolerance in the system, and also integrates recurrent neural networks to analyze and predict the behavior of nodes in the network. RNNs can be used to detect anomalies, predict system load, and analyze time series data related to node operation. The proposed combined approach opens up new prospects for the development of distributed systems, increasing their reliability, fault tolerance and adaptability to changing conditions. Further research in this direction could lead to more efficient and secure distributed systems that can efficiently handle complex real-world scenarios.

Keywords: PBFT · Raft · Recurrent Neural Networks · Reliability Ensuring · Distributed Systems

1 Introduction

The continuous search for new methods and algorithms is an integral part of the development of distributed systems. These methods must be able to ensure stable system operation even in the face of unexpected failures or attacks. Therefore, the development and application of mechanisms to ensure fault tolerance and data reliability becomes a key task for engineers and developers.

Fault tolerance in distributed systems is achieved through a number of methods, including data replication, backup mechanisms, and consensus algorithms.

O. Gervasi et al. (Eds.): ICCSA 2024 Workshops, LNCS 14815, pp. 226–237, 2024.
https://doi.org/10.1007/978-3-031-65154-0_14

Consensus algorithms such as PBFT (Practical Byzantine Fault Tolerance) and Raft play a critical role in ensuring data consistency in distributed environments [1,2].

However, recent research also shows that the use of neural networks, in particular recurrent neural networks (RNN), can significantly improve anomaly detection, system load forecasting, and time series analysis of node performance data.

Thus, the integration of consensus algorithms with recurrent neural networks represents a promising approach to improve the reliability and fault tolerance of distributed systems. This symbiosis of traditional methods and new technologies opens the door to the creation of more efficient, secure and adaptive distributed systems that can effectively cope with the challenges of the modern world [3].

2 Applications of Neural Networks for Analysis

The combined approach presented in this article combines two leading consensus algorithms - PBFT (Practical Byzantine Fault Tolerance) and Raft. PBFT is distinguished by its ability to provide data consistency in systems with a limited number of nodes, while Raft offers a simple and straightforward consensus mechanism for distributed systems (Fig. 1).

The inclusion of recurrent neural networks in this combined approach opens up new horizons for analyzing and predicting the behavior of nodes in the network. Recurrent neural networks can be used to detect anomalies, predict system load, and analyze time series data related to node activity. This innovative approach provides the ability to effectively detect and respond to changes in system operation.

In the context of distributed systems, recurrent neural networks can be used to detect anomalies in the operation of nodes. They are able to analyze time series of data related to node activity and identify deviations from normal behavior, which allows them to quickly respond to possible problems.

In addition, recurrent neural networks make it possible to predict the load on the system. By analyzing historical load and behavior data of nodes, they can predict future resource demands and temporary peaks in activity, which helps optimize system performance and warn of potential problems.

Integrating recurrent neural networks into a combination approach also provides the ability to analyze time series data, which allows us to better understand the dynamics of the system and identify hidden patterns or trends that can be useful for decision making.

The integration of PBFT, Raft and recurrent neural networks represents a promising path for the development of distributed systems. This symbiosis of traditional methods and new technologies opens the door to the creation of more reliable, secure and adaptive distributed systems that can effectively overcome the challenges of the modern world.

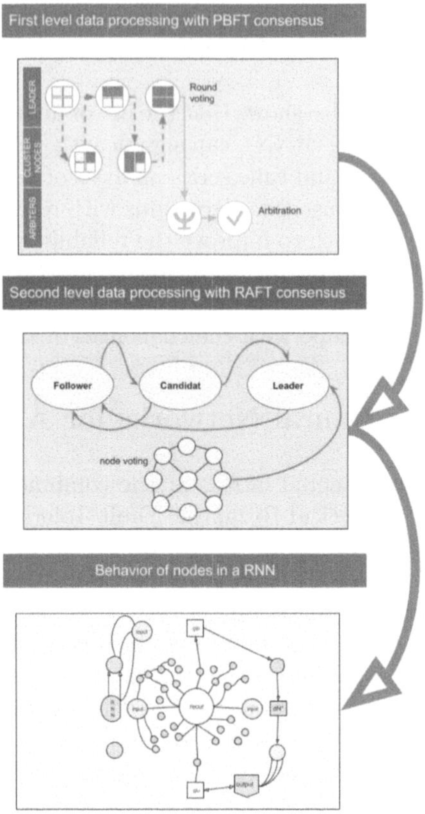

Fig. 1. Network process

3 Process of Operation of Recurrent Neural Networks

In the operation of recurrent neural networks (RNN), data is transferred through successive time steps, where each step includes input data and hidden layers [4]. RNNs have a special property called recurrence, which allows them to remember information about previous states and use this information for subsequent calculations.

Each hidden layer in an RNN has its own short-term memory, which allows the model to take into account the context and sequence of the input data [5]. This short-term memory allows the RNN to "remember" information about previous inputs and use it to make decisions in subsequent steps (Fig. 2).

When new data is input to an RNN, the model uses the current input value in combination with previous values stored in short-term memory to predict the next output or state. This process is repeated at every time step, making RNN a powerful tool for analyzing and processing sequential data such as time series, text, or audio signals.

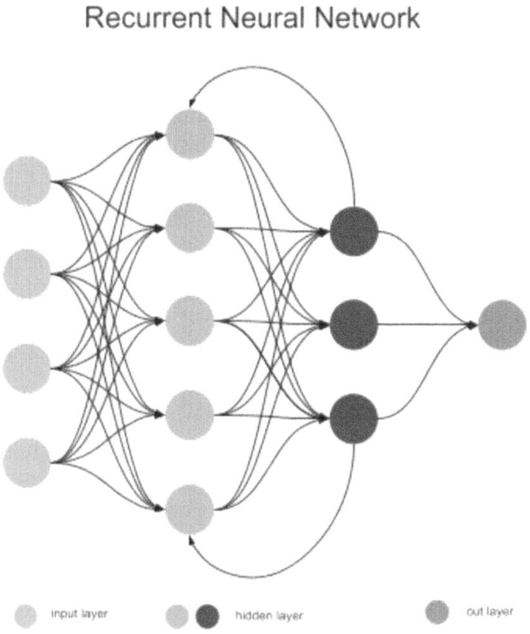

Fig. 2. RNN operation model

RNN There are different types of connections that define the interactions between nodes in the network [11,12]. Here are some of the main types of connections in RNN:

1. Unidirectional connections: Information is passed only in one direction, from input neurons to output neurons. This is a typical configuration in RNNs, where each neuron in the hidden layer is connected to the previous and subsequent layers;
2. Bidirectional connections: Information is passed both forward and backward through the neurons in the network. This allows considering context from both past and future when analyzing sequential data;
3. Self-connections: These connections allow a neuron to pass information to itself from previous time steps. They help maintain the neuron's state or detect long-term dependencies in the data.
4. Self-connections: These connections allow a neuron to pass information to itself from previous time steps. They help maintain the neuron's state or detect long-term dependencies in the data.
5. Fully connected layers: In this case, each neuron in one layer is connected to every neuron in the next layer. This is a typical configuration for fully connected layers used in neural networks.

They help determine the structure of the network and how information is transmitted and processed over time.

The introduction of RNNs into a combined approach represents a significant breakthrough in analyzing and predicting the behavior of nodes in a distributed network. RNNs have the unique ability to remember and use previous input data, making them a powerful tool for analyzing time series data.

The network analysis algorithm for a combination of the P-BFT and RAFT protocols may include the following steps:

1. Definition of network architecture:
   - Define the network structure, including the number of nodes, their types (leaders, match nodes, etc.), and the configuration of each layer (P-BFT and RAFT).
   - Determine the mechanisms for exchanging messages between nodes in the network.
2. Study of P-BFT and RAFT protocols:
   - Study the basic operating principles of each protocol, their leader selection algorithms, coordination and decision-making mechanisms.
3. Security analysis:
   - Evaluate the security level of each protocol and its suitability for a particular network.
   - Research vulnerabilities and possible attacks that could be directed at the network.
4. Determining network parameters:
   - Define network parameters such as number of nodes, timeout parameters, decision thresholds, etc.
5. Simulation and testing:
   - Create a network model using the selected parameters and protocols.
   - Conduct a series of test trials using various scenarios such as node failures, message delays, etc.
   - Evaluate network performance, its resilience to failures, and its ability to adapt to changing environmental conditions.
6. Optimization and improvement:
   - Identify weaknesses in the network and its protocols.
   - Propose and implement improvements to improve network performance, security and resiliency.
7. Monitoring and maintenance:
   - Install monitoring and tracking systems to continuously monitor the health of the network.
   - Perform periodic testing and maintenance of the network to ensure optimal operation.

This is the main network analysis algorithm for the combination of P-BFT and RAFT protocols. When implementing the algorithm, the specifics of a particular network and its goals should be taken into account.

With this ability, RNNs can effectively detect anomalies in node operation, predict system load, and analyze changes over time. This allows the system to quickly respond to changes in its operation and take the necessary measures to maintain stable and reliable operation.

Integrating RNNs into a combined approach opens up new horizons for improving the reliability, fault tolerance, and adaptability of distributed systems. Analyzing the data provided by RNN allows the system to more effectively adapt to changing conditions and successfully overcome complex scenarios encountered in the real world [6,7].

Research in this direction can lead to the creation of more efficient and reliable distributed systems that can effectively respond to changes in the environment and ensure stable operation in a wide variety of conditions. This opens up new prospects for developing technologies and improving the functioning of distributed networks in general.

4 Network Communication Model

A mathematical model of a combined approach using recurrent neural networks (RNN), PBFT and Raft in distributed systems can be represented as follows:

1. Recurrent neural networks (RNN):
   - RNNs are a class of neural networks in which information from past time steps is stored and passed on to the next steps;
   - Mathematically, RNNs are defined by the recurrence relation:

$$h_t = f(W_{xh}x_t + W_{hh}h_{t-1} + b_h)$$
$$y_t = g(W_{hy}h_t + b_y)$$

   - Where h_t is the hidden state at time step t, x_t is the input vector at time step t, W_{xh}, W_{hh}, W_{hy} are weight matrices, b_h, b_y are displacement vectors, f and g are activation functions.
2. PBFT (Practical Byzantine Fault Tolerance):
   - PBFT is a consensus algorithm for distributed systems that ensures data consistency in the face of asynchrony and unreliability;
   - Mathematically, PBFT relies on the idea of quorums and signature verification mechanisms.
   - PBFT uses quorums to make decisions. Let's assume there are N nodes in the system, and to reach an agreement, it's required that a majority of nodes ($N - f$, where f is the maximum number of faulty nodes) agree on a proposed value. Let M be the set of messages received by each node. Suppose $Q(m)$ is a function returning a quorum, where m is a message. Mathematically, the quorum $Q(m)$ can be defined as:

$$Q(m) = \{m' \in M : |\{m'' \in M : \text{m}'' \text{ supports m}'\}| > N - f\}$$

3. Raft:
   - Raft is also a consensus algorithm that offers a simple mechanism for leader election and log replication to maintain consistency [8,14].
   - Mathematically, Raft is determined by the logic of leader selection and the decision-making algorithm based on the majority of votes.

- Raft is based on leader election and log replication. Let N be the number of nodes in the system. To make a decision, each node votes for a leader candidate. If a candidate receives more than half of the votes (more than $N/2$), it becomes the leader. Mathematically, the leader election condition can be expressed as:

$$\text{If votes for candidate} > \frac{N}{2}, \text{then it becomes the leader}$$

The combined approach combines these algorithms using recurrent neural networks to analyze and predict the behavior of nodes in the network [9,13]. The mathematical model of the combined approach can include sharing the output of the RNN with the results of the PBFT and Raft algorithms for decision making and adaptation to changes in the distributed system [10]. PBFT and Raft ensure data consistency and efficient consensus management, while the integration of RNN complements their capabilities with analysis and prediction of node behavior in the network.

1. Reliability and Fault Tolerance: This refers to the system's ability to operate continuously and reliably even in the presence of faults or failures. A reliable system maintains its functionality and integrity despite adverse conditions.
2. Combined Approach: By combining PBFT, Raft, and RNN, we leverage the strengths of each component to enhance the overall reliability and fault tolerance of the system. This synergistic approach ensures that the system can withstand various challenges and continue functioning optimally.
3. PBFT and Raft for Data Consistency and Consensus Management:
   - PBFT is known for its ability to achieve consensus in distributed systems, even in the presence of Byzantine faults, where nodes may behave arbitrarily. It ensures data consistency by reaching agreement among a designated quorum of nodes;
   - Raft is another consensus algorithm that simplifies distributed system design while providing strong consistency guarantees. It elects a leader among the nodes, which coordinates the replication of the log and ensures data consistency across the cluster.
4. Integration of RNN for Node Behavior Analysis and Prediction: RNNs are a class of neural networks capable of modeling sequential data. By integrating RNNs into the system, we gain the ability to analyze and predict the behavior of nodes in the network over time. RNNs can detect anomalies, forecast node workload, and analyze temporal data patterns associated with node operations.
5. Complementary Capabilities: The integration of RNN complements the consensus algorithms (PBFT and Raft) by providing additional insights into the behavior of nodes. This combination enhances the system's ability to detect and respond to anomalies or deviations from expected behavior, thereby improving overall reliability and fault tolerance.

Formalizing an RNN algorithm for network analysis of a combination of P-BFT and RAFT protocols may involve defining mathematical expressions to evaluate the performance, security, and resilience of the network. The following are possible types of formulas that can be used in such an analysis:

1. Loss Function:
   - $L_{total} = L_{P-BFT} + L_{RAFT}$ - the total loss function, combining the loss functions for the P-BFT and RAFT protocols.
2. Performance:
   - $T^{P-BFT}_{round-trip}$ - the time taken to process one round-trip of consensus in the P-BFT protocol.
   - $T^{RAFT}_{round-trip}$ - the time taken to process one round-trip of consensus in the RAFT protocol.
   - $T^{total}_{round-trip} = T^{P-BFT}_{round-trip} + T^{RAFT}_{round-trip}$ - the total time taken to process one round-trip of consensus in the combination of protocols.
   - $Throughput_{total} = \frac{1}{T^{total}_{round-trip}}$ - the overall throughput of the network.
3. Security:
   - P^{P-BFT}_{attack} - the probability of a successful attack on the P-BFT protocol.
   - P^{RAFT}_{attack} - the probability of a successful attack on the RAFT protocol.
   - $P^{total}_{attack} = P^{P-BFT}_{attack} + P^{RAFT}_{attack}$ - the overall probability of a successful attack on the combination of protocols.
4. Resilience:
   - $T^{P-BFT}_{recovery}$ - the time taken to recover the network after a node failure in the P-BFT protocol.
   - $T^{RAFT}_{recovery}$ - the time taken to recover the network after a node failure in the RAFT protocol.
   - $T^{total}_{recovery} = T^{P-BFT}_{recovery} + T^{RAFT}_{recovery}$ - the total time taken to recover the network.

The loss function for the analysis of a network combining P-BFT and RAFT protocols depends on the specific task or objective being considered. In general, the loss function is used to quantify the discrepancy between the predicted output of the RNN model and the ground truth.

Here's a general form of the loss function for such an analysis:

Let's denote:

- $\hat{y}_i$ as the predicted output of the RNN model for the i-th example,
- y_i as the ground truth output for the i-th example.

The loss function L can be defined as the average loss across all examples in the dataset, and it can be calculated using various metrics such as mean squared error (MSE), mean absolute error (MAE), or cross-entropy loss (for classification tasks), among others.

For example, the mean squared error (MSE) loss function can be expressed as:

$$L = \frac{1}{N} \sum_{i=1}^{N} (\hat{y}_i - y_i)^2$$

where:

- N is the total number of examples in the dataset,
- $\hat{y}_i$ is the predicted output of the RNN model for the i-th example,
- y_i is the ground truth output for the i-th example.

This loss function quantifies the average squared difference between the predicted and actual outputs across all examples in the dataset. The goal during training is to minimize this loss function, typically using optimization algorithms like stochastic gradient descent (SGD) or its variants.

The performance of an RNN in analyzing a network combining P-BFT and RAFT protocols can be evaluated using various metrics. Here are some key performance metrics that can be considered:

1. Throughput: Throughput refers to the rate at which the network can process transactions or messages. In the context of RNN analysis, throughput can be measured as the number of transactions successfully processed per unit time.
2. Latency: Latency measures the delay between the initiation of a request and the completion of the corresponding operation. Lower latency indicates faster processing and better performance.
3. Accuracy: Accuracy measures how well the RNN model can predict or classify data. It is typically defined as the percentage of correct predictions or classifications made by the model.
4. Resource Utilization: Resource utilization evaluates how efficiently the computational resources (such as CPU, memory, and bandwidth) are utilized in the network. Higher resource utilization can lead to improved performance, while excessive utilization may result in bottlenecks and decreased performance.
5. Fault Tolerance: Fault tolerance measures the network's ability to continue operating correctly in the presence of faults or failures. This includes the ability to detect and recover from node failures, network partitions, or other types of disruptions.
6. Scalability: Scalability refers to the network's ability to handle an increasing number of transactions or users while maintaining performance. A scalable network can accommodate growth without significant degradation in performance.
7. Security: Security evaluates the network's resilience to attacks, unauthorized access, and data breaches. It includes measures such as encryption, authentication, and access control mechanisms to protect sensitive information and ensure the integrity of transactions.

These performance metrics can be quantitatively evaluated through simulations, experiments, or real-world deployments of the RNN model in the network environment.

1. Cryptographic Mechanisms: Evaluate the cryptographic mechanisms used by both P-BFT and RAFT protocols to ensure data confidentiality, integrity, and authentication. This includes assessing the strength of encryption algorithms, key management practices, and digital signature schemes.

2. Consensus Protocol Security: Analyze the security properties of the P-BFT and RAFT protocols, including resistance to various attacks such as Sybil attacks, Byzantine faults, and Denial of Service (DoS) attacks. Assess the robustness of the protocols in maintaining consensus and preventing malicious behavior by network participants.
3. Node Authentication: Verify the mechanisms for authenticating nodes in the network to prevent unauthorized access and impersonation attacks. This may involve using cryptographic certificates, public-key infrastructure (PKI), or other authentication methods to verify the identity of network participants.
4. Data Confidentiality: Ensure that sensitive data transmitted over the network is protected from eavesdropping and unauthorized access. Evaluate the use of encryption techniques such as Transport Layer Security (TLS) or Secure Socket Layer (SSL) to encrypt data in transit and protect it from interception.
5. Access Control: Implement access control mechanisms to restrict access to critical network resources and functions. This includes defining roles and permissions for network participants, enforcing authentication and authorization policies, and monitoring access logs for suspicious activity.
6. Resilience to Attacks: Assess the network's resilience to various types of cyber attacks, including distributed denial-of-service (DDoS) attacks, man-in-the-middle attacks, and insider threats. Implement measures such as intrusion detection systems (IDS), firewalls, and network segmentation to detect and mitigate potential security breaches.
7. Regular Audits and Security Updates: Conduct regular security audits and vulnerability assessments to identify and address potential security weaknesses in the network. Stay informed about security advisories and updates for the P-BFT and RAFT protocols, and promptly apply patches and fixes to mitigate known vulnerabilities.

By addressing these security considerations, researchers and practitioners can enhance the security posture of a network combining P-BFT and RAFT protocols analyzed using an RNN model, reducing the risk of security breaches and ensuring the integrity and confidentiality of network transactions.

This entire system is a complex mathematical model that requires the analysis and optimization of various parameters, such as weights and hyperparameters of neural networks, parameters of consensus algorithms.

5 Conclusions

In conclusion, the key aspects of the combined approach using PBFT, Raft and recurrent neural networks (RNN) for the development of distributed systems should be highlighted.

1. Reliability and fault tolerance: The combined approach allows you to create systems with a high degree of reliability and fault tolerance. PBFT and Raft provide data consistency and efficient consensus management, and RNN integration complements their capabilities by analyzing and predicting the behavior of nodes in the network;

2. Adaptability to changing conditions: The use of RNN allows systems to adapt to dynamic changes in the environment. Analysis of time series data and forecasting allow the system to quickly respond to changes and effectively adapt to new conditions;
3. Efficiency and Security: The combined approach helps to create more efficient and secure distributed systems. PBFT and Raft algorithms ensure stable system operation, and RNNs provide tools for detecting anomalies and preventing possible security threats
4. Potential for development: Further research in this direction could lead to the creation of more innovative and efficient distributed systems. Continuous improvement of algorithms and data analysis methods opens up new prospects for developing technologies and improving the functioning of distributed networks.

Security is a critical aspect of analyzing a network that combines P-BFT and RAFT protocols using an RNN model. Here are some considerations for evaluating the security of such a network:

So, a combined approach based on the joint use of PBFT, Raft and RNN is a promising direction for the development of distributed systems. It combines reliability, adaptability and security, making it an essential tool in the quest to create efficient and reliable infrastructures for various applications and industries.

References

1. Bogdanov, A., Shchegoleva, N., Khvatov, V., Dik, G., Kiyamov, J., Dik, A.: The Combination of P-BFT and RAFT: a new approach to building networks that provide reliability and security. In: Gervasi, O., et al. (eds.) Computational Science and Its Applications – ICCSA 2023 Workshops: Athens, Greece, July 3–6, 2023, Proceedings, Part I, pp. 572–583. Springer Nature Switzerland, Cham (2023). https://doi.org/10.1007/978-3-031-37105-9_38
2. Bogdanov, A., et al.: A multilayer approach to the security of blockchain networks of the future. In: Gervasi, O., Murgante, B., Misra, S., Rocha, A.M.A.C., Garau, C. (eds.) Computational Science and Its Applications – ICCSA 2022 Workshops: Malaga, Spain, July 4–7, 2022, Proceedings, Part I, pp. 205–216. Springer International Publishing, Cham (2022). https://doi.org/10.1007/978-3-031-10536-4_14
3. Ongaro, D., Ousterhout, J.: In search of an understandable consensus algorithm. In: Proceedings of the 2014 USENIX Annual Technical Conference (USENIX ATC), pp. 305–319 (2014)
4. Goodfellow, I., Bengio, Y., Courville, A.: Deep Learning. MIT Press (2016)
5. Hochreiter, S., Schmidhuber, J.: Long short-term memory. Neural Comput. **9**(8), 1735–1780 (1997)
6. Zhang, H., Juels, A., Reiter, M.K., Ristenpart, T.: Town Crier: an authenticated data feed for smart contracts. Proceedings of the 2016 ACM SIGSAC Conference on Computer and Communications Security, 270–282 (2016)
7. Chollet, F.: Deep Learning with Python. Manning Publications (2017)
8. Gilad-Bachrach, R., Navot, A., Reichental, O.: Machine Learning for Anomaly Detection. Springer (2020)

9. Bernstein, P.: Principles of Transaction Processing. Morgan Kaufmann (2017)
10. Haber, S., Stornetta, W.: How to time-stamp a digital document. J. Cryptol. **3**(2), 99–111 (1991)
11. Bahdanau, D., Cho, K., Bengio, Y.: Neural machine translation by jointly learning to align and translate. arXiv preprint arXiv:1409.0473 (2014)
12. Le, Q.V., Jaitly, N., Hinton, G.E.: A simple way to initialize recurrent networks of rectified linear units. arXiv preprint arXiv:1504.00941 (2015)
13. Rakhmatullaevich, R.I., Mardanokulovich, I.B.: Analysis of cryptanalysis methods applied to stream encryption algorithms. In: Artificial Intelligence, Blockchain, Computing and Security, vol. 1. - CRC Press, pp. 393–401 (2024)
14. Zaynalov, N.R., et al.: UNICODE for hiding information in a text document. In: 2020 IEEE 14th International Conference on Application of Information and Communication Technologies (AICT), pp. 1–5. IEEE (2020)

Application of Extended Bass Approach to Statistical Description of Some Cases of Distributed Finances on Example of Stablecoins

Victor Dostov[1,2](✉), Pavel Shust[2], and Svetlana Krivoruchko[1]

[1] Department of Banking and Monetary Regulation, Financial University Under the Government of the Russian Federation, 49 Leningradsky Prospekt, Moscow 125993, Russia
dostov@npaed.ru

[2] Russian Electronic Money and Remittance Association, Novoslobodskaya 20, Moscow 107078, Russia

Abstract. Financial instruments based on blockchain technologies known as Distributed Finances (DeFi), including cryptocurrencies, smart-contract based on tokens, central bank digital currencies (CBDC), are now actively spreading around the world. They acquire a visible share in financial ecosystems, and this share is growing fast. It is important to have some instruments to predict at least some of parameters of their growth. In the article we propose an extension of Bass innovation diffusion model to DeFi on example of widespread stablecoins to describe dynamics of their extension. Specifically, we consider how a number of active users (active addresses) evolve over time, basing on equation of extended Bass innovation diffusion model. The model results describe well qualitative trend and average quantitative behavior of two widespread stablecoins. We also provide a modification of extended Bass equations which is more convenient for stablecoins dynamic approximation and interpretation. Beside usefulness of results for DeFi market analysis, we confirm applicability of innovation diffusion model to payment markets once again. We also discuss limitations of model and possible ways of its development, including introducing competition between different stablecoins.

Keywords: Distributed finances · DeFi dynamics · Bass innovation diffusion · USDT · USDC

1 Distributed Finances Scope

DeFi is an umbrella term for wide class of payment, investing and other financial instruments [1] based on blockchain technology. In turn, blockchain is distributed leger (DL) technology which allow to build extremely reliable and untampered databases which do not depend on single entity, such as database server but store a huge number of database copies in independent nodes under control of blockchain participants. DeFi, correspondingly, relates to blockchains containing financially related information [2].

O. Gervasi et al. (Eds.): ICCSA 2024 Workshops, LNCS 14815, pp. 238–248, 2024.
https://doi.org/10.1007/978-3-031-65154-0_15

Some researchers [3] narrows this definition, limiting DeFi by smart-contract based products. Smart-contracts in this content are programs, which, using special technologies, are stored and executed in blockchain, processing financial information. However, we include in term DeFi all distributed financial services, specifically cryptocurrencies and CBDC.

First cryptocurrency, Bitcoin, was introduced in 2008 by Satoshi Nakamoto [4] and now is a biggest DeFi in the world in terms of capitalization [5]. A big number of clones and modification to follow, successful or not [2]. As a result, now we have almost ten thousand cryptocurrencies in circulation. For us, the following features of cryptocurrencies are important. First, cryptocurrencies are DL based, that means they are single level person to person (p2p) payment technologies without any centralized governance. All parameters such as emission, commissions, etc., are either defined algorithmically or defined by users. Second, in the lack of centralization, e.g. governmental control any person or company can start and run the own cryptocurrency, if he or she has enough competence and financial resources and related demand. In other worlds, cryptocurrencies are, opposite to traditional government-lead fiat money, the product which is determined in great extent by market demand [6]. To be exact, some government regulations of cryptocurrencies already exist [7], but their influence on market development is still relatively weak.

The basic property of bitcoin and other cryptocurrencies is sheer fluctuation of their price to fiat currencies. It may be considered as investment opportunity, but in terms of payments for goods and services often is not convenient as well as in other domains [2]. As a solution, stablecoin model was elaborates. Opposite to "classic" DL-based payment technologies, stablecoins are DL-based payment instruments under with (almost) fixed value to fiat currencies. They benefit from advances of DL technologies, from one side, from another allow to control exactly their monetary value.

2 Research Purpose

There are numerous attempts to model and predict DeFi behavior. Most efforts are put into modelling of behavior of price of cryptocurrencies. The prices are volatile and their knowledge would benefit far beyond academic purposes. A lot of approaches have been done using ARIMA [8], neural networks [9], Monte-Carlo simulations and other approaches [10, 11]. However, common believe is that DeFi markets generally fall under general stock market stochastic behavior [12] and there would be no chance for simple model academic advantages here.

Therefore, few years ago, the authors concentrated on prediction of user activity in cryptocurrencies basing on Bass innovation diffusion theory. Surprisingly, despite of exotic technologies underlining, growth of active users is described pretty well by classic approach, and shows similarity with model of "traditional" payment systems. Moreover, qualitative effects are explained even better, such as market saturation, differences of behavior of peer to peer (p2p) payment versus customer to business (c2b) payments and absence of correlation between early-stage success of payment schemes and long-term behavior [13].

In current paper we extend our consideration from "traditional" cryptocurrencies on stablecoin dynamics. We apply our modification of Bass model to dynamics of stablecoin audience. Stablecoins are cryptocurrencies connected to fiat currencies and contrary to bitcoin and other "classic" cryptocurrencies their values to US dollar and other fiat currencies oscillate in very narrow corridor or are fixed one to one. Here we apply approach early described in [11, 14] with predictable reasonably good results.

3 Stablecoin Definition

As it was briefly aforementioned, stablecoins are modification of cryptocurrencies connected to fiat currencies and contrary to bitcoin and other "classic" cryptocurrencies their values to US dollar and other fiat currencies oscillate in very narrow corridor or are fixed one to one. Here we apply approach early described in [13] with predictable reasonably good results. As it was mentioned, stablecoins are cryptocurrencies which have fixed exchange rate to fiat currencies, mostly to dollars. This may be secured by

- Special, usually oversighted, centralized institution (issuer) which guarantee exchange rate to fiat currencies
- By distributed guarantee supported in "traditional" cryptocurrencies
- By algorithmic trade
- or by combination of these mechanisms [15].

In other aspects stablecoins are pure DeFi, completely private and market driven.

Stablecoins plays important rule in DeFi ecosystems, providing reliable payments and investments, so users activity for them is very high.

4 Case of USDT

First, we consider Tether USDT [16] which first stablecoin announced as early as in 2014. It runs on the platform by Tether Limited and is pegged to US dollar. It is typical DeFi which runs on different DLs. It is issued by Fig. 1 describes dynamics and exchange rate of Tether stablecoin versus time.

Beside fluctuation we can easily identify three typical stages of Bass-complying systems. 2018–2019 we see slow gaining on traction, 2019–2020 sharp growth, 2020–2024 – fluctuation around saturation level.

Following our previous investigation, to descried system behavior we use modified Bass equation [18]:

$$\frac{dx}{dt} = a_p(N - x)x + a_b(N - x) - bx \tag{1}$$

Here the following assumption, mostly following original Bass article [19], are made:

1. There is a limited number of potential users of the product, USDT in our case. Let call it maximal size of audience, N. Number x of them are already active users, N-x are not.
2. In every moment a non-user made a random decision to become a user with probability a_b. This is a decision, independent on other user behavior. Bass associated it with early adoption and/or mass promotion effects, like advertisement.

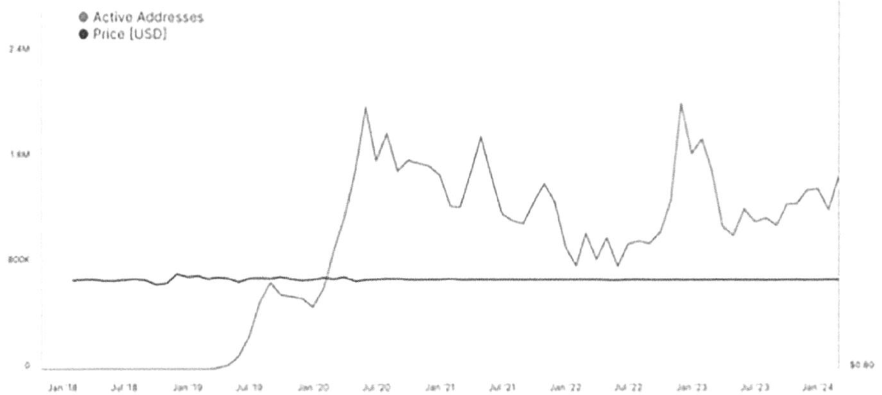

Fig. 1. Tether (USDT) price and active user number versus time [17].

3. In every moment a non-user also made a decision to become a user which is influenced by active users around. Bass called this following. The following probability is a_p. In payments it is especially important, as most of payments are peer to peer interaction.
4. In every moment a user makes a random decision to stop using the product with probability b, due to non-satisfaction, lack of need or any other reason.
5. Starting audience size at $t = 0$ is x_0. This parameter is introduced to describe systems, data for which is not available from very beginning. Actually, we can safely suppose x_0 negatively small for a lot of cases, including stablecoins.

Equation (1) is, actually, Ricatti equation [20]:

$$\frac{dx}{dt} = -a_p x^2 + lx + a_b N \tag{2}$$

where

$$l = a_p N - a_b - b \tag{3}$$

The solution of this equation gives

$$x = \frac{1}{2a_p}\left(D \tanh\left(\frac{1}{2}tD - C\right) + l\right) \tag{4}$$

where

$$D^2 = l^2 + 4a_b a_p N \tag{5}$$

which defines the reverse typical time of audience change. For $t \to \infty$ (11) transforms into

$$x_\infty = \frac{1}{2a_p}(D + l) \tag{6}$$

giving the maximum active audience size that the system aims for a long time.

The constant C can be found from the initial condition x(0) = x0

$$C = \operatorname{arctanh}((l - 2a_p x_0)/D)) \tag{7}$$

As it was shown earlier [18] we can formally also rewrite Eq. (1) in a more general dimensionless form redefining the values to dimensionless

$$\chi \to (2a_p x - l)/D \tag{8}$$

$$\tau \to \frac{Dt}{2} - C \tag{9}$$

and getting the most general form of the solution (11) as

$$\chi = \tanh \tau \tag{10}$$

This means that evolution of all payment systems, DeFi or "classic" falling under extended Bass conditions 1–5 comes along singe dimensionless trajectory. In Fig. 2 it is shown for different payment systems.

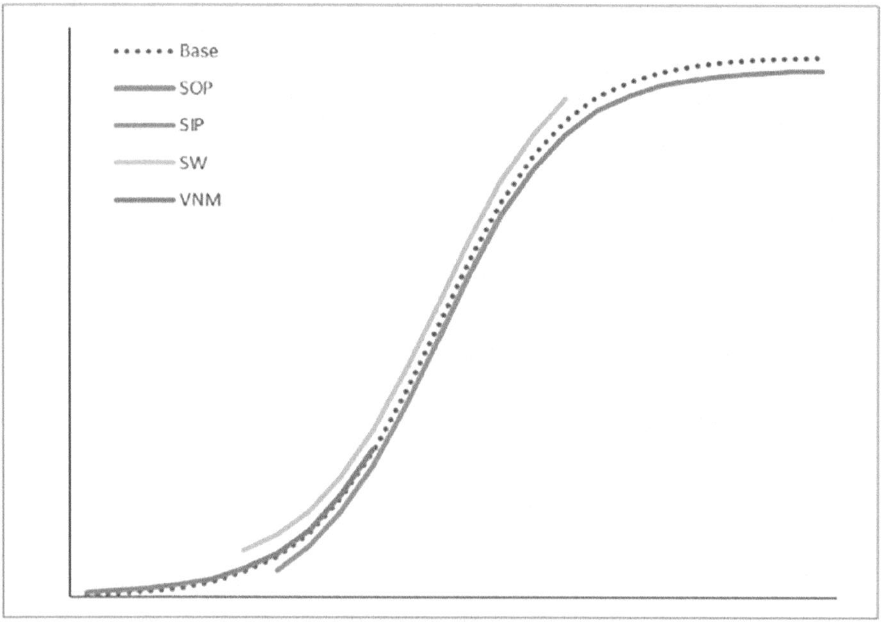

Fig. 2. Base trajectory (10) and different case of placement of payment system trajectories on it. Taken from [18].

Now, we can apply these equations to initial data of Fig. 1. For more evident interpretation we will use intermediate form between (4) and (10). We also can safely suppose $x_0 = 0$, thus obtaining

$$x = \frac{x_\infty}{2}(\tanh\left(\frac{Dt}{2} - C\right) + 1) \tag{11}$$

Here, evidently, C corresponds to time in which fastest growth occurs, t = 2s/D.

Sometimes, it is more convenient, to exclude high frequency oscillations due to high market volatility by analyzing quarterly values and/or taking average for long periods. Averages are given in Table 1.

Table 1. Active USDT addresses number, averaged by years.

Year	Average active USDT addresses number
2018	1044,667
2019	269669,6
2020	1352683
2021	1323774
2022	1047334
2023	1288761
2024	1349838

Here saturation effect is especially evident. To obtain parameters in (11) we can apply least square method both to initial data as well as to averaged data obtaining Table 2.

Table 2. Parameters for USDT.

x_∞	D	C
1380000	0,4 1/month	4,8

Correspondent curve is shown on Fig. 3.

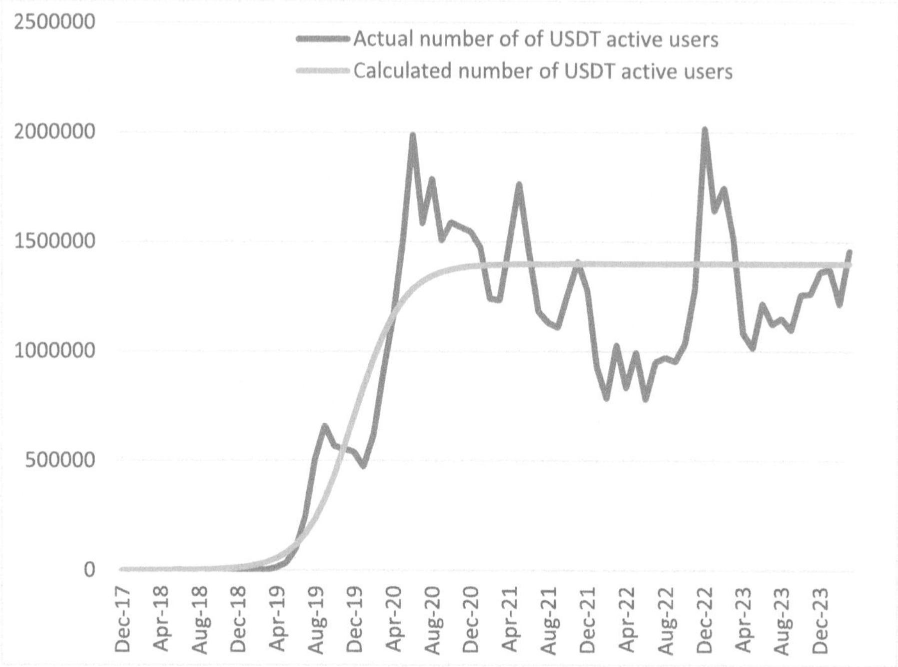

Fig. 3. Actual and calculated number of USDT active users.

Concerning empirical nature of Bass approach that parameters must be considered as qualitative, so fine fitting does not make sense. However, we see quite reasonable coincidence of model with real data and trend.

5 USD Coin

USD Coin is another example of popular stablecoins. It is run by consortium Circle [21] and is also pegged to US dollar. It is typical DeFi as well and as USDT it runs on different DLs. The dynamics demonstrated is similar to USDT. Applying the same approach as to USDT, we obtain similar results in Fig. 4, Tables 3 and 4.

As we see, parameters for USDC are close to USDT ones, but USDC has more slow penetration and less users. Qualitative but general in behavior is generally the same. Both curves are positioned on the same part of general trajectory on Fig. 5. Surprisingly, both real and calculated data supports the fact of saturation of size of audience, even if DeFi market is growing in total volume. This mean that specific sectors using these stablecoins lags from general market development.

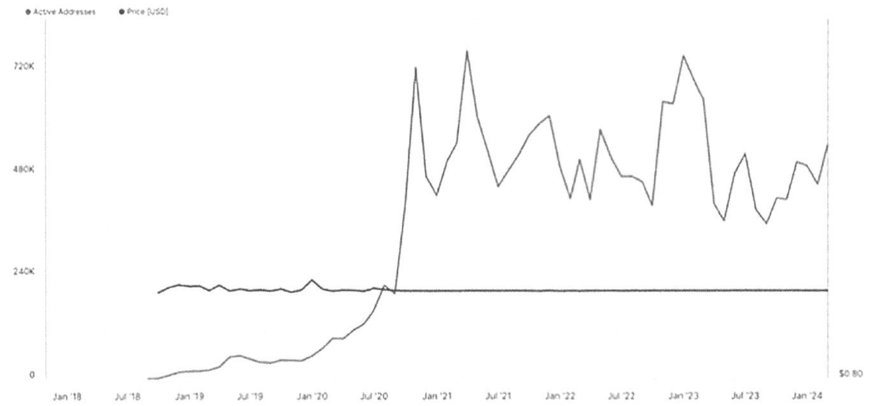

Fig. 4. USD Coin (USDC) price (gray line) and active user number (blue line) versus time [22].

Table 3. Active USDC addresses number, averaged by years.

Year	Average active USDC addresses number
2018	5881
2019	36602,83
2020	227520,4
2021	552035
2022	502833,5
2023	498207
2024	498078

Table 4. Parameters for USDC.

x_∞	D	C
500000	0,25 1/month	6

6 Some Common Outcomes

Another useful interpretation, common for both USDT and USDC arises from meaning of parameters of Eq. (1). As it was noted in [18] that relation between a_p which is responsible for peer-to-peer interaction and a_b, which is responsible for independent single person adoption is shifted to a_p in cryptocurrencies targeted to peer-to-peer payments. Value of $C > 0$ obtained from real data indicates clear peer to peer dominance in stablecoins which fit reality.

We may also note that deriving extended Bass equation, we assume that in average, the behavior of the masses, described by a huge set of parameters, is equivalent to

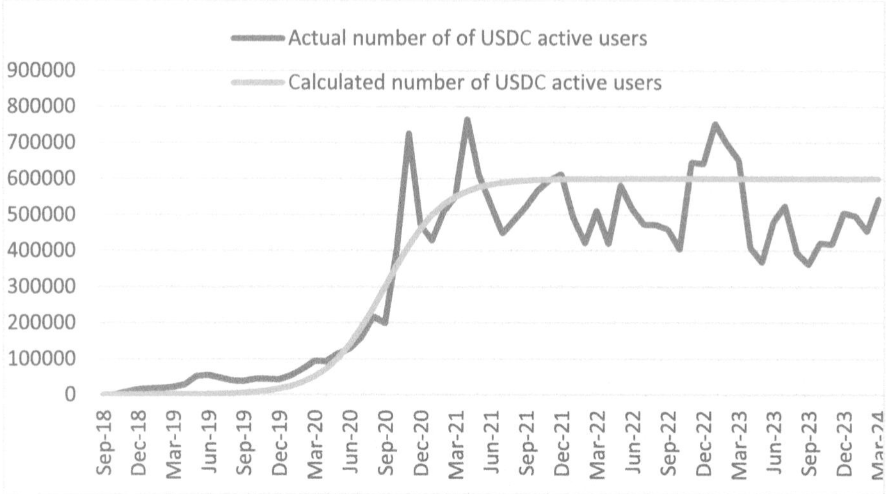

Fig. 5. Actual and calculated number of USDC active users.

the behavior of a single user, described by a small number of statistically measurable parameters. This may be called ergodic hypothesis [23] for payments. Note that the currently accepted approach to describing Bass-like diffusion of innovations explicitly or implicitly relies on a similar assumption about the possibility to empirically describe the behavior of complex systems by a small number of parameters. This paper introduces one more case which confirms basic Bass approach.

7 Conclusion

Here we see, that our model represents stablecoins trend pretty well. Evidently, it cannot predict external-driven fluctuation which are connected to general trends on cryptomarkets, but for average values we have good predictions. The generalized Bass model describes adequately the initial stage of getting traction, sharp growth stage and, eventually, slow move to saturation. Also, qualitative description is reasonably accurate. Previously, authors proposed a combination of Bass model and an ARMA statistical approach [24], which can also be used to develop the model for stablecoins. The model will also allow to describe some of the usage fluctuations.

Of course, the model has some limitation. Some of the parameters introduced into the model are constant. This is always true for the short periods of time and might be a good hypothesis for middle-term behavior. In longer-term horizons, technology modifications or regulatory changes may change usability and attractiveness of the product. Then, parameters will need to be changed accordingly. Also, competition between different stablecoins is not taken into account in the research: usually, stablecoins with big audience cannibalize those with smaller user base. More exact model must include a system of Bass equation with cross-terms which describe mutual influence. This may be subject of further studies.

Another interesting application of this approach is dynamics of central bank digital currencies, CBDC, which are being introduced now in different countries. In a sense, CBDC are also stablecoins, but issued by a government [25]. After accumulation of enough amount of statistic we can apply the model to analyze CBDC dynamics and its deviations from dynamics of private stablecoins.

References

1. Manda, V.K., et al.: Revolutionizing Finance with Decentralized Finance (DeFi). In: Decentralizing the Online Experience with Web3 Technologies, edited by Dina Darwish, pp. 127–150. Hershey, PA: IGI Global (2024). https://doi.org/10.4018/979-8-3693-1532-3.ch006
2. Birch, D.: The Currency Cold War: Cash and Cryptography Hash Rates and Hegemony. Publishing Partnership, London (2020)
3. Aquilina, M., Frost, J., Schrimpf, A.: Decentralized finance (DeFi): a functional approach. J. Fin. Regulation (2024). https://doi.org/10.1093/jfr/fjad013
4. Satoshi Nakamoto: Bitcoin: A Peer-to-Peer Electronic Cash System. https://www.bitgo.com/content-library/bitcoin.pdf
5. Today's Cryptocurrency Prices by Market Cap. https://coinmarketcap.com/
6. Dostov, V., Shust, P.: Cryptocurrencies: an unconventional challenge to the AML/CFT regulators? J Fin. Crime **21**(3), 249–263 (2014). https://doi.org/10.1108/JFC-06-2013-0043
7. Alekseenko, A.P.: Model framework for consumer protection and crypto-exchanges regulation. J. Risk Fin. Manage. **16**(7), 305 (2023). https://doi.org/10.3390/jrfm16070305
8. Gunawan, D., Febrianti, I.: Ethereum value forecasting model using autoregressive integrated moving average (ARIMA). Int. J. Adv. Soc. Sci. Hum. **2**(1), 29–35 (2023). https://doi.org/10.56225/ijassh.v2i1.151
9. Dempere, J.M., Il-Agure, Z., Allam, H., Ramasamy, L.K., Alqasemi, S.S.: The Influence of AI-identified consumer sentiment metrics on crypto-asset prices. In: 9th International Conference on Information Technology Trends (ITT), pp. 90–95. Dubai, United Arab Emirates, (2023). https://doi.org/10.1109/ITT59889.2023.10184246
10. Likitratcharoen, D., Chudasring, P., Pinmanee, C., Wiwattanalamphong, K.: The efficiency of value-at-risk models during extreme market stress in cryptocurrencies. Sustainability **15**(5), 4395 (2023). https://doi.org/10.3390/su15054395
11. Dostov, V., Pimenov, P., Shoust, P.: Comparison of deterministic, stochastic, and mixed approaches to cryptocurrency dynamics analysis. In: Gervasi, O., et al. Computational Science and Its Applications – ICCSA 2021. ICCSA 2021. Lecture Notes in Computer Science, vol. 12952. Springer, Cham (2021). https://doi.org/10.1007/978-3-030-86973-1_2
12. Tassopoulos, P., Protonotarios, Y.: Brownian motion & the stochastic behavior of stocks. J. Math. Finance **12**, 138–149 (2022). https://doi.org/10.4236/jmf.2022.121009
13. Dostov, V., Shoust, P., Popova, E.: Using mathematical models to describe the dynamics of the spread of traditional and cryptocurrency payment systems. In: Misra, S., et al. Computational Science and Its Applications – ICCSA 2019. ICCSA 2019. Lecture Notes in Computer Science, vol. 11620. Springer, Cham (2019). https://doi.org/10.1007/978-3-030-24296-1_36
14. Dostov, V., Pimenov, P., Shoust, P., Titov, V.: The influence of the effect of marketing incentives on the dynamics of the development of classic and cryptocurrency payment systems. In: Proceedings of the 3rd International Symposium on Automation, Information and Computing - ISAIC; ISBN 978–989–758–622–4; ISSN 2975–9463, SciTePress, pp. 580–585 (2023). https://doi.org/10.5220/0011961700003612

15. Nejadmalayeri, A., Molchanovsky, L., Paleo, B.W., Prescott, R.W.: Stablecoins: past, present, and future. In: Essex, A., et al. Financial Cryptography and Data Security. FC 2023 International Workshops. FC 2023. Lecture Notes in Computer Science, vol. 13953. Springer, Cham (2024). https://doi.org/10.1007/978-3-031-48806-1_13
16. Tether. https://tether.to/
17. Tether: Number of Active Addresses. Glassnode. https://studio.glassnode.com/metrics?a=USDT&m=addresses.ActiveCount&resolution=1month&s=1509494400&u=1709251200&zoom=
18. Dostov, V., Shust, P., Krivoruchko, S.: Fast payment systems dynamics: lessons from diffusion of innovation models. In: Abramowicz, W., Auer, S., Stróżyna, M. (eds) Business Information Systems Workshops. BIS 2021. Lecture Notes in Business Information Processing, vol. 444. Springer, Cham (2022). https://doi.org/10.1007/978-3-031-04216-4_31
19. Bass, F.: A new product growth for model consumer durables. Manage. Sci. **15**(5), 215–227 (1969). https://doi.org/10.1287/mnsc.15.5.215
20. Simmons, G., Robertson, J.: Differential Equations with Applications and Historical Notes, 2nd Edition. In: International Series in Pure and Applied Mathematics, McGraw-Hill (1991)
21. Jeremy Allaire: Ushering in the next chapter for USDC. https://www.circle.com/blog/ushering-in-the-next-chapter-for-usdc
22. USD Coin: Number of Active Addresses. Glassnode. https://studio.glassnode.com/metrics?a=USDC&ema=0&m=addresses.ActiveCount&mAvg=0&mMedian=0&resolution=1month&s=1509494400&u=1709251200&zoom
23. Birkhoff, G.D.: What is the ergodic theorem? Amer. Math. Monthly **49**(4), 222–226 (1942). https://doi.org/10.2307/2303229, JSTOR2303229
24. Dostov, V., Pimenov, P., Shoust, P., Fedorova, R.: Using an economically justified trend for the stationarity of time series in ARMA models. In: Gervasi, O., Murgante, B., Hendrix, E.M.T., Taniar, D., Apduhan, B.O. (eds.) Computational Science and Its Applications – ICCSA 2022: 22nd International Conference, Malaga, Spain, July 4–7, 2022, Proceedings, Part II, pp. 404–415. Springer International Publishing, Cham (2022). https://doi.org/10.1007/978-3-031-10450-3_35
25. Bindseil, U., Pantelopoulos, G.: Unbacked Crypto-Assets, Stablecoins and CBDC. In: Bindseil, U., Pantelopoulos, G. (eds.) Introduction to Payments and Financial Market Infrastructures, pp. 125–152. Springer Nature Switzerland, Cham (2023). https://doi.org/10.1007/978-3-031-39520-8_9

Computational and Applied Mathematics (CAM 2024)

A Nonlinear Variational Multiscale Stabilized Method for Compressible Navier-Stokes Equations

Elaine Bernine(✉), Isaac P. Santos, and Lucia Catabriga

Federal University of Espírito Santo, Vitória, Brazil
elaine.bernine@edu.ufes.br, {isaac.santos,lucia.catabriga}@ufes.br

Abstract. In this work, we solve the compressible Navier-Stokes equations using a nonlinear variational multiscale finite element methodology. The numerical scheme relies on decomposing the problem into macro and micro scales, wherein an artificial viscosity operator is incorporated into both scales of the discretization. The magnitude of artificial viscosity is adjusted based on the stabilization parameter of the Consistent Approximate Upwind (CAU) method. To assess the performance of the method, we solve some problems for compressible Navier-Stokes equations. The numerical results indicate that the new method yields solutions similar to those obtained with the CAU method, however, with a lower computational cost.

Keywords: Finite element method · Compressible flow problems · Stabilized methods · Nonlinear Multiscale Viscosity

1 Introduction

The compressible Navier-Stokes equations are used to model fluid flows with variation in density, being applied to model fluid transport problems, such as effects caused by pollution of rivers, seas and soil, flow around airfoils of cars and planes, and propagation of smoke in fires and industrial chimneys. In general, the analytical solutions of these equations are difficult to obtain. To overcome this difficulty, we can resort to the use of numerical methods such as finite differences, finite volumes and finite elements. In this work, we focus on the discretization of equations via finite element approximation.

The standard Galerkin finite element methods may present numerical instabilities for convective-dominated problems, mainly due to the hyperbolic nature of the equations, which is the case of the compressible Navier-Stokes equations. In order to correct these oscillations, stabilized finite element methods have been developed for more than four decades. We highlight the Streamline Upwind Petrov-Galerkin (SUPG) [1,8] and Consistent Approximate Upwind (CAU) [4] stabilization methods to solve the Navier-Stokes equations.

This work has been supported in part by CAPES.

O. Gervasi et al. (Eds.): ICCSA 2024 Workshops, LNCS 14815, pp. 251–267, 2024.
https://doi.org/10.1007/978-3-031-65154-0_16

The SUPG stabilization method is one of the most used for predominantly convective problems. This method is characterized by the addition of artificial viscosity only in the streamlines, obtaining good properties of stability and convergence, according to [8,13]. The SUPG stabilization matrix for the compressible Navier-Stokes equations, using conservative variables, was developed in [1,2] and later improved in [3]. In order to correct the oscillations of the SUPG method in the gradient elevation regions, the CAU non-linear stabilization method was developed in [10] for the advection-diffusion equation. This method inserts in a consistent way, besides the SUPG contribution, a discontinuity capturing operator that controls the derivatives in the direction of the gradient of the approximated solution. The CAU method was extended for compressible flows in [4], using entropy variables, and in [9], using conservative variables.

In the nineties, stabilized methods have been developed in the context of multiscale variational formulations, in order to obtain information contained at the micro scale. The multiscale variational stabilization (VMS) methods were introduced in [12] for the convection-diffusion equation and later [14] for compressible flow problems. These methods aim to decompose the problem of interest into two subproblems: one represented by the discretization of the domain used (macro scale - resolved scale) and the other by the smaller scales, sub-meshes (micro scale - unresolved scale). In [5,6] variations of the VMS method called Nonlinear Multiscale Viscosity (NMV) are developed, with the aim of numerically solving the system of compressible Euler Equations. The NMV methods add nonlinear artificial viscosity at both scales, defined by the YZβ method stabilization parameter [20].

In this work we redefine the NMV method for solving the compressible Navier-Stokes Equations. The artificial viscosity at both scales is defined by the discontinuity capture operator of the CAU method, that will be called NMVC. In order to validate the numerical implementation, we compared the results obtained between the NMVC and CAU methods in conservative variables for the Navier-Stokes equations. We emphasize that the temporal discretization was performed by the second-order predictor-multicorrector algorithm [6,11].

This work is organized as follows. In Sect. 2 the governing compressible Navier-Stokes equations are presented. In Sect. 3, the NMVC and CAU numerical formulations for the compressible Navier-Stokes equations are discussed. In Sect. 4 the predictor-multicorrect algorithm used as a time integration scheme is presented. Subsequently, in Sect. 5, numerical experiments on the compressible Navier-Stokes equation are presented in order to validate the numerical implementation of the NMVC method, in addition to showing the improvements in computational performance obtained. Finally, the conclusions of this work are presented.

2 Governing Equations

The compressible Navier-Stokes equations are obtained from a set of partial differential equations resulting from the laws of conservation of mass, motion and energy. These equations are given by

$$\frac{\partial \rho}{\partial t} + \nabla \cdot (\rho \boldsymbol{u}) = \mathbf{0}, \quad \text{in } \Omega \times (0, t_f] \tag{1}$$

$$\frac{\partial \rho \boldsymbol{u}}{\partial t} + \nabla \cdot (\rho \boldsymbol{u} \otimes \boldsymbol{u}) + \nabla p - \nabla \cdot \boldsymbol{\sigma} = \boldsymbol{f}, \quad \text{in } \Omega \times (0, t_f] \tag{2}$$

$$\frac{\partial E_t}{\partial t} + \nabla \cdot [(E_t + p)\, \boldsymbol{u} - \boldsymbol{\tau u} - \kappa \nabla T] = \mathbf{0}, \quad \text{in } \Omega \times (0, t_f] \tag{3}$$

where ρ, $\boldsymbol{u} = [u_1, u_2]^T$, $\boldsymbol{f}$, E_t, p, $\boldsymbol{\sigma}$, κ and T denote, respectively, density, velocity, source term, total energy, pressure, viscous stress tensor, thermal conductivity and temperature.

The viscous stress tensor $\boldsymbol{\tau}$ is defined as $\boldsymbol{\tau} = \lambda (\nabla \cdot \boldsymbol{u}) I + 2\mu\varepsilon(\boldsymbol{u})$, where $\mu = \rho\nu$ is the first viscosity coefficient, $\lambda = -\frac{2\mu}{3}$ is the second viscosity coefficient (considering the ideal gas - Stokes hypothesis), ν is the kinematic viscosity, and $\varepsilon(\boldsymbol{u})$ is the strain tensor: $\varepsilon(\boldsymbol{u}) = \frac{1}{2}\left((\boldsymbol{\nabla u}) + (\boldsymbol{\nabla u})^T\right)$.

When considering the fluid as a perfect gas and based on the definitions presented in [17], we have $E_t = \rho\left(e_{in} + \frac{\|\boldsymbol{u}\|_2^2}{2}\right) = \rho E$, where $e_{in} = c_v T$ is the internal energy, $p = \rho R T$ is the pressure, $k = \gamma R \mu/(\gamma - 1)Pr$ is the thermal conductivity, c_v is the specific heat at constant volume, c_p is the specific heat at constant pressure, $\gamma = c_p/c_v$ is the adiabatic exponent, $R = c_p - c_v$ is the specific gas constant and Pr is the Prandtl number.

The compressible Navier-Stokes equations, represented by Eqs. (1), (2) e (3), can be rewritten in vector form with $x_1, x_2 \in \Omega \subset \mathbb{R}^2$ and $t \in (0, t_f]$ as

$$\frac{\partial U}{\partial t} + \frac{\partial F_i}{\partial x_i} - \frac{\partial G_i}{\partial x_i} = \mathbf{0}, \quad \text{with} \quad i = 1, 2, \tag{4}$$

where $U = [U_1, U_2, U_3, U_4]^T = [\rho, \rho u_1, \rho u_2, \rho E]^T$ is the vector of conservative variables, F_i is the Euler vector (advective transport terms) and G_i is the viscous flow vector (diffusive transport terms), for $i = 1, 2$, defined by

$$F_i = \begin{bmatrix} u_i \rho \\ u_i u_1 \rho + \delta_{1i} p \\ u_i u_2 \rho + \delta_{2i} p \\ u_i (\rho E + p) \end{bmatrix} \quad \text{and} \quad G_i = \begin{bmatrix} 0 \\ \boldsymbol{\tau}_{i1} \rho + \delta_{1i} p \\ \boldsymbol{\tau}_{i2} \rho + \delta_{2i} p \\ -q_i + \boldsymbol{\tau}_{ik} u_k \end{bmatrix}.$$

We emphasize that δ_{ij} represents the components of the identity tensor $I_{2\times 2}$ and $\boldsymbol{q} = -\kappa \boldsymbol{\nabla} T$ the components of the temperature flow vector. Furthermore, the Eq. (4) can be rewritten in the quasi-linear form,

$$\frac{\partial U}{\partial t} + A_i \frac{\partial U}{\partial x_i} - \frac{\partial}{\partial x_i}\left(K_{ij} \frac{\partial U}{\partial x_j}\right) = \mathbf{0}, \quad \text{in } \Omega \times (0, t_f], \quad \text{with} \quad i, j = 1, 2, \tag{5}$$

where $A_i = \frac{\partial F_i}{\partial U}$ are the Jacobian matrices and $G_i = K_{ij} \frac{\partial U}{\partial x_j}$, with $i = 1, 2$. Related to Eq. (5) we have an appropriate set of initial and Dirichlet boundary conditions assumed to be

$$BU = Z, \quad \text{in } \Gamma \times (0, t_f], \quad \text{and} \quad U_0(x) = U(x, 0),$$

with Γ being the boundary of domain Ω, B the general boundary operator, and Z and U_0 given functions.

3 Numerical Formulations

In this section we present two stabilized numerical formulations used to obtain the solutions of the compressible Navier-Stokes equations for a perfect gas: CAU method and the Nonlinear Multiscale Viscosity method considering the artificial viscosity defined by CAU parameter (NMVC).

Consider the partition $\mathcal{T}_h = \{K\}$ of the domain Ω into nel linear triangular elements, where h^e is the element length. Let $\mathcal{V}_h$ be the space of test functions defined by

$$\mathcal{V}_h = \{U_h \in \left[H^1(\Omega)\right]^4; \quad U_h|\Omega_e \in \left[\mathbb{P}^1(\Omega_e)\right]^4, \quad BU_h = Z \in \Gamma\}, \tag{6}$$

where $H^1(\Omega)$ is a Hilbert space of square integrable functions with square integrable (in the weak sense) first derivative, $\mathbb{P}^1(\Omega_e)$ is the set of linear polynomials defined in Ω_e, and Γ is the boundary of Ω with Dirichlet conditions.

3.1 The Consistent Approximate Apwind (CAU) Method

The CAU formulation of the compressible Navier-Stokes equations, presented in [4], consists of finding $U_h \in \mathcal{V}_h$, such that

$$\begin{aligned}
&\int_{\Omega} \left[W_h \left(\frac{\partial U_h}{\partial t} + A_i^h \frac{\partial U_h}{\partial x_i} \right) + \frac{\partial W_h}{\partial x_i} \left(K_{ij}^h \frac{\partial U_h}{\partial x_j} \right) \right] d\Omega + \\
&+ \sum_{e=1}^{nel} \int_{\Omega^e} \boldsymbol{\tau}_{\text{cau}} \left(A_i^h \frac{\partial W_h}{\partial x_i} \right) \cdot R(U_h) d\Omega_e + \\
&+ \sum_{e=1}^{nel} \int_{\Omega_e} \delta_{\text{cau}} \left(\frac{\partial W_h}{\partial x_i} \frac{\partial U_h}{\partial x_i} \right) d\Omega_e = \mathbf{0}, \quad \forall W_h \in \mathcal{V}_h,
\end{aligned} \tag{7}$$

with initial condition $U_0(x) = U_h(x, 0)$, where

$$R(U_h) = \frac{\partial U_h}{\partial t} + A_i^h \frac{\partial U_h}{\partial x_i}$$

is the local residue of the Eq. (5), $\boldsymbol{\tau}_{\text{cau}}$ is the stabilization parameter of the CAU method, defined as in [3] by $\boldsymbol{\tau}_{\text{cau}} = \max\{\mathbf{0}, \boldsymbol{\tau}_t + \zeta \cdot (\boldsymbol{\tau}_a - \boldsymbol{\tau}_\delta - \boldsymbol{\tau}_d)\}$, with

$$\boldsymbol{\tau}_t = \frac{2}{3\,(1 + 2\alpha CFL)} \boldsymbol{\tau}_a, \qquad \boldsymbol{\tau}_a = \frac{h}{2\,(c + |\boldsymbol{u} \cdot \boldsymbol{\beta}|)} I, \qquad \boldsymbol{\tau}_\delta = \frac{\delta_{\text{cau}}}{(c + |\boldsymbol{u} \cdot \boldsymbol{\beta}|)^2} I$$

$$\text{and} \quad \boldsymbol{\tau}_d = \frac{\beta_1^2 \text{diag} K_{11} + \beta_2^2 \text{diag} K_{22}}{(c + |\boldsymbol{u} \cdot \boldsymbol{\beta}|)^2}.$$

Here, CFL is the Courant-Friedrichs-Lewy number, ζ is a weighting coefficient, and c is the acoustic velocity of the fluid, defined in [3] as

$$CFL = \frac{(c + |\boldsymbol{u} \cdot \boldsymbol{\beta}|)}{h} \Delta t, \quad \zeta = \frac{2\alpha CFL}{1 + 2\alpha CFL}, \quad c^2 = \gamma(\gamma - 1)\left(E - \frac{\|\boldsymbol{u}\|^2}{2}\right),$$

where $h^e = \sqrt{2A^e}$ is the element length, A^e is the area of the element Ω_e, and $\boldsymbol{\beta}$ is given by the expression

$$\boldsymbol{\beta} = \frac{\boldsymbol{\nabla} \|\boldsymbol{U}\|_2^2}{\left\|\boldsymbol{\nabla} \|\boldsymbol{U}\|_2^2\right\|_2}.$$

Finally, δ_{cau} is the discontinuity capturing parameter of the CAU method in conservative variables, defined in [9] as

$$\delta_{\text{cau}} = \begin{cases} \frac{\|R(U^h)\|}{\|\boldsymbol{\nabla}_\xi U^h\|_{\tilde{A}_0^{-1}}}, & \text{if } |\boldsymbol{\nabla} U^h|_{\tilde{A}_0^{-1}} > tol_\delta, \\ 0, & \text{otherwise}, \end{cases} \tag{8}$$

where

$$\|\boldsymbol{\nabla}_\xi U^h\|_{\tilde{A}_0^{-1}} = \left\| \frac{\partial x}{\partial \xi}\frac{\partial U^h}{\partial x} + \frac{\partial y}{\partial \xi}\frac{\partial U^h}{\partial y} \right\|_{\tilde{A}_0^{-1}} + \left\| \frac{\partial x}{\partial \eta}\frac{\partial U^h}{\partial x} + \frac{\partial y}{\partial \eta}\frac{\partial U^h}{\partial y} \right\|_{\tilde{A}_0^{-1}},$$

and tol_δ is a small positive real number used to prevent division by zero. In this work we use $tol_\delta = 10^{-8}$. The norm $\|\cdot\|_{\tilde{A}_0^{-1}}$ is defined as $\|\boldsymbol{w}\|_{\tilde{A}_0^{-1}} = \left(\boldsymbol{w}^T \tilde{A}_0^{-1} \boldsymbol{w}\right)^{1/2}$, for all vector $\boldsymbol{w}$ and $\tilde{A}_0^{-1}$ is the inverse of the Reimannian matrix tensor defined in [19].

The variational formulation described in Eq. (7) results in the global system of algebraic differential equations given by

$$M\dot{U}_h + KU_h = \mathbf{0}, \tag{9}$$

with U_h being the unknowns derived from each element Ω_e, $\dot{U}_h$ being their derivatives with respect to time, and M and K are matrices derived from Eq. (7).

3.2 The Nonlinear Multiscale Variational (NMVC) Method

Let $\mathcal{V}_E$ be the enriched space defined by the direct sum between the space of macro scales, $\mathcal{V}_h$, defined in Eq. (6), and space of micro scales, $\mathcal{V}_b$, spanned by bubble functions, $\mathcal{V}_E = \mathcal{V}_h \oplus \mathcal{V}_b$, where

$$\mathcal{V}_b = \{U_b \in \left[H^1(\Omega)\right]^4; \quad U_b|\Omega_e \in [\text{span}(\phi_B)]^4, \quad \forall \Omega_e \in \mathcal{T}_h\}.$$

The bubble function ϕ_B is defined in Ω_e as $\phi_B = 27N_1^eN_2^eN_3^e$, where $N_j^e = N_j^e(x, y)$ are the (local) basis function of space V_h.

The nonlinear multiscale variational (NMVC) method for the compressible Navier-Stokes equations consists of finding $U_E = U_h + U_b \in \mathcal{V}_E$, with $U_h \in \mathcal{V}_h$ and $U_b \in \mathcal{V}_b$, such that

$$\begin{aligned} &\int_{\Omega}\left[W_E \cdot \left(\frac{\partial U_E}{\partial t} + A_i^h \frac{\partial U_E}{\partial x_i}\right) + \frac{\partial W_E}{\partial x_i} \cdot \left(K_{ij}^h \frac{\partial U_E}{\partial x_j}\right)\right] d\Omega + \\ &+ \sum_{e=1}^{nel} \int_{\Omega_e} \delta_{\text{cau}}(U_h) \left(\frac{\partial W_E}{\partial x_i} \cdot \frac{\partial U_E}{\partial x_i}\right) d\Omega = \mathbf{0}, \quad \forall W_E \in \mathcal{V}_E, \end{aligned} \tag{10}$$

where $W_E = W_h + W_b \in \mathcal{V}_E$, whith $W_h \in \mathcal{V}_h$ and $W_b \in \mathcal{V}_b$, and $\delta_{\text{cau}}(U_h)$ is the discontinuity capturing parameter of the CAU method, defined in Eq. (8).

The variational formulation presented in the system (10) can be divided into two systems that concern the macro and micro scale, respectively. Thus, for the space of macro scales, we will have

$$\begin{aligned} &\int_{\Omega}\left[W_h \cdot \left(\frac{\partial U_h}{\partial t} + A_i^h \frac{\partial U_h}{\partial x_i}\right) + W_h \cdot \left(\frac{\partial U_b}{\partial t} + A_i^h \frac{\partial U_b}{\partial x_i}\right)\right] d\Omega + \\ &+ \int_{\Omega} \frac{\partial W_h}{\partial x_i} \cdot \left(K_{ij}^h \frac{\partial U_h}{\partial x_j}\right) d\Omega + \\ &+ \sum_{e=1}^{nel} \int_{\Omega_e} \delta_{\text{cau}}(U_h) \left(\frac{\partial W_h}{\partial x_i} \cdot \frac{\partial U_h}{\partial x_i}\right) d\Omega = \mathbf{0}, \quad \forall W_h \in \mathcal{V}_h. \end{aligned} \tag{11}$$

For the space of micro scales, we have

$$\begin{aligned} &\int_{\Omega}\left[W_b \cdot \left(\frac{\partial U_h}{\partial t} + A_i^h \frac{\partial U_h}{\partial x_i}\right) + W_b \cdot \left(\frac{\partial U_b}{\partial t} + A_i^h \frac{\partial U_b}{\partial x_i}\right)\right] d\Omega + \\ &+ \int_{\Omega} \frac{\partial W_b}{\partial x_i} \cdot \left(K_{ij}^h \frac{\partial U_b}{\partial x_j}\right) d\Omega + \\ &+ \sum_{e=1}^{nel} \int_{\Omega_e} \delta_{\text{cau}}(U_h) \left(\frac{\partial W_b}{\partial x_i} \cdot \frac{\partial U_b}{\partial x_i}\right) d\Omega = \mathbf{0}, \quad \forall W_b \in \mathcal{V}_b. \end{aligned} \tag{12}$$

When finite element approximations are used in the systems of Eqs. (11) and (12), considering homogeneous Dirichlet boundary conditions (i.e., $Z = \mathbf{0}$ in Γ), we obtain the following system of differential algebraic equations

$$\begin{bmatrix} M_{hh} & M_{hb} \\ M_{bh} & M_{bb} \end{bmatrix} \begin{bmatrix} \dot{U}_h \\ \dot{U}_b \end{bmatrix} + \begin{bmatrix} K_{hh} & K_{hb} \\ K_{bh} & K_{bb} \end{bmatrix} \begin{bmatrix} U_h \\ U_b \end{bmatrix} = \begin{bmatrix} \mathbf{0}_h \\ \mathbf{0}_b \end{bmatrix}, \tag{13}$$

with U_h and U_b being the unknowns derived from each element Ω_e, and $\dot{U}_h$ and $\dot{U}_b$ being their derivatives with respect to time. All matrices are defined based on Eqs. (11) and (12).

4 Time Integration Schemes

In order to solve the given system of differential equations by Eq. (9) we use the well known time integration scheme given by the predictor-multicorrector method based on implicit methods, as described in [11]. To solve the system of differential equations obtained by the NMVC method (Eq. (13)) we adapted the predictor-multicorrector method considering a static condensation, as described in Algorithm 1. In both systems, we consider $\alpha = 0.5$ in all experiments, thus obtaining a second order approximation for the time derivative of U_h and U_b, with U_h^n and U_b^n being the solution of the macro and micro scales of U in step of time n and Δt the time step.

Algorithm 1. NMVC Predictor-multicorrector algorithm

Input: U_h^n, $\dot{U}_h^n$, U_b^n and $\dot{U}_b^n$

$t = 0$

Predictor phase:

$t = t + \Delta t$

$U_h^{n+1,0} = U_h^n + (1-\alpha)\,\Delta t \dot{U}_h^n$

$\dot{U}_h^{n+1,0} = 0$

$U_b^{n+1,0} = U_b^n + (1-\alpha)\,\Delta t \dot{U}_b^n$

$\dot{U}_b^{n+1,0} = 0$

$i = 0$

Multicorrector phase:

Calculate residue:

$$R_1^{n+1,i} = -\left(M_{hh}\dot{U}_h^{n+1,i} + M_{hb}\dot{U}_b^{n+1,i}\right) - \left(K_{hh}U_h^{n+1,i} + K_{hb}U_b^{n+1,i}\right)$$

$$R_2^{n+1,i} = -\left(M_{bh}\dot{U}_h^{n+1,i} + M_{bb}\dot{U}_b^{n+1,i}\right) - \left(K_{bh}U_h^{n+1,i} + K_{bb}U_b^{n+1,i}\right)$$

Solve:

$M^*\dot{U}_h = F^*$,

with $M^* = M_1 - N_1 N_2^{-1} M_2$ and $F^* = R_1 - N_1 N_2^{-1} R_2$,

where $M_1 = M_{hh} + \alpha\Delta t K_{hh}$, $M_2 = M_{bh} + \alpha\Delta t K_{bh}$,

$N_1 = M_{hb} + \alpha\Delta t K_{hb}$ and $N_2 = M_{bb} + \alpha\Delta t K_{bb}$

Corrector:

$U_h^{n+1,i+1} = U_h^{n,i} + (1-\alpha)\,\Delta t \dot{U}_h^{n+1,i+1}$

$\dot{U}_h^{n+1,i+1} = \dot{U}_h^{n+1,i} + \Delta\dot{U}_h^{n+1,i+1}$

$U_b^{n+1,i+1} = U_b^{n,i} + (1-\alpha)\,\Delta t \dot{U}_b^{n+1,i+1}$

$\dot{U}_b^{n+1,i+1} = \dot{U}_b^{n+1,i} + \Delta\dot{U}_b^{n+1,i+1}$

with $\Delta\dot{U}_b^{n+1,i+1} = N_2^{-1}\left(R_2^{n+1,i} - M_2\Delta\dot{U}_b^{n+1,i+1}\right)$

5 Numerical Experiments

In this section, we present four numerical experiments, in order to compare the results obtained for the CAU and NMVC methods, described previously. The code was built in C Language based on the finite element library called FEM_CODES[1] - under development by the UFES Computational Optimization and Modeling Laboratory.

[1] Available in https://github.com/mod-comp-ufes/FEM_CODES.

In order to validate the numerical implementation, we present the oblique and reflected shock problems that use the compressible Euler equation, and the Carter's flat plate and compression corner problems that use the compressible Navier-Stokes equations. In all experiments, compressible gases are considered with specific heat at constant volume $c_v = 717.5$, specific heat at constant pressure $c_p = 1004.5$, gas constant $R = 287$, adiabatic exponent $\gamma = 1.4$ and Prandtl number $Pr = 0.72$. To carry out the experiments, we use the GMRES solver with a maximum number of cycles 100, 30 vectors in Krylov basis, solver tolerance 10^{-5}, 3 fixed nonlinear corrections, step-time 10^{-2}, BlockDiag preconditioner, element-by-element matrix-vector product and triangular meshes. The numerical experiments were carried out on a machine with an Intel®Core^{TM}i5-1035G1 CPU @ 1.00GHz processor, memory 8 GB of RAM and Ubuntu 20.04.5 LTS as operating system.

5.1 Oblique Shock Problem

The oblique shock problem, described in [7,19], consists of supersonic flow ($M = 2.0$) over a wedge located in the lower part of the domain $\Omega = [0.0, 1.0] \times [0.0, 1.0]$. The fluid enters at an angle of $-10°$ with respect to the wedge and the oblique shock occurs in the lower left corner with an angle of $29.3°$, as described in Fig. 1.

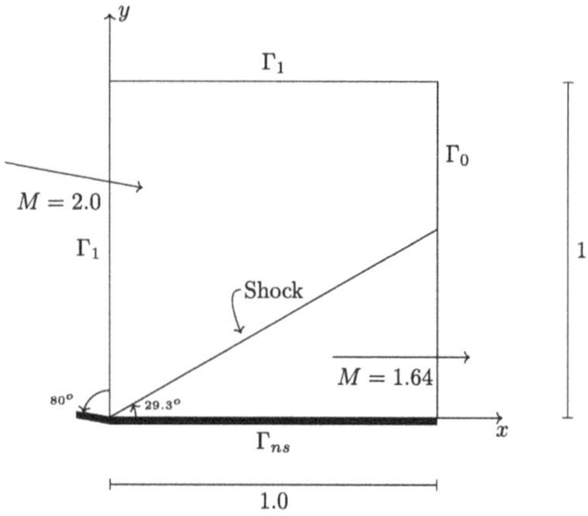

Fig. 1. Oblique shock problem description.

The specified boundary conditions are: in Γ_1 all variables are prescribed as $\{U_1, U_2, U_3, U_4\} = \{1.0, \cos 10°, -\sin 10°, 0.94643\}$; in Γ_{ns} the normal speed to the wall is zero, i.e., $U_3 = 0$; in Γ_0 no boundary conditions are prescribed.

The numerical results were analyzed at the time instant $t = 3.0\,\text{s}$ with an unstructured mesh with 474 nodes and 874 triangular elements. The Fig. 2 shows the density profile of the oblique shock problem along $x = 0.9$ comparing the

NMVC, CAU methods and their exact solution. Note that the results obtained by the NMVC and CAU methods are similar.

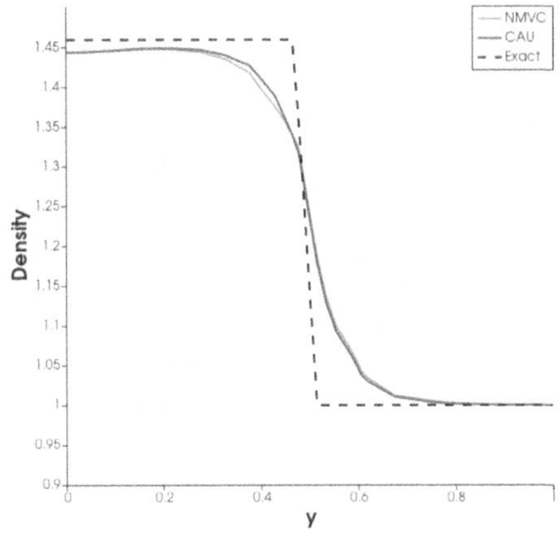

Fig. 2. Density profile along $x = 0.9$ of the oblique shock problem.

Figures 3a and 3b show the numerical results obtained by the NMVC method for the density and pressure, respectively, of the oblique shock problem. The numerical results can be compared with those presented in [5,9] with the CAU stabilization method.

Table 1 presents computational performance data between the NMVC and CAU methods with regard to the number of GMRES iterations and the CPU time spent. The NMVC method obtained the shortest time and the fewest number of iterations, being 19.56% faster than the CAU method.

Table 1. Computational performance of the oblique shock problem.

Methods	GMRES Iterations	CPU Time (s)
NMVC	06126	3.948
CAU	10325	4.908

5.2 Reflected Shock Problem

The reflected shock as describe in [19], is a two-dimensional stationary problem composed of three flow regions separated by an oblique shock and its reflection along the bottom wall. The computational domain is given by $\Omega = [0.0, 4.1] \times [0.0, 1.0]$, as shown in Fig. 4.

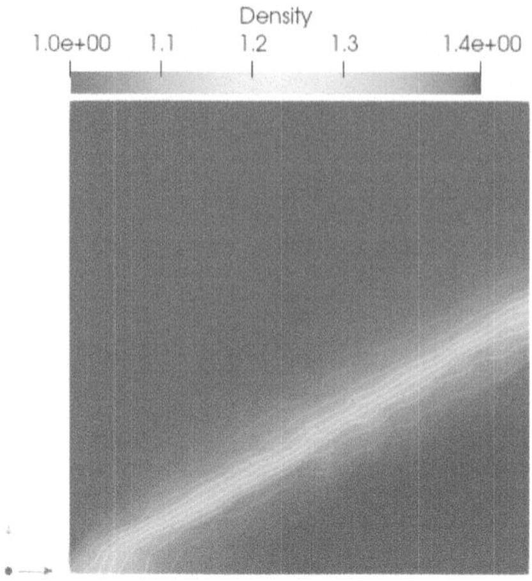

(a) Density.

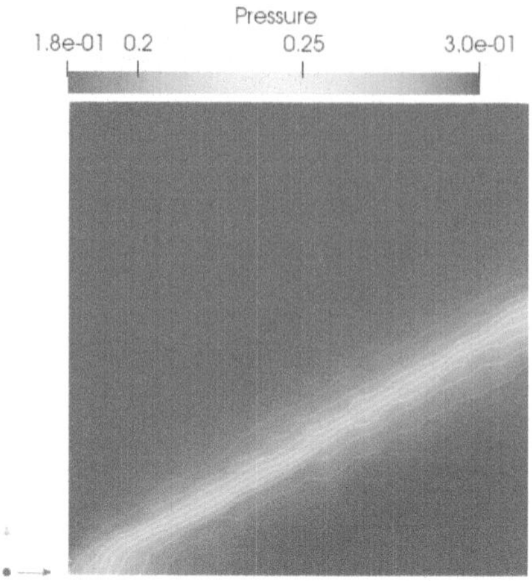

(b) Pressure.

Fig. 3. Numerical results of oblique shock problem.

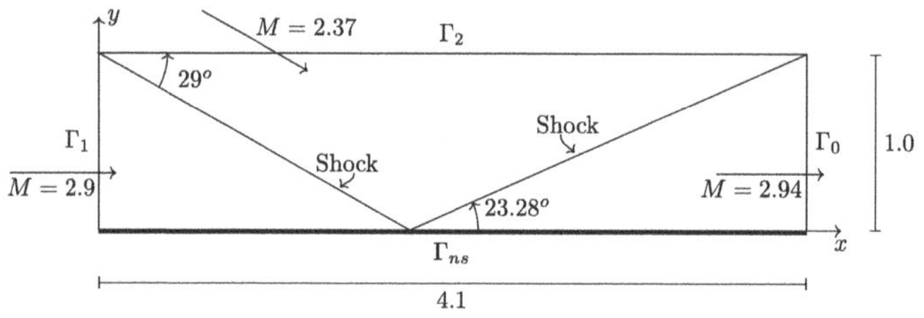

Fig. 4. Reflected shock problem description.

The prescribed boundary conditions are: in Γ_1 all variables are prescribed as $\{U_1, U_2, U_3, U_4\} = \{1.0, 2.9, 0.0, 5.990715\}$; in Γ_2 all variables are prescribed as $\{U_1, U_2, U_3, U_4\} = \{1.7, 4.452878, -0.860744, 9.870181\}$; in Γ_{ns} the normal speed to the wall is zero, i.e., $U_3 = 0$; in Γ_0 no boundary conditions are prescribed.

The results of the reflected shock problem were analyzed at time $t = 3.0$s with an unstructured mesh with 1404 nodes and 2646 triangular elements. The Fig. 5 presents the density profile of the reflected shock problem along $y = 0.25$ comparing the results obtained from the NMVC and CAU methods, and the exact solution of the problem. From the presented results of the density profile, we can verify the similarity between the NMVC and CAU methods.

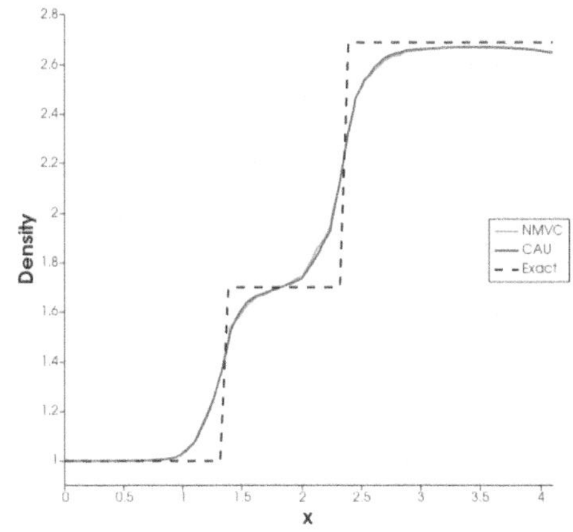

Fig. 5. Density profile along $y = 0.25$ of the reflected shock problem.

Figures 6a and 6b present the numerical results obtained by the NMVC method for the density and pressure, respectively, of the reflected shock problem. The computational performance data of the NMVC and CAU methods for the reflected shock problem are presented in Table 2. Note that the number of GMRES iterations and the CPU time of the NMVC method are better compared to the CAU method, leading the NMVC method to be 8.34% faster in this problem.

Table 2. Computational performance of the reflected shock problem.

Methods	GMRES Iterations	CPU Time (s)
NMVC	7515	13.136
CAU	9238	14.331

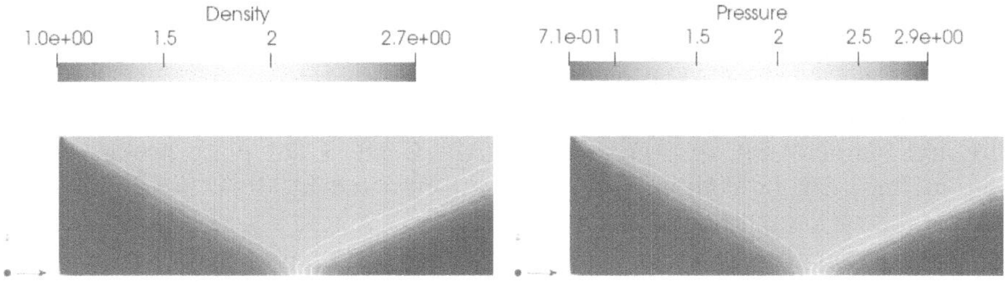

(a) Density. (b) Pressure.

Fig. 6. Numerical results of reflected shock problem.

5.3 Carter's Flat Plate Problem

The Carter's flat plate problem has a two-dimensional domain $\Omega = [-0.2, 1.2] \times [0.0, 0.8]$, Reynolds number $Re = 1000$ and Mach number $M = 3.0$. The flat plate is set in the range $0.0 \leq x \leq 1.2$, as shown in Fig. 7. We emphasize that thermal conductivity was defined as $\kappa = 1.395138$, as described in [16,21]. The viscosity is related to temperature through the equation $\mu = (0.0906T^{1.5})/(T + 0.0001406)$.

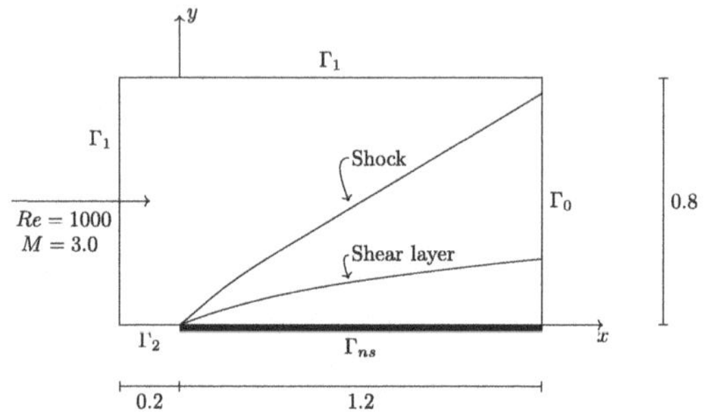

Fig. 7. Carter's flat plate problem description.

The specified boundary conditions are: in Γ_1 all variables are prescribed as $\{U_1, U_2, U_3, U_4\} = \{1.0, 1.0, 0.0, 0.698675\}$ and reference temperature $T_0 = 2.769 \times 10^{-4}$; in Γ_2 homogeneous Neumann boundary conditions are prescribed and $U_3 = 0$; in Γ_{ns} no-slip conditions are imposed $u_1 = u_2 = 0$ and stagnation temperature $T_{\text{stag}} = 7.7532 \times 10^{-4}$; in Γ_0 no boundary conditions are prescribed.

The numerical solutions were obtained at time $t = 3.5$s with a structured mesh with 1881 nodes and 3584 elements. Figures 8a and 8b present the density and velocity profile of the Carter's flat plate problem over $x = 1.0$ for the NMVC and CAU methods. Those numerical results can be compared with those presented in [15,16,18] with spectral elements and use SUPG stabilization method with the YZβ capture operator. The solutions obtained are similar, showing the effectiveness of implementing the NMVC method with the artificial viscosity operator given by the CAU discontinuity capture operator.

Figures 9a, 9b, 9c and 9d present the results of density, Mach number, pressure and temperature, respectively, from the Carter's flat plate problem. The contour lines can be compared with those presented in [4], where it uses the CAU stabilization method.

The friction coefficient of the Carter's flat plate problem is presented in Fig. 10, comparing the results obtained with the NMVC and CAU methods, and the modified Blasius solution [1]. Note that the solutions obtained by the NMVC and CAU methods are equivalent and close to the value of the modified Blasius solution.

The results of the computational performance of the NMVC and CAU methods for the Carter's flat plate problem are presented in Fig. 3. With the data

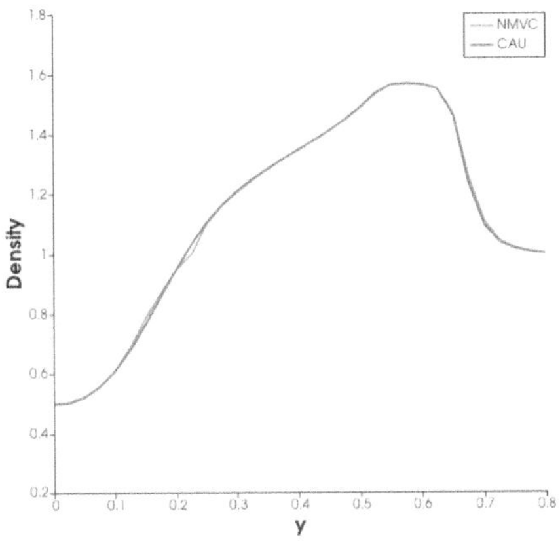

(a) Density.

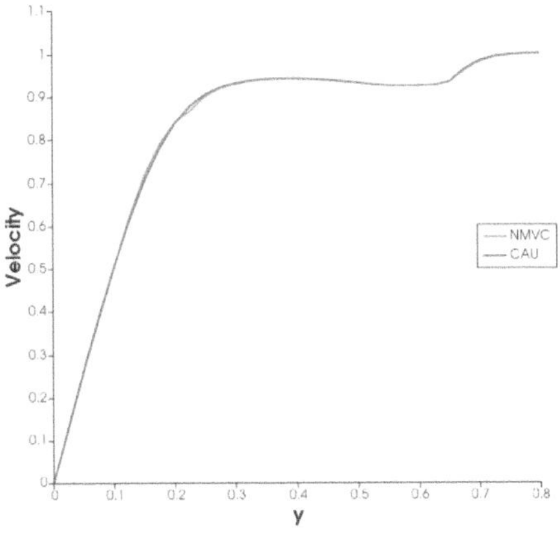

(b) Velocity.

Fig. 8. Profile along $x = 1.0$ of the Carter's flat plate.

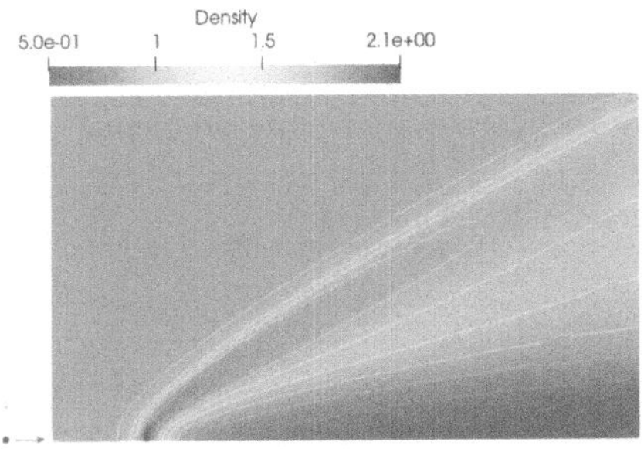

(a) Density.

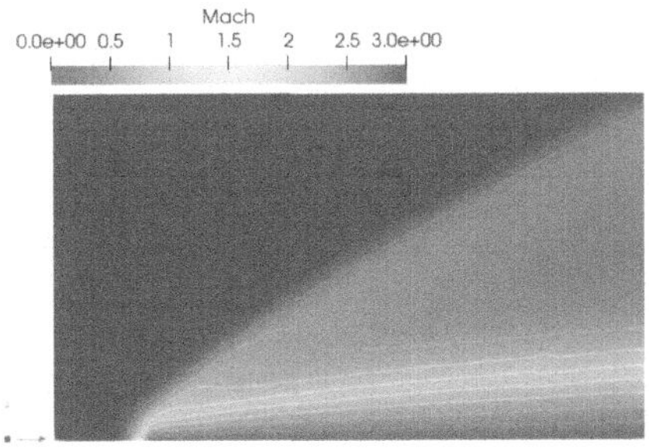

(b) Mach.

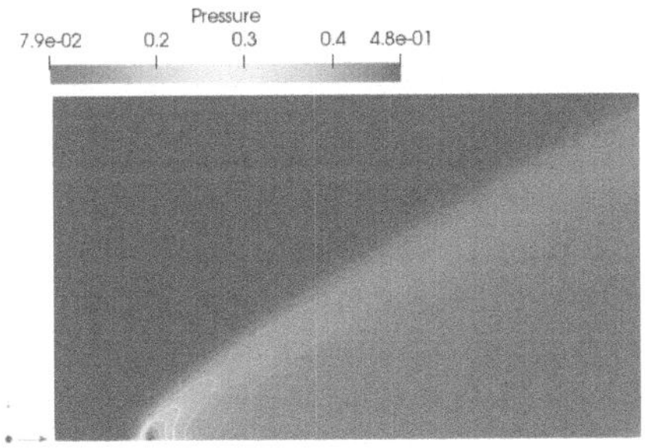

(c) Pressure.

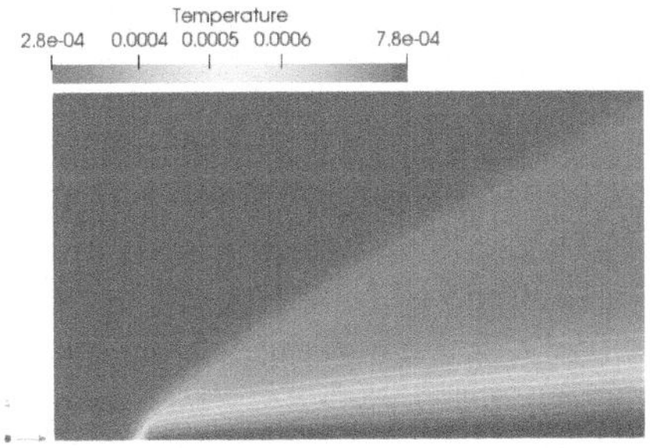

(d) Temperature.

Fig. 9. Numerical results of Carter's flat plate.

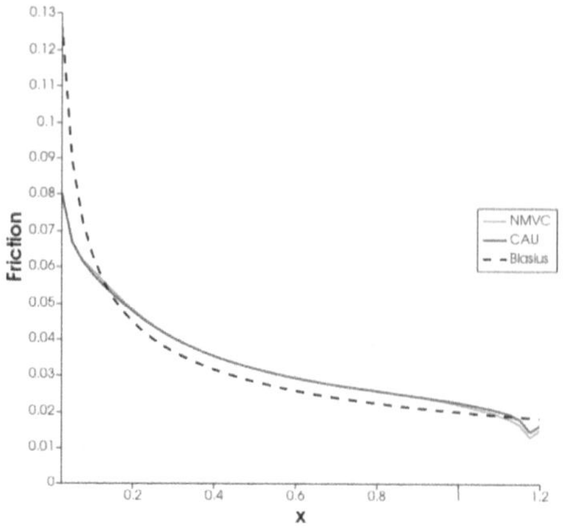

Fig. 10. Friction coefficient of Carter's flat plate problem.

we can verify the best performance of the NMVC method, obtaining the lowest number of iterations of the GMRES method and the lowest CPU time. In this way, we can see that the NMVC method is 24.86% faster than the CAU method for the Carter's flat plate problem (Table 3).

Table 3. Computational performance of the Carter's flat plate problem.

Methods	GMRES Iterations	CPU Time (s)
NMVC	07369	19.373
CAU	12475	24.481

5.4 Compression Corner Problem

The compression corner problem has a two-dimensional domain given by a rectangular part $[-0.2, 1.0] \times [0.0, 0.575]$ and by a part with slope of $10°$ given by $[1.0, 1.8] \times [0.8 \tan 10°, 0.575 + 0.8 \tan 10°]$, as shown in Fig. 11. According to [18,21], the flat plate is located after $x = 0.0$, and the following are considered at the input: Reynolds number $Re = 16800$, Mach number $M = 3.0$ and conductivity thermal $\kappa = 1.395138$. Viscosity is related to temperature through the equation $\mu = (0.00539T^{1.5})/(T + 0.0001406)$.

The specified boundary conditions are: in Γ_1 all variables are prescribed as $\{U_1, U_2, U_3, U_4\} = \{1.0, 1.0, 0.0, 0.698675\}$ and reference temperature $T_0 = 2.769 \times 10^{-4}$; in Γ_2 homogeneous Neumann boundary conditions are prescribed and $U_3 = 0$; in Γ_{ns} no-slip conditions are imposed $u_1 = u_2 = 0$ and stagnation temperature $T_{\text{stag}} = 7.7532 \times 10^{-4}$; in Γ_0 no boundary conditions are prescribed.

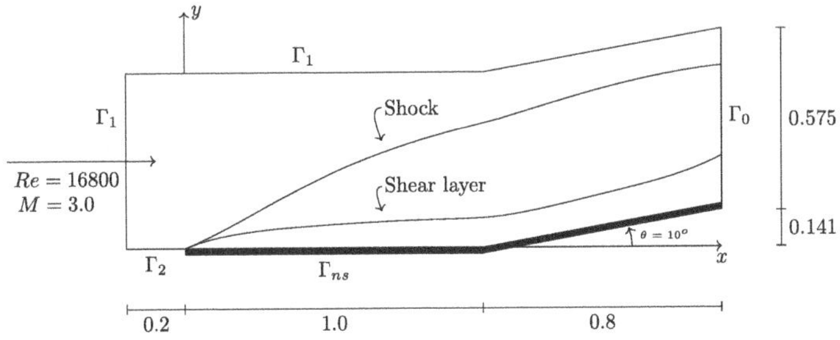

Fig. 11. Compression corner problem description.

The Figs. 12a, 12b, 12c and 12d present the density, Mach number, pressure and temperature for the compression corner problem, respectively. The results presented can be compared with those obtained in [21] using the SUPG stabilization method with the YZβ capture operator and [15] with a method based on the finite calculus (FIC). We emphasize that the solutions were obtained at the time instant $t = 3.0$s with a structured mesh with 1944 nodes and 3680 elements.

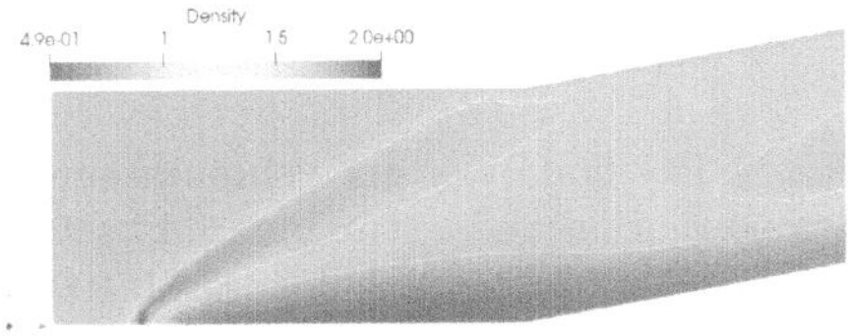

(a) Density.

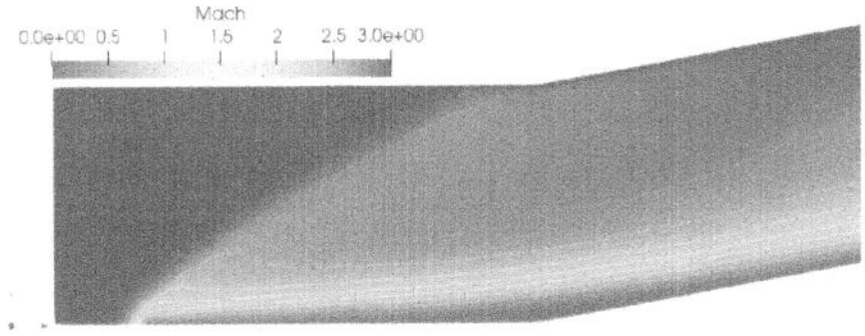

(b) Mach.

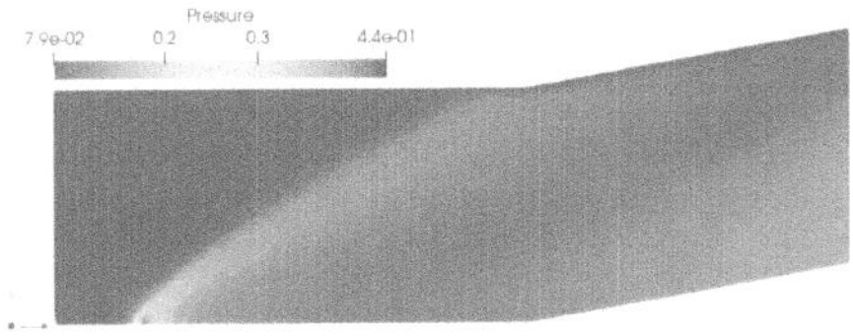

(c) Pressure.

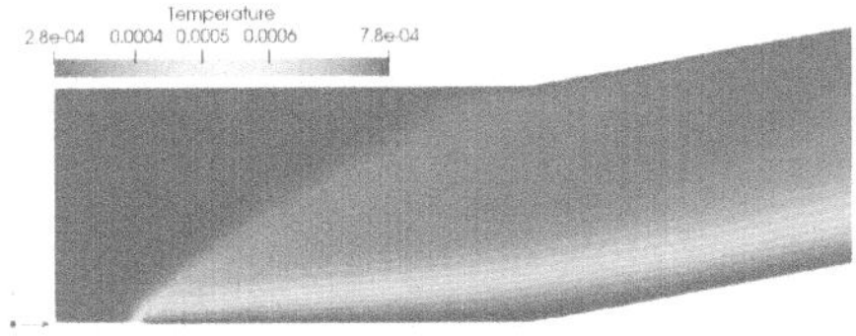

(d) Temperature.

Fig. 12. Numerical results of compression corner problem.

The results of the computational performance of the NMVC and CAU methods for the compression corner problem are presented in Table 4. With the tabulated data we can see that the NMVC method has better performance compared to the CAU method, with the NMVC method being 24.16% faster for the compression corner problem.

Table 4. Computational performance of the compression corner problem.

Methods	GMRES Iterations	CPU Time (s)
NMVC	07628	18.426
CAU	13274	24.299

6 Conclusions

In this work, we present the NMVC method of multiscale variational stabilization with nonlinear artificial viscosity for the compressible Navier-Stokes equations with the bubble functions scenario. This method adds artificial viscosity in the two discretization scales of the problem, which is defined by the discontinuity capture operator of the CAU method.

The NMVC and CAU methods were used to obtain the numerical solution of four problems comprising the Euler and compressible Navier-Stokes equations. The results obtained from the methods were compared and validated the implementation of the NMVC method, since the solutions obtained by the methods are similar. We also highlight the better computational performance obtained by the NMVC method, leading to faster solutions from 8 to 24%.

References

1. Aliabadi, S.K., Ray, S.E., Tezduyar, T.E.: SUPG finite element computation of viscous compressible flows based on the conservation and entropy variables formulations. Comput. Mech. **11**, 300–312. Springer (1993). https://doi.org/10.1007/BF00350089
2. Aliabadi, S.K., Tezduyar, T.E.: Space-time finite element computation of compressible flows involving moving boundaries and interfaces. Comput. Methods Appl. Mech. Eng. **107**(1-2), 209–223 (1993). https://doi.org/10.1016/0045-7825(93)90176-X
3. Aliabadi, S.K., Tezduyar, T.E.: Parallel fluid dynamics computations in aerospace applications. Int. J. Numer. Methods Fluids **21**(10), 783–805 (1995). https://doi.org/10.1002/fld.1650211003
4. Almeida, R.C., Galeão, A.C.: An adaptive Petrov-Galerkin formulation for the compressible Euler and Navier-Stokes equations. Comput. Methods Appl. Mech. Eng. **129**(1-2), 157–176 (1996). https://doi.org/10.1016/0045-7825(95)00858-6
5. Bento, S.S., de Lima, L.M., Sedano, R.Z., Catabriga, L., Santos, I.P.: A nonlinear multiscale viscosity method to solve compressible flow problems. In: Gervasi, O., et al. (eds.) ICCSA 2016. LNCS, vol. 9786, pp. 3–17. Springer, Cham (2016). https://doi.org/10.1007/978-3-319-42085-1_1
6. Bento, S.S., Barbosa, P.W., Santos, I.P., de Lima, L.M., Catabriga, L.: A nonlinear finite element formulation based on multiscale approach to solve compressible Euler equations. In: Gervasi, O., et al. (eds.) ICCSA 2017. LNCS, vol. 10409, pp. 735–743. Springer, Cham (2017). https://doi.org/10.1007/978-3-319-62407-5_55
7. Bento, S.S.: Nonlinear multiscale viscosity methods and time integration schemes for solving compressible Euler equations. DSc Thesis, Universidade Federal do Espírito Santo, Vitória - ES, Brasil (2018)

8. Brooks, A.N., Hughes, J.R.: Streamline upwind/Petrov-Galerkin formulations for convection dominated flows with particular emphasis on the incompressible Navier-Stokes equations. Comput. Methods Appl. Mech. Eng. **32**(1-3), 199–259 (1982). https://doi.org/10.1016/0045-7825(82)90071-8
9. Catabriga, L., Coutinho, A.L.G.A.: Implicit SUPG solution of Euler equations using edge-based data structures. Comput. Methods Appl. Mech. Eng. **191**, 3477-3490 (2002). https://doi.org/10.1016/S0045-7825(02)00285-2
10. Galeão, A.C., Do Carmo, E.G.D.,: A consistent approximate upwind Petrov-Galerkin method for convection-dominated problems. Comput. Methods Appl. Mech. Eng. **68**(1), 83–95 (1988). https://doi.org/10.1016/0045-7825(88)90108-9
11. Hughes, T.J.R., Tezduyar, T.E.: Finite element methods for first-order hyperbolic systems with particular emphasis on the compressible Euler equations. Comput. Methods Appl. Mech. Eng. **45**, 217–284 (1984). https://doi.org/10.1016/0045-7825(84)90157-9
12. Hughes, T.J.R.: Multiscale phenomena: Green's functions, the Dirichlet-to-Neumann formulation, subgrid scale models, bubbles and the origins of stabilized methods. Elsevier. Comput. Methods Appl. Mech. Eng. **127**(1-4), 387–401 (1995). https://doi.org/10.1016/0045-7825(95)00844-9
13. Knobloch, P.: Improvements of the Mizukami–Hughes method for convection–diffusion equations. Comput. Methods Appl. Mech. Eng. **196**(1-3), 579–594 (2006). https://doi.org/10.1016/j.cma.2006.06.004
14. Koobus, B., Farhat, C.: A variational multiscale method for the large eddy simulation of compressible turbulent flows on unstructured meshes-application to vortex shedding. Comput. Methods Appl. Mech. Eng. **193**(15-16), 1367–1383 (2004). https://doi.org/10.1016/j.cma.2003.12.028
15. Kouhi, M., Oñate, E.: An implicit stabilized finite element method for the compressible Navier-Stokes equations using finite calculus. Comput. Mech. **56**, 113-129 (2015). https://doi.org/10.1007/s00466-015-1161-2
16. Parada, S., Codina, R., Baiges, J.: A VMS-based fractional step technique for the compressible Navier-Stokes equations using conservative variables. J. Comput. Phys. **459**, 111–137 (2022). https://doi.org/10.1016/j.jcp.2022.111137
17. Quarteroni, A.: Numerical models for differential problems, 2nd edn. Springer, Milano (2009). https://doi.org/10.1007/978-88-470-5522-3
18. Ranjan, R., Catabriga, L., Yusheng, F.: High-Order Spectral/hp-Based Solver for Compressible Navier-Stokes Equations. AIAA J. **60**(5), 2972–2986 (2022). https://doi.org/10.2514/1.J060704
19. Shakib, F.T., Hughes, J.R., Johan, Z.: A new finite element formulation for computational fluid dynamics: X. The compressible Euler and Navier-Stokes equations. Comput. Methods Appl. Mech. Eng. **89**(1-3), 141–219 (1991). https://doi.org/10.1016/0045-7825(91)90041-4
20. Tezduyar, T.E., Senga, M.: Stabilization and shock-capturing parameters in SUPG formulation of compressible flows. Comput. Methods Appl. Mech. Eng. **195**, 1621–1632 (2006). https://doi.org/10.1016/j.cma.2005.05.032
21. Toro, J.B.: Implementation of finite element solvers for the compressible Navier-Stokes equations. Universitat Politècnica de Catalunya, Barcelona (2015)

The Zeros of Quadratic Coquaternionic Polynomials Revisited

Maria Irene Falcão, Fernando Miranda(✉), and Ricardo Severino

CMAT, Universidade do Minho, Braga, Portugal
{mif,fmiranda,ricardo}@math.uminho.pt

Abstract. In this paper, we address the problem of solving the quadratic equation $x^2 + bx + c = 0$, where b and c are elements of the algebra of coquaternions. The nature of this algebra leads, as expected, to results very different from the ones obtained in the classical complex case, making the root-finding problem much more demanding. In this paper we derive straightforward conditions to characterize the number and form of the non-isolated zeros of monic quadratic coquaternionic equations. Through carefully constructed examples and by leveraging the Mathematica system, we illustrate the core findings and showcase the array of scenarios that may emerge.

Keywords: Coquaternions · Quadratic Equation · Non-isolated Zeros · Computer Algebra System

1 Introduction

In 1849, James Cockle [5] introduced a non-commutative algebra whose elements – the coquaternions, also referred to as split quaternions – generalize the complex numbers. Although coquaternions have often been overlooked, in recent years one can find a growing interest in the use of this four-dimensional real algebra, not only from the theoretical point of view, but also from the applications standpoint [1–3, 10, 11, 14, 15, 18–21, 24, 25, 27, 28].

The motivation for this work came from previous studies on the dynamics of certain families of quadratic coquaternionic maps [8, 11, 12] which revealed that working on the coquaternion algebra setting leads to dynamics which are richer and even more extraordinary than the ones obtained in the classical real and complex cases. In fact, it was possible to show that, for some coquaternionic quadratics, non-isolated sets of fixed points appear: either lines, or even hyperboloids, of fixed points. Determining the fixed points of a quadratic dynamical system is inherently tied to the computation of the zeros of a quadratic polynomial. This connection underscores the importance of determining the zeros of generic quadratic polynomials and constructing polynomials with prescribed zeros.

O. Gervasi et al. (Eds.): ICCSA 2024 Workshops, LNCS 14815, pp. 268–284, 2024.
https://doi.org/10.1007/978-3-031-65154-0_17

The study of the zero-set of generic monic unilateral polynomials[1] was previously undertaken by the authors of this work in [10]. The idea follows the pioneer work of Niven for the quaternions [22] and led to a comprehensive characterization of the zeros of a unilateral coquaternionic polynomial of degree n, revealing three distinct types of zeros - isolated, linear or hyperboloidal - with the total *number of zeros* not exceeding $n(2n-1)$. However, the method proposed in [10,22] involves computing the zeros of a $2n$ degree real polynomial, typically resulting in only numerical approximations. Moreover, accuracy issues associated with classical rootfinding methods can hinder the identification of the type of the zero. Indeed, even for the $n = 2$ case, it is not possible to obtain a general expression of the zeros in terms of its coefficients nor to know easily how many zeros of each nature a quadratic polynomial has. The work [13] marked an initial effort to investigate the coexistence of non-isolated zeros of the aforementioned types. While the study provided valuable insights into this phenomenon, it fell short of establishing a direct correlation between the zeros and the coefficients of the polynomials.

In [26], the factorizability of quadratic polynomials was explored, presenting results relevant to this problem. Furthermore, explicit formulas for the roots of such polynomials were provided in [4]. It is worth noting that our approach diverges significantly from those in these two works, as well as from the methodology employed in [10] to establish results on polynomial zeros of arbitrary degree. Here, we draw inspiration from the work on quaternions presented in [17] to determine both the number and nature of zeros that a quadratic polynomial may possess, alongside providing explicit expressions for these zeros.

We must refer that, since the algebra of coquaternions is isomorphic to the algebra of 2×2 real matrices, the problem at hand, albeit approached differently, can be regarded as a specific instance of the broader problem of solving matrix polynomial equations [6,16,29]. By employing a coquaternionic formalism, we were able to derive explicit results that offer simple and direct applicability, often bypassing the need for numerical methods.

Due to the manifest intricate product between coquaternions, we believe that the development of symbolic computation techniques in this context plays an important role. In particular, we have used the software system Mathematica to avoid all the tedious computations and the add-on `CoqPolynomial`, complementing the package `Coquaternions` [7] to run all the examples. The current versions of these tools are described and available for download at the webpage https://w3.math.uminho.pt/Coquaternions.

The paper is organized as follows: Sect. 2 contains the basic results on the coquaternion algebra; Sect. 3 gives a matrix reformulation of the problem under consideration, while the main results of the paper are presented in Sect. 4. The paper ends with several examples carefully chosen to draw attention to some aspects of the theory.

[1] A polynomial in one formal variable x whose coefficients are coquaternions located on the left (or right)-hand side of the powers of x.

2 Basic Results and Notation

Let $\{1, \mathbf{i}, \mathbf{j}, \mathbf{k}\}$ be an orthonormal basis of the Euclidean vector space $\mathbb{R}^4$. The algebra of real coquaternions, which we denote by $\mathbb{H}_{\mathrm{coq}}$, is generated by the product given according to the following rules

$$\mathbf{i}^2 = -1,\ \mathbf{j}^2 = \mathbf{k}^2 = 1,\ \ \mathbf{ij} = -\mathbf{ji} = \mathbf{k}.$$

The multiplication of two coquaternions $p = p_0 + p_1\mathbf{i} + p_2\mathbf{j} + p_3\mathbf{k}$ and $q = q_0 + q_1\mathbf{i} + q_2\mathbf{j} + q_3\mathbf{k}$ is given by

$$\begin{aligned} pq = p_0q_0 - p_1q_1 + p_2q_2 + p_3q_3 + (p_0q_1 + p_1q_0 - p_2q_3 + p_3q_2)\mathbf{i} \\ + (p_0q_2 - p_1q_3 + p_2q_0 + p_3q_1)\mathbf{j} + (p_0q_3 + p_1q_2 - p_2q_1 + p_3q_0)\mathbf{k}. \quad (1) \end{aligned}$$

The expression (1) shows that the product pq can be computed using matrices as $L_p\mathbf{q}$, with

$$L_p = \begin{pmatrix} p_0 & -p_1 & p_2 & p_3 \\ p_1 & p_0 & p_3 & -p_2 \\ p_2 & p_3 & p_0 & -p_1 \\ p_3 & -p_2 & p_1 & p_0 \end{pmatrix} \quad (2)$$

and where, when performing the matrix multiplication, we identify q with the column vector $\mathbf{q} = (q_0\ q_1\ q_2\ q_3)^{\mathrm{T}}$.

The *conjugate* $\overline{q}$ of a coquaternion q is defined as $\overline{q} = q_0 - q_1\mathbf{i} - q_2\mathbf{j} - q_3\mathbf{k}$; the number q_0 is called the *real part* of q and denoted by $\mathrm{Re}\, q$ and the *vector part* of q, denoted by $\underline{q}$, is given by $\underline{q} = q_1\mathbf{i} + q_2\mathbf{j} + q_3\mathbf{k}$.

We recall that every coquaternion q can be represented by the real matrix

$$\begin{pmatrix} q_0 + q_3 & q_1 + q_2 \\ q_2 - q_1 & q_0 - q_3 \end{pmatrix}$$

and for this reason the quantities $\mathrm{tr}\, q = q + \overline{q} = 2\,\mathrm{Re}\, q$ and $\det q = q\overline{q} = q_0^2 + q_1^2 - q_2^2 - q_3^2$ are called the *trace* and *determinant* of q, respectively. We endow $\mathbb{H}_{\mathrm{coq}}$ with the *norm*[2] $\|q\| = \sqrt{|\det q|}$ and say that q is a *non-singular* coquaternion if $\|q\| \neq 0$ and call q a *unit coquaternion* if $\|q\| = 1$.

We identify the set of elements in $\mathbb{H}_{\mathrm{coq}}$ whose vector part is zero with the set $\mathbb{R}$ of real numbers. The subspace of $\mathbb{H}_{\mathrm{coq}}$ of coquaternions whose real part is zero (usually referred to as pure coquaternions) is identified with the $(2+1)$-Minkowski space $\mathbb{R}^{2+1}$. This is an inner product space consisting of the real vector space $\mathbb{R}^3$ equipped with the Lorentz inner product $\langle \underline{p}, \underline{q} \rangle_L = -p_1q_1 + p_2q_2 + p_3q_3$. We observe that $\langle \underline{q}, \underline{q} \rangle_L = -\det \underline{q}$.

The sign of $\det q$ determines the type of the coquaternion q; q is *space-like, light-like* or *time-like*, if $\det q < 0$, $\det q = 0$ or $\det q > 0$, respectively; the sets of such coquaternions will be denoted by $\mathbb{S}$, $\mathbb{L}$ and $\mathbb{T}$, respectively.

[2] Although this does not have all the properties of a true norm, it is still usually referred to as the norm of q.

We define now in $\mathbb{H}_{\text{coq}}$ the relation

$$p \sim q \iff \operatorname{Re} p = \operatorname{Re} q \text{ and } \det \underline{p} = \det \underline{q}. \tag{3}$$

This is an equivalence relation in $\mathbb{H}_{\text{coq}}$ and the corresponding equivalence class of q is the set

$$[q] := \left\{x_0 + x_1\mathbf{i} + x_2\mathbf{j} + x_3\mathbf{k} : x_0 = q_0 \text{ and } x_1^2 - x_2^2 - x_3^2 = q_1^2 - q_2^2 - q_3^2\right\}. \tag{4}$$

We can identify[3] $[q]$ with a hyperboloid in the hyperplane $x_0 = q_0$; this will be a hyperboloid of one sheet, a hyperboloid of two sheets or a degenerate hyperboloid (i.e., a cone), if $\underline{q} \in \mathbb{S}$, $\underline{q} \in \mathbb{T}$ or $\underline{q} \in \mathbb{L}$, respectively.

In a previous work [10] we presented a complete characterization of the zero-set $Z(P)$ of a unilateral coquaternionic polynomial P of degree n and proved that the zeros of P belong to, at most, $n(2n-1)$ equivalence classes. In the case of a quadratic equation, this result leads to the conclusion that such equation has at most six zeros. In this context, we have also showed that coquaternionic polynomials may have three different types of zeros, motivating us to introduce the following definition.

A zero z of a given coquaternionic polynomial P is said to be an *isolated zero* of P, if $[z]$ contains no other zeros of P; z is said to be a *hyperboloidal zero* of P, if $[z] \subseteq Z(P)$; z is said to be a *linear zero* of P, if z is neither an isolated zero nor a hyperboloidal zero of P.[4]

In what follows, we will treat all the zeros belonging to the same equivalence class as forming a single zero, i.e., we will refer to a whole hyperboloid of zeros or a line of zeros simply as a hyperboloidal zero or a linear zero, respectively.

3 Quadratic Polynomials in $\mathbb{H}_{\text{coq}}$

In what follows we consider the quadratic equation

$$x^2 + bx + c = 0, \tag{5}$$

where $x = x_0 + x_1\mathbf{i} + x_2\mathbf{j} + x_3\mathbf{k}$, $b = b_0 + b_1\mathbf{i} + b_2\mathbf{j} + b_3\mathbf{k}$ and $c = c_0 + c_1\mathbf{i} + c_2\mathbf{j} + c_3\mathbf{k}$ are in $\mathbb{H}_{\text{coq}}$. As mentioned before, equations of this form have at most six zeros; what remains to be seen is how many zeros of each type they may have.

3.1 Reformulation of the Problem

Recalling the so-called left representation of a coquaternion (2) and using the fact that any coquaternion $q = q_0 + q_1\mathbf{i} + q_2\mathbf{j} + q_3\mathbf{k}$ is a zero of the equation[5]

$$x^2 - \operatorname{tr}(q)x + \det q = 0, \tag{6}$$

[3] Contrary to what happens with quaternions, the relation (3) does not coincide with the usual similarity relation; coquaternions satisfying (3) are called quasi-similar; see e.g. [10] for details.

[4] The term linear zero is justified by the fact that, in this case, the zeros in the class $[z]$ form a line in a given hyperplane.

[5] The polynomial on the left-hand side of (6) is called the characteristic polynomial of q.

one can write the Eq. (5) in the matrix form

$$(2x_0 I_4 + L_b)\mathbf{x} = \mathbf{c},$$

where

$$\mathbf{x} = \begin{pmatrix} x_0 & x_1 & x_2 & x_3 \end{pmatrix}^T \text{ and } \mathbf{c} = \begin{pmatrix} -c_0 + x_0^2 + x_1^2 - x_2^2 - x_3^2 & -c_1 & -c_2 & -c_3 \end{pmatrix}^T.$$

We follow now the approach of [17] adapted to the coquaternionic setting. Assume that Eq. (5) has a solution x such that $\operatorname{Re} x = t$, i.e., that the following nonlinear system is solvable,

$$\begin{pmatrix} 2t+b_0 & -b_1 & b_2 & b_3 \\ b_1 & 2t+b_0 & b_3 & -b_2 \\ b_2 & b_3 & 2t+b_0 & -b_1 \\ b_3 & -b_2 & b_1 & 2t+b_0 \end{pmatrix} \begin{pmatrix} t \\ x_1 \\ x_2 \\ x_3 \end{pmatrix} = \begin{pmatrix} -c_0 + t^2 + x_1^2 - x_2^2 - x_3^2 \\ -c_1 \\ -c_2 \\ -c_3 \end{pmatrix}.$$

Such a system combines the nonlinear equation

$$(x_1 + \tfrac{b_1}{2})^2 - (x_2 + \tfrac{b_2}{2})^2 - (x_3 + \tfrac{b_3}{2})^2 = t^2 + b_0 t + \tfrac{b_1^2 - b_2^2 - b_3^2}{4} + c_0 \tag{7}$$

with the linear system

$$\mathcal{M}(t)\widetilde{\mathbf{x}}(t) = \widetilde{\mathbf{c}}(t), \tag{8}$$

where

$$\mathcal{M}(t) := \begin{pmatrix} 2t+b_0 & b_3 & -b_2 \\ b_3 & 2t+b_0 & -b_1 \\ -b_2 & b_1 & 2t+b_0 \end{pmatrix}, \; \widetilde{\mathbf{x}}(t) := \begin{pmatrix} x_1 \\ x_2 \\ x_3 \end{pmatrix}, \; \widetilde{\mathbf{c}}(t) := \begin{pmatrix} -c_1 - b_1 t \\ -c_2 - b_2 t \\ -c_3 - b_3 t \end{pmatrix}. \tag{9}$$

Observe that, for each value of t,

$$\begin{aligned} \mathcal{H}_t := \Big\{ & (x_0, x_1, x_2, x_3) \in \mathbb{R}^4 : x_0 = t, \\ & (x_1 + \tfrac{b_1}{2})^2 - (x_2 + \tfrac{b_2}{2})^2 - (x_3 + \tfrac{b_3}{2})^2 = t^2 + b_0 t + \tfrac{b_1^2 - b_2^2 - b_3^2}{4} + c_0 \Big\} \end{aligned} \tag{10}$$

can be identified with a hyperboloid with center $(-\frac{b_1}{2}, -\frac{b_2}{2}, -\frac{b_3}{2})$ in the hyperplane $x_0 = t$; this will be a hyperboloid of two-sheets, one-sheet, or a cone, depending on whether $t^2 + b_0 t + \frac{1}{4}\det \underline{b} + c_0$ is negative, positive or zero, respectively. The solvability of the system (7)-(8) is linked to the rank of the matrix $\mathcal{M}(t)$, as indicated in the next subsection.

3.2 Rank of $\mathcal{M}(t)$

Simple calculations show that

$$\det \mathcal{M}(t) = (b_0 + 2t)(\det \underline{b} + (b_0 + 2t)^2).$$

The set $\mathcal{S}$ of real solutions of $\det \mathcal{M}(t) = 0$ depends on the type of the vector part of b, namely:

1. if $\underline{b}$ is space-like, then

$$\mathcal{S} = \left\{-\tfrac{b_0}{2}, -\tfrac{b_0}{2} + \tfrac{\|\underline{b}\|}{2}, -\tfrac{b_0}{2} - \tfrac{\|\underline{b}\|}{2}\right\}$$

2. if $\underline{b}$ is time-like or light-like, then

$$\mathcal{S} = \left\{-\tfrac{b_0}{2}\right\}. \tag{11}$$

From now on and for simplicity we adopt the following notation.

$$N_1 := -\|\underline{b}\|;\ N_2 := \|\underline{b}\|;\ s_0 := -\tfrac{b_0}{2};\ s_1 := s_0 + N_1;\ s_2 := s_0 + N_2. \tag{12}$$

Case 1: rank $\mathcal{M}(t) = 0$

This is equivalent to saying that $b_1 = b_2 = b_3 = 0$ and $t = -\frac{b_0}{2}$. The system (8) is solvable iff $c_1 = c_2 = c_3 = 0$. In such case, the Eq. (5) reduces to the real quadratic equation

$$x^2 + b_0 x + c_0 = 0,\ x \in \mathbb{H}_{\mathrm{coq}},\ b_0, c_0 \in \mathbb{R}$$

whose solution $-\frac{b_0}{2} + x_1\mathbf{i} + x_2\mathbf{j} + x_3\mathbf{k}$ has to satisfy (7), i.e.,

$$x_1^2 - x_2^2 - x_3^2 = c_0 - \frac{b_0^2}{4}.$$

Case 2: rank $\mathcal{M}(t) = 1$

If rank $\mathcal{M}(t) < 3$, then det $\mathcal{M}(t) = 0$, i.e., $t \in \mathcal{S}$. Consider first the case where $\underline{b}$ is not space-like, i.e., $t = s_0$ (cf. (11)-(12)). Then

$$\mathcal{M}(s_0) = \begin{pmatrix} 0 & b_3 & -b_2 \\ b_3 & 0 & -b_1 \\ -b_2 & b_1 & 0 \end{pmatrix}.$$

The case $b_1 = b_2 = b_3 = 0$ was already considered. If one of the b_i is non-zero, then it follows that rank $\mathcal{M}(s_0) \neq 1$.

Assume now that $\underline{b}$ is space-like and consider the matrices

$$\mathcal{M}(s_k) = \begin{pmatrix} \frac{N_k}{2} & b_3 & -b_2 \\ b_3 & \frac{N_k}{2} & -b_1 \\ -b_2 & b_1 & \frac{N_k}{2} \end{pmatrix};\ k = 1, 2.$$

Since $N_k \neq 0$, it is easy to see that the systems

$$(N_k, b_3, -b_2) = \alpha(b_3, N_k, -b_1) = \beta(-b_2, b_1, N_k)$$

have no solution for $\alpha, \beta \in \mathbb{R}$, which in turn implies that rank $\mathcal{M}(s_k) \neq 1$. In conclusion, the case rank $\mathcal{M}(t) = 1$ never occurs.

Case 3: rank $\mathcal{M}(t) = 2$

In this situation the zero-set of the system (8) is an affine line L_t, provided that $\text{rank}([\mathcal{M}(t)\ \widetilde{\mathbf{c}}(t)]) = 2$; the discussion of the problem under consideration reduces to the discussion of the intersection of

$$\mathcal{L}_t = \{(x_0, x_1, x_2, x_3) \in \mathbb{R}^4 : x_0 = t, (x_1, x_2, x_3) \in L_t\} \tag{13}$$

with the hyperboloid $\mathcal{H}_t$ in (10), which, as it is well known, can be (in general): an empty set, one point, two points or $\mathcal{L}_t$ itself. We refer in this context the paper [27], where the intersection of a double cone and a line is studied in the coquaternionic setting.

Case 4: $\text{rank}\,\mathcal{M}(t) = 3$

In this case, $t \notin \mathcal{S}$ and for each t, the system (8) has a unique solution $(x_1, x_2, x_3) = (x_1(t), x_2(t), x_3(t))$ which can be obtained by using any computer algebra tools. Using the function `LinearSolve` of Mathematica, we end up in (7) with a sixth degree polynomial of the form

$$\begin{aligned} p_6(t) = &-16t^6 - 48b_0t^5 - 8(7b_0^2 + 2c_0 + \alpha)t^4 - 8(b_0(4(b_0^2 + c_0) + \alpha) + 2\beta)t^3 \\ &+ (-9b_0^4 - 2(12c_0 + \alpha)b_0^2 - 20\beta b_0 + 3\alpha^2 + 4c_0\alpha - 4\gamma)t^2 \\ &+ (-b_0^5 - 8c_0b_0^3 - 8\beta b_0^2 + (\alpha^2 + 4c_0\alpha - 4\gamma)b_0 + 4\alpha\beta)t \\ &+ \beta^2 - b_0^4c_0 - b_0^3\beta + b_0\alpha\beta + b_0^2(c_0\alpha - \gamma), \end{aligned} \tag{14}$$

where

$$\alpha := \langle \underline{b}, \underline{b}\rangle_L, \quad \beta := \langle \underline{b}, \underline{c}\rangle_L, \quad \gamma := \langle \underline{c}, \underline{c}\rangle_L. \tag{15}$$

This leads to the conclusion that there are at most six non-isolated solutions of the problem (5), which can be obtained, for each real solution t of (14), from

$$\begin{cases} x_0 = & t \\ x_1 = & -\dfrac{(b_3c_2 - b_2c_3)(b_0 + 2t) - (b_0 + 2t)^2(c_1 + b_1t) + b_1t\alpha + b_1\beta}{\det \mathcal{M}(t)} \\ x_2 = & -\dfrac{(b_3c_1 - b_1c_3)(b_0 + 2t) - (b_0 + 2t)^2(c_2 + b_2t) + b_2t\alpha + b_2\beta}{\det \mathcal{M}(t)} \\ x_3 = & \dfrac{(-b_2c_1 + b_1c_2)(b_0 + 2t) - (b_0 + 2t)^2(c_3 + b_3t) + b_3t\alpha + b_3\beta}{\det \mathcal{M}(t)} \end{cases} \tag{16}$$

4 Main Results

Based on the conclusions of the previous section, the approach to obtain and prove the results concerning the identification and computation of the linear zeros of a monic quadratic coquaternionic equation can be described in three steps:

Step 1: For each value of s, such that $\det \mathcal{M}(s) = 0$, determine conditions on b and c in order to guarantee that the linear system

$$\mathcal{M}(s)\widetilde{\mathbf{x}}(s) = \widetilde{\mathbf{c}}(s),$$

has infinitely many solutions; see (9);

Step 2: Determine the set L_s of solutions of such system and obtain the corresponding line $\mathcal{L}_s$ given by (13);

Step 3: Determine additional conditions, if any, on b and c in order to guarantee that $\mathcal{L}_s \subset \mathcal{H}_s$, i.e., that all the elements in $\mathcal{L}_s$ are also solutions of (7).

All the steps are based on computer algebra tools. In particular, we have used the software system Mathematica to avoid all the tedious computations. Details about such computations can be obtained in the notebooks available at https://w3.math.uminho.pt/QuadraticsTools.

The nature and number of non-isolated solutions of the quadratic equation (5) depend on the form of the coquaternions b and c. Next results give the explicit expressions of the linear (respectively, hyperboloidal) zeros that Eq. (5) may have and show that the co-existence of isolated and linear (respectively, hyperboloidal) zeros is possible, but the number of isolated zeros in such cases is at most two.

Theorem 1. *If $\underline{b} = 0$, the quadratic equation has non-isolated zeros iff $\underline{c} = 0$. In such conditions, the equation has* **one hyperboloidal zero** *given by*

$$\mathcal{H}_{-\frac{b_0}{2}} = \left\{(x_0, x_1, x_2, x_3) \in \mathbb{R}^4 : x_0 = -\tfrac{b_0}{2}, x_1^2 - x_2^2 - x_3^2 = c_0 - \tfrac{b_0^2}{4}\right\}. \qquad (17)$$

In addition, if $\underline{c} = 0$ and $b_0^2 - 4c_0 > 0$, there are also **two isolated real zeros,** *given by*

$$z_1 = \frac{-b_0 + \sqrt{b_0^2 - 4c_0}}{2} \qquad \text{and} \qquad z_2 = \frac{-b_0 - \sqrt{b_0^2 - 4c_0}}{2}. \qquad (18)$$

Proof. If $\underline{b} = \underline{c} = 0$, the result (17) follows at once from Case 1 of Sect. 3.2. In addition and under the assumption that $\underline{c} = 0$ and $b_0^2 - 4c_0 > 0$, we can conclude from (14) and (15) that the real part of the isolated zeros (different from $-\frac{b_0}{2}$) are the solutions of the equation $c_0 + t(b_0 + t) = 0$, and the result (18) follows. On the other hand, if $\underline{c} \neq 0$, then (14) reduces to

$$-(b_0 + 2t)^2 \left(\gamma + b_0^2 c_0 + (b_0^3 + 4b_0 c_0)t + (5b_0^2 + 4c_0)t^2 + 8b_0 t^3 + 4t^4\right),$$

and the result is proved, since $b_0 + 2t \neq 0$. □

Theorem 2. *If $\underline{b}$ is a time-like coquaternion, then the quadratic equation has no non-isolated zeros.*

Proof. If $\det \underline{b} > 0$, then $b_1 \neq 0$ and the unique value of s such that $\det \mathcal{M}(s) = 0$ is $s = s_0 = -\frac{b_0}{2}$ (cf. (11)). For $t = s_0$, the linear system (8) can be written in the equivalent form (cf. (12))

$$\left(\begin{array}{ccc|c} 0 & 0 & 0 & -\frac{\alpha b_0 - 2\beta}{2b_1} \\ b_3 & 0 & -b_1 & \frac{b_0 b_2}{2} - c_2 \\ -b_2 & b_1 & 0 & \frac{b_0 b_3}{2} - c_3 \end{array}\right).$$

This shows that the system is consistent iff $\alpha b_0 - 2\beta = 0$, i.e.,

$$c_1 = \frac{-\alpha b_0 + 2b_2c_2 + 2b_3c_3}{2b_1}. \tag{19}$$

The set L_{s_0} of solutions of the above system is given by

$$L_{s_0} = \left\{ \left(\lambda, \frac{b_0b_3 - 2c_3}{2b_1} + \frac{b_2}{b_1}\lambda, \frac{2c_2 - b_0b_2}{2b_1} + \frac{b_3}{b_1}\lambda \right) : \lambda \in \mathbb{R} \right\}. \tag{20}$$

The intersection of the corresponding line $\mathcal{L}_{s_0}$ with the hyperboloid $\mathcal{H}_{s_0}$ in (10) is the set of points such that

$$\begin{aligned} &\alpha b_0^2 + 4b_1(b_1c_0 - b_2c_3 + b_3c_2) - 4b_0(b_3c_3 + b_2c_2) + \\ &\qquad 4c_2^2 + 4c_3^2 + (8b_3c_2 - 8b_2c_3 + 4b_1\alpha)\lambda + 4\alpha\lambda^2 = 0. \end{aligned} \tag{21}$$

Since $\underline{b} \in \mathbb{T}$, it follows that $\alpha = -\det \underline{b} \neq 0$, i.e., this last equation has at most two real solutions which lead to isolated zeros of (5) with real part s_0. □

Theorem 3. *If $\underline{b} \neq 0$ is a light-like coquaternion, then the quadratic equation has non-isolated zeros iff*

$$c = mb - m^2, \quad \textit{for some } m \in \mathbb{R}. \tag{22}$$

In such conditions, the equation has **one linear zero**, *given by*

$$\mathcal{L}_{s_0} = \left\{ s_0 + \frac{s_0 + m}{b_1}(b_2\mathbf{k} - b_3\mathbf{j}) + \lambda\underline{b} : \lambda \in \mathbb{R} \right\}. \tag{23}$$

In addition to the assumption (22), *if $m \neq -s_0$, there are also* **two distinct isolated zeros**, *given by*

$$z_1 = -m \qquad \textit{and} \qquad z_2 = m - b. \tag{24}$$

Proof. If $\det \underline{b} = 0$ and $\underline{b} \neq 0$, relations (19)-(21) remain true; in particular, (21) reads as

$$b_1(b_0c_1 - b_1c_0 + b_2c_3 - b_3c_2) - c_2^2 - c_3^2 - -2(b_3c_2 - b_2c_3)\lambda = 0,$$

which means that $\mathcal{L}_{s_0} \subset \mathcal{H}_{s_0}$, iff

$$b_1(b_0c_1 - b_1c_0 + b_2c_3 - b_3c_2) - c_2^2 - c_3^2 = b_3c_2 - b_2c_3 = 0. \tag{25}$$

Combining (19) and (25) we obtain, after some manipulation,

$$c_0 = \frac{c_1(b_0b_1 - c_1)}{b_1^2}, \quad c_2 = \frac{b_2c_1}{b_1}, \quad c_3 = \frac{b_3c_1}{b_1}$$

and the first part of the result is proved. Using these relations together with (20), we obtain

$$\mathcal{L}_{s_0} = \left\{ -\frac{b_0}{2} + \lambda\mathbf{i} + \frac{b_0b_1b_3 - 2b_3c_1 + 2b_1b_2\lambda}{2b_1^2}\mathbf{j} + \frac{-b_0b_1b_2 + 2b_2c_1 + 2b_1b_3\lambda}{2b_1^2}\mathbf{k} : \lambda \in \mathbb{R} \right\}$$

and result (23) follows.

Concerning isolated zeros, if $t \neq s_0$ and $s_0 \neq m$, the polynomial (14) reduces, under the assumptions (22), to

$$-\frac{(b_0+2t)^4}{b_1^2}(c_1+b_1t)(-c_1+b_1(b_0+t))$$

whose real solutions are $t = -\frac{c_1}{b_1}$ and $t = \frac{-b_0b_1+c_1}{b_1}$, and the isolated zeros (24) follow from relation (16). Finally, in the general case, where the assumptions (22) are not valid and $t \neq s_0$, we end up with at most six isolated zeros of the quadratic equation (5), which can be obtained from (14) and (16). □

Theorem 4. *If $\underline{b}$ is a space-like coquaternion, then the quadratic equation has non-isolated zeros iff*

$$c = mb - m^2, \qquad \text{for some } m \in \mathbb{R}. \tag{26}$$

In such conditions, the quadratic equation has **two linear zeros** *$\mathcal{L}_1$ and $\mathcal{L}_2$ whose expressions are as follows:*

1. *If $b_1^2 \neq b_2^2$*

$$\mathcal{L}_k = \Big\{ s_k - \tfrac{s_k+m}{b_1^2-b_2^2}\big((b_2b_3-b_1N_k)\mathbf{i} + (b_1b_3-b_2N_k)\mathbf{j}\big) + \\ \lambda\big((b_1b_3-b_2N_k)\mathbf{i} + (b_2b_3-b_1N_k)\mathbf{j} + (b_1^2-b_2^2)\mathbf{k}\big) : \lambda \in \mathbb{R}\Big\};\ k=1,2.$$

2. *If $b_1 = (-1)^s b_2 \neq 0$ $(s=1,2)$*

$$\mathcal{L}_1 = \Big\{ \tfrac{-b_0+(-1)^s b_3}{2} + \tfrac{b_0-(-1)^s b_3-2m}{4b_2b_3}\Big((b_2^2-b_3^2)\mathbf{i} + (-1)^s(b_2^2+b_3^2)\mathbf{j}\Big) + \\ \lambda\Big((b_2^2+b_3^2)\mathbf{i} + (-1)^s(b_2^2-b_3^2)\mathbf{j} + 2(-1)^s b_2b_3\mathbf{k}\Big) : \lambda \in \mathbb{R}\Big\},$$

$$\mathcal{L}_2 = \Big\{ \tfrac{-b_0-(-1)^s b_3}{2} - (-1)^s\tfrac{b_0+(-1)^s b_3-2m}{2}\mathbf{k} + \lambda\big((-1)^s\mathbf{i}+\mathbf{j}\big) : \lambda \in \mathbb{R}\Big\}.$$

3. *If $b_1 = b_2 = 0$*

$$\mathcal{L}_k = \Big\{ s_k - \tfrac{s_k+m}{N_k}\underline{b} + \lambda(-b_3\mathbf{i} + N_k\mathbf{j}) : \lambda \in \mathbb{R}\Big\};\ k=1,2.$$

In addition to the assumption (26), if $m \neq -s_k$, there are also **two distinct isolated zeros**, *given by*

$$z_1 = -m \qquad \text{and} \qquad z_2 = m - b. \tag{27}$$

Proof. We first prove that when $\underline{b} \in \mathbb{S}$, there are no linear zeros with real part s_0. In fact, for $t = s_0$ and $b_3 \neq 0$, the linear system (8) can be written in the equivalent form

$$\left(\begin{array}{ccc|c} 0 & b_3 & -b_2 & \frac{b_0b_1}{2} - c_1 \\ b_3 & 0 & -b_1 & \frac{b_0b_2}{2} - c_2 \\ 0 & 0 & 0 & -\frac{\alpha b_0 - 2\beta}{2b_3} \end{array}\right).$$

This shows that the system is solvable iff $c_3 = \frac{\alpha b_0 + 2b_1c_1 - 2b_2c_2}{2b_3}$. The set L_{s_0} of solutions of the above system is given by (cf. (20))

$$L_{s_0} = \Big\{\Big(\frac{b_0b_2 - 2c_2}{2b_3} + \frac{b_1}{b_3}\lambda, \frac{-2c_1 + b_0b_1}{2b_3} + \frac{b_2}{b_3}\lambda, \lambda\Big) : \lambda \in \mathbb{R}\Big\}.$$

The intersection of the corresponding line $\mathcal{L}_{s_0}$ with the hyperboloid $\mathcal{H}_{s_0}$ in (10) is the set of points such that

$$\begin{aligned} &-\alpha b_0^2 + 4b_3(b_3c_0 - b_2c_1 + b_1c_2) - 4b_0(b_1c_1 + b_2c_2) + \\ &\qquad 4c_1^2 - 4c_2^2 + 4(2b_3c_2 - 2b_2c_3 + b_1\alpha)\lambda + 4\alpha\lambda^2 = 0. \end{aligned}$$

Since $\underline{b} \in \mathbb{S}$, it follows that $\alpha = -\det \underline{b} \neq 0$, i.e., this last equation has at most two real solutions which lead to isolated zeros of (5), with real part s_0. When $b_3 = 0$, the corresponding equation reads as

$$-\alpha b_0^2 + 4b_2(b_2c_0 - b_1c_3) - 4b_0b_1c_1 + 4c_1^2 - 4c_3^2 + (-8b_1c_3 + 4b_2\alpha)\lambda + 4\alpha\lambda^2 = 0$$

and the conclusion is the same.

The computation of the linear zeros with real part s_k requires the study of three distinct cases; observe that when $b_1^2 = b_2^2$ (Cases 2. and 3.), then $b_3 \neq 0$. We just give the proof of the first identity, for $k = 1$, using once more Mathematica capabilities for algebraic computation; the other identities can be proved in the same way (cf. notebook). For $t = s_1$ and under the assumption that $b_1^2 \neq b_2^2$, the linear system (8) can be written in the equivalent form

$$\left(\begin{array}{ccc|c} 2N_1 & 2b_3 & -2b_2 & b_0b_1 - b_1N_1 - 2c_1 \\ 0 & 2(b_1^2 - b_2^2) & -2b_2b_3 & b_3(b_0b_1 - 2c_1) + (2c_2 - b_1b_3 - b_0b_2)N_1 + \alpha b_2 \\ 0 & 0 & 0 & b_3(b_1c_1 - b_2c_2) + (b_2c_1 - b_1c_2)N_1 - c_3(b_1^2 - b_2^2) \end{array}\right),$$

which shows that the system is consistent iff

$$c_3 = \frac{b_3(b_1c_1 - b_2c_2) + (b_2c_1 - b_1c_2)N_1}{b_1^2 - b_2^2}. \tag{28}$$

The set L_{s_1} of solutions of the above system is given by

$$\begin{aligned} L_{s_1} = \Big\{\Big(&\frac{-b_3(c_2 + b_2s_1) + N_1(c_1 + b_1s_1)}{b_1^2 - b_2^2} + \frac{b_1b_3 - b_2N_1}{b_1^2 - b_2^2}\lambda, \\ &\frac{-b_3(c_1 + b_1s_1) + N_1(c_2 + b_2s_1)}{b_1^2 - b_2^2} + \frac{b_1b_3 - b_2N_1}{b_1^2 - b_2^2}\lambda, \lambda\Big) : \lambda \in \mathbb{R}\Big\} \end{aligned}$$

The intersection of the corresponding line $\mathcal{L}_{s_1}$ with the hyperboloid $\mathcal{H}_{s_1}$ in (10) is the set of points such that

$$(-b_1^2 + b_2^2)c_0 + (b_0b_1 + b_2b_3)c_1 - (b_0b_2 + b_1b_3)c_2 + c_2^2 - c_1^2 + 2(b_2c_1 - b_1c_2)\lambda = 0,$$

which means that $\mathcal{L}_{s_1} \subset \mathcal{H}_{s_1}$ iff

$$b_2c_1 - b_1c_2 = (-b_1^2 + b_2^2)c_0 + (b_0b_1 + b_2b_3)c_1 - (b_0b_2 + b_1b_3)c_2 + c_2^2 - c_1^2 = 0. \tag{29}$$

Combining (28) and (29) we obtain, after some manipulation,

$$c_0 = (b_0 - m)m, \quad c_1 = b_1 m, \quad c_2 = b_2 m, \quad c_3 = b_3 m$$

which leads to

$$\mathcal{L}_{s_1} = \left\{ s_1 + \frac{N_1(b_1 m + b_1 s_1 - b_2\lambda)}{b_1^2 - b_2^2}\mathbf{i} + \frac{N_1(b_2 m + b_2 s_1 - b_1\lambda)}{b_1^2 - b_2^2}\mathbf{j} + \lambda\mathbf{k} : \lambda \in \mathbb{R} \right\},$$

and the result in Case 1. (for $k = 1$) is proved.

Concerning now the coexistence of linear zeros and isolated zeros, we observe that, if $t \neq s_k$ and $s_k \neq m$, the polynomial (14) reduces, under the assumptions (26), to

$$-(b_0 - m + t)(m + t)(b_1^2 - b_2^2 - b_3^2 + (b_0 + 2t)^2)^2$$

whose real solutions are $t = -m$ and $t = -b_0 + m$, and the isolated zeros (27) follow from relation (16). Finally, in the general case, where the assumptions (26) are not valid and $t \neq s_k$; $k = 0, 1, 2$, we end up with at most six isolated zeros of the quadratic equation (5), which can be obtained from (14) and (16). □

As an immediate consequence of Theorems 1-4 we have the following results.

Corollary 1. *The zeros, if any, of the equation $x^2 = c$ (i.e., the square roots of c) are always either isolated or hyperboloidal.*

Corollary 2. *The equation $x^2 + bx + c = 0$ has linear zeros if and only if $\underline{b} \neq 0$ is a coquaternion in $\mathbb{L} \cup \mathbb{S}$ and $c = mb - m^2$, for some $m \in \mathbb{R}$. In particular, under these conditions, the equation $x^2 + bx = 0$ always has linear zeros.*

Corollary 3. *Concerning the number of non-isolated zeros, a quadratic equation of the form (5) can have at most:*

- *one hyperboloidal zero (and up to 2 isolated zeros);*
- *two linear zeros (and up to 2 isolated zeros).*

The results of Corollaries 1 and 3 align with the ones obtained in [9,23] and [13], respectively.

5 Examples

Recently we have developed a collection of Mathematica functions, `CoqPolynomial`, complementing the package `Coquaternions` whose current versions are described and available at http://w3.math.uminho.pt/Coquaternions for download. Details about the use of these tools together with several examples illustrating their performance can be found in [7].

With the help of `CoqPolynomial` we have developed a Mathematica m-file `QuadraticsAlgorithm.m` to implement the results of Theorems 1-4. In particular the function `ZerosQuadratic[b,c]` gives a list {`Izeros,Lzeros,Hzeros`} of the isolated, linear and hyperboloidal zeros of the polynomial $x^2 +$

$bx + c$, where b and c are coquaternions; these tools are available at https://w3.math.uminho.pt/QuadraticsTools.

We give now some examples illustrating the results of the previous section. For the first example we present all the details, including the use of the aforementioned Mathematica tools.

Example 1. Consider the polynomial

$$P(x) = x^2 + (3 + 5\mathbf{i} + 3\mathbf{j} + 4\mathbf{k})x + 2 + 10\mathbf{i} + 6\mathbf{j} + 8\mathbf{k}.$$

Since $\underline{b} = 5\mathbf{i} + 3\mathbf{j} + 4\mathbf{k} \in \mathbb{L}$ and $c = 2b - 4$, the polynomial P fulfills assumption (22) of Theorem 3 with $m = 2$. In this case, the matrix $\mathcal{M}(t)$ in (9) is

$$\mathcal{M}(t) := \begin{pmatrix} 2t+3 & 4 & -3 \\ 4 & 2t+3 & -5 \\ -3 & 5 & 2t+3 \end{pmatrix}$$

whose determinant is $(2t + 3)^3$. This means that $s_0 = -\frac{3}{2} = -\frac{b_0}{2}$ (cf. (11)-(12)) and the quadratic equation has one linear zero given by (23), i.e.,

$$\mathcal{L}_{-\frac{3}{2}} = \Big\{ -\tfrac{3}{2} + \tfrac{1}{10}(3\mathbf{k} - 4\mathbf{j}) + \lambda(5\mathbf{i} + 3\mathbf{j} + 4\mathbf{k}) : \lambda \in \mathbb{R} \Big\}.$$

In addition, since $m \neq s_0$, the equation also has the two distinct isolated zeros (24) -2 and $-1 - 5\mathbf{i} - 3\mathbf{j} - 4\mathbf{k}$.

All these calculations can be easily performed using the Mathematica add-on `CoqPolynomial` and the function `ZerosQuadratic` which implements the results of this paper.

```
In[1]:= <<QuadraticsAlgorithm`

In[2]:= b=Coquaternion[3,5,3,4]; c=Coquaternion[2,10,6,8]; Nature[Vec[b]]
          (* checks the nature of b *)

Out[2]= Lightlike

In[3]:= Solve[List@@(c-mb+m^2)=={0,0,0,0},m] (* checks the assumptions *)
Out[3]= {{m → 2}}
```

The zeros of P can be obtained as follows:

```
In[4]:= (zeros=ZerosQuadratic[b,c])// TraditionalForm
```

Out[4]= $\{\{-2, -1 - 5\mathbf{i} - 3\mathbf{j} - 4\mathbf{k}\}, \{-\frac{3}{2} + 5\mathbf{i}\lambda + \mathbf{j}\left(-\frac{2}{5} + 3\lambda\right) + \mathbf{k}\left(\frac{3}{10} + 4\lambda\right)\}, \{\}\}$

We can check the solution by constructing and evaluating the polynomial P at each computed zero.

```
In[5]:= P=Polynomial[1,b,c]; Eval[P,Flatten[zeros]]
Out[5]= {0,0,0}
```

Table 1. The number and nature (LZ-linear zeros; IZ-isolated zeros; HZ-hyperboloidal zeros) of the zeros of the polynomials of Example 2

Pol.	Coefficients	Type $\underline{b}$	Result	m	s_k	Number of zeros
P_1	$b = 2 + 4\mathbf{k}$ $c = 1 + 4\mathbf{k}$	$\underline{b} \in \mathbb{S}$	Th. 4 (3)	1	$s_1 = -3$ $s_2 = 1$	2 LZ 2 IZ
P_2	$b = 3 + 5\mathbf{i} + 3\mathbf{j} + 5\mathbf{k}$ $c = 0$	$\underline{b} \in \mathbb{S}$	Th. 4 (1)	0	$s_1 = -3$ $s_2 = 0$	2 LZ
P_3	$b = 4 + 2\mathbf{i} - 2\mathbf{j}$ $c = 4 + 4\mathbf{i} - 4\mathbf{j}$	$\underline{b} \in \mathbb{L}$	Th. 3	2	$s_0 = -2$	1 LZ
P_4	$b = 4$ $c = 3$	$\underline{b} \in \mathbb{L}$	Th. 1	-	$s_0 = -2$	1 HZ 2 IZ

Example 2. We consider now other four polynomials $P_i; i = 1, \ldots, 4$, with non-isolated zeros. The polynomials and some details about the structure of their zeros are listed in Table 1.

The result of using function `ZerosQuadratic` for each polynomial P_i, gives the following zeros:

$$\mathtt{P}_1 : \{\{-1, -1-4\mathbf{k}\}, \{-3-4\lambda\mathbf{i}-4\lambda\mathbf{j}-2\mathbf{k}, 1-4\lambda\mathbf{i}+4\lambda\mathbf{j}-2\mathbf{k}\}, \{\,\}\}$$

$$\mathtt{P}_2 : \{\{\,\}, -3+\left(\tfrac{45}{8}+34\lambda\right)\mathbf{i}+\left(\tfrac{51}{8}+30\lambda\right)\mathbf{j}+16\lambda\mathbf{k}, 16\lambda\mathbf{i}+16\lambda\mathbf{k}\}, \{\,\}\}$$

$$\mathtt{P}_3 : \{\{\,\}, \{-2+2\lambda\mathbf{i}-2\lambda\mathbf{j}\}, \{\,\}\}$$

$$\mathtt{P}_4 : \{\{-1, -3\}, \{\,\}, \{-2+\mathbf{j}\}\}$$

We remark that in the case of a hyperboloidal zero, the output is one representative of the equivalence class (4).

Example 3. Finally we consider four polynomials $Q_i; i = 1, \ldots, 4$, which have only isolated zeros. The polynomials and their zeros are listed in Table 2. We point out that in this situation, since the number of zeros of Q_i is at most 6, the nonlinear system corresponding to the quadratic equation (5), i.e.,

$$\begin{cases} c_0 + b_0x_0 + x_0^2 - b_1x_1 - x_1^2 + b_2x_2 + x_2^2 + b_3x_3 + x_3^2 = 0 \\ c_1 + b_1x_0 + b_0x_1 + 2x_0x_1 + b_3x_2 - b_2x_3 = 0 \\ c_2 + b_2x_0 + b_3x_1 + b_0x_2 + 2x_0x_2 - b_1x_3 = 0 \\ c_3 + b_3x_0 - b_2x_1 + b_1x_2 + b_0x_3 + 2x_0x_3 = 0 \end{cases} \tag{30}$$

can be easily solved (numerically, if necessary) by using the Mathematica function `Solve`.

Table 2. The zeros of the polynomials of Example 3

Pol.	Coefficients	Type of $\underline{b}$	Zeros
Q_1	$b = 2 - \mathbf{i} - \mathbf{j}$ $c = 3 - \mathbf{i} - \mathbf{j} - \mathbf{k}$	$\underline{b} \in \mathbb{L}$	$z_1 = -1 + 2\mathbf{i} + \mathbf{j}$
Q_2	$b = -1 + 2\mathbf{i} - \mathbf{j}$ $c = \mathbf{j} - 2\mathbf{k}$	$\underline{b} \in \mathbb{T}$	$z_1 = \mathbf{j}$ $z_2 = 1 - 3\mathbf{i} + 2\mathbf{j} + \mathbf{k}$
Q_3	$b = 2 - \mathbf{i} + 2\mathbf{j}$ $c = -1 + 2\mathbf{i} - \mathbf{j} - 2\mathbf{k}$	$\underline{b} \in \mathbb{S}$	$z_1 = \frac{1}{2}(-5 + 5\mathbf{i} - 5\mathbf{j} - 3\mathbf{k})$ $z_2 = -2 + 9\mathbf{i} - 6\mathbf{j} - 7\mathbf{k}$ $z_3 = \frac{1}{2}(-3 - 3\mathbf{i} - 3\mathbf{j} + 5\mathbf{k})$ $z_4 = \frac{1}{2}(-1 - 3\mathbf{i} + 3\mathbf{j} + \mathbf{k})$ $z_5 = \mathbf{k}$ $z_6 = \frac{1}{6}(3 - \mathbf{i} - \mathbf{j} + 3\mathbf{k})$
Q_4	$b = -2 - 2\mathbf{i} - 2\mathbf{j}$ $c = 3 + 2\mathbf{i} + 2\mathbf{j}$	$\underline{b} \in \mathbb{L}$	no zeros

6 Final Remarks

Solving the quadratic equation (5) in the variable x is equivalent to solving the system (30) of four nonlinear equations in the variables x_0, x_1, x_2, x_3. When the number of solutions is finite (i.e., ≤ 6), one can use a computer algebra system to obtain the isolated zeros (eventually with finite precision), but this turns out to be a very demanding approach when there are infinite solutions.

Nothing prevents the approach followed in this paper from being used also to determine isolated zeros. In this situation, the solution to the problem may involve solving 6th or 4th degree (real) equations, whose computational effort would be analogous to that of solving the system (30).

The results of Sect. 4 provide a very simple and elegant way to construct monic quadratic polynomials in $\mathbb{H}_{\text{coq}}$ with prescribed zeros, which can be a valuable help when performing numerical experiments such as those usually carried out in the study of the dynamics of the quadratic map.

Ackowledgment. Research at CMAT was partially financed by Portuguese funds through FCT - Fundação para a Ciência e a Tecnologia, within the Projects UIDB/00013/2020 and UIDP/00013/2020.

References

1. Ata, E., Yayli, Y.: Split quaternions and semi-euclidean projective spaces. Chaos, Solitons Fractals **41**(4), 1910–1915 (2009)
2. Bekar, M., Yaylı, Y.: Involutions of complexified quaternions and split quaternions. Adv. Appl. Clifford Algebras **23**(2), 283–299 (2013)
3. Brody, D.C., Graefe, E.M.: On complexified mechanics and coquaternions. J. Phys. Math. Theor. **44**(7), 072001 (2011)

4. Cao, W.: Quadratic equation in split quaternions. Axioms **11**(5), p.188 (2022)
5. Cockle, J.: On systems of algebra involving more than one imaginary; and on equations of the fifth degree. Phil. Mag. **35**(3), 434–435 (1849)
6. Dennis, J.E., Traub, J.F., Weber, R.P.: The algebraic theory of matrix polynomials. SIAM J. Numer. Anal. **13**(6), 831–845 (1976)
7. Falcão, Maria Irene, Miranda, Fernando, Severino, Ricardo, Soares, Maria Joana: Mathematica tools for coquaternions. In: Gervasi, O., et al. (eds.) ICCSA 2021. LNCS, vol. 12952, pp. 449–464. Springer, Cham (2021). https://doi.org/10.1007/978-3-030-86973-1_32
8. Falcão, M.I., Miranda, F., Severino, R., Soares, M.J.: Basins of attraction for a quadratic coquaternionic map. Chaos, Solitons Fractals **104**, 716–724 (2017)
9. Falcão, M.I., Miranda, F., Severino, R., Soares, M.J.: On the roots of coquaternions. Advances in Applied Clifford Algebras **28**(5) (2018)
10. Falcão, M.I., Miranda, F., Severino, R., Soares, M.J.: The number of zeros of unilateral polynomials over coquaternions revisited. Linear Multilinear Algebra **67**(6), 1231–1249 (2019)
11. Falcão, M.I., Miranda, F., Severino, R., Soares, M.J.: Iteration of quadratic maps on coquaternions. Int. J. Bifurcat. Chaos **27**(12), 1730039 (2017)
12. Falcão, M.I., Miranda, F., Severino, R., Soares, M.J.: Dynamics of the coquaternionic maps x^2+bx. Rend. Circ. Mat. Palermo, II. Ser. **72**, 959–975 (2023). https://doi.org/10.1007/s12215-021-00715-6
13. Falcão, M.I., Miranda, F., Severino, R., Soares, M.J.: Remarks on the zeros of quadratic coquaternionic polynomials. In: Computational Science and Its Applications – ICCSA 2022, vol. 13377 LNCS, pp. 466–477. Springer International Publishing (2022)
14. Gao, C., Chen, X., Shen, Y.G.: Quintessence and phantom emerging from the split-complex field and the split-quaternion field. Gen. Relativ. Gravit. **48**(11), 1–23 (2016)
15. Gogberashvili, M.: Split quaternions and particles in (2+1)-space. Eur. Phys. J. **74**(12) (2014)
16. Higham, N.J., Kim, H.M.: Numerical analysis of a quadratic matrix equation. IMA J. Numer. Anal. **20**(4), 499–519 (2000)
17. Jia, Z., Cheng, X., Zhao, M.: A new method for roots of monic quaternionic quadratic polynomial. Comput. Math. Appl. **58**(9), 1852–1858 (2009)
18. Jiang, T., Zhang, Z., Jiang, Z.: Algebraic techniques for Schrödinger equations in split quaternionic mechanics. Comput. Math. Appl. **75**(7), 2217–2222 (2018)
19. Kula, L., Yayli, Y.: Split quaternions and rotations in semi Euclidean space E_2^4. J. Korean Math. Soc. **44**(6), 1313–1327 (2007)
20. Marrani, A., Romano, L.: Orbits in nonsupersymmetric magic theories. Int. J. Mod. Phys. A **34**(32), 1950190 (2019)
21. Ni, Q.Y., Ding, J.K., Cheng, X.H., Jiao, Y.N.: 2×2 matrix representation forms and inner relationships of split quaternions. Advances in Applied Clifford Algebras **29**(2) (2019)
22. Niven, I.: Equations in quaternions. Amer. Math. Monthly **48**, 654–661 (1941)
23. Özdemir, M.: The roots of a split quaternion. Appl. Math. Lett. **22**(2), 258–263 (2009)
24. Özdemir, M., Ergin, A.: Some geometric applications of split quaternions. In: Proceedings 16th International. Conference Jangjeon Mathematics Society. 16, pp. 108–115 (2005)
25. Özdemir, M., Ergin, A.: Rotations with unit timelike quaternions in Minkowski 3-space. J. Geom. Phys. **56**(2), 322–336 (2006)

26. Scharler, D.F., Siegele, J., Schröcker, H.P.: Quadratic split quaternion polynomials: Factorization and geometry. Adv. Appl. Clifford Algebras **30**(1) (2020)
27. Serôdio, R., Beites, P.D., Vitória, J.: Intersection of a double cone and a line in the split-quaternions context. Adv. Appl. Clifford Algebras **27**(3), 2795–2803 (2017)
28. Simsek, H., Özdemir, M.: Rotations on a lightcone in Minkowski 3-space. Adv. Appl. Clifford Algebras **27**(3), 2841–2853 (2017)
29. Slusky, M.: Zeros of 2 × 2 matrix polynomials. Comm. Algebra **38**(11), 4212–4223 (2010)

Calculation and Geometric Interpretation of the Curvatures of Implicit Curves and Surfaces with Mathematica

Rolando E. Ipanaqué-Silva[1], Jhonny W. Eche-Antón[2], Elmer P. Díaz Contreras[2], Ricardo Velezmoro-León[2], and Robert Ipanaqué-Chero[2(✉)]

[1] Universidad Tecnológica del Perú, Av. Vice Cdra 1-Costado Real Plaza, Piura, Peru
c25335@utp.edu.pe

[2] Universidad Nacional de Piura, Urb. Miraflores s/n Castilla, Piura, Peru
jechea@posgrado.unp.edu.pe, {ediazc,ripanaquec}@unp.edu.pe
https://www.unp.edu.pe/pers/ripanaque/

Abstract. In this paper, based on the formulas proposed by Ronald Goldman, new functions are defined and encoded in the Wolfram Language using the Mathematica symbolic calculation system. With the coded functions, the curvature of implicit plane curves, the curvature and twist of implicit space curves, and the Gaussian and mean curvatures of implicit surfaces can be calculated. All of these functions are included in a Mathematica package. Finally, the package's functionality is shown by solving several exciting examples. The application of this package allows users to explore and understand the geometry of the analyzed implicit curves and surfaces. This results in a helpful computer tool of great value for educational purposes and to improve the visualization of these concepts.

Keywords: Curvature · implicit curves · implicit surfaces · Wolfram Language

1 Introduction

Formulas to calculate the curvature of curves and surfaces given in parametric form are common in classic Differential Geometry texts [1,4]. However, the same does not happen with the formulas to calculate the curvature of curves and surfaces given implicitly. The procedure to find the curvature of implicitly given plane curves can be found in the text of Bolgov and co-authors [5]. In this text, an algorithm is described to compute the curvature of spatial curves given implicitly; however, a specific formula is not shown. In the case of implicitly given surfaces, O'Neill presents two formulas (one for the Gaussian curvature and another for the average curvature) [4]. Still, obtaining the tangent vector fields to the said surface is not detailed.

O. Gervasi et al. (Eds.): ICCSA 2024 Workshops, LNCS 14815, pp. 285–301, 2024.
https://doi.org/10.1007/978-3-031-65154-0_18

Eighteen years ago, Goldman published the paper [2] presenting curvature formulas for implicit curves and surfaces. He establishes a bridge in that article by deducing curvature formulas for implicit curves and surfaces from the already-known curvature formulas for parametric curves and surfaces.

Based on Goldman's work, it is proposed to develop functions in the Wolfram Language [3,7] to implicitly calculate the curvatures of curves and surfaces given and group them in a new package of functions, ImplicitCurvatures.

This package allows users to immerse themselves in the world of implicit curves and surfaces, allowing them to observe their geometric properties more clearly and effectively. Additionally, it facilitates the teaching of these topics by providing an interactive platform that can be used to illustrate complex mathematical concepts in a more accessible and didactic way.

2 Mathematical Preliminaries

The formulas presented in this section have been derived and proven by Goldman [2].

2.1 Notations

1. Let $A_{n\times n}$ be a matrix. Then

$$A^{*} = (\mathbf{adj}(A))^{t} \ .$$

2. Let $C : f(x, y) = 0$ be an implicit curve. Then

$$\nabla f = (f_x, f_y) \, .$$

$$\nabla (\nabla f) = \nabla^2 f = H(f) = \begin{pmatrix} f_{xx} & f_{xy} \\ f_{yx} & f_{yy} \end{pmatrix} .$$

3. Let $M : F(x, y, z) = 0$ be an implicit surface. Then

$$\nabla F = (F_x, F_y, F_z) \, .$$

$$\nabla (\nabla F) = \nabla^2 F = H(F) = \begin{pmatrix} F_{xx} & F_{xy} & F_{xz} \\ F_{yx} & F_{yy} & F_{yx} \\ F_{zx} & F_{zy} & F_{zz} \end{pmatrix} ,$$

$$\Delta F = \mathbf{Tr}\,(H(F)) \ .$$

2.2 Parameterized Plane Curves

Let $\beta(s)$ be a plane curve parameterized by arc length. Then, the curvature κ is defined by

$$\kappa = -\frac{dN}{ds} \cdot T \, ,$$

where T is the tangent, and N is the normal to the curve.

2.3 Parameterized Spatial Curves

Let $\beta(s)$ be a spatial curve parameterized by arc length. Then, the curvature κ and torsion τ are defined by

$$\kappa = \left\| \frac{dT}{ds} \times T \right\|,$$
$$\tau = \frac{\mathbf{det}\left(T \; \frac{dT}{ds} \; \frac{d^2T}{ds^2}\right)}{\kappa^2},$$

where T is the tangent to the curve.

2.4 Parameterized Surfaces

Let $\mathbf{x}(u, v)$ be the parameterization of a surface. Let $\mathbf{x}_u$ and $\mathbf{x}_v$ be the first-order partial derivatives of $\mathbf{x}$ concerning u and v. Then, the normal N to the surface, the gaussian curvature K_G and mean curvature K_H are defined by

$$N(u, v) = \frac{\mathbf{x}_u \times \mathbf{x}_v}{\|\mathbf{x}_u \times \mathbf{x}_v\|},$$
$$K_G = \frac{\mathbf{x}_u \times \mathbf{x}_v \cdot N_u \times N_v}{\|\mathbf{x}_u \times \mathbf{x}_v\|^2},$$
$$K_H = \frac{\mathbf{x}_u \times \mathbf{x}_v \cdot (\mathbf{x}_v \times N_u - \mathbf{x}_u \times N_v)}{2\|\mathbf{x}_u \times \mathbf{x}_v\|},$$

2.5 Implicit Plane Curves

Let $C : f(x, y) = 0$ be an implicit plane curve. Then, the curvature κ is defined by

$$\kappa = -\frac{\nabla f \cdot (\nabla^2 f \cdot \nabla f^t)}{\|\nabla f\|^3}.$$

2.6 Implicit Spatial Curves

Let $C : \begin{cases} f(x, y, z) = 0, \\ g(x, y, z) = 0. \end{cases}$ be an implicit spatial curve. Then, the curvature κ and the torsion τ are defined by

$$\kappa = \frac{\|(\nabla f \times \nabla g \cdot \nabla(\nabla f \times \nabla g)) \times (\nabla f \times \nabla g)\|}{\|\nabla f \times \nabla g\|^3},$$
$$\tau = \frac{\mathbf{det}\left(T^I \; T^{II} \; T^{III}\right)}{\|T^I \times T^{II}\|^2},$$

where

$$\begin{aligned}
T^{I} &= \nabla f \times \nabla g\,, \\
T^{II} &= T^{I} \cdot \nabla T^{I} = \nabla f \times \nabla g \cdot \nabla(\nabla f \times \nabla g)\,, \\
T^{III} &= \left(T^{I} \cdot \nabla(\nabla T^{I})\right) \cdot T^{I} + \left(T^{I} \cdot \nabla T^{I}\right) \cdot \nabla T^{I} \\
&= (\nabla f \times \nabla g \cdot \nabla(\nabla(\nabla f \times \nabla g))) \cdot \nabla f \times \nabla g + \\
&+ (\nabla f \times \nabla g \cdot \nabla(\nabla f \times \nabla g)) \cdot \nabla(\nabla f \times \nabla g)\,.
\end{aligned}$$

2.7 Implicit Surfaces

Let $M : F(x, y, z) = 0$ be an implicit surface. Then, the gaussian curvature K_G and mean curvature K_H are defined by

$$\begin{aligned}
K_G &= \frac{\nabla F \cdot \left(\nabla^2 F^* \cdot \nabla F^t\right)}{\|\nabla F\|^4}\,, \\
K_H &= -\frac{\nabla F \cdot \left(\nabla^2 F \cdot \nabla F^t\right) - \Delta F\,(\nabla F \cdot \nabla F)}{2\|\nabla F\|^3}\,.
\end{aligned}$$

3 Geometric Interpretation of the Curvatures of Implicit Curves and Surfaces

3.1 Graph of a Function

Given the function $\Phi : \mathcal{D} \subset \mathrm{I\!R}^n \to \mathrm{I\!R}$, the graph of Φ is the set

$$\mathcal{G}(\Phi) = \{(\mathbf{p}, \Phi(\mathbf{p})) \,|\, \mathbf{p} \in \mathcal{D}\}\,.$$

This means that the graph of ϕ is in $\mathrm{I\!R}^{n+1}$.

3.2 Implicit Plane Curves

Let $C : f(x, y) = 0$ be an implicit plane curve. Then $\kappa : C \subset \mathrm{I\!R}^2 \to \mathrm{I\!R}$ (see Fig. 1) and

$$\mathcal{G}(\kappa) = \{(\mathbf{p}, \kappa(\mathbf{p})) \,|\, \mathbf{p} \in C\}\,.$$

3.3 Implicit Spatial Curves

Let $C : \begin{cases} f(x, y, z) = 0, \\ g(x, y, z) = 0. \end{cases}$ be an implicit spatial curve. Then $\kappa : C \subset \mathrm{I\!R}^3 \to \mathrm{I\!R}$ (see Fig. 2) and

$$\mathcal{G}(\kappa) = \{(\mathbf{p}, \kappa(\mathbf{p})) \,|\, \mathbf{p} \in C\}\,.$$

Similarly, $\tau : C \subset \mathrm{I\!R}^3 \to \mathrm{I\!R}$ (see Fig. 2) and

$$\mathcal{G}(\tau) = \{(\mathbf{p}, \tau(\mathbf{p})) \,|\, \mathbf{p} \in C\}\,.$$

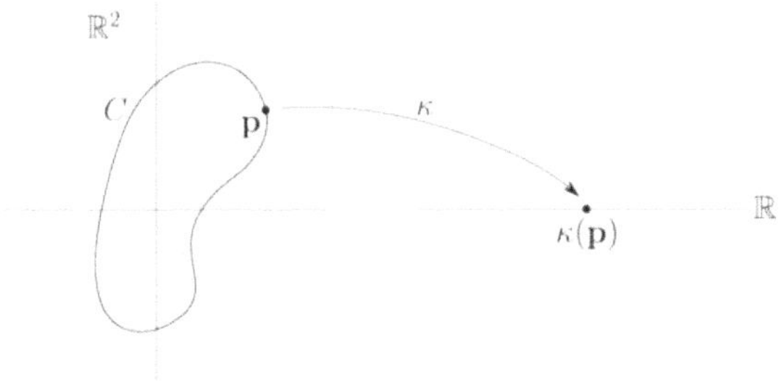

Fig. 1. Geometric interpretation of the curvature of an implicit plane curve.

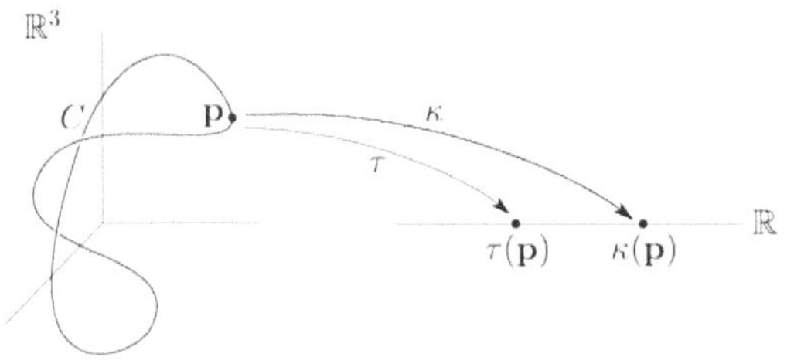

Fig. 2. Geometric interpretation of the curvature and torsion of an implicit space curve.

3.4 Implicit Surfaces

Let $M : F(x, y, z) = 0$ be an implicit surface. Then $K_G : M \subset \mathrm{I\!R}^3 \to \mathrm{I\!R}$ (see Fig. 3) and

$$\mathcal{G}(K_G) = \{(\mathbf{p}, K_G(\mathbf{p})) \,|\, \mathbf{p} \in M\} \,.$$

Similarly, $K_H : C \subset \mathrm{I\!R}^3 \to \mathrm{I\!R}$ (see Fig. 3) and

$$\mathcal{G}(K_H) = \{(\mathbf{p}, K_H(\mathbf{p})) \,|\, \mathbf{p} \in M\} \,.$$

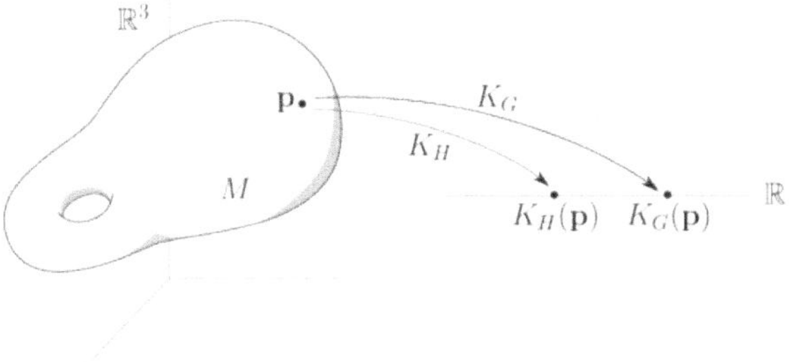

Fig. 3. Geometric interpretation of the Gaussian and mean curvatures of an implicit surface.

4 Implemented Code

According to [6], we will choose to use the three-dimensional model: $\{\mathcal{O}, \hat{\mathcal{B}}, \varphi\}$; where, $\mathcal{O} = (0,0,0)$, $\hat{\mathcal{B}} = \left\{\frac{3}{5\sqrt{3}}(-1,-1,-1),(1,0,0),(0,1,0),(0,0,1)\right\}$, and $\varphi(p_1,p_2,p_3,p_4) = \left(p_2 - \frac{3p_1}{5\sqrt{3}}, p_3 - \frac{3p_1}{5\sqrt{3}}, p_4 - \frac{3p_1}{5\sqrt{3}}\right)$. Based on this model, the following code will be used to visualize projections of curves and surfaces immersed in $\mathbb{R}^4$.

```
M={{-(3/(5*Sqrt[3])),-(3/(5*Sqrt[3])),-(3/(5*Sqrt[3]))},
 {1,0,0},{0,1,0},{0,0,1}};
P[{p1_,p2_,p3_,p4_}]:={p1,p2,p3,p4}.M
```

The following code has been created to show the coordinate axes that extend in the directions of the elements of $\hat{\mathcal{B}}$.

```
Vaxes[al_,M_,ah_:X]:=Graphics3D[{Gray,
 MapThread[Line[{{0,0,0},#1*#2}]&,{al,M}],
 MapThread[Text[Style[#1,Bold],#2]&,
 ({Array[Subscript[ah,#]&,Length[M]],al*M})]}]
```

The code for the five functions elaborated to calculate the curvatures is provided in the following subsections.

4.1 Implicit Plane Curves

```
Curvature[fxy_==0,{x_,y_}]:=
Module[{F=fxy,nablaF,HH,HHstar,nablaFt},
 nablaF=D[F,{{x,y}}];
 HH=D[F,{{x,y},2}];
 HHstar=Transpose[Adjugate[HH]];
 nablaFt=Transpose[nablaF];
 -nablaF.HHstar.nablaFt/Sqrt[nablaF.nablaF]^3//
 Simplify//Expand//Together
]
```

4.2 Implicit Spatial Curves

```
Curvature[{fxyz_==0,gxyz_==0},{x_,y_,z_}]:=
Module[{F=fxyz,G=gxyz,nablaF,nablaG,nablanablaFG,
  aux,norm},
 nablaF=D[F,{{x,y,z}}];
 nablaG=D[G,{{x,y,z}}];
 nablanablaFG=Transpose[D[Cross[nablaF,nablaG],{{x,y,z}}]];
 aux=Cross[Cross[nablaF,nablaG].nablanablaFG,Cross[nablaF,nablaG]];
 norm[v_]:=Sqrt[v.v];
 norm[aux]/norm[Cross[nablaF,nablaG]]^3//
 Simplify//Expand//Together//PowerExpand
]
```

```
Torsion[{fxyz_==0,gxyz_==0},{x_,y_,z_}]:=
Module[{F=fxyz,G=fxyz,nablaF,nablaG,T1,T2,T3,norm},
 nablaF=D[F,{{x,y,z}}];
 nablaG=D[G,{{x,y,z}}];
 T1=Cross[nablaF,nablaG];
 T2=T1.Transpose[D[T1,{{x,y,z}}]];
 T3=T1.Transpose[D[Transpose[D[T1,{{x,y,z}}]],{{x,y,z}}]].Transpose[T1]+
 T1.Transpose[D[T1,{{x,y,z}}]].Transpose[D[T1,{{x,y,z}}]];
 norm[v_]:=Sqrt[v.v];
 Det[Transpose[{T1,T2,T3}]]/norm[Cross[T1,T2]]^2//
 Simplify//Expand//Together
]
```

4.3 Implicit Surfaces

```
GaussianCurvature[fxyz_==0,{x_,y_,z_}]:=
Module[{F=fxyz,nablaF,HH,HHstar},
 nablaF=D[F,{{x,y,z}}];
 HH=D[F,{{x,y,z},2}];
 HHstar=Transpose[Adjugate[HH]];
 nablaF.HHstar.nablaF/Sqrt[nablaF.nablaF]^4//
 Simplify//Expand//Together
]
```

```
MeanCurvature[fxyz_==0,{x_,y_,z_}]:=
Module[{F=fxyz,nablaF,HH},
 nablaF=D[F,{{x,y,z}}];
 HH=D[F,{{x,y,z},2}];
 (nablaF.HH.nablaFt-Sqrt[nablaF.nablaF]^2 Tr[HH])/
  (2Sqrt[nablaF.nablaF]^3)//Simplify//Expand//Together
]
```

5 The New Package: `ImplicitCurvatures`

The new `ImplicitCurvatures` package incorporates the functions

`Curvature`, `Torsion`, `GaussianCurvature` and `MeanCurvature`.

The syntax of these functions is shown in Table 1.

Before describing the examples created with the help of the new package, it is necessary to initialize it.

Mathematica

Initialization of the `ImplicitCurvatures` package.

```
In[1]:= <<ImplicitCurvatures.m
```

Below are various and varied examples in which the new package is used.

Table 1. The syntax for functions is built into the `ImplicitCurvatures` package

`Curvature`$[f(x,y) == 0, \{x,y\}]$ gives the curvature of the implicit plane curve $C : f(x,y) = 0$.
`Curvature`$[\{f(x,y,z) == 0, g(x,y,z) == 0\}, \{x,y,z\}]$ gives the curvature of the implicit spatial curve $C : \begin{cases} f(x,y,z) = 0, \\ g(x,y,z) = 0. \end{cases}$.
`Torsion`$[\{f(x,y,z) == 0, g(x,y,z) == 0\}, \{x,y,z\}]$ gives the torsion of the implicit spatial curve $C : \begin{cases} f(x,y,z) = 0, \\ g(x,y,z) = 0. \end{cases}$.
`GaussianCurvature`$[F(x,y,z) == 0, \{x,y,z\}]$ gives the gaussian curvature of the implicit surface $M : F(x,y,z) = 0$.
`MeanCurvature`$[F(x,y,z) == 0, \{x,y,z\}]$ gives the mean curvature of the implicit surface $M : F(x,y,z) = 0$.

5.1 Implicit Plane Curves

The circumference $x^2 + y^2 - 1 = 0$.

Mathematica

We are obtaining the graph of the circumference.

```
In[2]:= f[x_,y_]:=x^2+y^2-1
        r=ImplicitRegion[f[x,y]==0,{x,y}];
        Graphics[mp=MeshPrimitives[DiscretizeRegion[r],1]]
Out[2]= See Fig. 4 (left).
```

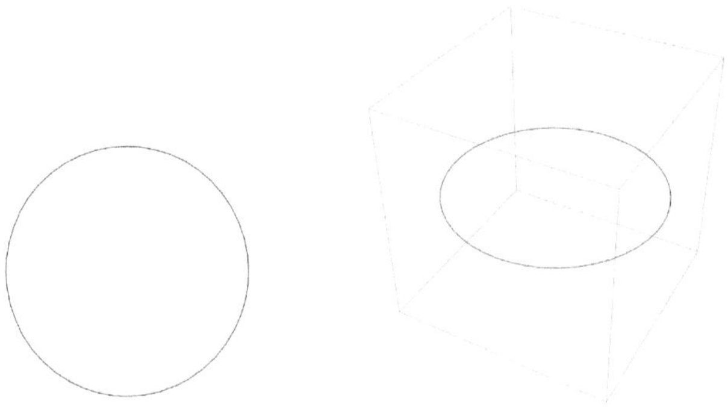

Fig. 4. The circumference and its curvature.

Mathematica

Function to obtain the value of the curvature of the circumference.

```
In[3]:= k=Curvature[f[x,y]==0,{x,y}]
```

Out[3]= $-\frac{1}{\sqrt{x^2+y^2}}$

Mathematica

We are obtaining the graph of the curvature of the circumference.

```
In[4]:= Graphics3D[mp/.Line[ps_]:>
          Line[{Sequence@@#,k/.MapThread[Rule,{{x,y},#}]}&/@ps]]
```

Out[4]= *See Fig. 4 (right).*

The fourth-degree Lamé curve $x^4 + y^4 - 1 = 0$.

Mathematica

We are obtaining the graph of the fourth-degree Lamé curve.

```
In[5]:= f[x_,y_]:=x^4+y^4-1
        r=ImplicitRegion[f[x,y]==0,{x,y}];
        Graphics[mp=MeshPrimitives[DiscretizeRegion[r],1]]
```

Out[5]= *See Fig. 5 (left).*

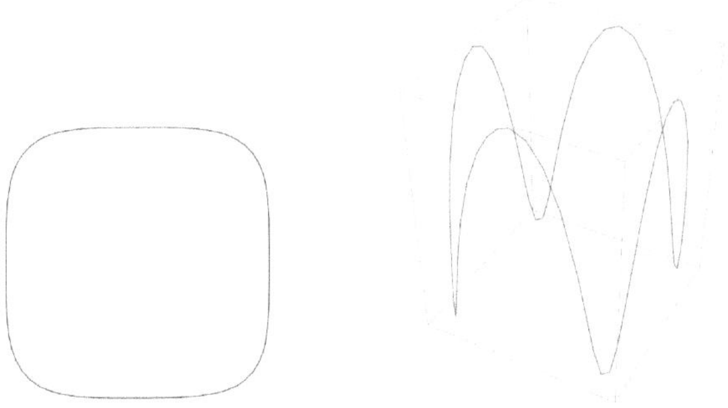

Fig. 5. Lamé's fourth-degree curve and its curvature.

Mathematica

Function to obtain the value of the curvature of the fourth-degree Lamé curve.

```
In[6]:= k=Curvature[f[x,y]==0,x,y]
```

Out[6]= $-\frac{3\left(x^6y^2+x^2y^6\right)}{\left(x^6+y^6\right)^{3/2}}$

Mathematica

We are obtaining the graph of the curvature of the fourth-degree Lamé curve.

```
In[7]:= Graphics3D[mp/.Line[ps_]:>
          Line[{Sequence@@#,k/.MapThread[Rule,{{x,y},#}]}&/@ps]]
Out[7]= See Fig. 5 (right).
```

The curve of lemniscatic trigonometry $x^2 + y^2 + x^2y^2 - 1 = 0$.

Mathematica

We are obtaining the graph of the lemniscatic trigonometry curve.

```
In[8]:= f[x_,y_]:=x^2+y^2+x^2y^2-1
        r=ImplicitRegion[f[x,y]==0,{x,y}];
        Graphics[mp=MeshPrimitives[DiscretizeRegion[r],1]]
Out[8]= See Fig. 6 (left).
```

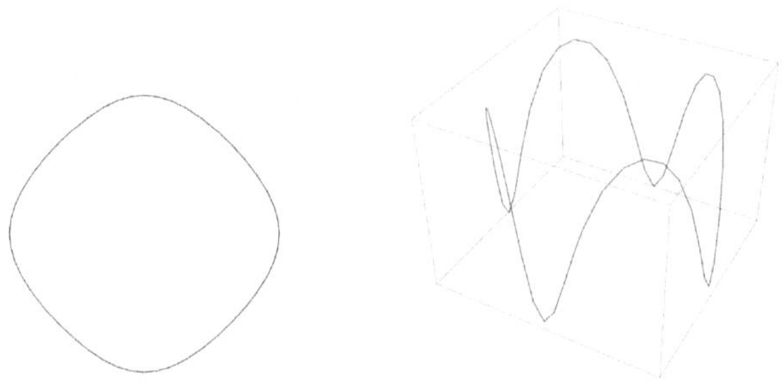

Fig. 6. The curve of lemniscatic trigonometry along with its curvature.

Mathematica

Function to obtain the value of the curvature of the lemniscatic trigonometry curve.

```
In[9]:= k=Curvature[f[x,y]==0,{x,y}]
```

Out[9]= $\frac{2x^4y^4+x^4y^2-x^4+x^2y^4-x^2-y^4-y^2}{(x^4y^2+x^2y^4+4x^2y^2+x^2+y^2)^{3/2}}$

Mathematica

We are obtaining the graph of the curvature of the lemniscatic trigonometry curve.

```
In[10]:= Graphics3D[mp/.Line[ps_]:>
           Line[{Sequence@@#,k/.MapThread[Rule,{{x,y},#}]}&/@ps]]
Out[10]= See Fig. 6 (right).
```

5.2 Implicit Spatial Curves

The curve of the circular and parabolic cylinders $\begin{cases} x^2+y^2-4=0, \\ z-x^2=0. \end{cases}$.

Mathematica

We are obtaining the graph of the curve of the circular and parabolic cylinders.

```
In[11]:= f[x_,y_,z_]:=x^2+y^2-4
         g[x_,y_,z_]:=z-x^2
         ContourPlot3D[{f[x,y,z]==0,g[x,y,z]==0},{x,-3,3},
           {y,-2,2},{z,0,4},Contours->0,ContourStyle->Opacity[0],
           Mesh->None,BoundaryStyle->{
            1->None,2->None,{1,2}->{
            AbsoluteThickness[1],Black}}]
```

Out[11]= *See Fig. 7 (left).*

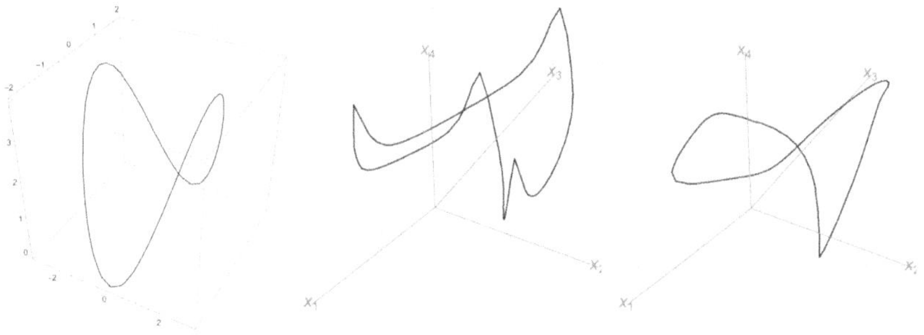

Fig. 7. The curve of circular and parabolic cylinders (left), their curvature (center), and torsion (right).

Mathematica

Function to obtain the value of the curvature of the curve of the circular and parabolic cylinders.

```
In[12]:= k=Curvature[{f[x,y,z]==0,g[x,y,z]==0},{x,y,z}]
```

Out[12]= $\frac{\sqrt{4x^6+x^4+2x^2y^2+4y^6+y^4}}{(4x^2y^2+x^2+y^2)^{3/2}}$

Mathematica

Function to obtain the value of the torsion of the curve of the circular and parabolic cylinders.

```
In[13]:= t=Torsion[{f[x,y,z]==0,g[x,y,z]==0},{x,y,z}]
```

Out[13]= $-\frac{2(4x^5y-x^3y+4xy^5-xy^3)}{4x^6+x^4+2x^2y^2+4y^6+y^4}$

Mathematica

We are obtaining the graph of the curvature of the parabolic cylinder curve.

```
In[14]:= al={6,4,6,4};
         Show[ContourPlot3D[{f[x,y,z]==0,g[x,y,z]==0},{x,-3,3},
           {y,-2,2},{z,0,4},Contours->{0},
           ContourStyle->Opacity[0],Mesh->None,
           BoundaryStyle->{1->None,2->None,
           {1,2}->{AbsoluteThickness[1],Black}},RegionFunction->
           Function[{x,y,z},x^2+y^2+4x^2y^2>0.1]]/.
           Graphics3D[{GraphicsComplex[p_,q_,r_],
           GraphicsComplex[p2_,q2_,r2_,t2_],{}},s_]:>
           Graphics3D[{GraphicsComplex[P[{Sequence@@#,k/.
           MapThread[Rule,{{x,y,z},#}]}]&/@p,q],{}},
           Boxed->False,PlotRange->All],Vaxes[al,M]]
```

Out[14]= *See Fig. 7 (center).*

Mathematica

We are obtaining the graph of the torsion of the parabolic cylinder curve.

```
In[15]:= al={6,4,6,4};
         Show[ContourPlot3D[{f[x,y,z]==0,g[x,y,z]==0},{x,-3,3},
           {y,-2,2},{z,0,4},Contours->{0},
           ContourStyle->Opacity[0],Mesh->None,
           BoundaryStyle->{1->None,2->None,
           {1,2}->{AbsoluteThickness[1],Black}},RegionFunction->
           Function[{x,y,z},x^4+4x^6+2x^2y^2+y^4+4y^6>0.1]]/.
           Graphics3D[{GraphicsComplex[p_,q_,r_],
           GraphicsComplex[p2_,q2_,r2_,t2_],{}},s_]:>
           Graphics3D[{GraphicsComplex[P[{Sequence@@#,t/.
           MapThread[Rule,{{x,y,z},#}]}]&/@p,q],{}},
           Boxed->False,PlotRange->All],Vaxes[al,M]]
```

Out[15]= *See Fig. 7 (right).*

5.3 Implicit Surfaces

The sphere $x^2 + y^2 + z^2 - 1 = 0$.

Mathematica

We are obtaining the graph of the sphere.

```
In[16]:= F[x_,y_,z_]:=x^2+y^2+z^2-1
         R=ImplicitRegion[F[x,y,z]==0,{x,y,z}];
         Graphics3D[MP=MeshPrimitives[DiscretizeRegion[R],2]]
```

Out[16]= *See Fig. 8 (left).*

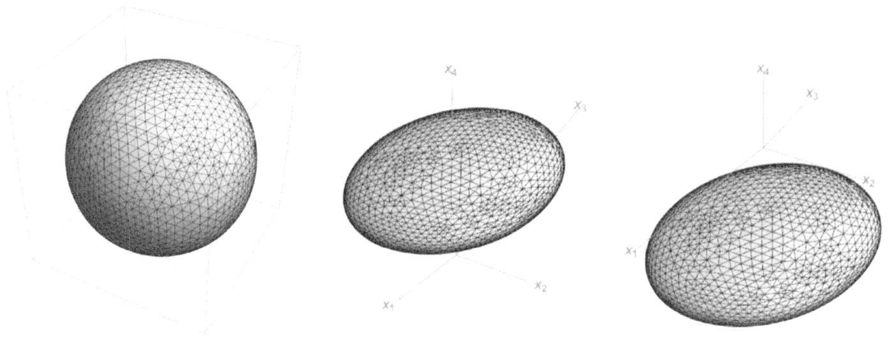

Fig. 8. The sphere and its Gaussian and mean curvatures.

Mathematica

Function to obtain the value of the gaussian curvature of the sphere.

```
In[17]:= KG=GaussianCurvature[F[x,y,z]==0,{x,y,z}]
```

Out[17]= $\frac{1}{x^2+y^2+z^2}$

Mathematica

Function to obtain the value of the mean curvature of the sphere.

```
In[18]:= KH=MeanCurvature[F[x,y,z]==0,{x,y,z}]
```

Out[18]= $-\frac{1}{\sqrt{x^2+y^2+z^2}}$

Mathematica

We are obtaining the graph of the gaussian curvature of the sphere.

```
In[19]:= al={1.5,1,3,2.25};
         Show[Graphics3D[MP/.Polygon[ps_]:>
             Polygon[P[{Sequence@@#,KG/.
           MapThread[Rule,{{x,y,z},#}]}]&/@ps]],Vaxes[al,M],
           Boxed->False]
```

Out[19]= *See Fig. 8 (center).*

Mathematica

We are obtaining the graph of the mean curvature of the sphere.

```
In[20]:= al={2.5,1,1,0.75};
         Show[Graphics3D[MP/.Polygon[ps_]:>
             Polygon[P[{Sequence@@#,KH/.
           MapThread[Rule,{{x,y,z},#}]}]&/@ps]],Vaxes[al,M],
           Boxed->False]
```

Out[20]= *See Fig. 8 (right).*

The fourth-degree surface of Lamé $x^4 + y^4 + z^4 - 1 = 0$.

Mathematica

We are obtaining the graph of the fourth-degree Lamé surface.

```
In[21]:= F[x_,y_,z_]:=x^4+y^4+z^4-1
         R=ImplicitRegion[F[x,y,z]==0,x,y,z];
         Graphics3D[MP=MeshPrimitives[DiscretizeRegion[R],2]]
```

Out[21]= *See Fig. 9 (left).*

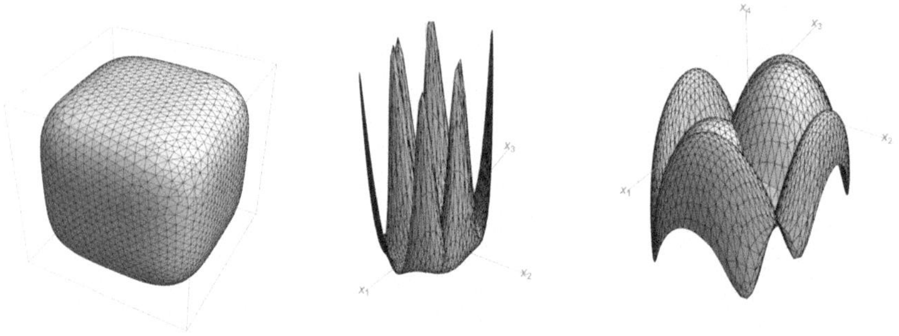

Fig. 9. The surface of Lamé and its Gaussian and mean curvatures.

Mathematica

Function to obtain the value of the gaussian curvature of the fourth-degree Lamé surface.

```
In[22]:= KG=GaussianCurvature[F[x,y,z]==0,{x,y,z}]
```

Out[22]= $\frac{9(x^6y^2z^2+x^2y^6z^2+x^2y^2z^6)}{(x^6+y^6+z^6)^2}$

Mathematica

Function to obtain the value of the mean curvature of the fourth-degree Lamé surface.

```
In[23]:= KH=MeanCurvature[F[x,y,z]==0,{x,y,z}]
```

Out[23]= $-\frac{3(x^6y^2+x^6z^2+x^2y^6+x^2z^6+y^6z^2+y^2z^6)}{2(x^6+y^6+z^6)^{3/2}}$

Mathematica

We are obtaining the graph of the gaussian curvature of the fourth-degree Lamé surface.

```
In[24]:= al={3.5,2.5,4,6.25};
         Show[Graphics3D[MP/.Polygon[ps_]:>Polygon[P[{Sequence@@#,KG/.
           MapThread[Rule,{{x,y,z},#}]}]&/@ps]],Vaxes[al,M],
           Boxed->False]
```

Out[24]= *See Fig. 9 (center).*

Mathematica

We are obtaining the graph of the mean curvature of the fourth-degree Lamé surface.

```
In[25]:= al={3.5,2,2,1.25};
        Show[Graphics3D[MP/.Polygon[ps_]:>Polygon[P[{Sequence@@#,KH/.
          MapThread[Rule,{{x,y,z},#}]}]&/@ps]],Vaxes[al,M],
          Boxed->False]
```

Out[25]= *See Fig. 9 (right).*

Descartes' surface $x^3 + y^3 + z^3 - 3xy - 3xz - 3yz = 0$.

Mathematica

We are obtaining the graph of the Descartes surface.

```
In[26]:= F[x_,y_,z_]:=x^3+y^3+z^3-3xy-3xz-3yz
        R=ImplicitRegion[F[x,y,z]==0,x,y,z];
        Graphics3D[MP=MeshPrimitives[DiscretizeRegion[R],2]]
```

Out[26]= *See Fig. 10 (left).*

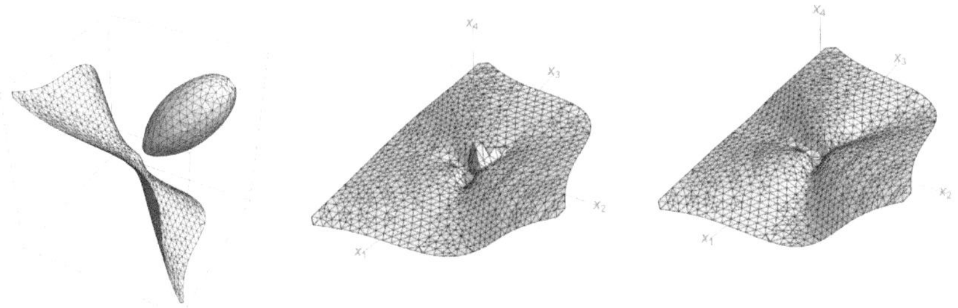

Fig. 10. The Descartes' surface and its Gaussian curvature.

Mathematica

Function to obtain the value of the gaussian curvature of the Descartes surface.

```
In[27]:= KG=GaussianCurvature[F[x,y,z]==0,{x,y,z}]
```

Out[27]= $(4x^4yz - x^4 - 12x^2y^2z + 2x^2y^2 - 12x^2yz^2 + 4x^2y + 2x^2z^2 + 4x^2z + 4xy^4z - 12xy^2z^2 + 4xy^2 + 4xyz^4 + 12xyz + 4xy + 4xz^2 + 4xz - y^4 + 2y^2z^2 + 4y^2z + 4yz^2 + 4yz - z^4)/(x^4 - 2x^2y - 2x^2z + 2x^2 - 2xy^2 + 2xy - 2xz^2 + 2xz + y^4 - 2y^2z + 2y^2 - 2yz^2 + 2yz + z^4 + 2z^2)^2$

Mathematica

Function to obtain the value of the mean curvature of the Descartes surface.

```
In[28]:= KH=MeanCurvature[F[x,y,z]==0,{x,y,z}]
```

Out[28]= $(x^4(-y) - x^4 z + 3x^2y^2 + 4x^2yz - 2x^2y + 3x^2z^2 - 2x^2z - x^2 - xy^4 + 4xy^2z - 2xy^2 + 4xyz^2 - 3xy - xz^4 - 2xz^2 - 3xz - y^4z + 3y^2z^2 - 2y^2z - y^2 - yz^4 - 2yz^2 - 3yz - z^2)/(x^4 - 2x^2(y+z-1) - 2x\left(y^2 - y + (z-1)z\right) + y^4 - 2y^2(z-1) - 2y(z-1)z + z^2\left(z^2+2\right))^{3/2}$

Mathematica

We are obtaining the graph of the gaussian curvature of the Descartes surface.

```
In[29]:= al={3.5,2.5,4,6.25};
         Show[Graphics3D[MP/.Polygon[ps_]:>Polygon[P[{Sequence@@#,KG/.
           MapThread[Rule,{{x,y,z},#}]}]&/@ps]],Vaxes[al,M],
           Boxed->False]
```

Out[29]= *See Fig. 10 (center).*

Mathematica

We are obtaining the graph of the mean curvature of the Descartes surface.

```
In[30]:= al={3.5,2,2,1.25};
         Show[Graphics3D[MP/.Polygon[ps_]:>Polygon[P[{Sequence@@#,KH/.
           MapThread[Rule,{{x,y,z},#}]}]&/@ps]],Vaxes[al,M],
           Boxed->False]
```

Out[30]= *See Fig. 10 (right).*

6 Conclusions

This paper has established a solid framework for defining and coding new features in the Wolfram Language. These functions allow the calculation of several vital geometric properties, such as the curvature of implicit plane curves, the curvature and twist of implicit space curves, and the mean and Gaussian curvatures of implicit surfaces. Including these functions in a Mathematica package gives users a powerful tool to explore and understand the geometry of the implicit curves and surfaces being analyzed. The resolution of several illustrative examples demonstrates this package's effectiveness and practical usefulness, both in the educational field and in improving the visualization of complex geometric concepts. Among the examples analyzed are the circumference, Lamé's fourth-degree curve, the curve of lemniscatic trigonometry, the curve of circular and parabolic cylinders, the sphere, Lamé's fourth-degree surface, and Descartes's surface.

References

1. Do Carmo, M.P.D.: Differential Geometry of Curves and Surfaces: Revised and Updated Second Edition. Courier Dover Publications (2016). google-Books-ID: uXF6DQAAQBAJ
2. Goldman, R.: Curvature formulas for implicit curves and surfaces. Comput. Aided Geom. Des. **22**(7), 632–658 (2005). https://doi.org/10.1016/j.cagd.2005.06.005. https://linkinghub.elsevier.com/retrieve/pii/S0167839605000737

3. Maeder, R.E.: Programming in Mathematica. Addison-Wesley Professional, Reading (1997)
4. O'Neill, B.: Elementary Differential Geometry, 2nd edn. Elsevier Academic Press, Amsterdam (2006). oCLC: ocm62493605
5. Bolgov, V., et al.: Problemas de las matemáticas superiores, vol. I. Mir (1983)
6. Velezmoro, R., Ipanaqué, R., Mechato, J.A.: A mathematica package for visualizing objects inmersed in $\mathbb{R}^4$. In: Misra, S., et al. (eds.) ICCSA 2019. LNCS, vol. 11624, pp. 479–493. Springer, Cham (2019). https://doi.org/10.1007/978-3-030-24311-1_35
7. Wolfram, S.: An Elementary Introduction to the Wolfram Language by Stephen Wolfram (2023). https://www.wolfram.com/language/elementary-introduction/3rd-ed/

On Appell-Vietoris Polynomials

Isabel Cação[2], M. Irene Falcão[1(✉)], Helmuth R. Malonek[2], Fernando Miranda[1], and Graça Tomaz[2,3]

[1] Centro de Matemática, Universidade do Minho, Braga, Portugal
{mif,fmiranda}@math.uminho.pt
[2] CIDMA, Universidade de Aveiro, Aveiro, Portugal
{isabel.cacao,hrmalon}@ua.pt, gtomaz@ipg.pt
[3] Polytechnic of Guarda, Guarda, Portugal

Abstract. In this paper we introduce a polynomial sequence $(\mathcal{V}_n(x))_{n\geq 0}$ involving the Vietoris' number sequence and satisfying the Appell property. We derive several equivalent representations of $\mathcal{V}_n(x)$ and we deduce important relations closely related to the aforementioned Appell property. Finally, we address the problem of the zeros distribution of $\mathcal{V}_n(x)$ and conclude that, when n is even, the polynomials $\mathcal{V}_n(x)$ have no real zeros, whereas for odd n, the unique real zero of $\mathcal{V}_n(x)$ lies within the interval $(-1, 0)$.

Keywords: Appell polynomials · Vietoris sequence · Combinatorial identities

1 Introduction

Some years ago, authors of this paper constructed sequences of multivariate generalized Appell polynomials [10,13] which involve the sequence of rational numbers

$$c_k := \frac{1}{2^k}\binom{k}{\lfloor \frac{k}{2} \rfloor}, \; k = 0, 1, \ldots, \tag{1}$$

where $\lfloor \cdot \rfloor$ is the floor function. In the context of positive trigonometric sums, in the celebrated paper [17], Vietoris considered a sequence that coincides with (1) from the second term onwards. For this reason, the sequence (1) came to be known as the *Vietoris sequence*.

In this work we focus on a sequence of real polynomials $(\mathcal{V}_n(x))_{n\geq 0}$ of the form

$$\mathcal{V}_n(x) = \sum_{k=0}^{n} \binom{n}{k} c_{n-k} x^k,$$

and study some of its properties. Since this sequence is constructed to fulfill the Appell property [3]

$$\mathcal{V}_n'(x) = n\mathcal{V}_{n-1}(x),$$

we designate it as the *Appell-Vietoris polynomial sequence*.

O. Gervasi et al. (Eds.): ICCSA 2024 Workshops, LNCS 14815, pp. 302–316, 2024.
https://doi.org/10.1007/978-3-031-65154-0_19

This paper is organized as follows: in Sect. 2 we recall some properties of the Vietoris sequence $(c_n)_{n\geq 0}$ and prove some new identities, needed for the sequel, including those related to its binomial inverse. In Sect. 3 we present important properties of Appell polynomials and derive the corresponding results for the Appell-Vietoris polynomials. Finally, the paper ends with some new results on the zeros of the polynomials under consideration.

2 Vietoris Sequence and Its Inverse

2.1 Combinatorial Identities Involving the Vietoris Sequence

One can find in the literature (see e.g. [11,12]) several well-known combinatorial identities involving the even-order terms c_{2k} of the Vietoris sequence (see also [6] and https://w3.math.uminho.pt/VietorisSequence). For example, identities (3.90), (3.91) and (3.85) of [11] can be rewritten, respectively, as

$$\sum_{s=0}^{k} c_{2\,s} c_{2k-2\,s} = 1,$$

$$\sum_{s=0}^{k} (-1)^s c_{2\,s} c_{2k-2\,s} = \begin{cases} 0, & \text{if } k \text{ odd} \\ c_k, & \text{if } k \text{ even} \end{cases},$$

and

$$\sum_{s=0}^{k} (-1)^s \binom{k}{s} c_{2k-2\,s} = (-1)^k c_{2k}.$$

For the purpose of this study, we now derive additional convolution identities involving all the terms of the Vietoris sequence. These identities emerge as we explore the sequence of coefficients associated with the introduced Appell-Vietoris polynomials. Within this framework, we examine an infinite array of numbers defined by:

$$\mathcal{T}_k^n = \binom{n}{k} c_{n-k}, \quad n = 0, 1, \ldots; \; k = 0, 1, \ldots, n. \tag{2}$$

These numbers form a triangular array with $n+1$ rows, ordered from $k=0$ to $k=n$. In Table 1, we present the first 10 rows of this triangular arrangement.

Theorem 1. *Let $\mathcal{T}_k^n$ denote the triangle* (2). *Then the following identities hold.*

Id$_1$ *Relations between adjacent elements:*

$$\mathcal{T}_k^n = \frac{n}{2\lfloor \frac{n-k+1}{2} \rfloor} \mathcal{T}_k^{n-1} = \frac{2\lfloor \frac{n-k+2}{2} \rfloor}{k} \mathcal{T}_{k-1}^n = \frac{n}{k} \mathcal{T}_{k-1}^{n-1}.$$

Table 1. The first 10 rows of $\mathcal{T}_k^n$

1									
$\frac{1}{2}$	1								
$\frac{1}{2}$	1	1							
$\frac{3}{8}$	$\frac{3}{2}$	$\frac{3}{2}$	1						
$\frac{3}{8}$	$\frac{3}{2}$	3	2	1					
$\frac{5}{16}$	$\frac{15}{8}$	$\frac{15}{4}$	5	$\frac{5}{2}$	1				
$\frac{5}{16}$	$\frac{15}{8}$	$\frac{45}{8}$	$\frac{15}{2}$	$\frac{15}{2}$	3	1			
$\frac{35}{128}$	$\frac{35}{16}$	$\frac{105}{16}$	$\frac{105}{8}$	$\frac{105}{8}$	$\frac{21}{2}$	$\frac{7}{2}$	1		
$\frac{35}{128}$	$\frac{35}{16}$	$\frac{35}{4}$	$\frac{35}{2}$	$\frac{105}{4}$	21	14	4	1	
$\frac{63}{256}$	$\frac{315}{128}$	$\frac{315}{32}$	$\frac{105}{4}$	$\frac{315}{8}$	$\frac{189}{4}$	$\frac{63}{2}$	18	$\frac{9}{2}$	1

Id$_2$ *Relation of elements in the k-column with the first column:*

$$c_k \mathcal{T}_k^n = \binom{\lfloor \frac{n+1}{2} \rfloor}{\lfloor \frac{k+1}{2} \rfloor} \binom{\lfloor \frac{n}{2} \rfloor}{\lfloor \frac{k}{2} \rfloor} \mathcal{T}_0^n .$$

Id$_3$ *Row sum:*

$$\sum_{k=0}^{n} \mathcal{T}_k^n = \sum_{k=0}^{n} \binom{n}{k} c_k = 2^{n+1} c_{2n+1}.$$

Id$_4$ *Alternating row sum:*

$$\sum_{k=0}^{n} (-1)^k \mathcal{T}_k^n = (-1)^n \sum_{k=0}^{n} (-1)^k \binom{n}{k} c_k = \frac{(-2)^n}{n+1} c_{2n}.$$

Proof. Identity **Id**$_1$ follows easily from the well-known properties of the binomial coefficients

$$\binom{n}{k} = \frac{n}{n-k} \binom{n-1}{k} = \frac{n+1-k}{k} \binom{n}{k-1} = \frac{n}{k} \binom{n-1}{k-1}.$$

Concerning Identity **Id**$_2$, we only consider here the case where n and k are both even; the proof in the other cases is similar. Simple calculations allow to write

$$\binom{2\,s}{s} \mathcal{T}_{2\,s}^{2m} = \binom{2\,s}{s} \binom{2m}{2\,s} c_{2m-2\,s} = \binom{2\,s}{s} \binom{2m}{2\,s} \binom{2m-2\,s}{m-s} 2^{2\,s-2m}$$

$$= \frac{\binom{2\,s}{s} \binom{2m}{2\,s} \binom{2m-2\,s}{m-s}}{\binom{2m}{m}} 2^{2\,s} c_{2m} = 4^s \binom{m}{s}^2 c_{2m} = 4^s \binom{m}{s}^2 \mathcal{T}_0^{2m}$$

and the result is proved.

To prove Identity $\mathbf{Id}_3$, we observe that the triangle $\widetilde{\mathcal{T}}_k^n = 2^n \mathcal{T}_{n-k}^n$ is the OEIS A051289 sequence [16], corresponding to the triangular array $\widetilde{\mathcal{T}}_k^n$ read by rows and whose row sum is

$$\sum_{k=0}^{n} \widetilde{\mathcal{T}}_k^n = \binom{2n+1}{n+1}.$$

Therefore

$$\sum_{k=0}^{n} \mathcal{T}_k^n = \sum_{k=0}^{n} \mathcal{T}_{n-k}^n = 2^{-n}\binom{2n+1}{n+1} = 2^{-n}\binom{2n+1}{n} = 2^{n+1}\frac{\binom{2n+1}{n}}{2^{2n+1}} = 2^{n+1}c_{2n+1}$$

and the second identity is proved. We now write

$$2^{n+1}c_{2n+1} = \sum_{k=0}^{n}\binom{n}{k}c_k = \sum_{k=0}^{\lfloor \frac{n}{2} \rfloor}\binom{n}{2k}c_{2k} + \sum_{k=0}^{\lfloor \frac{n-1}{2} \rfloor}\binom{n}{2k+1}c_{2k+1}.$$

Identity (3.99) of [11] can be rewritten as

$$\sum_{k=0}^{\lfloor \frac{n}{2} \rfloor}\binom{n}{2k}c_{2k} = 2^n c_{2n} \tag{3}$$

and this allows to conclude that

$$\sum_{k=0}^{\lfloor \frac{n-1}{2} \rfloor}\binom{n}{2k+1}c_{2k+1} = 2^{n+1}c_{2n+1} - 2^n c_{2n} = 2^n \frac{n}{n+1}c_{2n}, \tag{4}$$

since $c_{2n+1} = \frac{2n+1}{2n+2}c_{2n}$. Identity $\mathbf{Id}_4$ follows at once from (3)-(4). □

Remark 1. If $\mathcal{C}_n$ denotes the n-th Catalan number [7,12], then Identity $\mathbf{Id}_4$ can be written as

$$\sum_{k=0}^{n}(-1)^k \mathcal{T}_k^n = \sum_{k=0}^{n}(-1)^k\binom{n}{k}c_k = (-1)^n\frac{\mathcal{C}_n}{2^n}.$$

Theorem 2. *For each fixed n, the finite sequence $\mathcal{T}_0^n, \mathcal{T}_1^n, \ldots, \mathcal{T}_n^n$ is*

(i) *log-concave, i.e.,*

$$\left(\mathcal{T}_k^n\right)^2 \geq \mathcal{T}_{k-1}^n \mathcal{T}_{k+1}^n, \; k = 1, \ldots, n-1;$$

(ii) *unimodal, i.e.,*

$$\mathcal{T}_0^n \leq \mathcal{T}_1^n \leq \cdots \leq \mathcal{T}_{s-1}^n \leq \mathcal{T}_s^n \geq \mathcal{T}_{s+1}^n \geq \cdots \geq \mathcal{T}_n^n, \tag{5}$$

where $s = \lfloor \frac{n+2}{4} \rfloor + \lfloor \frac{n+3}{4} \rfloor$ by $s = \lfloor \frac{n+1}{2} \rfloor$.

Proof. Inequality **(*i*)** follows easily by using one of the identities in $\mathbf{Id}_1$, i.e.,

$$(\mathcal{T}_k^n)^2 - \mathcal{T}_{k-1}^n \mathcal{T}_{k+1}^n = \mathcal{T}_{k-1}^n \mathcal{T}_k^n \left(\frac{2}{k} \lfloor \frac{n-k+2}{2} \rfloor - \frac{2}{k+1} \lfloor \frac{n-k+1}{2} \rfloor \right) \geq 0.$$

It is well known that a log-concave sequence of positive numbers is unimodal [18], i.e., there exists s, $0 \leq s \leq n$, such that (5) holds. Therefore, it is enough to prove that for $s = \lfloor \frac{n+2}{4} \rfloor + \lfloor \frac{n+3}{4} \rfloor$ by $s = \lfloor \frac{n+1}{2} \rfloor$,

$$\mathcal{T}_{s-1}^n \leq \mathcal{T}_s^n \geq \mathcal{T}_{s+1}^n.$$

The repeated use of Identity $\mathbf{Id}_1$ allows to write

$$\begin{array}{lcl}
\mathcal{T}_{2m}^{4m} = \frac{m+1}{m} \mathcal{T}_{2m-1}^{4m} > \mathcal{T}_{2m-1}^{4m} & \text{and} & \mathcal{T}_{2m+1}^{4m} = \frac{2m}{2m+1} \mathcal{T}_{2m}^{4m} < \mathcal{T}_{2m}^{4m} \\
\mathcal{T}_{2m+1}^{4m+1} = \frac{2m+2}{2m+1} \mathcal{T}_{2m}^{4m+1} > \mathcal{T}_{2m}^{4m+1} & \text{and} & \mathcal{T}_{2m+2}^{4m+1} = \frac{m}{m+1} \mathcal{T}_{2m+1}^{4m+1} < \mathcal{T}_{2m+1}^{4m+1} \\
\mathcal{T}_{2m+2}^{4m+2} = \frac{m+1}{m+1} \mathcal{T}_{2m+1}^{4m+1} = \mathcal{T}_{2m+1}^{4m+1} & \text{and} & \mathcal{T}_{2m+3}^{4m+2} = \frac{2m}{2m+3} \mathcal{T}_{2m+2}^{4m+2} < \mathcal{T}_{2m+2}^{4m+2} \\
\mathcal{T}_{2m+2}^{4m+3} = \frac{m+1}{m+1} \mathcal{T}_{2m+1}^{4m+3} = \mathcal{T}_{2m+1}^{4m+3} & \text{and} & \mathcal{T}_{2m+3}^{4m+3} = \frac{2m+2}{2m+3} \mathcal{T}_{2m+2}^{4m+3} < \mathcal{T}_{2m+2}^{4m+3}
\end{array}$$

and the result **(*ii*)** follows at once. □

2.2 The Vietoris Binomial Inverse Sequence

Given two sequences $\mathbf{u} = (u_n)_{n\geq 0}$ and $\mathbf{v} = (v_n)_{n\geq 0}$, we recall that the binomial convolution of $\mathbf{u}$ and $\mathbf{v}$, here denoted by $\mathbf{u} \otimes \mathbf{v} = ((u \otimes v)_n)_{n\geq 0}$, is the sequence defined as

$$(u \otimes v)_n = \sum_{k=0}^{n} \binom{n}{k} u_k v_{n-k}.$$

Moreover, as it is well-known, if $f_{\mathbf{u}}(t)$ and $f_{\mathbf{v}}(t)$ are the exponential generating functions of the sequences $\mathbf{u}$ and $\mathbf{v}$, respectively, then the exponential generating function of the binomial convolution of the two sequences, $f_{\mathbf{u}\otimes\mathbf{v}}(t)$, is given by

$$f_{\mathbf{u}\otimes\mathbf{v}}(t) = f_{\mathbf{u}}(t) f_{\mathbf{v}}(t),$$

i.e., the multiplication of two exponential generating functions corresponds to the binomial convolution of sequences (see, for instance, [2]). We call $f_{\mathbf{u}}$ and $f_{\mathbf{v}}$ reciprocals if

$$f_{\mathbf{u}}(t) f_{\mathbf{v}}(t) = f_{\mathbf{v}}(t) f_{\mathbf{u}}(t) = 1.$$

We recall that the exponential generating function of the Vietoris sequence $(c_n)_{n\geq 0}$ is [4,6],

$$\boldsymbol{F}(t) = I_0(t) + I_1(t), \tag{6}$$

where I_0 and I_1 are the modified Bessel functions of the first kind, i.e.,

$$\boldsymbol{F}(t) = I_0(t) + I_1(t) = \sum_{k=0}^{\infty} c_k \frac{t^k}{k!}.$$

Therefore, the reciprocal $\boldsymbol{G}$ of $\boldsymbol{F}$ is such that

$$\boldsymbol{G}(t) = \frac{1}{I_0(t) + I_1(t)} = \sum_{k=0}^{\infty} d_k \frac{t^k}{k!}, \tag{7}$$

with

$$(c \otimes d)_n = \sum_{k=0}^{n} \binom{n}{k} c_k d_{n-k} = \delta_{n,0}, \tag{8}$$

where $\delta_{i,j}$ is the Kronecker delta function. We will call the sequence $(d_n)_{n\geq 0}$ the binomial inverse of the Vietoris sequence $(c_n)_{n\geq 0}$.

From (1) and (8), it follows immediately that the binomial inverse of the Vietoris sequence is defined recursively by

$$\begin{cases} d_0 = \dfrac{1}{c_0} = 1 \\ d_n = -\dfrac{1}{c_0} \displaystyle\sum_{k=1}^{n} \binom{n}{k} c_k d_{n-k} = -\sum_{k=1}^{n} \binom{n}{k} c_k d_{n-k}, \; n = 1, 2, \ldots. \end{cases} \tag{9}$$

Remark 2. Relations (1) and (8) also imply that

$$c_n = -\frac{1}{d_0} \sum_{k=1}^{n} \binom{n}{k} d_k c_{n-k} = -\sum_{k=1}^{n} \binom{n}{k} d_k c_{n-k}, \; n = 1, 2, \ldots,$$

with $c_0 = \frac{1}{d_0} = 1$.

Table 2 contains the first terms of the Vietoris sequence and its binomial inverse.

Table 2. The first terms of the Vietoris sequence and its binomial inverse

c_n	1	$\frac{1}{2}$	$\frac{1}{2}$	$\frac{3}{8}$	$\frac{3}{8}$	$\frac{5}{16}$	$\frac{5}{16}$	$\frac{35}{128}$	$\frac{35}{128}$	$\frac{63}{256}$	$\frac{63}{256}$	$\frac{231}{1024}$	$\frac{231}{1024}$
d_n	1	$-\frac{1}{2}$	0	$\frac{3}{8}$	$-\frac{3}{8}$	$-\frac{5}{16}$	$\frac{25}{16}$	$-\frac{175}{128}$	$-\frac{735}{128}$	$\frac{5607}{256}$	$-\frac{63}{16}$	$-\frac{223839}{1024}$	$\frac{703395}{1024}$

Observe that

$$d_k = \boldsymbol{G}^{(k)}(0), \; k = 0, 1, \ldots$$

(cf. (7)). The k-th derivative of the function $\boldsymbol{G}$ can be obtained by using the Faà di Bruno's formula in the form

$$\frac{d^n}{dx^n} f(g(x)) = \sum_{k=0}^{n} f^{(k)}(g(x)) \mathcal{B}_{n,k}\left(g'(x), g''(x), \ldots, g^{(n)}(x)\right), \tag{10}$$

where $\mathcal{B}_{n,k}$ are the incomplete exponential Bell polynomials [7, Th11.4]

$$\mathcal{B}_{n,k}(x_1, x_2, \ldots, x_n) = \sum_{\sigma(n,k)} \tfrac{n!}{k_1! k_2! \cdots k_n!} \left(\tfrac{x_1}{1!}\right)^{k_1} \left(\tfrac{x_2}{2!}\right)^{k_2} \cdots \left(\tfrac{x_n}{n!}\right)^{k_n},$$

$\sigma(n,k)$ denoting the set of all partitions of n into k parts.

Writing $g(x) = I_0(x) + I_1(x)$ and $f(x) = \frac{1}{x}$, and observing that $g^{(k)}(0) = c_k$ and $f^{(k)}(1) = (-1)^k k!$, we obtain from (10)

$$d_n = \sum_{k=0}^{n} (-1)^k k! \mathcal{B}_{n,k}(c_1, c_2, \ldots, c_n), \; n = 0, 1, \ldots. \tag{11}$$

Remark 3. The same reasoning leads to

$$c_n = \sum_{k=0}^{n} (-1)^k k! \mathcal{B}_{n,k}(d_1, d_2, \ldots, d_n), \; n = 0, 1, \ldots.$$

3 Appell-Vietoris Polynomials

3.1 Appell Polynomials Revisited

In this section we consider polynomials in x forming a sequence

$$\mathcal{A}_0(x), \mathcal{A}_1(x), \ldots, \mathcal{A}_n(x), \ldots,$$

whose term $\mathcal{A}_n(x)$ is a polynomial of degree n, satisfying the Appell property,

$$\mathcal{A}_n'(x) = n\mathcal{A}_{n-1}(x), \; n = 1, 2, \ldots, \tag{12}$$

with $\mathcal{A}_0(x) \neq 0$. The sequence $(\mathcal{A}_n(x))_{n\geq 0}$ is commonly referred to as Appell sequence and its terms as Appell polynomials. The following theorem summarizes some properties that characterize Appell polynomials.

Theorem 3. *Appell sequence of polynomials $\mathcal{A}_n(x)$ (of degree n) may be defined by either of the following equivalent conditions:*

1. *There exists a formal power series*

$$f(t) = \sum_{n=0}^{\infty} \alpha_n \frac{t^n}{n!}, \; (\alpha_0 \neq 0), \tag{13}$$

such that (again formally)

$$f(t)e^{tx} = \sum_{n=0}^{\infty} \mathcal{A}_n(x) \frac{t^n}{n!}, \tag{14}$$

i.e., (14) *is the exponential generating function of the sequence $(\mathcal{A}_n(x))_{n\geq 0}$.*

2. *There exists a sequence $(\alpha_n)_{n\geq 0}$, with $\alpha_0 \neq 0$, such that*

$$\mathcal{A}_n(x) = \sum_{k=0}^{n} \alpha_k \binom{n}{k} x^{n-k}, \; n = 0, 1, \ldots. \tag{15}$$

3. The sequence $(\mathcal{A}_n(x))_{n\geq 0}$ *satisfies the binomial identity*

$$\mathcal{A}_n(x+y) = \sum_{k=0}^{n} \binom{n}{k} \mathcal{A}_{n-k}(x) y^k, \ n = 0, 1, 2 \ldots . \tag{16}$$

4. There exists a sequence $(\beta_n)_{n\geq 0}$*, with* $\beta_0 \neq 0$*, such that*

$$\mathcal{A}_0(x) = \frac{1}{\beta_0} \tag{17}$$

$$\mathcal{A}_n(x) = \frac{(-1)^n}{\beta_0^{n+1}} \begin{vmatrix} 1 & x & x^2 & \cdots & x^{n-1} & x^n \\ \beta_0 & \beta_1 & \beta_2 & \cdots & \beta_{n-1} & \beta_n \\ 0 & \beta_0 & \binom{2}{1}\beta_1 & \cdots & \binom{n-1}{1}\beta_{n-2} & \binom{n}{1}\beta_{n-1} \\ 0 & 0 & \beta_0 & \cdots & \binom{n-1}{2}\beta_{n-3} & \binom{n}{2}\beta_{n-2} \\ \vdots & \vdots & \vdots & \ddots & \vdots & \vdots \\ 0 & 0 & 0 & \cdots & \beta_0 & \binom{n}{n-1}\beta_1 \end{vmatrix}, \ n = 1, 2, \ldots \tag{18}$$

The equivalence of (12), (14) and (15) was proved by Appell in [3], while the representation (17)-(18) was derived by Costabile and Longo [8], using a determinantal approach and also by Adell and Lekuona [2] using binomial convolutions. In both works we can find the proof that the sequence $(\beta_n)_{n\geq 0}$ in (17)-(18) is the binomial inverse of $(\alpha_n)_{n\geq 0}$ in (15), i.e.,

$$\begin{cases} \beta_0 = \dfrac{1}{\alpha_0} \\ \beta_k = -\dfrac{1}{\alpha_0} \displaystyle\sum_{s=0}^{k-1} \binom{k}{s} \alpha_{k-s} \beta_s, \quad k = 1, \ldots, n \end{cases} \tag{19}$$

(cf. (9)).

A proof that polynomials of exact degree n are Appell polynomials iff they satisfy the binomial identity (16) can be seen, for example, in [5, Th1].

Beyond Theorem 3, there exists a lesser-known unifying matrix approach, introduced in [1], for representing Appell polynomials. Considering the generating function (14) as well as the formal power series (13), the authors arrived at the representation of the Appell vector $\mathbf{a}(x) = [\mathcal{A}_0(x) \ \mathcal{A}_1(x) \ \cdots \ \mathcal{A}_n(x)]^T$ in the form

$$\mathbf{a}(x) = f(H)\xi(x),$$

where $\xi(x) = [1 \ x \ x^2 \cdots x_n]^T$, $H = (H_{ij})$ is the nilpotent matrix of order n defined by

$$H_{ij} = \begin{cases} i, & i = j+1 \\ 0, & \text{otherwise}, \quad i, j = 0, \ldots, n, \end{cases}$$

and

$$f(H) = \sum_{m=0}^{n} \alpha_m \frac{H^m}{m!}.$$

Since the matrix $M = f(H)$, called the transfer matrix for the Appell vector $\mathbf{a}(x)$, is nonsingular, the use of its inverse

$$M^{-1} = \sum_{m=0}^{n} \beta_m \frac{H^m}{m!}$$

enables the derivation of (19). Nevertheless, determining a closed form of the coefficients β_m in the matrix M^{-1} proves challenging. So far, such determination has been successful only in selected cases of Appell polynomials (cf. [1, p. 439]).

3.2 The Appell-Vietoris Polynomials

We consider now the sequence of polynomials $(\mathcal{V}_n(x))_{n\geq 0}$ of the form

$$\mathcal{V}_n(x) = \sum_{k=0}^{n} \mathcal{T}_k^n x^k = \sum_{k=0}^{n} \binom{n}{k} c_{n-k} x^k, \; n = 0, 1, 2 \ldots, \tag{20}$$

where $\mathcal{T}_k^n$ and c_k are respectively, the triangle (2) and the k-th term of the Vietoris sequence (1). This sequence inherently fulfills the Appell property stated in (12), (cf. (15)). This validation supports our choice of naming it the Appell-Vietoris sequence of polynomials. Table 3 and Fig. 1 present the initial polynomials of the Appell-Vietoris sequence.

Table 3. Appell-Vietoris Polynomials $\mathcal{V}_n$, $n = 0, 1, \ldots, 7$

n	$\mathcal{V}_n(x)$
0	1
1	$x + \frac{1}{2}$
2	$x^2 + x + \frac{1}{2}$
3	$x^3 + \frac{3x^2}{2} + \frac{3x}{2} + \frac{3}{8}$
4	$x^4 + 2x^3 + 3x^2 + \frac{3x}{2} + \frac{3}{8}$
5	$x^5 + \frac{5x^4}{2} + 5x^3 + \frac{15x^2}{4} + \frac{15x}{8} + \frac{5}{16}$
6	$x^6 + 3x^5 + \frac{15x^4}{2} + \frac{15x^3}{2} + \frac{45x^2}{8} + \frac{15x}{8} + \frac{5}{16}$
7	$x^7 + \frac{7x^6}{2} + \frac{21x^5}{2} + \frac{105x^4}{8} + \frac{105x^3}{8} + \frac{105x^2}{16} + \frac{35x}{16} + \frac{35}{128}$

Since $\mathcal{V}_n(0) = c_n$, $n = 0, 1, \ldots$, the exponential generating function of $(\mathcal{V}_n(x))_{n\geq 0}$ is (see (14) and (6))

$$(I_0(t) + I_1(t))e^{tx} = \sum_{n=0}^{\infty} \mathcal{V}_n(x) \frac{t^n}{n!}.$$

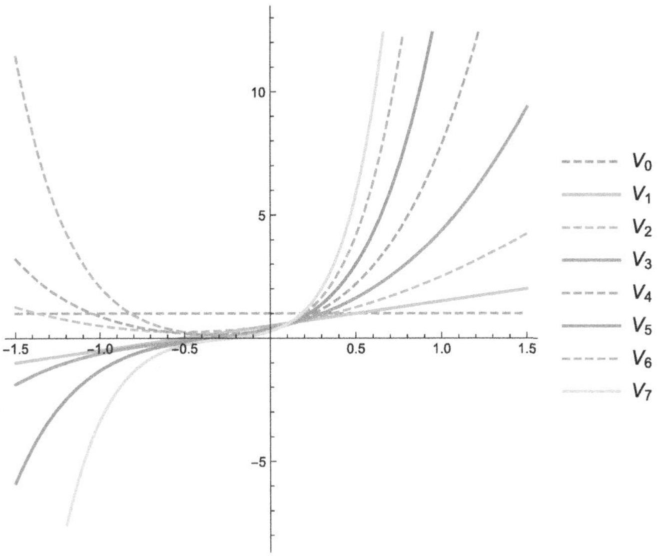

Fig. 1. First Appell-Vietoris Polynomials

The determinantal form of $\mathcal{V}_n(x)$ is (cf. (17)-(18))

$$\mathcal{V}_0(x) = 1$$

$$\mathcal{V}_n(x) = (-1)^n \begin{vmatrix} 1 & x & x^2 & \dots & x^{n-1} & x^n \\ 1 & d_1 & d_2 & \dots & d_{n-1} & d_n \\ 0 & 1 & \binom{2}{1}d_1 & \dots & \binom{n-1}{1}d_{n-2} & \binom{n}{1}d_{n-1} \\ 0 & 0 & 1 & \dots & \binom{n-1}{2}d_{n-3} & \binom{n}{2}d_{n-2} \\ \vdots & \vdots & \vdots & \ddots & \vdots & \vdots \\ 0 & 0 & 0 & \dots & 1 & \binom{n}{n-1}d_1 \end{vmatrix}, \quad n = 1, 2, \dots,$$

where $(d_n)_{n \geq 0}$ is the binomial inversion of the Vietoris sequence, given by (9) or (11). For example, when $n = 7$, we have

$$\mathcal{V}_7(x) = \begin{vmatrix} 1 & x & x^2 & x^3 & x^4 & x^5 & x^6 & x^7 \\ 1 & \frac{1}{2} & \frac{1}{2} & \frac{3}{8} & \frac{3}{8} & \frac{5}{16} & \frac{5}{16} & \frac{35}{128} \\ 0 & 1 & 1 & \frac{3}{2} & \frac{3}{2} & \frac{15}{8} & \frac{15}{8} & \frac{35}{16} \\ 0 & 0 & 1 & \frac{3}{2} & 3 & \frac{15}{4} & \frac{45}{8} & \frac{105}{16} \\ 0 & 0 & 0 & 1 & 2 & 5 & \frac{15}{2} & \frac{105}{8} \\ 0 & 0 & 0 & 0 & 1 & \frac{5}{2} & \frac{15}{2} & \frac{105}{8} \\ 0 & 0 & 0 & 0 & 0 & 1 & 3 & \frac{21}{2} \\ 0 & 0 & 0 & 0 & 0 & 0 & 1 & \frac{7}{2} \end{vmatrix}.$$

As an immediate consequence of last relation we can obtain the following recurrence relation [8, Th9] for the Appell-Vietoris polynomials

$$\mathcal{V}_n(x) = x^n - \sum_{k=0}^{n-1} \binom{n}{k} d_{n-k} \mathcal{V}_k(x), \; n = 1, 2, \ldots .$$

Finally, we consider the result obtained in [8, Th18], namely

$$\int_0^1 \mathcal{V}_n(x)dx = \frac{1}{n+1} \sum_{k=0}^{n} \binom{n+1}{k} \mathcal{V}_k(0),$$

which can be written as

$$\int_0^1 \mathcal{V}_n(x)dx = \frac{1}{n+1} \left(\sum_{k=0}^{n+1} \binom{n+1}{k} c_k - c_{n+1} \right).$$

Using now Identity $\mathbf{Id}_3$ in Theorem 1, we obtain

$$\int_0^1 \mathcal{V}_n(x)dx = \frac{1}{n+1} \left(2^{n+2} c_{2n+3} - c_{n+1} \right).$$

3.3 Zeros of the Appell-Vietoris Polynomials

The literature on the zeros of Appell polynomials is scarse. We can mention [9, Sect. 6.6], where one can find some results on the location of zeros of Appell sequences $(\mathcal{A}_n(x))_{n\geq 0}$ satisfying the condition that

$$\mathcal{A}_n(x), \; \mathcal{A}_{n-1}(x), \ldots, \mathcal{A}_0(x)$$

is a Sturm sequence [15].

We recall that a sequence of polynomials $P_0(x), P_1(x), \ldots, P_n(x)$ is called a Sturm sequence on an interval (a, b) if

1. $P_n(x) \neq 0$ in (a, b);

2. If $P_k(\zeta) = 0, \; k = 1, \ldots, n-1$, then

$$P_{k-1}(\zeta)P_{k+1}(\zeta) < 0.$$

By observing the first polynomials of the Appell-Vietoris sequence, it is easy to conclude that Condition 2 is not fulfilled.

Naturally, results connecting the zeros of a polynomial and its derivatives can be used, following e.g. [14]. In particular, the Gauss-Lucas Theorem allows to conclude that the zeros of $\mathcal{V}_{n-1}(x)$ are in the convex hull of the zeros of $\mathcal{V}_n(x)$, as illustrated in Fig. 2.

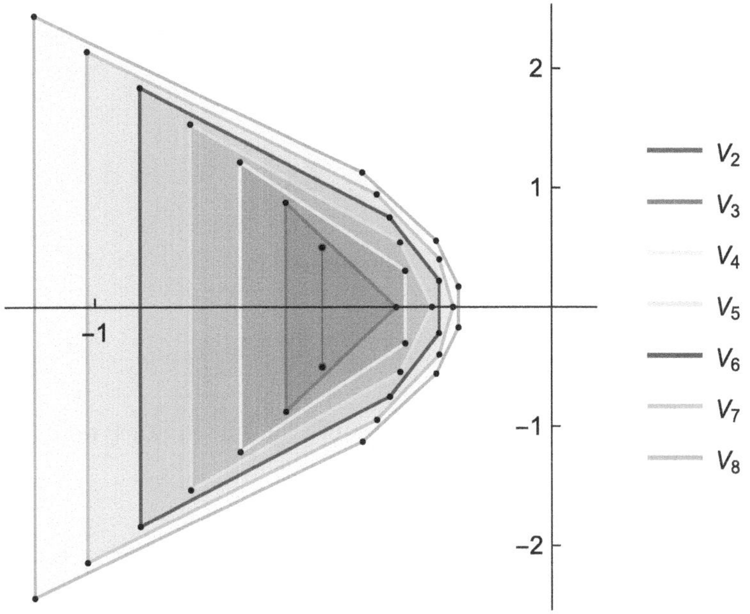

Fig. 2. The Gauss-Lucas Theorem for the first Appell-Vietoris polynomials

By construction, all the coefficients of the polynomials $\mathcal{V}_n(x)$ (20) are positive, which means, by Descartes' rule of signs, that the real zeros of $\mathcal{V}_n(x)$, if any, are negative. In addition, taking into account that

$$\mathcal{V}_n(0) = c_n > 0$$

and by Theorem 1 (**Id**$_3$)

$$\mathcal{V}_n(-1) = \frac{(-2)^n c_{2n}}{n+1} < 0, \text{ for odd } n,$$

we conclude that, when n is odd, there is at least a real root of $\mathcal{V}_n(x)$ in $(-1, 0)$.

We introduce now the $2n$ degree polynomial

$$\mathcal{W}_{2n}(x) = \mathcal{V}_n(x)\mathcal{V}_n(-x) = \sum_{k=0}^{2n} x^k \sum_{s=0}^{k} (-1)^s \mathcal{T}_s^n \mathcal{T}_{k-s}^n.$$

Observe that if ζ is a real zero of $\mathcal{W}_{2n}(x)$ then either ζ or $-\zeta$ is a zero of $\mathcal{V}_n(x)$. Consequently, if $\mathcal{W}_{2n}(x)$ has only nonreal zeros, the same holds for $\mathcal{V}_n(x)$.

The polynomial $\mathcal{W}_{2n}(x)$ can be expressed as

$$\mathcal{W}_{2n}(x) = \sum_{k=0}^{n} a_{k,n} x^{2k} + \sum_{k=0}^{n-1} b_{k,n} x^{2k+1},$$

where

$$a_{k,n} = \sum_{s=0}^{2k} (-1)^s \mathcal{T}_s^n \mathcal{T}_{2k-s}^n \tag{21}$$

and

$$b_{k,n} = \sum_{s=0}^{2k+1} (-1)^s \mathcal{T}_s^n \mathcal{T}_{2k+1-s}^n. \tag{22}$$

Changing s to $2k+1-s$ in (22), it follows that

$$b_{k,n} = -\sum_{s=0}^{2k+1} (-1)^s \mathcal{T}_{2k+1-s}^n \mathcal{T}_s^n = -b_{k,n},$$

which means that $b_{k,n} = 0$, for all values of k and n. In other words, we have proved that

$$\mathcal{W}_{2n}(x) = \sum_{k=0}^{n} a_{k,n} x^{2k}. \tag{23}$$

From the properties of the Vietoris sequence and (21), it becomes evident that for even values of n, (let's say $n = 2m$), the following relations hold:

$$a_{0,2m} = c_{2m}^2 \quad \text{and} \quad a_{1,2m} = 0.$$

The values of $a_{k,2m}$, for $k = 2, \ldots, 2m$ and $m = 1, \ldots, 5$ are presented in Table 4, arranged in a triangular way. It is noteworthy that this triangle inherits the properties of the triangle $\mathcal{T}_k^n$ that generated it, specifically the non-negativity of its elements and the log concavity of the finite sequence associated with each row, i.e., $a_{2,m}, a_{3,m}, \ldots, a_{2m,m}$.

Since $a_{k,2m} \geq 0$, it follows that both $\mathcal{W}_{2n}(x)$ and $\mathcal{W}_{2n}(-x)$ possess non-negative coefficients (cf. (23)). Consequently, neither $\mathcal{W}_{2n}(x)$ nor $\mathcal{V}_n(x)$ have real zeros, when n is even.

Table 4. The values $a_{2k,m}$, $m = 1, \ldots, 5$, $k = 2, \ldots 2m$

1								
$\frac{15}{4}$	2	1						
$\frac{525}{64}$	$\frac{35}{2}$	$\frac{45}{2}$	6	1				
$\frac{3675}{256}$	$\frac{2205}{32}$	$\frac{11655}{64}$	$\frac{343}{2}$	$\frac{161}{2}$	12	1		
$\frac{363825}{16384}$	$\frac{24255}{128}$	$\frac{3465}{4}$	$\frac{54747}{32}$	$\frac{112875}{64}$	$\frac{1725}{2}$	$\frac{855}{4}$	20	1

In the case of odd n, we know that $\mathcal{V}_n(x)$ has an odd number of real (negative) zeros. By Rolle's theorem, if $\mathcal{V}_n(x)$ has $k > 1$ zeros, then its derivative $n\mathcal{V}_{n-1}(x)$ has at least $k-1$ zeros, which is not possible, since this even-degree polynomial has no real zeros. Therefore we conclude that $\mathcal{V}_n(x)$ has only one negative zero ζ_n, which, as already proved, lies in $(-1, 0)$.

To illustrate the above considerations, we present in Table 5 the zeros of the first Vietoris polynomials (see also Fig. 1).

The numerical results obtained suggest the conjecture that all the zeros of $\mathcal{V}_n(x)$ lie in the open left half-plane. This property, very important in, for example, control theory or in the mathematical theory of differential and difference equations, deserves a more in-depth future study.

Table 5. The zeros of the first Vietoris polynomials

n	zeros of V_n
1	-0.5
2	-0.5 ± 0.5i
3	$-0.58055 \pm 0.87719i$ -0.33891
4	$-0.68090 \pm 1.21396i$ $-0.31910 \pm 0.30289i$

n	zeros of V_n
5	$-0.78934 \pm 1.53203i$ $-0.33012 \pm 0.54222i$ -0.26109
6	$-0.90193 \pm 1.83982i$ $-0.35274 \pm 0.75196i$ $-0.24534 \pm 0.21841i$

Acknowledgments. Research at CMAT was partially financed by Portuguese funds through FCT - Fundação para a Ciência e a Tecnologia within the Projects UIDB/00013/2020 (https://doi.org/10.54499/UIDB/00013/2020) and UIDP/00013/2020 (https://doi.org/10.54499/UIDP/00013/2020). Research at CIDMA has been financed by FCT within the Projects UIDB/04106/2020 (https://doi.org/10.54499/UIDB/04106/2020) and UIDP/04106/2020 (https://doi.org/10.54499/UIDP/04106/2020).

References

1. Aceto, L., Malonek, H., Tomaz, G.: A unified matrix approach to the representation of Appell polynomials. Integral Transform. Spec. Funct. **26**(6), 426–441 (2015)
2. Adell, J.A., Lekuona, A.: Binomial convolution and transformations of Appell polynomials. J. Math. Anal. Appl. **456**(1), 16–33 (2017)
3. Appell, P.: Sur une classe de polynômes. Ann. Sci. École Norm. Sup. **9**(2), 119–144 (1880)
4. Cação, I., Falcão, M.I., Malonek, H.R., Tomaz, G.: A Sturm-Liouville equation on the crossroads of continuous and discrete hypercomplex analysis. Math. Methods Appl. Sci. **47**, 7962–7987 (2024)
5. Carlson, B.: Polynomials satisfying a binomial theorem. J. Math. Anal. Appl. **32**, 543–558 (1970)
6. Cação, I., Falcão, M.I., Malonek, H.R., Miranda, F., Tomaz, G.: Remarks on the Vietoris sequence and corresponding convolution formulas. In: Gervasi, O., et al. (eds.) ICCSA 2023. LNCS, vol. 14104, pp. 677–692. Springer, Cham (2023). https://doi.org/10.1007/978-3-031-37105-9_45

7. Charalambides, C.A.: Enumerative Combinatorics, 1st edn. Chapman and Hall/CRC, Boca Raton (2002)
8. Costabile, F., Longo, E.: A determinantal approach to Appell polynomials. J. Comput. Appl. Math. **234**(5), 1528–1542 (2010)
9. Costabile, F.A.: Modern Umbral Calculus. De Gruyter (2019)
10. Falcão, M.I., Malonek, H.R.: Generalized exponentials through Appell sets in $\mathbb{R}^{n+1}$ and Bessel functions. In: AIP Conference Proceedings, vol. 936, pp. 738–741 (2007)
11. Gould, H.W.: Combinatorial Identities. Morgantown, West Virginia (1972)
12. Koshy, T.: Catalan Numbers with Applications. Oxford University Press, New York (2009)
13. Malonek, H., Falcão, M.: Special monogenic polynomials—properties and applications. In: Simos, T.E., Psihoyios, G., Tsitouras, C. (eds.) AIP Conference Proceedings, vol. 936, pp. 764–767 (2007)
14. Marden, M.: Geometry of polynomials. Mathematical Surveys and Monographs-1943-2010 Electronic Backfile Collection
15. McNamee, J.M.: Numerical Methods for Roots of Polynomials, Part I, vol. 16. Elsevier B. V, Amsterdam (2007)
16. OEIS Foundation Inc.: The on-line encyclopedia of integer sequences (2024). Published electronically at https://oeis.org
17. Vietoris, L.: Über das vorzeichen gewisser trigonometrischer summen. Sitzungsber. Österr. Akad. Wiss **167**, 125–135 (1958)
18. Wilf, H.: Generating Functionology, 2nd edn. Academic Press, San Diego (1994)

Computational and Applied Statistics (CAS 2024)

Categories's Churn: A Machine Learning Approach in Retail

Carlos Sousa[1,3], A. Manuela Gonçalves[1,2](✉), and Ana da Costa Freitas[3]

[1] Department of Mathematics, University of Minho, Guimarães, Portugal
mneves@math.uminho.pt
[2] Centre of Mathematics, University of Minho, Guimarães, Portugal
[3] Retail Chain, Lisbon, Portugal

Abstract. In the realm of business, the cessation of relations with a company by its customers can yield profound financial repercussions. Such consequences manifest as diminished revenue and profitability, while also bringing risk to the company's reputation. Thus, comprehending the roots of customer churn is of major importance. Equally crucial is the formulation of effective strategies to mitigate churn, thereby enhancing customer satisfaction, retention, and overall profitability. Within the framework of this work, clustering techniques were deployed alongside machine learning methodologies. This combination helped achieve a balance between accuracy and simplified model communication. In addition, data analysis techniques were deployed within the context of churn analysis, where total churn emerged as the optimal solution for the project, even if a case for partial churn could be made. The outcome was the development of a cohort of models capable of identifying the majority of churners within the selected pilot categories. Which empowers the retention department to implement more impactful retention campaigns, ensuring a more effective response to customer churn and bolstering overall business stability.

Keywords: Churn · Machine Learning · Clustering · Classification · Retail · Big Data

1 Introduction

There are a variety of factors that contribute to churn, including poor customer service, a lack luster customer experience, and a failure to provide value to customers. In addition, changing economic conditions, shifting consumer behavior, and evolving industry trends can all contribute to churn. Portuguese consumers have been gradually shifting towards online shopping, driven by convenience and changing consumer preferences. This forced companies to adapt in order to avoid losing customers.

In the Portuguese retail market, churn is a particularly important subject. According to a research made by The Consumer Goods Forum [1] 73% of Portugal retail customers bought in more than one supermarket banner per week,

O. Gervasi et al. (Eds.): ICCSA 2024 Workshops, LNCS 14815, pp. 319–336, 2024.
https://doi.org/10.1007/978-3-031-65154-0_20

with 21% shopping in more than two. The willingness of Portuguese consumers to change providers underlines the competitive nature of the retail landscape. This is particularly evident in the grocery sector, where consumers are often sensitive to price fluctuations and promotions. While price is a critical factor in consumer choice, it is not the sole determinant of customer loyalty [1]. Retailers need to consider a holistic approach to customer retention, addressing various aspects of the shopping journey.

The aim of this work is to create a set of predictive models capable of accurately predict and explain churn to a category level in a major Portuguese retailer. To do so, state of the art machine learning and data analysis techniques will be applied to the extensive existing customer and transactional databases and the derived results analysed, presented and implemented into production. Category churn will help in the creation of better focused promotional campaigns that current models do not allow for, while also allowing to individually approach categories that are more permeable to competitor influence. These models are also to be integrated into a bigger project aiming to develop an Advanced Diagnostic and Optimization Tool (ADOT), in order to assist higher management with decision making.

1.1 Data Imbalance

When the classes in a dataset are not represented equally, standard machine learning algorithms can have poor performance on under-represented classes. This is because, in such scenarios, the model is trained on mostly one class, leading to a bias towards the majority class and poor generalization to the minority class [2,3].

Resampling techniques, such as oversampling the minority class, undersampling the majority class, or a combination of both, can be used to balance the dataset. This can be done by either duplicating instances of the minority class or removing instances of the majority class. Random Oversampling (ROS) and Random Undersampling (RUS) are two well known sampling techniques, however, because of the random nature of the selection involved in duplicating and discarding the data values, these approaches lack consistency and show varying performance [2]. On top of that oversampling can lead to overfitting and a decrease in the diversity of the dataset, while undersampling can cause a loss of important information even in informed sampling techniques, like EasyEnsemble and BalanceCascade algorithms [3], therefore, a combination of oversampling and undersampling is often used. One such approach is to use SMOTE (Synthetic Minority Over-sampling Technique), capable of generating synthetic samples based on the feature space similarities between existing minority examples, in conjunction with a oversampling technique.

Cost-sensitive learning is another technique that can be used to address data imbalance. This approach incorporates the class imbalance into the learning algorithm by assigning different misclassification costs to different classes. Instead of creating balanced data distributions through different sampling strategies, cost sensitive learning targets the imbalanced learning problem by using different cost matrices that describe the costs for misclassifying any particular data example. This helps to ensure that the model pays more attention to the minority class during training [3]. Even though these techniques can be effective in addressing data imbalance, they are not a one-size-fits-all solution. Therefore, it is essential to thoroughly evaluate different approaches, before implementing them in a particular application.

1.2 Classification Tools

Classification is a fundamental problem in machine learning, where the goal is to predict the class of a given input based on its features. Churn prediction falls under this type of problem, usually trying to distinguish customers into two classes churner or not churner. In order to predict churn, several methods have been proposed and used during the years, being the most widely established and used ones Logistic Regression [5], Random Forest [6], Support Vector Machines (SVM) [7], Artificial Neural Networks [8], and Naive Bayes [4,9].

Boosting algorithms, that work by combining several base classifiers, sequentially estimated from perturbed versions of the calibration sample, have also been used to improve the classification performance of previously mentioned methods [10]. The biggest trade off between classification methods is that, usually, when performance increases the models tend to become less interpretable. This is mostly fine, as long as predictions are the sole purpose of the model. In more complex business environments, where identifying the roots behind the churn is important the performance/interpretability trade off must be considered more carefully. A business might be willing to trade some of the predictive performance of the model for the ability to better understand how each of the features interacts with the possibility of churn. Fortunately, over the years action has been taken in this regard and developers have built tools, like SHAP (Shapley Additive Explanations) or InterpretML, that look to bring to light more information out of these systems. The InterpretML package also included the first implementation of an Explainable Boosting Machine (EBM), a glassbox model that can be as accurate as many black-box models while remaining completely interpretable [11]. It works by building upon the principles behind Generalized Addictive Models with the use of techniques like boosting and bagging in conjunction with pair wise interactions that help to further boost accuracy.

2 Methodologies

2.1 Establishing Customer Representation and Churn

Customer definitions can vary depending on the context and objectives of the study. In industries where subscriptions are the norm, a customer may be defined as an individual or business entity that has an active subscription or contract with a service provider. On the other hand, in the retail sector, a customer may be defined as an individual who has made a purchase within a specific time frame or has reached a defined spending amount. While the specific criteria for identifying churn can differ based on the nature of the industry and the available data, by establishing clear definitions for customers and churn, it's possible to ensure consistency in the analyses and results, while minimising the risk of bias in the model. This section used data for the years of 2021 and 2022.

Defining Customer. In a company with the same dimensions as MCS, we may encounter a considerable number of customers who, despite being included in the database, exhibit shopping behaviors that are either sporadic or occur in such low volume that they can have a negative impact on the overall project results. To address this issue, a thorough analysis of the underlying data was conducted, and actions were taken to handle such customers. The first step involved identifying and excluding "*oneshot*" customers, those with only one purchase in a given time frame, in this case one year. Subsequently, the shopping behavior of the remaining customers was analyzed by plotting the number of customers under specific spending thresholds. A curve was then drawn, and its slope was measured. The objective was to identify points just before significant increases in the slope, which indicate potential changes in customer behavior. In this case there's two issues to be taken into consideration, the number of churners that would be removed and the cost of activation. There's also a balance to be struck in determining how much data should be sacrificed to reduce noise. The cut should ideally be made before reaching a point of acceleration to prevent the removal of essential churners from our dataset. Additionally, it's crucial to ensure that unprofitable customers are not inadvertently activated.

Two specific spending thresholds, 30€ and 50€, were identified as being particularly important, Fig. 1. The number of customers under each threshold was taken into consideration to determine how much data could be sacrificed to reduce noise in the dataset. Ultimately, the chosen threshold was 30€, which means only customers with at least two purchases and a minimum total spending of 30€ in the last 12 months were considered in this study. This selection ensured that the analysis focused on customers with more consistent shopping behavior and a higher level of engagement with the company, without risking losing data for customers that, in extreme cases, only buy a very small or even just one category.

Partial vs Total: Defining Customer Churn. To define churn we had to first isolate churners in order to observe their behaviour. To do this, a specific time frame was chosen, and T set as the target month. During this step, any customer who made a purchase on month T but did not make any further purchases between T+1 and T+6 (a six-month period) was considered a churner. This criterion ensures that T is the last month in which the customer made a purchase and confirms that they were not previously classified as a churner before that time, Fig. 2.

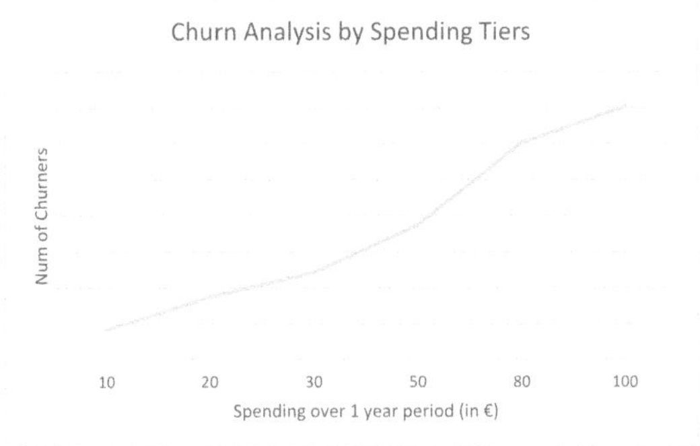

Fig. 1. Number of customers in a specific twelve month spending threshold that did not make a purchase in the following six months

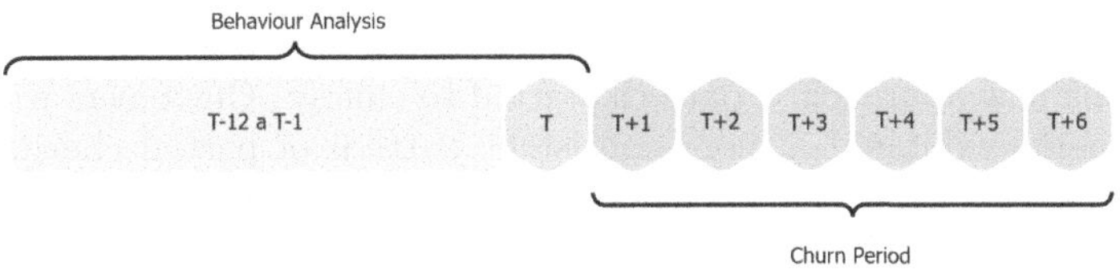

Fig. 2. Diagram of the process used to identify churners for behaviour analysis

Next, the transactional behavior of customers leading up to T (including month T) was analyzed to determine if there were any indications of partial churn prior to the actual churn event. This involved comparing each customer's monthly spending with their average monthly spending. A ratio was then crafted to observe the sales evolution over the year and the results aggregated and compared with non-churners to mitigate any potential bias caused by seasonal variations. This ratio was made by comparing a customer monthly spending to the average spending for the year, as follows

$$\text{Racio} = \frac{\text{Spending month X}}{\text{Average Spending for the Year}} \tag{1}$$

Initially, the findings of this analysis were underwhelming. There was a distinction in behavior between churners and non-churners, as seen in Fig. 3, but this wasn't as big as we had expected from analysing similar works. Due to these unexpected results, a different approach was adopted. The identified churners were categorized into groups based on their value segment, utilizing the industry-standard Recency, Frequency, Monetary (RFM) value system, and the transactional behavior was then reanalyzed using this approach. This are already existing segments of clients, previously created by MCS that group clients according to their overall value. Ranging from groups one to six, with one being the most valuable customers with the value progressively decreasing as the group increases.

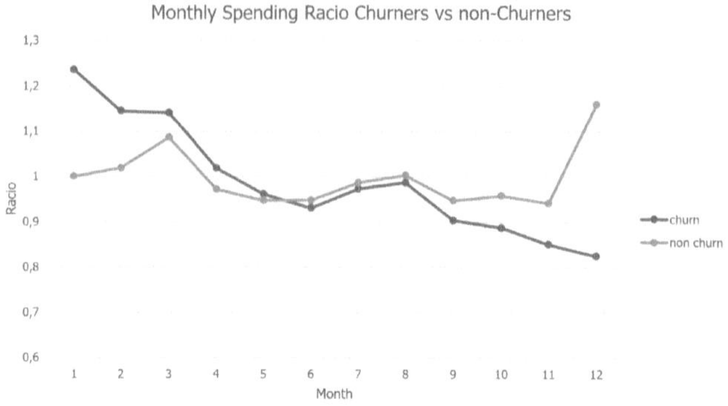

Fig. 3. Comparison of customer monthly spending vs it's average for churners and non-churners, leading up to the target month

With the new approach, a pattern started to emerge. Customers with higher value segments exhibited a more consistent pattern of partial churn, whereas those with lower value segments demonstrated more erratic behavior. This pattern of partial churn was particularly pronounced in the groups 2 and 3 of the RFM segments, loyal clients with medium and small spending, which showed a more pronounced decreased, Fig. 4. Thus, evidence supporting partial churn was emerging. However, upon further analysis, it became evident that the majority of churn cases were in the lower value groups of the customer base, where the partial churn behavior was less pronounced or non-existent. At the time, separating these groups of customers wasn't a feasible option for the company, because the increased complexity would complicate information sharing between different departments, the decision was made to adopt the definition of total churn.

2.2 Clustering Techniques

After reviewing literature for different techniques, we ultimately settled on K-Means and hierarchical clustering. Hierarchical clustering, utilizing the ward method, was employed to visualize the potential clusters. Multiple cuts were then applied to the cluster tree to explore different ways of dividing the clusters that could be created using K-Means. The resulting clusters from different cuts were used to modify the value of 'k' in K-Means, their quality was assessed using the silhouette method, and the outcomes were reviewed by business experts for confirmation and accuracy.

2.3 Performance Metrics and Validation Techniques

The assessment of machine learning model performance in scientific research hinges on the crucial elements of performance metrics and validation techniques. These indispensable tools serve to measure a model's effectiveness on a given dataset and to gauge its ability to generalize to new, unseen data. The selection of

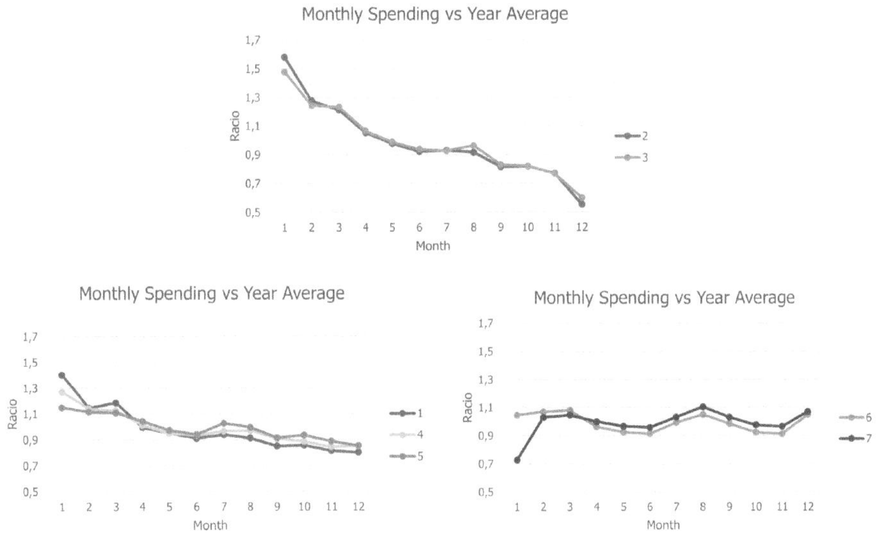

Fig. 4. Comparison of customer monthly spending vs it's yearly average, divided by value segment groups. Top left groups 2 and 3, top right groups 1, 4 and 5 and bottom groups 5 and 6.

appropriate performance metrics and validation techniques is a pivotal decision that warrants careful consideration, tailored to the specific nature of the machine learning task and the characteristics of the available data. A diverse array of performance metrics is at our disposal to assess machine learning models, with the choice contingent on the type of machine learning task under consideration. For this work a mix of metrics was employed, in specific accuracy, precision, recall, the F1 Score, as well as a careful analysis of the confusion matrix and the Area Under the Receiver Operating Characteristic Curve or Area Under the Curve (AUC).

2.4 Models

Explainable Boosting Machine: An Explainable Boosting Machine (EBM) is a machine learning algorithm that combines the principles of boosting and interpretable decision trees to create a predictive model that is easy to understand while maintaining competitive predictive performance. EBMs are based on Generalized Addictive Models (GAMs), but while GAMs were traditionally fit using smooth low order splines, EBMs learn shape functions using boosted decision trees. EBMs are especially interesting because they often match the accuracy of complex blackbox algorithms like XGBoost and random forests, while having a simple optimization procedure and final structure [12].

This restricted machine learning models that have the form:

$$g(E[y]) = \beta_0 + f_1(x_1) + f_2(x_2) + ...f_k(x_k) = \beta_0 + \sum_{j=1}^{k} f_j(x_j), \quad (2)$$

where β_0 is an intercept, each f_j is a univariate function that operates on a single input feature x_j, and g is a link function that adapts the model to different settings like classification and regression.

So, first EBMs learn each feature function f_j using machine learning techniques like gradient boosting or bagging, with the process being restricted in order to train on one feature at a time, in a round robin fashion, using a very low learning rate so that the order of the features does no matter and in order to mitigate co-linearity between features.

This following example shows how the model works each of the features: $y = a_0 + a_1(T_1^1(x_1) + ... + T_r^1(x_1)) + a_2(T_2^2(x_2) + ... + T_r^2(x_2)) + ... + a_k(T_1^k(x_k) + ... + T_r^k(x_k))$. Second this models can also include pairwise interaction terms of the form $g(E[y]) = \beta_0 + \sum f_i(x_i) + \sum f_{i,j}(x_i, x_j)$, which helps to further improve accuracy while maintaining intelligibility. In the context of crafting predictions on an individual basis, each function within the framework of Explainable Boosting Machines (EBMs) operates akin to a specialized lookup table corresponding to distinct features. The outcome of each function is a term contribution, representing the impact of the associated feature. By summing these term contributions and subsequently subjecting the aggregate to a designated link function, the ultimate prediction is computed. The key advantage of EBM lies in its modular structure, characterized by additivity. This structural property permits the sorting and visualization of term contributions, thereby facilitating the identification of features that wield significant influence over a particular prediction [12].

Decision Trees: Decision trees have emerged as a foundational and versatile tool for classification and regression tasks. Their roots trace back to the early days of artificial intelligence, making them one of the enduring pillars of data-driven decision-making.

In this work an optimized version of the CART algorithm was used, as implemented in the scikit learn python library and can be described as follows. Consider a specific node, denoted as m, which encapsulates a dataset denominated as Q_m, housing a count of n_m samples. The core decision centers on dividing this data into two distinct subsets: $Q_m^{\text{left}}(\theta)$ and $Q_m^{\text{right}}(\theta)$. Here, θ is instrumental in specifying the conditions for this partition: $x_j \leq t_m$.

The efficacy of a candidate split at node m hinges on evaluating the impurity function denoted as H. This function serves as a gauge of data homogeneity, ensuring the alignment of samples within the same class. The measure of the quality of the candidate split at node m is quantified as

$$G(Q_m, \theta) = \frac{n_m^{\text{left}}}{n_m} H(Q_m^{\text{left}}(\theta)) + \frac{n_m^{\text{right}}}{n_m} H(Q_m^{\text{right}}(\theta)) . \quad (3)$$

The objective is to identify the optimal candidate split, θ^*, which minimizes the impurity measure.

This process of selecting the best candidate split is reiterated, employing θ^*, and the data is further partitioned into left and right subsets ($Q_m^{\text{left}}(\theta^*)$ and $Q_m^{\text{right}}(\theta^*)$), until certain termination criteria are met. These criteria encompass reaching the maximum allowable depth or encountering nodes with an insufficient number of samples (i.e., $n_m < \min_{\text{samples}}$ or $n_m = 1$).

In scenarios where classification is the goal, involving target values ranging from 0 to $K-1$, the proportion of class observations in node m is quantified as $p_{mk} = \frac{1}{n_m} \sum_{(x,y)\in Q_m} I(y = k)$. Various measures of impurity are considered, with two common options being the Gini Impurity and Log Loss (or Entropy). The Gini Impurity is computed as $H(Q_m) = \sum_k p_{mk}(1 - p_{mk})$. The Log Loss (or Entropy) is represented as $H(Q_m) = -\sum_k p_{mk} \log(p_{mk})$.

Logistic Regression: Logistic regression is a statistical method widely used for modeling the relationship between a binary outcome variable and one or more predictor variables. Unlike linear regression, which aims to predict continuous numeric outcomes, logistic regression is particularly suited for scenarios where the dependent variable is categorical and takes on two possible outcomes, often referred to as "success" or "failure", "1" or "0".

In it's usual form, the simple logistic regression models is given by:

$$E(Y|x) = \pi(x) = \frac{exp(\beta_0+\beta_1 x)}{1+exp(\beta_0+\beta_1 x)} = \frac{1}{1+exp(-(\beta_0+\beta_1 x))}, \quad (4)$$

where β_0 is known as the intercept (the vertical intercept of the line $y = \beta_0+\beta_1 x$) and β_1 is the inverse scale parameter, $\beta_1 x = \frac{1}{s}$. These are the y-intercept and slope of the log-odds as a function of x.

When multiple explanatory variables are present, the model takes the form:

$$P(Y = 1|X) = \frac{1}{1 + exp^{-(\beta_0+\beta_1 X_1+\beta_2 X_2+\ldots+\beta_p X_p)}}. \quad (5)$$

The output of this equation is the estimated probability of the positive class. For modeling purposes, the β parameters that minimize the cost function must be found. The typical cost function is the log-loss function, which for two classes takes is defines as $J(\beta) = -\frac{1}{m} \sum[y_i log(\hat{p_i}) + (1 - y_i) log(1 - \hat{p_i})]$, where y_i is the actual class label and $\hat{p_i}$ is the predicted probability of the positive class for the ith instance.

3 Case Study

3.1 Data Collection and Methods

In this section, the data sources and methodologies employed are described, providing a comprehensive account of the research approach undertaken in the project.

Data. The collection and processing of data from *Cartão Co* database was done using a combination of Structured Query Language (SQL) and Pyspark, a Python API for Apache Spark that enables real-time, large-scale data processing in a distributed environment.

Several datasets were used for different parts of the project. Used transactional and product data from *Co* stores, *Co*, *Co Mo*, *Co Online* and *M Su*, transactional data from partner stores, like *Ga* and *Ib*, and DNA data. This was composed of hourly data, weekly, and monthly data (depending on specific dataset) retrieved for the period between January 2021 and February 2023, comprised of hundreds of millions of transactions and 4.2 million customers. Different parts of the project used different subsets of this data.

As for model training, do to computational effort required to analyze all the data, a representative sample of about 800.000 customers was collected for this purpose.

3.2 Category Clusters and Churn Periods

Data must be communicated across the company different departments, like sales or costumer retention, and so making complex problems simpler to understand helps with communication. With this in mind clustering was proposed as a way to reduce the number of necessary churn periods. By grouping categories we reduce the number of different churn periods mitigating some of the complexity behind the problem.

This section utilized data for the entire year of 2021, and initially the process involved identifying potentially irrelevant categories. Subsequently, we proceeded with the clustering process, which served two purposes: grouping categories with similar behaviors and identifying categories with distinct behaviors and potential outliers.

For this purpose a group of six variables, considered to be capable of representing category behaviour from the available data, were selected. This being Number of Transactions, Number of Customers, Sales, Mean Value Added Tax (VAT), Average Basket and Mean Frequency. All of the variables were grouped by category. Then, before proceeding to the clustering, a heat map was created to observe correlation between variables. This allows to identify variables that could be introducing bias into the models by bringing the same information, or very similar information, into the models and artificially increasing its weight.

After the analysis, highly correlated variables were excluded and a three variable set up was selected, these being Number of Transactions, Average Basket and mean VAT. The number of transactions helps to identify how frequently a customer visits the store, along with providing information on purchasing behaviour. More transactions suggest a higher frequency of visits. Average Basket size helps identify shopping behavior, while VAT serves as a measure of an item's essentially based on the different tax tiers. This setup also offers the advantage of visualization in a three-dimensional space, making it easily understandable by plotting cluster results. For this specific purpose plot was created with the package plotly, that allows for the plot to be freely moved in a digital 3 dimensional space and allows for a easier perception of cluster distribution, with each axis representing one of the three variables.

The clustering techniques were applied to a subset of 59 categories. To determine the optimal value for k in the K-Means algorithm, an elbow plot was created, and the most suitable value was selected. The resulting clusters were evaluated using the silhouette method and further analyzed by an expert. However, upon assessment, it was concluded that the clustering outcome was not satisfactory. As a result, hierarchical clustering (Fig. 5) was employed to establish a new k-value, and the process was repeated. Eventually, a 6-cluster configuration was settled upon, k = 7 was used, but one cluster contained only one category and so was merged into the closest cluster after validation with the respective business department, with the following clusters: Essentials, Side Characters, Pantry Completers, Budget Killers, Delights & Clean, and Beauty & Beyond.

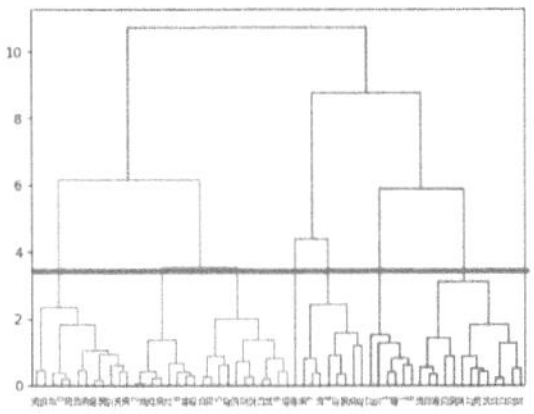

Fig. 5. Resulting dendrogram

Churn Periods. The selection of an optimal churn period is a delicate balancing act, where an excessively short period can lead to inefficient allocation of resources, while an overly extended one may render intervention efforts too late to effectively retain the customer. To ascertain the most appropriate churn periods, a comprehensive analysis of customer behavior spanning the years 2021 and 2022 was undertaken. This analysis involved an examination of the average time intervals between transactions within distinct product or service categories for each individual customer. From this intervals outliers were analyzed using Z-scores and the interquartile range.

3.3 Model Training

The study involved the evaluation of various models to ascertain their efficacy in classifying churners. Three distinct models - Logistic Regression, Decision Trees (DT), and EBM - were tested. To enhance the precision of the analysis, a subset of the training data was addressed, excluding customers with zero sales (0€) in the previous twelve months for the specific category under consideration. This step is crucial in eliminating the potential misclassification of customers who had never engaged in transactions within that category, thus preserving the integrity of the churner classification process. Otherwise, customers who never bought the category before, would be flagged as churners, but this would in fact be a false positive.

Then the dataset was organized chronologically. Subsequently, it was partitioned into distinct training and validation sets, with the training dataset encompassing the initial 80% of observations and the remaining 20% reserved for validation purposes, around 110 million and 27 million transactions respectively. This partitioning prevents any overlap between the training and validation and avoids training on data occurring after the events in the validation set, thereby helping ensure model's robustness and providing better reliability and validity of the findings presented.

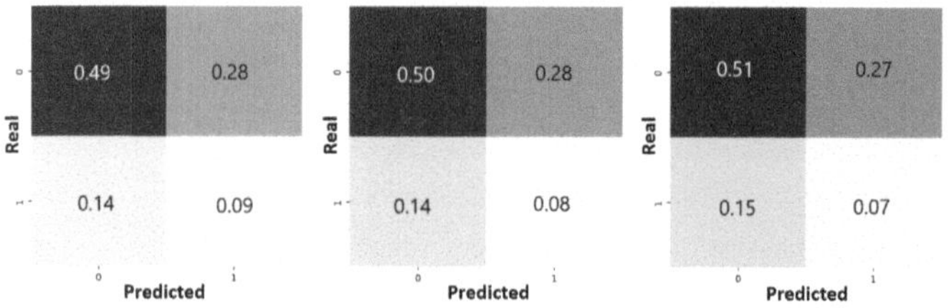

Fig. 6. (From left to right) Confusion matrix for Logistic Regression, Decision Tree and Explainable Boosting Machine

All of the models presented accuracies just above 50% given their particularly poor performance predicting the positive category, with more information available in Fig. 6.

Upon reanalyzing the data a problem was found in one of the features. The mistake was corrected and models were retrained. After some adjustments to hyperparameters the results improved greatly. Despite all of the models performing in line with each other, the EBM is particularly worthy of mention because of it's better ability to correctly predict churners and overall better accuracy. Bellow is shown the comparison of confusion matrix for fruits' models (Fig. 7).

The results remain similar for the other categories with the EBM being more robust and having overall superior performance, closely followed by logistic regression (Fig. 8). For this models, accuracy ranges from around 70% to 78% and AUC scores ranging from 82% to 86%, with very good precision and good recall for the negative class (0). As for the positive class, recall is good, but, except for beers, precision is weak remaining below the 60% mark. This happens because the models have a tendency to over-predict the positive class. This can be problematic, because customers classified as churners will be flagged so the retention department can take action and prevent churn, and that has a cost associated with it. In order to work around this limitation a small code snippet was created in order to allow for a change in the classification threshold. This way, by increasing the threshold we can increase the precision of the positive

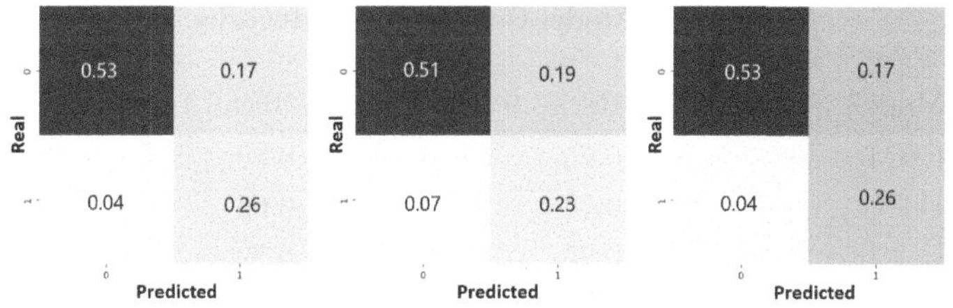

Fig. 7. (From left to right) Confusion matrix for Logistic Regression, Decision Tree and Explainable Boosting Machine, after corrections

class at the cost of recall, and increasing the return on investment. And so, after waiting the results for all the models and categories EBM was the chosen model for all the categories. Even if Logistic Regression could perform in line with EBM, when looking at the AUC metric, EBM is the clear winner.

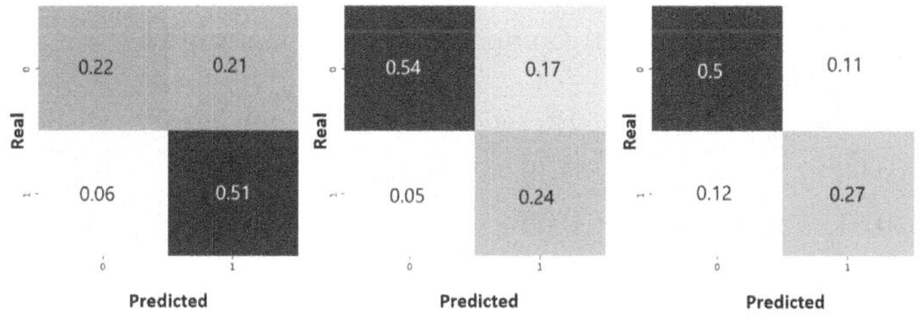

Fig. 8. (From left to right) Confusion matrix for Beers, Cheeses and Clothing Care and Cleaning

Looking into the evaluation metrics previously discussed, the models compare as displayed in Tables 1, 2 and 3, with the 0 and 1 next to recall and precision representing the relevant class.

3.4 Feature Importance

In order to extract feature importance from the model, the interpret package integrates two measures of importance, global and local.

Global importance gives the weight of the fifteen most important features for the model. The first plot is a general score and works by calculating average of the absolute predicted value of each feature for the training dataset. This is, for each feature, it calculates what each training data point would be scored by that feature alone. Then it takes the absolute value of all of these scores, and averages the result, because EBM is an additive model, this method corresponds with which features have the largest impact on predictions in the training set (Fig. 9).

Table 1. Model Comparison Categories

Category	Model	Precision 0	Recall 0	Precision 1	Recall 1	Accuracy	F1 Score
Fruits	EBM	0.93	0.75	0.49	0.80	0.76	0.61
	DT	0.88	0.73	0.42	0.66	0.71	0.51
	Logistic	0.92	0.75	0.48	0.79	0.76	0.60
Cheeses	EBM	0.91	0.77	0.59	0.81	0.78	0.69
	DT	0.70	0.59	0.30	0.41	0.54	0.34
	Logistic	0.70	0.56	0.30	0.44	0.52	0.36
Beers	EBM	0.79	0.52	0.71	0.90	0.73	0.79
	DT	0.58	0.51	0.66	0.73	0.63	0.69
	Logistic	0.75	0.56	0.72	0.86	0.73	0.78
C.C.C.	EBM	0.91	0.57	0.57	0.91	0.70	0.70
	DT	0.80	0.59	0.55	0.78	0.66	0.64
	Logistic	0.90	0.56	0.57	0.90	0.69	0.70

Table 2. EBM Comparison Across Categories

Category	Precision 0	Recall 0	Precision 1	Recall 1	Accuracy	F1 Score	AUC
Fruits	0.93	0.75	0.49	0.80	0.76	0.61	0.86
Cheeses	0.91	0.77	0.59	0.81	0.78	0.69	0.86
Beers	0.79	0.52	0.71	0.90	0.73	0.79	0.82
C.C.C	0.91	0.57	0.57	0.91	0.70	0.70	0.85

Table 3. Model AUC Comparison

Model	Fruits	Cheeses	Beers	C.C.C
EBM	0.86	0.86	0.82	0.85
DT	0.69	0.46	0.69	0.68
Logistic	0.77	0.50	0.71	0.73

By analyzing this features it's possible to derive hypothesis about the behaviour of different categories, specially when the focus is set on the differences between the plots. One very good case is the plot for the Beer category model, Fig. 10. For all of the tested categories the most important feature is gross sales for the specific category, and for all of them but Beers, the second most important feature is *h_month_trx_racio*. For the category Beers the most important feature is *year_month*. This is very interesting information, because the *year_month* feature represents the month of the year signifying that the specific month for which we are running the model has a higher importance than for the other three features, hinting to a more seasonal behaviour in this case.

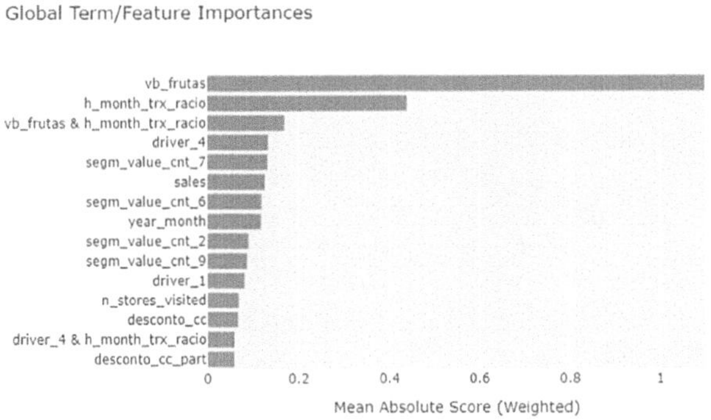

Fig. 9. Summary of the feature importance plot for the model for category Fruits

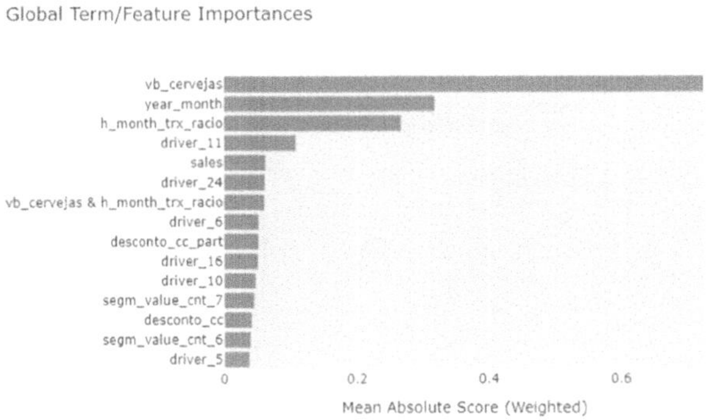

Fig. 10. Summary of the feature importance plot for the model for category Beers

The package also generates individual plots for each of the variables explaining their contribution to the final score. The X axis represents the value taken by the feature and Y-axis represents the log odds, these get then passed through a logit link function to get probability scores at prediction time (Fig. 11).

For the local importance, the package allows the user to see how each of the variables influenced a specific prediction. For each data point the fifteen more important features, for that case, are shown, and for each feature it's corresponding weight. So for each data point the weights would be added and the final value passed through a logit link function to get the probability score. As an example, for the example seen in Fig. 12.

One case where we could see the model reasoning clearly at work is on the wrong predictions. Bellow we see the example of a customer wrongly classified as churner by the model.

In this case (Fig. 13) we can see how a low value for *sales* (6,66€) in *vb_frutas* coupled with a high racio of spending in one month (40% of all expenditure in a month) and the fact that it belongs to the lowest value segment (*segm_value_cnt_9*) pushed the model to classify the customer as a churner with a probability of

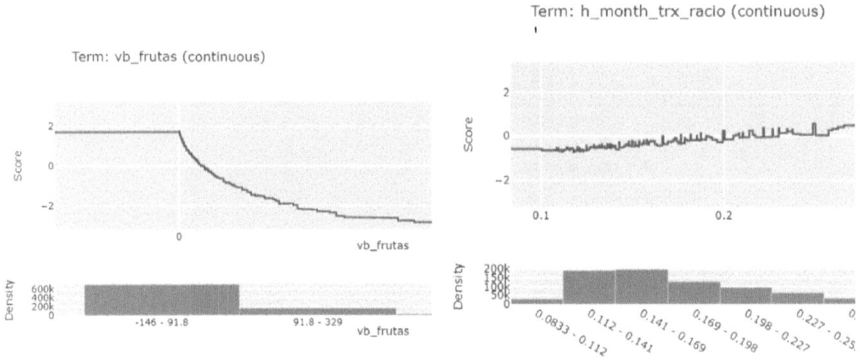

Fig. 11. Snippets of the behaviour for features *vb_frutas* and *h_month_trx_racio*

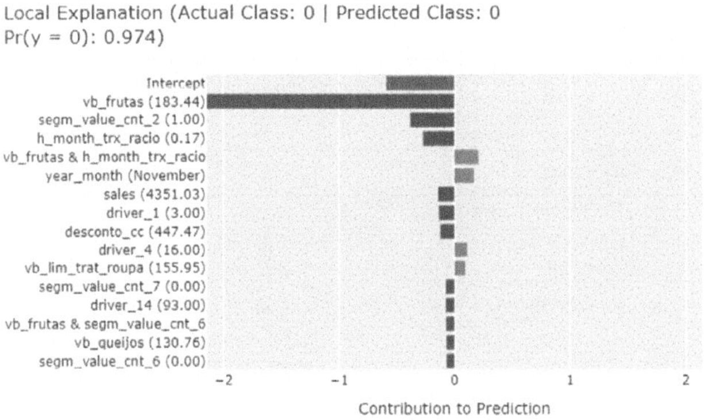

Fig. 12. Local plot for the 3rd observation in the test dataset

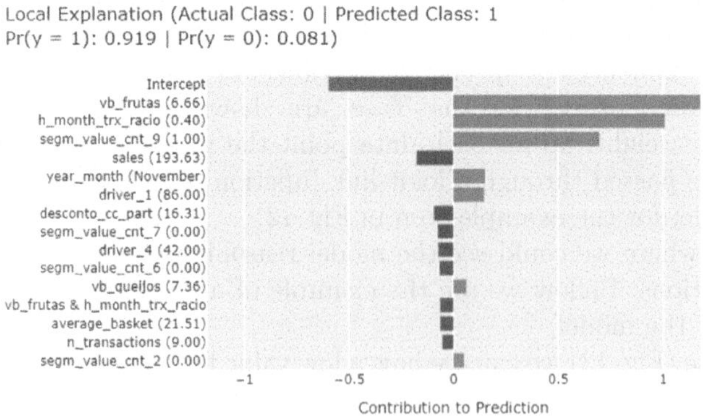

Fig. 13. Local plot for miss classified observation.

91.9%. This kind of errors, even if not optimal, are fairly easy to understand from a decision stand point. Also helps to set the importance of model interpretability for businesses and decision making. This allows the different teams to easily identify factors behind churn and focus on the constructions of micro strategies oriented towards this specific factors for specific customers.

4 Conclusions

As discussed before, the ability to predict churn is of great value for a company. This allows for more efficient retention campaigns and better leverage of customer data. In this work, the proposed approach was to seek accurate predictions for churn while retaining explainability.

In the first phase of the project we set the foundations of the project. Churn and customer were defined by analyzing transactional data for the customers in the retail stores and then clusters of categories were created, going from 196 categories at the start to 6 clusters by the end, in order to decrease the number of churn periods required. Churn periods were calculated and a sample was collected. Secondly, 4 pilot categories were selected and models were trained and its results compared using several metrics. Given it's superior performance over the selected categories EBM was the selected model. All models created had a good accuracy, with values between 70% and 78%, and AUC score, between 82% and 86%, despite some weaknesses in the positive class precision. Even then the models were good in capturing the bulk of the churners.

The low precision in classifying the positive class could be problematic in the future, and so a simple to implement, preemptive work around was created to mitigate this problem, by allowing the classification threshold to be manipulated in order to warrant a more precise allocation of funds, should the need arise. Finally the feature importance was analyzed and it's predictive ability validated by opposing the models decision process to a human decision process with the access to the same data.

5 Future Work

After analysing the variable importance for the models one thing is notorious. The variables the model uses to predict churn are the ones that better describe the behaviour of a bad customer. Low sales, a high amount of total sales in just one month, low value segment, amongst others. This means that the performance of the model in predicting churn for the higher value customers is probably going to be lower, and some light preliminary testing seems to point in that way. This means that in the future a new model should be trained on just this subsection of customers, or if, like in this case, it's the goal to have one model for all of the customers, then the features should be revised. Features that describe the behaviour around competitors, like distance to competitors stores, change in the number of competitors stores in the customer place of residence, can be a good starting point. This approach was attempted during the project, but the lack of suitable data at the time prevented its implementation.

Acknowledgements. A. Manuela Gonçalves was partially financed by Portuguese Funds through FCT (Fundação para a Ciência e a Tecnologia) within the Projects UIDB/00013/2020 (https://doi.org/10.54499/UIDB/00013/2020) and UIDP/00013/2020 (https://doi.org/10.54499/UIDP/00013/2020) of CMAT-UM.

References

1. The Consumer Goods Forum *Portugal: A Retail Snapshot.* The Consumer Goods Forum (2018). https://www.theconsumergoodsforum.com/blog/2018/03/14/portugal-retail-snapshot/. Accessed 18 Feb 2023
2. Idris, A., Rizwan, M., Khan, A.: Churn prediction in telecom using Random Forest and PSO based data balancing in combination with various feature selection strategies. Comput. Electr. Eng. **38**(6), 1808–1819 (2012). https://doi.org/10.1016/j.compeleceng.2012.09.001
3. He, H., Garcia, E.A.: Learning from imbalanced data. IEEE Trans. Knowl. Data Eng. **21**(9), 1263–1284 (2009). https://doi.org/10.1109/tkde.2008.239
4. Vafeiadis, T., Diamantaras, K.I., Sarigiannidis, G., Chatzisavvas, K.C.: A comparison of machine learning techniques for customer churn prediction. Simul. Model. Pract. Theory **55**, 1–9 (2015). https://doi.org/10.1016/j.simpat.2015.03.003
5. Hastie, T., Tibshirani, R., Friedman, J.: The Elements of Statistical Learning: Data Mining, Inference, and Prediction, 2nd edn. Springer, New York (2009). https://doi.org/10.1007/978-0-387-84858-7
6. Breiman, L., Schapire, R.: Random forests. Mach. Learn. **45**, 5–32 (2001)
7. Cortes, C., Vapnik, V.: Support-vector networks. Mach. Learn. **20**(3), 273–297 (1995). https://doi.org/10.1007/bf00994018
8. Goodfellow, I., Bengio, Y., Courville, A.: Deep learning. Genet. Program Evolvable Mach. **19**, 305–307 (2017). https://doi.org/10.1007/s10710-017-9314-z
9. Zhang, H.: The optimality of Naive Bayes. In: American Association for Artificial Intelligence. Seventeenth International Florida Artificial Intelligence Research Society Conference (2004)
10. Lemmens, A., Croux, C.: Bagging and boosting classification trees to predict churn. J. Mark. Res. **43**(2), 276–286 (2006). https://doi.org/10.1509/jmkr.43.2.276
11. InterpretML Team: Documentation. interpret.ml (n.d.). https://interpret.ml/docs/getting-started. Accessed 11 Jan 2023
12. Nori, H., Caruana, R., Bu, Z., Shen, J., Kulkarni, J.: Accuracy, Interpretability, and Differential Privacy via Explainable Boosting (2021). http://proceedings.mlr.press/v139/nori21a/nori21a.pdf. Accessed 22 Aug 2023

Cluster Analysis for Two HoReCa Channels of a Large Grocery Retail Company

Sandra M. Aleixo[1,2](✉), Bruno Pereira[1], Tiago Fernandes[1], José Rodrigues[3], and Miguel Pina[3]

[1] Department of Mathematics, ISEL – Instituto Superior de Engenharia de Lisboa, IPL – Instituto Politécnico de Lisboa, Rua Conselheiro Emídio Navarro, 1, 1959-007 Lisboa, Portugal
{sandra.aleixo,bruno.pereira}@isel.pt, A48695@alunos.isel.pt

[2] Faculdade de Ciências da Universidade de Lisboa, CEAUL – Centro de Estatística e Aplicações da Universidade de lisboa, Bloco C6, Piso 4, 1749-016 Lisboa, Portugal

[3] Jerónimo Martins, Rua Actor António Silva, 7, 1649-033 Lisboa, Portugal
{jose.manuel.rodrigues,miguel.pina}@jeronimo-martins.com

Abstract. This work was developed within the scope of industrial mathematics, in partnership with a large grocery retail company in the Portuguese market, Jerónimo Martins, in particular with Recheio, the largest chain of Cash&Carry stores in Portugal. The objective was to segment the Families (groups of products in the marketing structure) in Recheio's HoReCa channel, into disjoint sets that can be interpreted by the business. Initially, database manipulation, preprocessing and choice of variables to use were carried out. Then followed the segmentation phase carried out in two ways: through the total HoReCa channel and through the online HoReCa channel. A clear separation of the company's products was achieved using various Cluster Analysis methods such as K-Means, K-Medoids and Hierarchical. Different groups were obtained, based on common characteristics of the Families, with the aim of better understanding the company's market, helping to make strategic decisions and develop more effective marketing and production plans. The work involved the use of several types of software, namely Excel, SQL, Python and R.

Keywords: Cluster analysis · Database manipulation · Preprocessing · Retail · HoReCa channel · Industrial mathematics

1 Introduction

In order to strengthen their market position during recent years, the main challenge for retail companies is to maintain a sustained growth in customers and sales of both the Traditional Retail and HoReCa (Hotels, Restaurants and Catering) channels, in very competitive market conditions, due to the uncertainty

O. Gervasi et al. (Eds.): ICCSA 2024 Workshops, LNCS 14815, pp. 337–356, 2024.
https://doi.org/10.1007/978-3-031-65154-0_21

caused by the economic environment. This can be achieved using different marketing strategies, namely those that improve customer experience, achieve customer retention and grow their customer base. Thus, there is a growing significance placed on customer-oriented marketing. The rise of individual-focused approaches, particularly in online commerce, is rendering conventional mass marketing in this sector progressively outdated, given the feasibility of tailoring efforts to specific customer needs. This approach underscores the necessity of cultivating a profound comprehension of the customer's buying behavior instead of its demographics or location, for example.

One of the biggest companies in Portugal is Jerónimo Martins, which operates in the food distribution and specialized retail business. The group is present in Portugal, Poland and Colombia and, currently, around 70% of revenue comes from Biedronka, in Poland. The present work is based on data provided by the Market Analysis and Studies section of the Marketing Department of Recheio, one of the businesses of Jerónimo Martins, which has 4% of the revenue of the group. The company set two goals when they proposed this study: the purchasing behavior of its clients in the two HoReCa channels and the comprehension of the distinction in performance of the online HoReCa channel in comparison to the total HoReCa channel.

Instead of dividing a company's customer base into distinct and homogeneous groups or segments based on shared characteristics to develop a suitable marketing strategy [2], the pandemic has caused retailers to focus on product grouping based on customer buying pattern, in order to adapt to changes in customers lives and work, since most corporations encouraged remote work and online collaboration [3]. There are three main requirements that retailers must comply with if they want to analyze customer behavior: the ability to collect and store customer data, a suitable algorithm to characterize the collected data, and an efficient strategy to apply the extracted characterization successfully into the business model. We will focus on the first two items using suitable preprocessing methods and cluster analysis, based on the data provided by Recheio.

Cluster analysis is a data analysis technique applied in several fields of study, in which its main goal is to organize collected datasets or observations into groups or clusters based on the similarity between them, i.e. it identifies underlying groupings and patterns into subsets in a way that members within the same subset are more similar to each other than to those in other subsets [7].

The process of cluster analysis involves assigning data points to non overlapping clusters so that the within-cluster similarity is maximized, while the between-cluster similarity is minimized. This is achieved analysing how two data points or objects are alike with respect to certain attributes or characteristics such as the euclidean distance or the correlation coefficient, among others [10]. Various algorithms are used to perform cluster analysis. In this article, we focus on K-means, K-medoids, and Hierarchical clustering.

K-means clustering works by iteratively assigning data points to groups based on their distance to the cluster centroid and then minimizing the within-cluster variance by optimizing the centroids. In the end, the sum of squared distances between data points and their assigned centroids is minimum [8,11]. Since this approach is sensible to outliers, an alternative approach designed to identify representative data points, known as medoids, can be used within each cluster [9]. Defining a predetermined number of medoids, the algorithm aims to minimize the sum of distances between those points and the remaining data, selecting, in each iteration, the optimal medoids. This algorithm offers robustness to outliers and noise in the data. Hierarchical clustering is a technique used to organize large datasets to form hierarchical groups of mutually exclusive subsets, each of which has members that have maximally affinity with respect to a specific attribute or property, in order to better consider and understand relations within those datasets [14], producing a nested set of clusters, where the relationship between them is represented in a dendrogram. This clustering method may assume that all data are in the same cluster and, in each step, separates the clusters until each data point forms its own cluster (divisive), or starts with individual data points as separate clusters and iteratively merges the most similar clusters until all data points belong to a single cluster (agglomerative).

This paper is organized as follows. In Sect. 2, we detail which variables are present in the data collected by Recheio, the preprocessing method and data refining using Python, detailing the variables and the reasoning behind the decision of considering some of the product Families as outliers, as well as establishing the optimal number of clusters. In Sect. 3, we implement the aforementioned clustering methods to valid data and obtained a clear segmentation of Recheio Families, based on descriptive metrics of their behavior. Finally, in Sect. 4, we discuss the results and draw some conclusions which helped the decision making process of more effective marketing and production plans.

2 Data Wrangling

The original data provided by Recheio for both HoReCa channels consists of transactions, made during a period of twelve months in 2022 and 2023, of each product sold by the company, which we call the Families, that can be linked to individual customers. These customers are defined in two different ways: a paying customer, who is uniquely identified by a reference (the NIF) across all Recheio stores, or as a profiled customer where an internal code is used per store to identify the customer. Hence, one paying customer can have multiple customer profiles in the same store since Recheio treats them as a different customer due to different delivery addresses, for example.

Some variables of interest are summarized in Table 1, some of which are related with the paying customer and others with the profiled customer. All variables are numerical except "family_id" and "family", which are categorical.

Due to their relevance in this work, we single out two variables. The first one is freq_payer, a ratio between the total amount of purchases from customers (payer or profiled) divided by the total number of days in the analyzed period. It represents the average amount of days between purchases in a given Family. We also define pene_cust, which is the customer penetration, a measure which gives the percentage of Recheio's customers (payer or profiled) who purchased

Table 1. Variables of the Case Study.

Name	Description
family_id	Unique value to represent each Family
family	Description of each Family
tot_sales	Total sales by Family, in euros
nm_tickets	Number of tickets, meaning purchases per Family
cust_payer	Number of paying customers per Family
spent_payer	Average spending per payer, in euros, within the specific Families
cust_profile	Number of registered customers per Family
freq_profile	Time difference, in days, between purchases per Family
spent_profile	Average spending per customer, in euros, within the specific Families

a given Family during the analyzed period. It ranges between 0 and 1, and if it is related with a payer customer, the variable is called pene_cust_payer. On the other hand, if it is associated to a profiled customer, the variable is designated by pene_cust_profile. For example, if pene_cust_payer for some Family is zero it means that no Recheio's customers payer purchased any product of this Family.

The values of the variables were obtained from the database through queries in SQL language. Then, it was necessary to preprocess them, analysing missing data, duplicate values and the existence of outliers. We found out that there were no null or repeated values, enabling the start of outlier search after the variables selection. The organized data was used in the applied methodologies. For each variable (column in the matrices), we had 155 and 124 Families (number of rows in the matrices, one for each Family), for the total and the online channel, respectively.

3 Statistical Analysis

We begin this statistical study by selecting variables that are not highly correlated, since this can help to reduce redundancy and multicollinearity in the data, improving the performance of the clustering algorithm, [6]. Subsequently, we performed a brief descriptive statistical analysis to characterize those variables and identify extreme outliers, which are under consideration for removal. Finally, we apply the K-Means, K-Medoids, and Hierarchical unsupervised machine learning clustering algorithms to obtain a segmentation of the Families of both HoReCa channels.

The focus of Recheio was on the payer customers, therefore this work will only involve the variables "cust_payer", "freq_payer" and "spent_payer", beside the general ones "tot_sales" and "nm_tickets". Since the variable "pene_cust_payer" is proportional to cust_payer, we also replace the latter by the former.

3.1 Total HoReCa Channel

Variable Selection. In cluster analysis, it is important not to use highly correlated redundant variables. The selection of variables to include in cluster analysis regulate the characteristics of the clusters themselves. If the variables exhibit significant multicollinearity, they interfere with the calculation of dissimilarity measures, namely Euclidean distance, hence the reliability of the results is not guaranteed [13].

Not all variables observed in a study are always interesting for cluster analysis. Some do not contribute to the objective of the study and others are redundant as the characteristic they represent is strongly correlated with other variables. Taking this argument into account, these redundant variables can be eliminated [1]. The inclusion of redundant variables complicates or even masks the clustering process [5].

In cluster analysis, when variables exhibit collinearity, certain variables wield greater weight than others. In instances where two variables are perfectly correlated, they are essentially similar. Consequently, they are duplicated within the dataset, doubling the weight they carry compared to other variables in cluster analysis. As a result, the resultant solution may skew disproportionately towards these variables, potentially posing new problems if this isn't taken into consideration.

Using Shapiro-Wilk test, we conclude that the normality assumption for the five variables is not verified. In fact, the histograms of the main diagonal of Fig. 1 already suggested that this was the outcome. Therefore, we opted for Spearman's coefficient to evaluate the correlation of each pair of variables among the five existing ones [13], and the associated test to the correlation significance. The p-values being close to zero leads to the rejection of the null hypothesis so we can conclude that we have significant correlations.

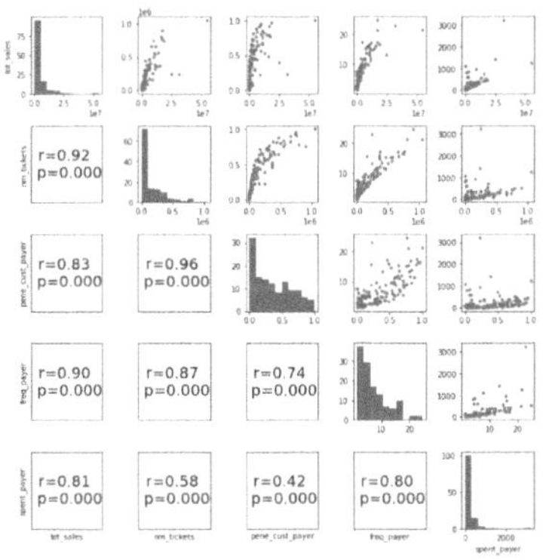

Fig. 1. Correlations Matrix.

Above the diagonal of the correlation matrix in Fig. 1, there are scatter plots which relate every possible pair of variables. In the lower triangular part, we have the value of sample correlation coefficient between each pair of variables with the p-value associated with the hypothesis test for the nullity of the population correlation coefficient, to assess the significance of their correlation.

As previously mentioned, there are two very important variables in this study from the Recheio company's perspective, namely freq_payer and pene_cust_payer. These variables were chosen to build the clusters due to their historical relevance and wide acceptance as key business metrics in internal decision business making by the company's functional teams, for example, when making decisions about the positioning in store of a specific line of products. It is also important for the company to be able to easily and consistently measure the impact of these business decisions, so having available a small set of consensual variables is crucial for that objective.

It can be assumed that two variables are highly correlated if the correlation coefficient between them exceeds 0.8 [4]. In Fig. 1, the correlation coefficient value for the aforementioned variables is 0.74, hence we conclude that they are not strongly correlated for cluster analysis. Note that the variable spent_payer is also not strongly correlated with pene_cust_payer ($r = 0.42$), but it is strongly correlated with the variable freq_payer, thus it should not be included in this analysis. Similarly, the variables nm_tickets and tot_sales are strongly correlated with the variables freq_payer and pene_cust_payer ($r = 0.87$ and $r = 0.96$, respectively, for nm_tickets; $r = 0.90$ and $r = 0.83$, respectively, for tot_sales), therefore they should also be excluded from the cluster analysis.

Descriptive Analysis. A descriptive analysis of the two variables is conducted to characterize them and to check for the existence of outliers. In Fig. 2 and Table 2 we have the boxplots and the descriptive metrics of the two variables.

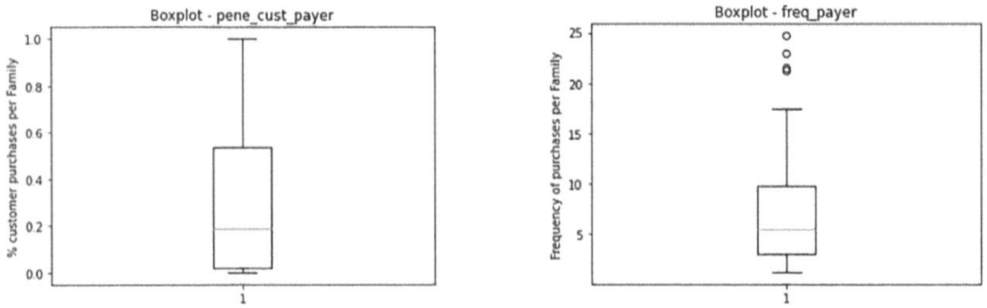

Fig. 2. Boxplots for pene_cust_payer and freq_payer for the total HoReCa channel.

Regarding the variable pene_cust_payer, the average is 0.208, which means that the average percentage of Recheio's customers payer who purchased a given Family during the analyzed period is around 21% in the total channel. Also in location terms, data round about 0.185, being 50% of the observations less

Table 2. Descriptive metrics of total HoReCa channel variables.

pene_cust_payer	value	freq_payer	value
Average	0.208		
Median	0.185	Median	5.446
Standard Deviation	0.291		
Minimum	0.000	Minimum	1.199
Maximum	1.000	Maximum	24.683
1st Quartile	0.020	1st Quartile	2.990
3rd Quartile	0.536	3rd Quartile	9.694
Inter-Quartile Range	0.516	Inter-Quartile Range	6.704
Coefficient of variation	101.301%	Coefficient of variation (resistant)	78.948%
Skewness coefficient	0.720	Bowley coefficient (resistant)	0.267
Kurtosis coefficient	−0.786	Kurtosis coefficient (resistant)	1.500

than this value and the other half greater than it. Since the median value is closer to the first quartile and the right tail is longer, the data exhibit positive skewness, confirmed by the value of the skewness coefficient, indicating that pene_cust_payer data are concentrated at lower values. For dispersion, data show a strong variability as 50% of the central values vary 0.516 at most (high IQR value length of the box), confirmed with the high value of the variation coefficient around 101%. Furthermore, in boxplot, there are no outliers. So, to characterize the sample, other nonresistant measures that use all the information contained in the data can be calculated. For the observed data, the value of the pene_cust_payer variable is on average 0.208, with a variability of 0.291 around this value. About sample location for the Freq_payer variable, the values are around 5 and a half days, with 50% of the observations being lower than this value and the rest higher. Regarding dispersion, the values present a great deal of variability, increased by the existence of outliers, and confirmed by the high value of the coefficient of variation of around 79%. The asymmetry is clearly positive since median is closer to left side of the box, right tail is much longer and there are outliers on the right, confirmed by the positive value of the Bowley coefficient. We use resistant measures to characterize the sample, since outliers exist.

Thus, as outliers are present for the variable freq_payer, a Python program was created to find which Families are outliers, to wit: fresh vegetables, fresh fish from aquaculture and basic products. Since these outliers are all mild (as they fall within the bounds of the inner fences of the boxplot) and these Families are actually very relevant to Recheio, it was decided to keep these observations in the sample. The relevance is due to the corresponding high number of sales and to follow the business strategy.

On the other hand, due to low sales (less than €10000), the company decided to remove all Families that don't reach this sales threshold, as these are indeed insignificant for the company's business. The number of Families removed is around 30 and they are mostly related to leisure, hygiene and personal care products, food and appliances.

Cluster Analysis. We made the segmentation of Families resorting to the aforementioned cluster analysis algorithms. One of the first things we need to determine is the most appropriate number of clusters to use. There aren't clear rules, just a comprehensive set of guidelines we can use. For example, if the main goal is to identify market segments, a certain number of clusters proposed by management is the way to go. The number of clusters can also be decided using a dendogram, for hierarchical clustering, or plotting the ratio of total within-group variance against variance between each group, for non-hierarchical clustering [12]. In the present case, we will use the Elbow Method to guide us. According to Fig. 3, we can observe that the "elbow" is verified for three clusters, and the inertia is decreasing more slowly above this number, until the reduction in inertia becomes much less considerable from six clusters onwards. We are going to consider six clusters even because this number of clusters enable internal comparison in Recheio with similar cluster analysis in the companies of the group, which are focused in segmenting groups of products which also use penetration and frequency as variables. In fact, this result was in line with the view of the retail company in business context, since it is suitable for the subsequent comparison between HoReCa channels.

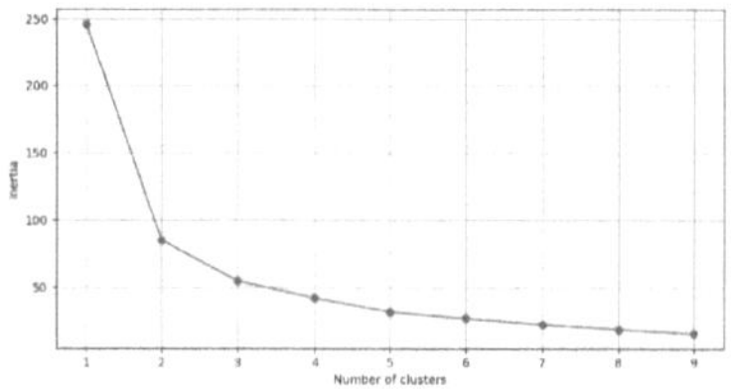

Fig. 3. Elbow method - total channel

In Fig. 4, we plot the graphical representations of the six clusters obtained by the several methods used. The main goal is to analyze which method provides a better separation of groups, which correspond to the best segmentation. Observing the scatter plots, there are two methods that seem to produce good clusters, cohesive and well separated: the Hierarchical with Ward Linkage criteria and the K-Medoids. But let's validate the results by analysing the silhouette graphs and the average silhouette score values presented in Fig. 5. Each observation or element i from each cluster has its own silhouette score $s(i)$. A large $s(i)$ (almost 1) means that this element is very well clustered, a small $s(i)$ (around 0) means that the observation i lies between two clusters and a negative $s(i)$ means that the element i is probably placed in the wrong cluster. After computing the silhouette coefficient for each point from each cluster, the average of all elements scores is the average silhouette score (red line in the Silhouette Plots on Fig. 5).

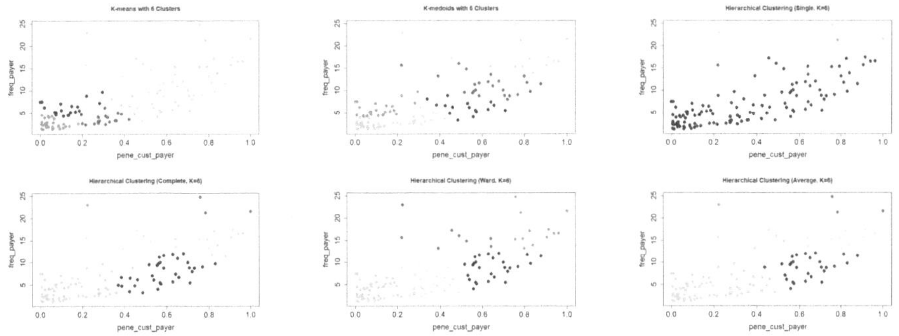

Fig. 4. K-Means, K-Medoids, Hierachical Clustering with Single, Complete, Ward and Average linkage, in the total HoReCA channel - 6 clusters.

Analysing the silhouette plots for the six methods in Fig. 5, we can take some conclusions. The Hierarchical Method with Single Linkage is the worst choice because there is a cluster with almost all elements which has many points with negative scores (misclassified) and each of the other five clusters has only one element with null score, besides that the average silhouette score is low (0.22). The K-Means Method has a low average silhouette score (0.13) and there are many misclassified elements in all clusters, so it is not a good choice. The Hierarchical Methods with Complete and Average Linkage, although having good average silhouette scores (0.48 and 0.5), higher than the Hierarchical Method with Ward Linkage, have a cluster much bigger than the others and have also some misclassified elements. From the analysis of both: the scatter plots and Silhouette plots, the two methods that produce the most cohesive and well separated clusters are the Hierarchical with Ward Linkage Criteria and the K-Medoids. For these clustering methods, all clusters have several points above the average score (red line), even if there are a few points with negative scores (misclassified) and both methods allow to obtain more homogeneous width for almost all the clusters, which means that the clusters have similar sizes. However, we consider that the clusters obtained by the Hierarchical Method with Ward Linkage are our choice in this work for the total channel, because the average silhouette score for this method (0.41) is slightly higher than for the K-Medoids (0.38).
Analysing the distribution of Families across clusters obtained by the best chosen method, it can be seen that: Cluster 1 includes the following Families: frozen fish and seafood, ready-made food products, breakfast goods, snacks and cafeteria products, accessories and cleaning products, packaging/preserving products and raw materials, and body hygiene products; Cluster 2 has Families of fish and dried cod, more specific meats (lamb and goat, small animals and special beef), meals, cold cuts, pastries, daily milk and vegetable drinks, cat/dog products, restaurant drinks and foreign wines; the Families in Cluster 3 cover body hygiene products, kitchen and household items, packaged cakes, stationery products, air fresheners, disinfection, cleaning and extermination products, and health and healthy food items; Cluster 4 aggregates grocery products, beauty

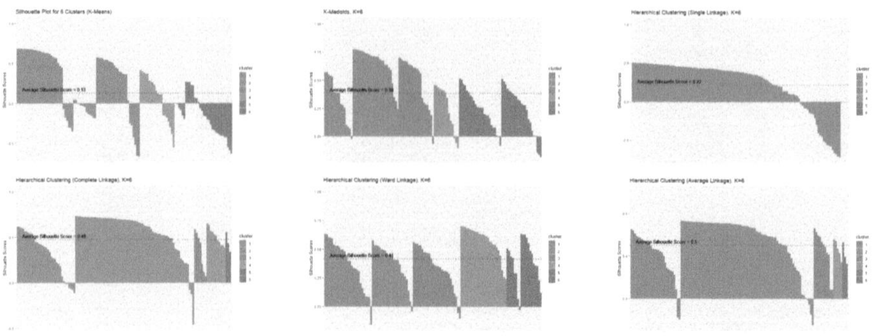

Fig. 5. Silhouette Plots for total HoReCa channel with 6 clusters, for the six cluster analysis methods.

and personal hygiene products, uniforms and clothing, pet products, refreshing drinks, natural flowers and field/beach and garden items, household appliances, lighting, image and car items, and facility cleaning products; Cluster 5 has fresh products, namely poultry, beef and pork meat, fresh wild fish, fresh aquaculture fish, eggs, cold cuts, fruit and vegetables, drinks, preserved products, conservation vegetables, sweet desserts; Cluster 6 contains current and still wines, beers, spirits, coffee shop drinks, water, festive and disposable items, paper products, dish and household cleaning products, icecreams, bakery, dairy products and food fats.

For each of the six clusters, we computed statistical metrics for each variable to characterize each of these clusters and to understand their properties. The statistical metrics in Table 3 provide an overview of trends and distributions of values in each cluster. Also, in Fig. 6a, we plot two parallel boxplots about the 6 clusters concerning the variable pene_cust_payer. The Clusters 5 and 6 stand out for having the highest medians, 0.772 and 0.665, respectively. Therefore, Families belonging to these two clusters have higher values for the weight of each Family relative to the total weight of the total channel Families. On the other hand, Clusters 2 and 4 have very low medians, 0.074 and 0.059, respectively. In terms of dispersion, it is noteworthy that the Cluster 5 has the highest dispersion followed by Cluster 1. In Clusters 2, 3 and 4, the dispersion is similar. These three clusters have the median closest to the first quartile, indicating positive skewness i.e., concentration of the pene_cust_payer variable in low values. Conversely, Clusters 1, 5 and 6 have negative skewness i.e., concentration in high values. Cluster 5 has the greatest inter-quartile range equal to 0.339, meaning that 50% of the sample central values vary, at most, approximately 0.34. None of the clusters have outliers.

The parallel boxplots and statistical metrics for the variable freq_payer are presented in Fig. 6b and Table 3, respectively.

Table 3. Statistical Metrics of pene_cust_payer and freq_payer in HoReCa total

Cluster	Mean_p	Med_p	Min_p	Max_p	St Dev_p	IQR_p	Med_f	Min_f	Max_f	IQR_f
1	0.478	0.497	0.221	0.709	0.146	0.221	6.574	4.011	9.666	1.539
2	0.090	0.074	0.000	0.196	0.061	0.099	5.069	3.665	7.460	1.513
3	0.334	0.316	0.257	0.485	0.066	0.090	3.262	2.352	4.980	1.103
4	0.070	0.059	0.005	0.216	0.061	0.078	2.108	1.199	2.881	0.665
5	0.693	0.772	0.219	1.000	0.237	0.339	15.812	13.188	24.683	2.140
6	0.669	0.665	0.516	0.877	0.106	0.155	9.886	7.981	12.040	2.267

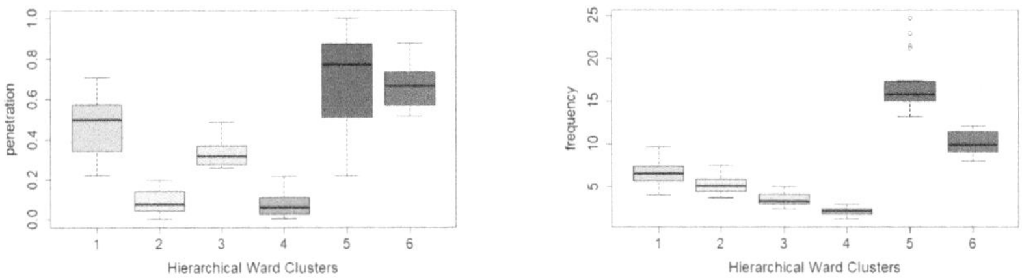

(a) total_channel - pene_cust_payer (b) total_channel - freq_payer

Fig. 6. Boxplots of the total channel.

Analysing Fig. 6b and Table 3, the Cluster 5 is emphasized in localization terms because it has the highest median and it is the only one that has outliers. The median value is about 16 days, which means that half of the Families in this cluster have a time between two purchases (for the payer customer) that is a maximum of 16 days and the rest have times longer than that value. Clusters 3, 5 and 6 exhibit positive skewness, meaning the data concentrates on lower values. The Clusters 5 and 6 are the ones that show the greatest inter-quartiles ranges, therefore, they are the clusters in which the variable freq_payer presents the highest variability. These inter-quartiles ranges with values of 2.140 and 2.267, respectively, mean that an half of the products related to Families in these clusters, corresponding to central values of the freq_payer variable, are purchased by payer costumers at most with a difference of around 2 days.

3.2 Online HoReCa Channel

Variable Selection. Regarding the variable selection process for the online HoReCa channel, we obtained the same results and selected the same two variables for the study: pene_cust_payer and freq_payer.

Descriptive Analysis. A descriptive analysis of the two variables is performed to characterize them and to check for the existence of outliers. Here we make only a brief analysis because it is analogous to the other made for the total channel. In mean terms, the values of pene_cust_payer for the online channel round about 0.12, and have a high variability (coefficient of variation of 139%) and there are some outliers to the right). For the variable freq_payer, the times between product sales are around 4 days but there is also high variability (coefficient of variation of 81%). Both variables have a positive skewness, meaning a higher concentration on small values.

In Fig. 7, we show the boxplots for the two variables, and in Table 4 we have the comparable descriptive metrics.

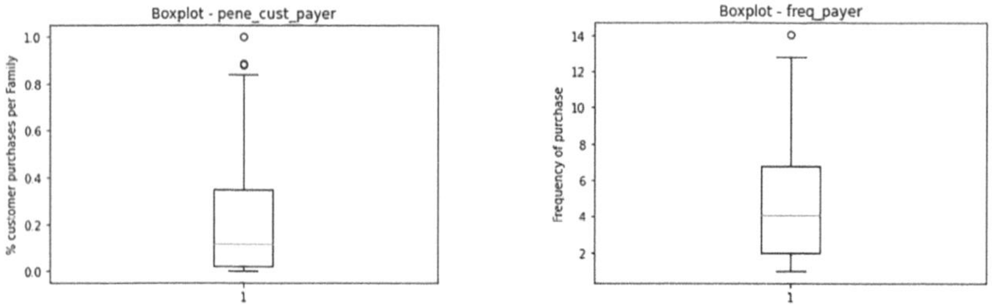

Fig. 7. Boxplots for pene_cust_payer and freq_payer for the online HoReCa channel.

Table 4. Descriptive metrics of online HoReCa channel variables.

pene_cust_payer	value	freq_payer	value
Median	0.117	Median	4.076
Minimum	0.002	Minimum	1.000
Maximum	1.000	Maximum	14.034
1st Quartile	0.020	1st Quartile	2.000
3rd Quartile	0.351	3rd Quartile	6.799
Inter-Quartile Range	0.331	Inter-Quartile Range	4.799
Coefficient of variation (resistant)	139.390%	Coefficient of variation (resistant)	81.114%
Bowley coefficient (resistant)	0.412	Bowley coefficient (resistant)	0.135
Kurtosis coefficient (resistant)	1.500	Kurtosis coefficient (resistant)	1.500

Cluster Analysis. Now with data of online HoReCa channel, we want also to group Families in separate clusters, using the same analysis algorithms used before for the data of total HoReCa channel: K-Means, K-Medoids, and Hierarchical.

Once again, the number of clusters to use will be defined based on the Elbow Method in Fig. 8 attending also to the business needs and objectives.

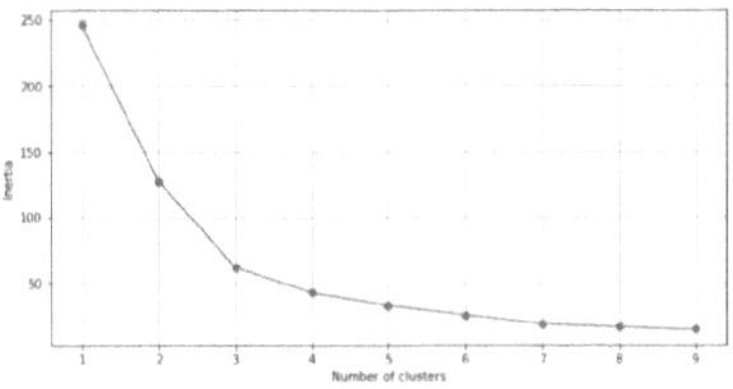

Fig. 8. Elbow method - online channel

Based on Fig. 8, the conclusion about the number of clusters is similar to the one made for the total channel. So by the same reasons presented before we choose to use six clusters, even to later be able to compare the results obtained for the two channels as intended.

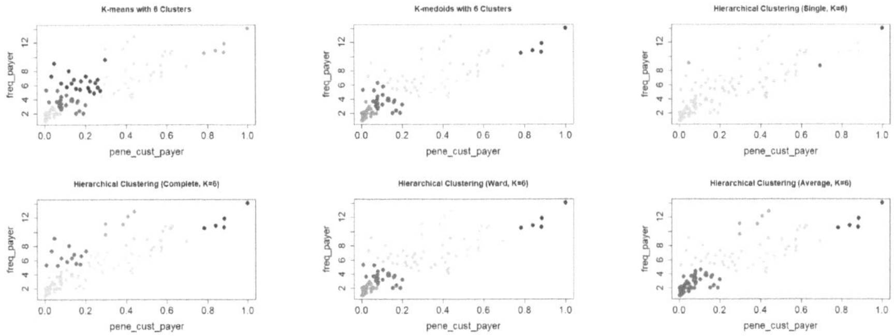

Fig. 9. K-Means, K-Medoids, Hierarchical Clustering with Single, Complete, Ward and Average Linkage, in the online HoReCA channel - 6 clusters. (Color figure online)

For the online channel, observing the scatter plots of Fig. 9, the choice of the most efficient method to obtain the best clusters is not so clear. Almost all methods seems to produce reasonable results, except the Hierarchical Method with Single Linkage. In fact, this method does not clearly produce acceptable results again, as it produces a huge cluster and the others with very few elements. However, looking more closely, the K-Means Method has some elements that do not clearly belong to a given cluster and there is a certain mix. The K-Medoids Method has two clusters (green and blue) whose elements are more dispersed. The Hierarchical Method with Ward Linkage has a group (the yellow one) that is separated in two parts with another cluster in the middle (the cyan one). The Hierarchical Method with Average Linkage is better but some elements of the yellow cluster are surrounded by cyan points of another cluster. In reality, the Hierarchical Method with Complete Linkage seems to be the one that has more cohesive clusters but well separated from each other, so it appears to be the best method for the online HoReCa data.

We will use Silhouette Plots on Fig. 10 to validate these conclusions. In this case the plot related to the Hierarchical Method with Single Linkage confirms the bad results and it is similar to the correspondent plot in the total HoReCa case. For the other five methods all the Silhouette plots are quite similar, they have a bigger cluster and some of them have clusters with many points below the red line (average silhouette score), but the values of the average silhouette score are all very alike, however it is really the Hierarchical Method with Complete Linkage which has the highest value (0.5). So we consider the clusters produced by this method for the online channel.

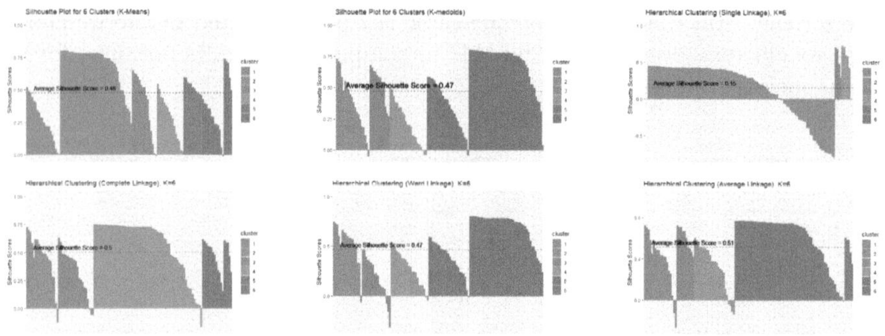

Fig. 10. Silhouette Plots for online HoReCa channel with 6 clusters, for the six cluster analysis methods. (Color figure online)

The composition of the clusters obtained from Hierarchical method with Ward Linkage is as follows: Cluster 1 has essentially Families related to fresh fruits and vegetables, preserved vegetables and some type of desserts; Cluster 2 is formed by Families of healthy food and vegetable drinks, poultry, beef and pork, appetizers, food fats, fresh aquaculture fish, packaged cakes, seafood, meals, bakery, ice-creams, still wines, beers, spirits and water. The cluster also includes cleaning accessories and products for dishes and clothes, as well as party items and packaging and conservation products; some of the Families in Cluster 3 are refreshing and warm drinks, current wines, dairy products, eggs, breakfast goods; Cluster 4 comprises a wide variety of Families, namely food Families as whole dried cod, more specific meats (small animals, special breed beef, lamb and goat), fresh wild fish and frozen fish, seafood, frozen meals, grocery and delicatessen products, pastries and milk of the day; cleaning Families such as air fresheners, disinfectants, extermination products and various types of cleaning. It also holds other types of items, specifically for the home and kitchen, pets, country/beach and garden items, hygiene, beauty and health products, uniforms and clothing, household appliances, lighting, image and automobile items; Cluster 5 owns Families of products for cats and dogs and coffee shop drinks; Cluster 6 carries Families of preserved products, basic products, condiments, milk and sweet desserts.

As was done for the total HoReCa channel, an analysis was carried out regarding the two variables under study for each of the six clusters defined for the HoReCa online channel. Firstly, for the variable pene_cust_payer, Fig. 11a and Table 5 can be observed. In terms of location, Families in Cluster 1 are those that clearly reach the highest values for the pene_cust_payer variable (median of 0.882), followed by cluster 2 (median of 0.571). For Families in Clusters 3 and 6, the pene_cust_payer values are relatively close despite being higher for Families in Cluster 6 (median of 0.384). The lowest pene_cust_payer values are very identical and smaller for Families in Clusters 4 and 5. With regard to dispersion, it can be said that the Families belonging to Cluster 3 are the ones that show greater variability in terms of the values they assume for the variable pene_cust_payer. In fact, the box length of that cluster, which corresponds to the largest IQR (around 0.16), is the biggest. Furthermore, all other clusters show low variability, which means that for the Families that belong to each of these clusters, the pene_cust_payer values are relatively close. The Families included in each cluster can be consulted as described above.

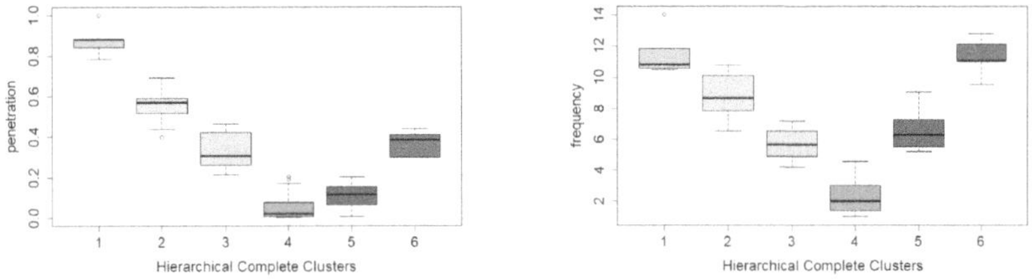

(a) online_channel - pene_cust_payer (b) online_channel - freq_payer

Fig. 11. Boxplots of the online channel.

In relation to the other variable freq_payer, it can be analyzed Fig. 11b and Table 5, to compare its values for the six clusters obtained for the online HoReCa channel. The Clusters 1 and 6 stand out in terms of the highest median, with about 11 days. This means that, in mean terms, products from Families in these clusters are purchased at most every 11 days by a customer payer, with half of these products being purchased within this time difference at most, while the remainder are purchased with a temporal difference greater than that number of days. On the other hand, the Cluster 4 has a very low median of 2 days, indicating that, in mean terms, products from Families in this cluster are purchased at most every 2 days by a customer payer, which means that they are purchased more frequently than all other products from Families in other clusters. When we compare the dispersion of the values of the variable freq_payer in the several clusters, there is greater variability in the temporal difference, in days, between purchases per Family in Clusters 2, 3, 4 and 5. Half of the products of Families in these clusters vary at most in two days in relation to the period of time between two purchases of that product. In Clusters 1 and 6, the variability is similar and lower, at most around a day, for half of the products in these clusters.

Table 5. Statistical Metrics of pene_cust_payer and freq_payer in HoReCa online

Cluster	Med_p	Min_p	Max_p	IQR_p	Med_f	Min_f	Max_f	IQR_f
1	0.882	0.783	1.000	0.042	10.837	10.512	14.034	1.252
2	0.571	0.398	0.694	0.068	8.687	6.537	10.780	2.011
3	0.306	0.215	0.465	0.159	5.646	4.198	7.160	1.635
4	0.022	0.002	0.201	0.071	2.000	1.000	4.565	1.625
5	0.117	0.007	0.203	0.091	6.277	5.216	9.071	1.723
6	0.384	0.298	0.440	0.110	11.057	9.545	12.819	1.084

3.3 Comparison Between HoReCa Total and HoReCa Online

As previously stated, we choose six as the number of clusters for both HoReCa channels to ensure that a meaningful comparison that is relevant for Recheio. The clusters are numbered from 1 to 6 in decreasing order of importance related to the penetration and frequency variables. Hence, Cluster 1 will have higher values for these variables.

After obtaining the segmentations for both HoReCa total and HoReCa online data, a renaming of the clusters was performed to make it more intelligible in business context (AF1 to AF6 to substitute Clusters 1 to 6). However, it should be noted that the composition of the clusters remains the same. In Table 6, we link the AF_i groups and C_j clusters to simultaneously identify the Families belonging to each cluster and their respective variable values. AF1 represents the most important Families for the business, while AF6 represents the least important ones. Table 6a explains the renaming criteria for the Families in the HoReCa total channel, and Table 6b for the HoReCa online channel. To make things easier, we will designate the variables pene_cust_payer and freq_payers respectively as Penetration and Frequency.

Figure 12 aims to assist in the comparison between the results obtained for the two channels. On the left, we have the scatter plot and pie chart of the clusters formed using the Hierarchical Method with Ward Linkage for the HoReCa total channel. On the right, the same for the HoReCa online channel, obtained through the Hierarchical Method with Complete Linkage. We can conclude that Penetration vs. Frequency plot for the online channel indicates less frequency in this channel, and indicates fewer Families with Penetration above 50%. It is also noteworthy that in the online channel, there is a greater concentration of Families in AF6 (+32%) and a lower concentration of Families of the others AFs, specially in AF2 (−11%), AF5 (−8%), AF1 (−6%), and AF4 (−5%), when compared to the total channel. In fact, the groups AF2, AF5, AF1 and AF4 lost a significant amount of weight from total HoReCa to online HoReCa data, AF3

Table 6. Family analysis in both channels

(a) Total channel				(b) Online channel			
Group	Cluster	Penetration	Frequency	Group	Cluster	Penetration	Frequency
AF1	6	[0.750, 1.000]	[12.500, 25.000]	AF1	1	[0.780, 1.000]	[10.510, 14.035]
AF2	1	[0.515, 0.880]	[3.000, 12.500]	AF2	2	[0.395, 0.695]	[6.535, 10.785]
AF3	5	[0.220, 0.700]	[12.500, 25.000]	AF3	6	[0.295, 0.445]	[9.540, 12.820]
AF4	3	[0.200, 0.500]	[0.000, 10.500]	AF4	3	[0.215, 0.465]	[4.200, 7.200]
AF5	2	[0.000, 0.220]	[3.000, 8.000]	AF5	5	[0.005, 0.205]	[5.215, 9.075]
AF6	4	[0.000, 0.250]	[0.000, 2.900]	AF6	4	[0.000, 0.205]	[1.000, 4.600]

relatively maintained the same number of elements on the two channel. Finally, it should be noted that in the online channel, AF6 represents about half of the elements.

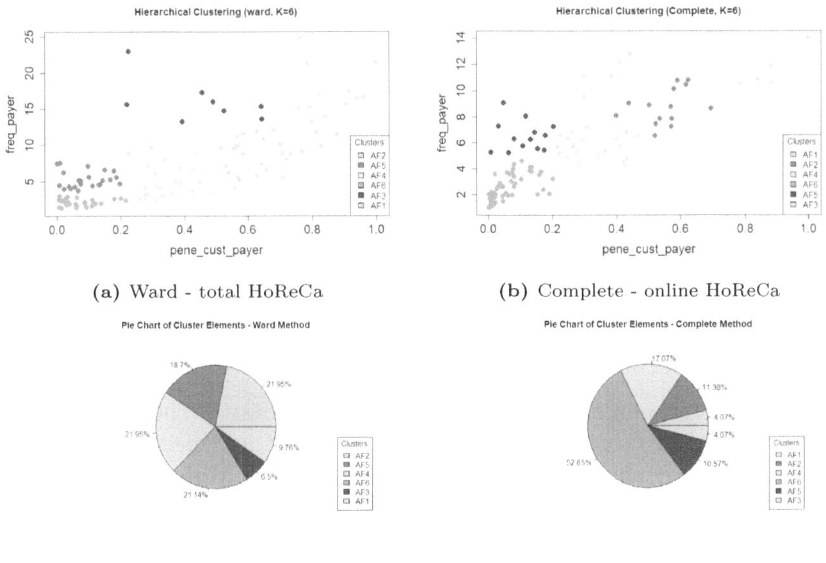

(a) Ward - total HoReCa

(b) Complete - online HoReCa

(c) Pie chart - total HoReCa

(d) Pie chart - online HoReCa

Fig. 12. Comparison between channels.

In Table 7, the defined levels for each variable are necessary to compare the behavior of Families across both channels. The quantitative levels from 1 to 5 correspond, respectively, to the qualitative levels: low, medium-low, medium, medium-high, high. These classifications contribute to a meaningful comprehension of the Penetration and Frequency of consumer activities inside each channel, enabling insightful comparisons and analyses across several customer categories.

Subsequently, we wanted to understand every substantial changes in behavior occurring between the total channel and the online channel. These changes were deemed significant if Families shifted by two or more levels in any of the variables. For example, if some Family was at level 5 in the total channel and moved to level 3 in the online channel, this would be considered a significant change. Let's present some examples of significant changes for two Families.

Table 7. Levels for both variables on each HoReCa channel.

(a) Total channel

Level	Penetration	Frequency
1	$[0, 0.2[$	$[0, 5[$
2	$[0.2, 0.4[$	$[5, 10[$
3	$[0.4, 0.6[$	$[10, 15[$
4	$[0.6, 0.8[$	$[15, 20[$
5	$[0.8, 1[$	$[20, 25]$

(b) Online channel

Level	Penetration	Frequency
1	$[0, 0.2[$	$[0, 3[$
2	$[0.2, 0.4[$	$[3, 6[$
3	$[0.4, 0.6[$	$[6, 9[$
4	$[0.6, 0.8[$	$[9, 12[$
5	$[0.8, 1[$	$[12, 15]$

Table 8. Examples of Families with significant changes between channels

Families	total channel			online channel		
	Pene	Freq	AF	Pene	Freq	AF
Fresh wild fish	0.22 (level 2)	15.62 (level 4)	AF3	0.05 (level 1)	2.63 (level 1)	AF6
Water	0.91 (level 5)	15.67 (level 4)	AF1	0.51 (level 3)	10.74 (level 4)	AF2

In Table 8, examining the transition from the total to the online channel, Family Fresh wild fish had a difference of one level in Penetration and three levels in Frequency, shifting from group AF3 to AF6, the Water Family decreases two levels in Penetration but remains in the same level for Frequency, moving from AF1 to AF2.

4 Conclusions

This study derived a comprehensive segmentation of Recheio's data, using the K-Means, K-Medoids, and Hierarchical algorithms, allowing the firm to find meaningful heterogeneous groups of products from the company's HoReCa sales channel, separating between physical and online transactions, and establishing a clear profile of its customers.

It was also possible to reveal variations in purchasing profiles when isolating transactions made through both channels. This highlights the importance of considering these two channels separately, as customers exhibit different behaviors in each channel, and of creating effective strategies for each channel separately.

The amount and nature of the variables used in the study were purposely set to be respectively small and business descriptive in order to allow quickly actionable conclusions. The groups formed with the clustering techniques are being used to: 1) discover the main differences and similarities between the pattern of purchases found in the HoReCa online and physical channel of sales and better decide what to offer in each context; 2) organize the HoReCa physical and online levels of assortment, taking advantage of the clear separation between the groups; 3) identify opportunities for recommending products to customers which have already demonstrated interest for other products within the group.
This can be a strategic advantage, allowing Recheio to make quicker and better decisions when selecting the assortment of products to be made available through each channel. Recheio can also personalize its marketing strategies, optimize product offerings, and enhance the customer experience.

Finally, some suggestions for future work are presented: 1) to carry out a similar study for the customer profile; 2) to automate the code developed to turn this study into a recurring segmentation exercise, periodically refreshing with new transactional data; 3) to apply the same methodology to other Recheio channels (non-HoReCa) to quickly segment and detect differences between the total channel and the online channel; 4) to enrich the clustering ensemble with other unsupervised methods; 5) to use this model for classifying new Families when adding/reorganizing the market structure.

Acknowledgements. Research partially funded by FCT - Fundação para a Ciência e a Tecnologia, Portugal, under the project UIDB/00006/2020, DOI: 10.54499/UIDB/00006/2020 (CEAUL) and ISEL. The authors thank the company Recheio from the Jerónimo Martins group for authorizing the publication of the information in this paper.

References

1. Branco, J.A.: Uma Introdução à Análise de Clusters. Sociedade Portuguesa de Estatística (2004)
2. Chen, Y., Guozheng, Z., Dengfeng, H., Chua, F.: Customer segmentation based on survival character. J. Intell. Manuf. **18**(4), 513–517 (2007)
3. Chen, N., Yang, Y.: The impact of customer experience on consumer purchase intention in cross-border E-commerce - taking network structural embeddedness as mediator variable. J. Retail. Consum. Serv. **59**, 102344 (2021)
4. Edwin, P.C.: Beyond the Numbers: Making Sense of Statistics. National Science Teaching Association (2012)
5. Everitt, B.S., Landau, S., Leese, M., Stahl, D.: Cluster Analysis, 5th edn. Wiley, Hoboken (2011)
6. Farahani, A., Rahiminezhed, H., Same, A., Immannezhed, K.: A comparison of partial least square (PLS) and ordinary least square (OLS) regressions in predicting of couples mental health based on their communicational patterns. Procedia Soc. Behav. Sci. **5**, 1459–1463 (2010)
7. Grabmeier, J., Rudolph, A.: Techniques of cluster algorithms in data mining. Data Min. Knowl. Disc. **6**, 303–360 (2002)

8. Hartigan, J.A., Wong, M.A.: A K-means clustering algorithm. J. Roy. Stat. Soc. Ser. C (Appl. Stat.) **28**(1), 100–108 (1979)
9. Kaufman, L., Rousseeuw, P.J.: Finding Groups in Data: An Introduction to Cluster Analysis. Wiley, New York (1990)
10. Kettenring, J.R.: The practice of cluster analysis. J. Classif. **23**(1), 3–30 (2006)
11. MacQueen, J.B.: Some methods for classification and analysis of multivariate observations. In: Proceedings of the Fifth Berkeley Symposium on Mathematical Statistics and Probability, vol. 1: Statistics, pp. 281–297. University of California Press, Berkeley (1967)
12. Malhotra, N., Birks, D., Wills, P.: Marketing Research - An Applied Approach, 5th edn. Pearson Education, London (2017)
13. Pestana, M.H., Gageiro, J.N.: Análise de dados para ciências sociais: a complementaridade do SPSS, 6th edn. Edições Sílabo (2014)
14. Ward, J.H.: Hierarchical grouping to optimize an objective function. J. Am. Stat. Assoc. **58**(301), 236–244 (1963)

CATPCA in R: Application to Sensorial Data of Wine-Tasting

Andreia Gomes[1(✉)] and Ana Cristina Braga[2]

[1] School of Engineering, University of Minho, 4710-057 Braga, Portugal
andreiagomes_6@outlook.com

[2] ALGORITMI Research Centre, LASI, University of Minho, Campus de Gualtar, 4710-057 Braga, Portugal
acb@dps.uminho.pt

Abstract. Analyzing large volumes of categorical data presents a recurring challenge in the social, behavioral, and biological sciences. Therefore, there is a necessity to reduce these data while maintaining minimal loss of information. CATPCA serves as an alternative to conventional Principal Component Analysis (PCA), enabling the reduction of dimensionality for variables measured on different scales. To elucidate the underlying principles of this statistical method, a review of bibliographic sources was undertaken. This search also highlighted the `Gifi` and the `Homals` packages, identified as the sole packages equipped with functions supporting the implementation of CATPCA. Both packages were explored to assess and compare their functionalities and features. The `Gifi` package is derived from the `Homals` package, aiming for enhanced user-friendliness and flexibility. To further delve into the functionalities and constraints of the `Gifi` package and to demonstrate the handling of biological data, an analysis of sensory data from wine-tasting trials was additionally conducted. In order to enable users to perform an intuitive and simplified CATPCA, a web application named ***Gify***, available at https://andreiagomes.shinyapps.io/Gify/, based on the `princals()` function from the `Gifi` package, has been developed.

Keywords: Categorical variables · PCA · CATPCA · R · Shiny

1 Introduction

Large datasets are increasingly prevalent in many areas of the sciences, such as social, behavioral, and biological fields. To interpret such datasets effectively, methods are required to significantly reduce their dimensionality in an interpretable manner while preserving a substantial amount of the information contained within them [3,11].

This work has been supported by FCT - Fundação para a Ciência e Tecnologia within the R&D Units Project Scope: UIDB/00319/2020.

O. Gervasi et al. (Eds.): ICCSA 2024 Workshops, LNCS 14815, pp. 357–374, 2024.
https://doi.org/10.1007/978-3-031-65154-0_22

This reduction will be able to remove the noise, but retaining the signal of interest that can be crucial for understanding hidden patterns. On the other hand, the original, high-dimensional data may contain non-informative or redundant variables [17].

Many techniques have been developed for this purpose. Principal Component Analysis (PCA) is one of the oldest and most commonly used techniques of multivariate analysis [1]. Its principle is simple: to reduce the dimensionality of a dataset while simultaneously preserving the maximum variability possible [5]. This dimensionality reduction reveals the underlying structure, sometimes hidden and simplified, that often exists within it [22].

This technique allows for explaining the variance-covariance structure of a set of dependent variables, which are typically correlated, in order to transform them into a set of new, uncorrelated orthogonal variables called principal components (PCs). These PCs are linear combinations of the original set [1,4].

The PCs resulting from the decomposition of the covariance matrix are presented in descending order of their importance. That is, the first principal component (PC) explains the maximum variability in the data, the second PC explains the maximum variability remaining in the set after removing the first component, and so on, until the last PC, which expresses the least contribution to explaining variations in the initial variables. In this case, PCs with lower variability can be eliminated without leading to a significant loss of information in the initial dataset. The quality of PCA results improves as fewer linear combinations are needed to explain the total variance of the data [2,5,23].

However, this analysis is only suitable for continuous variables that are measured on a numeric level, assuming the existence of a linear relationship between them. Additionally, it requires a large sample size for accurate results. Therefore, it is not an appropriate method for dimensionality reduction when dealing with categorical variables that exhibit non-linear relationships [10,15].

Thus, the categorical principal component analysis (CATPCA), also known as nonlinear principal component analysis (NLPCA), emerges as an alternative to traditional PCA [11]. This approach aims at the same objectives as PCA, which is to reduce a dataset consisting of many variables and complicated correlation patterns to a smaller number of uncorrelated summary variables (PCs) that closely represent the information in the data. However, in this case, CATPCA is suitable for mixed-level measurement variables (nominal, ordinal, and numeric) that may not be linearly related to each other [11,15,20].

CATPCA technique quantifies categorical variables using optimal scaling, assigning numerical quantifications to the categories of each qualitative variable so that the maximum variance of the quantified variables is accounted for [24].

Therefore, the main motivation of this paper is to explore the multivariate statistical analysis tools for qualitative variables, particularly CATPCA, available in R. The utility of this methodology will be demonstrated by applying it to a real dataset of wine-tasting trials.

This paper is organized into 5 sections. Section 2 presents the theoretical and mathematical foundations of concepts related to CATPCA that support this research. Section 3 explores the `Gifi` and `Homals` packages available in the R software, which enable the execution of CATPCA. Section 4 presents a CATPCA analysis utilizing the `princals()` function from the `Gifi` package, applied to a dataset comprising wine-tasting evaluations. In Sect. 5, the ***Gify*** application, developed in R Shiny to simplify the implementation of the `princals()` function from the `Gifi` package, is introduced. Finally, Chap. 6 encapsulates the key findings described in this paper, accompanied by future outlooks for this research.

2 Methods

In CATPCA, all variables are considered categorical, however, the quantification assigned to each category takes into account the nature of these variables [11, 18]. This quantification is based on the optimal scaling process, which relies on minimizing the loss function of Alternating Least Squares (ALS) [11]. The loss to be minimized is the information loss associated with the fact that variables are now represented by a smaller number of components.

After the quantification of the variables, the $\mathbf{Q}_{n \times m}$ matrix is obtained, replacing the original data matrix $\mathbf{H}_{n \times m}$, and it contains the transformed variables $\mathbf{q}_j = \phi_j(\mathbf{h}_j)$, where j represents the index of the variables in the matrix $\mathbf{H}$, and $\mathbf{h}_j$ is vector of size $n \times 1$, with $j = 1, ..., m$ [11]. The minimization criterion is then applied through the $\mathbf{Q}$ matrix [21]:

$$tr(\mathbf{Q} - \mathbf{Y}\mathbf{B}^T)^T(\mathbf{Q} - \mathbf{Y}\mathbf{B}^T) \tag{1}$$

Concerning the $\mathbf{Y}_{n \times p}$ matrix, where the columns represent linear functions of the columns of the $\mathbf{Q}$ matrix, this matrix is composed of the coordinates (scores) of the first p PCs, where p is the number of PCs defined for the analysis [11]. Regarding the $\mathbf{B}^T_{p \times m}$, where the (orthogonal) columns represent the eigenvectors of the variance-covariance matrix of $\mathbf{Y}$ [11,21]. In the case of the latter, the matrix is composed of the coefficients (loadings) of the first p PCs [21].

2.1 Analysis Levels

Nominal Analysis Level. In this analysis level, objects with the same category in the original dataset obtain the same optimal quantification. Orders or distances between categories are not considered [6,11].

Ordinal Analysis Level. Considers the original order of categories, in addition to taking into account objects belonging to the same category, as described in the nominal analysis. All quantifications must be less than or equal to the quantification of the category with the highest value in the original data [6,11].

Numeric Analysis Level. It is considered the most restrictive since it takes into account the objects belonging to each category while also maintaining the order and distance between categories. This distance is always equal [6].

Spline Analysis Level. Ordinal and nominal levels of analysis may lead to irregular quantifications due to the use of step functions, while spline functions offer a smoother and more stable alternative [6,10,11].

This spline transformation involves dividing the x-axis of the transformation plot into pre-defined intervals and adjusting these intervals using individual low-degree polynomial functions [10,16]. The locations where these curves intersect are called knots [7].

Various authors [11,12] recommend applying ordinal analysis when the number of categories is small and monotonic spline analysis when the number of categories exceeds the number of samples or is greater than 10. In these cases, linear transformation is too restrictive, and ordinal transformation is too specific, while monotonic spline transformation allows for maintaining the order of categories.

2.2 CATPCA Metrics

Component Loadings. Allows the quantification of the influence of the transformed variables in creating the PC [7,16]. In CATPCA, the component loading corresponds to the correlation between the transformed (quantified) variables and the retained non-linear PCs, so its value varies between -1 and 1 [11].

Variance Accounted for (VAF). It is the most important measure for quantifying the effectiveness of the method [6,18].

Nominal and ordinal level analyses are based on maximizing the p largest eigenvalues of the correlation matrix between the transformed variables $\mathbf{q}_j$. Each eigenvalue (which corresponds to the sum of the squared component loadings of each dimension) represents the amount of variance explained by each PC, and the sum of these eigenvalues divided by the number of analyzed variables is equivalent to the cumulative VAF [16]. The cumulative VAF results from the sum of the VAF of the considered components [18]. Calculating the VAF for each PC (dividing each eigenvalue by the number of analyzed variables) allows understanding the relative importance of each component in explaining the overall variance of the data, aiding in determining which PCs contribute more to its structure [10].

Crohnbach's Alpha (α_s). The most commonly used coefficients to measure internal consistency in applied psychometrics [16]. The higher its value, the closer to 1 (varies in between 0 and 1), the greater the reliability of the model and each dimension [18]. The relationship between the eigenvalue and Cronbach's alpha is used to assess the internal consistency of each dimension [16].

Principal Components Number. The number of chosen components depends on the information that can be excluded and the interpretation of these components themselves.

Its choice can be defined through the *Scree plot*, which represents the eigenvalues and the PCs. In this case, these plots show a break, or an elbow, that indicates the number of components to be considered [11,18]. Alternatively, the choice can be based on the eigenvalue, where PCs with eigenvalues greater than 1 are selected [18].

3 R Packages

The exploration of the R software, combined with the literature review, was essential to investigate which tools are currently available and enable the execution of CATPCA, thereby facilitating the handling of data with categorical variables.

The `Gifi` [14] and the `Homals` [13] packages stand out as the only ones equipped with functions (`princals()` and `homals()`, respectively) that allow the application of CATPCA. Both functions were explored using the same set of sample data, and a detailed analysis of their arguments and the values and graphs obtained was carried out to compare the functionalities and features that both packages offer.

3.1 Gifi

The `Gifi` package [14], developed in R by Patrick Mair, Jan de Leeuw, and Patrick J. F. Groenen, allows for the implementation of CATPCA (PRINCALS), multiple correspondence analysis (HOMALS), and monotone regression analysis (MORALS).

In this package, there are 12 example datasets and 9 functions, with the main function being the `princals()` command. This function adjusts the CATPCA and allows the user to define a total of 14 arguments. Simpler analysis levels such as metric, ordinal, and nominal can be specified through the `levels` argument, and the corresponding spline transformations are internally created [14].

The auxiliary function `knotsGifi()` enables the implementation of spline functions, allowing the specification of the type and number of knots for each variable. The type of knots (type) is "Q" when the knots are quantiles of the variables, "R" when the knots are equally spaced, "E" when there are no internal knots, and "D" when the internal knots correspond to data points. In the case of type = "E" and type = "D", it is not necessary to define the number of knots [9]. Similarly, it is essential to determine the degree of the spline function using the `degrees` argument [12].

The `copies` argument, generating as many copies as the number of PCs, allows for the relaxation of linear constraints on nominal variables, enabling the categories of variables to spread freely in the p space, where p is the number of PCs defined for the analysis [9,12].

The `missing` argument allows the user to choose the treatment for missing values (NAs). Regarding the `active` argument, when a variable is considered passive, it is not optimized and therefore does not contribute to the loss function, but can be included in the plots either way [9].

The plots depicting the results can be generated using the `plot.princals()` function, also included in the `Gifi` package [14].

3.2 Homals

The `Homals` package [13], currently available in R, was developed by Patrick Mair, with co-authorship by Jan De Leeuw.

This package allows for the conduct of a homogeneity analysis, multiple correspondence analysis, and, by imposing *rank-1* constraints on the quantifications of categories (setting the `rank` argument to 1), it can be extended to perform NLPCA [8].

This package comprises a total of 4 functions and 11 example datasets, with the most important function being `homals()`.

The graphic results can be obtained using the `plot.homals()` function [13].

3.3 Comparison Between Packages

The `Gifi` package is derived from the `Homals` package, designed to be an improved version that is more user-friendly and flexible. This is primarily due to a slight difference in the formulation of the loss function and the utilization of B-splines, which provide computational and conceptual advantages to the `Gifi` package [9].

Also, the `princals()` function in the `Gifi` package is specifically tailored for CATPCA, leading to more perceptible and interpretable results in line with the initial objective.

The graphical results obtained by each package exhibit differences. It's noteworthy that while the `Homals` package offers a broader range of plots for result interpretation, the `Gifi` package encompasses the essential plots crucial for understanding the CATPCA results.

Table 1 summarizes the similarities and differences between the packages.

Table 1. Comparison table: `Gifi` vs. `Homals` package

	Gifi	Homals
Version	0.4–0	1.0–10
Last update	October 2022	June 2022
Function	princals()	homals()
Aplication	Developed for CATPCA, descends from the `Homals` package	Developed for MCA, executes CATPCA by applying a *rank-1* restriction
Methodology	• Performs the minimization of the following loss function through the ALS algorithm: $\sigma(\mathbf{X}, \mathbf{H}, \mathbf{A}) = \sum_{j=1}^{m} \mathbf{SQQ}(\mathbf{X} - \mathbf{H}_j \mathbf{A}_j)$ • Uses B-splines • Allows the presence of missing values.	• Performs the minimization of the following loss function through the ALS algorithm: $\sigma(\mathbf{X}, \mathbf{Y}) = \frac{1}{m} \sum_{j=1}^{\mathbf{m}} SQQ(\mathbf{X} - \sum_{\ell \in \mathbf{K}_j} \mathbf{G}_\ell \mathbf{Y}_\ell)$ • Uses binary matrices • Allows the presence of missing values.
Graphic results	• *Scree plot* - all components • *Transformation plot* - all graphs in a figure • *Loadings plot* • *Joint plot* - loadings and category quantifications • *Object plot* • *Biplot* - loadings and object scores	• *Scree plot* - defined number of components • *Transformation plot* - graphs in separated figures • *Loadings plot* • *Joint plot* - category quantifications and object scores • *Object plot* • *Category plot* • *Discrimination plot*
Utilization	• Computationally advantageous • More flexible • Easier to use	• Less intuitive

4 Results and Discussion

To further explore the functionalities and limitations of the `princals()` function from the `Gifi` package, chosen for its suitability in CATPCA, an analysis was conducted on a dataset comprising sensory data collected from wine-tasting trials.

In this study, a sensory dataset was utilized, collected by a research group affiliated with the Center of Biological Engineering at the University of Minho, coordinated by Professor José Oliveira. The dataset compiles information on evaluations of seven distinct wines categorized from A to G, featuring qualitative sensory descriptors determined by a panel of six wine tasters. Following the processing and elimination of non-essential variables, the dataset comprises 126 observations and 25 variables, with five of those variables having missing values. The variables are categorized into Olfactory Assessment, Gustatory Assessment, and Appearance groups, a more detailed description of the variables can be accessed on *Github*.

For the variables "Wine" and "Taster", a nominal level of analysis was chosen since they correspond to the type of wine evaluated and the respective taster, and therefore, the order is irrelevant.

The same analysis was applied to the variables "Clarity", "Color", "Intensity" and "Evolution".

For the remaining variables that have an ordinal qualitative measurement scale, an ordinal level of analysis was defined, as the number of categories does not exceed the number of observations, and each variable does not have more than 10 categories (7 is the maximum value). Therefore, the decision was made not to apply a spline level of analysis, as this level of analysis tends to be more restrictive, leading to lower VAF values [11].

The nominal variables were automatically encoded into dummy variables by the `princals()` function. For instance, the variable "Wine" initially had 7 categories ("A" to "G") and was transformed into 6 dummy variables labeled "Wine.1', "Wine.2', "Wine.3", "Wine.4", "Wine.5" and "Wine.6". The same approach was applied to the remaining nominal variables.

For the analysis, 7 PCs were specified based on the *Scree plot*, Fig. 1.

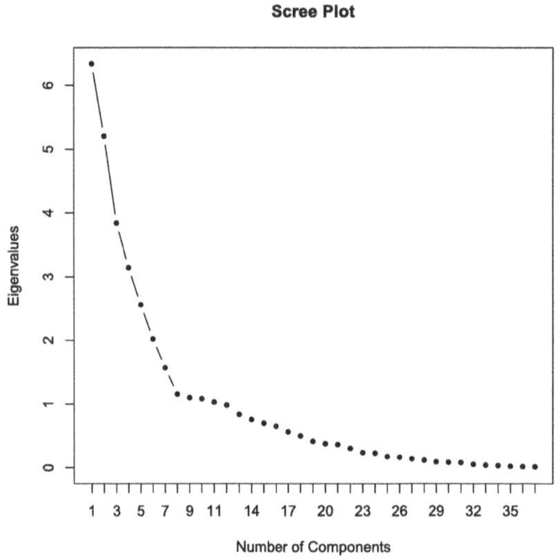

Fig. 1. *Scree plot* obtained through the `plot.princals()` function.

The argument `copies` was set equal to the number of components for nominal variables to ease linear restrictions on this type of variable [12]. Regarding missing values, option `a` was chosen within the `missing` argument of the `princals()` function.

The initial 7 components collectively explained 66.64% of the total variance in the original variables, with the top two components contributing the highest percentage of VAF. The first PC has a percentage of VAF of 17.12%, an eigenvalue of 6.335, and a Cronbach's alpha of 0.877, while the second PC has a VAF of 14.07%, with an eigenvalue of 5.205 and a Cronbach's alpha of 0.842.

It is relevant to emphasize that, since the first two PCs, together, explain the majority of the variance, with a cumulative VAF value of 31.19%, the subsequent plots will only illustrate the first and second dimensions. Therefore, the results will be based on the first two PCs.

To illustrate the impact of choosing a specific quantification level for variables, *Transformation plots* were applied. In this paper, for example purposes, only the plots for the variables "Wine" and "Taster" are represented in Fig. 2.

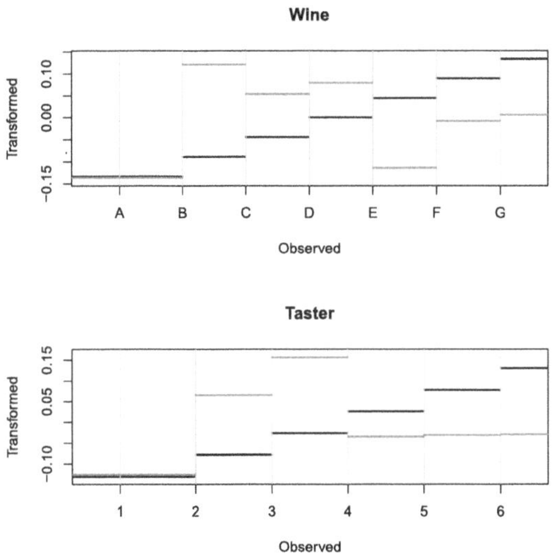

Fig. 2. *Transformation plots* for the "Wine" and "Taster" variables obtained through the `plot.princals()` function.

This graph represents the optimal transformations assigned to the categories of each variable based on the optimal scaling technique and provides insights into the relationships between variables. On the x-axis, the real values of the categories are displayed, and on the y-axis, the corresponding optimal quantifications [10].

The black lines depict the transformation in the first dimension and the red lines in the second dimension. Due to the *rank-1* restriction [12], only the transformations in the first dimension are significant.

The obtained component loadings, along with the VAF(%), eigenvalues, and Cronbach's alpha for each PC, are summarized in Table 2. Component loadings greater than 0.5 are considered significant for the analysis [24] and are highlighted in bold in the table.

Considering the values of the component loadings together with the *Joint plot*, in Fig. 3, which represents in a single plot the component loadings of ordinal variables and the quantifications of the categories of nominal variables, it is possible to establish the most important relationships between variables for the first two components.

The variables "Bitterness", "Carbon_dioxide" and "Dry_fruit" are overlapped, indicating a positive correlation among them. This suggests that wines tend to exhibit these characteristics together. However, they are in opposite

Table 2. Principal components extracted from CATPCA, with their respective component loadings, Cronbach's alphas, eigenvalues, and VAF(%).

	Principal Components						
Variables	1	2	3	4	5	6	7
"Wine.1"	–0.044	–0.020	–0.090	–0.044	0.200	–0.279	0.439
"Wine.2"	0.015	0.098	0.061	0.140	–0.099	0.170	0.356
"Wine.3"	0.032	0.047	0.021	0.021	–0.129	0.186	–0.258
"Wine.4"	–0.025	–0.155	–0.143	–0.102	0.144	–0.425	–0.197
"Wine.5"	0.039	0.047	0.063	0.055	–0.146	0.306	–0.250
"Wine.6"	0.018	0.125	0.120	0.071	-0.101	0.303	0.384
"Taster.1"	0.053	-0.517	0.268	**0.635**	–0.226	–0.255	–0.070
"Taster.2"	**0.831**	0.108	0.360	–0.102	0.233	–0.113	0.003
"Taster.3"	0.093	0.342	0.034	–0.243	**-0.689**	–0.436	–0.039
"Taster.4"	–0.414	**0.529**	0.511	0.264	0.223	–0.210	–0.126
"Taster.5"	–0.231	–0.447	**0.604**	–0.500	–0.055	0.072	0.098
"Citrus_fruit"	**–0.532**	-0.369	–0.398	–0.412	0.125	0.027	0.154
"Tree_fruit"	0.285	–0.131	**0.520**	–0.207	0.112	–0.494	–0.146
"Tropical_fruit"	0.003	0.094	–0.448	**0.523**	0.439	0.109	0.020
"Dry_fruit"	0.173	**0.583**	0.325	0.115	0.376	0.017	–0.141
"Floral"	–0.422	0.096	–0.566	**–0.593**	–0.199	0.120	–0.001
"Fresh_vegetable"	–0.249	**–0.791**	0.394	–0.006	0.142	0.254	0.046
"Dry_vegetable"	0.159	**–0.530**	0.355	0.084	–0.374	0.209	–0.171
"Honeyed"	0.047	–0.399	0.263	0.198	–0.278	0.091	–0.257
"Mineral"	0.185	–0.011	0.014	0.132	–0.352	0.074	0.354
"Carbon_dioxide"	0.185	**0.633**	0.541	–0.034	0.060	0.292	0.014
"Sweetness"	–0.523	**0.647**	0.000	–0.329	0.196	0.077	–0.023
"Acidity"	**–0.768**	0.025	0.467	–0.200	–0.274	–0.100	0.009
"Heat"	–0.361	–0.038	0.418	-0.441	–0.114	–0.182	0.017
"Bitterness"	0.244	**0.805**	0.154	–0.305	–0.189	0.123	0.022
"Astringency"	–0.217	0.199	–0.331	–0.211	–0.255	0.205	–0.056
"Structure"	**–0.891**	0.154	0.102	0.249	–0.019	–0.066	–0.018
"Balance"	**–0.941**	0.062	0.126	0.238	0.040	-0.057	–0.038
"Persistence"	**–0.863**	0.078	0.145	0.362	0.040	–0.049	–0.031
"Clarity.1"	0.291	**0.693**	–0.410	–0.073	–0.052	–0.255	–0.207
"Clarity.2"	–0.006	–0.289	0.059	–0.276	**0.527**	0.058	–0.440
"Color"	**0.569**	0.474	0.443	–0.136	–0.181	–0.173	0.089
"Intensity.1"	**–0.755**	0.108	0.211	–0.162	0.004	0.034	–0.099
"Intensity.2"	–0.225	0.141	–0.157	**0.564**	–0.433	–0.361	0.166
"Color_quality"	0.067	**–0.585**	–0.095	–0.431	–0.123	–0.109	0.093
"Evolution.1"	–0.095	–0.255	–0.466	–0.065	-0.091	-0.435	–0.302
"Evolution.2"	0.075	0.172	–0.150	0.161	**-0.531**	0.408	–0.474
Cronbach's alpha	0.877	0.842	0.770	0.710	0.634	0.525	0.377
Eigenvalue	6.335	5.205	3.838	3.138	2.555	2.017	1.568
VAF(%)	17.12	14.07	10.37	8.48	6.90	5.45	4.24

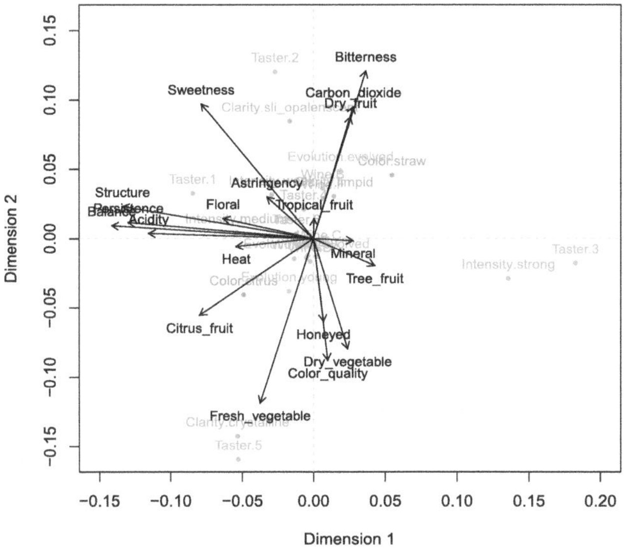

Fig. 3. *Joint plot* for the first two components obtained through the `plot.princals()` function.

positions compared to the variable "Fresh_vegetable" implying a strong negative correlation. In other words, wines with a fresh vegetable olfactory characteristic did not exhibit a bitter taste, nor did they have an aroma of dry fruits and carbon dioxide.

Similarly, the variables "Structure", "Persistence", "Balance" and "Acidity" are positively correlated, as is the group comprising the variables "Honeyed", "Dry_vegetable" and "Color_quality".

Geometrically analyzing the plot it is possible to see that the variables "Structure", "Persistence", "Balance", "Acidity" and "Citrus_fruit" contribute more to the first PC/dimension, as they have an angle $\beta < 45°$ with the axis representing it (x-axis). Also, the variables "Floral", "Heat", "Mineral" and "Tree_fruit" meet this condition; however, their contribution is much smaller as their vectors are shorter and closer to the origin of the plot.

On the other hand, the second PC is more influenced by the variables "Bitterness", "Carbon_dioxide" and "Dry_fruit", with positive values on the second PC/dimension, and by the variables "Honeyed", "Dry_vegetable", "Color_quality" and "Fresh_vegetable", with negative values. The variable "Tropical_fruit" also has an angle $\beta < 45°$ with the y-axis, however, it does not have a significant influence on its formation.

The variable "Sweetness" exhibits an angle $\beta \approx 45°$ with the axes and therefore has a similar influence on both components. The variable "Astringency" has the same characteristic, however, its influence is residual.

Regarding the points of the categories of nominal variables, and since the position of these points reflects their relationship with ordinal variables [11], it was possible to conclude that the "Intensity" and "Color" variables are discriminants in the first PC, the "Clarity" variable discriminates in the second PC, and the "Evolution" variable does not have a significant influence on either of the components. As for the categories "A", "C", "D", "E" and "G" of the "Wine" variable, they are mainly accumulated at the origin and are not associated with any of the components. Wines "B" and "F" are similarly related to the variables "Bitterness", "Dry_fruit", "Carbon_dioxide" and "Sweetness". The tasters can be grouped according to the characteristics they evaluated, as the variables they are close to in the plot are highly influential in their assessments. Thus, tasters "1" and "3" are associated with the first PC, tasters "2" and "5" with the second PC, and tasters "4" and "6" are close, indicating similar evaluations, however, they are located near the origin of the plot, which does not allow for significant conclusions.

Based on the interpretation, the first PC can be defined as "Wine Quality", as many variables contributing to its formation describe fresh characteristics and a persistent and balanced flavor, where color intensity has a significant influence. The second PC is moderately influenced by wines with olfactory characteristics of fruits, dried vegetables, and carbon dioxide, and a sweet taste, and strongly influenced by the aroma of fresh vegetables and a bitter taste. Thus, this PC can be defined as "Wine Aroma". The *Object plot* in Fig. 4, represents the scores of the objects in this analysis, which reveals the existence of three different groups highlighted with circles. Objects from the same group, meaning those closer geometrically, share identical scores on the PCs [18].

The cluster of points in the graph complicates its interpretation, but this division into 3 groups seems to be related to the tasters' rating patterns. The group on the right consists mostly of evaluations made by taster "3" where the choice of the "strong" category predominates for the "Intensity" variable. Meanwhile, the group located in the third quadrant is mostly evaluated by taster "5" and includes evaluations where only the "crystalline" category of the "Clarity" variable was chosen. The larger group brings together the remaining tasters "1", "2", "4" and "6" being abstract regarding the selection of categories and the influence of the evaluated variables, as it encompasses numerous observations.

Additionally, it is possible to relate the object scores to the component loadings through the *Biplot*, shown in Fig. 5.

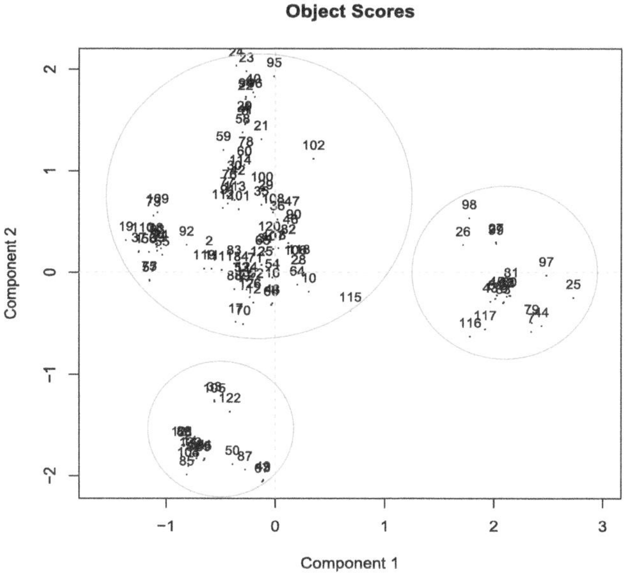

Fig. 4. *Object Plot* for the first two components obtained through the `plot.princals()` function.

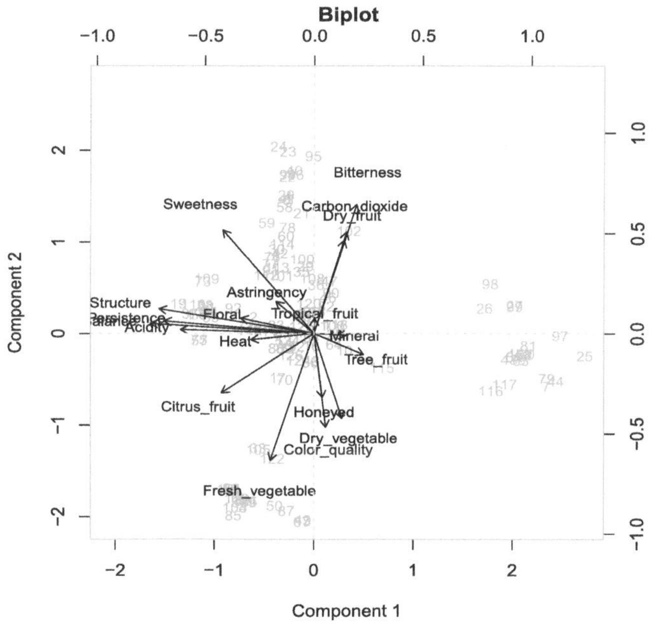

Fig. 5. *Biplot* for the first two components obtained through the `plot.princals()` function.

This plot only allows representing the loadings of ordinal variables, following the vector model. Therefore, it is not possible to relate the object scores to the quantifications of categories for nominal variables, which follow the centroid model.

Nevertheless, this plot reinforces the previously explained observations. The larger group located at the origin and in the second quadrant is overlapped by most loading vectors, explaining the heterogeneous characteristics of this group. The group located in the third quadrant is more influenced by the variable "Fresh_vegetable" and the group of observations on the right does not experience a considered significant influence from any ordinal variable. As observed, the vectors do not reach the area where the scores of the objects in this group are located.

4.1 Shiny: Gify App

To enable users to perform CATPCA without writing a single line of code, a web application in R Shiny was developed [19]. Named ***Gify***, this application provides a more intuitive and simplified way for users to utilize the `princals()` function from the `Gifi` package.

This application can be accessed at https://andreiagomes.shinyapps.io/Gify/ from any internet-enabled device.

It was created to allow users to upload their dataset to the web page, define analysis parameters, execute the CATPCA, and review the results, all processed through selection buttons and input spaces.

A user guide is provided in the application, containing information about the operation of the entire application and links to CRAN support documents.

In the Upload file section, represented in Fig. 6, the user is prompted to upload the data file (.csv or .txt) that he/she plans to analyze. The user is also requested to specify necessary parameters for reading the file, such as indicating whether the file contains a header, if the first column represents row names, and selecting the separator used in the original file ('.', ';', or ',').

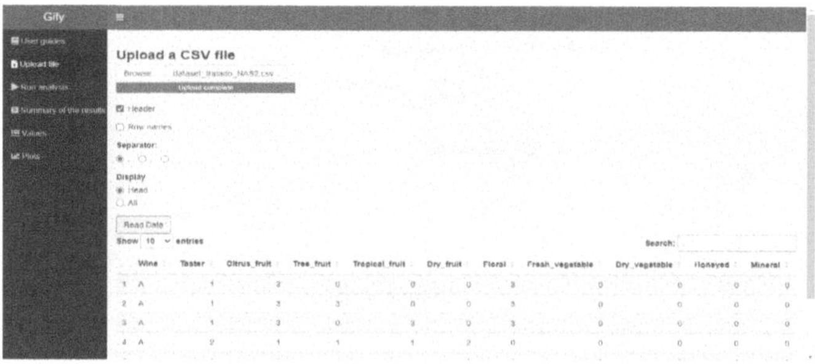

Fig. 6. Uploading the dataset file in the ***Gify*** app.

The Run analysis tab, Fig. 7, allows the user to set the analysis parameters. The parameters in the left column are fixed and refer to the number of dimensions to be computed, handling ties and missing values, whether object scores are z-scores, the maximum number of iterations, and the convergence criteria.

Meanwhile, the parameters in the right column only appear after uploading the data file. In this case, the first question allows the user to choose what type of analysis they want to perform, similar to what happens in the original function.

If the user chooses the "predefined levels" option, Fig. 7, they should, for each variable in the dataset, choose the analysis level ("ordinal", "nominal" or "metric"), spline degree (this argument is maintained in this type of analysis as it does in the original function), the number of copies, and whether the variable is considered active for analysis.

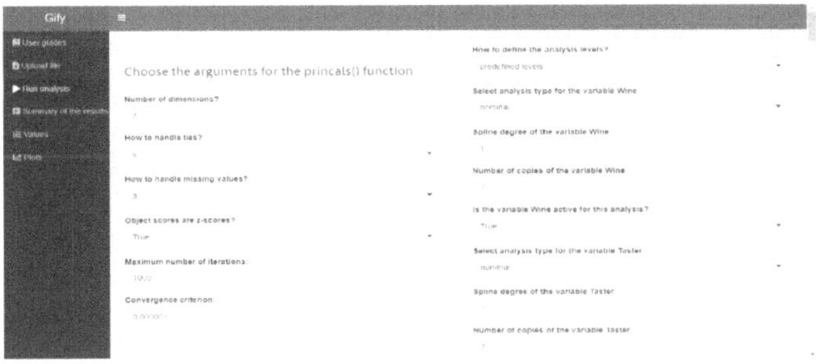

Fig. 7. Specifying the analysis parameters within the ***Gify*** app.

There is also the possibility to configure a spline analysis manually, choosing the "manual splines" option, for that option only the question regarding the selection of the analysis type is replaced by questions specifying whether the variable in question follows an order, the type of internal knots for the variable ("D", "E", "Q", and "R"), and the number of knots for that variable [14]. The remaining questions regarding the spline degree, number of copies, and whether the variable is active persist unchanged.

All initially presented values correspond to the default values of the function.

After defining all parameters, the user will reach the end of the page where the "Run Analysis" button is located, which will automatically redirect the user to the next tab containing a summary of the analysis results.

In the Summary tab, shown in Fig. 8, summaries of the obtained results can be accessed. This includes the function, loss function value, number of iterations, eigenvalues, component loadings (with a cutoff of 0.5), VAF, and cumulative VAF.

At the Values tab, Fig. 9, it is possible to check all the values obtained through the `princals()` function. Among the options are commands such as `transform`, `rhat`, `evals`, `objectscores`, `scoremat`, `quantifications`, `dmeasures`, `lambda`,

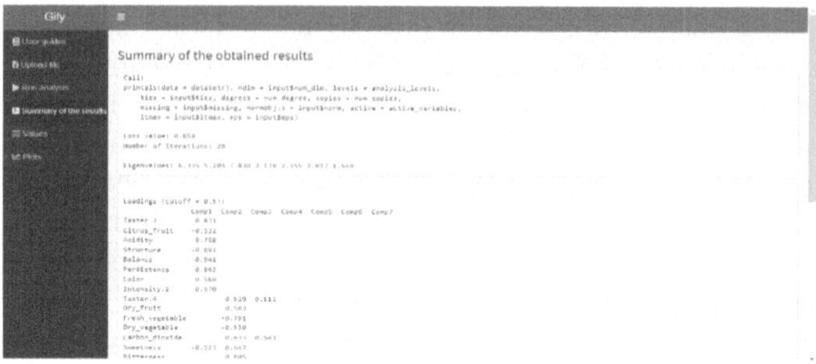

Fig. 8. Summary of the results obtained, displayed in the Summary tab in the ***Gify*** app.

`weights`, `loadings`, `ntel`, `f`, `data`, `datanum`, `ndim`, and `call`, all of these commands and their respective descriptions can be found at [14].

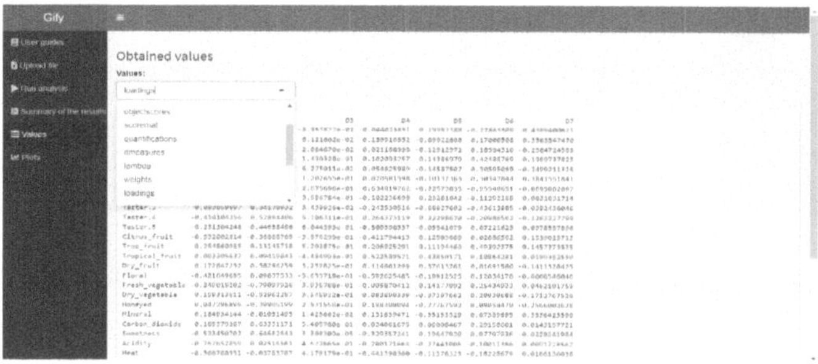

Fig. 9. Overview of the values obtained, displayed in the Values tab in the ***Gify*** app.

Additionally, users can utilize the application for accessing and downloading graphical results such as the *Scree plot, Transformation plot, Loadings plot, Joint plot, Object plot* and *Biplot* generated from the analysis.

5 Conclusion and Future Work

This study aimed to explore the currently available tools in R for applying CAT-PCA. A comprehensive search identified the `Gifi` and `Homals` packages, with their respective functions `princals()` and `homals()`, as the only ones capable of achieving this objective.

By studying these packages, the `Gifi` package was selected as the most flexible and comprehensive. To investigate the capabilities of the `Gifi` package, an analysis of a wine-tasting dataset was also conducted. This analysis provided valuable insights into the dependency structure of the wine data, which holds promise for future research within the wine industry.

Subsequently, based on the `princals()` function of this package, a web application in R Shiny, named ***Gify***, was developed. ***Gify*** streamlines the execution of CATPCA through a dynamic and simplified interface, making it accessible to users without programming or R software expertise.

In the future, it would be highly interesting to explore the inclusion of other software tools for performing CATPCA, as well as testing additional functionalities of this package. Improving the dynamics of the application and keeping it up-to-date would also be of great interest, given its utility across various fields.

References

1. Abdi, H., Williams, L.: Principal component analysis. Wiley Interdisc. Rev. Comput. Stat. **2**, 433–459 (2010). https://doi.org/10.1002/wics.101
2. Barth, J., Katumullage, D., Yang, C., Cao, J.: Classification of wines using principal component analysis. J. Wine Econ. **16**(1), 56–67 (2021). https://doi.org/10.1017/jwe.2020.35
3. Carreño, E.R., et al.: Study of risk factors for healthcare-associated infections in acute cardiac patients using categorical principal component analysis (catpca). Sci. Rep. **12**(1), 28 (2022). https://doi.org/10.1038/s41598-021-03970-w
4. Jolliffe, I.: Principal Component Analysis, 2nd edn. Springer, New York (2002). https://doi.org/10.1007/b98835
5. Jolliffe, I.T., Cadima, J.: Principal component analysis: a review and recent developments. Phil. Trans. Roy. Soc. A: Math. Phys. Eng. Sci. **374**(2065), 20150202 (2016). https://doi.org/10.1098/rsta.2015.0202
6. Lavado, N.: Análise em Componentes Principais Não - Linear. Master's thesis, Universidade Nova de Lisboa (2004)
7. Lavado, N.: Extensões via splines da Análise em Componentes Principais. Master's thesis, Universidade Nova de Lisboa (2012)
8. de Leeuw, J., Mair, P.: Gifi methods for optimal scaling in r: the package homals. J. Stat. Softw. **31**(4), 1–21 (2009). https://doi.org/10.18637/jss.v031.i04
9. de Leeuw, J., Mair, P., Groenen, P.: Multivariate Analysis with Optimal Scaling (2016)
10. Linting, M., Kooij, A.V.D.: Nonlinear principal components analysis with catpca: a tutorial. J. Pers. Assess. **94**(1), 12–25 (2012). https://doi.org/10.1080/00223891.2011.627965
11. Linting, M., Meulman, J.J., Groenen, P.J., van der Kooij, A.J.: Nonlinear principal components analysis: introduction and application. Psychol. Methods **12**(3), 336–358 (2007). https://doi.org/10.1037/1082-989X.12.3.336
12. Mair, P.: Modern Psychometrics with R, vol. 62 (2018)
13. Mair, P., de Leeuw, J.: homals: gifi methods for optimal scaling (2022). https://CRAN.R-project.org/package=homals. Accessed 28 Jan 2023
14. Mair, P., de Leeuw, J., Groenen, P.J.F.: Gifi: multivariate analysis with optimal scaling (2022). https://CRAN.R-project.org/package=Gifi. Accessed 28 Jan 2023
15. Manisera, M., van der Kooij, A.J., Dusseldorp, E.: Identifying the component structure of satisfaction scales by nonlinear principal components analysis. Qual. Technol. Quant. Manag. **7**(6), 97–115 (2010). https://doi.org/10.1080/16843703.2010.11673222

16. Meulman, J., Kooij, A., Heiser, W.: Principal Component Analysis with Nonlinear Optimal Scaling Transformations for Ordinal and Nominal Data, pp. 49–70. Sage Publications, Thousands Oaks (2004). https://doi.org/10.4135/9781412986311
17. Nguyen, L.H., Holmes, S.: Ten quick tips for effective dimensionality reduction. PLoS Comput. Biol. **15**(6), e1006907 (2019). https://doi.org/10.1371/journal.pcbi.1006907
18. Ribeiro, C.: Estudo de estratégias de valorização económica do Alto Douro Vinhateiro: Aplicação de Técnicas Multivariadas Qualitativas. Master's thesis, Universidade de Trás os Montes e Alto Douro (2015)
19. Satyahadewi, N., Perdana, H.: Web application development for inferential statistics using r shiny. In: Proceedings of the 1st International Conference on Mathematics and Mathematics Education (ICMMEd 2020), pp. 425–429. Atlantis Press (2021). https://doi.org/10.2991/assehr.k.210508.099
20. Saukani, N., Ismail, N.A.: Identifying the components of social capital by categorical principal component analysis (catpca). Soc. Indic. Res. **141**(2), 631–655 (2019). https://doi.org/10.1007/s11205-018-1842-2
21. Sebastião, F.J.: Técnicas multivariadas de redução de dados: comparação, aplicabilidade e convergência de resultados. Ph.D. thesis, UL, Lisboa (2016)
22. Shlens, J.: A tutorial on principal component analysis. Educational **51** (2014). https://doi.org/10.48550/arXiv.1404.1100
23. Todorov, H., Fournier, D., Gerber, S.: Principal components analysis: theory and application to gene expression data analysis. Genom. Comput. Biol. **4**(2), 100041 (2018). https://doi.org/10.18547/gcb.2018.vol4.iss2.e100041
24. Vilela, A., Monteiro, B., Correia, E.: Sensory profile of port wines: categorical principal component analysis, an approach for sensory data treatment. Ciência e Técnica Vitivinícola **30**(1), 1–8 (2015). https://doi.org/10.1051/ctv/20153001001

Predictive Application for Early *Delirium* Detection Subtypes Using GLM's

Alexandra Coelho[1](✉) and Ana Cristina Braga[2]

[1] School of Engineering, University of Minho, 4710-057 Braga, Portugal
alexmcoelho11@gmail.com
[2] ALGORITMI Research Centre, LASI, University of Minho, Campus de Gualtar, 4710-057 Braga, Portugal
acb@dps.uminho.pt

Abstract. *Delirium* is an acute neuropsychiatric dysfunction prevalent in patients admitted to inpatient and intensive care hospital settings. As a multifactorial manifestation, it is typically underdiagnosed and overlooked. *Delirium* can be categorized, based on motor activity profile, into hypoactive and hyperactive subtypes. Multinomial logistic regression predictive models are often implemented to identify the most influential variables, as they allow for modelling the relationship between predictors and a multinomial dependent variable. In this context, the goal of this paper arises, aiming to develop an application capable of predicting the occurrence of *delirium* and its subtypes using the GLMs methodology. Subsequently, variable selection was performed using various techniques, with the *Elastic Net* method having an *alpha* value of 0.1 showing the best performance. The model achieved combines the multinomial logistic regression algorithm with the *elastic net* method, which is included in the web application. For the hypoactive subtype, it allowed the selection of 27 variables, resulting in an AUC-ROC of 0.691. The most influential variables include the length of hospitalization in days, alcoholism, analgesics, cardiotonics, as well as the diagnostic group related to toxicity and drugs. Regarding the hyperactive subtype, the model identified 29 relevant variables, with an AUC-ROC of 0.531. The most impactful variables include PCR, age, pO_2, SIRS criteria, and the ER source, specifically UDC1 (Clinical Decision Unit identifies high-priority patients with assigned yellow wristbands). The application is available at https://alexandra-coelho.shinyapps.io/Delirium_detection_app/. While further enhancements are possible, this predictive model remains a valuable tool for healthcare professionals diagnosing *delirium* in emergency rooms.

Keywords: *delirium* · Generalized linear model · Multinomial logistic regression

This work has been supported by FCT - Fundação para a Ciência e Tecnologia within the R&D Units Project Scope: UIDB/00319/2020.

O. Gervasi et al. (Eds.): ICCSA 2024 Workshops, LNCS 14815, pp. 375–392, 2024.
https://doi.org/10.1007/978-3-031-65154-0_23

1 Introduction

In recent years, advancements in medical technology have played a crucial role in early disease detection and improved treatment outcomes, contributing to a noteworthy increase in life expectancy and overall well-being. However, the ageing demographic has led to a rise in neurocognitive decline, impacting both physical and cognitive functions.

The natural ageing process, or senescence, is influenced by a combination of biological, psychological, and social factors. While positive strides have been made, mental disorders continue to be a significant global health concern, affecting a quarter of the population. Consequently, there is a heightened medical focus on developing tools that can predict and detect mental illnesses early on, leveraging symptoms and associated risk factors for more effective intervention and management of mental health issues [33].

Currently, based on the DSM-V (*Diagnostic and Statistical Manual of Mental Disorders*) definition, *delirium* is a severe neuropsychiatric syndrome characterized primarily by disturbances in consciousness, incoherent thoughts, attention deficit, and cognitive dysfunction, sometimes accompanied by psychotic symptoms and mood alteration with fluctuations throughout the day [5–7,29].

Generally, it develops over a short period of hours or days [21], and there is evidence that the disturbance is a direct physiological consequence of a medical condition or multiple etiologies [5,6,28]. The symptomatology reflects deficits in three domains: the cognitive, which is related to orientation, attention, short and long-term memory, and visuospatial perception; the domain of higher-level thinking, which is involved in language impairment and thought processes; and the circadian, which includes the sleep-wake cycle and motor activity disturbance [15,18].

In general, the disorder is associated with adverse outcomes, reflecting increased mortality, prolonged hospitalization, functional and cognitive decline, as well as the exacerbation of a pre-existing clinical picture of dementia [14,36]. As the population ages, the prevalence of chronic diseases increases. In parallel to this fact, *delirium* is a common acute illness in elderly individuals [25], requiring urgent attention. It is often underdiagnosed and can lead to mortality rates exceeding 25%, accelerate the onset of dementia, decrease independence, and consequently, reduce the quality of life, with a significantly high associated hospitalization cost [20,26]. The prevalence of *delirium* varies from 3 to 52% depending on the studied population, their environment [2,19], the type of hospitalization, and the detection method applied [21]. The occurrence rate in the general community is less than 2%, but it increases with age [21].

According to Lipowski [24], *delirium* can be categorized into three clinically defined subgroups based on the motor activity profile. These subgroups differ in terms of pathophysiology, detection rates, and the duration of the episode [34]. Individuals with the hyperactive subtype exhibit a state of hyperalertness, often characterized by hypervigilance, agitation, hallucinations, verbal and physical confusion, aggression, hyperexcitability, and restlessness [4,12]. It is estimated to occur in approximately 15 to 25% of all cases, mainly manifesting in *delirium tremens* and other syndromes resulting from substance withdrawal [8,10].

In contrast, the hypoactive subtype shows a decrease in alertness, lethargy, reduced awareness of the surrounding environment, apathy, and slow and inappropriate speech [32]. This form of *delirium* is the most common; however, it significantly presents a worse prognosis, resulting in a higher associated mortality rate [8,35]. Patients most prone to developing this phenotype are typically older individuals, anaemic, and more susceptible to injuries during hospitalization [32].

Currently, there are studies and clinical assessment tools, such as the Confusion Assessment Method, for the study and prediction of the disease based on a set of risk factors. However, in the context of a hospital emergency, the patient is subject to various risk factors that make them more susceptible to the progression of the disorder. In these circumstances, time is crucial, as well as the correct and early diagnosis to intervene as quickly as possible. Therefore, there is a pressing need for an effective tool capable of predicting the occurrence of *delirium* and its subtypes to minimize the detrimental consequences of this disease. In this regard, to achieve a more accurate diagnosis, we aim to develop an application based on the Generalized Linear Models (GLM) methodology, specifically multinomial logistic regression [1,17,27].

Predictive models of multinomial logistic regression are commonly implemented to determine the variables that have the greatest influence, as they allow modelling the relationship between multiple independent variables and a categorical dependent variable [9]. In the present case study, it will be used to estimate the probability of an individual presenting one of the subtypes of *delirium*.

After identifying the set of most influential independent variables to include in the model, the statistical significance level of the estimated parameters should be evaluated. To obtain robust results for this classification problem, validating the developed model is essential.

The main motivation for the development of this study stems from the increasing incidence of neuro and psychological disorders, coupled with the negligence associated with their diagnosis due to a lack of appropriate tools in a hospital emergency setting. In light of this, leveraging the data available upon a patient's admission to the emergency department (ED) of a portuguese hospital, the proposal is to develop a computer application that determines the probability of a patient presenting one of the subtypes of *delirium* in this context. The aim is to assist healthcare professionals in the diagnostic process and, consequently, restore the well-being of the patient.

This paper is divided into five sections, with the first part dedicated to contextualizing the subject. It offers a thorough examination of *delirium* and its prevalence, emphasizing the need to develop a predictive model for precisely determining its occurrence. The second section provides a comprehensive account of the methodology implemented, intricately explaining the modelling process, which encompasses strategies for feature engineering and variable selection.

In the third section, we present and discuss the results obtained from the implementation of the multinomial logistic regression models using different variable selection techniques. The aim is to identify the model that exhibits the most effective classificatory performance in predicting the occurrence of the disorder and its subtypes. An in-depth analysis of the most influential variables for each subtype is then presented. Subsequently, we introduce the developed application designed to aid in the diagnosis. The fourth section presents the deduced conclusions derived from the case study. Finally, the last section delves into prospects for improving the model to attain improved predictions, therefore enhancing the performance of the predictive model.

2 Material and Methods

2.1 Generalized Linear Models

Many data science models provide the option to specify the relationship used to describe the response variable. For instance, a generic family of models that can represent a wide variety of relationships between input and response variables is the Generalized Linear Model (GLM) [22]. GLMs follow the structure of a linear model but allow the response variable to have an arbitrary error distribution (rather than simply normal distributions). They enable the estimation of regression models for univariate response data that follow a very general distribution known as the exponential family, which includes Gaussian, Binomial, Poisson, and Gamma distributions. Each serves a different purpose, and depending on the distribution and the choice of the link function, it may be used for prediction or classification, resulting in various types of models [11].

In this case study, the focus will primarily be on multinomial logistic regression models, as they are frequently implemented to identify the most influential variables. These models capture the relationship between multiple independent variables and a multicategorical dependent variable to determine the most contributive variables for each subtype of delirium, thereby estimating the probability of an individual presenting one of the disorder's subclassifications.

2.2 Multinomial Logistic Regression

Given the exponential growth in data volume driven by technological advancements and the widespread use of digital devices, the application of machine learning techniques has become crucial for extracting knowledge from vast amounts of information. In the extensive field of machine learning, the goal is to predict an outcome based on available data, a task also known as a classification problem. When the outcome represents more than two different classes, it is referred to as multinomial. Regression methods have long been a fundamental part of any multivariate data analysis, essential for describing the relationship between an outcome variable and one or more explanatory variables.

Multinomial logistic regression (MLR) is an approach that allows the analysis of relationships between variables, both independent and dependent, when the values of the dependent variable are categorical and have more than two categories. Typically, the dependent variable is nominal, and independent variables can be categorical and/or continuous. This method aims to identify distinctive characteristics among groups in the dependent variable based on the distribution of data from independent variables. Ultimately, it seeks to identify the factors or variables that most influence the clustering of data in both independent and dependent variables [3]. The impact of predictor variables is usually explained in terms of odds ratios (OR). Multinomial logistic regression is not the only estimation methodology available for situations involving unordered categorical dependent variables. However, it stands out for three significant advantages over other methods. Firstly, this technique is widely accessible as it is incorporated into almost all commonly used statistical packages. Additionally, computational efficiency allows for relatively quick calculations, particularly in scenarios with numerous categories. Finally, it is worth noting that the results obtained through this model are easily interpretable [23].

2.3 Modulation

As outlined in the preceding investigation [13], the initial dataset comprised 112 variables and 434 patients. Following thorough pre-processing, a standardized dataset was derived, featuring a reduced set of 29 independent variables. These variables encompass details pertaining to patient origin, admission category, patient characteristics, duration of stay in the emergency department, diagnostic group, blood test results, administered pharmacological groups, and alcohol dependence.

Feature Engineering. Recognizing the imbalanced distribution within the dataset, a stratified split methodology was adopted to maintain proportional class representation in both the training and testing sets. Post-split, the training set featured 238 instances characterized by the absence of delirium, 56 instances of the hypoactive subtype, and 10 instances of the hyperactive subtype. The residual examples were systematically assigned to the test dataset.

Nevertheless, to address the imbalance within the training dataset, methodologies were implemented to rectify this issue, with oversampling deemed the most appropriate approach in the context of limited data. Oversampling involves the generation of synthetic samples for the minority class. Consequently, two techniques were considered: SMOTE (Synthetic Minority Over-sampling Technique) and ADASYN (Adaptive Synthetic Sampling).

In contrast to SMOTE, ADASYN consistently achieved higher levels of precision, sensitivity, and discriminative capacity. This enhancement is perceptible in the superior values observed for the F_1 score, precision, AUC-ROC, and AUC-PR as achieved with ADASYN. These outcomes substantiate compelling evidence affirming the superiority of ADASYN in augmenting the performance of classification models within scenarios characterized by imbalanced data [13].

Variable Selection. The challenge posed by high-dimensional data is evident in machine learning methods. When confronted with a multitude of variables, models tend to overfit, resulting in a diminished performance. Variable selection is a widely employed approach to alleviate data dimensionality. Its objective is to identify the subset of variables that are most relevant and informative, leading to enhanced performance, reduced computational cost, and a better understanding of the model. Additionally, it results in more robust models with improved generalization capabilities when confronted with new data.

The process of variable selection holds paramount significance in the training phase of classification problems. Initially, this method discerns a subset comprising the most contributive variables, which are subsequently fed into the multinomial logistic regression model. The overarching objective of the optimal regression model is to fine-tune the relationship between the response variable and explanatory variables, striving to minimize the number of explanatory variables pivotal in distinguishing between different classes. Variable selection techniques are broadly classified into three categories: filtering, *wrapper*, and *embedded* methods.

Based on the characteristics of the data, filtering models evaluate variables without the need for implementing classification algorithms. Variables are classified according to specific statistical criteria, assigning a score to each one. However, due to its univariate nature, the individual calculation of scores for each variable does not consider their interactions, leading to a reduction in classification performance. This reduction is primarily attributed to the fact that the combination of numerous variables may result in the development of one of the subtypes of *delirium*. Consequently, predominantly due to this drawback, this method was not considered.

Wrapper methods are an approach involving the creation of variable subsets and the evaluation of their performance using a predictive model during the training phase. These methods include simple techniques such as sequential search. During training, multinomial logistic regression assesses the accuracy rate to determine the relevance of variables. Sequential search strategies are particularly computationally advantageous and robust against overfitting. This method includes commonly implemented techniques such as *forward*, *backward*, *bidirectional*, and Recursive Feature Elimination (RFE).

The *forward* strategy initiates the process with one predictive variable and iteratively incorporates a variable only if it leads to improved model performance. When the potential inclusion of a new variable does not enhance performance, the procedure concludes. The method continues until none of the remaining variables provides a significant improvement or until specific stopping criteria are met.

In the *backward* method, the model initially includes all variables, and in each iteration, it progressively eliminates the least significant variable until reaching a reduced model that still adequately describes the data and improves model performance. The variable elimination procedure occurs sequentially until a predefined stopping rule is satisfied. A common example of a stopping rule is when all remaining variables in the model are statistically significant at a predefined significance level, meaning that each remaining variable is statistically relevant to the model.

The bidirectional method, in turn, combines the two aforementioned methods. At each step of the process, it chooses the best predictor to add to the model and removes the least relevant variable from the remaining ones. This method reevaluates both the addition and removal of attributes as the procedure advances. To implement the first three sequential search methods for variable selection in multinomial logistic regression, it is necessary to use the `MASS` package in combination with the `multinom` function from the `nnet` package [30,31].

The RFE is a technique aimed at selecting variables iteratively. Initially, the model is trained with all variables, and the importance of each is assessed through a specific attribute. Then, the less relevant attributes are removed from the current set of predictors. This process is repeated recursively until the desired number of variables is reached.

The *embedded* method combines variable selection with the construction of the learning algorithm, similar to *wrapper*. Moreover, it is seen as the merger of the advantages of *wrapper* models, as it involves interaction with the classification model, and filtering models, which assume lower computational power. These models implement regularization techniques, seeking to minimize model fitting errors while continuously forcing the coefficients to be small or even equal to zero, penalizing them if they are too far from this value. In this way, it reduces the complexity of the model, leading to the elimination of variables whose coefficients approach zero. Some examples of predictive methods that perform *embedded* variable selection include *Least Absolute Shrinkage and Selection Operator* (LASSO) regularization, *Ridge* regularization, and *Elastic Net*.

The LASSO regularization is based on the use of $L1$ penalty to assess coefficients. This technique imposes penalties on the non-zero coefficients of predictors, penalizing the sum of their absolute values.

On the other hand, *Ridge* regularization penalizes the sum of squared coefficients, which corresponds to the $L2$ penalty. This method adds a penalty associated with the coefficients to the logistic regression cost function, aiming to minimize multicollinearity issues and overfitting to the data. Thus, it is possible to reduce the complexity of the model while including all variables. As a consequence, in cases of significantly high values of *lambda*, several coefficients exhibit precisely zero in the LASSO method, a situation that never occurs in *Ridge* regularization.

It is common for some variables to be highly correlated. In these situations, the LASSO method tends to choose only one of the correlated attributes. Thus, *Elastic Net* arises as the combination of *Ridge* and LASSO, which applies penalties to the coefficients of the variables using two hyperparameters, one related to the $L1$ penalty and the other to the $L2$ penalty. This results in the fusion of the advantages of the aforementioned techniques, i.e., automatic variable selection ($L1$) and control of multicollinearity ($L2$). The values of *alpha* control the type of regularization. When *alpha* is set to 0, it corresponds to *Ridge* regularization,

1 refers to LASSO, and values between 0 and 1 represent *Elastic Net*. It is noteworthy that the *alpha* parameter in the *Elastic Net* algorithm is responsible for balancing variable selection and overfitting by combining $L1$ and $L2$ penalties.

3 Results

This section discusses the results derived from the statistical analysis of different models, as per the methodology detailed in Sect. 2. The model selected for implementation in a web application, to predict the occurrence of *delirium* and its subtypes, is the one exhibiting optimal results based on performance evaluation metrics.

The primary outcome of this investigation is the formulation of a comprehensive pipeline for multinomial logistic regression, which elucidates essential procedural steps and outcomes (see Fig. 1) [13].

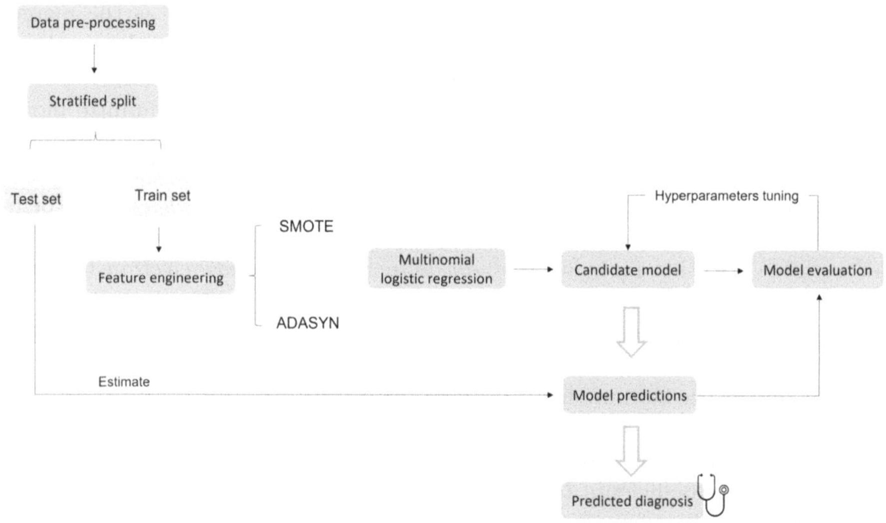

Fig. 1. Main steps of the pipeline for deploying multinomial logistic regression to forecast *delirium* outcome.

The implementation of various variable selection techniques was carried out, aiming to address the challenge of high-dimensional features by excluding less contributive attributes for the model's performance. In the context of the training dataset, it is crucial to identify which attributes will be incorporated into the model based on their impact on the correct and accurate classification of individuals with the absence or presence of one of the subtypes (hypoactive or hyperactive) of *delirium*.

Thus, after an analysis of the respective strategies as described in Subsect. 2.3, the implementation of *wrapper* and *embedded* selection methods took place, which will be analysed and compared. The preference for these methods over filtering methods is due to the fact that these approaches take into account the existence of interactions between variables.

To seek the best subset of variables for the classifier (multinomial logistic regression), for the *wrapper* method, strategies such as *forward*, *backward*, *bidirectional*, and RFE were employed.

The implementation of cross-validation, specifically stratified repeated *k-fold*, for the first three techniques did not show improvements in the model's performance. Therefore, they were not considered for the comparison of selection techniques, and it was decided to opt for methods without cross-validation. This may be attributed to variations in the training and testing sets, the dataset dimensions, the model configuration, and the inherent randomness in the data. However, stratified repeated cross-validation was used for the RFE algorithm.

On the other hand, for the *embedded* method, regularization strategies such as *Ridge*, LASSO, and *Elastic Net* were implemented, coupled with stratified repeated k-fold cross-validation with 10 validation folds and 3 repetitions.

Specifically, for the *Elastic Net* regularization strategy, different values were considered for the *alpha* parameter, which can vary between 0 and 1, to obtain a more viable comparison with other methods. This parameter is crucial in allowing control over the balance between variable selection and preventing overfitting of the model to the training data. Values of *alpha* close to 0 result in a more generalizable model with more features, while values closer to 1 emphasize a more stringent selection of more contributive predictors. Note that the choice of the ideal *lambda* value is determined by the cross-validation approach and depends on numerous factors, such as the dataset and the nature of the problem.

To compare the various models of multinomial logistic regression (MLR) with different subsets of variables resulting from feature selection, it is necessary to construct a reference model, denoted as Model 0, without any selection technique. This model includes all 39 dummy variables, and the prediction results obtained through evaluation metrics have been recorded.

Thus, the aforementioned selection methods, both sequential search and regularization methods, use coefficients to decide which variables to include or exclude in the final model. Predictors with statistically significant coefficients are retained, while non-significant ones may be removed to simplify the model. In addition to indicating the direction (positive or negative) of the relationship between each independent variable and the classes of the dependent variable, they also reveal the magnitude of this relationship.

In multinomial logistic regression, one category of the response variable is selected as the reference, while the other classes are compared to this reference. The choice of the reference category is arbitrary and does not affect the predictive ability of the model. The coefficients for the reference category are set to zero, while the coefficients for the remaining classes represent the logarithm of the odds ratio of belonging to each category compared to the reference category.

However, it is important to note that in the case of an imbalanced dataset, with a greater emphasis on the test set, which has only 18 observations for the

Hypoactive class and 8 for the Hyperactive subtype, the metric related to the AUC-ROC (Area Under the Receiver Operating Characteristic curve) should be given greater consideration. This specific metric is more robust, as it is particularly useful in discriminating between different classes during classification (higher values indicating better distinction).

As observed from the analysis of Table 1, the models related to sequential search contribute little to the improvement of predictive performance compared to the reference model. Specifically, the forward method does not show any improvement, yielding the same estimates as the model without variable selection, suggesting that selection based on this method did not bring discernible benefits to the model.

Similarly, the *backward* and bidirectional methods reduced the number of attributes used, providing a slight improvement in predictive capability. Results for the *backward* method were similar or even superior for most evaluation metrics. On the other hand, for the model implementing the RFE (Recursive Feature Elimination) technique with stratified cross-validation and repetitions, the number of predictors significantly decreased to 27, and the results approached those of the reference model.

As mentioned earlier, the *Ridge* regularization ($alpha = 0$) is designed to prevent overfitting; consequently, the resulting model is more generalizable. This characteristic was observed as the model exhibits a high number of features (36) and, therefore, a lower predictive capacity as expected. On the other hand, the LASSO regularization ($alpha = 1$) aims to implement a more rigorous selection, reflected in a substantial reduction of variables to only 12. The estimates are similar to the reference model; however, it is still not sufficient to surpass the performance of the model without variable selection.

Finally, several models were implemented for *Elastic Net* regularization with different values of *alpha* (models 7 to 11). The model with $alpha = 0.1$ emerged as the one showing the best results compared to others, including the reference model, with superior and noticeable values, particularly for the AUC-ROC metric and a slight increase for AUC-PR and F_1. These results align with expectations, as lower values for the *alpha* parameter tend to retain more variables in the model, while higher values perform a more meticulous and selective variable selection, more aggressively reducing multicollinearity.

Although models 8, 10, and 11 show results very similar to model 7, with a smaller set of variables and reasonable values for AUC-ROC, model 7 was chosen as it placed more emphasis on the higher value achieved by the evaluation metrics. This was a decisive criterion, considering the problem involves a relatively low number of observations.

It is noteworthy that when comparing models 2, 3, and 7, although the first two implement wrapper methods and the last one employs an *embedded* method, all reflect similar performances. Therefore, the model that showed a greater reduction in dimensionality and different predictive variables for each category, corresponding to model 7, was selected.

Table 1. The results obtained by the classifier algorithm, multinomial logistic regression, for variable selection.

Multinomial logistic regression							
Model	Variables	Accuracy	Sensibility	Precision	F1	AUC-PR	AUC-ROC
0	**Reference model (without selection methods)**						
Hypoactive	39	0.662	0.242	0.444	0.320	0.227	0.638
Hyperactive	39	0.662	0.195	0.333	0.241	0.086	0.493
1	**Forward**						
Hypoactive	39	0.662	0.242	0.444	0.320	0.227	0.638
Hyperactive	39	0.662	0.195	0.333	0.241	0.086	0.493
2	**Backward**						
Hypoactive	34	0.654	0.333	0.500	0.301	0.232	0.620
Hyperactive	34	0.654	0.226	0.389	0.186	0.070	0.513
3	**Bidirecional**						
Hypoactive	34	0.652	0.367	0.500	0.222	0.287	0.669
Hyperactive	34	0.652	0.154	0.167	0.205	0.070	0.585
4	**RFE**						
Hypoactive	27	0.659	0.284	0.456	0.243	0.249	0.641
Hyperactive	27	0.659	0.106	0.158	0.176	0.066	0.483
5	**Regularization *Ridge***						
Hypoactive	36	0.631	0.253	0.333	0.286	0.254	0.646
Hyperactive	36	0.631	0.158	0.125	0.071	0.056	0.457
6	**Regularization LASSO**						
Hypoactive	12	0.569	0.242	0.444	0.314	0.265	0.643
Hyperactive	12	0.569	0.145	0.258	0.105	0.072	0.595
7	**Regularization *Elastic Net* (*alpha* = 0.1)**						
Hypoactive	27	0.638	0.320	0.500	0.367	0.307	0.691
Hyperactive	29	0.638	0.189	0.251	0.121	0.074	0.531
8	**Regularization *Elastic Net* (*alpha* = 0.3)**						
Hypoactive	25	0.600	0.290	0.444	0.372	0.270	0.669
Hyperactive	27	0.600	0.145	0.125	0.067	0.056	0.467
9	**Regularization *Elastic Net* (*alpha* = 0.5)**						
Hypoactive	15	0.562	0.313	0.556	0.400	0.239	0.646
Hyperactive	20	0.562	0.138	0.168	0.059	0.058	0.492
10	**Regularization *Elastic Net* (*alpha* = 0.7)**						
Hypoactive	11	0.592	0.333	0.667	0.444	0.246	0.660
Hyperactive	12	0.592	0.137	0.125	0.057	0.054	0.513
11	**Regularization *Elastic Net* (*alpha* = 0.9)**						
Hypoactive	7	0.569	0.265	0.450	0.346	0.255	0.652
Hyperactive	8	0.569	0.165	0.217	0.103	0.061	0.594

Furthermore, it is worth emphasizing that model 7 exhibits a relatively reasonable AUC-ROC value, with 0.691 and 0.531 for the hypoactive and hyperactive classes of the disorder, respectively. A value of AUC above 0.5 indicates that the classifier is capable of classifying the different categories. However, concerning the AUC-PR metric, only values of 0.307 and 0.074 were obtained for the hypoactive and hyperactive categories, respectively. This highlights that the predictive model faced significant difficulty in classifying hypoactive cases and, more specifically, hyperactive cases with the test data, where it showed very low values, indicating its limited classification ability for this subtype. This suggests that the model is less sensitive and more specific, capturing more information related to the absence of the syndrome.

These results are explained by the low representation of these classes in the data, as out of 438 records, only 12.90% of cases pertain to the hypoactive subtype, and only 2.30% to the hyperactive subtype. In the context of limited data, there may also be information gaps regarding the combinations between different classes.

It is important to note that when fitting the multinomial logistic regression model with the `nnet` package, it is common to observe that the same independent variables are used for all categories of the response variable. The artificial neural network package models the relationships between the independent variables and the various categories of the response variable. During training, all predictors are considered relative to all categories of the dependent variable, resulting in the use of the same independent variables for all classes.

However, the regularization approach of the `glmnet` package identifies only some dummy variables as relevant for certain categories [16]. This reflects that the categorical variable as a whole has some impact on the outcome, but not all categories have the same effect. The discrepancy arises from the methodology adopted by the packages.

Although there was not a substantial decrease in the number of initial variables, the model's dimensionality was reduced by only two predictors. The variables excluded for not demonstrating significance in this dataset, according to the *Elastic Net* method of model 7, correspond to pCO_2 and the pharmacological group of antihypertensive drugs.

3.1 Most Contributing Variables

After selecting the best model, there is a pressing need to interpret the coefficient values. The results returned by the model are in logarithmic form, adding complexity to their comprehension. To simplify the interpretation of the coefficients concerning the dependent variable "Outcome" related to the diagnosis of *delirium*, a transformation was performed by exponentiating the model's coefficients by 7, resulting in odds ratios (OR). This conversion, as represented in Table 2, aims to interpret the variable effects more accessible and understandable within the model context.

For the Hypoactive category compared to the reference category (Absent), the result indicates that for a one-unit change in blood pH, the probability of a patient developing the hypoactive subtype of *delirium* increases by 1.351 times. However, it is noteworthy that an increase of one day in the attribute related to hospitalization days shows a 9.044 times increase in the occurrence of this subtype. Regarding categorical predictors such as alcoholism, analgesic drugs, and cardiotonics, individuals exhibiting these habits and consuming these medications are shown to have 2.203 times, 2.018 times, and 1.806 times, respectively, greater probability of exhibiting this phenotype compared to those without the habit or not taking these pharmacological groups.

On the other hand, for male individuals, the probability of developing this subtype decreases by about 48.8% (0.512 times), meaning that the reference class, the absence of the disorder, is more likely. If there is a one-unit change in pO_2, the probability of the hypoactive subtype occurring decreases by 72.2%. In other words, the likelihood of an individual developing this subtype is 0.278 times lower when pO_2 increases by one unit, while the other attributes remain constant.

Similarly, for the Hyperactive category, in contrast to the Absent class, the result shows that a one-unit increase in PCR increases the probability of an individual exhibiting the hyperactive subtype by 14.856 times. A one-unit change in age implies that the probability of this subtype occurring increases by 9.650 times compared to the absence of the disorder. However, a one-unit change in glucose and sodium values reveals a decrease of 84% and 79.2%, respectively, in the development of the hyperactive phenotype.

In summary, it can be concluded that the best predictive model implemented for multinomial logistic regression leaned towards the *Elastic Net* technique with an *alpha* of 0.1. This model will lead to the achievement of the main goal of this dissertation, which is a web application capable of predicting *delirium* diagnosis based on 26 independent predictors (which includes 27 dummy variables for hypoactive and 29 for hyperactive) and the utilized hyperparameters, corresponding to a *lambda* value of 0.1.

3.2 Web Application

As previously verified, the multinomial logistic regression model that demonstrated superior predictive capability was Model 7, which implemented an *embedded* method, *Elastic Net* with an *alpha* of 0.1. Therefore, considering the goal of this study, we proceeded to build a web application using the `shiny` package, aiming to facilitate the use of this predictive model to estimate the diagnosis of *delirium* in the emergency department.

This tool allows real-time access from any device to the prediction estimates. The estimates are generated by filling out the fields in the application form, which correspond to the 26 independent variables selected previously, as mentioned. In this way, it aims to efficiently calculate the probability of the occurrence of one of the subtypes of *delirium* in individuals admitted to the emergency department, assisting healthcare professionals in the diagnostic process.

Figure 2 represents the form developed for data collection to be filled out by the user, which is included in the "Form" section. To obtain the prediction of the

Table 2. Interpretation of the estimated coefficients of the independent variables in the selected model (Model 7) for each category of the outcome variable, according to the odds ratios.

Logit	Variables	Coef.	OR	Logit	Variables	Coef.	OR
0	**(The reference category corresponds to Absent.)**						
	Intercept	0.146	1.157		Intercept	-0.942	0.390
	OriginHome	0.007	1.007		OriginHome	-0.606	0.546
	OriginInter-Hospitalar	-0.026	0.974		OriginIntra-Hospitalar	0.288	1.334
	ConditionUDC1	-0.217	0.805		OriginLar	0.302	1.353
	Age	0.087	1.091		ConditionUCI	-0.314	0.731
	GenderMale	-0.669	0.512		ConditionUDC1	0.591	1.806
	Hospitalization_Days	2.021	9.044		ConditionUDC2	-0.004	0.996
	Diagn_GroupGastrointestinal	-0.045	0.956		Age	2.267	9.650
	Diagn_GroupHemato-oncologic	-0.044	0.957		GenderMale	0.404	1.498
	Diagn_GroupNeurologic	-0.276	0.759		Diagn_GroupHemato-oncologic	-0.143	0.867
	Diagn_GroupOther	0.087	1.091		Diagn_GroupGeniturinary	-0.009	0.991
	Diagn_GroupRespiratory	0.075	1.078		Diagn_GroupNeurologic	0.058	1.060
	Diagn_GroupToxi	0.544	1.723		Diagn_GroupOther	-0.348	0.706
	SIRS	-0.493	0.611		SIRS	0.545	1.725
1 Hypoactive	Glicose	0.325	1.384	**2 Hyperactive**	Glicose	-1.833	0.160
	Creatinine	-0.099	0.906		Sodium	-1.572	0.208
	PCR	-0.764	0.466		Urea	0.511	1.668
	pH	0.301	1.351		Creatinine	0.451	1.570
	Ionized_calcium	0.046	1.047		PCR	2.698	14.856
	pO2	-1.279	0.278		pH	-0.041	0.960
	Antidyslipidemics	0.481	1.618		Ionized_calcium	-0.608	0.544
	Anxiolytics	0.405	1.499		pO2	1.346	3.844
	Analgesics	0.702	2.018		HCO3	-0.310	0.733
	Antipsicotics	0.183	1.201		Antidyslipidemics	-0.221	0.802
	Anticoagulants	0.327	1.387		Anxiolytics	-0.327	0.721
	Cardiotonics	0.591	1.806		Analgesics	-0.578	0.561
	Other_Med	0.400	1.492		Antidepressants	0.164	1.178
	AlcoolicYes	0.790	2.203		Corticosteroids	0.269	1.309
					Cardiotonics	-0.480	0.619
					AlcoolicYes	-0.332	0.718

occurrence of the disorder subtypes, it was essential to include the same variables as those in the training model, corresponding to 26 independent variables. Note that the application displays default values that need to be modified by the user to make the prediction. Each variable is restricted to a certain range of values, similar to those in the training dataset. Thus, the user cannot input values that exceed the limits otherwise, it would hinder the use of the application based on the multinomial logistic regression model for prediction.

A tabular section was created considering how crucial it is to verify the data entered in the form by the user, as a small change can significantly influence the obtained results, aiming to mitigate errors. The prediction result will only be generated when the "Estimate" button is pressed. The prediction result obtained through the implementation of the multinomial logistic regression model is returned as 0, 1, or 2 according to the corresponding category of the response variable (diagnosis outcome of *delirium*). To enhance the readability and intuitiveness of the result interpretation, values have been categorized to prevent confusion for the user.

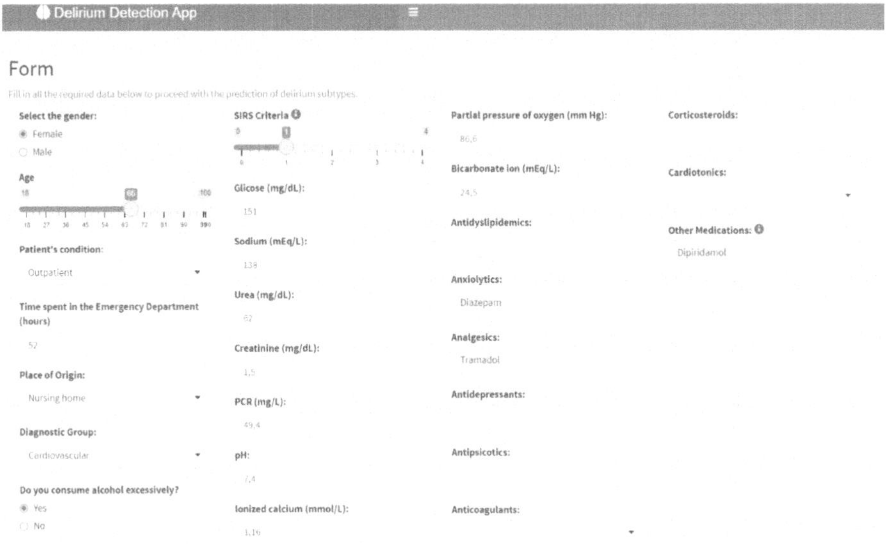

Fig. 2. The web application form for collecting data from individuals in the emergency department.

4 Conclusion

This study demonstrated the importance of data preparation along with data modulation to predict a previous diagnosis outcome. During the modelling process, the variable selection was performed to reduce the model's complexity and facilitate data understanding. Among the various techniques implemented for both the wrapper and *embedded* methods, the technique that produced the best performance for the predictive model was *Elastic Net* with an *alpha* value of 0.1. The model removed the variables pCO_2 and the group of antihypertensive drugs, as they did not prove significant in this dataset. The exclusion of this pharmacological group raised some perplexity; however, it is concluded that it may result from its low representativeness in the population sample.

Specifically, this *embedded* method allowed the selection of 27 dummy variables for the hypoactive subtype, achieving an AUC-PR of 0.307 and an AUC-ROC value of 0.691. The most contributive variables for its development include the length of hospitalization days in the emergency department (ED), alcoholism, drugs from the analgesic and cardiotonic groups, as well as the diagnostic group related to toxicity and drugs. The analgesic group consists of codeine, morphine, and tramadol, while the cardiotonic group includes digoxin. The fact that these pharmacological groups prove to be the most influential for predicting the hypoactive subtype is consistent with expectations since analgesics showed 14 records, of which 6 exhibited this phenotype (42.86%). In turn, from the population sample of 28 individuals regularly taking cardiotonic glycosides, 35.71% (10 people) exhibit hypoactive *delirium*. Due to these statistics, it is reasonable to conclude that these variables have a significant impact on predicting this subtype, as the probability of such cases occurring is substantially higher when one of these drugs is present.

Regarding the hyperactive subtype, the selected model determined 29 dummy variables as the most relevant, obtaining an AUC-PR value of 0.074 and an AUC-ROC value of 0.531. It is speculated that the low values associated primarily with the hyperactive subtype are due to its low representation in the data, making the model unable to accurately predict this class. Among the variables that have the most impact on predicting this subtype are PCR, age, pO_2, SIRS criteria, and the place of origin in the ED, specifically UDC1 (patients assigned the yellow bracelet).

Although the predictive capacity is reasonable, it is assumed to stem from the small number of observations and a high number of predictors. Consequently, the classifier faces increased difficulty in detecting patterns in the data due to gaps in combinations between different categories of the response variable. If the number of records were substantially higher, it is postulated that the prediction process would result in a higher accuracy rate.

After the process of selecting the best predictive model and adjusting the hyperparameters accordingly, the development of the web application using the `shiny` package was undertaken. This application implements the selected model and is built on a total of 26 independent variables. While there is potential for enhancement, this predictive model could prove valuable to assist healthcare professionals in diagnosing *delirium* and its respective subtypes in the context of the emergency department through an intuitive and easily interpretable interface.

5 Future Work

In future work, exploring alternative machine learning algorithms and implementing different variable selection methods is suggested to enhance the predictive capability of the model for the imbalanced and multicategorical variable. Integrating the predictive model into the hospital system would automate the process, offering healthcare professionals timely information about an individual's probability of developing *delirium* subtypes upon admission to the emergency department, potentially reducing underdiagnosed cases and improving patient outcomes. However, to substantially augment the predictive capacity of the model, it is imperative to augment the volume of records in the training set, focusing particularly on the hypoactive and hyperactive subtypes of *delirium*.

References

1. Field, A.: Discovering Statistics Using R. SAGE, Thousands Oaks (2012)
2. Adamis, D., McCarthy, G., O'Mahony, E., Meagher, D.: Motor disturbances in elderly medical inpatients and their relationship to delirium. J. Geriatr. Psychiatry Neurol. **30**(4), 214–219 (2017)

3. Ai, M.T., Sumiati, S., Rosalina, V.: Predictive model for heart disease diagnosis based on multinomial logistic regression. Inf. Technol. Control **50**(2), 308–318 (2021)
4. Ali, S., et al.: Insight into delirium. Innov. Clin. Neurosci. **8**(10), 25–34 (2011)
5. Asken, M.J., Grossman, D., Christensen, L.W.: American psychiatric association. diagnostic and statistical manual of mental disorders. American psychiatric publishing, Arlington (2013)
6. Archibald, H.C., Tuddenham, R.D.: persistent stress reaction after combat: a 20-year follow-up. Arch. Gener. Psy. Therapy **45**(10), 2317–2325 (2007)
7. Assefa, M.T., Chekol, W.B., Melesse, D.Y., Nigatu, Y.A., Bizuneh, Y.B.: Incidence and risk factors of emergence delirium in elderly patients after general or spinal anesthesia for both elective and emergency surgery. Ann. Med. Surg. **84**, 104959 (2022)
8. Bellelli, G., Speciale, S., Barisione, E., Trabucchi, M.: Delirium subtypes and 1-year mortality among elderly patients discharged from a post-acute rehabilitation facility. J. Gerontol. Series A **62**, 1182–1183 (2007)
9. Boateng, E.Y., Abaye, D.A., Boateng, E.Y., Abaye, D.A.: A review of the logistic regression model with emphasis on medical research. J. Data Anal. Inf. Process. **7**, 190–207 (2019)
10. Boettger, S., Breitbart, W.: Phenomenology of the subtypes of delirium: phenomenological differences between hyperactive and hypoactive delirium. Palliat. Support. Care **9**, 129–135 (2011)
11. Breslow, N.E.: Generalized linear models: checking assumptions and strengthening conclusions. Statistica Applicata **8**(1), 23–41 (1996)
12. Bulic, D., et al.: Cognitive and psychosocial outcomes of mechanically ventilated intensive care patients with and without delirium. Ann. Intensive Care **10**, 1–10 (2020)
13. Coelho, A., Braga, A.C., Mariz, J.: GLM's in data science as a tool in the prediction of delirium. In: Optimization. Learning Algorithms and Applications, pp. 591–606. Springer, Cham (2024). https://doi.org/10.1007/978-3-031-53025-8_40
14. Davis, D.H., et al.: Delirium is a strong risk factor for dementia in the oldest-old: a population-based cohort study. Brain **135**(9), 2809–2816 (2012)
15. Franco, J., et al.: Three core domains of delirium validated using exploratory and confirmatory factor analyses. Psychosomatics **54**(3), 227–238 (2013)
16. Friedman, J., et al.: Package 'glmnet'. CRAN R Reposit. **595** (2021)
17. Garson, G.D.: Logistic Regression: Binary and Multinomial, 2014th edn. Asheboro (2014)
18. Harrington, C.J., Vardi, K.: Delirium: presentation, epidemiology, and diagnostic evaluation (part 1). RI Med. J. **97**(6), 18–23 (2014)
19. Hosie, A., Davidson, P.M., Agar, M., Sanderson, C.R., Phillips, J.: Delirium prevalence, incidence, and implications for screening in specialist palliative care inpatient settings: a systematic review. Palliat. Med. **27**(6), 486–498 (2013)
20. Huson, K., Stolee, P., Pearce, N., Bradfield, C., Heckman, G.A.: Examining the hospital elder life program in a rehabilitation setting: a pilot feasibility study. BMC Geriatr. **16**(1), 1–12 (2016)
21. Inouye, S.K., Westendorp, R.G., Saczynski, J.S.: Delirium in elderly people. Lancet **383**(9920), 911–922 (2014)
22. Karpatne, A., et al.: Theory-guided data science: a new paradigm for scientific discovery from data. IEEE Trans. Knowl. Data Eng. **29**(10), 2318–2331 (2017)
23. Kwak, C., Clayton-Matthews, A.: Multinomial logistic regression. Nurs. Res. **51**(6), 404–410 (2002)

24. Lipowski, Z.J.: Delirium: how its concept has developed. Int. Psychogeriatr. **3**(2), 115–120 (1991)
25. Maldonado, J.R.: Delirium pathophysiology: an updated hypothesis of the etiology of acute brain failure. Int. J. Geriatr. Psychiatry **33**(11), 1428–1457 (2018)
26. Marcantonio, E.R., et al.: Outcomes of older people admitted to postacute facilities with delirium. J. Am. Geriatr. Soc. **53**(6), 963–969 (2005)
27. Milewska, A.J., Jankowska, D., Więsak, T., Acacio, B., Milewski, R.: The application of multinomial logistic regression models for the assessment of parameters of oocytes and embryos quality in predicting pregnancy and miscarriage. Stud. Logic Gram. Rhetoric **51**, 7–18 (2017)
28. Morandi, A., et al.: Clinical features associated with delirium motor subtypes in older inpatients: results of a multicenter study. Am. J. Geriatr. Psychiatry **25**(10), 1064–1071 (2017)
29. Rabinowitz, T.: Delirium: an important (but often unrecognized) clinical syndrome. Curr. Psychiatry Rep. **4**(3), 202–208 (2002)
30. Ripley, B., et al.: Package 'mass'. Cran R **538**, 113–120 (2013)
31. Ripley, B., Venables, W.: Package 'nnet': feed-forward neural networks and multinomial log-linear models (2023)
32. Robinson, T.N., Raeburn, C.D., Tran, Z.V., Brenner, L.A., Moss, M.: Motor subtypes of postoperative delirium in older adults. Arch. Surg. **146**, 295–300 (2011)
33. Ruano, L., et al.: Prevalence and causes of cognitive impairment and dementia in a population-based cohort from Northern Portugal. Am. J. Alzheimer's Dis. Other Dementias® **34**(1), 49–56 (2019
34. Slor, C.J., et al.: Delirium motor subtypes in elderly hip fracture patients: risk factors, outcomes and longitudinal stability. J. Psychosomatic Res. **74**, 444–449 (2013)
35. Yang, F.M., et al.: Phenomenological subtypes of delirium in older persons: patterns, prevalence, and prognosis. Psychosomatics **50**, 248–254 (2009)
36. Zamoscik, K., Godbold, R., Freeman, P.: Intensive care nurses' experiences and perceptions of delirium and delirium care. Intensive Crit. Care Nurs. **40**, 94–100 (2017)

Regression Models in Lubricant Oil Quality Assessment

Sandra M. Aleixo[1,2(✉)], Ricardo Enguiça[2,3], Francisco Sedas[1], Paulo Ferreira[4], and André Silva[4]

[1] Department of Mathematics, ISEL – Instituto Superior de Engenharia de Lisboa, IPL – Instituto Politécnico de Lisboa, Rua Conselheiro Emídio Navarro, 1, 1959-007 Lisboa, Portugal
sandra.aleixo@isel.pt

[2] CEAUL – Centro de Estatística e Aplicações da Universidade de lisboa, Faculdade de Ciências da Universidade de Lisboa, Bloco C6, Piso 4, 1749-016 Lisboa, Portugal
ricardo.roque@isel.pt

[3] CEMAT Ciências – Centro de Matemática Computacional e Estocástica - Instituto Superior Técnico, Av. Rovisco Pais, 1049-001 Lisboa, Portugal

[4] Galp, Quality & Technical Product Care, Avenida da Índia, 8, 1349-065 Lisboa, Portugal
{paulo.miguel.ferreira,andre.c.silva}@galp.com

Abstract. After a suitable data analysis, we adjust two types of regression models to support decision-making when monitoring lubricants in an industrial environment. The target variable is the remaining useful life of a lubricant, as it is an essential process in preventing damage to associated equipment. The main objective of this work is to predict at an early stage how long will an oil load still perform correctly.

The first model is a multiple linear regression, adjusting coefficients using cross-validation on several subgroups of the data set. Though the performance of this model is satisfactory, the corresponding adjustment is compromised by the fact that the observations are not independent, as they are grouped taking into account the oil loads to which they belonged. For this reason, a second type of regression was adjusted: a linear regression model with mixed effects. After adjusting the models, a *Python* algorithm was created to determine an optimal interval regarding the oil service hours after which the lubricant should be replaced.

Keywords: Predictive maintenance · Lubricants · Predictor selection · Correlation · Multiple linear regression model · Mixed effects linear regression · Stepwise selection methods · Optimal range

1 Introduction

Within the scope of a particular project, the Quality & Technical Product Care Department of the main Portuguese energy company (Galp) intends to carry out predictive maintenance of industrial equipment, in particular through a thorough data analysis and a corresponding assembly of a model to support decision-making when monitoring lubricants in service.

O. Gervasi et al. (Eds.): ICCSA 2024 Workshops, LNCS 14815, pp. 393–411, 2024.
https://doi.org/10.1007/978-3-031-65154-0_24

Evaluating the remaining useful life of a lubricant is essential to prevent damage in the equipment. It is important to provide the customer with a forecast of the condition of the lubricant so that damage does not occur. This can be accomplished by means of data modeling of the lubricants in service.

In what follows we make a brief review of some literature on this subject and also on the techniques that were applied.

In [8], Pinheiro *et al.* perform several multiple linear regressions on the available predictors for assessing lubricant oil properties, where it was shown that there is no overall superior regression method and the choice is dependent on the predicted property. Also on the maintenance of lubricants framework, Wakiro *et al.* [9] develop a maintenance decision support system that automatically quantifies the influence of lubricant parameters on the unhealthy state of the machine using alternative classifiers. The classifiers are compared for robustness from which decision-makers select an appropriate classifier given a specific lubricant data set. In our framework, we want to use a reduced set of explanatory variables and keep the most relevant ones through all models. Note that we used a stepwise selection method to choose the best explanatory variables.

Another aspect that we enhance in our work is the determination of the confidence interval of service hours where we get the minimum wrong diagnosis, that is, getting a warning to change oil when it is still in good condition (false positive) or a tag considering that the oil is functional when it should be changed (false negative). An interesting applied study on this matter can be found in [7], where Malo *et al.* screen several chemical compounds to identify candidate "hits" accurately. This work also has its focus on finding hits' thresholds and the importance of minimizing false-positive and false-negative rates.

Recently, machine learning techniques are getting a much broader attention in all domains, and our framework is not an exception. For example, in the paper by Malaguti *et al.* [5], some of these tools are used to analyse lubricant oil data, enabling better information in the condition based maintenance approach to the process of diagnosing and predicting failures in diesel-powered vehicle fleets. The results presented in this analysis show that to explain 90% of the variation in the original data only a few number of variables are needed, just as is our case. After evaluating the quality of the variables, an experimental study to analyse the performance of various machine learning algorithms was conducted, taking into account the number of features as input data. In [3], we can find an application of machine learning tools to calibrate real-time condition monitoring of lubricating oil. The methods used are ensembles of regression trees. Ensembles are combinations of models that often are able to improve the results of individual models. Several ensemble methods were studied and the best results were obtained with Rotation Forests. In [6], Mota *et al.* explore Predictive Maintenance systems as an enabler to predict a machine's condition/lifespan, allowing for maintenance-effective manufacturing. This paper aims to address these issues by proposing a novel methodology to improve this performance, by proposing a machine learning training methodology, an automatic hyperparameter optimizer, and a retraining strategy for real-time application. To validate the proposed methodology a random forest and an artificial neural network model are implemented as well as explored. A synthetic dataset, that replicates industrial machine data, was used to show the robustness of the proposed methodology. In our approach we opted not to consider advanced machine learning methods, namely neural networks in order to obtain an explicit model, which is harder to find using those tools.

For a generic reference on Regression Diagnostics, we mention the book by Belsley *et al.* [2], where we can find good practices to assess quality and reliability of regression estimates. This book emphasizes diagnostics and includes suggestions for remedial action. Another reference for the impact of different undesirable scenarios is the paper by Afreixo *et al.* [1], where issues like collinearity, Simpson's paradox, variable interaction or Freedman's paradox are analysed in order to find criteria for adequate feature selection and coefficients' estimation, namely through traditional methodologies, such as automatic selection (e.g., stepwise using Akaike criterion and Bayesian criterion) and penalized regression (e.g., least absolute shrinkage and selection operator (LASSO), elastic net, relaxed and adaptive LASSO, minimax concave penalty and smoothly clipped absolute deviation penalty, penalized regression with second-generation p-values).

In this work, we perform two different regression models applied to a data set, using the accumulated service hours of the lubricating oil as the response variable. First, we considered a multiple linear regression model, where to estimate coefficients we applied cross-validation. Given that the observations are not independent (since they can naturally bee grouped taking into account the oil load to which they belonged), in a second approach we opted to adjust the data to a linear regression model with mixed effects.

Comparing the results of the two models, we conclude that the linear regression model with mixed effects seems to be more appropriate, due to the relevance given to the grouping structure present in the data.

On the subject of regression models mixed linear effects, we indicate the reference book by Galecki and Burzykowski [4].

This paper is organised in the following way: in Sect. 2 we explore the considered data set, in Sect. 3 we detail the associate models, in Sect. 4 we built the optimal intervals that minimize misclassified observations and we end by stating the main conclusions in Sect. 5.

2 Data Set

Galp's Quality & Technical Product Care department deals with issues related to quality, technical assistance and services associated to sold products, whether fuels, chemicals or lubricants.

This work focuses on monitoring lubricants, with the primary objective being to make a decision regarding the time interval in which oil renewal should occur, through the analysis of laboratory data. Thus, data samples were collected from the equipment and sent to the laboratory, where they were classified according to the recorded values in each of the physicochemical tests.

Each test corresponds to the results for several independent variables (of a total of m), and the results for each of these variables can be seen as a vector represented by $\mathbf{X_j}$, corresponding to one of the columns in the data matrix $\mathbf{X}$. The last column will correspond to the response variable, y, which is the number of service hours the oil has been in use. Each of the analysed samples corresponds to a line in the matrix, thus being considered as a single observation, of a total of n.

The included explanatory variables result from laboratory analysis, carried out on lubricant samples, and can be grouped into three categories: variables related to the physicochemical state, variables resulting from the wear of a metal and variables linked to another type of contamination.

The variables in the first group are those that constitute the physicochemical composition of the lubricant. Throughout the useful life of the oil, these values are compared with the initial condition of the oil. The considered variables are:

- Oxy, the generic term oxidation is a chemical reaction of the lubricant with oxygen. Oxidation corrosion results in serious effects on both the oil and the equipment's engine. In this context, oxidation is a measure of the byproducts of this reaction in the oil, whose unit of measurement is Abs/cm.
- pH, a dimensionless numerical scale used to specify the acidity or basicity of a substance. Over time, the lubricant degrades, making the pH more acidic.
- Sul, sulfation is a chemical reaction of the lubricant with sulfur. This reaction results in acidic compounds. This variable is measured in Abs/cm.
- TAN, the total acid number evaluates the amount of acidic compounds present in the lubricating oil. This variable is measured in mg_{KOH}/g.
- TBN, the total basic number evaluates the amount of alkaline reserve present in the lubricating oil. This variable is measured in mg_{KOH}/g.
- Ca, the calcium content indicates the concentration of Calcium present in the lubricating oil. This variable is measured in ppm.
- P, the phosphorus content indicates the concentration of phosphorus present in the lubricating oil. This variable is measured in ppm.
- S, the sulphur content indicates the concentration of Sulfur present in the lubricating oil. This variable is measured in ppm.
- Zn, the zinc content indicates the concentration of Zinc present in the lubricating oil. This variable is measured in ppm.
- Vis_{40} and Vis_{100}, the viscosity at 40 °C and at 100 °C, reflect the dispersion of the lubricant in a given area over a given period of time. They are both measured in cSt.

The second group of variables reflect oil contamination due to wear:

- PQ Index, an indirect measure of the concentration of ferromagnetic metals in the lubricating oil, capturing particles from 14 microns. This variable is dimensionless;
- Al, aluminium content that measures the concentration of this metal in the lubricating oil, and a high value may indicate that there is wear on pistons, bearings, pumps and rotors. This variable is measured in ppm;

- Cu, copper content that measures the concentration of this element in the lubricating oil. This variable is also measured in ppm;
- Fe, iron content that measures the concentration of ferrous material in the lubricating oil. This variable is also measured in ppm.

The last group of explanatory variables concern external contamination:

- Na, sodium content that frequently originates from the refrigerant. A high value of this variable may indicate leaks in the cooling system. This variable is measured in ppm.
- Si, silicon content that can come from dust, the wear of the rubber that seals the oil compartments and the gas used in the gas engine. This variable is also measured in ppm.

The response or dependent variable is the one that we indent to be explained by all previously described. Within the scope of the project developed, this variable will be the number of hours that the lubricating oil is at service, h_{oil}.

The lubricating oil in service is only removed and, consequently completely renewed, when after a sample analysis, it is diagnosed as being in danger. This means that observations corresponding to the same oil load follow an increasing function in the variable h_{oil}, which is only interrupted when the next observation corresponds to another load. When this happens, it is possible to verify that the next observation will have a lower oil service hours value. This lubricant total lifetime can be influenced by several factors, namely the quality of the lubricant, the environment outside the engine, or the operation of the equipment itself. Therefore, the periodic analysis of lubricant samples in service is due to the variability of these factors, allowing us to determine when the lubricant should be replaced.

We also considered a non-numerical information resulting from laboratory analysis, which is the diagnosis category. This categorical variable is represented by C_i for the ith observation and admits three possible states: "Normal", "Watch" or "Risk". This variable will later be associated to the number of hours of service of a given load, being this association the one that reduces most wrong diagnosis.

The data set on which we based our model comes from a biogas motor generator. A biogas motor generator consists of an internal combustion engine that generates heat and electrical energy and, as in any other type of engine, the correct functioning of the lubrication system plays a critical role, for example in reducing friction between parts and protecting against corrosion.

The data set involves 172 observations, analysed between April 2018 and December 2021. As stated before, since new oil charges are always topped up and when considered obsolete are fully removed, the majority of sequential observations belong to the same lubricant charge.

3 Modeling Approaches

In a first and more simplistic approach, a multiple linear regression model was adjusted using the entire amount of samples. This was made with the awareness that it is not the most appropriate model, due to the fact that observations belonging to the same oil load are not independent. However, in order to mitigate effects of dependence in observations, coefficients for this regression were estimated using a cross-validation technique.

In a second approach, a linear regression model with mixed effects was adjusted, accommodating observations dependent on each oil load, and also removing observations that belonged to loads with two or fewer observations (in order to avoid the performance of a regression with probable outliers, that did not represent the standard population of oil loads).

All the results stated ahead were obtained through algorithms developed in *Python* programming language and using appropriate available packages.

3.1 Multiple Linear Regression Model

In a first phase, a multiple linear regression model was adjusted. The first model must include independent explanatory variables that contribute to the best explanation of the response variable.

An analysis of correlations between all variables (explanatory and response) was initially carried out (using Pearson correlation coefficient) (see the matrix in Fig. 1). Below the main diagonal we have the sample correlation values between each pair of variables and the corresponding p-values associated to the significance test of the population correlation coefficient (p-values are presented with two decimal places).

Significantly high sample correlation coefficient values (greater than 0.7) were identified. These correspond to p-values lower than the 5% significance level, leading to the rejection of the respective null hypothesis. For each pair of variables under these conditions, that is, for each two linearly correlated explanatory variables, the one with a lower correlation coefficient value with the response variable is removed.

After the execution of this process, only five explanatory variables remained, namely Sulfation, Aluminium Content, Silicon Content, Viscosity at 100 °C and Viscosity at 40 °C.

The first model was adjusted following two different procedures. In the first, variable selection was made through hypothesis tests for each model's coefficients, while in the second, a stepwise variable selection algorithm was used.

For the first case, the regression model was adjusted with the five explanatory variables determined previously, obtaining a globally significant model, since the p-value of the F test is practically null. Subsequently, those variables whose p-value relative to the significance test of the respective coefficient was higher than the significance level of 5% were excluded, implying the exclusion of two more variables: Al content and Viscosity at 40 °C.

Alternatively, using the stepwise method with the Both Forward-Backward algorithm, the variables that better explained the response variable were selected among the five remaining ones, optimizing the number of variables. The algorithm returned the same three previously found by the other selection method.

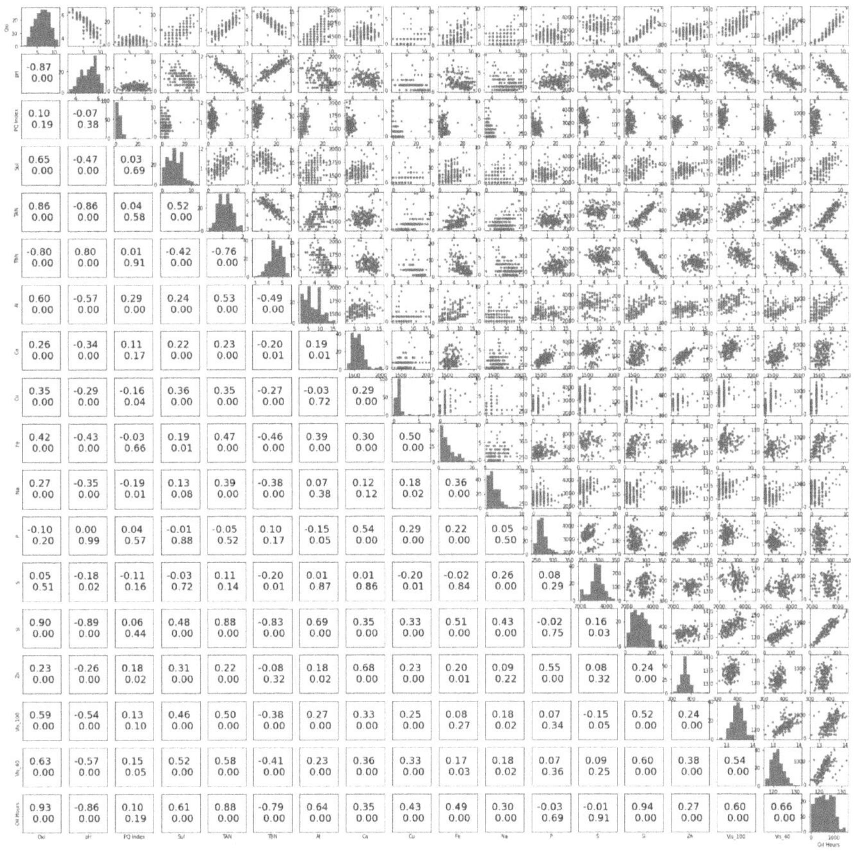

Fig. 1. Correlation matrix.

Therefore, the following explanatory variables were set as predictors for the multiple linear regression model: Sulfation, Silicon Content and Viscosity at 100 °C.

To estimate the coefficients we used cross-validation. The initial sample was divided into five groups and five multiple regressions were carried out, considering data from four of these groups, allowing a random effect in the calculation of these coefficients. Each coefficient was calculated as the arithmetic mean of the coefficients obtained in the five regressions. The estimated model equation is the following:

$$\hat{h}_{oil} = -2150.996 + 4.975Sul + 24.574Si + 157.606Vis_{100}$$

For each coefficient, the obtained value represents the change in the number of oil service hours per unit of the corresponding independent variable, keeping the values of the other independent variables constant. For example, if Sulfation increases 1 Abs/cm, the number of hours that the lubricating oil remains in service increases about 5 h (considering that the values Silicon Content and Viscosity at 100 °C remain constant).

To validate the estimated model, an analysis of residuals and of the existence of influential observations was carried out.

For the adjusted model to be valid, the residuals must meet three assumptions: independence, homoscedasticity and normality. Through Fig. 2, a brief graphical analysis of the residuals can be made.

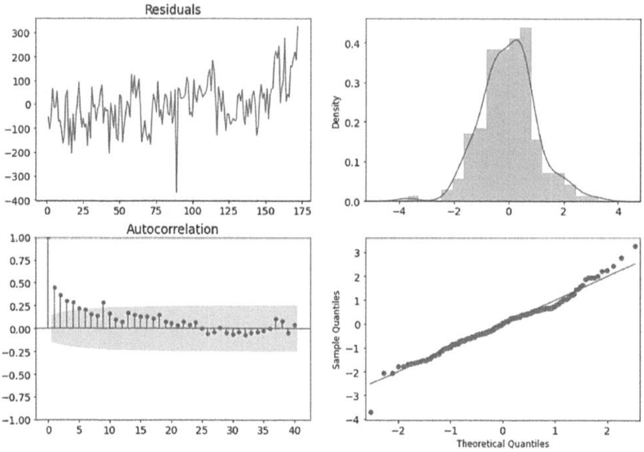

Fig. 2. Graphs for Residuals Analysis.

Concerning residuals independence, given that all observations come from the same equipment and that many of them belong to the same oil load, it is known a priori that this assumption will not be verified. If the observations are dependent, then the residuals must be dependent as well. When analysing the correlogram, in the bottom left corner of Fig. 2, it can be seen that not all points are within the blue band, which is an indicator of correlation between residuals. This graphical analysis can be validated by performing the Durbin-Watson test, whose null hypothesis states that the residuals are independent. The test value obtained was 1.04, so the fact that it is below 1.5 means that the null hypothesis is rejected, and therefore the existence of positive autocorrelation between the residuals can be assumed.

On the residuals homoscedasticity assumption, we need to see if the residuals variance is constant.

Through the scatter diagram, it can only be concluded that this variance is constant if the points are dispersed randomly, without presenting any type of pattern. Additionally, to analytically confirm what is observed in the graph, the Breusch-Pagan homoscedasticity hypothesis test can also be carried out. In Fig. 3 we have the Residuals vs Fitted graph, and it can be seen that an increase in residual variability is observed for higher adjusted values. Performing the Breusch-Pagan hypothesis test, a p-value of 0.65 was obtained, which is higher than the significance level of 5%, so we can conclude that the variance of residuals appears to be constant.

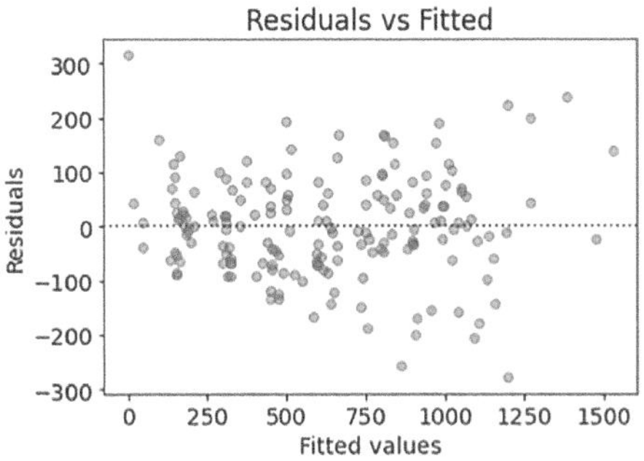

Fig. 3. Dispersion diagram between residuals and adjusted values.

To check the normality of residuals, we initially carry out a graphical analysis of the QQ-Plot, in the bottom right corner of Fig. 2. It seems reasonable to conclude that the residuals follow a normal distribution, as most of the blue points are on the red diagonal line. This analysis can be complemented by analysing the shape of the histogram and the respective frequency polygon, that resembles the normal density curve (in the top right corner of Fig. 2). To complement this analysis, Shapiro-Wilk hypothesis test was carried out to evaluate the hypothesis that residuals come from a population with normal distribution. For this test, a p-value of 0.036 was obtained, which is below the significance level of 5%. Therefore, the null hypothesis is rejected, concluding that the residuals do not appear to come from a normal distribution. (Note that if the significance level considered was 1%, normality would already be verified).

With this, we can only conclude that the homoscedasticity assumption is verified. Regarding independence, given the presence of samples from the same oil cargo, it was known from the beginning that it would not be verified. The non-validation of the assumption of normality would not invalidate the model in its whole if it was the only assumption not verified, which was not the case.

In the Residuals vs Fitted graph in Fig. 3, it is possible to see two values with absolute value close to 300, and, therefore, potentially consisting in influential observations.

Observing the graph of Residuals vs Leverage in Fig. 4, it is possible to see that all points are within the dashed lines. Combining the information on the two

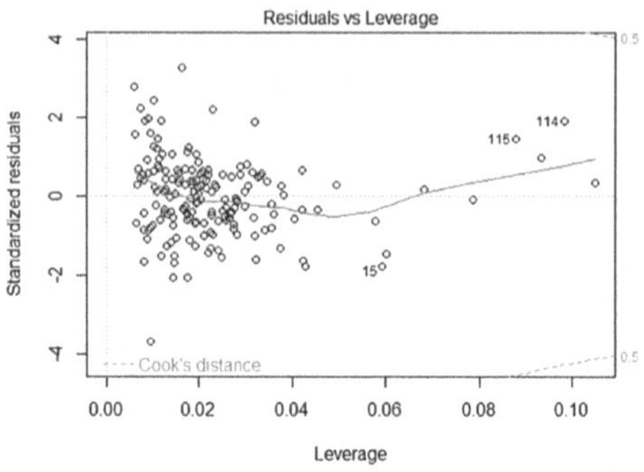

Fig. 4. Scatter diagram between residuals and fitted values.

graphs, the existence of two influential observations can be assumed, even if the Cook distance is not very high for them. The details of these observations are stated in Table 1.

Table 1. Influential observations noted.

Index	Sulfation	Silicon Content	Viscosity to 100 °C	Oil Hours
89	3	70	13.31	0
172	4	154	13.68	1196

These observations were consequently removed and the multiple linear regression model was readjusted to the data, without these observations, following the same procedure, and the following formula was obtained:

$$\hat{h}_{oil} = -2004.012 + 4.930Sul + 25.183Si + 146.869Vis_{100}$$

For the first adjusted linear multiple regression model, the R_a^2 value is 0.913, meaning a good adjustment, explaining about 91.3% of the response variable. The corresponding AIC coefficient is 2078. For the adjusted model without influential observations, R_a^2 improved to 92.3% and the AIC to 2029, enabling us to conclude that the quality of this new model is slightly better.

In Fig. 5, we find a representation of the estimated values and real observations. The resemblance is evident, confirming that the model is well adjusted.

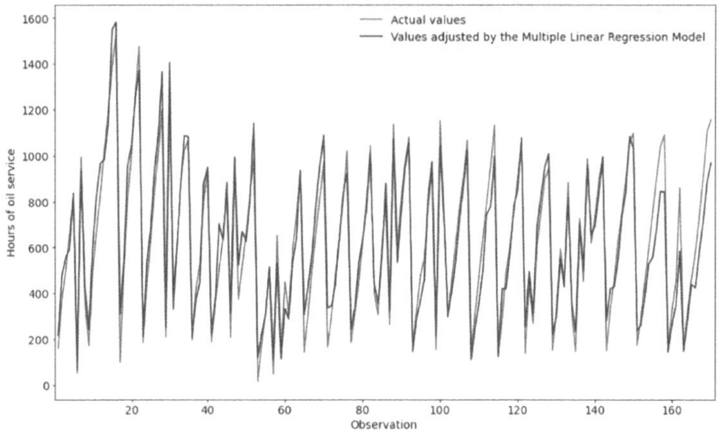

Fig. 5. Comparison between the values estimated by the model and the real values.

In terms of residuals analysis, the assumption of independence remains unverified. However, the assumption of normality of residuals was already been verified (the p-value for the Shapiro-Wilk test is 0.133).

This improved Multiple Linear Regression Model is well adjusted, however, it is not the most suitable for this data set due to the non independence of observations. Therefore, we proceed to find another model, that better fits the properties of our data: the Multiple Linear Regression Model with Mixed Effects.

3.2 Multiple Linear Regression Model with Mixed Effects

By the reasons already stated above, it is clear that observations are dependent within the same oil load, so, in order to built an alternative model, we opted to consider groups of observations taking into account the lubricating oil load to which they belong. To improve the statistical relevance of the data set, it was decided to remove groups with a total of observations smaller than three, resulting in a slight decrease in the total number of observations. Furthermore, influential observations previously identified and removed were taken into account, none of which influenced the removal of groups. The final data set consists of 144 observations, split into 26 groups (we kept the original id's of each group in the original set), corresponding to different oil loads.

Mixed-effects linear regression models can include random intercepts, random slopes, or both, so, in the following we will settle which is more appropriate.

We started with a procedure analogous to that previously described. Through the correlation matrix and the respective tests on the correlation coefficients, the uncorrelated variables were chosen to enter the model, which were the same: Sulfation, Aluminium Content, Silicon Content, Viscosity at 100 °C and Viscosity at 40 °C. After that, using variable selection methods, three more variables were removed: Aluminium Content, Viscosity at 100 °C and Viscosity at 40 °C. So, the model will only include two variables: Sulfation and Silicon Content.

In order to understand whether it makes sense to introduce random intersections, we analysed the boxplots relating to the response variable, taking into account the group to which observations belong, which are represented in Fig. 6.

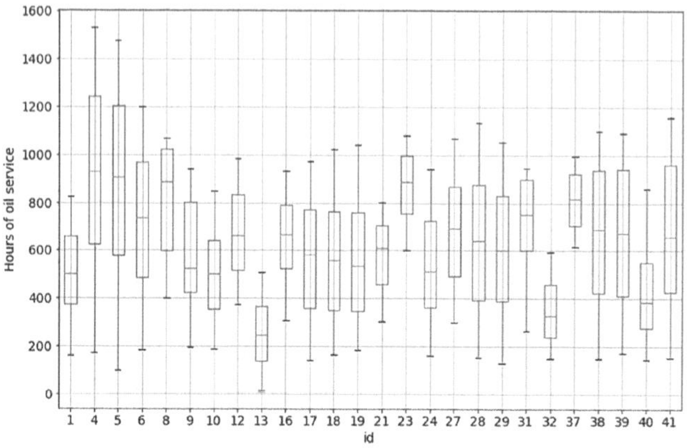

Fig. 6. Boxplots of the response variable grouped by id.

It can be seen that there is a clear difference in the number of oil service hours between groups: some are around 1000 h, while others around 300 h. Due to these differences, it makes sense to insert random intersections for each group, meaning that the mixed model will estimate a different random intersection for each group. For each group we will consider an equation of this type:

$$h_{oil} = \beta_0 + \beta_1 Sul + \beta_2 Si + (u_0)_{id=i} + \epsilon$$

where $i = 1, \cdots, 26$ and $(u_0)_{id=i}$ represents the random intersection for i^{th} group. To investigate the possibility of introducing random slopes, we analyse the graphs containing simple linear regressions between a predictor and the output variable, for each of the groups. In Fig. 7, the left graph refers to simple linear regressions between the variable Silicon Content and the output variable for each of the groups; on the right we have the same for the Sulfation variable.

For Silicon Content, all regressions present similar slopes, so there will be no need to apply a random element to the coefficient of this variable. For Sulfation, it can be seen that some regressions' slope are quite different from the majority, but in general most regressions are similar. Therefore, it was considered that the increase in model complexity inherent in the estimation of many more parameters if random slopes were introduced is not justifiable and, therefore, the considered model for each group i is:

$$\hat{h}_{oil} = -106.116 + 12.946 Sul + 5.999 Si + (\hat{u_0})_{id=i}$$

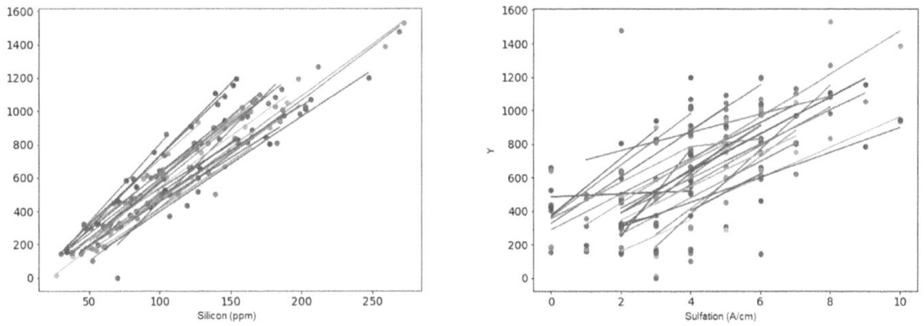

Fig. 7. Simple regressions between a predictor and the output variable for each group.

The range of random intersection values for the linear mixed model vary from −139.01 in group 6 to 152.19 in group 39. For example, for the group with *id* 1 of the first oil load, whose random intercept value is -18.24, the equation would be:

$$\hat{h}_{oil} = -124.356 + 12.946 Sul + 5.999 Si$$

To validate the estimated model, an analysis of the residuals and the existence of influential observations was carried out.

As already mentioned, the model will have to verify three assumptions. Contrary to what was previously observed in the adjustment of the multiple linear regression model, it is expected that the assumption of independence will be verified. When analysing the correlogram, in the lower left corner of Fig. 8, it can be seen that only the first and third points are not within the blue band, with the third point being very close to the limit. This means that there appears to be no correlation between the residuals. This interpretation can be validated by using the Durbin-Watson test. An observed test statistic value of 1.91 was obtained, which is in the interval [1.5, 2.5], so the null hypothesis is not rejected and it can be assumed that there is no autocorrelation between the residuals.
To graphically verify the assumption of homoscedasticity of the residuals, we proceed to analyze the Residuals vs Fitted graph, presented in Fig. 9.
As can be seen, the points are dispersed randomly without, apparently, presenting any type of pattern. Thus, the variance of the residuals appears to be constant. To confirm this suspicion, the Breusch-Pagan hypothesis test was carried out, obtaining a p-value of 0.22, which is higher than the significance level of 5%, so that the variance of the residuals appears to be, in fact, constant.

To assess the normality of the residuals, we analyze the QQ-Plot, in the bottom right corner of Fig. 8, and it seems possible to conclude that the residuals come from a population with normal distribution, because most of the blue points are on the red line. To analytically confirm this suspicion, the Shapiro-Wilk hypothesis test was carried out, obtaining a p-value of 0.57, which is higher than the significance level of 5%. In this way, the normality of residuals is confirmed.

It is therefore concluded that all assumptions were verified when adjusting the multiple linear regression model with mixed effects, contrary to what happened when adjusting the multiple linear regression model.

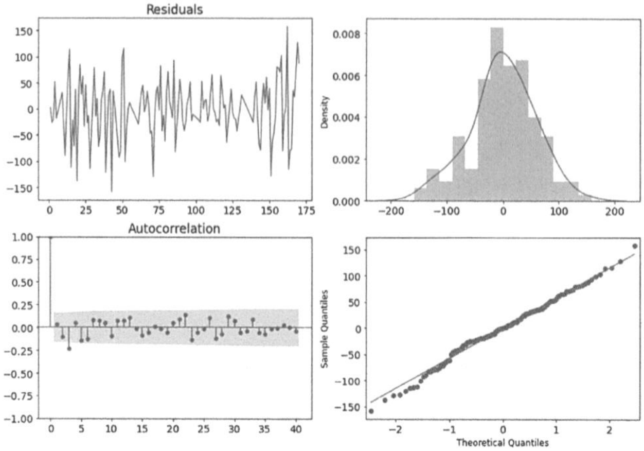

Fig. 8. Graphs for residuals analysis.

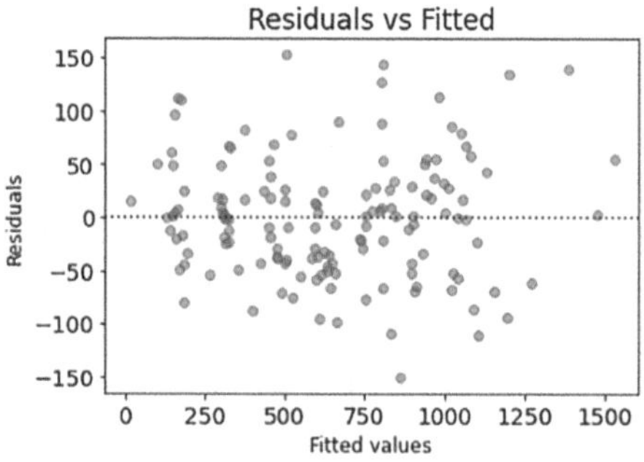

Fig. 9. Scatter diagram between residuals and fitted values.

Analysing the Residuals vs Fitted graph in Fig. 9 there do not appear to be any values that differ significantly from the others. Therefore, there do not appear to be any influential observations.

Through the quotient between the variance of the random intercept and the sum between this and the error variance, it is possible to evaluate the quality of fit of the model. The value of this indicator must be in the range [0,1], with a value closer to 1 meaning that the estimation of the random effect for the group is relevant. In this specific case, the following result was obtained:

$$\frac{7158.44}{7158.44 + 3990.80} = 0.642\,,$$

and given that it is larger than 0.5, the grouping of data taking into account the oil load can be considered significant.

For this mixed effects model with random intercepts, the AIC value is 1674, which can be assumed to be a better option compared to the multiple linear regression model, where the AIC is 2029. Therefore, this model is better suited to this data than the multiple linear regression model without mixed effects.

Another way to evaluate the quality of this type of model with mixed effects is through two determination coefficients. A first one, the Adjusted Marginal Coefficient of Determination, which concerns the proportion of variance that is explained by the fixed effects. This coefficient is the quotient between the variance of the fixed effects and the total variance of the model (sum of the variances of the fixed effects, the mixed effects and the error), which in this case is given by:

$$\frac{113779.16}{124928.41} = 0.911\,.$$

The second is the Conditional Adjusted Coefficient of Determination, which concerns the proportion of variance that is explained by both fixed effects and mixed effects, that is, the quotient between the sum of the variances of the fixed and mixed effects and the total variance of the model, being for the data under study given by:

$$\frac{113779.16 + 7158.44}{124928.41} = 0.968\,.$$

Given the high values of both coefficients (above 0.9), it can be considered that the model is well adjusted.

For the multiple linear regression with random intersections (MLRRI), the results were much better when compared to the results of multiple linear regression (MLR). The main validation and quality measures of the models are presented in Table 2.

Table 2. Linear Regression Model Comparison Table.

Validation and Quality Indicators	MLR	MLRRI
Number of Predictors	3	2
R_a^2	92.3 %	91.1 % (Marginal)
AIC	2029	1674
Residuals Independence	No	Yes
Residuals Normality, Residuals Homoscedasticity	Yes	Yes

4 Optimal Intervals for Lubricant Replacement Based on Regression Results

In this section we find an optimal confidence interval, through which it is possible to infer from the total service hours when to renew the lubricating oil, avoiding the performance of extra testing.

Note that the correct diagnoses are only guaranteed by laboratory analysis, and that our goal is to be able to provide an estimate for how long should a load remain on a machine using preliminary laboratory analysis values.

Although the multiple linear regression model is not the most suitable for adjusting this type of data, we opted to consider it as the basis to find the optimal interval for renewing the lubricating. Later we will also consider a version using the mixed effects model.

The first step consisted in representing the total number of anomalous diagnoses if the classification was defined by a single threshold value concerning the total number of hours at service of a given oil load.

Anomalous diagnosis can be split in diagnoses considered Normal above an Upper Control Limit (UCL) and diagnoses labelled as Watch or Risk but below the Lower Control Limit (LCL). If $UCL = LCL$, Fig. 10 shows us the corresponding numbers of misclassifications.

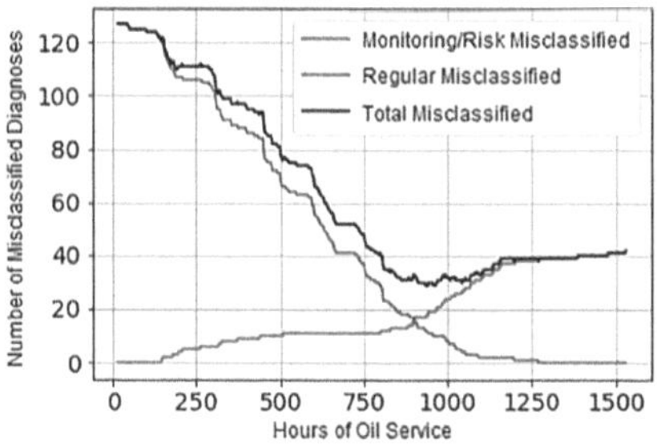

Fig. 10. Graphic Representation of the Number of Anomalous Diagnoses

The minimum of total misclassifications is located at the 932 h mark (for a total of 29 misclassified diagnoses). This value is the natural choice for our threshold, but since it is important to give the customer some room for maneuver, we consider a 95% confidence interval centered at it. To calculate the limits of the confidence interval it is necessary to have a vector with the values of the explanatory variables.

An algorithm was created in *Python*, which checks all possible combinations of integer values of the explanatory variables and returns the one whose value of the response variable is closer to a target value. For example, considering a target value of 932 h, we get a Sulfation value of 11, a Silicon Content of 152 and a Viscosity at 100 °C equal to 13.

Having the values of the explanatory variables, it is now possible to determine the limits of the 95% confidence interval for the 932 h forecast: [726, 1136]. Using this interval, the number of anomalous diagnoses is 13, with 2 Normal diagnoses above the upper limit of the range, 9 Watch diagnoses below the lower limit of the range, and 2 Risk diagnoses below the lower limit of the range.

In the next step, we allow for a shift of this interval, maintaining its amplitude and search for the minimum number of anomalous diagnoses. On the considered case, if we add 59 hours to our interval, we avoid one extra misclassification, getting the optimal interval [785, 1195].

The last step consists in reusing the algorithm to find the predictors integer values for the new center of the interval.

To obtain the optimal range of oil service hours using linear regression with mixed effects, the optimization algorithm underwent some changes.

The grouping of observations must be taken into consideration when setting the interval for a future observation.

As an example, in order to explain the changes made to the optimization algorithm, we consider a sample with 299 hours of service, with a Sulfation level of 5 and Silicon content equal to 41.

This is a sample that was taken from a very "young" oil, which makes it a suitable example as you can compare it to the available data for subsequent samples of the same load.

Unlike the multiple linear regression case, it is not necessary to find values for the predictors. However, the first step is to understand which of the 26 groups should the interval will be calculated for. To do this, with the associated model and the values of the new observation, the random intersection value is determined. For observation mentioned above, a value of 94.42 was obtained. Then, the absolute difference between this value and that of the random intersections of all groups was calculated and the one whose difference was minimal considered. This guarantees that if the new observation is inserted into the group, its random intersection would not change significantly. In this case, the association was with group 16, which contains only 4 observations.

This first step is the main difference in the algorithm, as the following steps are similar to the previous case.

The associated threshold of hours that minimizes anomalous diagnoses is 932 h, where no anomalous diagnoses were recorded. Then, as had already been done, the combination of integer values to be given to the predictors was calculated, so that the model responded with a value close to 932 h. For Sulfation, the value was 9 and for Silicon Content, the value was 126.

With these values, the 95% confidence interval is [807, 1020], and there was no need to implement the optimization algorithm for this interval, since if it had zero amplitude there would not be any anomalous diagnoses, therefore, located at the same value with a greater amplitude, the number of anomalous diagnoses will also be zero.

Comparison with the Real Sample. A good methodology for validating the range will be to compare it with the real sample. As mentioned, this observation belongs to a data set with 24 observations grouped into 4 groups. This way we can compare the interval with the later observations of the oil load corresponding to this observation.

When analyzing the Table 3, it appears that the last two samples already indicated a possible degradation of the lubricating oil. However, it was only replaced

Table 3. Oil Load to which the observation belongs.

Oil Service Hours	Status
299, 452, 595, 750	Normal
906	Risk
1094	Watch

at 1094 h. However, the calculated interval defines a maximum value for renewal of 1020 h, with the central value located at 913 h.

5 Conclusions and Future Work

Conclusions regarding the relevance of each of the considered models were stated in previous sections, but we enhance that the dependence of observations between samples from the same load implied that a mixed effects multiple linear regression model with random intersections was the most appropriate for our framework.

Obviously, a larger dataset, not necessarily for oil cargoes always associated to the same machine could allow us to draw better conclusion for our mixed effects regression model, eventually with a clearer influence of random slopes, instead of only on random intersections. Somehow we feel that different values for the intersection can be associated to an oil that degrades at a similar pace, but starts working with different level of quality. On another hand, random slopes can be related to a degradation speed, maybe associated to the lubricant's purpose on different machines, or even to different types of oil. We find that there is still room to improve results by applying these type of models.

The determination of the appropriate thresholds for the categorical classification (Normal, Watch and Risk) can also follow the mixed effects version, by assuming different intervals depending on the first analysis on the corresponding load. We provided a grounding work on this subject, but we feel that improvements can be made in a future work.

Acknowledgements. Research partially funded by FCT - Fundação para a Ciência e a Tecnologia, Portugal, under the projects UIDB/00006/2020, DOI: 10.54499/UIDB/00006/2020 (CEAUL), UIDB/04621/2020, DOI: 10.54499/UIDB/04621/2020 (CEMAT) and ISEL.

References

1. Afreixo, V., Cabral, J., Macedo, P.: Comparison of feature selection methods in regression modeling: a simulation study. In: Gervasi, O., et al. (eds.) ICCSA 2023. LNCS, vol. 14112, pp. 150–159. Springer, Cham (2023). https://doi.org/10.1007/978-3-031-37129-5_13
2. Belsley, D.A., Kuh, E., Welsch, R.E.: Regression Diagnostics: Identifying Influential Data and Sources of Collinearity. Wiley, Hoboken (2005)

3. Bustillo, A., Villar, A., Gorritxategi, E., Ferreiro, S., Rodríguez, J.J.: Using ensembles of regression trees to monitor lubricating oil quality. In: Mehrotra, K.G., Mohan, C.K., Oh, J.C., Varshney, P.K., Ali, M. (eds.) IEA/AIE 2011. LNCS (LNAI), vol. 6703, pp. 199–206. Springer, Heidelberg (2011). https://doi.org/10.1007/978-3-642-21822-4_21
4. Galecki, A., Burzykowski, T.: Linear mixed-effects model. In: Galecki, A., Burzykowski, T. (eds.) Linear Mixed-Effects Models Using R. Springer Texts in Statistics, pp. 245–273. Springer, New York (2013). https://doi.org/10.1007/978-1-4614-3900-4_13
5. Malaguti, R., Lourenço, N., Silva, C.: A supervised machine learning model for determining lubricant oil operating conditions. Expert Syst. **40**(5), e13116 (2023). https://doi.org/10.1111/exsy.13116
6. Mota, B., Faria, P., Ramos, C.: Machine learning applied to industrial machines for an efficient maintenance strategy: a predictive maintenance approach. In: Jorgensen, B.N., da Silva, L.C.P., Ma, Z. (eds.) Energy Informatics. LNCS, vol. 14467. Springer, Cham (2024). https://doi.org/10.1007/978-3-031-48649-4_17
7. Malo, N., Hanley, J., Cerquozzi, S., et al.: Statistical practice in high-throughput screening data analysis. Nat. Biotechnol. **24**, 167–175 (2006). https://doi.org/10.1038/nbt1186
8. Pinheiro, C., Rendall, R., Quina, M., Reis, M., Gando-Ferreira, L.: Assessment and prediction of lubricant oil properties using infrared spectroscopy and advanced predictive analytics. Energy Fuels **31**(1), 179–187 (2017). https://doi.org/10.1021/acs.energyfuels.6b01958
9. Wakiru, J., Pintelon, L., Muchiri, P., Chemweno, P.: A data mining approach for lubricant-based fault diagnosis. J. Qual. Maint. Eng. **27**(2), 264–291 (2021). https://doi.org/10.1108/JQME-03-2018-0027
10. Yu, J.: A hybrid feature selection scheme and self-organizing map model for machine health assessment. Appl. Soft Comput. **11**(5), 4041–4054 (2011). https://doi.org/10.1016/j.asoc.2011.03.026. ISSN 1568-4946

Beyond the Cox Model: Applying Machine Learning Techniques with Time-to-Event Data

Francesca Pierri[1](✉), Damiano Perri[2], and Chrys Caroni[3]

[1] Department of Economics, University of Perugia, Perugia, Italy
francesca.pierri@unipg.it

[2] Department of Mathematics and Computer Science, University of Perugia, Perugia, Italy
damiano.perri@unipg.it

[3] Department of Mathematics, National Technical University of Athens, Athens, Greece
ccar@math.ntua.gr

Abstract. The enhancement of data storage capacity over the years and the advancement of various technologies that enable data acquisition and support big data have increased interest in collecting information and its variation over time. In many different disciplines, the aim of monitoring this kind of observations is to analyse and predict the time until the occurrence of an event of interest.

For 50 years, Cox's semi-parametric proportional hazards regression model has been the statistical methodology most widely used for survival analysis (the analysis of time-to-event data). However, nowadays, machine learning techniques are becoming more popular and several studies assert their supremacy from the predictive point of view.

The purpose of the present research is the application of new methodologies related to the Cox model and their comparison with the classic survival model in the field of corporate default risk prediction. In particular, *scikit survival* [1], a Python module for survival analysis designed to be compatible with *scikit-learn* [2] Application Program Interface (API), will be evaluated as a machine learning technique and the results compared with those obtained by applying classical survival analysis techniques implemented with the SAS® PHREG procedure.

Keywords: Survival Analysis · Machine Learning · Penalised methods · Prediction · Bankruptcy · scikit-survival

1 Introduction

The increased ability to acquire and store data has enhanced over time the interest in longitudinal studies in the most diverse fields of application, from medicine and engineering to economics, with the aim of predicting the time of the occurrence of the event object of study. In such studies you fix a start and an end of the observational period along with collecting for all the subjects the

O. Gervasi et al. (Eds.): ICCSA 2024 Workshops, LNCS 14815, pp. 412–427, 2024.
https://doi.org/10.1007/978-3-031-65154-0_25

information about the variables of interest; however, only for some, due to various reasons (duration of study, loss of contact with the subject), will you observe an event. When you are in the presence of censored data it is not appropriate to straightaway apply predictive algorithms using standard statistical or machine learning approaches.

For about 50 years, Cox's semi-parametric proportional hazards regression model [3] and its extensions (for a detailed review see [4,5]) have been applied to analyse survival data and handle censored data problems. Over the last few decades, machine learning techniques have become increasingly popular and comparison among the classic and new models is of interest [6]. In the medical field, Cruz and Wishart [7] and Kourou et al. [8] discuss applications in cancer prediction and provide a comparison of several machine learning techniques. Wan et al. [9] assess the effectiveness of machine learning methods for time-to event recurrence prediction and Spooner [10] states that the latter may be a valid alternative to Cox proportional hazards model in the presence of high dimensional data. The purpose of the present research is to expand previous researches in the field of corporate default risk prediction, applying machine learning methodologies developed for survival analysis and comparing results with the classical survival model. In particular, *scikit survival*, a Python module for survival analysis designed to be compatible with *scikit-learn* API, will be evaluated as a machine learning technique and the results compared with those obtained by applying classical survival analysis techniques implemented with the SAS® PHREG procedure. It would also have been possible to apply SAS using Python libraries, which would have allowed all calculations to be performed with a single script. Instead, we preferred to use SAS ® PHREG procedure as in our workflow its report was easily obtainable and required no additional code. The rest of the paper is structured as follows: a brief review of the Cox proportional hazards model and Cox model-based penalised regression approaches; description of data used for the analysis; results and discussion.

2 Survival Analysis

Survival analysis is designed to connect covariates with the time of an event. The concept of survival analysis is derived from clinical research [11–14], where the primary goal is to predict the time of death, which is survival. In engineering, it is also referred to as reliability analysis [15,16], which is applied to assess the time-to-failure of mechanical items or products. In economics and finance, it is used in the credit scoring field [17–23] to understand the causes of financial distress and identify the main predictors of the probability of business failure within a given time frame. In survival analysis, unlike traditional regression, parts of the training data are only partially observed due to censoring. The survival function is a key measure that relates time to the probability of surviving past a certain time point.

Let T denote a continuous non-negative random variable corresponding to a subject's survival time. The survival function $S(t)$ returns the probability of survival beyond time t and is defined as $S(t) = P(T > t)$. The survival function decreases monotonically with time t, and its initial value at $t = 0$, when all observed subjects are alive, is 1.

The cumulative distribution function $F(t)$, which represents the probability that the event of interest occurs before t, is defined as $F(t) = 1 - S(t)$.

The hazard function $h(t)$ representing the rate of event at time t given that no event occurred before time t has the form shown in Eq. 1.

$$h(t) = \lim_{\delta t \to 0} \frac{P[t < T \leq t + \delta t | T > t]}{\delta t} = \frac{f(t)}{S(t)} \tag{1}$$

2.1 Cox's Semi-parametric Regression Model

Cox's semi-parametric proportional hazards model defines the dependence of the hazard function on the values of a vector of covariates $\mathbf{x}$ as shown in Eq. 2,

$$h(t|\mathbf{x_i}) = h_0(t)e^{\mathbf{x_i}'\boldsymbol{\beta}} \tag{2}$$

where $h_0(t)$ is the baseline hazard function. The parameter β in the hazard ratio expression ($e^{\mathbf{x_i}'\boldsymbol{\beta}}$) is estimated through the partial likelihood method shown in Eq. 3,

$$L(\boldsymbol{\beta}) = \prod_{i=1}^{n} \left\{ \frac{e^{\mathbf{x_i}'\boldsymbol{\beta}}}{\sum_{j \in R(t)} e^{\mathbf{x_j}'\boldsymbol{\beta}}} \right\} \tag{3}$$

which requires no specification about h_0.

2.2 Penalised Methods

Correlation among variables and high-dimensional data often suggests the use of penalised methods, that include Lasso [24], Ridge [25], and Elastic Net [26]. The mathematical problem caused by matrix inversion in the presence of high correlation is solved by introducing a penalty that shrinks the coefficients to 0. The Lasso (Least Absolute Shrinkage and Selection Operator) penalty allows the selection of a small subset of features that are most predictive of the event object of study. The so called $l1$ penalty is given by Eq. 4.

$$\arg\max_{\boldsymbol{\beta}} \quad l(\boldsymbol{\beta}) - \frac{\alpha}{2} \sum_{i=1}^{n} |\beta_i| \tag{4}$$

In Eq. 4, $l(\boldsymbol{\beta})$ is the log likelihood partial function of the Cox model, $\beta_1, ...\beta_k$ are the k parameters for the k features and $\alpha \geq 0$ is a hyper-parameter that controls the amount of shrinkage. Therefore, when α is set to 0 you obtain the standard Cox model.

The Ridge method solves the mathematical problem in the presence of correlation; the penalty used, known as $l2$, is given by the following Eq. 5.

$$\arg\max_{\boldsymbol{\beta}} \quad l(\boldsymbol{\beta}) - \alpha \sum_{i=1}^{k} \beta_i^2 \tag{5}$$

The Elastic Net penalty uses a weighted combination of the $l1$ and $l2$ penalty by solving Eq. 6.

$$\arg\max_{\boldsymbol{\beta}} \quad l(\boldsymbol{\beta}) - \alpha(r \sum_{i=1}^{k} |\beta_i| + \frac{1-r}{2} \sum_{i=1}^{k} \beta_i^2) \tag{6}$$

In Eq. 6, $r \in [0; 1]$ is the relative weight of the $l1$ and $l2$ penalty. Consequently, it is clear that the subset selection property of the Lasso is combined with the regularisation strength of the Ridge penalty.

3 Data

Data used in this paper were extracted from the Orbis [27] database, which offers a collection of information and tools for searching and analysing over 400 million private companies. The same data were used in previous research [28] where different variable selection methods in binary regression model are compared. The sample extracted consist of 37875 Italian firms operating in the manufacturing sector during the period 2000–2018.

For each firm we know the financial data, the legal form, the current legal status and the geographical location. From the whole sample we selected the firms still active at the end of the observational period (34046) and those closed as a result of bankruptcy (3312). The low incidence of the default event (8.86%) in the total sample, suggested/required a data balancing operation, randomly choosing a number of active firms (3312) equal to the ones closed (3312) due to bankruptcy. Therefore, the pre-processing phase resulted in reducing the sample size from 37358 to 6624 observations, taking all the bankrupt firms and an equal number of active enterprises chosen through random selection without replacement. The final data, consisting of 6624 observations, was then split randomly into training (80% of the total sample, 5299 observations) and validation (20% of the total sample, 1325 observations) data sets. The first is used to develop the model and the second to test its predictive ability.

From the financial data extracted from the database, a series of indexes with economic and financial relevance were computed, according to their deemed appropriateness and literature evidence [29–32]. A detailed description of the statistical distribution for the indexes representative of the overall firms' performance status including profitability, efficiency, solvency and liquidity, can be found in the appendix, specifically, in Table 5, Table 6 and Table 7 (data in the appendix is organised into three tables to improve readability).

The firms' distribution (in the training set) by geographical area (Table 1) and Legal form (Table 2) shows that the bankruptcy event is more frequent in the

Table 1. Distribution of firms in the training set, by geographical area

		North West	North East	Centre	South	Insular	Total
Active	N	1064	858	1728	220	74	2657
	%	20.08	16.19	8.32	4.15	1.40	50.14
Bankruptcy	N	956	744	489	325	113	2642
	%	18.04	14.04	9.51	6.13	2.13	49.86
	Column %	36.18	46.44	53.33	59.63	60.43	
Total	N	2020	1602	945	545	187	5299
	%	38.12	30.22	17.23	10.28	3.53	100.00

South (59.63%) and Insular (60.43%) areas and in Private Limited Companies (51.33%).

Table 2. Distribution of firms in the training set, by legal form (LC = limited company)

		Partnerships	PrivateLC	PublicLC	Total
Active	N	58	2188	411	2957
	%	1.09	41.29	7.76	50.14
Bankruptcy	N	46	2308	288	2642
	%	0.87	43.56	5.43	49.86
	Column %	44.23	51.33	41.20	
Total	N	104	4496	699	
	%	1.96	82.87	15.17	100.00

4 Results

4.1 Classic Survival

We performed regression analysis of survival data based on the Cox proportional hazards model applying the SAS® PHREG procedure to the training data set. First of all, correlation problems among indexes were checked and among those indexes with correlation higher than 0.70 we included only one. The selection of one index rather than another is influenced by its broader applicability or its lack of correlation with other indexes.

The stepwise model selection method was applied: variables are entered into and removed from the model in such a way that each forward selection step can be followed by one or more backward elimination steps [33].

The resulting model incorporates significant variables such as Legal Form, Geographical Area, and 17 indexes (Table 3). It is noted that concerning the geographical area, the variable holds overall significance; however, the significant comparisons are those excluding the number 1 within the HR confidence interval. As regards the Legal Form, Private Limited Companies are more susceptible to bankruptcy (HR = 1.387) compared to Partnerships, which have a lower risk (HR = 0.689). Indexes with negative estimated coefficients are associated with a decreased probability of bankruptcy, whereas those with positive coefficients are linked to an increased risk. The interpretation of the estimated hazard ratio (HR) is the rate of progression to bankruptcy among firms. For example, a one-unit increase in ind007 (current ratio index) results in the probability of bankruptcy rising by 2.762 times, with a 95% confidence interval ranging from 2.386 to 3.198. Additionally, a one-unit increase in ind029 (short-term debt ratio) causes the same probability to increase more than tenfold. Conversely, ind042 (equity ratio) and ind068 (Net income/Total Debts) are associated with a protective effect against the default event, reducing its likelihood by factors of 0.994 (HR = 0.006) and 0.983 (HR = 0.017), respectively.

The concordance index for the training and validation datasets is 0.7925 and 0.7818, respectively. The area under the ROC curve (AUC) increases from 0.7215 to 0.8025 over a period of 2 to 10 years in the validation data, whereas in the training dataset, it rises from 0.7846 to 0.8245.

4.2 Penalised Methods

The subsequent analyses are performed using *scikit-survival* [1], a Python module specifically designed for survival analysis. It is constructed on top of the widely-used open-source *scikit-learn* library [2], which incorporates a broad array of cutting-edge machine learning algorithms for medium-scale supervised and unsupervised problems.

Lasso. The use of the Lasso penalty in the training set returns a model with concordance index equal to 0.8052. This index experiences a slight decrease to 0.7947 in the validation set. At first, we calculated an α value that does not take into account any features, and then gradually decreased it until it was only about 1% of the initial value. The final $l1$ value, which is used for selecting the optimal model, is not returned by the software. In Fig. 1 you see that this method for larger α values selects a smaller subset of features. On the left you may notice among the most important features ind042 and ind082.

Ridge. Various α values were evaluated, and the minimum viable value was determined to be 0.5; any value lower than this caused the system to crash. When training the model with $\alpha = 0.5$, we achieve the highest concordance index of 0.8141. The validation results also show a satisfactory concordance index (0.7943), which reaches its best value (0.7954) for $\alpha = 8$. In Fig. 2, it is evident that as the penalty weight increases, all coefficients are reduced to zero. Additionally, Fig. 3a illustrates that ind042 and ind082 are once again deemed significant predictors of bankruptcy. The selected indexes for $\alpha = 0.5$ and $\alpha = 8$ are displayed in Fig. 3a and Fig. 3b respectively. Here, only a change in the first five significant features can be observed.

Table 3. Estimated regression coefficients, Hazard Ratio (HR) and 95% Confidence Interval (CI) in survival analyses. Reference category: *Private Limited Companies, **Centre

	Est. Coefficient	HR	95% HR CI
Legal Form *			
Partnerships	−0.373	0.689	0.51–0.929
PublicLC	0.327	1.387	1.215–1.583
Geographical Area **			
North West	0.020	1.020	0.915–1.138
North East	−0.069	0.934	0.832–1.047
South	0.252	1.286	1.116–1.482
Insular	0.181	1.199	0.973–1.476
ind001	−0.026	0.974	0.960–0.989
ind079	−0.076	0.926	0.879–0.977
ind007	1.016	2.762	2.386–3.198
ind083	−0.098	0.907	0.880–0.935
ind084	0.060	1.062	1.038–1.087
ind042	−5.071	0.006	0.004–0.010
ind092	−0.281	0.755	0.686–0.832
ind094	−0.003	0.997	0.995–0.999
ind055	0.305	1.357	1.223–1.506
ind116	−0.015	0.985	0.982–0.989
ind060	0.470	1.600	1.254–2.041
ind117	−0.012	0.988	0.980–0.997
ind124	−0.495	0.610	0.513–0.724
ind132	0.389	1.475	1.343–1.621
ind029	2.329	10.268	7.838–13.451
ind068	−4.049	0.017	0.010–0.029
ind082	5.280	196.461	80.239–481.027

Elastic Net. The weighted combination of $l1$ and $l2$ regularisation displays a coefficient plot (Fig. 4) with a shape closely resembling those in Fig. 1 and Fig. 2. However, the most significant features differ (Fig. 5). The top-performing model achieved a concordance index of 0.8006 in the training set and 0.7943 in the

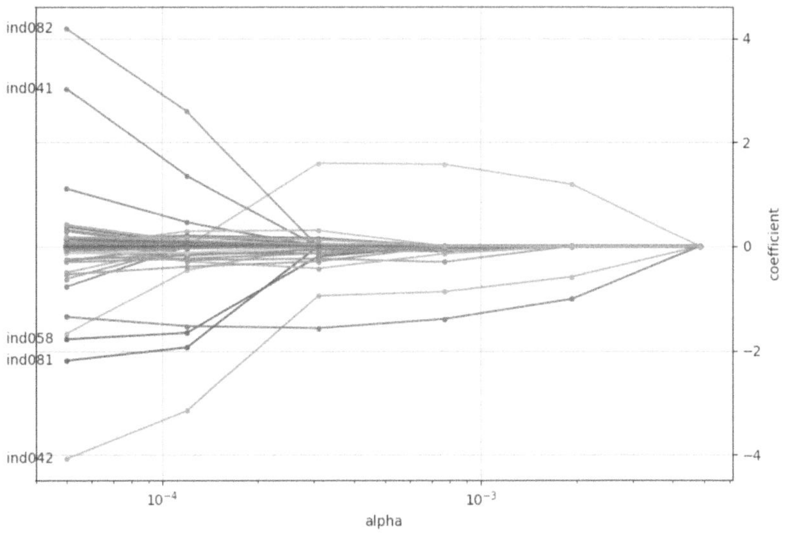

Fig. 1. Lasso coefficient plot

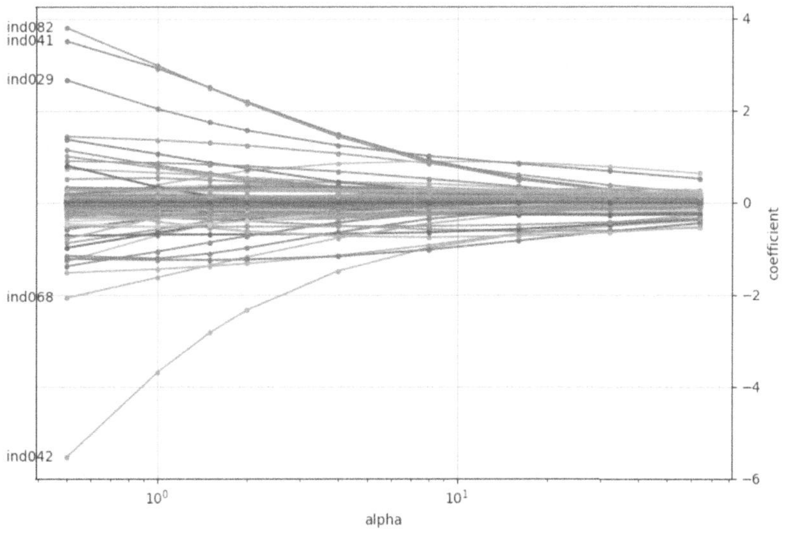

Fig. 2. Ridge coefficient shrinkage for varying α

validation set. As in Lasso in the output, besides the most important features, the value chosen for the penalty parameters are not shown.

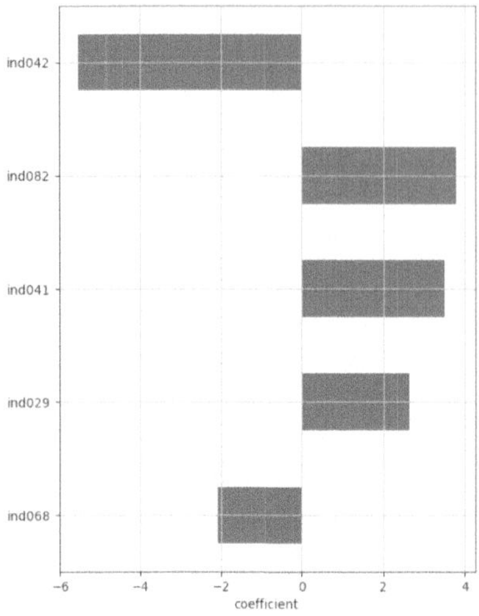

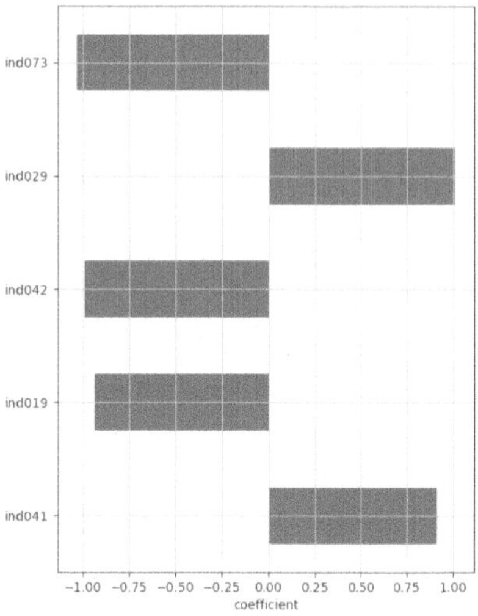

(a) Ridge's best coefficients for $\alpha = 0.5$ (b) Ridge's best coefficients for $\alpha = 8$

Fig. 3. Comparison of Ridge's best coefficients for different α values

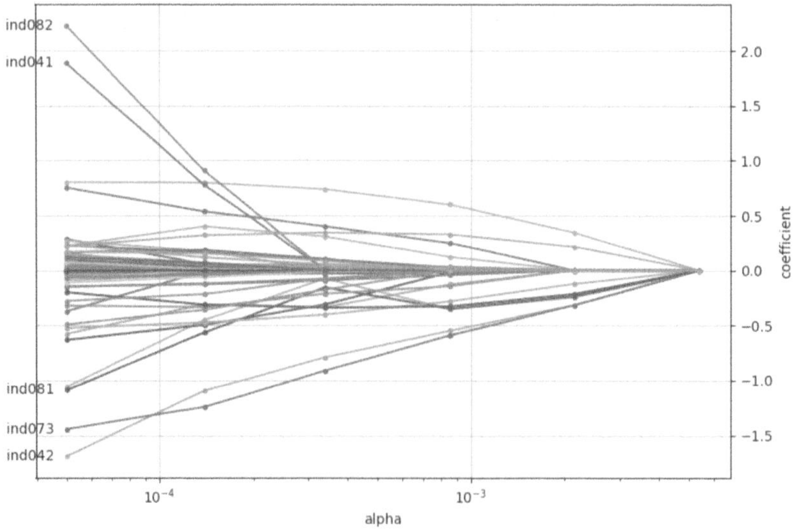

Fig. 4. Elastic Net Coefficients

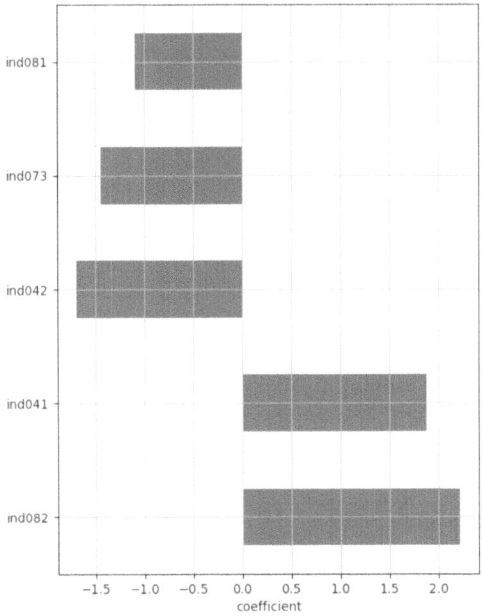

Fig. 5. Elastic Net Features importance

5 Conclusions

The growing interest in machine learning applications has led to the adoption of a user-friendly package such as *scikit-learn* [2], which now includes a module specifically for survival analysis. This module is being employed across diverse research domains, as evidenced by [34–37] and in this paper, we have implemented it in the context of predicting corporate default risk. Utilising the same dataset, divided into training and validation sets, we developed a classical Cox proportional hazards model using SAS software. Subsequently, employing *scikit-survival*, we focused on penalised methods to perform a comparative analysis.

Examining the concordance index within the validation dataset, the optimal results are achieved with ridge penalisation, registering a score of 0.7954 when the penalty parameter is set to 8. Fixing an α value equal to 0.5 Lasso and Ridge methods select the same five significant features, the first with a slightly lower concordance index in the training set, while there is almost parity in the validation set, with the difference being only in the fourth decimal place.

Among the penalised methods, the Elastic Net yields the lowest concordance index in the training set (0.8006) incorporating only a subset of the features chosen by the other two models. In the validation set, the difference occurs at the fourth decimal place.

On the other hand, the classical survival model has the lowest concordance index in the validation set (0.7818) compared to others, yet it demonstrates an increasing predictive ability over time, achieving an AUC value of 0.8025 at 10 years. Additionally, the PHREG output (Table 3) clearly presents coefficients' values, their hazard ratios, and confidence intervals. Moreover, while penalised methods focus solely on indexes, classical survival analysis also emphasises the significance of Legal Form and Geographical Area, in line with prior research on similar data in Europe [38] and Italy [39].

Table 4. Description of the indexes chosen as predictors of bankruptcy events through the four analysed methods

ID	Formula	ID	Formula
ind001	ln (EBITDA)	ind079	Quick Assets/Sales
ind007	Cash flow/Current Liabilities	ind081	Return On Assets
ind019	Ln(Sales)	ind082	EBIT/Total assets
ind029	Current Liabilities/Total Liabilities	ind083	Return On Equity
ind041	EBITDA/Total Assets	ind084	Net Income /Shareholder's Equity
ind042	Total sharholder's Equity/Total Assets	ind092	Sales/Total Assets
ind055	Long Term Debts/Sales	ind094	Shareolders Funds/Capital
ind058	Long Term Liabilities /Total Assets	ind116	EBIT/Interest Paid
ind060	(Long Term Debt + Loans)/Total Assets	ind117	Long Term Debts/Equity
ind068	Net Income/Total Debts	ind124	Receivables/Current Assets
ind073	Other shareholders fund/Total assets	ind132	Equity/Sales

For a clearer understanding of the results, Table 4 provides a description of the indexes selected by the four methods analysed. The Results section shows agreement on the significance of ind042, which indicates the firm's capacity to manage its debt. However, the coefficient's value, representing its relative importance, differs across models: it is higher in the classical survival model (-5.071) and in Ridge penalisation with $\alpha = 0.5$ (< -5.5) and less than half in the alternative methods. Another index consistently present among the penalised models is ind041, which assumes a value of approximately 3 in both Lasso and Ridge for $\alpha = 0.5$ while its importance decreases to 1.5 in Elastic Net and to less than 1 in Ridge when $\alpha = 8$. In the classical survival model, the information provided by ind041 is echoed by indexes ind082 and ind116, albeit with distinct nuances.

In conclusion, penalised methods appear to be more concise and provide an immediate insight into the most significant variables. The classical model offers more detail and may be easier to interpret, yet it has in this case a marginally lower concordance index. Given that there are no significant differences in predictive ability between the models, the selection of one method over another should not be predetermined but should always be based on a comparative analysis.

Appendix

Table 5. Indexes evaluated as potential predictors of the bankruptcy event

Variable	Mean	Coeff. Var	Std Dev	Min	Max
Age	14.11	88.24	12.45	0.01	123.07
ind001	3.98	94.05	3.74	−11.32	13.53
ind004	18.05	354.38	63.97	0.08	1138.55
ind006	813.21	1629.90	13254.49	−15697.00	820789.00
ind007	0.11	338.08	0.37	−11.05	8.08
ind009	0.20	617.46	1.25	−9.01	16.24
ind010	0.03	382.14	0.11	−1.06	0.85
ind011	0.20	615.29	1.26	−9.01	16.24
ind012	0.03	214.60	0.07	−0.76	0.63
ind013	0.07	247.45	0.17	−2.43	2.74
ind019	7.91	18.05	1.43	0.65	16.16
ind020	8.08	16.83	1.36	−0.02	15.28
ind021	78.44	118.99	93.33	0.00	2534.44
ind022	13.99	1257.93	176.00	−170.20	12440.85
ind023	0.94	105.40	0.99	0.08	43.20
ind024	0.71	29.47	0.21	0.04	1.01
ind025	0.89	65.98	0.59	0.01	17.76
ind027	13.04	257.69	33.60	−16.96	1115.02
ind028	0.57	39.55	0.23	0.01	1.20
ind029	0.73	24.92	0.18	0.02	1.00
ind030	5.74	340.46	19.55	−25.38	891.18
ind031	1.74	213.32	3.71	0.06	98.83
ind032	114.35	118.74	135.79	−0.03	3849.12
ind033	0.32	118.74	0.38	0.00	10.69
ind034	605.57	1666.80	10093.66	−108113.60	582932.00
ind036	0.38	677.09	2.60	−79.24	48.97
ind037	0.02	541.31	0.11	−0.89	0.77
ind038	3.16	1447.60	45.70	−885.89	2569.31
ind040	0.06	175.71	0.11	−0.86	0.98
ind041	0.06	130.37	0.08	−0.62	0.55
ind042	0.23	90.34	0.20	−0.52	0.96
ind043	0.49	199.35	0.98	−0.34	23.30
ind044	2.32	370.51	8.60	−7.84	284.47
ind048	0.29	70.68	0.21	−0.01	0.96
ind049	0.31	65.54	0.21	0.00	0.98
ind050	0.32	152.15	0.49	0.00	12.36
ind051	0.22	76.26	0.17	0.00	0.94
ind052	−23.81	−7835.09	1865.48	−135728.00	3989.01
ind053	0.13	111.69	0.15	0.00	0.90

Table 6. Indexes evaluated as potential predictors of the bankruptcy event

Variable	Mean	Coeff. Var	Std Dev	Min	Max
ind055	0.11	255.97	0.28	−0.02	7.69
ind056	7.37	1890.81	139.33	−1.51	9708.55
ind057	0.06	147.73	0.10	−0.03	0.72
ind058	0.20	72.85	0.15	0.00	0.98
ind059	0.24	92.42	0.23	0.00	0.99
ind060	0.20	96.91	0.19	0.00	0.90
ind062	0.07	422.38	0.30	−4.32	4.13
ind063	1.32	5115.09	67.58	−625.97	4833.35
ind064	0.00	−3091.34	0.15	−3.43	1.14
ind065	0.04	5563.24	2.14	−83.31	21.87
ind066	−0.25	−435.83	1.11	−9.67	7.03
ind068	0.02	743.22	0.16	−3.68	2.32
ind070	0.33	193.32	0.65	−0.39	26.10
ind071	0.55	252.35	1.38	0.00	61.30
ind072	0.32	161.58	0.52	0.00	11.80
ind073	0.17	117.88	0.20	−1.09	0.94
ind074	1.55	94.01	1.46	0.66	44.79
ind075	449.36	2125.39	9550.61	−68634.00	588170.00
ind076	0.10	367.33	0.37	−6.76	3.60
ind077	6335.94	931.93	59046.78	0.48	3116481.00
ind078	1.21	212.25	2.57	0.01	71.63
ind079	0.62	114.82	0.71	0.02	35.52
ind080	0.48	42.82	0.21	0.01	0.99
ind081	0.00	2102.16	0.07	−0.77	0.54
ind082	0.03	248.92	0.08	−0.63	0.52
ind083	−0.26	−433.47	1.11	−9.67	7.03
ind084	0.29	551.23	1.58	−9.33	25.60
ind085	−0.01	−921.59	0.11	−1.19	0.83
ind086	14888.96	1224.12	182258.40	1.93	10396912.00
ind087	2.61	73576.65	1920.59	−126093.49	36075.41
ind088	1.46	57.26	0.84	0.02	13.33
ind089	−114.15	−6547.40	7473.91	−518257.00	3572.02
ind090	98735.21	608.35	600660.45	−65395.79	27873248.41
ind091	13.05	377.57	49.29	−96.09	1385.69
ind092	0.98	53.70	0.53	0.02	6.24
ind093	−1.11	−25450.52	282.00	−17549.90	4834.21
ind094	20.05	631.81	126.65	−14.62	7432.27
ind097	17.62	220.42	38.83	−23.53	1128.00
ind098	1.46	102.97	1.51	0.16	43.32
ind100	1.13	108.41	1.22	0.01	36.87

Table 7. Indexes evaluated as potential predictors of the bankruptcy event

Variable	Mean	Coeff. Var	Std Dev	Min	Max
ind101	16.62	233.37	38.78	−24.53	1127.00
ind102	0.77	27.07	0.21	0.02	1.52
ind104	−2537.90	−732.76	18596.80	−542334.00	387454.07
ind105	2328.83	1591.49	37062.97	−153109.15	2368921.00
ind107	0.74	502.24	3.71	−0.94	97.83
ind108	0.14	439.03	0.60	−7.55	11.52
ind109	0.13	187.05	0.25	−0.83	0.93
ind113	15.91	223.10	35.49	−21.37	722.96
ind114	−0.15	−879.21	1.30	−9.96	9.43
ind115	1076.49	1293.82	13927.92	−82402.99	752554.00
ind116	21.38	384.14	82.15	−207.69	994.97
ind117	1.01	408.01	4.11	−0.52	131.60
ind118	0.55	265.23	1.46	−0.34	43.79
ind119	0.23	90.97	0.21	−0.52	0.98
ind121	1.08	103.46	1.12	0.04	33.59
ind122	0.94	105.40	0.99	0.08	43.20
ind123	13.03	257.37	33.54	−16.96	1115.02
ind124	0.36	71.83	0.26	0.00	0.98
ind132	0.33	194.94	0.64	−0.39	26.10
ind136	2.75	44.67	1.23	0.00	9.04

References

1. Pölsterl, S.: Scikit-survival: a library for time-to-event analysis built on top of scikit-learn. J. Mach. Learn. Res. **21**(212), 1–6 (2020). http://jmlr.org/papers/v21/20-729.html
2. Pedregosa, F., et al.: Scikit-learn: machine learning in Python. J. Mach. Learn. Res. **12**, 2825–2830 (2011)
3. Cox, D.R.: Regression models and life-tables. J. Roy. Stat. Soc.: Ser. B (Methodol.) **34**(2), 187–202 (1972)
4. Kalbfleisch, J.D., Schaubel, D.E.: Fifty years of the cox model. Annu. Rev. Stat. Appl. **10**(1), 1–23 (2023)
5. Andersen, P.K.: Fifty years with the Cox proportional hazards model: history, influence, and future. J. Roy. Stat. Soc. Ser. A Stat. Soc. qnad114 (2023). https://doi.org/10.1093/jrsssa/qnad114. eprint: https://academic.oup.com/jrsssa/advance-article-pdf/doi/10.1093/jrsssa/qnad114/51361152/qnad114.pdf. https://doi.org/10.1093/jrsssa/qnad114. ISSN 0964-1998
6. Perri, D., Simonetti, M., Lombardi, A., Faginas-Lago, N., Gervasi, O.: Binary classification of proteins by a machine learning approach. In: Gervasi, O., et al. (eds.) ICCSA 2020. LNCS, vol. 12255, pp. 549–558. Springer, Cham (2020). https://doi.org/10.1007/978-3-030-58820-5_41

7. Cruz, J.A., Wishart, D.S.: Applications of machine learning in cancer prediction and prognosis. Cancer Inform. **2**, 117693510600200030 (2006)
8. Kourou, K., Exarchos, T.P., Exarchos, K.P., Karamouzis, M.V., Fotiadis, D.I.: Machine learning applications in cancer prognosis and prediction. Comput. Struct. Biotechnol. J. **13**, 8–17 (2015)
9. Wan, G., et al.: Prediction of early-stage melanoma recurrence using clinical and histopathologic features. NPJ Precis. Oncol. **6**(1), 79 (2022)
10. Spooner, A., et al.: A comparison of machine learning methods for survival analysis of high-dimensional clinical data for dementia prediction. Sci. Rep. **10**(1), 20410 (2020)
11. Fleming, T.R., Lin, D.Y.: Survival analysis in clinical trials: past developments and future directions. Biometrics **56**(4), 971–983 (2000)
12. Jänne, P.A., et al.: Twenty-five years of clinical research for patients with limited-stage small cell lung carcinoma in North America: meaningful improvements in survival. Cancer **95**(7), 1528–1538 (2002)
13. Hosmer, D.W., Jr., Lemeshow, S., May, S.: Applied Survival Analysis: Regression Modeling of Time-to-Event Data. Wiley, Hoboken (2008)
14. Collett, D.: Modelling Survival Data in Medical Research. Chapman and Hall/CRC, Boca Raton (2023)
15. Huang, X., Aslett, L.J.M., Coolen, F.P.A.: Reliability analysis of general phased mission systems with a new survival signature. Reliab. Eng. Syst. Saf. **189**, 416–422 (2019)
16. Karim, M.R., Islam, M.A., et al.: Reliability and Survival Analysis. Springer, Singapore (2019). https://doi.org/10.1007/978-981-13-9776-9
17. Narain, B.: Survival analysis and the credit-granting decision. In: Thomas, L.C., Crook, J.N., Edelman, D.B. (eds.) Credit Scoring and Credit Control, pp. 109–122. Oxford University Press, Oxford (1992)
18. Shumway, T.: Forecasting bankruptcy more accurately: a simple hazard model. J. Bus. **74**(1), 101–124 (2001)
19. Bellotti, T., Crook, J.: Credit scoring with macroeconomic variables using survival analysis. J. Oper. Res. Soc. **60**(12), 1699–1707 (2009)
20. Lee, M.-C.: Business bankruptcy prediction based on survival analysis approach. AIRCC's Int. J. Comput. Sci. Inf. Technol. **6**, 103–119 (2014)
21. LoPucki, L.M., Doherty, J.W.: Bankruptcy survival. UCLA L. Rev. **62**, 969 (2015)
22. Pierri, F., Caroni, C.: Bankruptcy prediction by survival models based on current and lagged values of time-varying financial data. Commun. Stat. Case Stud. Data Anal. Appl. **3**(3–4), 62–70 (2017)
23. Zelenkov, Y.: Bankruptcy prediction using survival analysis technique. In: 2020 IEEE 22nd Conference on Business Informatics (CBI), vol. 2, pp. 141–149. IEEE (2020)
24. Tibshirani, R.: The lasso method for variable selection in the Cox model. Stat. Med. **16**(4), 385–395 (1997)
25. Hoerl, R.W.: Ridge regression: a historical context. Technometrics **62**(4), 420–425 (2020)
26. Zou, H., Hastie, T.: Regularization and variable selection via the elastic net. J. Roy. Stat. Soc. Ser. B Stat. Methodol. **67**(2), 301–320 (2005)
27. Orbis. Orbis. Bureau van Dijk. https://orbis.bvdinfo.com/. Accessed June 2020
28. Pierri, F.: Variable selection in binary logistic regression for modelling bankruptcy risk. In: Kitsos, C.P., Oliveira, T.A., Pierri, F., Restaino, M. (eds.) ICRA 2022, pp. 143–155. Springer, Cham (2022). https://doi.org/10.1007/978-3-031-39864-3_12

29. Beaver, W.H.: Financial ratios as predictors of failure. J. Account. Res. **4**, 71–111 (1966)
30. Altman, E.I.: Financial ratios, discriminant analysis and the prediction of corporate bankruptcy. J. Finance **23**(4), 589–609 (1968)
31. Mossman, C.E., Bell, G.G., Swartz, L.M., Turtle, H.: An empirical comparison of bankruptcy models. Financ. Rev. **33**(2), 35–54 (1998)
32. du Jardin, P.: Predicting bankruptcy using neural networks and other classification methods: the influence of variable selection techniques on model accuracy. Neurocomputing **73**(10), 2047–2060 (2010). Subspace Learning/Selected papers from the European Symposium on Time Series Prediction. ISSN 0925-2312. https://doi.org/10.1016/j.neucom.2009.11.034. https://www.sciencedirect.com/science/article/pii/S0925231210001098
33. SAS. SAS/STAT® 9.22 User's Guide. https://support.sas.com/documentation/cdl/en/statug/63962/HTML/default/viewer.htm#phregtoc.htm. Accessed 15 Mar 2024
34. Belounnas, A., Brissaud, F., Jardon, G.: Analysis of reliability factors of gas transport industrial assets using supervised machine learning (2022)
35. Ashfaq, A., et al.: Survival analysis for pediatric heart transplant patients using a novel machine learning algorithm: a UNOS analysis. J. Heart Lung Transplant. **42**(10), 1341–1348 (2023)
36. Peng, Z.-H., Huang, Z.-X., Tian, J.-H., Chong, T., Li, Z.-L.: The application of time-to-event analysis in machine learning prognostic models. J. Transl. Med. **22**(1), 146 (2024)
37. Cherukuri, L.S., Rajput, R.S., Neema, S.: Unveiling the impact of demographic factors on disease survival: a multifaceted examination across diverse medical conditions. Int. J. Health Sci. **7**(2), 1–14 (2024)
38. Caroni, C., Pierri, F., Restaino, M.: A comparison of variable selection methods in competing risks models for business failures. Statistica Applicazioni (2023). https://doi.org/10.26350/999999_000053
39. Caroni, C., Pierri, F.: Different causes of closure of small business enterprises: alternative models for competing risks survival analysis. Electron. J. Appl. Stat. Anal. **13**(1), 211–228 (2020)

Author Index

O. Gervasi et al. (Eds.): ICCSA 2024 Workshops, LNCS 14815, pp. 429–430, 2024.
https://doi.org/10.1007/978-3-031-65154-0

The manufacturer's authorised representative in the EU is Springer Nature Customer Service Centre GmbH, Europaplatz 3, 69115 Heidelberg, Germany. If you have any concerns regarding our products, please contact ProductSafety@springernature.com

Printed and bound by CPI Group (UK) Ltd, Croydon, CR0 4YY
30/09/2026
02225585-0016